ESALEN

$\mathcal{E}salen$

AMERICA AND THE RELIGION OF NO RELIGION

Jeffrey J. Kripal

The University of Chicago Press
Chicago and London

JEFFREY J. KRIPAL is the J. Newton Rayzor professor of religious studies at Rice University.

The University of Chicago Press, Chicago 60637
The University of Chicago Press, Ltd., London
© 2007 by Jeffrey J. Kripal
All rights reserved. Published 2007
Printed in the United States of America

16 15 14 13 12 11 10 09 08 07   1 2 3 4 5

ISBN-13: 978-0-226-45369-9   (cloth)
ISBN-10: 0-226-45369-3   (cloth)

Library of Congress Cataloging-in-Publication Data

Kripal, Jeffrey John, 1962–
    Esalen : America and the religion of no religion / Jeffrey J. Kripal.
        p.   cm.
    Includes bibliographical references and index.
    ISBN-13: 978-0-226-45369-9 (cloth : alk. paper)
    ISBN-10: 0-226-45369-3 (cloth : alk. paper)
        1. United States—Religion.   2. Religion and culture—United States.
    3. Esalen Institute.   I. Title.
      BL2525.K75   2007
      150.71′179476—dc22

                                    2006029913

Frontispiece: Hieronymus Bosch (c. 1450–1516), central panel of *The Garden of Earthly Delights*. Museo del Prado, Madrid, Spain. Photo: Scala / Art Resource, NY.

for Mike

bhukti-mukti

sensual delight spiritual flight

and for Dick

na samsarasya nirvanat kimchid asti visheshanam
na nirvanasya samsarat kimchid asti visheshanam .

There is the slightest difference between the world and nirvana.
There is not the slightest difference between nirvana and the world.

Now the revising of *The Interpretation of Dreams* for the Collected Edition was a spur to reconsider the problem of telepathy. Moreover my own experiences...won such a convincing force for me that the diplomatic considerations on the other side had to give way. I was once more faced with a case where on a reduced scale I had to repeat the great experiment of my life: namely, to proclaim a conviction without taking into account any echo from the outer world.

private letter of SIGMUND FREUD to ERNEST JONES

The siddhi [supernormal power] of the vijnana [gnostic faculty] and the siddhi of the body belong... to that range of experience and of divine fulfillment which are abnormal to the present state of humanity.... they are denied by [the reason of] the sceptic and discouraged by [the faith of] the saint.... [But there is no] great man with the divine powers at all manifest in him who does not use them continually in an imperfect form without knowing clearly what are these supreme faculties that he is employing. If nothing else, he uses the powers of intuition & inspiration, the power of ishita [synchronistic desire] which brings him the opportunities he needs and the means which make these opportunities fruitful and the power of vyapti [psychic permeation, likened to telepathy] by which his thoughts go darting & flashing through the world & creating unexpected waves of tendency both around him and at a distance. We need no more avoid the use of these things than a poet should avoid the use of his poetical genius which is also a siddhi unattainable by ordinary men or an artist renounce the use of his pencil.

SRI AUROBINDO in his private diaries, *Record of Yoga*

Contents

Illustrations

Acknowledgments, Sins, and Delight

I am indebted to the many individuals I have had the privilege of meeting and working with over the last eight years on this and related projects. In particular, there were all those brave enough to trust an already controversial interpreter with analyses of their own books and lives, and who graciously responded to my eroticized readings with uncensoring criticisms, helpful suggestions, and more, not less, humor and eros (much of it way sexier than anything I had written—even pictures). Thank you all for putting up with me, and for egging me on. I apologize for not using the pictures.

I must first and foremost thank Michael Murphy, cofounder of Esalen, deep reader of my earlier books, and fellow X-Man. Steven Donovan, John Heider, and George Leonard also deserve special mention. Steve was a constant source of insight, humor, historical information, and invaluable archival material. I doubt I have ever seen such an organized being. John graciously offered me his unpublished Esalen journals, novels, and human potential essays, welcomed me into his Kansas home for a weekend visit, and bore my countless questions with patience and humor. George gave his expert eye to the manuscript, offered critical feedback, and taught me, through example, "to take the hit as a gift."

I must also thank the community and leaders of the Esalen Institute itself, not only for their constant hospitality and generosity over the years, but also for their willingness to accept my proposal to hold an academic conference on the history of the place at the place. On the Edge of the Future: Locating Esalen in the Histories of American Religion, Psychology, and Culture was held from March 30 to April 5, 2003. This gathering featured approximately twenty historians of American religion and major Esalen figures, each of whom delivered papers and all of whom helped me think through my own initial book outline. Select papers from this gathering were subsequently published by Glenn Shuck and me as *On the Edge of the Future: Esalen and the Evolution of American Culture* (Indiana University Press, 2005).

Numerous other individuals also played significant roles in my research and thinking. Some receive major treatment here. Others work their magic behind the scenes. All of these include, in alphabetical, that is, random order: Walter Truett Anderson, Bill Barnard, John Barrie, Steve Beck, Bill Benda, Marcia Brennan, George Brown, Antonella Cappuccio, Fritjof Capra, Seymour Carter, Dorothy Charles, Chungliang Al Huang, Adam Crabtree, Eric Erickson, Anita Eubank, Jorge Ferrer, Robert Forte, Robert Fuller, James Garrison, Christina Grof, Stanislav Grof, Jessica Grogan, Joan Halifax Roshi, Wouter Hanegraaff, Steve Harper, Jane Hartford, Gil Hedley, Peter Heehs, James Hickman, Laura Huxley, Don Hanlon Johnson, Cynthia Johnson-Bianchetta, Sam Keen, Ed Kelly, Emily Williams Kelly, Rondi Lightmark, Bob Love, Nancy Lunney-Wheeler, Brian Lyke, Edward Maupin, Sukie Miller, Joseph Montville, Katriona Munthe-Lindgren, the late Dennis Murphy, Dulce Murphy, Claudio Naranjo, Andy Nussbaum, Jay Ogilvy, Frank Poletti, Chris Price, David Price, Pennell Rock, Marina Romero, Henry Stapp, Rick Strassman, Jeremy Tarcher, Russell Targ, Richard Tarnas, Charles Tart, Ann Taves, Keith Thompson, Bill Torbert, Andrew Weil, and Gordon Wheeler.

I also want to express my gratitude for a colleague, friend, and spiritual brother, Robert C. Gordon, whose vision of things American and mystical connects intriguingly, uncannily, with my own. Robert's essential claim in *The Open Road* is that much of modern American mysticism can best be thought of as a creative fusion of Tantric sensibilities from Asia and the humanist-individualist ethos of American democracy, especially as the latter is revealed by Emerson, Whitman, and Thoreau.[1] His integral fusions render the resonances between our visions astonishingly close at times. I simply want to confess that resonance here.

I am also especially grateful to my editor at the University of Chicago Press, T. David Brent. David encouraged my early, undeveloped thoughts on Esalen and enthusiastically embraced a book proposal that was both quite sketchy in terms of content and a long ways off in terms of a real delivery date. His moral, intellectual, and professional support over the last ten years has been simply invaluable to me. Most authors can only dream about having such an editor. I would also like to thank my literary agent, Anne Borchardt, who helped guide me through the long process of conception, proposal, negotiation, and completion; the thirty-two undergraduate and graduate students of my 2005 fall Rice course on Esalen whose critical inquiries ("You can't possibly mean . . . "), shared altered states ("I was floating above my body . . . "), and editorial skills ("This sentence is *way* too long . . . ") tightened and deepened the final manuscript; Al, Lydia, and Patrick Dugan, for their generous help in underwriting the production and promotion costs; Daniel Bianchetta, whose gracious help with the photos (and whose own photos) added immeasurably to the book; and, finally, Gary Wihl, dean of the Humanities at Rice University, who generously supported various stages of the research, which often required both money to travel and time away from my teaching and administrative duties. My Rice colleagues often joked about me "working" in Big Sur (the scare quotes being theirs), as if working and traveling to Big Sur were mutually exclusive dimensions of reality. I'm not challenging that.

Finally, I must say this. As a young boy, I used to recite, rather obsessively, a Catholic prayer of penitence that asked for forgiveness for sins committed, knowingly or not. That little prayer seems relevant here again, as I am absolutely certain that I have committed minor historical errors and failed to acknowledge someone somewhere in the pages that follow, even if I have no idea whom or where (or about what). As with my earlier books (and life itself), the plot was simply too thick, my conversations too many, my sources too diverse to keep absolute track of everything everywhere always. I could have easily worked on this book for another ten (or twenty) years, and there still would have been mistakes, gaps, stories not told, people missed, interpretations to debate. In truth, there is no end to the stories (because there is no end to the human potential), and the ideal of perfection is a false one: even the biological mutation, after all, begins as an apparent mistake.

I will leave it at that. Guilt or penitence can never be the guiding sign of a robust book, much less a robust book about Esalen. Creative freedom and what William Blake called Energy and Delight take over from here, as they have in everything else I have written—the *corpus mysticum* taking a form between and betwixt this world "in here" and that world "out there," which, if the present story means anything at all, are really the same world.

I

Openings

On Wild Facts and Altered Categories

If there is anything which human history demonstrates, it is the extreme slowness with which the ordinary academic and critical mind acknowledges facts to exist which present themselves as wild facts with no stall or pigeonhole, or as facts which threaten to break up the accepted system.

WILLIAM JAMES, "What Psychical Research Has Accomplished"

For the Eye altering alters all.

WILLIAM BLAKE

Categories are containers for storing experience in symbolic form.

JOHN HEIDER in his Esalen journals

Go ahead. Turn at the little white wooden sign on the cliff highway marked, "Esalen Institute by Reservation Only." It already hints of secrecy, or at least privacy, promising the knowing week-long initiations into ancient mysteries and modern revelations uniting science and religion. The sensuality of the place, it is true, is as palpable as it is primordial. The hot baths down by the sea bob day and night with naked flesh, but the geology of the waters themselves bespeaks more of the almost limitless energy of the earth. At last count, there are approximately sixty different springs on the property that together pump out six hundred gallons of mineral-rich water every minute, and it's *hot*—an impressive but also somewhat nervous sign of just how volatile the land itself is here in this sacred place.

Humpback blue and grey whales can often be seen playing just off the coast as they migrate to and from Baja. At the right time of year, tens of thousands of monarch butterflies can also be seen fluttering through the air and clustering just out of reach in the eucalyptus trees—they've come to winter here. Do not be fooled, though, by their beautiful bright colors. The flapping shapes signal to potential predators that these bodies are poisonous to the palate.

A whiff of personal danger adds to all of this mystical, geological, and biological excitement. One inevitably encounters a small sign on the way down to the rocks that reads something like this: "Dangerous riptides. Swim at your own risk." The sign could just as well be placed at the front gate and be read metaphorically, as both the personal risks and the promises of adventure are quite real here, and the powerful currents that flow just under the surface of things, like the explosive hot springs, should never be underestimated.

Then there are all those legends and rumors. Was the banned eroticist Henry Miller really a regular at the baths? Did the novelist and psychedelic seer Aldous Huxley give the founders their initial language? Did a young Hunter Thompson wield a billy club and tote a gun here in the early days only to get fired by a woman named Bunny? Is it true that Beatle George Harrison landed on these grounds in his own private helicopter to jam with Ravi Shankar? Did Joan Baez, John Denver, and Billy Joel all really sing in the Esalen story? And what, exactly, was the institute's relationship to the FDA, the PGA, the NFL, NASA, the KGB, the FBI, and the CIA, that is, what do illegal drugs, golf, football, space flight, and cold war espionage all have in common? One may have heard that Esalen was in the crosshairs of the Nixon administration. One may have also heard that it was admired and quietly supported by the Reagan administration, Mikhail Gorbachev's Kremlin, and a touring Boris Yeltsin. How can this be? Did Esalen really help end the cold war?

Our story will answer all of these questions in due time, but for now, all of this seems a bit remote as we make our way to Big Sur. The forty-mile drive down from Monterey and Carmel, past Pebble Beach on a famous road whose twists and turns along an ocean mountainside could easily end your life at any moment has already slightly altered your state of consciousness and made you a bit nauseous. You feel funny, a bit disoriented. You are grateful to step out of the car and stand on land that is not moving or, worse yet, *falling.*

You have heard about this beautiful place, at once sacred, sexy, and slightly disreputable. You think you know what Esalen is about, what it is. You probably do not. But there are those who do, and you will soon meet them, at least as I have come to know them through my own winding, falling, rising road to Esalen . . .

Cofounder Richard Price often called Esalen the Rorschach or Ink Blot Institute. He was thinking of those funny looking ink-blot pictures (so many of which vaguely resemble sexual organs) that psychologists use to test a person's projections. "I see a butterfly, or maybe it's a black bat . . . that looks sort of like a vagina." That sort of thing. Price thought that Esalen, rather like the ink blots, somehow encourages people to see themselves in it, and that there are as many Esalens as there are people deeply engaging the place as spiritual presence, as therapeutic refuge, as sensual spa, and so on. Dick was right. Before we begin our story, then, I need to be very clear about what I think I am seeing in all this ink and about how exactly I am seeing it. I also need to be clear about when and how I am projecting— that is, I need to own up to my own bat and vagina sightings—and why this is not such a bad thing.

As a historian of religions with particular interests and questions, I have naturally made choices. Or, more reflective of my experience of the mysterious processes of thinking and writing (and of the psychological language of Esalen), I have put a series of life events, odd coincidences, and thousands of "random" flashes of insight into conversation with a practice of disciplined reading and writing to create or discover (it is impossible to tell which) a new *gestalt* or meaningful whole. As I hope will become clear, this is neither fantasy nor science, but a mystical art through which one interprets a phenomenon and is in turn interpreted by it. Words like "subjective" and "objective" cease to have much meaning here. Something far more interesting, and far weirder, is at play. It is as if the world itself has become fantastically plastic, infinitely plural and, above all, radically *open*.

I mean this in not just a metaphorical sense, but also in a metaphysical one. Michael Murphy, cofounder of Esalen, might compare this sense to his "occult realism," that is, a particular genre of novel writing whose imaginative fusing of the mystical ("occult") and empirical ("realism") dimensions of anomalous experiences ends up conjuring for the reader a fantastic world in which many strange and marvelous things can (and oddly do) happen.[1] Such anomalous events are what one of Murphy's favorite authors, the Harvard psychologist and philosopher William James, called the "wild facts" of history in our opening epigraph. These wild facts were apparent to James both in his spiritual experiments with nitrous oxide, which revealed to him that consciousness was not single but multiple, and in his psychical researches with the gifted Boston medium Mrs. Leonara E. Piper, which convinced him that consciousness cannot be reduced to material processes. James approached all of these wild facts with great philosophical seriousness and what he himself called a "radical empiricism," that is, a faithfulness to the full data of human experience that refuses to ignore anomalies simply because they can not be fit into the reigning scientism of the day.

The history and cultural influence of a place like Esalen resemble as much the occult realism of Murphy's novels and the wild facts of James's radical empiricism as they do any linear or causal model of cultural change. That anyway is what I intend to demonstrate here. I intend to explore the wild facts and altered states of Esalen's history.

But also its reasons. Murphy, after all, has produced as many analytical pages as he has occult ones, and Esalen's relationship to the university has always been a very intimate one. Indeed, the story of Esalen is very much a living out in the realm of elite and popular culture some of the deepest implications of what many scholars of religion have long taught and thought in their classrooms. The Esalen "story" (or *mythos*), in other words, encodes and expresses the intellectual "theory" (or *logos*), if not always in exactly the way that this or that academic might prefer.

Such a thesis will be counterintuitive for many, but it is quite easy to establish historically. To begin with, Esalen's invitational conferences, which go back to its founding and have consistently attracted both world-class scientists and humanist scholars, echo and develop in some fascinating ways the more well-known Eranos conferences led by C. G. Jung in the early countercultural heart of Europe (that is, Ascona, Switzerland) in the first half of the twentieth century. The latter Eranos meetings, by all accounts, had a major impact on the comparative study of religion.[2] Eranos and Esalen are related European and American countercultural weavings of radical religious experimentation, technical scholarship, and popular culture that provided the intellectual substance for broad cultural transformations: Eranos for the comparative study of religion that appeared in American universities and colleges in the 1960s and '70s; Esalen for the human potential movement that built on the intellectual foundation of this same comparative method to fashion a new American mysticism. Key bridge figures between Eranos and Esalen, moreover, such as Frederic Spiegelberg and Joseph Campbell render this historical narrative of the transformation of comparative religion from European academic method to practiced American mysticism particularly apt.

The currents flow both ways. Much of the modern study of religion is a rationalized expression of the kinds of social activism and countercultural mysticism that have flowed through American life in the last fifty years. In effect, the altered states of the counterculture became the altered categories of the university.[3] It is no accident, for example, that the explosion of "comparative religion" in American universities coincided *exactly* with the counterculture and its famous turn East. Nor is it an accident that race, class, and gender have come to define much of the field. These, after all, were precisely the concerns of the 1960s via the civil rights movement, the sexual revolution, and the definitive birth of feminist and gay consciousness in that still reverberating decade. To the extent that intellectuals still insist on placing these forms of thought at the very heart of their critical thinking, they still inhabit what is essentially a countercultural state of consciousness.

The same counterculture, of course, also helped produce Esalen. It would be a serious mistake, though, to conflate the two. A broad view of this place and its people shows that the inspirations of Esalen well predate the counterculture, and that most of the institute's history—and virtually all of its social activism—came well after the counterculture had closed. I have tried to reflect this "bigger story" through a broader view of the place and its people. Earlier discussions of Esalen, including Walter Truett Anderson's classic *The Upstart Spring* (1983), naturally centered their narratives in the 1960s and '70s and focused on therapeutic encounter as the core principle of the place. This was the right thing to do in 1983, but it's only half the story in 2007. My story finds its deeper keel in the early 1970s to the mid-1990s, that is, in the years that witnessed the appearance of Michael Murphy's occult and analytic corpus and Esalen's psychical and political activism with the Soviet Union.

Which is not to say that this is the whole story. *Any* focus that provides otherwise unavailable insights also necessarily fades or blurs other important aspects. There is simply no way around this. A historian has to choose a specific lens and accept that one's vision will be both focused and limited accordingly.[4] For my own part, I have chosen to approach Esalen as an American mystical tradition that "changed the rules of the game." Those who made Esalen recognized that the deepest problems of the world could not be solved by moving the religious pieces around on the board here or there, or by pointing a finger at this or that player. The problem was not the players. The problem was *the religious game itself.* The old rules had to go. Esalen thus chose to operate with modern democratic principles, individualist values, a celebration of science, secular notions of religion as a primarily private affair of personal choice and creativity, and socially liberal agendas, all of which together effectively set it apart from any traditional religious system in either the West or Asia. In the enigmatic phrase of Frederic Spiegelberg, Murphy's professor of comparative religion at Stanford University in the '50s, Esalen set out to embody a "religion of no religion."[5]

The Religion of No Religion

Which is also the religion of all religions. The paradox is a common one in the history of religions, where it is usually found in a select number of individuals whom we have come to call "mystics." One thinks here, for example, of the medieval Muslim philosopher, Ibn al-Arabi, and his celebration of religious difference in the Christian, Muslim, Jew, and Hindu as the beautiful play of the divine; of the sixteenth-century Indian poet, Kabir, who worshipped the formless God beyond all sectarian categories; and of the nineteenth-century Indian saint Sri Ramakrishna, who embraced all faiths as effective paths to the divine. Closer to home, one might invoke the American poet Walt Whitman, whose erotic celebration of a kind of cosmic consciousness and shocking insistence that all scriptures originate in the human inspired him to sing in his *Leaves of Grass* about how "my faith is the greatest of faiths and the least of faiths."[6] Perhaps this same mystical humanism, the ground of all religious revelation, helped supply the base metaphors of his most famous poem, that of the human as plant and of creative activity as leaves. Listen:

> We consider the bibles and religions divine.... I do not say they
> are not divine,
> I say they have all grown out of you and may grow out of you still,
> It is not they who give the life.... it is you who give the life;
> Leaves are not more shed from the trees or trees from the earth
> than they are shed out of you.[7]

Walt Whitman was a poet of the future, not of the past. He is thus easily the closest in spirit, place, and time to what will become Esalen. Walt would have been at home on that cliff in Big Sur, and they would have loved him. But his and Esalen's profound poetic resonances with what came before, in both the West and Asia, should not be overlooked or underestimated. It is important to point out, for example, that one of Whitman's most famous interpreters, the literary critic Malcolm Cowley, invoked Ramakrishna and especially the eroticism of Hindu and Buddhist Tantra as the closest analogues to the forms of consciousness and eros celebrated in *Leaves of Grass*.[8] I will make a similar argument with respect to Esalen and Tantric Asia.

Tantra aside for the moment, figures such as Ibn al-Arabi, Kabir, and Ramakrishna, by refusing to identify exclusively with any single dogmatic truth and by assuming a metaphorical or symbolic understanding of all religious language, have been able to inhabit different existential positions within their own religious systems in which they could affirm that all religious worlds are symbolically "true" expressions of an infinitely expressive mystery that nevertheless overflows the social boundaries and relative truths of each and every religion: a religion of no religion; a religion of all religions.

What sets apart Esalen's (and Whitman's) religion of no religion from these earlier forms is that it locates itself within no single historical tradition and rejects the game of religion itself. Such a move may initially *look* innocent enough, and often, particularly in some of its recent New Age forms, it may often devolve into a kind of anemic anti-intellectualism that cannot apprehend real and important differences. But the potential deconstructive power of such a worldview remains powerfully in place, even when it is not fully activated. After all, from the perspective of ethnic nationalism or religious literalism, it is a deeply heretical move, since a religion of no religion refuses to recognize any boundary drawn on a map or inscribed within a political identity.

A religion of no religion is also deeply "American." Like the constitutional separation of church and state, which effectively carves out a secular space in which almost any religious form can find legal protection and so flourish within American society, Esalen's religion of no religion has no official alliance with *any* religious system. It can provide, like a kind of American Mystical Constitution, a spiritual space where almost any religious form can flourish, provided—and this is crucial—that it does not attempt to impose itself on the entire community or claim to speak for everyone. As an early Esalen motto put it, "No one captures the flag."

When successful, such a democratic pluralism ends up having a kind of secret metaphysical function, as people who live with other people with very different worldviews, none of which are privileged, end up realizing that *all* cultural systems are relative and constructed. To speak sociologically for a moment, the plausibility structures of the individual religious systems break down. They are no longer completely believable; they have become in-credible. People, in effect, see through them. Hence literalisms of all kinds are flatly rejected, not only because it is now patently obvious that they are not literally true, but also because they encroach on the freedom of this democratic mystical space and so endanger the flourishing of multiple religious symbols and forms. Thus we arrive at a second early Esalen motto and defining principle: "We hold our dogmas lightly." It is something of this same mystical secularism, this same symbolic understanding of religious language that so many Americans are embracing when they insist on describing themselves as "spiritual but not religious."

It is no accident that a similar move, now more rigorously theorized as an intellectual practice, lies at the heart of the modern comparative study of religion. A basic democratic dynamism advances through a simultaneous embrace of all religious systems as symbolic expressions and a deconstructive urge to deny ultimacy to any one of them. Indeed, so strong are the subversive analogies between the comparative study of religion and the mystical traditions that the modern study of religion can be thought of as a modern mystical tradition in its own right. Mysticism here is not some transcendent abstraction without political or moral content. It is the modern liberal West's, and certainly the Western academy's, most well-known religion of no religion.[9] Hence the Esalen phrase was first coined not by a traditional religious authority or a revered saint, but by a professor of comparative religion in exile from Nazi Germany.

In two previous works, I made the case for a particular symbiosis between traditional mystical forms of thought—in both the West and Asia—and the comparative study of religion as it is practiced in our modern universities.[10] Here I want to extend that project by exploring (a) how these two countercultural forces—mysticism and comparativism—have also flourished within American culture on more popular levels, and (b) how these mystical movements have drawn heavily on academic actors and ideas for much of their inspiration and direction. I also want to radicalize and politicize this project by asking what all of this might tell us about the spiritual potentialities of American democracy, not, mind you, about what religion in America is today or generally has been in the past, but about what it yet *might be* in the future.

Admittedly, my case here is more utopian than actual. What I will end up suggesting, after all, is that the deepest psychological, social, and spiritual implications of democracy are *far* more radical than any society—including our own—has yet realized. Certainly no major religious tradition of which I am aware—with the possible exception of a group like the Quakers—has been able to translate these potentialities into stable ritual, iconic, or theological terms. Thus even as we speak of human rights, of individual freedoms and civil liberties, and of the inviolable integrity of the individual, many religious traditions continue to obey, worship, bow down to, and piously submit to a whole panoply of divine lords and kings, so many oppressive monarchies in the sky.

Much of the planet, in other words, lives within one immense anachronism or super-stition, literally a "left-over" in this sense: whereas our political ideals have evolved over the last three hundred years into different democratic and egalitarian forms, many of our most popular images of the divine remain stuck in the political past and so continue to encourage and justify grossly hierarchical, authoritarian, and violent practices. Despite its many faults and shortcomings, the same cannot be said about Esalen. Even if it remains as only a utopian hope or ideal, such a dream prophetically counters precisely that which we now suffer: religion itself.

The Altered States of History

How might we go about imagining such a modern American mystical religion of no religion? And how can we write a history of Esalen in such a way that honors, or at least understands, Esalen's own understandings of history and cultural change?

Even otherwise quite rational philosophers of history understand that the art of writing history is not really about relating a series of external events and explaining their causal and linear relationships. Since the foundational work of Wilhelm Dilthey, humanists have understood that the goal of the humanities is a distinct type of interpretive or aesthetic understanding that works through the principles of intellectual consistency, explanatory reach, and aesthetic shock or beauty, not the rational or causal explanation of the natural sciences, which work through experimental verification, falsification, and replicability. Put much too simply, the humanist is after pattern, beauty, and *meaning,* whereas the natural scientist is after *cause;* the humanist is after the openness of *wonder,* whereas the scientist is after the closure of *explanation.*

This is all true enough and quite helpful as a beginning, but this initial severing of the humanistic and the scientific is definitely not the

FIGURE 1. Front cover of the first quadrifold brochure, September 1962. Printed with permission of the Esalen Institute.

mode of history to which most Esalen visionaries subscribe. From the very beginning, from the very first brochure featuring on its cover an infinitesimal calculus equation from Bertrand Russell and an iconic lotus from Buddhist and Hindu symbolism, Esalen has dedicated itself to the fusing or synthesizing of the spiritual and the scientific, of wonder and reason, or what an academic might call the humanities and the sciences. Science, after all, is also an expression of the human, and Esalen is first and foremost about *the integral,* about the whole human being, infinitesimal calculus and all. Bertrand, here, is as holy as the Buddha.

Those early brochures could have just as easily quoted British psychical researcher Frederic Myers, an author Murphy was just beginning to read as Esalen began but who would come to play a more and more important role in his vision of things as the decades ticked by. At the turn of the twentieth century, just before he died (in 1901), Myers wrote the following:

> Bacon foresaw the gradual victory of observation and experiment— the triumph of actual analysed fact—in every department of human study;—in every department save one. The realm of "Divine things" he left to Authority and Faith. I here urge that that great exemption need be no longer made. I claim that there now exists an incipient method of getting at this Divine knowledge also.... The authority of the creeds and Churches will thus be replaced by the authority of observation and experiment. The impulse of faith will resolve itself into a reasoned and resolute imagination, bent upon raising even higher than now the highest ideals of man.[11]

Esalen would pursue just such "an incipient method," just such a fusion of reason and faith into a higher gnosis beyond both the orthodoxies of science and the creeds of the churches. Certainly it would make mistakes along the way, become too enthused about this or that facile conflation of science and religion, but its deepest vision would remain as constant as it is understandable—to embrace and celebrate the fullest scope of human knowledge and experience, even and especially if these mediating fusions were subversive to both traditional "science" and traditional "religion." Of course, they often were.

To understand such a place, it seems wise to begin with a model of writing history that is as comfortable with the metaphors of modern science as it is with the symbols and myths of the history of religions. One, for example, that can employ the terms of quantum physics or evolutionary biology, certainly not as physics or biology per se (I am no scientist and claim no authority here), but as an interpretive strategy, a mode of intellectual beauty with which to interpret the final strangeness of who we are and how we appear to inhabit a historical space, a space-time, as the scientists—who are looking more and more like poets—now say.

Altered states of consciousness and energy, which are also often altered states of space-time (and so of history), are as common as the leaping whales and flapping butterflies at Esalen. There are many languages with which to express these events, but certainly one of the most common is through the Jungian category of synchronicity. Any history of the place, then, will have to come to terms quickly with the kinds of human experiences that are crystallized by this single term.

Synchronicity is a word first coined by the depth psychologist C. G. Jung, who fused the term, partly out of his correspondence with the physicist Wolfgang Pauli, to capture the spirit of those moments in a human life where some seeming coincidence signals to the person a kind of spiritual guidance or meaning (an "omen," if you will). Technically defined, synchronicity represents "a noncausal connecting principle" or "meaningful coincidence" through which the psyche establishes or detects meaning between what are otherwise presumed to be the "external" and "internal" worlds. So, for example, a friend, who will later confess to me his own profound homosexual orientation and its cruel condemnation by his beloved Catholicism, relates how he is always getting into minor car accidents and physical mishaps. As we sit on the church steps and he tells me about a bird that recently shat on him as it flew over, a pigeon nest falls from the bell tower and literally lands on his head. Neither of us quite saw it then, but the Church was indeed "shitting on him" from its own imagined heavens. It would soon be time for him (after an attempted suicide) to leave the Church or suffer more dangerous disconnections with his own deepest nature and reality.

As this example makes clear, synchronicity, very much like a dream, is both a physical and a linguistic phenomenon (and often an erotically charged one) that works through metaphor, puns, and symbolism that in turn require active interpretation. To employ the classical psychological language of early Esalen, synchronicity reveals the world to be a *gestalt*, that is, a meaningful whole that is co-created by a subject and an environment within a particular moment of awareness. A focused "figure" thus leaps from the "ground" of the total perceptual field. And "when the figure is present and the ground fraught with energy and excitement," Esalen teacher John Heider wrote, "all creation reveals meaningful interconnectedness."[12] Such synchronistic revelations are neither fully "subjective" (for external things really and truly appear to behave in meaningful ways) nor fully "objective" (for these meaningful ways really and truly require human interpretation to become meaningful). In a word, they reveal the world to be *nondual.* They are thus both subjective and objective, and they are neither subjective nor objective.[13] This is the Tao or Way of Esalen.

Such paradoxical events have profound implications for how we understand the history of a phenomenon like Esalen (or most any other religious movement, for that matter). After all, history is not experienced here as simply causal or linear, much less as random or meaningless. Rather, history is experienced as something fundamentally creative, metaphorical, and linguistic, as something through which the world is revealed as a mystery we interpret into being and are in turn interpreted by. This is why, I would suggest, within any experienced synchronistic moment, space-time looks very much like a text and physical objects begin to function more like words or symbols than like the lifeless objects we assume them to be. Birds don't just poop, and nests just don't fall from the sky within this sort of time: they *represent,* they *speak,* they *connect.* But only if we are listening and are willing to engage them as such. What we have in the end, then, is a kind of modern magical time in which human intention and the powers of the imagination somehow have real effects in the real world. We are back, that is, to the intuition that sometimes the world works as much like an occult novel as a mechanical clock.

There is another point to make here. Because the altered states of history's synchronicity rely so much on language and symbols, they are also often *literally* textual phenomena, that is, they are often connected quite directly to the reading of texts. Arthur Koestler, an author popular at early Esalen, for example, went so far as to claim his own "library angel," his term for all those otherwise inexplicable moments in a researcher's life when a book or passage appears, as if out of nowhere, to provide the next insight (I doubt there is a single intellectual who has not known dozens of such angelic irruptions).

So too, some of the most famous events in the history of religions were essentially synchronistic events, that is, lucky finds involving a passage or a page. Consider, for example, Augustine's oft-cited story in his *Confessions* of hearing a child's singing voice repeating *tolle, lege* (take and read) as he lay under a fig tree weeping over the state of his soul. At the song's literal prodding, he took up a text of Paul that he had been reading earlier and was struck dumb by the passage on which his eyes first fell. Few conversions have had a greater impact on Western history. Similar moments can easily be found in Asia as well. To take just one example, the great nineteenth-century Hindu reformer Debendranath Tagore began his own religious quest when he caught a page of Sanskrit literally flutter by him on the street, had it translated by a pundit, and was delightfully shocked to learn that it spoke directly to his own spiritual crisis over how to reconcile God and the world (which the synchronistic event had just done in its own symbolic way).

The reader, of course, is free to object to such musings and anecdotes. What cannot be denied, however, is that the history of Esalen is filled with similar synchronistic patterns, and that this is precisely how many Esalen figures "read" the nature of space, time, and consciousness (not to mention the practice of reading itself). Indeed, the category of synchronicity was so central in Esalen's early history and inspiration that Michael Murphy actually kept what he called a Journal of Synchronicities in which he listed all the synchronistic occurrences that defined and helped guide Esalen's early beginnings. Like Augustine and Debendranath before them, Murphy and his colleagues acted on their own altered states of history. And so they made history.

The Tantric Transmission

My own experience writing this book was punctured by both quiet and dramatic synchronicities, of such pages flapping by on the street, as it were. Synchronicity, then, was not just an object of study. It also became a subject, a mode of writing history, and an intimate part of my own interpretive and creative processes.

Fundamental to these processes was my own Esalen-as-Rorschach, that is, my desire to read this history at least partly through the lens of Asian Tantra. Here is where my bats-that-look-like-vaginas begin to appear. I am aware of this, and I certainly do not intend such readings to be taken as normative or exhaustive. Nothing would be less faithful to the spirit of Esalen than trying to locate the meanings of its history in a particular religious frame. I do, however, wish to make the more humble claim that Asian Tantra provides us with a unique lens into Esalen's history that can reveal—in a way other lenses cannot—some unusually coherent patterns and meaningful coincidences that deserve our consideration. In this, my interpretive strategy is similar to Malcolm Cowley's literary method with respect to Walt Whitman's Leaves of Grass: "Since the Indian mystical philosophies [by which he meant Tantric philosophies] are elaborate structures, based on conceptions that have been shaped and defined by centuries of discussion, they help to explain Whitman's ideas at points in the first edition where he seems at first glance to be vague or self-contradictory."[14] So too with Esalen—Asian Tantra helps us to see and interpret some of the meaningful structures and patterns of Esalen's history that would otherwise remain invisible, or simply chaotic, odd, and accidental.

Put differently, the Tantra is my own comparative magic, my own interpretive system of synchronicities, my own world-as-text. The clearest marker of this magic is the fact that the creative origin of this book lies not in any intentions on my part, but in the reading event of another human being, that is, Michael Murphy's reading-recognition of my first book, on the Tantric experiences and teachings of Ramakrishna—*Kali's Child*. Someone wrote that a writer does not find a truly great subject; a truly great subject finds him. Certainly this is how I feel about the present book. This being found, however, was hardly accidental, as both of our lives had been formed by a textual-spiritual encounter with a Bengali saint. Murphy's spirit had been awakened and guided by the revolutionary turned retiring visionary and metaphysical writer, Sri Aurobindo (1872–1950). Mine had been transformed by a textual encounter with the Bengali Tantric saint, Sri Ramakrishna (1836–1886). On one level at least, Mike and I understood each other precisely because we had been through very similar religious experiences with two different modern Indian mystics and subsequently had to struggle with very similar cross-cultural, ethical, and psychological problems as we tried to make sense of these experiences and the insights they generated in an American context.

In a word, we *recognized* one another, particularly in our parallel attempts to express something we both understood as a kind of imperfect but very real fusion of Western and Asian esoteric traditions that turns to the potentials of the human body as the most potent site of spiritual transformation and intellectual insight. Murphy followed Aurobindo's synthesis of Indian metaphysics and Darwinian science and drew deeply on his own occult experiences of the human body (the final black-hole of the present text to which all light-words flow but from which none escapes). He thus stressed the "integral" nature of his own "evolutionary panentheism" and the central role of the *siddhis* or "supernormal powers" signaled by this book's opening epigraph. I, on the other hand, was inspired by Ramakrishna's Shakta Tantra, Freud's psychoanalysis, and the gnostic empowerment of a single Night in Calcutta.[15] I thus stressed the erotic, noetic, and transgressive qualities of what the Tantric traditions call the *shakti* or "empowering energy." In the end, though, whether through Darwin or Freud, we could both see that such *siddhis* and *shakti* were parallel embodiments of a very similar vision and vocation. Hence our friendship. And hence this book.

It was this friendship in turn that provided me with some very specific insights into the ways that the history of Esalen can be read as an American moment in a much broader Tantric transmission from Asia to the West that different cultural actors have been catalyzing for well over a century now. Arnold Toynbee, the philosopher of history who gave one of the earliest seminars at Esalen, once famously predicted that when future generations look back on the twentieth century, they will understand that one of the most significant global transformations of that era was the transmission of Buddhism to the West. I am taking a similar, but broader position here: what is transmitted to the West in our age is wider and deeper than Buddhism; it is the Tantra.

But how in turn to define this Tantra? The term has come to mean something like "sacred sex" and has taken on distinct interpersonal and romantic dimensions that it probably never had in Asia.[16] Although I consider such cultural transformations to be entirely normal, the very stuff of the history of religions, this is not quite how I will be using the term in the present book. I intend something more metaphysical and more reflective of the Asian traditions themselves. Most of all, though, I am interested in exploring the intercultural voices that speak simultaneously in American and Asian tongues and so poetically, and erotically, create a third cultural space that can accommodate what Geoffrey Samuel has so aptly called "the attractions of Tantra" in the modern world. In short, I am not interested in historical cultural essences; I am interested in contemporary intercultural fusions and how the "visionary state" of California can be playfully transformed into the "Tantric state" of Kalifornia.[17]

And why not? Literally, the Sanskrit word *Tantra* refers to something woven together, usually an ordered philosophical and ritual system or, more simply, a *text* (which, by the way, also literally means "something woven," hence the English *textile*). For our purposes here, Tantra is an altered category that scholars of Hinduism, Buddhism, and Taoism have forged over the last century (but particularly in the last four decades, that is, since Esalen and the American counterculture) to describe a broad pan-Asian deep worldview that weaves together such local traditions as Hindu Shakta Tantra, some forms of Indian Jainism, Tibetan or Vajrayana Buddhism, much of Chinese Taoism and Mahayana Buddhism, as well as various forms of esoteric Japanese Buddhism, including and especially many aspects of Zen.[18] The doctrinal features of this super tradition have been debated endlessly, but I will adopt two classic definitions for my own Tantric readings of Esalen: those of David Gordon White and André Padoux. For White, "Tantra is the Asian body of beliefs and practices which, working from the principle that the universe we experience is nothing other than the concrete manifestation of the divine energy of the godhead that creates and maintains that universe, seeks to ritually appropriate and channel that energy, within the human microcosm, in creative and emancipatory ways."[19] For Padoux, moreover, Tantra is "an attempt to place *kāma,* desire, in every sense of the word, in the service of liberation . . . not to sacrifice this world for liberation's sake, but to reinstate it, in varying ways, within the perspective of salvation."[20]

To speak in Sanskrit terms with Padoux for just a moment, whereas ascetic Asian traditions such as Advaita Vedanta or Theravada Buddhism tend to privilege strongly the transcendent order (as *brahman* or *nirvana,* respectively) and consequently denigrate or renounce the everyday world (*samsara*) as illusory (*maya*) or as impermanent (*anitya*), the Tantric traditions tend to insist rather on the essential unity of the transcendent and the immanent orders and in fact often privilege the immanent over the transcendent in their rituals and meditations.

One of the clearest statements of this most basic feature of Tantric logic is from the ancient Buddhist philosopher Nagarjuna (and echoed in the dedication of this book): "There is not the slightest difference between the world and *nirvana.* There is not the slightest difference between *nirvana* and the world." The implications of such a claim are immense and explain much of the Tantric traditions' most (in)famous characteristics, that is, their turn to the sexual body as the most potent site of spiritual enlightenment and occult energy. Here we might paraphrase Nagarjuna: "There is not the slightest difference between the erotic and the mystical. There is not the slightest difference between the mystical and the erotic." The Hindu Tantric compound *bhukti-mukti,* also quoted in my dedication, affirms in just two words the potent unity of sensual pleasure (*bhukti*) and spiritual liberation (*mukti*). Once again, from the perspective of the realized Tantric practitioner or philosopher, "there is not the slightest difference."

Now what is so striking is the fact that the modern scholarly definitions of Tantra by White and Padoux, or for that matter the ancient line from Nagarjuna, could easily function as a perfectly accurate description of Esalen, particularly as it is has been conceived and envisioned by Murphy. These Tantric emphases on the mystical potentials of the human body, on a structured universe seen as the manifestation of divine energies and processes, on the uses of sexual desire as spiritual force, and on a type of salvation in and as this life and this world—these are *all* classical features of Esalen's history. Murphy's life-long interest in what he calls the *siddhis* or supernormal powers also fit beautifully here.

Perhaps the best way to understand this astonishing correspondence is to note that, historically speaking, Esalen sits at the very center of a broad countercultural shift with respect to the American reception of the Asian religions. This shift begins in the 1950s, explodes in the '60s, develops in the '70s, and matures in the '80s and '90s. Whereas the reception of Hinduism before 1950, for example, was dominated by a highly ascetic and monastic tradition like Advaita Vedanta, the reception of Hinduism after 1950 was catalyzed largely by charismatic gurus and powerful deities whose "countercultural" energies were fundamentally Tantric in orientation. So too with the American reception of Buddhism, which sees a quite dramatic shift after 1950 toward a warm embrace of Zen and Tibetan Buddhism, both fundamentally Tantric in philosophical orientation again. When I write of "Tantra" below, then, it is this entire twentieth-century shift, conversion, or Tantric transmission that I have in mind, not any historical variant or local expression.[21]

There is a further interpretive payoff here with respect to the traditional division of Indian Tantric cultures into conservative or "right-handed" traditions and radical or "left-handed" traditions. Generally speaking, whereas left-handed Tantric traditions (which almost certainly originated the lineages) are those that insist on the actual performance of the transgressive acts and sexual rituals of the texts and iconographies, right-handed Tantric traditions are those that have sublimated these same acts and rituals into internal contemplative exercises, pure spiritual metaphors, and elaborate metaphysical systems that still bear the stamp of the original erotic union but are now quite removed from any literal act or "polluting" sexual fluid. Thus whereas a left-handed Tantrika might really smoke *ganja* (marijuana), eat meat, drink wine, and engage in real ritual intercourse (and a whole lot else), a right-handed Tantrika can be a vegetarian orthodox Brahmin whose contemplative sexuality exists only in the realm of the icon or *yantra* (an abstract geometric symbol) he worships as a physical expression of the divine.[22]

Such a left-right symbolism is quite useful with respect to the American lineage of Esalen. First, it helps us to affirm and explain both the interconnections and the tensions that exist between these two schools of thought and practice at Esalen. For example, as we will see below, the main Indian influence on Murphy, Sri Aurobindo, was certainly a right-handed Tantric philosopher who renounced actual sexuality but nevertheless developed an elaborate metaphysical system deeply informed by the bipolar structure of heterosexual intercourse and the Tantric embrace of the physical world. On the other hand (pun intended), much of the 1960s counterculture—from its sexual revolution and psychedelia to its explicit and consistent borrowing from Tantric Asia—can easily be read as a left-handed American Tantric tradition. These two Esalen hands certainly did not always get along—tensions in fact abounded, and still abound—but there they were nevertheless, polar parts of the same single Esalen body.

Secondly, such a left-right symbolism fuses nicely with an indigenous ordering symbolism at early Esalen, that is, the Nietzschean rhetoric of the Dionysian and the Apollonian. Nietzsche called on the two archetypal Greek gods of Dionysus and Apollo in his first book, *The Birth of Tragedy* (1872), to name the two major tendencies of Greek mystical art and drama: the wild, sexualized, and violent ecstasies of Dionysus (of whom he proclaimed himself to be a gnostic initiate), and the cool, cerebral, and rational contemplations of Apollo. It was probably Claudio Naranjo, the Chilean psychoanalyst and eventual gestalt psychologist, who popularized this Nietzschean trope in the Esalen community of the mid-1960s, just after the community had moved out of its initial Apollonian phase of academic seminars and into its ecstatic Dionysian phase of body work, encounter groups, and psychedelics. The language stuck and became one of the main ways that Esalen actors explained to themselves the "opposite" but related currents that constituted the tensile core of their community and tradition.

Even Nietzsche, though, must become a kind of Western Tantrika in this Esalen story. Hence Naranjo himself pointed out to me that Nietzsche's beloved Dionysus and the Indian god Shiva (who is central to many Tantric traditions) share numerous characteristics and may in fact be historically related expressions of the same ancient Indo-European mythology. India's Tantric Shiva and Esalen's Nietzschean Dionysus, then, meet in places well beyond my own projecting mind. They meet (and dance together) at the left hand of Esalen.

The Enlightenment of the Body

Fundamental to most Asian Tantric systems is a bipolar model of reality that is also heavily sexualized, hence all those beautiful Hindu and Buddhist Tantric icons of copulating deities. In the Hindu Shakta tradition, for example, the pure transcendent Consciousness that is the god Shiva can never be separated from the occult Energy and mystical matter that is the goddess Shakti. *Shaktihin shib shab,* goes the Bengali Tantric saying, "Shiva without Shakti is just a corpse." That is, Consciousness without Energy is a dead abstraction. But Shakti without Shiva, Energy without Consciousness, is equally incomplete (and equally dead).

In my earlier writings, the fundamental polarity of consciousness and energy within the history of religions is described as the unity of the mystical and the erotic. What I call *the enlightenment of the body* is a development of that previous work, here extended into modern American religious history—from Bengal to Big Sur, as it were—and into the broader but analogous question of the relationship of mind and matter.[23] The elaborate witness of the history of mysticism (here the history of Esalen) renders inadequate the philosophical options of *both* dualism (consciousness/mind/spirit and energy/matter/sex are fundamentally separate independent entities) *and* monism (consciousness/mind/spirit and energy/matter/sex are the same thing).

As the psychologist and Esalen regular Emily Williams Kelly has argued so eloquently, what we need to be working toward is a model at once more paradoxical and more humble, that is, one that can recognize that precisely because our present pictures of both mind (through abnormal psychology and psychical research) and matter (through quantum physics) are so thoroughly surprising and frankly puzzling, we should also expect that the real relationship of mind and matter radically overflows our present philosophical options and psychological models.[24] Hence all those altered states of Esalen's history that are neither exactly mind nor purely matter, but somehow both, rather like a synchronistic event, an occult novel, or a supernormal power (*siddhi*).

My own approach to mind and matter also participates in another seeming paradox to the extent that it is both comparative and historical or, if you prefer, both universal and contextual. With respect to my comparative or universal convictions, I will suggest that the cross-cultural correspondences and actual borrowings that we can see between Asian Tantra and American counterculture can best be explained by one simple but astonishingly complex fact, namely, that both the phenomenology of consciousness as witness of all human experience and the anatomical, hormonal, sexual, molecular, genetic, and subatomic processes of the human body display similar dynamics and structures across all known human cultures and recorded times. This is why human beings in different cultures and times can experience similar, if probably never identical, forms of the enlightenment of the body. This is also why Tantric traditions can and do migrate from culture to culture: everywhere they go, they find the same psychosomatic base.

In no way, however, do I want to deny the relativities of historical context or the profound, even metaphysical effects that social forces have on human consciousness and the body. Nor, by the way, do my sources. The whole Esalen principle of evolution, after all, demands both an appreciation of profound continuity and real metamorphosis. Still, the differences and effects of culture and history should not blind us to the similarities and continuities, that is, to the fact that *context* literally implies a "weaving together" (*con-textus* or *tantra*) of *both* universal *and* local processes, and that every development is also a continuity.[25]

Here we might point to the fundamental Esalen category of *the human potential* and the ways that it implicitly recognizes universality (human), particularity (potential), and, above all, development. The more sophisticated writers of the human potential realize fully that the supernormal dimensions of consciousness and the body that they seek typically lie dormant or undeveloped and require specific cultural practices or beliefs (that is, cultural particularity) to be fully actualized and sustained. They also realize that, once stabilized in culture and the body, such practices tend to have permanent and long-lasting effects on future forms of experience. The principle of the human potential, like that of evolution, thus again demands both universalism and contextualism to work at all.

In this same spirit, it is worth noting that the enlightenment of the body I seek to realize in the following pages relies as much on the contexts of cultural history as it does on the universalisms of modern psychology, biology, and physics. More specifically, it depends on the European Enlightenment, the Oriental Renaissance (that is, the meeting of "East" and "West" over the last three hundred years), the historical experiment of American democracy, and the cultural dominance of "the atom" during the cold war. Through all of these paths, I seek to portray Esalen as what I believe it in fact is, namely, a utopian experiment creatively suspended between the revelations of the religions and the democratic, pluralistic, and scientific revolutions of modernity. As such, Esalen's enlightenment of the body encompasses something of both the European Enlightenment, with its emphasis on reason, individual integrity, and liberty, and the corporate enlightenment of Asia, with all those remarkable psychophysical techniques of accessing and cultivating contemplative states of consciousness and energy. Again, as with every other altered category of the present book, the enlightenment of the body is both of the West and the East. And it is neither.

These, then, are the altered categories of my four-fold art and storytelling: the religion of no religion, the altered states of history, the Tantric transmission, and the enlightenment of the body. Three of these faithfully reflect Esalen's understanding of itself. The other finds solid grounding in that same history but is fundamentally both a creative projection of my own creative processes and a comparative "term of art" of contemporary scholarship. Entering these four altered states again and again, I will argue that it is Esalen's religion of no religion, which simultaneously affirms and denies each and every religious tradition, and its turn to the universal and yet ever-particular evolving body-mind that, together, make Esalen one of America's most sophisticated mystical expressions.

II

Geographic, Historical, and Literary Orientations (1882–1962)

Slate's Hot Springs

HOMESTEAD, FAMILY SPA,
LITERARY PARADISE

As to whether the sexual and the religious are conflicting and opposed, I would answer thus: every element or aspect of life, however necessitated, however questionable (to us), is susceptible to conversion.... The effort to eliminate the "repulsive" aspects of existence, which is the obsession of moralists, is not only absurd but futile. One may succeed in repressing ugly, "sinful" thoughts and desires, impulses and urges, but the results are patently disastrous. (Between being a saint and being a criminal there is little to choose.) To live out one's desires and, in so doing, subtly alter their nature, is the aim of every individual who aspires to evolve.

HENRY MILLER, *The World of Sex*

Likewise they created among themselves a peculiar mode of discourse by which they call the act of sexual union "the joy of Paradise" or, by another name, "the way to the heights" (*acclivitas*). And in this manner they speak of such a lustful act to others who do not understand it, in a favourable sense.

indictment from the heresy trial of the Brethren of the Free Spirit (1411),
in Wilhelm Fränger's *The Millennium of Hieronymus Bosch*

Esalen is on the edge. Located in Big Sur, California, just off Highway 1 on approximately one hundred and fifty acres of stunning natural beauty, Esalen is, geographically speaking, a cliff suspended about one hundred feet above the crashing surf and kelp-congested tides of the Pacific Ocean. By all measures, it is a stunning place, replete with natural beauty and a certain physical paradox, partly produced by the proximate presence of mountains and ocean; indeed, the rocky heights seem to drop directly into the watery depths here or, more true to the place's primeval geological history, it is as if the heights rise up *out of* the depths. Henry Miller called Big Sur "a religion where extremes meet."[1] Indeed. The physical paradox of the land is deepened further by a simple, but somehow profound, historical and geographic fact: these, after all, are grounds that both constitute the very edge of the American frontier and look due west to see the East. Certainly Walter Truett Anderson had it right when he wrote, "If a place can have charisma, then surely this one has it."[2]

Little wonder, then, that Don Lattin began his recent history of the 1960s and the spiritual revolutions it wrought in the American soul with the appearance of the Esalen Institute.[3] The place and its history are indeed mythical in that deeper symbolic sense of which historians of religion and mythologists speak, that is, as "founding story" or "world-defining narrative." The place has both heralded and significantly advanced for many the establishment of a new world of meaning, a new vision of human possibilities, a "New Age,"[4] even if few can quite agree on exactly what this newness means or how this age should be brought into more effective practice.

What, then, *is* Esalen? The Esalen catalogs of the 1960s often included a brief mission statement at the back: "ESALEN INSTITUTE is a center to explore those trends in the behavioral sciences, religion and philosophy which emphasize the potentialities and values of human existence." A recent issue of the *Friends of Esalen Newsletter* defined it as "an alternative educational center devoted to the exploration of the human potential."[5] That is all fair enough, but it hardly does justice to the place's richness, and it leaves begging the question as to how to define "the human potential." Just about everything hinges on that single telling phrase, first coined by George Leonard and Michael Murphy in 1965.

How many times have I searched for some memorable sound bite to capture the essence of what Leonard and Murphy were after with those three words. It is surely significant that I have never found any, except perhaps for my little five-word koan or mystical riddle, "the enlightenment of the body." But alas, it will take me the rest of the book to perform such a paradox, so it is perhaps better to begin in the beginning, as it were, with the region's Amerindian and colonial histories and Esalen's more immediate origins in twentieth-century Big Sur literary culture.

The Esselen

The land itself is ancient, unimaginably older than any human habitation. Ten to fifteen million years ago the coastline was in fact some miles east of where it crashes now, at least until one of the area's infamous fault lines gave way and thrust up to the sky what Spanish settlers would call the Santa Lucia Mountains.

Big Sur. The Big South. Already we are in the realm of an obvious linguistic and cultural hybrid, this one of English and Spanish colonial origins. Historically speaking, this hundred-mile stretch of coast running between Carmel and San Simeon was named after a river that has been flowing for over a million years. The native Americans who lived in the area called it the Jojopan. The Spanish renamed it El Rio Grande del Sur, the Big River of the South.

Numerous Amerindian tribes, including the Costanoan, Rumsen, Salinan, and Esselen, lived along this mountain coast for thousands of years, probably moving back and forth from the coast and rugged inlands from season to season for fishing, hunting, and shelter. Burial sites have been discovered up and down the coast and dated with radiocarbon tests at about 3,000 years.[6] Other sites, however, are far older. A skeleton recently found on Santa Rosa Island, off the Santa Barbara coast, has been dated at around 13,400 years old, and recent DNA tests with samples from Monterey County suggest a similar general period, leading scholars to speculate that the theorized early migrations from Siberia and the Asian Pacific coast across the Bering Straits and down the west coast of what is now Canada and the United States probably occurred earlier than previously expected.[7] In any case, the archaeological point remains the same: the cultural origins of these original American cultures was originally an East Asian one. In other words, the East was here long before the West.

Rock shelters, petroglyphs, and pictographs have been found in the area. Distinctive "hand paintings"—abstract forms that resemble striped ghostlike shadows of the human hand—are particularly striking and have recently entered the logo of the Esselen Tribe of Monterey County.[8] Theories abound on their meaning. One of the most interesting involves an immense slab of sandstone that juts up near one of the main sites of the hand-paintings: it looks very much like a huge human hand.[9]

As for the Esselen themselves, local Big Sur legend has it that they used the very hot springs that are now enjoyed by Esalen's inhabitants, that they ate strange foods, mostly fruits and vegetables, and that they loved to go about naked. Some say the hand paintings are products of puberty initiation rituals involving the ingestion of local psychotropic plants. In other words, the Esselen were a bit odd in ways that uncannily resemble the habits of Esalen inhabitants today. Although there is good ethnographic evidence to suggest that the Esselen did at times go about naked, we are almost certainly dealing here with more of a wishful projection backwards than an accurate historical memory.[10] The truth is that the Esselen are one of the least studied tribes of California, that we know very little about their culture, and that what we do know comes primarily from the letters and journals of early explorers, missionaries, and settlers.

In any case, one thing is clear enough: Esalen was named after the Esselen. So too was much else. Michael Murphy remembers that, long before there was an Esalen Institute, the Murphys' Big Sur milk cow was named Essie and the local Boy Scout campgrounds was called Camp Esselen. It was actually Harry Dick Ross, a local Big Sur personality, who suggested to Price and Murphy that they name their dream after the Esselen Indians. There were certainly other possibilities. Murphy's grandmother wanted to call the grounds Tokitok Lodge after the alleged Esselen word for "the god in the springs" (*tokitok*). The very sound of the word causes Murphy to break into laughter over the term's weirdly appropriate English resonances (the baths are famously loquacious). He also notes a postcard from 1940 that actually carried the designation Tokitok Lodge.[11]

Michael Murphy's grandfather, Dr. Henry Murphy, believed that the meeting of three kinds of waters here (mineral, sea, and fresh) rendered the place nearly unique. In fact it was some kind of burial ground. Around fifty skeletons have been discovered over the years, primarily around the Big and Little House and up near the Middle Point House, always buried in the fetal position and looking toward the sea. Michael Murphy believes the Esselen worshiped and buried their dead here because of the natural "power points" created by the meeting of these waters. As a boy Murphy remembers that the land was full of arrowheads, spear points, mortars, and pestles, and that its greasy dirt was difficult to wash off—it was composted over the centuries from thousands of abalone guts that the Esselen Indians had piled up here.

As for the original Indian name itself, according to Thomas Roy Hester, "the rubric Esselen is probably derived from the name of a major village, perhaps Exse'ein or the place called Eslenes, which was the site of the San Carlos Mission. In any event, the early Spanish extended the term to include the entire linguistic group."[12] We certainly do not know what the Esselen called themselves. Like so many other cultural designations—from "Christian" and "Hindu" to "American Indian"—these native peoples were originally named by others.

The colonial past was a particularly cruel one for these native peoples. The first European contact appears to have occurred in 1602, when

Sebastian Vizcáino visited the Amerindians of the Monterey area.[13] When New Spain (Mexico) took control of California in 1770, these same peoples were Christianized, baptized, clothed, and acculturated into European ways. According to Breshchini and Haversat, the first direct historical reference we have to the Esselen occurs in a letter of Father Junípero Serra, dated August 24, 1774. It reads: "there are some who come from *Eslen*, called La Soledad, a place about halfway on the road between this mission and that of San Antonio, about twelve leagues distant from both."[14] On May 9, 1775, Father Serra baptized the first Esselen as Mission San Carlos Baptism number 350, "a man about 40 years old, in danger of death, married, the headman of the territory of *Excelen* and its rancherias, named *Pach-hepas*." "I gave him the name Miguel Gregorio," Serra wrote.[15]

Sadly, however, Father Serra and his comrades were not simply baptizing the native peoples. They repressed their native beliefs and customs, eliminated their spiritual leaders, used them for hard labor, separated parents from their children, and, perhaps most disastrously, unwittingly infected them with multiple diseases for which they had no natural immunities.[16] The Franciscans also attempted to impose a quasi-monastic lifestyle on their baptized converts. Women in the missions were often locked up each night after dinner to prevent any sexual activity.[17] Some accounts even have the Spanish priests and soldiers forcibly segregating the natives by gender and imprisoning them in cagelike structures in order to effect a kind of slow generational genocide. Whatever the causes, most agree that the Mission Era (1770–1834) saw a 90 percent drop in population among the local tribes.

In any case, between 1770 and 1803, estimates of the actual numbers of Esselen ran between 500 and 1300, although by most accounts no Esselen could be found in Big Sur by the time the place was homesteaded in the early 1880s. Alfred Kroeber, for example, estimated their numbers at five hundred in 1770 and zero by 1910 in his authoritative *Handbook of California Indians*.[18] This is probably too pessimistic. The Esselen are not completely extinct. But neither do they any longer constitute an independent culture. Indeed, even their Web site more or less fuses their identities with the Ohlone and Costanoan tribal nations.[19] By the time novelist Helen Hunt Jackson visited these populations in the early 1880s, most of the land had already been appropriated by the European settlers. Jackson asked the Bureau of Indian Affairs to protect the lands of the Monterey group, invoking the warning of a local parish priest who, speaking in code about a local rancher, had warned that the Indians "have their homes there only by the patience of the thief."[20]

Homestead, Vacation Home, and the Pacific Coast Highway

This is all tragically true enough. But these are not the only truths. In the words of William Everson, "that California is little more than an American exploit, something taken from the Mexicans, and that strangeness and the exotic between them sum up its relevance to the national experience, can never constitute the way [the Californian] sees himself. Rather, he feels that his situation as term of the westward migration places him at the center, rather than on the periphery, of the American experience." Put succinctly, "the Californian knows that the expansiveness of attitude in the West is simply the well-known national expansiveness carried to its ultimate."[21] And indeed, that is what Big Sur will become—the frontier of the frontier, if you will, the furthest edge of the spirit of the West. If the once wagon-wheel rutted Nebraska prairies where I grew up can be described on billboards and bumper stickers as the place "Where the West Begins," this California coast, where only the bravest and most hardy of the pioneers reached, can well be described as "Where the West Ends." This, in other words, was the final goal and destination of the American expansion and colonization of the West.

A Missouri native named Thomas Benton Slate homesteaded the grounds of what is now Esalen in 1882, hence the local designation of the place until the early 1960s: Slate's Hot Springs. Local memory has it that Slate had actually arrived in the region in 1869, brought there by the already strong coastal reputation of the mineral springs. He had come from Santa Cruz to Big Sur in hopes of a cure for his painful arthritis; he came, in other words, to be healed. The Esselen were gone by this point, and the bubbling chemistry of the colorful hot springs—arsenic grays, soda whites, and lovely blue and red coppers—were already being used for their therapeutic promise. Perhaps they always had been.

Slate owned the property for eleven years, finally selling it to the Little family in 1893. Tom Slate still lives on in memory and in the forms of the now immense nonindigenous eucalyptus trees that he planted on the grounds in the 1880s. The Little family was more successful still. They became prominent in Big Sur and now have a local state park named after their clan.

In 1910, the Little family sold the property to Dr. Henry Murphy, a successful doctor from Salinas, who, according to local legend delivered half the town's population, including a certain John Steinbeck. Dr. Murphy dreamed of establishing a European-style health spa down the coast at his newly purchased property. In 1914 he had two large claw-footed bathtubs shipped in via a Chinese fishing vessel to replace the previous tubs, which probably went all the way back to 1869.

Transporting bathtubs was the least of their worries. Who, after all, could actually get to a remote cliff in good health, much less in bad? At this point, it was a three-day journey by horse from Salinas to Big Sur, not an easy feat even for the most fit and hardy. Thus the cultural future of Murphy's spa would depend almost entirely on a single and still future engineering marvel: the building of the Pacific Coast Highway. Dr. Murphy would have to wait over two decades.

The project began in the south, just north of Los Angeles around 1918, when the technology and engineering art of building bridges and roads had matured enough to venture up the winding coast of California. The crews started there and worked their way north. Although they met many dangers, and although death by burial in a landslide was both a constant possibility and an occasional grim reality, their greatest challenge in fact lay hundreds of miles ahead, in Big Sur. Dramatic canyons, steep cliffs, and a young, shifting geological environment made work extremely hazardous here. Beware indeed a coast with road sections that would win names like Rain Rock Cliff and The Devil's Slide or, for that matter, a state that would become known as "the theme park of disasters."

Raining rocks and sliding devils aside, the crews reached San Simeon, the southernmost point of Big Sur, in 1921. By 1927 they were hiring prison crews, who could work for reduced sentences and/or pay. Professional contractors handled the heavy equipment, and the convicts did the brunt of the brutal back-work. Together, it took them ten years to blast, dig, and pray their way through the next sixty miles, as other crews worked their way south from the north. The southern crew reached the Murphy property in Big Sur sometime in 1935. By 1937, they had broken through to Carmel and the Carmel-San Simeon highway was finally opened.[22] In one of those light-hearted synchronistic moments that define so much of Esalen's history, the intrepid truck driver who first braved his way through the pass with a load of dynamite had a familiar name: Michael Murphy.

Archetype West: California as a Literary Event

Both the image of the rough homesteading mountain man and the tough prison highway crews risking their lives for a road, a bit of money, and some real outdoor freedom would come to define the Outlaw Country image of Big Sur and, subsequently, the radical spiritualities of experimentation, psychological risk, and psychedelic transgression of early Esalen. Much of this early homesteading and criminal culture, however, would first be filtered through and transformed by the "obscene" eroticism, nature mysticism, experimental poetry, and adventure novels of a Pacific Coast literary culture defined by people like John Steinbeck, Aldous Huxley, Robinson Jeffers, Robert Duncan, Michael McClure, Kenneth Rexroth, Henry Miller, Lawrence Ferlinghetti, Allen Ginsberg, Jack Kerouac, and Gary Snyder. It is this same California literary culture that formed the cultural bedrock of Big Sur and helped eventually produce Esalen. George Leonard has said the human potential movement that developed out of Esalen will, in the end, be thought of as a literary movement, since so many of its central figures were first and foremost writers. Certainly its earliest roots run deep in precisely these literary and poetic directions.

And in Asian ones. The Beat poets Ginsberg, Kerouac, and Snyder all turned to different forms of Buddhism to develop and express their artistic gifts. In some sense, the Buddhist writer Alan Watts—brought out to California by Frederic Spiegelberg, Murphy's Stanford mentor—was the Beats' initial guru here, if certainly not their final master.[23] Another Englishman, William Blake, the radical poet and visionary, also played a special role in this era, despite the fact that he had been dead for over a hundred years. Huxley, for example, would name his "mescaline Bible" (*The Doors of Perception*) after a single line from Blake's stunning *The Marriage of Heaven and Hell* (1793). More Blakean still, Ginsberg came to his poetic vocation in an altered state of consciousness and energy in which he believed he became possessed by the spirit of the English bard. Induced by "a sort of dull postorgasmic blankness resulting from his having read Blake's poetry while he was idly masturbating," the young Columbia student claimed that he heard Blake recite one of his poems through his own voice and so call him to his own vatic vocation as "howling" muse and prophet of the coming counterculture—an altered state of history, if ever there was one.[24]

Ginsberg was hardly alone in his mystically induced poetic convictions. The poet William Everson, who participated in the same regional literary culture, identifies a literary genre he calls Archetype West, his term for the muse or genius of the American West that came to possess the cultural figure of the creative writer in order to forge a unique regional spirit of expansiveness, pantheism, eroticism, and radical artistic freedom. For Everson, at least, such forces are an expression of both "the mystery of place"[25] and the spiritual implications of democracy itself. Everson is clear that the political order of democracy tends inevitably toward what he calls Apotheosis, that is, Divinization, the revelation of the divine in the here and now and everyone beyond every ruse of traditional hierarchy, mediation, or official authority. Within such an immediate empowering experience, the author becomes, in effect, the model and extreme type of democracy itself, that is, his or her own author-ity.

Everson is also convinced that the impulses of such a mystical democracy are fundamentally erotic, even occasionally and especially obscene. Indeed, "recognizing the apotheosis of pantheism in the incarnational instance," that is, realizing the degree to which original Christianity collapses all stable distinctions between God, humanity, and nature, Everson himself left his California literary world for the confines of a Dominican monastery, where he would pursue what he calls an incarnational erotic mysticism for eighteen years.[26] There he learned what I learned in a very similar setting, that is, that "the ancient aegis of erotic mysticism" found in European Catholicism "had not been effectively realized by any man,"[27] that is to say (in my own words now), by any heterosexual man.

How could it? The literary voice of this erotic mysticism was unmistakably feminine. God or Christ was male, the Bridegroom, and every soul was imagined to be his bride, a woman in relation to "Him." Historically and symbolically speaking, then, such an erotic mysticism was psychosexually possible only within the celibate confines of sublimation, be it of the "unmanned" homoerotic male or the cloistered heteroerotic female. *Nowhere* in the orthodox Western world do we ever find a male mystic sexually uniting with a female deity. Nowhere, that is, do we find a male mystical heterosexuality. The California writers, and alongside them Esalen, would help to change all of this, but they would need Asia, and particularly Tantric Asia, to catalyze such a heretical project.

Henry Miller's Garden of Earthly Delights (1944–1962)

Not that there were no resources for such a project in the West. There most certainly were. Western religious history is filled with erotic forms of mysticism, from the biblical accounts of having sex with angels, through the early and medieval gnostic "heresies," to the nineteenth-century American Oneida community of John Humphrey Noyes in New York state. Oneida converts employed free love and arrested orgasms ("male continence," as they called it) to re-create the Edenic state of Jesus's kingdom in which no one is given in marriage and everything (read *everyone*) is shared.

But such angels, gnostics, and erotic Christians had been suppressed, cen-sored, tortured or (in the case of Noyes himself) chased out of the country. Obviously, to re-activate something of such a love would require more than a little boldness, more than a little imagination, and more than a few cultural battles.

Enter Henry Miller. In February of 1944, the fifty-three-year-old banned author, fresh from his tumultuous break with the brilliant and lovely Anaïs Nin in Paris, retreated to Big Sur. In 1946, he settled near Anderson Creek in what was originally a shack for the prison work crews, and then moved, in February of 1947, to Partington Ridge, where he lived until 1962, when he would move down the coast, often to his great regret, to Los Angeles.

One of the first things Miller did on his arrival in Big Sur was visit the baths of Slate's Hot Springs, which he insisted on misspelling Slade's Hot Springs.[28] He loved the baths and wrote hilariously of their colorful characters, including a large and arrogant Indian gentleman who claimed to be of the famously tolerant and universal Bahai faith ("the *only* religion," he observed, with more than a little unintended irony).[29] Later, Miller would actually help rebuild the bath structures of which Henry Murphy had earlier dreamed. He would also do things like play ping-pong with a young Michael Murphy and slog three miles down the road to wash his children's stinky diapers in the hot springs: "To walk six miles with a bucketful of diapers is no joke," he once wrote. "Especially if it's raining."[30] Neither was getting the groceries and mail, which Miller did with a little child's car that he pulled a mile and a half up a steep hill until, by the time he reached Roosevelt's driveway, he had to divest himself "of everything but a jock-strap."[31] That must have been quite a sight.

Miller would also, almost despite himself, establish a legendary lit-erary presence in Big Sur that would stamp the place as a mecca of sex, banned literature, and political anarchy. Although much of this, as we will soon see, was grossly distorted for polemical purposes by Miller's en-emies, some of it was also quite true, even if the multiple bans on his books more or less prevented many Big Sur locals, including the Murphy family, from actually understanding the famous writer in their midst. Miller, in other words, was something of a public secret, and his censored works did as much as anyone's to transform the legal and cultural shape of Amer-ica's attitudes toward sexuality. Indeed, at one point, there were no less than forty-one legal battles being fought over Miller's *Tropic of Cancer*.[32] This same book, along with D. H. Lawrence's *Lady Chatterley* and John Cleland's *Fanny Hill*, all successfully defended by Charles Rembar, would

FIGURE 2. Henry Miller at what would become the Esalen baths, 1950. Photo by Emil White, printed with permission of the Henry Miller Memorial Library.

together eventually spell what one author has called "the end of obscenity" in the American legal system and lay the cultural and legal foundations for the Beat Generation, the counterculture, and the sexual revolution of the 1960s and '70s.[33] Henry Miller, perhaps more than any other single figure, was the grandfather of all of this.

But those victories would come later. As Miller moved into the Outlaw Country, he was himself still something of an outlaw. Hence there is something appropriate about his early stay in a convict cabin. Such a reputation would not fade easily, despite the author's weary frustration with it late in life. As late as 1957 he could calmly note seven of his titles that were available in various languages but still banned in the States. He did have a bit of humorous advice for the insistent reader: "As to how and where to get the banned books, the simplest way would be to make a raid on the customs house in any of our ports of entry."[34] So when Miller turned up in Big Sur in 1944, he created something of a sensation. Local bookstores dedicated entire window displays to his works, and the young Bohemian writers and surrealists who admired him were even called Millerites.[35]

For his part, Miller was not after more fame. He seemed tired of the constant battles over what could and could not be published, and he would warn the young writers who sought him out in his cabin bearing gifts that the "fruit of their labors" might well turn out bitter to their taste, regardless of the purity of their intentions or the skill of their pens. No, Henry Miller was not after more of this. He had learned to play all that "as a game," and to say *Amen!* to whatever experience came to him.[36] Now he was after some humble modicum of peace, friendship, love, and the reconciliations of nature.

All of this he found, and found in abundance, in Big Sur. This magical place was a true paradise for Miller, a paradise of love, kindness, paranormal synchronicity, and preternatural beauty that he found in Wilhelm Fränger's *The Millennium of Hieronymus Bosch.* Fränger was a German art critic who had sought to interpret Bosch's famous triptych, including its central panel of *The Garden of Earthly Delights,* in the light of the medieval heresy of the Brethren of the Free Spirit.[37] The Brethren were known (or said to be known) for any number of spiritual and sexual excesses, including ritual nudity, the practice of free love, and the attempted sublimation of orgasm into mystical ecstasy (the *acclivitas* of our opening epigraph). Sex was no sin for Fränger's free spirits. Modeled on the divine image of Adam and Eve in Paradise, who were created to be "of one flesh," sexual intercourse for the Brethren became, in Fränger's words now, a "deification of the flesh," a "premonition of its divine nature," and a "mystery at once sensual and suprasensual" that could reunite what the Fall had since separated, that is, the genders and the human-divine order.[38] This was a kind of Christian Tantra that, had it been allowed to take root and develop in Western culture, could have well met the spiritual needs of the early Esalen actors and countercultural visionaries. Such mysteries, however, had all been effectively repressed, and so the modern visionaries turned East, where they could more easily find—or so they thought—what it was they were seeking, that is, a deification of the flesh, an enlightenment of the body.

Henry Miller had not yet made that turn East, but he had read Fränger. Hence when he sought to express something of his own enlightenment, he turned to Bosch and the Brethren. Indeed, he wrote an entire book on Big Sur that was inspired—rhetorically and spiritually—by Fränger's study, *Big Sur and the Oranges of Hieronymus Bosch* (1957). In the course of this text, Miller encourages his readers to go out and buy Fränger's book, and he uses both the Free Spirit paradise of love and Bosch's painting to explore his own mystical and occult experiences of Big Sur and its motley little community.

Bosch's triptych is relevant to our story, and not just because Henry Miller wrote a book about Big Sur through its oranges. The same painting appears in Michael Murphy's *Golf in the Kingdom* opposite the title page, here as a kind of playful satire. The frontispiece inscription claims Hieronymus Bosch played an early form of golf, and that his Hell scene is a representation of his frustrations with that game! On a more serious (but not too serious) note, Murphy has hung the same triptych in all of his homes—from Big Sur, to Mill Valley, to Sausalito—for over forty years now (since 1966) as an image that speaks deeply to him of Esalen, of its earthly delights, of its sexual-spiritual syntheses, and of its moral hells. I stood before the painting with him in his kitchenette (an oddly appropriate place, given the painting's clear conflation of food and sex) and asked him about why he has kept it so long. "Just look at it," he answered. "Just look at it. Those are clearly altered states, and highly erotic ones at that. There is paradise. And there is hell. It's just like Esalen."

Henry would have agreed. For him Bosch acquired a "magic vision" that "saw through the phenomenal world, rendered it transparent, and thus revealed its pristine aspect. Seeing the world through his eyes it appears to us once again as a world of indestructible order, beauty, harmony, which it is our privilege to accept as a paradise or convert into a purgatory."[39] For his part, Miller had chosen to accept the world of Big Sur as a Bosch paradise, as a Garden of Earthly Delights. By 1957 Henry Miller had transmuted his earlier pornographic sexuality, for which he had become so (in)famous, into a kind of panerotic nature mysticism, in which he could see that "living and dying are one, that all is one, and that it makes no difference whether we live a day or a thousand years."[40] The usual divisions of good and bad, of pure and impure, were no more in such a realization, and everything became transvalued: "When we are one with ourselves the most insignificant blade of grass assumes its proper place in the universe. Or a piece of manure, for that matter. Properly attuned, it's all one come Christmas, as we say. One thing becomes just as important as another, one person as good as another. Lowest and highest become interchangeable."[41]

Miller had begun to embody the religion of no religion. "I am a deeply religious man without a religion," he once wrote. "I don't believe in a god, and yet I feel that life and everything in it is holy . . . God is within you."[42] Here in this same nonreligious religiosity that recognized no "low" or "high," no "good" or "bad" Miller had found the secret spirit of all of his earlier "obscenities." They were all reaching for this, it now seemed, intuiting the fundamental unity of all human experience. Elayne Wareing Fitzpatrick is thus certainly onto something important when she describes Miller's later life in Big Sur as a kind of spiritual maturation in which the author settled down into a type of nature mysticism within which he could "do it with the cosmos."

Banned Books, Censored Sex, and "the Mystics of India"

Not everyone was terribly pleased about such free spirits. Ironically, most of the objections to Miller's corpus served only to increase his legend and help eventually make him a small fortune once the bans were finally removed by the courts. To ban, after all, is also to advertise.

Consider, for example, the appearance of an early polemical piece clearly designed to damn the literary likes of Miller and his Big Sur company, Mildred Edie Brady's *Harper's Magazine* essay, "The New Cult of Sex and Anarchy" (1947). The essay is remarkable for a number of historical and theoretical reasons, none of which Brady intended. Indeed, reading her enthusiastic descriptions of all that "sexual mysticism," which she vehemently condemns in such delicious colors, is an especially illuminating exercise.

Brady begins by describing the shacks of the numerous writers who had set up their shops and typewriters along Highway 1 as "an obvious rash on the countryside." Already we are in one of the traditional languages of heresy, that of the infectious disease. She then goes on to note that the logic-transcending language of poetry is the preferred medium of these writers, and she insightfully observes the centrality of sexuality and psychoanalysis in their worldviews. She even has an interesting historical thesis: the present West Coast bohemia, Brady claims, is a broad cultural reaction to the aftermath of World War II, just as the decadent 1920s were a reaction to the devastation of World War I. But there is an important difference between the two periods for Brady, and this revolves around the obscene ways in which the West Coast writers dare to unite sex and religion:

> These builders of the new Paris in the nineteen-forties would profoundly shock their agnostic predecessors of the twenties with their sentimental mysticism; for bohemia today is proudly religious. Its creeds, however, would certainly terrify any good Methodists.... [for] when they turn on the word "love" your Sunday School background falls down on you no matter how many times you may have sung "Love Lifted Me" in a Billy Sunday revival. Even less would a sojourn in the Greenwich Village of the twenties prepare you for

love as "the ecstasy of the cosmos" or for "the sexual sacrament"
as the acme of worship. Back in the postwar of World War I, sexual emancipation was stoutly defended and practically furthered
by the younger generation... but it never got mixed up with the
deity. Sex in those days was a strictly worldly affair and nobody's
business but our own. "The great oneness," however, is an intimate
participant in the sexual emotions of his worshippers. In fact, he
reveals himself fully only in the self-effacing ecstasy of the sexual
climax. This, they hold, is the moment of deepest spiritual compre-
hension of "the other reality," the one moment when there is living
communication between "the vital force" and the individual.[43]

Such mystically orgasmic climaxes—which Brady explicitly traces back
to "the mystics of India,"[44] that is, to a still unnamed Tantra—are also the
physiological secret of poetic and literary creativity, that moment when
the "fecund" or "orgastic" being experiences himself as the channel of
mysterious cosmic energies and forces.

Enter the renegade psychoanalyst, social reformer, and "mad scientist," Wilhelm Reich. By almost anyone's standards, Reich was in a category all by himself. Among many other astonishing accomplishments,
he managed, for example, to get himself kicked out of both Freud's Psychoanalytic Society in Vienna and, a bit later, Hitler's Nazi Germany, the
latter for trying to loosen up the authoritarian German personality with a
program of sexual clinics. Drawing on such educational experiments, Reich wrote in 1933 his *The Mass Psychology of Fascism,* arguing, in effect,
that fascism and the authoritarian personality are products of massive
sexual repression.[45] Predictably, the Nazis banned the book on September
4, 1935, along with anything else on "sexual politics," since such texts, according to the Gestapo order (#41230/35), "constitute a danger to public
security and order."[46]

I mention such matters here, not to dwell on the horrors of European
fascism, but to flag a series of important themes that will become important for us as we proceed: the intellectual presence of Reich among later
Esalen practitioners and theoreticians, the relationship between political
authoritarianism and sexual repression ("The more I revolt, the more I
make love," as the hippies would so succinctly put it[47]), the post–World
War II, cold-war context of most of Esalen's history, and the recurring
theme of the censored or banned author.

Mildred Edie Brady, it seems, was implicitly arguing for more, not
less, censorship. She identified Reich's *The Function of the Orgasm* as

the most likely popular text of this group of writers and linked its central thesis—that, in her words now, "all physical and spiritual ills, from cancer to fascism, stem from 'orgastic' (*sic*) impotence," that is, from a person's inability to achieve full orgasm—to political anarchism, the destruction of the family, and, one gathers, the potential fall of civilization itself. Brady, in other words, saw Reich, Miller, and the latter's bohemian followers as a real threat, and she was out to help contain their infectious influence on American society.

She was partly successful. One year later, Brady published a second essay in the *New Republic* called "The Strange Case of Wilhelm Reich."[48] Walt Anderson summarizes the essay and its influence this way: "it denounced [Reich's] subversive sexual and political ideas and demanded that somebody do something about him. Somebody did.... officials of the Food and Drug Administration began an investigation of Reich and the orgone accumulator—an investigation that led ultimately to that tormented man's death in a federal prison."[49] William Everson also points to Brady's earlier essay as the beginning of a kind of McCarthyism directed at his band of writers that would culminate ten years later, in 1957, in the obscenity trials of Ginsberg's famous 1956 poem, "Howl." Significantly, it was at this point that the image of the Beatnik was definitively born.[50]

Henry Miller, however, unlike Reich and Ginsberg, escaped Brady's prudish dragnet. He had, after all, been through this before—many, many times. He also had his own take on Mildred and his own ideas about how her *Harper's* essay came about. According to him, Mrs. Brady and her husband showed up at his house one day with his friend and astrologer, Gavin Arthur. Miller disliked the Bradys immediately and refused to offer them the same wine that he so generously poured for Gavin. Mrs. Brady was livid and, at least according to Miller, later wrote the piece for *Harper's* to get even.[51]

Which is not to say that there was not more than a little truth in her essay. Certainly her focus on sexual mysticism, the occult, and the psychoanalytic were all more or less accurate, even if her valuation of these matters could not be further from the experiences of the human beings she so phobically portrayed there. Altered states of consciousness and synchronicity were common in the Big Sur life of Henry Miller. Like so many other American authors, Miller was a firm believer in the occult dimensions of the human mind, especially as it manifested in the mysterious processes of literary creativity.[52] He certainly believed in astrology. He once had a waking vision of Madame Blavatsky, the enigmatic Russian founder of Theosophy, who proceeded to predict to him, quite accurately it later turned out, the traveling fate of one of his close friends.[53]

There are some beautiful passages in *Big Sur and the Oranges of Hieronymus Bosch* on Miller's experiences of occult dictation, literary inspiration, and even automatic writing. Miller confesses that "this business has been going on ever since I got the happy thought about the oranges of Hieronymus Bosch."[54] He tries to take a nap, but the messages start coming; first whole sentences pour into him; then paragraphs; then pages. The oranges sing. The painting comes alive.

It was a common experience for the writer, who describes writing *Tropic of Capricorn* as the direct dictation of a "voice" and then bemoans his fate of having to listen and write down whatever the muses sing: "When I began the Interlude called 'The Land of Fuck'—meaning 'Cockaigne'—I couldn't believe my ears. '*What's that?*' I cried, never dreaming of what I was being led into. 'Don't ask me to put *that* down, please. You're only creating more trouble for me.' But my pleas were ignored." The muses apparently loved raunchy sex, and so they continued to sing their dirty ditties to the astonished writer. And he, in faith and obedience, continued to write them out. Miller at least recognized that his lines were not entirely his own. "It takes courage to put one's signature to a piece of pure ore which is handed you on a platter straight from the mint."[55] Along similar lines, Miller also reports on a type of precognitive writing in which he encounters a Big Sur landscape that he had years before described in a book,[56] as well as a kind of synchronistic correspondence in which letters appear in the day's mail from dear friends with whom he had been remotely communing in his mind just then.[57]

Both Miller's erotic nature mysticism and his occult experience of literary inspiration would more than survive his death and wind their ways through Esalen's story, but only after they had been energized by the sexual revolution of the Beat poets of the 1950s, by the hippies of the '60s, and by the Asian Tantra that was only hinted at in Brady's *Harper's* tirade against California's modern-day incarnations of those ancient "mystics of India." Tom Slate had homesteaded the land, the state of California had carved out a road to it, and Dr. Murphy had developed the property. But it was Wilhelm Reich, Henry Miller (with a little Hieronymus Bosch), the Buddhist Beats, and all those erotic mystical poets who laid the literary, psychological, and visionary foundations for what would now become Esalen.

III

The Empowerment of the Founders (1950-1960)

The Professor and the Saint

THE EARLY INSPIRATIONS OF MICHAEL MURPHY

Wisdom never puts enmity anywhere. All those pointless cockfights between Man and Nature, between Nature and God, between the Flesh and the Spirit! Wisdom doesn't make those insane separations.... Darwin took the old [totemic Wisdom] and raised it to the level of biology... And now it's up to us to take another half turn up the spiral.... The new conscious Wisdom—the kind of Wisdom that was prophetically glimpsed in Zen and Taoism and Tantra—is biological theory realized in living practice, is Darwinism raised to the level of compassion and spiritual insight.

ALDOUS HUXLEY, *Island*

Given Esalen's natural beauty and the centuries-long presence of the coastal Amerindians, one would think the initial inspirations for the place must have taken place somewhere on these Edenic grounds—on the crashing beach, perhaps, or in the ancient forest, or at least before a spectacular sunset... or something.

And one would be quite wrong. In fact, one of the earliest and most important events in Esalen's prehistory, an event without which Esalen would have never been, occurred in a large university lecture hall. It was April, the spring quarter of 1950, the second day of classes to be exact, and a young Stanford sophomore and fraternity brother named Michael Murphy was sitting in the wrong classroom. Cubberly Auditorium was supposed to be the place for a social psychology class, but there had been a room change, and what the young Murphy was actually sitting in was Frederic Spiegelberg's popular comparative religion course. Indeed, this particular course was so popular that Spiegelberg needed a large auditorium to hold all those who showed up the first day, hence the last-minute switch. "I'm just going to stay here and listen to the guy," Murphy thought to himself. That decision would turn out to be one of the most important of his life. It all began, in other words, with a bit of good luck, providential guidance, or, if you prefer, a scheduling mistake.

From a Walk in the Wheat to the Religion of No Religion (1917–1948)

Oddly, however, the experiences that Murphy would later have with Spiegelberg in that lecture hall had everything to do with nature, or more precisely, with a powerful form of nature mysticism that had erupted in a young Spiegelberg in 1917 when he had been a theology student thirty-three years earlier. Frederic Spiegelberg (1897–1994) came from a wealthy aristocratic family. He was one of a generation of talented intellectuals who fled Hitler's Germany for safe haven in the American university system. Spiegelberg finally got out in 1937, four years after his close friend and older colleague, Paul Tillich, had fled before him.

The Nazis at this point were sending thought police to academic conferences. Spiegelberg was warned by some friends not to attend a particular conference. He went anyway. When he returned, his university president called him in and fired him on the spot. He had just a few hours to clear out his office. He fled Germany soon after. It was Tillich who arranged for his employment in the American university system. It was Tillich again who eventually introduced him to the woman who would become his wife, a beautiful dancer named Rose Muhlemann. Finally, it was Tillich who gave Spiegelberg his life-long language of the Ground of Being and helped him to answer, or at least better address, the mysterious question he remembers his mother always asking when he was a boy: Why? Why is there anything at all? Why is there not nothing?[1]

All of this life-threatening censorship and personal romance would come later, though. In 1917, Frederic Spiegelberg was, very much like Michael Murphy in 1950—a young man in search of a more adequate and deeper understanding of God. More specifically, he was studying Latin theology at the University of Holland and, in the process, losing his simple Christian faith to the rigors of thought. One bright spring day, he took a walk through a wheat field laced with blue corn flowers and red poppies. The clouds shone brightly above him, and the field was filled with bird song. Like so many other altered states of Esalen's history, what happened on this walk would profoundly affect, like lightning in one blow, both the rest of Spiegelberg's life and, indirectly through him, much of the early inspiration of Esalen. We can piece together the event through two sources: a recorded lecture Spiegelberg gave in Steve Donovan's San Francisco apartment on January 24, 1983, and an earlier textual account of the same experience that Spiegelberg camouflaged in the form of a thought experiment involving a boy walking along a seashore.

The earlier textual account occurs in the second chapter of Spiegelberg's *The Religion of No-Religion* (1948). The story is structurally bracketed by two poems: the first by Rainer Maria Rilke, whom the young Spiegelberg seems to have been reading intently at the time; the second a Bengali song translated by Rabindranath Tagore from the Baul tradition, a highly eclectic spiritual lineage deeply informed by Tantric ideas and practices. I suspect strongly that it was the Rilke poem that synchronistically connected to the events of the walk, which in turn led to a Tantric destination, here a Bengali Baul song. We are back, in other words, to a kind of literary or poetic occultism grounded in a nature mysticism and richly resonant with the "mystics of India." In Rilke's lines is a kind of German foreshadowing of the later Big Sur bohemians. They read

> All will again be great and Mighty
> And no churches which clasp Him tight
> As though a fugitive, then wail over Him
> As over a captive and wounded deer

Spiegelberg follows these lines with a thought-experiment, a third-person account of his own mystical experience in 1917. "I see a boy running along the seashore, across meadows and green fields, looking at trees and bushes," he begins, noting in particular the boy's recent reading "for the first time some songs of the mystic poet Rainer Maria Rilke." As the ideas of the visionary poet fill the young man's heart and the bright swirling clouds overhead delight him, something begins to happen. An altered state erupts and enters remembered and now recorded history, coming to inform, shape, and guide it. Here is how Spiegelberg put it:

> His usual, every-day consciousness has vanished, and he feels instead something deep, something holy. He calls it his higher Self. And this, his new, better transmuted Ego, feels in the so-called world nothing but holiness. These waves of the ocean and the blowing of the wind are the voice of God; all these flowers and trees are full of his glory; like Moses he sees each bush burning in sacred fire, and like the mystic shoe-maker, Jakob Boehme, after having looked for a long time at his shoe-maker's globe, he sees the bright glance of

some super-cosmic sun shining from the centre of every creature around him. This whole reality has become perfect and holy. Secular life has faded away, or it has changed to some better life, more real and bright now that the former things have passed away.

Then, while still enjoying God's glory in everything that is, something stops him in his tracks, something both religious and disturbing, something that recalls the Rilke poem:

he suddenly approaches around the corner of the road—a church. And the sight of the church gives him a shock. For what on earth is a church doing in his glorified world? What can be behind these stone walls, what means this coloured light behind the windows, and what these strange sounds of music which reach his ears? All the world around has been holy, has been God's eternal nature, has been His face and His expression. Therefore—and this is what shocks him— if there is really anything else, anything peculiar behind those walls, it could only be a matter outside God, in contrast with, or even in opposition to this eternal bliss of the all-penetrating holiness.

"And no churches which clasp Him tight . . ." After having deconstructed and rejected the Christian church, Spiegelberg proceeds to quote a Baul song on a similar theme. Through these lines, he denies as well that there is anything particularly holy about the pilgrimage sites of Mecca or Medina for the Muslim or Kashi (Benares) for the Hindu. There is only One who counts: the divine Friend, the Beloved, that immanent presence whom the Bauls knew and loved as the "man of the heart" (*maner manush*). And so those lovers of the Human One sing with and through Spiegelberg now:

I would not go, my heart, to Mecca or Medina,
For behold, I ever abide by the side of my Friend.
Mad would I become, had I dwelt afar, not knowing Him.
There's no worship in mosque or temple or special holy day.
At every step I have my Mecca and Kashi; sacred is
     every moment.

"Now such a feeling and such an experience," Spiegelberg tells us, has always meant the birth of the religion of no religion.[2]

The religion of no religion. It is at once a potent phrase, a paradox, and a poetic expression of Spiegelberg's walk through the wheat and existential collision with the gray church. It also will function as the theological foundation of Esalen, hence it is worth our time to dwell on its connotations for a moment. These five seemingly simple words encode an entire mystical or dialectical theology for Spiegelberg, a mystical theology that is also a comparative vision of the whole history of religions.

For Spiegelberg, historical religions have consistently made two major mistakes: they have consistently misread their own symbolic statements as literal truths, and they have traditionally devalued one side of reality (the natural world) for the sake of the other (the transcendent divine). Only rarely—usually at the prophetic beginning, or at the very end of their historical development—have the religions seen that the relationship of the divine to the natural world is an essentially paradoxical one, and that all profound religious claims are in fact symbolic expressions of this same paradox.[3] Hence, for example, the traditional Christian understandings of Christ (traditionally misread as a literalism applicable to only one historical individual) as *both* fully human *and* fully divine.

With these two moves, Spiegelberg in effect reverses the meanings of "orthodoxy" and "heresy," retaining the former for the mystical traditions that preserve a paradoxical and symbolic understanding of God and the world, and the latter term for the naïveté of the conservative traditions that mistake symbolism for literalism and dismiss the natural world as somehow distinct or distant from God: "Whenever it means anything else but sustaining the paradox and the questionableness of its own statements, orthodoxy means heresy."[4]

The revolt against such orthodox heresy, against such literal nonsense, is the religion of no religion. It is at once a deeply religious iconoclasm and, according to Spiegelberg, the fruit of a long historical development or spiritual maturation. The process begins with monotheism (which denies the gods of every other tradition), breaks out in pantheism (which sees that God "lives in everything and everywhere"), develops further in an abstract impersonal mysticism (which denies any ultimate divisions between self, cosmos, and God), and finally ends in what Spiegelberg calls *psychological inversion*, that is, a certain gnostic or mystical insight into how the gods are manifestations or psychological projections of the human spirit. "What has been treated in the past as a reality standing before men, becomes now an inner reality to the mind. To put it in one sentence: The background of any religion of non-religion, which leads always to the conception of new names for God, can be seen in a pantheistic feeling of mystic all-oneness which is formulated in an abstract and quite neutral way, and which means a psychological inversion of former ideas of some objective reality."[5]

There is no personal God here, no imaginary father or mother in the sky to talk to or, more problematically still, to bow down to. All such hierarchical systems are "demonic" for Spiegelberg. No, the entire natural universe is divine: it makes no more sense to bow down to a lord in the clouds than it does to build a church in the midst of a shimmering wheat field. Everything that *is* is holy. This is what Spiegelberg, following the theological language of his German colleagues and friends Paul Tillich and Martin Heidegger, would later call the astonishment of Being or, alternately and echoing Meister Eckhart now, the ground of Being beyond every god.

Paradoxically, this denial of the gods and this astonishment of Being itself "leads always to the conception of new names for God." And this too is central, for the religion of no religion may be a kind of mystical secularism, but it is certainly not an atheism that denies the essential holiness of Being.[6] It is a kind of fertile emptiness, a creative void that denies and deconstructs the old to create the new. It is the deepest source, at once full and empty, of the history of religions. As such, the religion of no religion sits in paradoxical tension with every religious tradition, at once functioning as its ontological or most real origin *and* as its fundamental denial.

Obviously, this is quite heady and dangerous stuff. Spiegelberg knew this. During his 1983 lecture in Donovan's apartment, he spoke openly about "our blasphemy" and the nature of their apartment lectures as a ritual of "unworship." He also spoke openly about how his theological studies in Holland destroyed his naïve childhood faith within a few weeks, and about the need to laugh at the illusions that exist in the churches. In 1983, in other words, he was still thinking and speaking in the afterglow of the Dutch wheat field and the foolish church.

Significantly, there are three historical traditions that Spiegelberg singles out as particularly suggestive of the religion of no religion: Zen Buddhism, which he always saw as a prototype of the religion of no religion; western alchemy, which recognizes that salvation is ultimately a matter of matter and the body; and Indian yoga, which recognizes, particularly in its Tantric forms, that the final temple of the divine is, again, the human body.

Spiegelberg, it must be said, was never comfortable with Tantra as a category. And, indeed, the term is not a particularly salient one in *The Religion of No-Religion*. However, many, if not most, of the Asian examples he cites are classically Tantric ones in precisely the sense contemporary scholars now use the term. Consider the Baul song Spiegelberg cites to explain the "young boy's" enlightenment on the seashore; the story of the Tantric adept, Siddha Ghantapada, who is enlightened through his seductive wife, child, and whiskey bottle and whom Spiegelberg uses to illustrate the radical holiness of all of existence beyond all notions of purity and impurity; his Jungian reading of Tibetan *mandalas* as "creative patterns of the soul"; his vague but real treatment of female blood and male semen as basic to Indian and Western alchemy; and, of course, the fundamental presence of Zen Buddhism as prototype of the religion of no religion.[7] Whether named as such or not, Spiegelberg's Asia was most definitely a Tantric Asia. Moreover, it was this same Asia that he saw as most appropriate for a Westerner, hence his later highlighting of *hatha* and *kundalini* yoga as "spiritual exercises which are best suited to the Western temperament" and his chapter title for *kundalini* yoga as "The Serpent *in Us.*"[8]

Spiegelberg also singles out two Western practices as approaching the symbolic and paradoxical gnosis of the religion of no religion: art and psychoanalysis (and by the latter he means both the Freudian and the Jungian streams). Both art and psychoanalysis, after all, recognize symbols as symbols, encourage the focusing of consciousness toward greater insight, and delight in the mystery of human creativity. In the end, though, it was probably artistic creativity that Spiegelberg most appreciated. Steve Donovan remembers well his elderly mentor repeating often a single mantra late in life: "Art is our only salvation." Perhaps this is why his descriptions of that initiatory walk through the wheat return repeatedly to a language of divine beauty "expressing" itself through the natural world. The cosmos *is* art for Spiegelberg, and the Ground of Being is best thought of in terms of a kind of infinite creativity or flux that must constantly destroy old forms of beauty in order to create new ones.

It seems finally fitting, then, to represent Spiegelberg in the present book not as a historical photo, but as a living work of art. The Italian artist, Antonella Cappuccio (who also painted Michael Murphy and most recently was commissioned to do a portrait of Pope Benedict XVI), had this to say about her vision of Spiegelberg: "He is *eros.* I felt so strongly his ability to embrace all that was sensual, all that was pleasure, his deep understanding of the flesh. . . . In him I saw a spiritual form of pantheism, or an erotic and an aesthetic form of spirituality."[9] Such is the nature of the religion of no religion—God in a vine and a good glass of wine.

Brahman! *A Transmission from Pondicherry to Stanford (1949–1950)*

Spiegelberg was also intensely interested in the meeting of East and West and believed that immense cultural transformations awaited the world

FIGURE 3. Portrait of Frederic Spiegelberg, 1993. Oil painting by Antonella Cappuccio, printed with permission of Steven Donovan for the Frederic Spiegelberg Estate.

just around the corner. He had edited, for example, *The Bible of the World,* an early source reader whose title implicitly challenged the exclusivity of Christianity by extending its scriptural code ("the Bible") into all the world's major religions. In 1949 he traveled throughout India, taking *darshan* (a kind of sacramental "seeing" in which the essence of the god or guru is transmitted into the viewer through the mystical medium of sight) with both the South Indian sage, Ramana Maharshi, and the famous philosopher-saint of East-West synthesis, Sri Aurobindo (1872–1950). He took *darshan* with Aurobindo at Pondicherry in South India, where he spent two weeks living in the saint's ashram.

Murphy has noted that Spiegelberg was never as influenced by Aurobindo as much as he was (though the guru's presence cured the professor permanently and inexplicably of a lifetime of nightmares), and that in fact he could be quite critical of the ashram, particularly for its sexual puritanism and the authoritarian style of the Mother, Aurobindo's spiritual partner and successor. Spiegelberg had nevertheless received some kind of spontaneous *diksha* or initiation from the Indian guru during the few seconds of the *darshan* he had with Aurobindo and was somehow able to charismatically transmit this energy in his lectures. In one of his prefaces he dedicates a book, "To Sri Aurobindo for having X-rayed the author for five seconds lasting an eternity and for thereby calling forth the atman [immortal Self] within as the only reality which he notices in any visitor."[10]

Although he does not tell his readers, this inscription is based on an argument Spiegelberg had with the Indian gentleman who was in charge of the *darshan* line at Pondicherry. There were 2,200 people in line that afternoon. Aurobindo was sitting for *darshan* just four times a year, from 1:00 to 5:00 in the afternoon, that is, for exactly four hours. Spiegelberg did the math in his head—that would leave each devotee only about 6.5 seconds before the guru! Spiegelberg tried to negotiate more time with the gentleman in charge of the line. Had he not come the farthest? Should he not get just a little more time? The man would have none of this, gently pointing out that if he were paying for an X-ray exam, five seconds would be plenty, and a few minutes would burn him severely. Spiegelberg was not convinced by such a clever analogy, but it turned out that the man was exactly right. Sri Aurobindo "X-rayed" him in five seconds flat, penetrating, as Spiegelberg himself put it, down to the very ground of his own being.[11]

The professor had been zapped. He had also received a transmission. And now he was about to transmit it in turn. Spiegelberg's comparative religion course in the spring of 1950 very much reflected this Indian trip and this initiatory event. The course began with the ancient Brahmanical scriptures, the Vedas and Upanishads, then moved on to Buddhism, Saint Paul, and Plotinus, and ended with the Hindu mystic Sri Ramakrishna as the exemplar of the unity of world religions and Sri Aurobindo as the philosopher of the future. Looking back on the experience, Murphy has no doubt that the course was designed to be crowned by Aurobindo and what Spiegelberg considered to be one of the greatest works of twentieth-century philosophy, Aurobindo's *The Life Divine*.

Murphy, it turns out, was hooked from the very beginning of that first course, from the Upanishads, to be precise. To this day, he considers Spiegelberg to be the "number one door opener" into that realm of the metaphysical, the mystical, and the psychical that would define the rest of his own eventful life. Clearly, that course was a kind of initiatory event for him. From an Indian perspective, Spiegelberg was the guru, the course was the teaching, and a single potent Sanskrit word resonating through the large auditorium was the initiatory mantra: "*Brahman!*" The moment Murphy heard Spiegelberg utter this single word, his entire world changed. He knew that, "it was all over." "Wake up!" Spiegelberg shouted to his class. "The *brahman* is the *atman*." Roughly, "The cosmic essence and the human spirit are one." Here is how Spiegelberg remembered the same event forty-three years later:

> In my lecture, I spoke the term "Brahman" with what one might call fullness of inflection, aided by the tremendous acoustics of the hall. Unbeknownst to me, this young Michael Murphy sat in the back, amidst the Hindi reverberation, wondering what strangeness he had happened upon. Some time later Michael paid a visit to my office to meet me, saying his life had not been the same since that moment. I offered my condolences, but he said, no, it was all to the good, and could he please study philosophy and religion at my direction for the rest of his academic career?[12]

The impact, in other words was both immediate and gradual. It would take about nine months for everything in the young Murphy's life to change.

Or evolve. This was not, after all, the first religious thought Michael Murphy had ever been moved by. His childhood was a happy one. The world was a good place to live. Perhaps this was one reason that by the age of fourteen or fifteen he had already begun to develop what he calls an emanationist worldview, that is, a philosophy that understands the universe to be an overflowing or spontaneous expression of the divine. Not everything, of course, was perfect about such overflowings. He had begun to realize, for example, that one cannot really cure a neurosis; the best one can do is transform it into something else, what he would later call, drawing on the yogic and Tantric traditions, a *siddhi* or "superpower." But that would come later. At fifteen, he may have been an aspiring Neoplatonist, even a potential Tantric philosopher, but he was also still a good Episcopalian boy, an altar boy no less. Each summer he would go off to church camp and return with the conviction that he wanted to become a priest.

Sometime between his freshman and sophomore year at Stanford, however, he formally broke with his Episcopalian faith. By his own account, a college-class exposure to Darwinian evolution was the "knock-out punch" (Murphy is predisposed to use athletic metaphors). But a resolution of the crisis was not long in coming. Toward the end of that first spring class, Spiegelberg suggested to the class that they read Aurobindo's *The Life Divine*. Murphy began reading the eleven-hundred page tome immediately. The shocks of recognition and inspiration were intense, like a "fire burning underground," as he puts it. But such fires did not burst into the surface immediately. That would take time.

Murphy went home for summer and played a good deal of golf. His younger brother, Dennis, was the first to notice that his brother seemed to be meditating as he played and called him a "golfing yogi." Toward the end of the summer, Murphy went on his usual summer retreat, this time with the Jesuits. The religious anomalies of the situation did not go unnoticed. Fathers Ryan and Cavanaugh, the retreat directors, asked Murphy to stand up before the group at the end of the three-day retreat: "We want you to behold Mr. Michael Murphy. This man is an Episcopalian. Behold him!" "Yes, but I'm also a Hindu," the young Murphy quipped back. "A Hindu-Episcopalian named Murphy!" exclaimed the fathers, as the room burst into affectionate laughter.

That next fall, Murphy, now a junior, enrolled in Spiegelberg's Indian philosophy course and met Duncan Bazemore and Rob Crist. Crist had organized a study group led by a handsome and extremely charismatic young man named Walt Page. Murphy spent time with this little intense group but also kept a bit of distance. It struck him as a terribly exciting but also somehow cultish group. Page would shoot himself in 1965.[13] Meanwhile, Spiegelberg was explaining to his students in more detail what he had only sketched out in the previous course. The Indian philosophical systems of Samkhya, Vedanta, and Tantra: one by one, he led them through the different systems. Later Murphy would describe his reading of *The Life Divine* in the context of these larger intellectual adventures as the "big climax" in which "it all came together" for him.

FIGURE 4. Brothers Dennis and Michael (with an Army buzz cut), on their parents' back porch in Salinas, California, 1953. Printed with permission of Michael Murphy.

The winter quarter saw Murphy quitting his fraternity (for, among other reasons, the fact that it was practically impossible to meditate there). He also dropped out of his premed track and took a private but formal religious vow that he speaks of to this day. Inspired by both Spiegelberg and Aurobindo, he had in essence converted to a new spiritually conceived evolutionary worldview. Accordingly, he made a vow to both himself and the divine by Lake Lagunitas on January 15, 1951, to dedicate the rest of his life to this Aurobindonian vision.

Not everyone was pleased by the young Murphy's transformation. Murphy's father, for example, was less than amused. Indeed, worried that his son would abandon a successful career track for what he no doubt thought of as eastern cults, Mr. Murphy, who was a lawyer, threatened to do something about Spiegelberg. The philosophers at the university, it turns out, would have been equally happy to see the Indologist go. As one university administrator explained to Murphy at that time, "Parents want their children to learn about these things, not become excited about them." Education was one thing; conversion quite another. Father or no, however, the young Murphy had been converted, and he was determined to persist in his newfound vow and vocation.

In the late 1940s, a wealthy gentleman by the name of Louis Gains-
borough had donated some money to help found the American Academy
of Asian Studies in San Francisco. He asked Spiegelberg to be its first
president. The two of them then approached Alan Watts to teach there.
Watts, who eventually became the new institution's dean, would later
describe Spiegelberg as the "*de facto* mastermind of the project."[14] Also
teaching at the new academy was a Bengali philosopher by the name of
Haridas Chaudhuri. Speigelberg had asked K. D. Sethna, an eminent Parsi
intellectual and poet who lived at the Aurobindo ashram, to join his faculty, but Sethna had just begun editing and publishing the journal *Mother
India* and so did not want to leave the country. Instead, Sethna proposed
Haridas Chaudhuri, a young academic star from Calcutta University who
had taken *darshan* with Aurobindo many times and had adopted his philosophy as a new form of Vedanta that he called *purnadvaita*, literally
"complete (*purna*) nondualism (*advaita*)."

Toward the end of the winter quarter of 1951, Spiegelberg set up a
table on the Stanford campus to recruit students for this new educational
venture. According to the oral legend advanced repeatedly by Spiegelberg
himself, Michael Murphy was the first to sign up. He immediately dropped
out of Stanford for a quarter to attend the academy that same spring. Dick
Price would also eventually attend. During this same time, Spiegelberg,
Chaudhuri, and Watts were holding colloquia every other Friday night in
a Pacific Heights mansion they had been given for their work.

After a summer of playing catch-up, Murphy was back at Stanford
the next fall and graduated on schedule in June of 1952. After taking
some more classes at the American Academy of Asian Studies, he joined
the army and was assigned various duties that he managed to transform
into *de facto* retreat sessions. He in fact spent most of his time reading
and meditating or playing baseball, basketball, and golf. He would get up
before reveille and meditate in the chapel in the mornings and return to
it in the evenings. Most of his tour of duty he spent in Puerto Rico until
he was discharged in January of 1955.

He then attempted a doctorate at Stanford in the philosophy department, but things did not work out. To begin with, the faculty was not well
disposed to Murphy's metaphysical interests. Even more tellingly, Murphy began to manifest all sorts of neurotic symptoms, including shortness
of breath and rushes of anxiety. He read these as meaningful signs, warnings that he was on the wrong path. He thus abandoned the doctoral
program to do what he had long wanted to do anyway: go to India. He set
off in April of 1956. On his way, ever the avid golfer, he stopped over in

Scotland to play a round on the famous links of St. Andrews, the legendary origin-site of the game. It was this pilgrimage and this round of golf that would later become fictionalized in Murphy's popular novel, *Golf in the Kingdom*.

Aurobindo had died in 1950, but the Mother was still alive and active, running an ashram that Aurobindo had called his "laboratory of evolution." Murphy stayed for about sixteen months (from June of 1956 to October of 1957), meditating, reading, organizing a softball team, and observing, with some concern, the deep ambiguities of communal life that these traditional hierarchical systems inevitably produce on the ground: spiritual monarchies, as we have repeatedly learned over the last forty years, do not do well with democratic values like radical individualism, human equality, and the freedom of expression. Long before the American guru scandals of the 1970s and '80s, Murphy was worrying about similar problems in the '50s. When he returned to the States and helped found Esalen, he would make sure that institutional principles were in place and were honored to prevent similar things from happening there. They did anyway, of course, but no one ever "captured the flag."

Still, issues of authority aside, there was something *there* at the ashram, something Murphy felt to be tangibly present. When he was finally allowed, for example, to meditate in Aurobindo's apartment, he lost consciousness of the outer world almost immediately and quite completely. So powerful was this contemplative experience that he could speculate in F. W. H. Myers's terms that the room was a kind of "phantasmogenetic center," or, in Rupert Sheldrake's later terms, that the master's long decades of spiritual practice had created in effect a kind of "morphic field" in that holy room. In a pattern that would become definitive in the American experience of these Asian spiritualities, serious reservations about the authoritarian nature of the guru-disciple relationship could go hand-in-hand with profound mystical experiences of the guru's occult presence and power.

Reading as a Transformative Practice

What did Murphy read when he lost himself in Aurobindo's *The Life Divine* that spring, summer, and fall of 1950? And what inspired him so in that room in Pondicherry, sending him into a blissful state of deep meditative absorption? What in the text saved him from his Darwinian crisis and inspired him to make a religious vow that he has kept until this very day?

The first thing that we need to appreciate Michael Murphy's reading of *The Life Divine* is a model of writing, reading, and understanding that is deeply hermeneutical—a model that recognizes a truly profound engagement with a text can alter *both* the received meaning of the text *and* one's own meaning and being (this, by the way, is also physiologically true in regards to the "subtle body" of the brain's neural pathways—reading is an embodied practice that literally changes some of the body's most subtle processes). That is, we need to recognize that the act of reading, far from being a mechanical, disembodied exercise of vocabulary and grammar, is in fact an immeasurably complex psychophysical event in which two horizons of meaning and being (the reader and the read) are "fused" and transfigured in a mysterious process that we do not, and perhaps cannot ever, fully understand. Elsewhere, I have referred to a *hermeneutical mysticism* in the life and work of twentieth-century scholars of mysticism—a disciplined practice of reading, writing, and interpreting through which intellectuals actually come to experience the religious dimensions of the texts they study, dimensions that somehow crystallize or linguistically embody the forms of consciousness of their original authors. In effect, a kind of initiatory transmission sometimes occurs between the subject and object of study to the point where terms like "subject" and "object" or "reader" and "read" cease to have much meaning. And this, of course, is a classically mystical structure—a twoness becoming one, or, perhaps better, a not-two. Reading has become an altered state of consciousness.

We must, I believe, recognize a similar hermeneutical mysticism in Murphy's life-long interaction with Aurobindo's text. Michael Murphy did not simply read *The Life Divine*. The text also read him.[15] To use a later Esalen terminology, deep reading became an effective transformative practice for him. From here on, Murphy would live within this text's metaphysical mutations. Just as importantly, Aurobindo's text would take on a new American life through Murphy and his own writings—corpus morphed into corpus within a life-long transformative practice.

Reading The Life Divine *as a Tantric Practice*

Because no text is as central as *The Life Divine* in inspiring the young Michael Murphy—or to the Tantric transmission that passed through

Aurobindo, Spiegelberg, and Murphy into Esalen—it is important that we come to some understanding of its nature and content before we proceed any further.[16]

Let me begin with the text as a text, and more specifically with one of its most obvious but probably least appreciated features, namely, the simple fact that it was conceived and written *in English*. This has, or at least should have, profound consequences for how we read and understand it, particularly since it was also originally written and revised during the four final decades of India's successful struggle for self-rule and independence from British colonialism, and this while Aurobindo was under intense surveillance from British intelligence as one of India's most dangerous men (Aurobindo was a famous political revolutionary in Calcutta before he received his religious vocation and retreated/escaped to the French enclave of Pondicherry).[17] Together, this English of the text and this struggle against the English suggest strongly that *The Life Divine* is *already* a cross-cultural translation, an encounter and negotiation, a boldly creative colonial moment through which Aurobindo attempted a metaphysical union of Indian spiritual philosophy and Western scientific and social thought. It is too easy to forget this.

Aurobindo's translation also happens to be a fundamentally Tantric one in the sense that his most important category, that of the Supermind, suggests an enlightenment of the body or "double affirmation" that insists on the nondual reality of both spirit and matter, consciousness and energy. This, of course, is precisely what I have defined as "the Tantra."[18] We are also very close here to Spiegelberg's insistence on the essentially paradoxical union of God and the world.

From a purely lexical standpoint, it must be admitted that we have to be very careful about calling Aurobindo's system a form of Tantra. He certainly did not write in these terms, and he clearly saw his own "integral yoga" as encompassing and transcending (that is, *integrating*) both the consciousness of *brahman* (generally associated with Advaita Vedanta) and the occult energy of *shakti* (generally associated with Tantra).[19] Still, it is patently obvious that this very integralism is deeply indebted to the Tantric traditions of India.

It is also worth pointing out that Aurobindo's understanding of the Tantra foreshadows all sorts of later Esalen themes. For example, he explicitly links his central category of potentiality to the sleeping *kundalini* or coiled serpent power lying dormant at the base of the spine that is "struck" by breathing exercises and Tantric yoga so that it can "straighten up" and ascend (or descend, for Aurobindo) through the central channel of the subtle body (roughly coterminous with the spinal cord), awaken various dimensions of human being, and finally unite with the divine above the brain.[20] Moreover, when he discusses the psychical powers lying dormant within the human mind, Aurobindo invokes a psychological concept that will become very dear to Michael Murphy—Frederic Myers's category of the subliminal self, which he then links to the *chakras* or "psychological planes" of Tantric yoga.[21] Finally, "psycho-physical methods" (an apt description of virtually every major technique that became popular at Esalen in the 1960s and '70s) and "Tantric practices" are analogous or related terms for Aurobindo, who freely (and correctly) observes that "all religions and philosophies in India which use largely the psycho-physical method, depend more or less upon it [the Tantra] for their practices."[22] The Tantric roots of what has come to be called Hinduism (a very modern category constructed during the colonial period of the nineteenth and twentieth centuries) do not get much more acknowledged than this, at least until the modern writings of scholars like Agehananda Bharati and David Gordon White.

There are good historical reasons why Aurobindo avoided any explicit alliance with the Tantras. We must never forget that he was writing in a political context and time period in which the terms "Tantra" and "Tantric" carried overwhelmingly pejorative meanings, partly because they had long been controversial within orthodox Brahmanical circles, more recently because they had been savaged by Christian missionaries who saw in the sexual rituals and animal sacrifices of the Tantric traditions the epitome of human depravity, violence, and religious folly. Murphy himself is clear that these same categories still evinced reactions of deep ambivalence and cultural embarrassment from Bengalis at the ashram in the 1950s.[23] Simply because we lack the centrality of the term "Tantra" in his text, then, does not mean that we cannot or should not use the term in our own precise ways; it simply means that Aurobindo chose not to do the same for his own perfectly sensible and very defensible historical and cultural reasons. He had his own audience. So do we.

What, then, constitutes the Tantric features of Aurobindo's *The Life Divine?* The strongest evidence lies in the text's explicit doctrinal content. Abstractly put, that content is consistently and rigorously determined by a dialectical worldview that identifies Reality as bipolar. Aurobindo invokes numerous terms to express this dialectical nature (the One and the Many, the Transcendent and the Immanent, Consciousness and Energy, Spirit and Nature, Being and Becoming, Father and Mother, Shiva and Shakti), but his vision is always the same: the ultimate Reality is best understood as a dialectical process within which neither pole can be effaced, denied, or renounced.

In another classically Tantric move, Aurobindo insists that desire is not something to be repressed or, worse yet, extinguished (a code word in his text meant to evoke the *nirvana* of Buddhism). Indeed, it is essentially divine, a manifestation of the evolutionary energy of the cosmos itself: "Desire is the lever by which the divine Life-principle effects its end of self-affirmation in the universe and the attempt to extinguish it in the interests of inertia is a denial of the divine Life-principle, a Will-not-to-be which is necessarily ignorance." Desire, then, is not to be denied. It is to be sublimated and fulfilled in the Infinite: "Desire too can only cease rightly by becoming the desire of the infinite and satisfying itself with a supernal fulfillment and an infinite satisfaction in the all-possessing bliss of the Infinite."[24] Not surprisingly, one of the three highest terms Aurobindo can give the nature of Reality is that of a capitalized Delight (*ananda*).

Aurobindo was not writing of "symbols" or "pure spiritual metaphors" here. He was speaking of a kind of (meta)physical pleasure rooted deeply in the human body, itself an ecstatically evolved expression of the cosmos. Indeed, according to the *Taittiriya Upanishad,* a text Aurobindo loved, *ananda* or Bliss is the source and origin of everything in the universe. This same cosmic bliss became, in the saint's own words now, "the base" of his practice.[25] Hence he did not hesitate to emphasize (at least in his private diaries) the physical, even sexual, dimensions of his own experience of this *kamananda* or "erotic bliss," "equal to the first movements of the actual maithuna ananda," literally, the bliss of sexual intercourse.[26] This latter description is from Aurobindo's *Record of Yoga,* a recently published two-volume tome whose highly experimental and nondogmatic qualities make it Michael Murphy's "new favorite Aurobindo." According to Aurobindo's biographer Peter Heehs, one of the most common themes of the *Record* is that of *ananda.*

"The secret," Aurobindo once wrote of the Goddess Shakti, "is to enjoy her in the soul as one enjoys a woman with the body."[27] He also clearly associated "the way of Ananda" with the "left-handed" path of Tantra.[28] And here he was being entirely faithful to the ancient Sanskrit texts, which in a much more explicit way link the bliss of *ananda* with the physical pleasures and ecstasies of the penis.[29] Though Aurobindo is clear that such mature spiritual events carry very physical dimensions (his entire system insists on this), there is no evidence that after his wife died he acted physically on what he called his *kamananda* or "bliss of sexual desire," which, as Heehs points out, often came upon him spontaneously, for example, while he was writing or walking.[30] Aurobindo's mature Tantric system, in other words, was a right-handed, sublimated vision rooted in his own occult body, its bliss expressed primarily through textuality and spirituality, not a genitally expressed sexuality.

Still within this same Tantric affirmation of the world and the erotic body, Aurobindo rejects what he calls the "refusal of the ascetic." A bit later he will criticize "the pessimistic and illusionist philosophies," almost certainly a reference to "the Nihil of the Buddhists" and to Advaita Vedanta's famous dismissal of the phenomenal world as *maya*, a word that can be variously translated as "illusion," "magical trick," or "perceptual mistake."[31] Aurobindo points out that such doctrines may often be necessary to the Spirit's struggling freedom, but they can have extremely negative social effects (for if the social world is an illusion, why bother?). Such doctrines are also dangerous and ultimately false half-truths on the road to the greater syntheses of the Supermind, that descending Power, influx, or catalyst of occult evolution that will eventually rend the veil between the subliminal Self and the surface consciousness and so effectively reunite the spiritual and material dimensions of reality within the human soul. The eventual result will be what Aurobindo calls the Superman, his term for a diversely gifted race of "gnostic beings" or "cosmic individuals" who consciously embody a full integration of Matter, Mind, and Spirit. None of this, the saint insists, annuls the basic principles of biological evolution. Such occult influences rather harmonize, steady, "and to a great extent hedonise the difficult and afflicted process of the evolutionary emergence."[32]

Aurobindo's notion of an evolutionary understanding of the body—here only hinted at in his notion of an evolutionary *ananda* or hedonism—is perhaps the most original aspect of his thought. Indian history is rich with dreams of transforming the flesh. Many of these are connected to the practice of alchemy—the attempt to transfigure the human body into an immortal one, often through hydraulic and pneumatic techniques of sublimation involving the sexual fluids and the breath. Aurobindo's writings certainly know nothing of actual sexual fluids, although he does appear to have been perfectly aware that his attempted spiritual transmutations of the physical body relied on the suppression and sublimation of actual sexual energies: "I for one have put the sexual side completely aside," he said on December 13, 1923, "it is lying blocked so that I can make this daring attempt at physical transformation."[33] He too, in other words, was something of an occult alchemist.

But Aurobindo's original contribution does not lie in the erotic or the alchemical. That was all old news. Aurobindo's original contribution lies rather in his synthesis of these ancient Indic systems with a modern scientific worldview. In essence, he transformed the earlier erotic alchemy into a Western-influenced, future-oriented, evolutionary mysticism—Tantra and Darwinism raised another half turn up the evolutionary spiral, as Huxley put it in our opening epigraph. For Aurobindo, then, it is the process of evolution, now rendered rationally conscious through science and gnostically catalyzed by the grace or "the descent of the Force,"[34] that will eventually produce the full integration of the cosmos in and as the Superman. This fully integral cooperation and communion with the natural and spiritual forces of evolution is precisely what constituted, for him, "the life divine." And for this, the Supermind and the Superman must evolve what we might now call a Superbody.[35]

In the meantime, it is the *siddhis* or superpowers, so prominent in the Tantric traditions, that offer us a glimpse of the occult biology of this mystical body and its emergent potentialities.[36] Aurobindo can thus write of "psychic" or "supernormal" phenomena that derive from "an occult subtle physical energy."[37] We are also told that, "our life energies while we live are continually mixing with the energies of other beings," and that "there is a constant dissolution and dispersion and a reconstruction effected by the shock of mind upon mind with a constant interchange and fusion of elements."[38] In contemporary terms, we are all in constant, if largely unconscious, telepathic contact. Here he draws on "new-born forms of scientific research" into telepathy and other similar phenomena (no doubt a reference to the London Society for Psychical Research) whose evidence "cannot long be resisted except by minds shut up in the brilliant shell of the past."[39] It is precisely this evolutionary mysticism and this interest in the psychical superpowers that Michael Murphy will pick up and develop in his own Aurobindonian ways.

If I may gloss all of this with a modern American mythology, we might better speak here not of a Superman but of the X-Men, those gifted mutants whom evolution has graced with supernormal powers that need to be affirmed, nurtured, and trained by the telepath Professor Xavier in his secret Westchester Academy. Oddly—synchronistically?—at almost the exact same cultural moment the West Coast evolutionary mysticism of early Esalen was introduced to the public (in the fall of 1962), so too was the East Coast evolutionary mythology of the X-Men (in the fall of 1963). Both cultural visions, moreover, imagined an esoteric or alternative academy where the human potentialities of mystical and psychical experience could be protected, educated, disciplined, and eventually stabilized within a set of transformative practices. Finally, as with Aurobindo's

Pondicherry ashram, both Professor Xavier's Westchester Academy and Michael Murphy's early Esalen vision insisted that it is evolution that produces these metaphysical mutations, these uncanny superpowers (*siddhis*) that signal the mutant forerunners of the species's superhuman future and its life divine.

So it was a professor of comparative religion and an Indian saint who rescued Michael Murphy from his Darwinian faith-crisis and set him on a path back home that would, very much like Aurobindo's system, always insist on the basic unity of the transcendent consciousness of *brahman,* which first overwhelmed him so in that Stanford classroom, and the ever-changing, constantly evolving *shakti* or occult energy of the human body, which he would later encode in his mystical novels and theorize in his analytic works. Such a vision was not simply a metaphysical union of the Supermind and the universe, of Shiva and Shakti, of consciousness and energy. It was also a potential cultural union of East and West, of India and America.

There was and still is a certain hidden radicalism here that often goes unrecognized. Michael Murphy is a charming man, but he is a revolutionary nonetheless. He insists, after all, that religious truth changes, that the divine itself *evolves,* that the human species and human nature itself is neither stable nor complete—we are a being in process, a temporary marker on the road to a much greater and fuller life. We are subliminal superheroes, X-Men and X-Women in disguise, our supernormal powers and true identities hidden even from ourselves.

Murphy has long remained agnostic, even skeptical about some of the bolder speculations of Aurobindo's thought, particularly those revolving around the descent of the Supermind and the nature of the Superman in *The Life Divine.* As William James might have said, in doctrines such as the Supermind a set of exaggerated public "overbeliefs" have replaced a set of private and perfectly empirical psycho-physical experiences.[40] Overbeliefs aside, Murphy has never abandoned Aurobindo's teaching that physical, cultural, and religious change are real, that the body's energies are involved as much as the spirit's grace in these natural and occult processes, and that this is precisely how the Divine progressively incarnates in the world. Hence his most recent enthusiasm for Aurobindo's private diaries only recently released as the *Record of Yoga* in which Aurobindo experimentally tests, affirms, or rejects thesis after thesis with a disarming honesty and a matter-of-fact empiricism. Murphy reads the diaries as a striking confirmation, late in life, of what he has always been trying to express through "fictional" characters like Jacob Atabet, that is, an experimental and self-reflexive practice that "holds its dogmas lightly" in order to advance toward a deeper and deeper engagement with the very real supernormal powers of evolution and the human form.

After reading my work on the Tantric dialectical structure of Ramakrishna's teachings, this is what Murphy first described to me in 1998 as his own "evolutionary Tantra." It is a jarring phrase, particularly for the cultural purist, but it captures well what I am trying to say here. Anachronistically speaking, it was through just such an evolutionary Tantra that Aurobindo came to early Esalen.

Buddhism, Breakdown, Breakthrough

THE EARLY INSPIRATIONS OF RICHARD PRICE

Madness need not be all breakdown. It may also be breakthrough. It is potentially liberation and renewal as well as enslavement and existential death.

R. D. LAING, *The Politics of Experience*

The situation is hopeless, but not serious.

DICK PRICE

When we turn to the life of the other founder of Esalen, Richard Price, we are immediately met with a series of challenges. To begin with, Price died in 1985. I never met him, never spoke to him, never sat in his gentle but firm company. Just as serious for a historian, Price did not write much, not even letters. This choice seems to have been an intentional one. When Eric Erickson asked Price how he could afford to be so available to everyone and answer all the correspondence he received, he immediately quipped back, "Easy, I don't write."[1]

This was no doubt the right decision given Price's priorities and considerable administrative, therapeutic, and business skills. Dick Price more or less ran Esalen from the mid-1960s, when Murphy moved off the grounds, to his own sudden death in 1985. In so many obvious and not so obvious ways, the Esalen of Big Sur of this formative period was shaped after the image of Dick Price.

But this reasonable choice to leave a legacy in action and not letters creates real challenges for the historian. How to explore a personality who is no longer with us and who left precious few historical documents to consult? Fortunately, the same man left some rather massive waves in his historical wake in the form of human memory, loved ones, friends, students, and associates, many of whom have much to say about the man and his work at Esalen. Chris Price, who was Dick's wife, for example, still gives gestalt workshops at Esalen, as do Steve Harper, Dorothy Charles, and Seymour Carter, all of whom together carry on Price's legacy. John Heider, whom we will hear more from later, should also be mentioned in this context. As should Price's son (through an earlier relationship), David Price, who helped administer the business of Esalen for years.[2] Also especially helpful for our present task is the fact that Dick Price has recently enjoyed the sustained historical attention and psychological analysis of one of his own students, Barclay (Eric) Erickson, whose dissertation on the life and work of Price stands as our only full study of the man's biography and work.

The latter text, like most psychobiographical studies, is controversial for some. Chris Price, for example, has expressed serious reservations about some of Erickson's analytic methods and conclusions, mostly on the grounds that any methods that rely on digging into the speculative past violate Price's own profound sense that psychological truth is best encountered in the immediate awareness of the present. Chris is certainly correct to point out this tension between Price's gestalt present, which he adamantly refused to interpret and analyze, and the psychobiographical past, which can only be a product of interpretation and analysis.

Having said that, it must also be admitted that the past is precisely the focus of the historian, and that no history can be written without focusing on a speculatively reconstructed past. I see no way around this tension. I can only proceed in a way that I hope can honor something of both Price's spirituality of awareness in the present and the psychobiographer's commitment to the meanings and forces of the past.

Family Histories

Price's father, Herman, was born on Yom Kippur in 1895 in Lithuania, at that point still a part of Russia. The family's name was most likely Preis or Preuss, and Herman was born not as Herman, but as Hymie, into an orthodox Jewish family and a strict kosher household. Hymie's father died when the boy was just twelve, and three years later his mother, Mary, moved the entire family (four sons and three daughters) out of Russia to America. They landed at Ellis Island in 1911, where their surname was changed to Price and Hymie became Herman. Erickson tells us that the main reason for the move was male survival: Jewish boys were being conscripted into the Imperial Army at alarming rates, where they were sent to the front lines and quickly disappeared in the slaughter of battle.[3]

The family stayed in New York City for two years and then moved to Chicago when Herman was seventeen. Herman joined the Coast Guard and then the Navy during World War I and returned from the service to work in business in the Chicago area. In 1930, he joined Sears and Roebuck and within a short time became merchandise manager for the major appliance division. Eventually, he would climb all the way to executive vice-president of the company. His transformation from Lithuanian boy in danger of an early and violent death on the front lines to successful American businessman in the heart of a prosperous United States was now complete.

Audrey Myers, Dick Price's mother, was born in Litton, Indiana, on April 19, 1895, and grew up in Auburn, Illinois, where her father owned a general store. The Myerses were of Dutch, Irish, and English extraction. Family members described Audrey as "extremely superstitious." More specifically, she was a firm believer in astrology, which, it turns out, made her very successful on the stock market. If her stars told her not to sell, she would not sell, even if her husband's expert advice told her otherwise. As an adult she was recognized for her strong will, and even her children later came to see her as dominating and tyrannical. But no one could dispute her investment success. By this literally stellar method, her estate would grow over the years and eventually exceed that of her husband.[4] So much for superstition.

Richard Price was born on October 12, 1930, in Chicago, Illinois, along with his twin brother, Bobby, by caesarean section. Their parents were both thirty-five years old at the time. Their sister Joan had arrived two years earlier, on January 9, 1929, via an emergency caesarean, a month early and at a mere four pounds. "Bobby was always the leader in our playing," Joan said of their childhood trio, "he took charge of the toys—and Dick and I were the followers."[5]

In 1933, though, two of the three children became ill: Joan came down with ethmoiditis, and Bobby, only three-years old at the time, was misdiagnosed and then suffered a burst appendicitis. Bobby did not survive. Within a few days, the little boy was gone, and the family was crushed into a kind of quiet despair that, by most accounts, was never fully worked through. Little Dick kept looking for his playmate; Herman retreated into his business affairs; and Audrey refused to process the tragic loss at all. As an adult, Joan acknowledged that the trauma of Bobby's death affected everyone very deeply, and that it "also served to emphasize the differences in my parents' characters."[6] In Erickson's reading, those same differences would play havoc on Price's character and later emotional stability.

As much as Herman was broadly liked in the extended Price family, Audrey was almost universally disliked. Since his teenage years, Price referred to his mother as "the bitch" and "the witch" for her rigid expectations.[7] David Price, Dick's son, recalls his father telling him about how his mother insisted on such an immaculately clean house that he had to back out of her kitchen with rags under his feet to prevent making any marks.[8]

Dick's father Herman had renounced his mother's orthodox Jewish ways and did not attend any regular synagogue services. Still, the German American Bund was on the rise in the States, and Hitler had come to power in Germany. The Prices reasonably feared for their safety and so kept a very low profile. In 1941, they even moved to Kenilworth, a wealthy suburb of Chicago, which forbade the selling of property to Jews. Audrey informed her children to keep their Jewishness secret and insisted that they join the Episcopalian Church. Joan was baptized, and Dick would take confirmation classes. Erikson reads this event as a protection strategy. Chris Price reads it as an expression of Audrey's own anti-Semitism and her deep concerns about image control and social status.

In the meantime, Price had become a real athlete. who excelled in both football and especially wrestling. He placed second at the Illinois State Wrestling Championships. In 1948, he graduated from New Trier High School and left for California to attend Stanford University. Looking back, his motives appeared clear enough: he wanted to get as far away from his family as he could.[9]

Dick Price's Buddhism (1955)

At Stanford in the fall of 1948, Price pledged Chi Psi and began to participate immediately in the rich social life of the university. He also had the luxury of beginning his college career with a new Studebaker his father had given him and a bank account that could never be exhausted: it was set up to replenish itself to $1,000, regardless of what the young man chose to spend. He began his studies under the expectations of his father and so chose an economics major. He would quickly switch to psychology, however, after becoming fascinated with mental illness and the ways that different cultures shape, address, and define such experiences. Today we would say that Dick Price was interested in ethnopsychiatry or cultural psychology.

His long-term goal was to become an analyst. To this end, he graduated from Stanford in 1952 and enrolled in Harvard's recently created program in social relations. Harvard was an immense disappointment. He had left Stanford's "rats and questionnaires" approach to psychology in disgust only to walk into Harvard's professional bickering and internal politics. When he criticized the department's workings in an exam, he received a C (Harvard code for F). He left at the end of the year, completely disillusioned and sorely confused. After a brief stop in Kenilworth, where he was quickly reminded why he had left the place, he departed for California again and enrolled in some courses at the University of California, Berkeley, including one with Carl Rogers. He was not impressed. He then applied for an army commission as a psychological tester and soon found himself in the air force. After basic training and a few initial assignments that bored him silly, he applied for a transfer to Parks Air Force Base in Pleasanton, California.

In the spring of 1955, Price enrolled in more courses at Stanford, including one taught by Spiegelberg on the *Bhagavad Gita* (literally, *The Song of the Lord,* one of the most popular scriptural texts of classical Hinduism). Spiegelberg worked his magic again. Until now, Price had shown no real interest in religion, but Spiegelberg's lectures sparked something in him: "For the first time, I began thinking there was something in religion; it was more than a system of deceit and enforcement of social rules."[10] Price, in other words, had begun to sense the deeper truths of the religion of no religion, particularly as it was expressed through Spiegelberg's interpretations of the Asian religions.

Spiegelberg encouraged his students to visit the Vedanta Society and to attend both the sermons of Swami Ashokananda and the charismatic lectures of Alan Watts. Price was moved, particularly by Watts and his unique brand of Beat Zen Buddhism and countercultural Taoism.[11] Price was, as he himself put it, "immensely impressed, it was like nothing I'd ever touched into."[12] These Buddhist and Taoist streams of thought, first catalyzed by Watts and the Beat poets, would continue through the rest of his life, flowing in turn into Esalen.

Soon Price began taking classes at the American Academy of Asian Studies that Spiegelberg had just helped found, Michael Murphy had attended, and where Watts was the principal teacher and dean. Price took a room there and began studying Buddhism in earnest, particularly the writings of the Theravada Vipassana teacher Nyanaponika Thera.[13] What appealed to Price, Erickson has suggested, was Nyanaponika Thera's emphasis on relying on personal experience in the absence of any external authority. In his own reading of Thera's *The Heart of Buddhist Meditation,* Erickson was struck by how similar it was to Price's own meditation practice. There are, then, some grounds to consider this text as one of the earliest teachers of Dick Price on the principles and theory of meditation.[14] Chris Price confirms this and puts the year of the Buddhist influence at around 1955, that is, while Price was still in the air force.

Price was also hanging out in the North Beach district, which had become the epicenter of the burgeoning Beat scene. Gary Snyder, Jack Kerouac, Allen Ginsberg, and Lawrence Ferlinghetti: Price knew them all. And everyone was attending Watts's famous lectures. It was a heady time. Looking back on it, Price could not help but notice that the North Beach Beat scene and the birth of his own spiritual practice emerged more or less together.[15] He certainly did not fully understand the latter. Indeed, much of what emerged confused and troubled him: "I just started doing the practice and all this stuff started to happen."[16] Moreover, no one at the academy seemed to be able to help him. Only the Beat poets, particularly Snyder, seemed to know anything about the experiential dimensions he was encountering in his meditation.

In December of 1955, one of his friends, a Chinese-American businessman by the name of Gia-fu Feng, came by the academy with a woman named Bonnie (Gia-fu would later end up at Esalen). Bonnie had studied at London's Academy of Dramatic Art and had grown up, like Price, in Chicago. The three met and went to dinner. Price was pondering the Buddhist monastic life and was still reeling from the emotional horrors of his early family life, which hardly put a positive light on marriage and what he described later as his "avoidance thing with women."[17] Still, during the dinner he heard an actual voice speaking to him in a matter-of-fact sort of way, "There is your wife." He would later describe the voice to Walt Anderson as an "auditory hallucination," and one that he argued with beneath his breath at that.[18] Whatever the point of his argument was, it didn't work. A few months later, in February of 1956, the two were married in an elaborate Japanese Buddhist ceremony at the Soto Zen Temple in San Francisco, the same temple where Price would sometimes meditate.

The ceremony was performed in Japanese. The best man was Japanese. The bridesmaid was black. The ritual was designed partly, Price later admitted, to horrify his middle-America Episcopalian parents who were attending but objected to the marriage (Price would also later admit that they were partly right to question the union).[19] The ceremony, though, was no doubt testimony to the early Buddhist influences on Price's own self-understanding. Also central here was the altered state of the original voice that informed him of the fact of his future marriage to Bonnie. Such an experience bespoke of what Anderson calls "a new concept of self," that is, an intuition that Price's "old self—the compact knot of rational ideas and conflicted needs he had heretofore identified as Richard Price—was only a fragment of a much larger being, who was stronger and smarter and not entirely trustworthy."[20] Before long, that larger, "untrustworthy" being would threaten to take over completely.

Dick Price's Taoism (1955)

If Michael Murphy's early Asian inspirations were derived primarily from the Indian philosophy of Sri Aurobindo,[21] it was the general nontheistic worldviews of Sinhalese Theravada Buddhism, Japanese Zen, and Chinese Taoism that attracted and inspired Richard Price. Price was not one for whom the idea of a personal divinity, of any sort, held much attraction. As Erickson put it to me, Price, despite his paternal Jewish background, was naturally drawn to worldviews without a personal God, particularly when they expressed strong unitive themes with the natural world. Seymour Carter has shared the same with me. In his mind, Price's lineage at Esalen was a Buddhist path of *anatman* or no-self, "no special status for anything."

Price's dedication to no-self has made it uncomfortable for Chris Price to witness the postmortem mythologization of her former beloved husband and the patriarchal theology much of it implies. Price has become a minor god of sorts, at least at Esalen, and this despite the fact that he found all such gods distasteful and ultimately unbelievable. Price wanted none of that. In Chris's own words, "God" for Price was "life unfolding itself." "We are each a part of God's unfoldment," and gestalt is "learning to say Yes to that unfoldment," to that "sourcing." Also relevant here is Chris's deep sense that humor was fundamental to Price's spiritual life, or what she calls his "alignment with the greater Source." Price took an almost cosmic delight in this Source, and his laughter was an expression of a certain equanimity that could see humor in almost any situation through the bigger picture, through the cosmic gestalt, if you will. Thus little glimmers of amusement would often ripple across Price's face, and his deep bond with Murphy was often expressed precisely through their shared sense of humor.

In addition to his early Buddhism, Price was also inspired by Taoism, an ancient Chinese religion whose most basic teaching involves the Tao or Way as a mysterious, paradoxical, and finally indescribable balance between two cosmic forces: the female *yin* and the male *yang*. It is unclear when exactly Price became attracted to Taoism, though it is almost certain his earliest exposure came through two men: Alan Watts, who wrote about Taoism for the public, and Gary Snyder, the Beat poet who later went on to become a Zen practitioner (Zen Buddhism is clearly influenced by Chinese Taoism). Chris Price believes that Price was first attracted to Taoism sometime around 1955, in tandem with the February appearance of R. B. Blakney's translation of Taoism's central scriptural text, the *Tao Te Ching*.

Much like Zen Buddhist meditation is a practice that claims not to be a practice and Spiegelberg's religion claims to be a non-religion, the *Tao Te Ching* is a text that attempts not to be a text. Thus it insists (in words) that the Tao or Way can never be adequately captured in words. Text or no text, religion or no religion, words or no words, there is no doubt that the *Tao Te Ching* was one of the most significant Asian influences on Dick Price. Chris Price gave Steve Donovan the same edition of Price's Blakney translation and marked for him the passages that Price had marked in his own copy. Here are a few examples of highlighted passages:

Thirty spokes will converge
In the hub of a wheel;

But the use of the cart
Will depend on the part
Of the hub that is void.[22]

Those who know do not talk
And talkers do not know.[23]

The troubles of the world
Cannot be solved except
Before they grow too hard.[24]

It does not seem much of an exaggeration to observe that Dick Price tried to model himself on the empty Taoist sage, the wise man who conformed his nature to nature, governed by not governing, spoke by not speaking, and gained lasting fame precisely through renouncing it. If this was not yet true of him in the mid-1950s, then it certainly was in the mid-1960s. Murphy had it right, then, when he reflected back on his late friend and cofounder, remembering that "there was in him something of both John Muir and a wild Taoist monk."[25]

It bears repeating: Chinese Taoism and Indian Tantra are very close, if they are not actually local expressions of a deeper pan-Asian supertradition. Both broad traditions, after all, work through a very similar vision of reality as ontologically gendered and sexualized. Nonspecialists often miss the fundamental erotic dimensions of Taoist symbolism and are simply unaware of the rich fund of Taoist sexual yoga. The famous *yin-yang* symbolism, for example, is almost certainly rooted, like Aurobindo's metaphysics, in the act of heterosexual intercourse. Alan Watts once described the image as the embrace of two copulating fishes.[26] In essence, then, as long as we recognize the mystical depths of the erotic, that is, as long as we understand human sexuality to be much more than simply "sex," we can say with Douglas Wile that, "sex is *yin* and *yang* in action; *yin* and *yang* are sex writ large."[27]

Indeed, so strong and ancient are the erotic dimensions of Taoism that some scholars have argued that Tantrism actually originated in China and migrated from there into India and the rest of Asia. Dick Price's Taoism, in other words, may very well be a distant development of what was once the *Ur*-Tantra of all of Asia. Hence the wild popularity of the *yin-yang* symbol in the American counterculture: *they* at least knew what they were looking at—sex writ large, sex become metaphysics, the pan-Asian supertradition of Tantra.

Mystical Mania and Institutionalization

The year 1955 may have been the *annus mirabilis,* the year of miracle, marking the beginning of Dick Price's inspiration by both the Theravada Buddhism of Nyanaponika Thera and the Taoism of Blakney's translation. The next year, however, things began to go terribly wrong.

Things were not quite right, or perhaps they were too right. Price was entering a manic stage, going on only two hours of sleep a night as he experienced tremendous rushes of energy and enthusiasm that he feared he could neither contain nor control: "At the time, especially with almost Bonnie catalyzing this, I started to go crazier and crazier. But in a way for me it was just this immense expansion and excitement which I was having trouble containing."[28] He had recalled an incipient awareness of this in his recollection of his marriage ceremony: "My experience was very much like, hey, you know there's another me that's somehow vaster and greater, that I can't quite trust, that's running the conscious Dick and there is the conscious Dick up at the altar being married by Reverend Tobasi."[29] Walt Anderson remembers how things culminated in a seminal life-event, an altered state of history when "finally, one night in a bar in North Beach, all the energy came to a head. He felt a tremendous opening-up inside himself, like a glorious dawn. The place he was in had a fireplace, and he thought it would be appropriate for them to light a fire there, in celebration of this great and mysterious event. 'Light the fire,' he kept saying; 'light the fire.'"[30] The bartender saw it differently. Price's behavior concerned him and he called the police. Six of them arrived and manhandled Price into a paddy wagon (it took all six). With the manic enlightenment now transformed by the circumstances into a state of immense anxiety, fear, and pain, Price lost consciousness.

He was taken to Letterman's Army Hospital in the city, where he would spend three spiritually eventful months in a state that was, as he put it later, "opening up all sorts of kind of suppressed possibilities for me."[31] His energy level was still so high that the drugs that they administered him had no noticeable effect. Price was also passing through various visionary states. He experienced, for example, a "whole regression through history," during which he "was leaping through all sorts of past lives" that ended with a previous life as some sort of monk, a Buddhist one he assumed.[32]

Other experiences were more physical, if no less unusual. When he violently threw himself against the padded walls of his room to release the incredible rage he felt burning inside him, a kind of "energy field" would surround his body and protect him from injury. During this same hospitalization, he was also spontaneously healed of a very serious back injury that he had suffered in wrestling: "Anyway this injury, in the process of this energy flow, just completely cleared up. So I recognized I was having some type of experience that was in some way healing, because I was into my life and vitality in a way that I organically recognized as correct. I felt fully alive for the first time in my memory."[33]

Other experiences were more painful and emotionally conflicted. He felt, for example, "a kind of an early shut-up in my genitals," which he recognized as an important sign or symptom of his sexuality and its stunting around childhood prohibitions against touching his genitals. Price did not masturbate until he was twenty-two years old. Erickson glosses the sexual expression of Price's psychosis this way: "He felt the experiences he was having were an attempt to restore some of that life energy in a way that would allow it to flow freely, rather than having to remain bottled up and restricted."[34] The mystical and the erotic were manifesting themselves, and, as is so often the case, they were emerging into consciousness *together*. This, we might say, was an expression of the Tao or Way, the eroticized life-force that was now manifesting itself in his altered states.

Ecstatic energies, past life regression, protecting energy fields, spontaneous healing, and an acute sense of his own psychosexual development and arrest: they were all here, and they were all coming out. And he knew it. Chris Price remembers Dick telling her about this seminal period in his life: "He'd had a little enlightenment experience as part of all of this, he had a lot of psychological stuff too, and he knew that it was mixed." Mixed or no, Price emerged from the psychotic episode "washed clean." He would later describe it as a "transitional psychosis,"[35] but we could just as easily see it as a type of modern American shamanic initiation for what would become a life of healing (himself and others), altered states of consciousness, and strong communal leadership. Price, though he probably did not know it quite yet, would have from this time a distinctly mystical vocation. He had been marked and called.

But the trauma of his sufferings was by no means over. Price asked his old Stanford professor, Gregory Bateson, to suggest a therapist for him. He pointed Price to Steven Schoen, a psychiatrist Price had in fact known in the North Beach district as Allen Ginsberg's therapist. But Price would never be discharged from the hospital. His father had worked out an arrangement with the military brass, and Price was moved to another air force hospital just fifteen miles from Kenilworth. He was given certain privileges, including freedom on the weekends to visit Bonnie, who was living with his parents now, but he was still very much under someone else's control.

Bonnie did not get along well with Price's mother. Audrey had in fact gone through some of Bonnie's mail, whose content further convinced her that this was no proper wife for her son. Price was outraged, and for the first time in his life angrily confronted his mother for her domineering, meddling ways. He moved Bonnie out.[36] Now Herman, at the insistence of his wife according to Joan, had lunch with his son and gave him what was essentially an ultimatum: either Dick would go willingly to the Institute of Living in Hartford, Connecticut, a mental hospital for the wealthy and privileged, or he himself would commit his son. Thinking he had no choice, Price went. What he did not know but later discovered was that he had actually been discharged from the air force while he was still in the California hospital. He could have walked out then. No one, moreover, really had the power to move him to the hospital near Chicago.

He did not have to go to the Institute of Living, as his father claimed. Price's institutionalizations, in other words, were enforced by a series of deceptions orchestrated by his own parents.

Price entered the Institute of Living on December 7, 1956. His parents immediately had his marriage legally annulled. Audrey offered Bonnie a sum between $10,000 and $25,000 if she promised to disappear. Bonnie disappeared.

Over the next nine months Dick Price would receive fifty-nine insulin shock treatments, approximately ten electroshock treatments (ECT, electroconvulsive therapy), and large doses of phenothiazines. The physiological and psychological effects on Price were all unspeakably brutal. Indeed, an autopsy performed at the time of his death in 1985 showed residual organic brain damage, probably from the electroshock treatments. Much later, Price would reflect back on the experience and describe it to Wade Hudson, a fellow psychiatric survivor with these words:

> There was a fundamental mistake being made and that mistake was supposing that the healing process was the disease, rather than the process whereby the disease is healed. The disease, if any, was the state previous to the "psychosis." The so-called "psychosis" was an attempt toward spontaneous healing, and it was a movement toward health, not a movement toward disease. . . . It's a little difficult to talk about. Certainly a range of experience. In some categories it would be called mystical, really a re-owning and discovery of parts of myself where I set myself in relation to a larger cosmos. But don't try to talk to a psychiatrist in these terms; to them, this is simply a symptom of "very deep lying illness."[37]

The torture became so extreme that Price came to the conclusion that he would either escape or perish within the trauma. He climbed over a wall and escaped, only to find that he was not psychologically capable of surviving in the outside world. He asked a homeless man living on the street for a dime and called his father.

Herman requested an open ward this time. Price's recovery began, and he left the Institute of Living on Thanksgiving Day, 1957. For Erickson, Price "had paid a very high price for deviating from the acceptable path of behavior that had been established for him by the values of his parents and upheld by their very long and authoritative reach. The lesson was exceedingly simple: conform or be punished."[38] For Chris Price, the move back home was much more about resting, running in the cold fresh air,

FIGURE 5. Richard Price and Michael Murphy shortly after their first meeting in the fall of 1960. Printed with permission of the Esalen Institute.

enjoying some good live jazz music in a local bar, and rebuilding his body. In either reading, Price now had no illusions about his family relationships. They were essentially dead to him. He moved back home, took a job at Price Brothers, and began making illuminated beer signs for his uncle Louis's business. But this was by no means a permanent solution. It was a resting place on the way to a life's teaching: Price would never again let anyone or any institution become the authority over his own experience and truth. He would be fearless.

The Stage Is Set

After three years in Kenilworth, Price heard that Gia-fu and some of his other friends were forming something called the East-West House in San Francisco. And so in May of 1960, Price got on a plane and flew back to his old haunt. That same fall, he attended a public lecture of Haridas Chaudhuri. Chaudhuri, we might recall, had come to the States to teach in the American Academy of Asian Studies. Unfortunately, the academy's principle donor experienced some serious business losses. By 1952, just one year after it opened its doors, the academy was effectively out of funds. Alan Watts, as dean, ran it on a shoestring for the next four years, until it was finally closed in 1956.[39] After the academy's collapse, Chaudhuri founded the Cultural Integration Fellowship, essentially a more humble institution closer to his own Aurobindonian vision of an "integral philosophy" and the practice of an "integral yoga."[40] It was there, at Chaudhuri's meditation house on Fulton Street, that Murphy first met Price. Murphy was living there. Murphy invited Price to move in. He did.[41]

Thus in 1960, both men found themselves living at Chaudhuri's Cultural Integration Fellowship on Fulton Street on the edge of Golden Gate Park. Each had been through a great deal. Murphy had lost his Episcopalian faith after encountering the science of evolution at Stanford, only to rediscover a new spirituality in the evolutionary and occult mysticism of *The Life Divine* and the charismatic lectures of Spiegelberg. Price had just survived the trauma of family manipulation and psychiatric mistreatments. Now, after experiencing hints of the supernormal enlightenment inspired by his encounters with Buddhist meditation and Taoism, he was back in his beloved San Francisco, and he had met Murphy.

Erickson paints the following picture. Murphy and Price were both athletes. Both were Stanford graduates and psychology majors. Both had spent time in the military and had dropped out of graduate school. Both were profoundly shaped by Asian religious thought and influenced by the same professor of Asian and comparative religion. And, perhaps most importantly, both had had life-altering "breakout" experiences in 1955–56: Murphy's trip to Aurobindo's ashram and Price's psychotic breakdown as breakthrough.[42]

The stage was set.

The Outlaw Era and the American Counterculture (1960-1970)

"Totally on Fire"

THE EXPERIENCE OF FOUNDING ESALEN

There is reason to suppose that in man, and in him alone, there lies the possibility of further evolution: that this further stage must be through evolution of new faculties; that man is offered the possibility of emerging on to a new level of conscious being, as much above his present powers and apprehensions as they transcend an amphibian's; that the symptoms of this latent creative energy, pent within him, are the peculiar intensities and persistencies of both his pain and his lust.

GERALD HEARD, *Pain, Sex and Time*

I want to tell you about Big Sur Hot Springs. The operative word is *hot*. This place is hot.

ABRAHAM MASLOW

In 1960 Price went to hear Aldous Huxley deliver a lecture called "Human Potentialities" at the University of California, San Francisco Medical Center.[1] Although "we are pretty much the same as we were twenty thousand years ago," said Huxley, we have "in the course of these twenty thousand years actualized an immense number of things which at that time for many, many centuries thereafter were wholly potential and latent in man." He went on to suggest that other potentialities remain hidden in us, and he called on his audience to develop methods and means to actualize them. "The neurologists have shown us," said Huxley, "that no human being has ever made use of as much as ten percent of all the neurons in his brain. And perhaps, if we set about it in the right way, we might be able to produce extraordinary things out of this strange piece of work that a man is."[2]

Price was listening. Murphy would soon write Huxley asking for advice on how to go about doing something about that other ninety percent. Murphy and Price asked to visit Huxley in his Hollywood Hills home on their way down to Mexico to return a pick-up truck they had borrowed from one of Price's friends. Huxley apologized for being away at that time but strongly encouraged them to visit his old friend, Gerald Heard, who lived in Santa Monica. He also suggested that they visit Rancho La Puerta, a burgeoning growth center in Mexico that featured health food, yoga, and various and sundry alternative lifestyles that Huxley thought they would find conducive to their own developing worldviews.

In June of 1961, Murphy and Price drove down to Santa Monica to visit Gerald Heard, a reclusive visionary British intellectual who had arrived in the States with his partner, Christopher Wood, as well as with Aldous and Maria Huxley, and their son Matthew on April 12, 1937. Hollywood screen writer and novelist Christopher Isherwood would follow not long after. Huxley, Heard, and Isherwood would eventually have a major impact on the American countercultural appropriation of Hinduism. All three would be influenced by the Vedanta philosophy of Swami Prabhavananda, the charismatic head of the Vedanta Society of Southern California. All three finally would spend much of their mature years reflecting on what this Indian philosophy could offer the West in a long series of essays, books, and lectures. Quite appropriately, Alan Watts and Felix Greene called them "the British Mystical Expatriates of Southern California."[3] It was Huxley and Heard, however, who would have the most influence on the founding of Esalen.

Aldous Huxley, the Perennial Philosophy, and the Tantric Paradise of Pala

Although Murphy and Price actually met Aldous Huxley only once, in January of 1962 when the author visited them briefly in Big Sur shortly before his death on November 22, 1963 (the same day, it turns out, that JFK was assassinated), his intellectual and personal influence on the place was immense. His second wife, Laura, would also become a longtime friend of Esalen, where she would fill any number of roles, including acting as a sitter for one of Murphy's psychedelic sessions.

Aldous Huxley's writings on the mystical dimensions of psychedelics and on what he called the perennial philosophy were foundational. Moreover, his call for an institution that could teach the "nonverbal humanities" and the development of the "human potentialities" functioned as the working mission statement of early Esalen. Indeed, the very first Esalen brochures actually bore the Huxley-inspired title, "the human potentiality."

This same phrase would later morph in a midnight brainstorming session between Michael Murphy and George Leonard into the now well-known "human potential movement." When developing the early brochures for Esalen, Murphy was searching for a language that could mediate between his own Aurobindonian evolutionary mysticism and the more secular and psychological language of American culture. It was Huxley who helped him to create such a new hybrid language. This should not surprise us, as Huxley had been experimenting for decades on how to translate Indian ideas into Western literary and intellectual culture.

One of the ways he did this was through his notion of perennialism put forward in his 1944 work *The Perennial Philosophy*. Perennialism referred to a set of mystical experiences and doctrines that he believed lay at the core of all great religions, hence it is a philosophy that "perennially" returns in the history of religions. The book laid the intellectual and comparative foundations for much that would come after it, including Esalen and, a bit later, the American New Age movement. By the 1980s and '90s, Esalen intellectuals were growing quite weary and deeply suspicious of what was looking more and more like facile ecumenism and an ideological refusal to acknowledge real and important differences among the world's cultures and religions. But this would take decades of hard thinking and multiple disillusionments. In the 1940s, '50s, and '60s, it was still a radical and deeply subversive thing to assert the deep unity of the world's religions.

And this is precisely what Huxley was doing. After mistakenly attributing the Latin phrase *philosophia perennis* to Leibniz, Huxley defines the key concept this way in his very first lines: "PHILOSOPHIA PERENNIS... the metaphysic that recognizes a divine Reality substantial to the world of things and lives and minds; the psychology that finds in the soul something similar to, or even identical with, divine Reality; the ethic that places man's final end in the knowledge of the immanent and transcendent Ground of all being—the thing is immemorial and universal."[4]

In essence, Huxley's perennial philosophy was a form of what historians of Indian religion call neo-Vedanta, a modern religious movement inspired by the ecstatic visionary experiences of Sri Ramakrishna (1836–1886) and the preaching and writing of Swami Vivekananda (1863–1902), Ramakrishna's beloved disciple who brought his master's message about the unity of all religions to the States in the last decade of the nineteenth century. It was Huxley who wrote the foreword to this same tradition's central text in translation, *The Gospel of Sri Ramakrishna* (1942). It was within this same spiritual lineage again that Huxley, Heard, and Isherwood found much of their own inspiration and through which a general Hindu perennialism was passed on to early Esalen and American culture.

Such cultural combinations, of course, did not always work. As with all intellectual systems, there were gaps, stress points, contradictions. Nowhere was this more apparent than in the realm of ethics. Thus, for example, Huxley seems personally puzzled over the strange moral conditions of his hybrid vision, that is, the suppression or destruction of the personality, whose very existence the perennial philosophy understands as the "original sin."[5] But he accepts the textual facts for what they in fact seem to be and then illustrates them with a telling chemical metaphor that we might now recognize as an early traumatic model for the mystical, perhaps best expressed in this story in the mystical life and psychological sufferings of Dick Price. Here is how Huxley put it in 1944:

> Nothing in our everyday experience gives us any reason for supposing that water is made up of hydrogen and oxygen; and yet when we subject water to certain rather drastic treatments, the nature of its constituent elements becomes manifest. Similarly, nothing in our everyday experience gives us much reason for supposing that the mind of the average sensual man has, as one of its constituents, something resembling, or identical with, the Reality substantial to the manifold world; and yet, when that mind is subjected to drastic treatments, the divine element, of which it is in part at least composed, becomes manifest.[6]

But it was not quite these mystical-ethical dilemmas or this psychology of trauma that Huxley would pass on to Esalen. It was, first, his Hindu-inspired notion of the perennial philosophy; second, his firm belief that psychedelic substances can grant genuine metaphysical insight; and, third, his central notion of the latent and manifest "potentialities." We will get to the psychedelic soon enough. Here is how Huxley introduced the concept of potentialities, with a little help from an unacknowledged Freud, in *The Perennial Philosophy:* "It is only by making physical experiments that we can discover the intimate nature of matter and its potentialities. And it is only by making psychological and moral experiments that we can discover the intimate nature of mind and its potentialities. In the ordinary circumstances of average sensual life these potentialities of the mind remain latent and unmanifested." A few pages later, Huxley writes of "the almost endless potentialities of the human mind" that have "remained for so long unactualized," foreshadowing the later language and psychology of

Abraham Maslow's notion of self-actualization, another major conceptual influence on the founding of Esalen.

Even more relevant to the history of Esalen—indeed, prophetic of that future story—was Huxley's very last novel, *Island,* which appeared in March of 1962, just one month after he had introduced a still unknown Timothy Leary to "the ultimate yoga" of Tantra, and just two months after he met Michael Murphy and Richard Price in Big Sur. The novel's pragmatic celebration of Tantric eroticism and its harsh criticism of ascetic forms of spirituality (which the novel links to sexual repression, a guilt-ridden homosexuality, and aggressive militarism) marks a significant shift in Huxley's spiritual worldview, at least as he was expressing it in print. After all, if in 1942 he could write a carefully diplomatic foreword to a book about a Hindu saint who considered all women to be aspects of the Mother Goddess and so would have sex with none of them (*The Gospel of Sri Ramakrishna*), now he was suggesting openly in 1962 that "to think of Woman as essentially Holy" was an expression of a conflicted male homosexuality anxious to avoid any and all heterosexual contact.[7] It is much better, the novel now suggests, to think of the erotic union of man and woman as holy, that is, to see the sacred in the sexual and the sexual in the sacred. Hence "the cosmic love-making of Shiva and the Goddess."[8] Late in life Huxley appears to have been moving away from his earlier ascetic Vedanta, so prominently featured in *The Perennial Philosophy,* toward a new psychologically inflected Tantra.

Laura Huxley considers *Island* to be her husband's final legacy, the place where he put everything he had learned. When I asked her about the novel's obvious focus on Tantra, she was quick to point out that Aldous was not particularly friendly to traditional religion, and that he considered Tantra to be a technique, not a religion. Everything written in *Island,* she insisted, had been tried somewhere. The novel thus laid down a real and practical path to follow, not just a dream or another impossible religious claim. The novel was Aldous's blueprint for a good society, even, Laura pointed out, if that "island" is one's own home or private inner world. It can be done. That is the point.

The story itself involves a jaded journalist, Will Farnaby, who lands by accident on a forbidden island called Pala. Pala culture had been formed a few generations earlier by two men—a pious Indian adept in Tantric forms of Buddhism and Hinduism and a scientifically enlightened Scottish doctor. The culture thus embodied both a literal friendship between and a consequent synthesis of Tantric Asia, with its lingams, deities, and yogas, and Western rationalism, with its humanism, psychology, and science.

Farnaby quickly learns that Pala's two principle educational practices involve a contemplative form of sexuality called *maithuna* (the Tantric term for sexual intercourse) and the ingestion of a psychedelic mushroom the inhabitants called *moksha* (the traditional Sanskrit word for "spiritual liberation"). The sexual practice, which was also consciously modeled on the Oneida community of nineteenth-century America and its ideal of male continence (a form of extended sexual intercourse without ejaculation), functioned as both a contemplative technique and as an effective means of birth control. The psychedelic practice initiated the young islanders into metaphysical wisdom, that is, into the empirical realization that their true selves could not be identified with their little social egos, which were understood to be necessary but temporary "filters" of a greater cosmic consciousness.

The novel meanders lovingly through and around both this *maithuna* and this *moksha*—which are manifestly the real point and deepest story of the novel—as the Rani or Queen Mother of Pala and her sexually repressed homosexual son, Murugan, take the utopian island further and further toward Westernization, industrialization, capitalism, and a finally violent fundamentalism organized around notions of "the Ideal of Purity," "the Crusade of the Spirit," and "God's Avatars" (the Queen liked to capitalize things). The ending is as predictable as it is depressing: the forces of righteousness and religion win out over those of natural sensuality, pantheism, and erotic wisdom.

Strikingly, virtually all the markers of the later Esalen gnosis are present on Huxley's "imagined" utopian island. Laura Huxley's observation about her late husband's rejection of organized religion, for example, are played out in full. "We have no established church," one of the islanders explains, "and our religion stresses immediate experience and deplores belief in unverifiable dogmas and the emotions which that belief inspires." Hence the humorous prayer of Pala: "Give us this day our daily Faith, but deliver us, dear God, from Belief."[9] The islanders even integrated this religion of no religion into their agricultural affairs: the scarecrows in the fields were thus made to look like a Future Buddha and a God the Father, so that the children who manipulated the scarecrow-puppets with strings to scare off the birds could learn that "all gods are homemade, and that it's we who pull their strings and so give them the power to pull ours."[10] Altered states, of course, were also central to Pala's culture through the *moksha*-medicine, and the techniques of Tantra were omnipresent in their sexual lives. Perhaps most strikingly, Huxley saw very clearly that Zen, Taoism, and Tantra were all related expressions of a deeper transcultural gnosis or supertradition—what he called "the new conscious Wisdom." More astonishingly still, he even linked this supertradition to the scientific insights of Darwinian evolution and proposed that the latter should now be realized through conscious contemplative practice in a way that uncannily foreshadows Murphy's own "evolutionary Tantra."[11]

Somehow, Aldous knew what Esalen would come to know. And then he died. An earthquake struck Big Sur that day.

Gerald Heard and the Evolutionary Energies of Lust

Gerald Heard also played a significant role in the founding of Esalen. It was his charismatic presence and advice that finally tipped the scales for Murphy and Price and pushed them to jump in. Heard would also go on to give no less than four separate seminars in the early years. Appropriately, Anderson actually begins *The Upstart Spring* with Heard and has this to say about the writer's influence on the two young men: "Huxley had so diffidently advocated a research project, had so hesitantly suggested its revolutionary possibilities. He thought something of that sort *might* happen. Heard thought it *had* to happen."[12]

Murphy has reminisced about his and Price's first four-hour visit with Heard and its profound effects on him in both a brief essay titled "Totally on Fire" and in various personal communications with me. He described Heard as "archetypally Irish, like a big leprechaun, with red hair and flashing eyes," and as "tremendously charismatic." He also spoke of that original meeting with Heard as a real "tipping point" in his life, comparable to those first few class lectures with Spiegelberg. In the essay, moreover, he mentions Heard's institutional presence in California, particularly his founding of Trabuco College, a small quasi-monastic educational experiment that lasted five years (1942–47) before Heard turned it over to the Vedanta Society of Southern California in 1949, as well as his strong presence in the Sequoia Seminars on the San Francisco peninsula. Both Trabuco and the Sequoia Seminars were clear precedents for Esalen.[13]

So were a number of Heard's ideas. Murphy was reading Heard's *Pain, Sex and Time* and *The Human Venture* just before he and Price met him in 1961. Murphy is clear that Heard was not a significant intellectual influence on his own thought, but he also points out that the connections were real ones. Hence the Fire. Heard, for example, was very conversant in psychical research. Indeed, he had spent ten years working closely with the Society for Psychical Research in London (1932–42). Like Murphy, he had also lost his Christian faith over the convincing truths of science. Indeed, in his late twenties, he appears to have experienced a nervous breakdown over this intellectual revolution. But like Murphy again, Heard returned to a transformed faith refashioned around a new evolutionary mysticism. Physical evolution of the human species, Heard believes, has ceased, but human consciousness is still evolving; indeed, with the advent of the human species and the awakening of the human psyche through civilization, the evolutionary process has actually *quickened* and, perhaps most importantly, become conscious of itself. And here Murphy finds connection with Heard's thought: "Part of his vision that appealed to me was seeing the mystical life in an evolutionary context, which put him squarely on par with Aurobindo."

Heard had also written about the spiritual potentials of mind-altering drugs (like Huxley), about the complementarity of science and religion, even about UFO phenomena—all topics that would reappear at Esalen.[14] And indeed, his books, rather like the UFOs, seem to swarm with strange and charming speculations, like the utterly preposterous and yet oddly attractive idea that the European witchcraft trials had eliminated a large gene pool of real psychical faculties, but that the centuries had since replaced the pool and we are now on the verge of a new "rare stock" of gifted souls endowed with evolutionary powers.[15] All we need now is a small community, an esoteric subculture, to nurture and protect the gifted. In a talk at Esalen in 1963, he wondered out loud whether Esalen might become such an occult school. Another X-Men scenario.

Whatever one makes of such a claim, one thing seems clear enough: Heard knew what he was saying was heretical. He was aligning himself and his friends, after all, with the genes of witches. He was certainly as hard on religious orthodoxy as Spiegelberg had been. Heard could thus admit that humanity may have once needed its gods to keep in touch with the subconscious (and it was this same subconscious that supplied "the basis and force of the religious conviction" for him). Still, such anthropo-morphic religions have now taken on largely "degenerative forms" that are hopelessly out of date with our science and psychology.[16] It is time to move on, *to evolve.*

Finally, Heard, like his fellow British expatriate and brother Vedantist, Christopher Isherwood, was quite clear about his homosexuality. In other words, two of the three British expatriates (Huxley, Heard, and Isherwood) were self-described homosexuals, even if they chose to express this sexual-spiritual orientation in very different ways. Isherwood wrote openly about his own active homosexuality, his (failed) attempts at celibacy, and his sexuality's defining effect on his devotional relationship to the tradition's founding saint, Sri Ramakrishna, who he suspected (correctly) was also homoerotic in both his spiritual and sexual orientations.[17]

Heard chose a different path. In *Pain, Sex and Time* he wrote about the oddly abundant energies of pain and lust in the human species as reservoirs of evolutionary energy and explored the possibilities of consciously controlling, channeling, and using this energy to cooperate with evolution and so enlarge the aperture of consciousness, to implode through spacetime. Interestingly, when Heard turned to a historical sketch of these energetic techniques in the West, he began with Asia and various Tantric techniques of arresting the orgasm to alter consciousness and transcend time. Tantric Asia, in other words, functioned as something of an archetypal model for Heard in his search for a type of asceticism that was not life-denying but consciously erotic, a lifestyle that could embrace the evolutionary energies sparkling in sex, build them up through discipline, and then ride their spontaneous combustions into higher and higher states of consciousness and energy.

These Tantric moments reappear repeatedly throughout his writings. In one of his last books, for example, *The Five Ages of Man* (his forty-seventh book), he included an appendix: "On the Evidence for an Esoteric Mystery Tradition in the West and Its Postponement of Social Despair." Once again, he begins a Western historical sketch not with the West, but with Tantra. Tantra, he tells us here, is the esoteric tradition of India that was subsequently persecuted and censored by both a puritan Islam and a prudish Brahmanism. Such a persecution of the mystical as the erotic was even more extreme in the West, where the esoteric often functioned as a kind of spiritual-sexual underground. Hence Heard's reflections on an already familiar painting, Bosch's *The Garden of Earthly Delights* as explored by Wilhelm Fränger. Much like Henry Miller before him, Heard celebrates Fränger. Not that he does not have his own contribution to make: "Here, too," he writes with reference to the same painting, "are unmistakable Tantra pictures of the rousing of Kundalini."[18]

He was even more explicit in his private letters. In one letter to W. J. H. Sprott (a gay friend, I presume, loosely involved with the Bloomsbury group), Heard playfully describes the yogic practices of drawing water up through the anus and penis. He recounts in rather flip terms how the *kundalini* comes out through the top of the skull, and then jokes of Tantra's use of sexual-spiritual double meanings, offering his own very funny examples in the process. And that was not all. He goes on to claim that homosexuality is the norm among Tibetan Buddhist saints, and confesses that fetishism has become his own chosen path of spiritual sublimation. It was a version of this wild theory involving the spiritual fetish that he promised Sprott to read someday to an erotic comedic club to which they both apparently belonged.[19] Club or no club, bawdy laughter and real insight are impossible to distinguish in such moments, and it is the private letter, the secret talk, not the published text, that most reveals.

In midlife, probably around 1935, Heard seems to have followed his own speculations about the evolutionary sublimation of erotic energies (just after he began "turning East," around 1932–33). He quite intentionally chose a celibate lifestyle and lived with his Platonic life-partner and personal secretary Michael Barrie. But he certainly never gave up his belief in the evolutionary potentials of sexual desire and the mystical privileges of homosexuality. Thus in the mid to late 1950s, he wrote, under the pseudonymn of D. B. Vest, about homosexuality as a potent spiritual force that might have some important role in the evolution of human consciousness. Two such essays appeared in *One: The Homosexual Magazine* as "A Future for the Isophyl" and "Evolution's Next Step," and a third would appear in *Homophile Studies: One Institute Quarterly* as "Is the Isophyl a Biological Variant?"[20] Both the former magazine's title ("One") and its Carlyle motto ("a mystic bond of brotherhood makes all men one") strongly suggest Heard's own Vedantic monistic metaphysics and mystical reading of homosexuality.

Heard's mature homosexuality, however, was also "made sublime," a kind of homoeroticism alchemically transmuted into a metaphysical force. Those who knew Heard often commented on these related ascetic and charismatic qualities of his personal presence (though seldom on the erotic dimensions that he himself consistently identified). His austerity was as palpable as his charisma. Indeed, Heard's major differences with Swami Prabhavananda of the Hollywood Vedanta Society involved his strong criticisms of the Swami's "moral lapses," such as enjoying an occasional smoke and a nightly drink. Scandalous indeed.

Enter Hunter Thompson (1961)

Murphy and Price had already arrived at Big Sur Hot Springs before they met Heard and decided to found a new institution. When they arrived in their red Jeep pick-up in April of 1961, they found what can only be called a surreal mixture of people and worldviews. Murphy and Price pulled in late, well after dark. It was not a terribly auspicious first night. Murphy reports waking up in the middle of the night in the Big House to an angry young man pointing a gun at him: "Who the hell are you, and what are ya' doing here?"

Enter Hunter Thompson. Bunny Murphy, Michael Murphy's grandmother, had hired a young, billy-club-toting Thompson to guard the property and keep order. Unfortunately, she had neglected to tell her zealous guard that her grandson and friend were coming down to stay that night. Thompson, a young aspiring writer still finding his voice, had arrived to seek out the presence and inspiration of Dennis Murphy, Mike's younger brother, whose literary work he deeply admired. Dennis had published a very successful novel in 1958, *The Sergeant* (about a homosexual affair in the U.S. Army), which had won the acclaim of John Steinbeck and would eventually be made into a Hollywood movie starring Rod Steiger, for which he would write the screenplay.

In 1967 Hunter Thompson published his first book, *Hell's Angels,* and went on to create Gonzo journalism, a new style of American literature. Gary Trudeau immortalized his place in American literary culture as Duke in his *Doonesbury* series, but this would all happen later. At this point in 1961, Thompson was a young man of twenty-two living in the Big House and making copious notes in the margins of Dennis Murphy's *The Sergeant,* learning the art of the pen, the sentence, and the turn of the phrase.

Thompson was hardly the only colorful character on the Murphy property, though. The folksinger Joan Baez lived in one of the cabins, where she often gave small concerts. The guest hotel on the grounds, moreover, was being managed by a certain Mrs. Webb, a fervent Evangelical Christian who had hired her fellow church members from the First Church of God of Prophecy to help her manage the day-to-day running of the place, which they leased from Bunny on a month-to-month basis. The bar, on the other hand, was patronized by what Price and Murphy called the Big Sur Heavies, locals known for their rough manners, their penchant for marijuana (which they grew in the mountains), and their quasi-criminal (or just criminal) tendencies. Then there were the baths, frequented on most weekends by homosexual men who would drive down from San Francisco or up from Los Angeles to gather in the hot waters and explore the limits of sensual pleasure. These men had even developed a kind of simple Morse code to help them manage their sexual activities: on the path leading down to the baths they would post a guard, who would switch on a blinking light at the baths to signal to the bathing lovers the approach of straight people coming down the path. Anderson paints the following humorous picture with his usual verve: "And so it went through the spring and summer of 1961: sodomy in the baths, glossolalia in the lodge, fistfights in the parking lot, folk music in the cabins, meditation in the Big House."[21]

Bunny had long turned down her grandson's repeated requests to hand the grounds over to him. She was particularly concerned that Michael would "give it away to the Hindoos." But things were getting out of hand at Big Sur Hot Springs, and she would soon change her mind after events that have since become legendary. Much of it, unsurprisingly with hindsight, revolved around Hunter Thompson.

Thompson, it turns out, sometimes picked verbal fights with the homosexual bathers. One night, he returned to the property with his girlfriend and two hitchhiking soldiers from Fort Ord (a base just north of Monterey). Thinking it was safe to go down to the baths in such a crowd, Thompson ventured down the dark path. But some of the bathers jumped him, the soldiers and his girlfriend ran away, and Thompson was left alone to slug it out. As the story goes, most of the slugging was done by the bathers. The men beat Thompson up and came very close to throwing him off the cliff that night. Bloodied and bruised, he got back to his room in the Big House, where he spent the next day sulking and shooting his gun out a window, which he never bothered to open.[22]

Not long after this incident, Bunny would read one of Thompson's early published essays in *Rogue* magazine, "Big Sur: The Tropic of Henry Miller," in which he described the folks of Big Sur as "expatriates, ranchers, out-and-out bastards, and genuine deviates."[23] Such language did not go down well with Bunny. She may have been in her eighties, but she was also tough. According to Anderson, she then "made one of her rare trips down to Big Sur, in her black Cadillac with her Filipino chauffeur, for the specific purpose of firing Thompson."[24] Exit Hunter Thompson.

The Night of the Dobermans

Then in October came what is known in Esalen legend as the Night of the Dobermans. Thompson may have been gone, but the baths remained in the control of the gay men. Things had gotten so out of control that even

Dennis Murphy's friend Jack Kerouac looked askance. If this veritable archetype of the American Beat scene, so immune to the pettiness and damning comforts of middle-America, could visit and leave the Hot Spring baths disgusted with their moral and fluid state (he saw a dead otter bobbing in the waves and sperm floating in his bath), clearly, something had to be done.[25]

It was not always like this. When Henry Miller wrote about Esalen's homosexual bathers in the late 1950s, it was with real affection and a certain playful humor. For Miller at least, these were elegant artists and dancers who belonged to that "ancient order of hermaphrodites." They reminded him of "the valiant Spartans—just before the battle of Thermopylae." He doubted, though, that "the Slade's Springs type would be ready to die to the last man. ('It's sort of silly, don't you think?')"[26] That was in 1957. Things were different now. These men were acting much more like Miller's imagined Spartans. They were ready to fight.

Murphy and Price began by erecting a gated steel fence around the baths and announcing that they would be closed from now on at 8:00 p.m.—not exactly a popular move. One night they walked down the path to close the gate and encountered a group of men who simply refused to leave. Everyone knew what had happened to Hunter. Murphy and Price returned to the lodge to gather the troops, which in the end amounted to five people, including Joan Baez and three Doberman pinschers. The dogs, it turns out, were the key. As the small band walked down the path, the three dogs began to bark viciously at each other as the owner yelled, "Choke him! Choke him!" It was all the group could do to keep the dogs apart. When the growling and snarling group finally arrived at the baths, the place was completely empty. Cars were starting and lights could be seen in the parking lot as the men made their anxious retreat. Later that evening, as Murphy walked around the property, he noticed a young man and woman kissing in the moonlight up on the highway. For Murphy, Anderson reports, the young couple synchronistically signaled a shift in the atmosphere and a new day (and night) at Esalen.[27]

The proverbial guard had now literally changed. Mrs. Webb and the charismatic Christians would soon leave. The baths were no longer synonymous with the rowdy gay men of the cities. There was a meditating American yogi and an aspiring Buddhist shaman-healer on the grounds. And Joan was still singing in her cabin. Big Sur Hot Springs was on its way to becoming, as the white wooden sign still says, "Esalen Institute by Reservation Only."

FIGURE 6. The first staff, 1962. From left to right: Robert Breckenridge, Richard Price, Robert Nash, Alice Sellers, James Sellers, and Michael Murphy. Printed with permission of the Esalen Institute.

The Early Brochures (1962–1964)

In almost every way, Esalen was defined by the spirits of its two founders and their families. Even in terms of pure numbers, those two founders constituted exactly one-third of the original Esalen staff of six. Without either personality the project would not have developed the way it did. This was certainly true financially. Michael Murphy, with the help of his dad John Murphy, managed to convince Bunny to lease the property to them. Price managed to convince his father to release his share of some stocks so that he could borrow $10,000 of start-up capital.[28] Murphy's family would continue to be generous with both the property and the project (John, for example, acted as their lawyer in the early years), and Price would generously continue to fund numerous individuals and Esalen projects out of his own pocket.

This is not to say that Murphy and Price agreed on everything (they did not), or that their visions were identical (they were not), or that there would not be serious tensions and disagreements (there would be). What made Esalen Esalen lay precisely in the two founders' differences and the distinct interpersonal and institutional ways they found to balance these, to keep them in productive tension, and to generate institutional creativity out of their respective energies and tensions.

One can only suspect that both the real success and the real tensions of their friendship were set up, at least partially, by their family backgrounds. Erickson speculates that the nuclear patterns of Price's original twinship and subsequent early loss of his twin brother (recall that Bobby died of a misdiagnosed appendicitis at the age of three) had something to do with his psychological kinship with Murphy.[29] Murphy too had known a strong fraternal bond to his brother, Dennis, and this relationship, not unlike his later relationship to Price, was defined by a distinct polarity. Whatever the psychological origins of Price and Murphy's kinship, it was foundational for the beginning of Esalen. In the early years, Murphy would quickly take over the tasks of programming, while Price would take over the business and administrative operation of the place. By all accounts, it was an effective sharing of duties.

There was also real humor here. Anderson confesses that his own experience leading a few seminars on group encounter at Esalen led him to marvel at how he could "stumble through with a group process that was accepted before it was invented." Abe Maslow reportedly quipped that if Satan himself showed up at Esalen, Murphy would have invited him to lead a seminar.[30] Murphy's hospitality and charm are both legendary, so there is, no doubt, more than a little grinning truth to this tradition, even if Satan himself never did actually show up at the front gate (that I know of).

So who did? Fortunately, we can answer this question with significant precision through the early brochures of Esalen. Other than the actual grounds, buildings, and hot springs themselves, the first material artifacts of the Esalen Institute were a series of brochures created by Michael Murphy and Peter Bailley. The institute's mailing list was composed of two earlier lists—one provided by the Beat Zen philosopher and popular writer, Alan Watts, and the other from the famous Sequoia Seminars partly inspired by Gerald Heard and run by Harry Rathbun, a professor of business at Stanford, and his charismatic wife Amelia, both of whom had decidedly liberal religious views. Murphy and Bailley worked on these brochures for some time, and they were expressly designed to embody the ideals and visions of the new venture.

Although there were two early test-run seminars in January and April of 1962 featuring Alan Watts and Kenneth Rexroth respectively, the first official Esalen seminar took place on September 22–23, 1962. From the fall of 1962 through the winter of 1965, the brochures are dominated by a single iconic image that morphs slightly from year to year but nevertheless remains obviously consistent: a line drawing of a lotus to suggest traditional Hindu and Buddhist notions of the pristine and pure enlightenment that arises out of the fertile mud. The name "Aurobindo," by the way, translates literally as "lotus," hence a lotus is featured on the logo of the Aurobindo ashram and in all of its publications. Consciously or unconsciously, there is a definite association being set up here between the founding of Esalen and the lotus-teachings of Sri Aurobindo.

A new conception of human nature is emerging in the field of psychology, a conception that is gradually superseding the views of classical psychoanalysis and strict behaviourism, a conception oriented toward health, growth and the exploration of our psychic potentialities. Creativity research, work with the "mind-opening" drugs and the discoveries of parapsychology (psychical research) complement this development, pointing as they do toward a profounder human possibility.

Some scientists and philosophers believe that this quiet reformulation of psychological thought will bring the greatest change in the vision of western man since Copernicus and the Renaissance. It will certainly affect our most basic attitudes toward human possibility and human destiny.

Each seminar will explore a different aspect of this development. The panel discussion on December 1 will summarize the previous three seminars and relate the topics they will have covered. It is hoped that some of the participants will attend more than one session, thus lending a continuity to the entire discussion.

The charge for each seminar: $16.00 per person per day for a single occupancy, $13.00 for a double (two persons in a room), $12.00 for a triple. This charge covers room, all meals, use of the mineral baths and the seminar itself. Each seminar will begin on Saturday morning at 9:00 A.M. and conclude Sunday afternoon. Participants are advised to spend Friday night at the Hot

A SEMINAR SERIES EXPLORING RECENT
DEVELOPMENTS IN PSYCHOLOGY, PSYCHICAL
RESEARCH AND WORK WITH
THE "MIND-OPENING" DRUGS

FIGURE 7. The second and third pages of the first quadrifold brochure setting out the original triple mission statement, September 1962. Printed with permission of the Esalen Institute.

The first two brochures, both entitled "the human potentiality," also feature a mathematical equation marked "INFINITESIMAL CALCULUS, Bernard Russell." On the inside flap is a Thai Buddha sculpture; the Buddha is smiling, rapt in the bliss of meditation.

Over the Buddha of the first brochure appears the following synopsis of this new venture: "A seminar series exploring recent developments in psychology, psychical research and work with the 'mind-opening' drugs." A kind of mission statement follows: "A new conception of human nature is emerging in the field of psychology, a conception that is gradually superseding the views of classical psychoanalysis and strict behaviorism, a conception oriented toward health, growth and the exploration of our psychic potentialities. Creativity research, work with the 'mind-opening' drugs and the discoveries of parapsychology (psychical research) complement this development, pointing as they do toward a profounder human possibility."

The first two events announced the visionary projects of Murphy and Price that would come to define the dual (para)psychological nature of Esalen and remain remarkably constant through the decades. The Expanding Vision seminar was in fact "a review of the current conceptual revolution in psychology. The discoveries of parapsychology. An examination of the resistance to these developments on the part of scientists and academicians. The resistance within ourselves. The implications for our personal beliefs and values." It was, in other words, pure Michael Murphy.

Not that there wasn't also a good deal of skepticism expressed. There was, mostly by Joe K. Adams, a Princeton-trained psychologist, Texan, and friend of Gregory Bateson who had done psychical research at Stanford. Adams was skeptical of the whole field. He participated in the October and again in the December panel. Murphy had invited Adams precisely for his skepticism, and probably for his connections to Stanford.

To this day, Murphy takes delight in the fact that Thomas Welton Stanford, a member of the original donor family, had endowed the university with a $50,000 grant to fund psychical research. The psychology department barely obliged this original bequest by occasionally inviting a skeptic to go through the motions, as it were, and Adams was one of these.[31] In 1961 and 1962, he had also experienced two psychotic episodes, probably connected to LSD. He would become a popular countervoice in Big Sur and play an important role there as friend, counselor, and local critic against any totalizing system. Murphy often describes him as a kind of "freedom fighter" or "early Foucault"—as someone who saw power and authority posing as knowledge just about everywhere (including in Sri Aurobindo).

If the first seminar was pure Mike Murphy, the second seminar was a barely concealed philosophical discourse on the institutional sufferings of Dick Price, this time led by Adams and Bateson. Bateson was described in his by-line as an ethnologist working at the Veteran's Hospital in Palo Alto (probably the only hospital in the country to have an anthropologist on staff). The earliest recorded statement of Dick Price's worldview is well worth quoting in full:

In every society the individual is taught to perceive the world (including himself) in ways which are asserted to be objectively correct. Individuals who indicate that they do not perceive the world in these ways are likely to be labeled "irrational." Western civilization is now in the process of rapid change in which different ways of perceiving the world are in strong competition, with great dangers to individual freedoms. A somewhat comparable period in history is the period 1200–1700. The field of mental health is one of the important areas in which ideological conflict occurs.

The third announced event was a special lecture by Gerald Heard on art and religion. It sought to define a sense of "religion" that could work again for modern individuals: "RELIGIO—the force that bound him to nature and to his fellow beings and kept him whole." Heard was playing with one common etymology of "religion" here, from the Latin *religare*, "to bind." A series of particularly dramatic events immediately preceded this last lecture. They finally culminated in a life-threatening car accident that Michael Murphy immediately read as synchronistic. The synchronicities this time involved the erotic.

Murphy had taken a vow of celibacy in the 1950s. He had always found it easy to keep this vow, perhaps because, unlike so many other ascetics, his early family life was a happy one and he was not conflicted about his sexuality. More importantly, he had realized the sublime secret of both psychoanalysis and mystical practice, namely, that a practice like deep meditation requires a certain energetic momentum, and that a celibate lifestyle can effectively supply these reservoirs of energy for spiritual transformation (another point on which he no doubt found himself in deep agreement with Aurobindo and Heard). Still, he was thirty-two. He was young, dashing, and the coleader of an exciting new institution that was attracting many talented and attractive young people, including a certain Erica Weston, a beautiful twenty-five-year-old woman who happened to be the granddaughter of the great American photographer, Edward Weston.

Michael broke his vow of celibacy with Erica on the night of October 25, 1962. More positively, Murphy and Weston spent the entire night making love. The next day Weston and Murphy were traveling in a Volkswagen Bug driven by an Indian woman, all on their way to Heard's lecture, which Murphy was to introduce. The two women sat in the front seat. Murphy was in the back. As they turned a blind curve on Highway 1, they found themselves rushing toward another car coming straight at them in their lane. It was too late and too fast. The two cars collided. The Bug spun in circles until it hit the guard-rail, which kept the trio from plunging hundreds of feet to the rocks below. This was all bad enough.

It would get worse. When Murphy came to, he saw the drunk driver of the other car crawling down the highway toward him, yelling, "Murphy! Murphy! I found you!" The scene was beginning to look like a bad dream, all aimed at him personally and orchestrated by none other than his own punishing superego.

The ambulances arrived, the highway was closed for some time, and an investigation followed. As the pieces fell into place, it was discovered that the drunken driver, a character of somewhat ill repute in the community, had in fact been looking for Murphy all that day. Earlier, he had bought a drink for a man he thought was Michael Murphy at the Nepenthe restaurant. "But I'm not Michael Murphy," he was told, "Murphy works down at the Hot Springs." So he went to the Hot Springs, where he then confused Dennis Murphy, who was tending the bar there, with his older brother. Dennis kicked him out. It was at this point that the man, now quite drunk, sped north on Highway 1.

Despite a few broken ribs and some very shaky knees, Murphy refused to go to the hospital. He insisted on being driven to Esalen so that he could introduce Gerald Heard. He had met Heard twice now, once in 1961 and once in 1962, and both times the meetings were connected to life-changing events—it was two for two. He could not help but connect the car accident with his breaking his vow of celibacy. The night, the day, and their synchronistic signs all felt "like death" to him.

This feeling would eventually wear off, but there was something *there* that day, something that signaled a new stage in Murphy's life, a certain decision or "command" to incarnate, to descend into the flesh and the world in order to fulfill the deeper vow, that is, the calling to cofound Esalen and help create the human potential movement. If the accident meant anything, this was not an easy or particularly safe decision to make. Indeed, it was quite nearly fatal.

The fourth seminar of the fall of 1962 was on drug-induced mysticism. It announced yet another revolution in the history of human civilization and religion:

> There seems to be no question in anyone's mind who has experienced it, that the so-called "psychedelic" drugs, such as LSD and mescalin, produce a kind of mystical experience. The question that worries many people is, "Is the drug-induced mysticism religion?" It is altogether possible that drug-induced mystical experiences will force us to study and revise all of our previous definitions of religion. Those who are interested in expanding the boundaries of

their own religious faith should be interested in a discussion of these questions.

We can hear echoes again here of Spiegelberg's religion of no religion, a new religiosity that is not particularly religious, a new spirituality being awakened not by authoritative scriptural texts, but by "mind-opening drugs." The anxieties are as apparent as the enthusiasms.

Twelve other seminars appeared in the second brochure, including two more on drug-induced mysticism (already the most popular topic), one on Sri Aurobindo (led by Murphy), a seminar on the joining of theology and psychology into a kind of external synchronicity in which the intentions of inner and outer events are linked "just as one can read one's own dreams" (exactly like Murphy's sexual car wreck), and a retreat with Evelyn Underhill via her little book, *Practical Mysticism.*

The following year saw these same patterns repeated and others added. Up till now, these were very much intellectual gatherings, respectable "Apollonian" events, to use a later Esalen language. In 1963, however, we begin to encounter the first experiential-based offerings. February saw Paul S. Kurtz introducing Leadership Training in Group Dynamics, perhaps the earliest instance of an Esalen encounter group experience. March saw Mary Whitehouse teaching Physical Movement as a Revelation of the Self. And October saw Charlotte Selver offering an Introduction to Non-Verbal Experience. Charlotte Selver and her husband Charles Brooks would come to play an important role at Esalen. So too would their sensory awareness exercises. Experiential seminars increased each year until, by the end of the decade, almost 90 percent of Esalen seminar offerings were experience-based—the Apollonian had given way to the Dionysian.

In 1963 there was also a seminar on the photography of Erica's grandfather, Edward Weston (co-led by the American nature photographer Ansel Adams), a lecture on the study of contemporary history by Arnold Toynbee, three more lectures by Gerald Heard (including one in which he observed that the word *evolution* is derived historically from a medieval Latin term for the unfolding of a robe), and one by Michael Murphy on the varieties of religious experience.

It was in Murphy's comparative seminar on religious experience that is particularly significant for our present purposes, as here we encounter the first occurrence of the word "Tantra" (as "the Tantras") in the Esalen literature. At the same time, we are also introduced to the formative intellectual influence of William James and his central category of "mystical experience." The seminar's content is described in terms that display the influences of Frederic Spiegelberg and Aldous Huxley and more or less crystallize Murphy's mystical vision of early Esalen, just as the very first brochure encapsulated Dick Price's antipsychiatric therapeutic approach:

> A comparative study of some of the mystical traditions within the great world religions, combining discussion with practice of meditation exercises derived from these traditions. The seminar will explore the possibility of applying these ancient ideas and exercises to our present religious life, in ways appropriate to our individual temperaments, capacities, and circumstances. Special attention will be given to the Upanishads, the Tantras, the Christian contemplative life as exemplified by Ruysbroeck and St. John of the Cross, Hasidism, and the lives and teachings of Ramana Maharishi and Sri Aurobindo.

Esalen was becoming a place of combination and convergence—a nexus of intellectual and spiritual influences where Christian and Jewish mystics mixed freely with the Tantras and Aurobindo. Science was also beginning to play a role. On the first brochure of 1964 the equation $E = MC^2$ is superimposed over the Aurobindonian lotus, signaling again a certain distinct mysticism of energy. Here too a number of thinkers and figures who came to play a major role at Esalen made their first appearances. Frederick (Fritz) Perls introduced a small group to gestalt therapy and thus related gestalt to both existentialism and Zen Buddhism. Haridas Chaudhuri led a seminar on the internal yoga of Sri Aurobindo. Finally, Michael Harner, Joseph Henderson, and Charles Savage spoke on "shamanism," a topic already associated with the central early Esalen theme of psychedelic substances, hence the title of the seminar—Shamanism: Supernaturalism and Hallucinogenic Drugs.

The summer 1964 brochure announced the place's new name, Esalen Institute, and continued to attract figures that would become iconic in this era of American history and counterculture. There was A Trip with Ken Kesey, whose psychedelic exploits would soon be immortalized in Tom Wolfe's *The Electric Kool-Aid Acid Test;* a seminar on creativity by the psychologist Frank Barron; and a folk music concert, which would become a more or less annual event throughout the 1960s. "I had had no

FIGURE 8. Poster for fifth annual Big Sur Folk Festival at Esalen, c. 1969. Artist unknown.

idea," MIT historian William Irwin Thompson wrote of his 1967 summer visit to Esalen, "that the seminar I came up for was to be followed by a festival with Joan Baez *and* Judy Collins *and* Simon and Garfunkel *and* the Chambers Brothers."[32] Bernard Gunther taught Body Awareness. Charlotte Selver taught Sensory Reawakening. And a paralyzed and bed-bound Anthony Sutich lectured on humanistic psychology, that "third force" of American psychology that sought to move beyond both Freudian psychoanalysis and Skinnerian behavioralism toward a better "understanding of health, self-actualization, creativity and human potentiality in general."

In October Richard Alpert and Timothy Leary led a lecture on the ecstatic experience after their recently published *The Psychedelic Experience*. For legal or comedic reasons (it is not clear which), the last line of the seminar description reads: "No drugs will be used." In November Beat Buddhist poet Gary Snyder appeared after seven years studying Zen Buddhist meditation in Tokyo. A few weeks later in December, the Duke parapyschologist J. B. Rhine gave a seminar entitled Parapsychology and the Nature of Man. The year 1965 began with two seminars on American international relations (with the Soviet Union and China, respectively) framing a fascinating seminar offered by Frederic Spiegelberg called The Face of Enlightenment. Using slides of religious art from around the world

FIGURE 9. Ravi Shankar and George Harrison on the front lawn, c. 1968. Printed with permission of the Esalen Institute.

and a special study of the Hindu female saint, Ma Anandamayi, Spiegelberg sought to explore "the physical aspects of the enlightened state"—
again, the enlightenment of the body, now in the form of a slide-show.[33]
So ended 1964 and so began 1965.

Questions of Sex and Self

There are many ways to read Esalen's founding. Certainly, via Huxley and
Heard's American brand of Vedantic Hinduism and perennial philosophy, there is an emphasis on the Self as the immortal, eternal base of all
such experience, and with it, a certain ascetic tendency. But Heard in particular certainly understood this asceticism as fundamentally erotic. More
importantly, though, was the fact that this American encounter with Asia
was turning less and less to ascetic themes and more and more to erotic
ones. Hence Heard's explicit invocation of Tantric sexual sublimation and
Watts's consistent turn to Tantrism as a subject of his lectures and writing. Understood or not, something had begun to resonate between Tantric
Asia and the early beginnings of the American counterculture.

This makes good sense from a structural point of view. After all, both
the American Esalen and the Asian Tantric traditions were "counters"
to their respective normative or conservative cultures. This perhaps best
explains their various cross-cultural harmonies and echoes. There are
other more literal connections, however. The historian Theodore Roszak,
for example, who first brought the expression "counterculture" into popular consciousness in 1968 in a four-part article in the *Nation,* saw clearly
that in order to make sense of the American counterculture one also had
to understand its new erotic relationship to Asia. Here is what he wrote
in 1969, shortly after he had named the counterculture:

> The amorality of Zen, as one might imagine, was rapidly given
> special emphasis where sex was concerned. And in this respect,
> the latest European-American journey to the East *is* a new depar-
> ture. The Vedantism of the twenties and thirties had always been
> severely contemplative in the most ascetic sense of the term. One
> always has the feeling in looking through its literature that its fol-
> lowing was found among the very old or very withered, for whom
> the ideal swami was a kindly orientalized version of an Irish Je-
> suit priest in charge of a pleasant retreat....But the mysteries of

the Orient we now have on hand in the counter culture have broken entirely from this earlier Christianized interpretation. In fact,
nothing is so striking about the new orientalism as its highly sexed
flavor. If there was anything Kerouac and his colleagues found especially appealing in the Zen they adopted, it was the wealth of hyper-
bolic eroticism the religion brought with it rather indiscriminately
from the *Kama-sutra* and the tantric tradition.[34]

Speaking in my own terms, Roszak understood that *Tantra had overtaken Vedanta through the American counterculture.* In this, he simply
expressed sociologically in 1969 what Huxley had earlier imagined as Pala
in 1962, that forbidden island where the erotic pleasures of *maithuna* and
the mystical revelations of the *moksha*-medicine made life reasonably
happy and more or less peaceful, in striking contrast to—that is, *against*
(counter-)—the arrogant militarism, dogmatic beliefs, and repressed prud-
eries of Nation, God, and True Religion. Speaking in political terms, Roszak
understood that consciousness, not class, had become the new root and
generator of social revolution. Speaking in academic terms, he understood
that Freud had overtaken Marx, that psychology was more important to
these countercultural actors than sociology, and that the key was personal
experience. Significantly, of the seven figures he offered to demonstrate
such a multiple thesis—Norman O. Brown, Allen Ginsberg, Alan Watts,
Aldous Huxley, Timothy Leary, Paul Goodman, and Herbert Marcuse—the
first five had connections to Esalen, and the sixth (Goodman) had strong
indirect connections (through Fritz Perls). Whatever Roszak was naming
with his counterculture and erotic orientalism theses, Esalen seemed to
sit at the center of both.[35]

Again, though, it was not simply about energy or sex. There was also
the question of the self, of the very nature of subjectivity and identity—of
consciousness itself. Thus one of the most pressing questions in Big Sur
could be framed in this way: what model of human subjectivity would
dominate the countering culture of Esalen? The *soul* of traditional Christian theology that is created, fallen, and in need of salvation? The *psyche*
of modern psychology that is as conflicted as it is creative, all the while
controlled largely by hidden unconscious forces beyond the surface ego?
Or the Indian *atman* or Self, already immortal, divine and somehow sen-
suously blissful? Or perhaps there is no such thing as a self or a soul, as we
find, for example, in the Theravada no-self Buddhism that was so important to Dick Price. In any case, the nondual bliss (*ananda*) remained, and

this Delight was continuously posing other, equally important questions, such as: What of the body? And whither and whether sex?

This, of course, was Gerald Heard's question as well back in 1939. "We may ask," he wrote, "Have we here another and far more extensive example of the discharge of evolutionary energy? May we, by studying sex, hope to find how that energy might be channeled and, held from escape on more rudimentary levels, give rise to a higher degree of consciousness?"[36] Like (but well before) so many other Esalen intellectuals, Heard turned almost immediately to Tantric Asia for his initial answer. It is clear, he claimed, that, "in the Shakti form of Laya Yoga there was made a step in man's attempt to understand spastic sensation and to employ paroxysm to rise above Time to enlarge, and not to diffuse or to arrest, consciousness."[37]

Still, he was not finally happy with this answer, since he believed that the nervous energies of both pain and sex were in the end secondary manifestations of the primary force of evolution, which was, for him anyway, consciousness itself. Within our developing model of consciousness and energy, then, Heard clearly put the accent on consciousness and sought to suppress and sublimate energy. Accordingly, he turned to the subtleties and exquisite pleasures of an ascetic lifestyle and the fetish, not to deny sexuality or to renounce the world, but as a hyperconscious technique to channel his (homo)sexual evolutionary energies into a fuller and fuller life of the spirit.

In many ways, Gerald Heard's answer was very traditional both in the West and Asia: male homoerotic asceticism and sublimation have historically produced the model norms, repressions, and energies of sanctity.[38] It would not, however, be Esalen's answer, as the defining early presence of the banned Henry Miller, the panerotic painting of Hieronymus Bosch, the kissing couple on the cliff after the Night of the Dobermans, and Michael Murphy's first sexual experience and subsequent car accident all suggested. Such "accidents" were not experienced as accidents. They were interpreted as both ruptures with the familiar past and as signals of a different kind of future.

But there is also something more—the altered states of history signaling that this story would be neither traditional nor orthodox, especially in terms of gender and sexuality. Holiness would not take yet another sublimated homoerotic path here. It would be heterosexual or, better, pansexual. Recall that Murphy "crashed" immediately after his night of heterosexual delight and precisely on his way to introduce the homoerotic ascetic mystic Gerald Heard. I take that car accident as a powerful and potentially deadly struggle between the traditional and the new, between the way of male homoerotic sublimation and the way of heterosexual expression.

There would, of course, be real dangers on such a heterosexual heretical path, as the spinning car on the cliff suggested. It is not an easy or safe thing to break with the past. But there was also a firm guard rail to hold the new energy "on the road," so to speak. And it held. Most of all, though, there was an immense reservoir of pent-up pain and passion that could simply not be suppressed any longer. The place was about to burst into flames. It would not take long now.

/Mind /Manifest

PSYCHEDELIA AT EARLY ESALEN AND BEYOND

Spiritual practice is necessary in order to attain the essence. If one only repeats the scriptural verses with the mouth, nothing will happen. If one only says *"siddhi siddhi"* [bhang or cannabis], one will not become intoxicated. One must eat the *siddhi.*

RAMAKRISHNA in the *Kathamrita* 5.118

I could look back and see my body on the bed. I relived my life, and re-experienced many events I had forgotten. More than that, I went back in time in an evolutionary sense to where I was aware of being a one-celled organism . . . . The discovery that the human brain possesses an infinity of potentialities and can operate at unexpected space-time dimensions left me feeling exhilarated, awed, and quite convinced that I had awakened from a long ontological sleep.

TIMOTHY LEARY, *The Politics of Ecstasy*

From the mescaline-rich peyote buttons of traditional Amerindian cultures to what the first Esalen brochure calls the "drug-induced mysticism" of the early 1960s, mind-altering plants and substances have been a crucial part of American religious history for centuries, if not millennia.[1] Similar patterns, moreover, can be reasonably, if still often speculatively, located in the general history of religions. Such patterns—often advanced and developed by nonprofessional scholars—constitute one of the grand theories of religion that have come out of the mystical American counterculture that we are exploring here through the prism of Esalen.

Simply put, this theory of religion locates the origins of many paradigmatic religious revelations in the ingestion of mind-altering plants that open the psyche up to alternative realities that are otherwise closed off from it by the utilitarian filters of the brain. The latter filters, as theorists from Myers to Huxley have argued, are carefully designed by evolution to focus in on the tiniest sliver of the energy spectrum (that picked up by the five senses) in order to help us survive, that is, hunt, kill, and eat other animals and generally get along in the natural and social worlds so that we can procreate and pass our genes on to the next generation. Certain plants, as "natural" as nature itself, appear to shut such adaptive filters and concerns out and open us, as part of their same nature, to the most extraordinary realities. They *reveal*.

Somewhat surprisingly, this particular grand theory about the origins of religion did not arise from the counterculture, but from the American mainstream, with a New York banker and his wife no less. R. Gordon Wasson and his wife, Russian émigré Valentina Pavlovna, were amateur mycologists (mushroom experts). In a series of journal articles and books, Wasson has described their mycological researches within multiple cultural domains, including Amerindian and Siberian shamanism, ancient Vedic India, and the Eleusinian mysteries of classical Greece. In each case, Wasson provided ideas to experts in the field and asked them for confirmation or correction. As it turned out, he received more of the former than the latter, even on a psychopharmacological level. When he sent Albert Hofmann samples of mushrooms and morning glory seeds that Mexican shamans were using for their trance states, Hofmann ran the tests. Hofmann, the Swiss chemist and original synthesizer of LSD-25, found that both the mushrooms and the seeds produced chemicals of the same family that were in turn related to ergot, the "mold" or "tiny mushroom" similar to LSD that grows on rye and other grains and can induce visionary phenomena or, in high doses, death.

Over the decades, Wasson employed this same chemistry of consciousness to reread the history of religions: first in Mexico with the local *Sabia* (wise woman or gnostic) María Sabina in the 1950s, then in the ancient Indian texts with classicist Robert Graves and Sanskritists Wendy O'Flaherty and Stella Kramrisch in the '60s, and finally in ancient Greece with Carl Ruck in the '70s. Wasson was always particularly proud of his first *Velada* with María Sabina on the Saturday night of June 29, 1955 in Huautla de Jiménez, Oaxaca. His research team filmed and photographed the ritual as a kind of transmission event of these powerful religious substances from the indigenous Mesoamerican peoples to the Euro-American culture of Wasson and his later readers and successors— Timothy Leary, Michael Harner, Carlos Castaneda (whom Wasson was the first to denounce[2]), and Terence McKenna. All these men were connected to Esalen in some way.[3] Wasson also wrote about this event in 1957 in a widely read and richly illustrated essay for *Life* magazine—more evidence of the mainstream nature of the original hypothesis.[4]

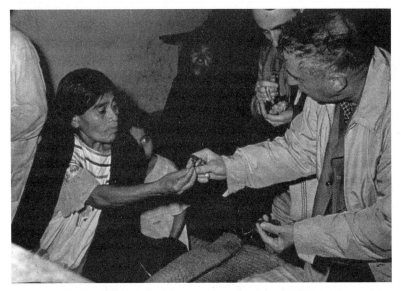

FIGURE 10. "Mexican Transmission," June 29, 1955. Photo by Allan Richardson, printed with permission of the R. G. Wasson Estate, with thanks to Robert Forte.

After these Mexican revelations, Wasson himself began to wonder about other cultures and other visionary phenomena. His mind soon settled on the historical mystery of the *soma* of ancient India, the plant whose crushed and carefully prepared essence seems to have granted the ancient *rishis* or seers their poetic flights that in turn helped produce the *Rig Veda,* the foundational revealed text of what would eventually become classical Hinduism. Working primarily with classicist Robert Graves (whose major collaboration was probably not sufficiently acknowledged by Wasson) and finally with Wendy O'Flaherty, then a graduate student at Harvard studying with Daniel Ingalls, Wasson became convinced that the Vedic *soma* was in fact a particular strain of mushroom from Eurasia, the *Amanita muscaria* (or fly agaric), whose powers, Wasson felt, had been widely worshipped under different forms across a broad global belt of cultures from the Americas through Europe and Asia.[5]

In the following decade, classicist Carl Ruck, following Wasson's lead and the chemical studies of Albert Hofmann, provocatively argued that the ancient Greeks had used a drink derived from ergot in their famous Eleusinian mysteries. In these hushed secret rituals, in which both Socrates and Plato allegedly participated, initiates were required "to keep shut" (*muein*) about the precise details of the ceremonial rites that gave us the Greek term *mustikos* or mystical.[6] In other words, according to Wasson and Ruck, the mystical possesses psychedelic origins in Western culture.

Although often fantastically overextended and forced (like all meta-theories), Wasson's hypothesis remains an important, if often conveniently neglected, theory that, for our own purposes, undoubtedly played a major role in the psychedelic subcultures of the 1960s, including that of Esalen. Whether established or not, Wasson's mycological theory of the origin of religion was unquestionably one of the major narratives of the American counterculture, providing one of its most important and lasting mythological structures. By the founding of Esalen in 1962, Wasson's historical and chemical hypotheses, catalyzed again by Huxley's *The Doors of Perception* (1954), had begun to pass over into the realm of religious revelation. America was no longer dealing with just the eccentric theory of an established banker and his wife. America was now witnessing the birth of a religious phenomenon with immense appeal and broad cultural, artistic, musical, medical, metaphysical, political, and legal implications. Wasson was being co-opted by Leary. As it turned out, like so many other mystical traditions concerned with the production of altered states of consciousness, the movement would eventually crash on the rocks of pressing social needs and moral concerns. The filters always return.

Altered Words

As with all temporary revelations, though, this one left its mark in language, through which we can still trace its lightning-like paths, as in a burned retina. Words encode ideologies, and there are few words that encode more entrenched ideologies than those surrounding the naming and use of mind-altering plants and synthesized substances. Gordon and Valentina Wasson were especially aware of this. Indeed, they developed an entire cultural theory (partly out of their Anglo-Saxon/Russian marriage) that divided the world roughly into mycophobic or "mushroom fearing" zones (like England) and mycophiliac or "mushroom loving" zones (like Russia).[7] One, after all, would expect something very different from the English "toadstool" than from the Mexican "flesh of the gods"!

The same issue is already encoded in our opening nineteenth-century epigraph on Ramakrishna's *siddhi* or cannabis. This Sanskrit term normally refers to the magical, psychic, or supernormal powers that yogic and especially Tantric practice is said to generate spontaneously. In the present passage, however, *siddhi* functions as a code word, as a descriptor of both cannabis and the parapsychological states that such a substance can effect in the consciousness of the one who ingests it. This connection between the psychic and the psychedelic is both an ancient and a modern one and certainly respects no cultural or political boundaries. Wasson, for example, recounts how the very next day after his first *Velada* with María Sabina he received detailed and impossibly accurate information about his son in New York City by parapsychological means from a Mexican shaman, and this despite his constitutional horror of the chicanery of so many of these claims.[8] Similarly, Terence McKenna would later also comment on the telepathic and psychical components of his own psychedelic trips. The Bengali or Sanskrit *siddhi,* in other words, is a very wise word—more altered states of history, here posing as an altered word.

Similar linguistic complexities and cultural connotations are apparent in a small set of newly coined words that the ingestion of mushrooms and synthesized substances has produced over the last half century within the English language. The journey began with two playful poems penned by psychiatrist Humphry Osmond and Aldous Huxley in correspondence. Huxley began: "To make this trivial world sublime. Take half a gramme of phanerothyme." To which Osmond responded: "To fathom hell or soar angelic. Just take a pinch of psychedelic." Obviously, it was the second Greek neologism—meaning roughly "mind-manifesting" or "soul-revealing"— that stuck and became the preferred term in the 1960s over the general banality of "drug" and the more technical but too psychiatrically loaded *hallucinogen* (hallucination-generating).

The Psychedelia of Early Esalen

Excesses and enthusiasms aside, it is most certainly true that powerful mind-altering plants have been informing human culture since before the beginning of recorded time. It is also certainly true that there are particular moments in a society's history where this intimate connection between plant and culture becomes particularly transparent, and sometimes particularly contentious. In modern Western literary and artistic culture, what Paul Schimmel calls "the relationship between the creative act, the exploration of altered states, and the inducement of such states through mind-altering substances" can be traced back to the late eighteenth century, when Europe's intellectual elite began employing everything from opium and hashish to absinthe (a green liquor) and mescaline to spark their creative visions.[9] The Orientalist poem "Kubla Khan," for example, came to Coleridge in an opium-induced dream, and Van Gogh's love of absinthe was legendary. And on and on we could go.

In America, the early 1960s marks a chemical-religious watershed in which drug use "forms part of a tradition that privileges immediacy, from gnosis to rock and roll."[10] And Esalen, as with so many other things, seemed to sit at the center of this American gnosis. Indeed, as Anderson notes, it is no small matter that every one of the leaders of the first brochure had participated in LSD experiments,[11] and that Aldous Huxley, the Esalen literary figure who inspired the psychedelic movement, also inspired the human potential movement. Esalen, in other words, had some distinctly psychedelic beginnings.[12]

And this psychedelic pattern, this public secret, would continue down through the decades. From Aldous Huxley and Humphry Osmond, to Stanislav Grof, the Czech psychiatrist who used LSD to map the human psyche, to the shamanistic mushroom explorer Terence McKenna, many of the major figures of the movement have either given workshops at Esalen or have lived there for extended periods of time. Indeed, Huxley bestowed the all-important central category of the place ("human potentialities") and has an important seminar room named after him on the grounds; Grof lived and taught there for fourteen years; and McKenna lived in the Little House for some time, stayed with former Esalen president Steve Donovan when he was undergoing brain surgery and dying, and willed his entire literary estate to Esalen. Obviously, if we are to understand Esalen, we must also understand its psychedelia, however many ethical challenges this presents within our present legal and cultural milieus.

As it turns out, such a temporary focus takes us into the very heart of any number of traditional themes, including that Indic linkage of the psychic and the psychedelic through the yogic and Tantric vocabulary of the *siddhi*. The same psychic-psychedelic connections appears quite explicitly in the very first Esalen brochure, which actually names "psychical research" and "work with the 'mind-opening' drugs" as two of its three major foci (the third being psychology, that is, the study of the mind itself as the basis of the other two). As we have already seen in the previous chapter, moreover, the fourth seminar given at Esalen was dedicated to "drug-induced mysticism," which soon became one of the most popular and frequently offered topics.

To my knowledge, there are no records of that first formative seminar, so we cannot determine with any certainty exactly what was said there. But we do know what they were reading. Three authors are listed alphabetically: Aldous Huxley, Alan Watts, and R. C. Zaehner. In order to get some idea of the early Esalen debates and dialogues about "drug-induced mysticism," we will look at each in turn here, not in their alphabetized arbitrariness, but in the chronological order in which their books historically appeared and so defined the cultural debates that Esalen was now entering.

Aldous Huxley and R. C. Zaehner: Debating The Doors of Perception (1954–1957)

In the spring of 1953, a few months before Wasson's historical encounter with María Sabina in Mexico, Huxley swallowed four-tenths of a gram of mescaline in the hills above Los Angeles under the supervision of his friend and fellow wordsmith Humphry Osmond and in the company of his wife Maria. Huxley's objective was to explore the mystical potential of the hallucinogen, for "short of being born again as a visionary, a medium, or a musical genius," how else "can we ever visit the worlds to which, to Blake, to Swedenborg, to Johann Sebastian Bach, were home?" he asked.[13] In essence, Huxley wanted to know "from the inside" those altered states of history from which the mystics, artists, and musical masters had been writing, painting, and composing their visionary works.

What the writer expected from the drug was an elaborate visionary show within the solipsistic confines of his own chemical brain. What he got instead was an apocalyptically tinged revelation of the external world—"The great change was in the realm of objective fact"[14]—and the creative genesis of his little Blakean tract, *The Doors of Perception*. It was Huxley's fortieth book, written during one of the most conservative and repressive moments in American history. Eisenhower was in office, the races were segregated, gender roles were fixed and unquestioned, and McCarthyism was the order of the day. Huxley couldn't have known his book would become a kind of cult classic for the 1960s counterculture, inspire a generation of writers on the mystical, and provide a catchy name for a popular rock band (the Doors). Huxley was not thinking about the '60s or rock music at the time. He was thinking about ancient Greek philosophy, Platonism to be exact, and medieval German Christian mysticism:

Istigkeit—wasn't that the word Meister Eckhart liked to use? "Is-ness." The Being of Platonic philosophy—except that Plato seems to have made the enormous, the grotesque mistake of separating Being from becoming and identifying it with the mathematical abstraction of the Idea. He could never, poor fellow, have seen a bunch of flowers shining with their own inner light and all but quivering under the pressure of the significance with which they were charged . . . a transience that was yet eternal life, a perpetual perishing that was at the same time pure Being, a bundle of minute, unique particulars in which, by some unspeakable and yet self-evident paradox, was to be seen the divine source of all existence.[15]

This dialectical experience of the unity of Being and Becoming—of the unity of consciousness and energy, we might say—was also a profoundly hermeneutical one, that is, it was very much related to Huxley's reading practice. The experience, after all, clearly both issued from his intimate knowledge of Hindu and Buddhist mystical literature and in turn impacted on those same texts, now transfigured in the light shining through the doors thrown open by the mescaline.

Even more interesting, the books of twentieth-century scholar of Zen Buddhism D. T. Suzuki appear to have mediated Huxley's interpretation of the experience *within the experience itself*. No one has said it, but it is worth saying: Aldous Huxley's psychedelic mysticism was exceedingly bookish.

The Beatific Vision, Sat Chit Ananda, Being-Awareness-Bliss—for the first time I understood, not on the verbal level, not by inchoate hints or at a distance, but precisely and completely what those prodigious syllables referred to. And then I remembered a passage I had read in one of Suzuki's essays, "What is the Dharma-Body of the Buddha?" . . . the Master answers "The hedge at the bottom of the garden." . . . It had been, when I read it, only a vaguely pregnant piece of nonsense. Now it was all clear as day, as evident as Euclid. Of course the Dharma-Body of the Buddha was the hedge at the bottom of the garden.[16]

Much of *The Doors of Perception* concerns itself, not with the experience itself, but with Huxley's speculations on what it all might mean. Huxley wonders, as we have already noted, whether the brain's function might be primarily eliminative, filtering out every sensation and bit of information that is not important to human physical and social survival. Through mystical or psychedelic experience, however, something Huxley calls Mind at Large "seeps past the no longer watertight valve" and "all kinds of biologically useless things start to happen."[17]

Among these useless things are an apocalyptic entrance into reality itself beyond the cozy symbols and linguistic signs and a subsequent indifference to human relationships and social concerns. This kind of mystical state, Huxley admits, cannot be reconciled with active charity and practical compassion.[18] Under the influence of mescaline, Huxley confesses that he knew contemplation "at its height, but not yet in its fullness."[19] In the end, a more dialectical position is needed, one that knows the ontological ground but can still insist on the integrity, even holiness, of the individual and human reason: "But the man who comes back through the Door in the Wall will never be quite the same as the man who went out. He will be wiser but less cocksure, happier but less self-satisfied, humbler in acknowledging his ignorance yet better equipped to understand the relationship of words to things, of systematic reasoning to the unfathomable Mystery which it tries, forever vainly, to comprehend."[20] Huxley, in other words, recognized very early that the altered states of mescaline could be both mystically profound *and* morally wanting. He understood that the psychedelic is not the ethical (although, as many have argued, it can deeply inform ethical and social sensibilities), and he was wise enough to make room for both human concerns in his broad humane worldview.

Like Huxley, the early Esalen seminar leaders and participants were very much aware of the religious dilemma that the psychedelic substances posed. Put in Christian terms, what was essentially at stake was the theology of grace and the necessity of the sacraments and community life. The Oxford don R. C. Zaehner put the matter as succinctly as anyone in his famous rejection of Huxley's thesis.

Zaehner begins *Mysticism Sacred and Profane* (1957): "It should be said at the outset that this book owes its genesis to Mr. Aldous Huxley. Had *The Doors of Perception* never been published, it is extremely doubtful whether the present author would have been rash enough to enter the field of comparative mysticism. Mr. Huxley left us no choice."[21] The claim of Huxley that his own mescaline-induced mystical experiences were of the same nature and order of the classical mystics of the history of religions strikes "at the roots of all religion that makes any claim to be taken seriously," Zaehner argued.[22] Why? Because "if mescalin can produce the Beatific Vision here on earth . . . the Christian emphasis on morality is not only all wrong but also a little naive." Mescaline thus "presents us not only with a social problem,—for how on earth could a society composed exclusively of ecstatics possibly be run?—but also with a theological problem of great magnitude."[23]

Zaehner, of course, was right to point to these problems. The writers and seminar leaders of Esalen would often come to different answers than those offered by the pious Zaehner, but all had to struggle with the questions he so poignantly posed. Zaehner's own answer was a kind of typological dualism between what he called "profane mysticism," which is produced from entirely natural psychological and biological processes and leads usually to some form of monism or nature mysticism (and of which the drug-induced variety was one example), and "sacred mysticism," which involves real transcendence and love and requires the grace-filled actions of the one and only personal God of Zaehner's Catholic faith (or some Muslim, Jewish, or Hindu version thereof).

Alan Watts: From Skepticism to Cosmic Joy (1958–1962)

Alan Watts was definitely not a monotheist, but he was not so sure either about all this drug stuff. He had certainly read his share of Huxley, Heard, and Isherwood, and he was quite grateful for the ways their discovery of mind-manifesting substances had relieved Huxley and Heard of their ascetic, if not actually prudish and Victorian, prejudices.[24] But he was frankly skeptical when it came to Huxley's claims about the mystical potential of something like mescaline. How could this be?

But Watts was an adventurer by nature, and, very much unlike the pious Zaehner, he had so few inhibitions that he did not hesitate to describe himself as a hedonist and Bohemian, as "a disreputable epicurean who has had three wives, seven children, and five grandchildren—and I cannot make up my mind whether I am confessing or boasting."[25] By his own confession, he could only follow his own way (Tao) and so be quite literally perverse: "although you must remember that this word means *per* (through) *verse* (poetry), out-of-the-way and wayward, which is surely towards the way, and that to be queer—to 'follow your own weird'—is wholeheartedly to accept your own *karma,* or fate, or destiny, and thus to be odd in the service of God."[26]

This odd Godly service took Watts right to the Blakean door Huxley had opened for his readers and Zaehner had tried to shut, that is, the door of psychedelic substances. Watts walked through six times with three different substances (300 milligrams of mescaline, 100 micrograms of LSD, and 20 milligrams of psilocybin) before he put down on paper what he found inside in a little essay called "The New Alchemy" (1958) and, a bit later, in a widely read and richly illustrated book, *The Joyous Cosmology: Adventures in the Chemistry of Consciousness* (1962). Erickson has noted that both this book and Huxley's *The Doors of Perception* were widely circulated at Esalen in the 1960s. It is not difficult to see why. *The Joyous Cosmology* constitutes a kind of "textualized experience" in which Watts synthesizes his various trips into a beautifully written vision of things—yet another example of the literary and textual nature of this countercultural mystical tradition. Indeed, the literary quality of this text, like Huxley's, is quite striking. There is no doubt about it: *these men could write.* And, if we are to believe their own confessions, part of this literary success was due to the psychedelic substances themselves, which, according to Watts, act as impressive catalysts for creative, associative, and theoretical thought. Certainly, as McKenna would later remind his readers, opium (that is, the *siddhi* of our opening epigraph) had long been used in Western culture to inspire poetry and literature.

Still, however inspired, there is something provocatively reductive about this kind of text, something that suggests that the secret of religious revelation and mystical experience lies in our bodies, not in the heavens. This no doubt is what a writer like R. C. Zaehner was reacting to, and even Watts recognized its force: as a self-confessed comparative mystic who had taken the time and energy to meditate and read his way into the grace of such states, he was "at once gratified and embarrassed by a development in Western science which could possibly put this unitive vision of the world, by almost shockingly easy means, within the reach of many who have thus far sought it in vain by traditional means."[27]

This in fact actually happened to the comparativist of religion and Esalen participant Huston Smith. Smith meditated for years to little effect and even argued that Westerners could not access the mystical experiences Asians seemed so prone to until Aldous Huxley passed him Leary's phone number at an MIT event. Smith then contacted Leary on his own and arranged for an experimental mescaline session with Leary on New Year's Day, 1961, under the auspices of the Center for Personality Research at Harvard University. The effect was overwhelming and deeply, deeply religious: Smith uses expressions like "terrifying beyond belief" and "emanationism" to capture what he calls the "empirical metaphysics" of the stunning event. He had read plenty of Vedanta and Plotinus.

Now he was experiencing these systems as empirical truths.[28] He could perceive at least five different bands of consciousness, and he could now make sense of Henri Bergson's notion of the brain as a kind of reducing valve. Smith would become one of the most eloquent and important writers on the religious legitimacy and historical significance of psychedelics, which he prefers to call entheogens (literally, substances that "generate God within"). He also effectively tried to "cleanse the doors of perception" that Huxley had so dramatically opened and Leary had just as efficiently muddied for so many. Among other points, Smith would insist that such experiences were not sufficient taken alone, and that the true religious import of entheogens was their ability to catalyze an entire religious *life*, not just a single religious experience.[29]

As for Watts's *Joyous Cosmology*, the subtitle alone suggests that the enlightenment of the body was quickly entering the chemical, and even molecular and genetic, levels through a kind of micromysticism. With Leary, moreover (who co-wrote the foreword to *The Joyous Cosmology* with his Harvard colleague Richard Alpert), it would not be long before an entire genetic mysticism of DNA strands was set loose in the culture. A very small number of writers, artists, and intellectuals were transforming an entire generation, and they were doing it with what were essentially chemical-spiritual tracts infused, more often than not, with a kind of subtle reductionism of the sacred to the chemical.

What, then, constitutes the joyous cosmology that Watts claimed to see within this chemistry of consciousness? Most fundamentally, it was an enlightenment of the body in our own terms, that is, a dissolution of the division of the mind and body that has haunted Western culture down through the ages. Indeed, Watts's text begins with this sentence: "Slowly it becomes clear that one of the greatest of all superstitions is the separation of the mind from the body."[30] Ultimately, Watts will reject all hyphenated compromises (like "mental-physical") and turn to the language of energy instead: "Whether it is organic or inorganic, we are learning to see matter as patterns of energy—not *of* energy as if energy were a stuff, but as energetic pattern, moving order, active intelligence."[31]

The book is generously illustrated with twenty-one photographs of abstract geometric patterns taken entirely from the natural world: the polished surface of an agate, the patterned back of a goliath beetle, the squiggly but strangely symmetrical feeding patterns of a caterpillar, the fireworks-like skeleton of star coral, platinum crystal magnified 750,000 times, and finally, as if to signal the cosmic perspective of the final lines of the book, the spiral galaxy Messier 81. The implied message of the photographs is the same message of the text itself, namely, that we are inseparable parts of a greater whole.

Moreover, the world is not happening to us; we are happening as intimate parts of the world. We should thus fret no more about a death or loss than our wise body worries about the death of a skin cell, the destruction of an invading bacterial organism, or the dropping of another hair follicle: it is all a matter of perspective.[32] In short, the world is a nondual hierarchy, a vast coincidence of opposites,[33] a hyperdimensional history whose basic nature is joy.

There is something terrifying, even inhuman, about such a vision, and one wonders if Watts is an entirely reliable guide here (the practical details of his own life would suggest not). Like McKenna after him, Watts was unbelievably articulate, but not entirely trustworthy. One wonders, in particular, if his eloquence has not swamped his moral vision here, or whether he even has one at this moment. Perhaps this is why, like so many mystical writers before him, Watts realizes that he has a secret that must be revealed, regardless of whether or not anyone "has ears to hear." And so, toward the end of the book, he speaks to his readers directly:

> Listen, there's something I *must* tell. I've never, never seen it so clearly. But it doesn't matter a bit if you don't understand, because each one of you is quite perfect as you are, even if you don't know it. Life is basically a gesture, but no one, no thing, is *making* it. There is no necessity for it to happen, and none for it to go on happening.... It's a gesture of motion, of sound, of color, and just as no one is making it, it isn't *happening* to anyone. There is simply no problem of life; it is completely purposeless play—exuberance which is its own end... There is no reason whatever to explain it, for explanations are just another form of complexity, a new manifestation of life on top of life, of gestures gesturing. Pain and suffering are simply extreme forms of play, and there isn't anything in the whole universe to be afraid of because it doesn't happen to anyone! There isn't any substantial ego at all. The ego is a kind of flip, a knowing of knowing, a fearing of fearing. It's a curlicue, an extra jazz to experience, a sort of double-take or reverberation, a dithering of consciousness which is the same as anxiety.[34]

Watts's bending of the English language to express such a vision often involved a related gender-bending that played havoc with the usual American assumptions about gender identity and heterosexuality. Within such a universe, life, Watts tells us, "seems to resolve itself down to a tiny germ or nipple of sensitivity. I call it the Eenie-Weenie—a squiggling little nucleus that is trying to make love to itself and can never quite get there. The whole fabulous complexity of vegetable and animal life, as of human civilization, is just a colossal elaboration of the Eenie-Weenie trying to make the Eenie-Weenie. I am in love with myself, but cannot seek myself without hiding myself. As I pursue my own tail, it runs away from me."[35] A vague sort of Taoism finally enters the picture: "The principle is that all dualities and opposites are not disjoined but polar; they do not encounter and confront one another from afar; they exfoliate from a common center. Ordinary thinking conceals polarity and relativity because it employs *terms*, the terminals or ends, the poles, neglecting what lies between them."[36]

Timothy Leary and the Origins of Psychedelic Orientalism (1962)

What is particularly striking from a comparative perspective is the degree to which such a psychedelic vision, very much like Huxley's, turns to Asian philosophies in order to express these metaphysical realizations. Except for a final vision of cosmic love involving "angels with wings of golden fire" and a face that reminds Watts of a Byzantine icon of Christ as Ruler of the Universe,[37] the joyous cosmology of the text is almost entirely of Buddhist, Taoist, and especially Hindu extraction. Indeed, years later, when Watts was writing his memoirs and looking back on the writing of this same text, he would identify this "joyous cosmology" as fundamentally Hindu, and this despite his own conscious leanings toward Japanese Zen and Chinese Taoism. He would also comment on its "simultaneously holy and disreputable" quality, perhaps a reference to the amorality or transmorality of this nondual worldview and its dramatic sexual expressions:[38]

> But oddly, considering my absorption in Zen at the time, the flavor of these experiences was Hindu rather than Chinese. Somehow the atmosphere of Hindu mythology and imagery slid into them, suggesting at the same time that Hindu philosophy was a local form of a sort of undercover wisdom, inconceivably ancient, which everyone knows in the back of his mind but will not admit. This wisdom was simultaneously holy and disreputable, and therefore necessarily esoteric, and it came in the dress of a totally logical, obvious, and basic common sense.[39]

"Undercover wisdom," "simultaneously holy and disreputable," "esoteric"—none of these terms reflect the self-understanding of orthodox Hinduism, then or now. They are all rather code words that Watts used to refer to his own experience of the Tantric transmission.

This psychedelic turn to Asia is worth commenting on for a moment. Often, this Asian turn is read as a kind of foolish Western projection on cultures somehow completely devoid of such meanings. I think such a reading is both demeaning and mistaken. The truth of the matter is that the American visionaries saw their own altered states accurately, fantastically reflected in the mythologies and mystical systems of Asia. That is why so many young Americans traveled there in the 1960s and '70s. That is why they loved India, Tibet, Nepal, and Japan. Yes, they were projecting (but so was everyone else, including the Indians, Tibetans, Nepalese, and Japanese). Yes, they missed the ascetic and conservative orthodoxies of these ancient cultures. But they also found something very real and very important there. They found the Asian countercultures, that is, the "undercover wisdom" of Tantra.

It should hardly surprise us, then, to learn that many contemporary American Buddhist meditators found their first taste of enlightenment in psychedelic states.[40] Nor should we be shocked to discover that the archetypal American guru Ram Dass identified three organic stages in his transformation from "Dr. Richard Alpert, PhD" into "Baba Ram Dass": the social science stage (as a Harvard psychologist), the psychedelic stage (psilocybin and LSD), and the yogi stage (under the tutelage of his Indian guru, Neem Karoli Baba). Nor finally should we flinch to find William Blake and Hieronymus Bosch showing up yet again, this time as a "huge red wave" that resembled both of their arts and encoded all of "Alpert's" identities.[41] In any case, created by the psychology, the psychedelics, the visionary art, and the Indian guru, "Baba Ram Dass" makes what is perhaps one of his first public appearances in May of 1969 in the Esalen catalog with these words: "Richard Alpert had been on the faculties of Stanford, Harvard, and the University of California. His search has led from the academic to the psychedelic to the traditional, but obscured, mystical practices of the East. In 1967 Dr. Alpert started by Land Rover in Iran in search of men who might still retain the keys to the knowledge of enlightenment. Finally his search found fruit in relationship to a Master of Raja Yoga. He returns to the United States as BABA RAM DASS."[42]

As Michael Murphy points out in an interview, it would certainly be a serious mistake to reduce America's turn East to the use of psychedelics.[43]

There were other important factors, from a deep disillusionment with the mainline churches and synagogues, to the lifting of immigration barriers for Asian peoples, to the simultaneous appearance of charismatic gurus in the cities and talented Indologists in the universities (Heinrich Zimmer at Columbia, Mircea Eliade at Chicago, and Frederic Spiegelberg at Stanford, to name just a few).

But it would also be a mistake to ignore the psychedelic catalyst or dismiss it as nothing more than Western projection and postcolonial gazing. After all, similar mind-altering substances have been used in Asia for millennia. No, America's psychedelic orientalism may have been naïve at times, but it was definitely not simply pure projection. It was much more a combination of partial observation, an intuitive sympathy for Asian countercultures, selective borrowing, and almost perfect timing.

This psychedelic orientalism hardly escaped the notice of any number of counterculture actors. Few, however, were so taken with it than the Harvard psychologist turned 1960s guru Timothy Leary (1920–1997), who more or less defined the movement—for better and for worse—throughout the next decade. Leary, unlike Huxley and Watts, was not a major actor at Esalen. Indeed, during one of his visits he decided to "escape" the grounds for more exciting venues by hiding in the trunk of a friend's car. Still, he and Richard Alpert were guides for Murphy's third LSD trip in 1964 on the grounds.[44] It is probably safe to say that Leary's intellectual presence at Esalen was palpable in the late '60s, and that there is no one—with the possible exception of Richard Alpert—who did more to turn the chemical mysticism of the '60s "East."

Predictably, this East was a Tantric East. To mention just a few of the dozens, indeed hundreds, of textual examples, we might notice that traditional images of the Tantric *chakras,* including an abstract triangular *yoni* (or vagina), were painted on the house at Millbrook where much of Leary's early experimentation took place;[45] that Leary wrote a poem on the *chakras* in 1965 while he was living at Millbrook; and that the same text, at least in its present edition, includes a playful line-drawing of Leary as a Tantric *mahasiddha* or "great perfected being," complete with the traditional Tibetan skull cup and the modern ritual implements of an LSD trip.[46] Little wonder, then, that when Leary, Alpert, and Ralph Metzner set out to create a manual for their psychedelic rituals, they chose a Vajrayana Buddhist text, *The Tibetan Book of the Dead,* as their model.[47] Or that Leary's ecstatic *High Priest* is filled with Tantric texts, images, doctrines, and even guides (for his last trip Leary lists the Hindu god Krishna as his!), all translated here through Leary's evolutionary mysticism.

Leary arrived at his LSD Tantra only gradually. By his own confession, in 1961, when he first realized the extraordinary sexual potential of the drug, he was much too Irish Catholic "to realize that God and Sex are one, that God for a man is woman, that the direct path to God is through the divine union of male-female." It would not be until 1964 that he really awoke to his own "sexual yoga," and this only after he had listened to his "tantric guru with the Siva tiger skin, . . . resurrected my body, and moved on the journey to the East."[48]

There were at least two important steps along the way in Leary's Tantric journey to the East. The first is recorded in a letter from Huxley to Leary that Robert Forte has preserved for us. According to Forte and as evidenced by this letter, there is little doubt that Timothy Leary's turn to Asia stems finally back to Aldous Huxley. The two had been corresponding throughout 1961 on the subject of LSD. At some point, Leary seems to have asked Huxley about the subject of Tantra. On February 2, 1962, Huxley answers by suggesting the works of Sir John Woodroffe, an early Calcutta judge who pioneered Tantric Studies, Heinrich Zimmer's chapter on Tantra in *Philosophies of India* (ghostwritten by Joseph Campbell), and the scholarly works of Mircea Eliade and Edward Conze.

Then Huxley launches into his own interpretations of Tantra. He praises it as the highest ideal possible, explicitly links it to Zen Buddhism, invokes psychoanalysis and gestalt therapy to explain its psychological mechanisms, offers some rather pointed criticisms of Asian traditions that ascetically reject the world (in a sentence that makes no grammatical sense), and finally suggests that it is Tantra that supplies the best context for the ritual use of psychedelics:

> the basic ideal [of Tantra] seems to me the highest possible ideal—
> enlightenment achieved, essentially, through constant awareness.
> This is the ultimate yoga—being aware, conscious even of the
> unconscious—on every level from the physiological to the spiritual.
> In this context see the list of 112 exercises in awareness, extracted
> from a Tantrik Text and printed at the end of "Zen Flesh Zen Bones"
> (now in paperback. The whole of gestalt therapy is anticipated in
> these exercises—and the world) as the Vedantists and the Nirvana-
> addicts of the Hinayana School of Buddhists. Tantra teaches a yoga
> of sex, a yoga of eating (even eating forbidden foods and drinking
> forbidden drinks) . . . . LSD and the mushrooms should be used, it
> seems to me, in the context of this basic Tantrik idea of the yoga of

total awareness, leading to enlightenment within the world of everyday experience—which of course becomes the world of miracle and beauty and divine mystery when experience is what it always ought to be.[49]

The second step in Leary's Tantric journey occurred just a few weeks after this letter, and this time it is Leary who locates the event both temporally and spatially and interprets its (now Hindu) significance for us. Leary dates the event in the spring of 1962 and precisely locates it in a Boston Vedanta ashram dedicated to Ramakrishna. Although the presence of Huston Smith down the river at MIT was important as well, it all began, Leary claims, with Fred Swain, a former World War II air force major turned Vedanta Hindu monk. Swain was living in the ashram near Boston and telling Leary, then still teaching at Harvard, about "the psychedelic pantheon of gods and his guru and yoga." Leary began visiting the ashram and reading the Hindu scriptures as psychedelic manuals. "The Hindu myths," he concluded, "were session reports."

Soon Leary was asked by members of the ashram to guide them through an LSD session. The psychedelic substance was mixed with Ganges holy water in chalices and ritually drunk in the sacred confines of the Vedanta Society temple, just as five years earlier Wasson had witnessed the Mexican female shamans approach their sacred mushrooms as a kind of esoteric Christian "communion" service. As "the Holy folk got high," Leary reports, the temple room morphed into a living Purana or Hindu mythological text. Leary himself became Shiva, the erotic deity of so many of the Tantric traditions. Not surprisingly, Shiva's consort Shakti quickly manifested herself as well, this time as a beautiful Vedantic nun named, appropriately, Shakti. According to Leary, Shakti crawled over to Leary, put her head in his lap, and began to adoringly address Leary as Shiva.

The candles burned. The incense wafted. And the parliament of avatars represented in the temple shone forth in approval: "Ramakrishna's statue breathed and his eyes twinkled the message. Vivekananda's brown face beamed and winked. Christ grinned to be joined again by his celestial brothers." The effect of all of this on Leary was transformative, a kind of initiation into his own Hindu supernature: "I was a Hindu from that moment on. No, that's not the way to say it. I recognized that day in the temple that we are all Hindus in our essence. We are all Hindu Gods and Goddesses. Laughing Krishna. Immutable Brahma. Yes and

Asiatic-sensual Siva. Stern Kali with bloody hands. Undulant flowering Laxmi. Multi-armed Vishnu. Noble Rama. That day in the temple I discovered my Hindu-ness."

This was also the day that Leary began to realize that he had a real religious vocation, that he was being called by both his own chromosomes and the historical times to become a guru, even perhaps, in his own words, a saint. His analytical mind, however, never left him: "Is it reincarnation? Or just the living-out of adolescent fantasies of messiahism? It makes no difference how you explain it—it's as real as rain." In any case, the monks and nuns of the ashram saw clearly that Leary was a guru now, and they treated him accordingly. Leary would soon abandon his identity as a Harvard lecturer (in the end he was fired for failing to show up for his own classes) and become a countercultural saint. Still, he was sophisticated enough to see that this vocation, like all genetic reality, was "a combination of internal protein potentiality and external pressure. Seed and sun. And so with man's spiritual evolution. Inner potential plus external social pressure." Leary, in other words, had his own understanding of the altered states of history, one that combined the enlightenment of the body down to its tiniest DNA spirals (predictably often likened to the coiled *kundalini* serpent of Tantric yoga) and the broader contexts of culture, politics, and religion.[50]

Extreme caution is in order, however, when dealing with anything Timothy Leary said or wrote. Even his closest friends often recognized that he donned and shed metaphors and religious identities like a snail with a series of shells. Hindu and Buddhist Tantra were two of these shells he donned and shed for his own purposes. One wonders if he took any of it seriously in the long run.

More seriously still, Leary was prone to make things up when it suited him. The highly publicized 1966 *Playboy* interview "She Comes in Colors" is a good example of this fiction-on-the-spot. In this interview, Leary famously claims that a woman can have several hundred orgasms in a properly prepared LSD session. "Several hundred?" the *Playboy* interviewer asked in disbelief. "Yes, several hundred."

No, not several hundred. As Leary confessed years later to a young female German talk-show host (who was understandably interested in the claim), he was simply making this up.[51] Which leads one to suspect other aspects of the *Playboy* interview and, indeed, by extension, Leary's entire corpus.

"Several hundred orgasms" aside, the link between psychedelics and eroticism was quite real and was often noted by other writers. Leary, then, was probably not exaggerating too much when he had the following exchange:

> PLAYBOY: And this rapture was erotic?
>
> LEARY: Transcendentally. An enormous amount of energy from every fiber of your body is released under LSD—most specifically including sexual energy.... The three inevitable goals of the LSD session are to discover and make love with God, to discover and make love with yourself, and to discover and make love with a woman.... The sexual impact is, of course, the open but private secret about LSD, which none of us has talked about in the last few years. It's socially dangerous enough to say that LSD helps you find divinity and helps you discover yourself. You're already in trouble when you say that. But then if you announce that the psychedelic experience is basically a *sexual* experience, you're asking to bring the whole middle-aged, middle-class monolith down on your head.[52]

As with his orientalism, so too with his mystical eroticism, Leary was probably remembering something that Huxley had once told him, that is, "to not let the sexual cat out of the bag," that is, to not link psychedelics with sexuality in a public forum, even if, as everyone in the know knew, they were in fact linked. Gerald Heard had told him the same thing, invoking the earlier examples of "Tantric cults" and "medieval sects," the latter most likely a reference to the Brethren of the Free Spirit whose erotic mysticism both Henry Miller and Heard had seen in Bosch's *The Garden of Earthly Delights*.[53]

Huxley and Heard guessed correctly what would happen in such a situation. And Leary spectacularly ignored their advice. He was, after all, speaking to *Playboy*. As Leary gave the interview, he faced a series of court appearances that would eventually land him in federal prison for years and, through a dramatic prison escape, turn him into an international fugitive. President Nixon went so far as to call Timothy Leary "the most dangerous man in America." The sexual cat was out of the bag. And it was having sex with the psychedelic cat. And it would be a long time before anyone could get these two cats back in the bag again.

The Law and Esalen's Choices

As much as Price and Murphy were fascinated with the intellectual implications of what they called drug-induced mysticism in their early seminars, and as much as they affectionately liked "Tim," (Murphy, after all, even shared a deep pool of Irish genes with this weaver of outrageous tales), they were becoming increasingly concerned about what excessive drug use on the grounds could do to their fledgling institute. Legally, it could very well sink it. Even Price, who used psychedelics throughout his life, saw the dangers of Leary's excessive methods and public ways. When Leary later got into computers and various Internet enthusiasms, Price joked that "Tim will be the first person to get computers made illegal!"[54] John Heider was just as clear about the problem in his private Esalen journals, where he observed that the "public taking of pot" "threaten[s] the community."[55]

There were also real spiritual and psychological problems to worry about. Put most simply, the leaders eventually realized that such substances as mescaline and LSD may act as effective initial catalysts into altered states, but their social and personal side effects rendered them dubious at best as long-standing transformative practices. If psychedelics were initiatory—and they seemed to be in fantastic proportions—the initiates were still in need of a stable practice that could engage both nonordinary states of consciousness and the ordinary concerns of culture, politics, and ethics. There were also real tragedies here, human lives destroyed and ravished by the drugs. Murphy mentions at least three suicides in the larger Esalen orbit in which being stoned accentuated the depression and led to a self-inflicted death.[56] There were probably more.

There was a real historical development here. Murphy observes that psychedelics were simply not a major part of the Esalen culture in its first two years. By 1965, however, things had started to cook up, and by 1966 and especially 1967, the Summer of Love, events were quickly spinning beyond the original meditative order of the place: "our canyons were full—I mean it *exploded,* and to some extent we lost control of the place. I would say—'66 through '70—that was the most tumultuous, out-of-control time. It's a miracle Esalen survived that period."

Things could get very dark indeed. Charles Manson was forming his own cult down at Lime Kiln Canyon, and stoned bands of the Hell's Angels would roar through Highway 1, at one point threatening to take over the Esalen grounds with their motorcycles and weapons.[57] Moreover, in an aggressive attempt to discredit Esalen, what Murphy calls "the Dirty Tricks Department" of the Nixon administration went so far as to claim that Charles Manson had been indoctrinated at Esalen, and that Esalen was therefore somehow implicated in the murders. The opposite was in fact closer to the truth. Seymour Carter remembers being awakened by a young woman in the middle of the night in the waterfall house, where he was living with his girlfriend. The waking woman wanted to get her friends into Esalen. Sleepily, Carter agreed to meet the group, which turned out to be three women, a baby, and a scruffy hippie man in a bread truck van parked up on Highway 1. After offering Seymour some grass to smoke, the man began playing his guitar and singing, both badly. Carter sensed that something was wrong, that they were, in his own words, "bad news." He thus refused them entry and sent them on their way. Within two weeks, the murders happened, and within another two Esalen was receiving phone calls about rumored links. Carter realized then just whom he had sent away that night.

It was true, though, that Abigail Folger, the coffee heiress who was among the murdered, had attended an Esalen seminar. It was also true that Sharon Tate happened to be at Esalen the night before the gruesome events. Both were there to work with Perls. But there certainly was no causal link between Esalen and the Manson crimes. The connection was not fact, but rather the work of a misinformation campaign apparently under the direction of White House aides.[58] With events such as these, Esalen knew that it had to be careful. It had enemies in very high places.

There were also personal differences between the two founders regarding the use of psychedelics. Murphy became much more circumspect about psychedelics than Price ever did. Whereas Murphy ended his trips in 1966 after just eight of them (with an elite list of guides, from Aldous and Laura Huxley to Timothy Leary and Richard Alpert), Price continued to use the substances in his spiritual journeying until the day of his death (and perhaps even that very day) in 1985. Still, Price and Murphy were both very much in agreement that the policies of Esalen needed to take a clear stance against the public sale or consumption of anything illegal. And here they took a very proactive path.

They knew, for example, that they were under surveillance by any number of federal agencies, including and especially the Food and Drug Administration. Willis Harman, who was doing legal LSD research at the time, knew many of these government officials and often warned Esalen of possible raids.[59] With the counsel of Harman and other like-minded friends, Murphy met twice with the Northern California FDA to clarify what the issues were and how they, as an institute dedicated to both spiritual adventures and the law, could respond most effectively and humanely. What Murphy learned was that the law protects institutions from being legally responsible for what goes on in the privacy of, say, a hotel room. Murphy explains: "So we were clear with everybody, our lawyers, everyone, that we were not obliged to go Gestapo-like into the seminarian rooms. But the great reason that our institute never went under—because there was a huge amount of drug use on the grounds—was, we prohibited any sale of drugs there or the use of any in workshops."[60] Murphy's "a huge amount of drug use" is no exaggeration. As Anderson humorously put it, "in reality, Esalen's official policy about drugs had about as much relevance to what went on at Big Sur as the nineteenth amendment had to do with American drinking habits in the 1920s."[61]

Still, signs were clearly posted. And they were backed by action. They kicked out anyone whom they caught selling drugs or using them in the seminars. It was a sane and legal compromise worked out with the federal authorities that certainly did not please everyone. But it worked.

/Mesmer to /Maslow

ENERGY AND THE FREUDIAN LEFT

Mysticism is the obscure self-perception of the realm outside the ego, of the id.
SIGMUND FREUD's final jotting in *The Complete Psychological Works*

If Aldous Huxley was the early literary philosopher of Esalen who set down the all-important concept of *human potentialities,* Abraham Maslow (1908–1970) was the early psychologist of Esalen who explained how human beings *self-actualize* these potentialities, that is, realize them in their own personal lives (and it is certainly no accident that Maslow loved Huxley's writings). Moreover, if the psychedelic—and by extension, the neurological and biochemical—dimensions of religious experience was one of the two grand theories of religion advanced at early Esalen, the psychological nature of religion was the second. Esalen figures knew, like few religious figures before them, that religious experiences are co-creations of the human psyche. They thus turned, with enthusiasm, to both earlier and contemporary psychological theories to help them form their own religious community and self-understanding. Religion and the psychology of religion had seldom, if ever, come closer.

Despite the quick public dominance of gestalt psychology at Esalen, mostly through the charismatic presence of Fritz Perls, whom we will meet in our next chapter, there is probably no psychologist who was more influential on the early Esalen vision than Abraham Maslow. The influence seems to have gone both ways. Esalen was clearly an example—perhaps *the* example—of what Maslow imagined as Eupsychia (roughly "good souled"), his term for a small community of individuals whose social lives are more or less synergistic with the physiological, psychological, and spiritual requirements of self-actualization. Esalen, in effect, was Abe Maslow's utopia.[1] It was also something of a spiritual home for him. Twice a year,

FIGURE 11. Abraham Maslow in the lodge, c. 1967. Printed with permission of the Esalen Institute.

he would leave Brandeis University and travel across the country to spend time on the grounds.

There is an oft-told textual synchronicity involving the book as magical spell again, an event within Esalen's history that did as much as anything to unite the visions of Abraham Maslow and Esalen Institute. It involved Abe and Bertha Maslow driving down Highway 1 one night looking for a motel. Anyone who has driven the same road in darkness can appreciate their plight—the road curves precariously around cliff after cliff, and many of the road's establishments, tucked well below the highway behind small forests on their own private cliffs, are difficult to find in broad daylight, much less in the blackness of a Big Sur night.

It was June of 1962, when Maslow was a visiting fellow at Western Behavioral Sciences Institute in La Jolla, California. At this time a very young Esalen community was reading with great enthusiasm Maslow's recently published *Toward a Psychology of Being* (1962), a treatise on self-actualization and the peak experience, in whose pages many of these readers saw their own forming ideas reflected, theorized and, most importantly, culturally sanctioned by a major intellectual.[2] It was as if Abraham Maslow and this book had appeared on the cultural horizon just for them.

And then he actually did. Abe came to the front desk of the lodge that night. Gia-Fu was manning the desk. A former businessman in China,

Gia-Fu kept Esalen's early finances on an abacus. He was also the keeper of the baths and taught the locals Tai Chi. Later, he would become an important teacher of the same martial art in the broader culture. Gia-Fu's English was not perfect, but when he asked the stranger to write down his name on the guest list, he recognized it immediately. "Abraham Maslow? Abraham Maslow? Abraham Maslow!" Murphy remembers Gia-Fu repeating the name over and over as he bounced around the lodge and ran to find the others to tell them that Abraham Maslow was actually standing at the front desk and needed a room. One can only imagine Maslow's reaction. It is a rare experience to go looking for a motel in the dark only to find one run by a small band of American visionaries reading your latest book.

However the reader chooses to read such an event, it is clear that both the Esalen community and Maslow himself embraced the coincidence as deeply meaningful. Maslow frequented Esalen often throughout the '60s as his professional and publishing careers became more and more successful. Maslow and Murphy also grew quite close. Indeed, Abraham Maslow came to understand and treat a young Michael Murphy as the son he never had. The affection was clearly mutual.

It is important to appreciate Maslow's cultural cache at this time. During the heady '60s, it was not unusual for his books to sell over 100,000 copies. He was elected president of the American Psychological Association in 1967–68. He also founded, with Anthony Sutich, both the *Journal of Humanistic Psychology* (in 1961) and the American Association of Humanistic Psychology (in 1963) in an attempt to establish what he called the Third Force in American psychology. In this popular model, Freud's reductive depth psychology of the unconscious was said to constitute the First Force; the behaviorism of John B. Watson and B. F. Skinner, which denied subjectivity and recognized only observable behaviors, constituted the Second Force; and Maslow's humanistic psychology, focused now on human beings in their future-oriented and self-actualizing "peak experiences" instead of in their past-oriented neuroses, announced the appearance of the Third Force. Behaviorism was particularly acidic to Esalen's interest in the depths of human experience, a fact captured in the joke I once heard there about the two behaviorists having sex: after the act, the one behaviorist turns to the other and says, "It was good for you. Was it good for me?" So much for the Second Force.

This Three Force model, which would quickly become the Four and then even the Five Force model, carried its own ideological weight. It certainly made sense to the early Esalen participants, whose deep and positive interests in various altered states of consciousness and energy—that is, in what Maslow would call peak experiences—were routinely diagnosed by the Freudian medical establishment as signs of mental disorder and completely dismissed by the behaviorists as both unreal and inconsequential. Maslow's Third, and then Fourth, and then Fifth Force gave the Esalen actors a culturally sanctioned way of rejecting this professional rebuke, of asserting their own ecstatic vision of the human potentialities.

The force model, of course, works through a kind of subsumption thesis in which later forces are said to subsume and transcend earlier forces, rather like what the early Christians did when they dubbed their own texts the New Testament and the Jewish Torah the Old Testament (the Jewish traditions have certainly never seen it that way). Ideological usefulness aside, there are real historical problems with all such moves. Very much as biblical scholarship has increasingly shown just how Jewish Jesus, Paul, and the early Christians were—that is, how "old" the "new" was—historians of psychology have demonstrated in increasingly convincing detail how psychoanalysis found many of its origin-points in altered states of consciousness. In Maslow's terms, the Third and Fourth Forces actually preceded, indeed helped *create,* the First Force.

With respect to Esalen, the psychological situation is even more complex, since Esalen has found a remarkably consistent use for psychoanalytic ideas in some of its most famous thinkers and central body practices. Put simply, the Four Force model served important cultural needs in the '60s for the fledgling institution that was Esalen, but in the end it is very much an ideological construct, not an accurate descriptor of what actually transpired either in western psychological theory or at Esalen.

Psychologically speaking, Esalen is better seen as a flowing together of two separate but connected lineages: the psychoanalytic stream, which focused on various mystical, occult, and erotic understandings of *energy;* and the gestalt stream, which focused on the nature, creative constructions, and awakening of *consciousness.*[3] I treat the former energy-lineage in the present chapter and the latter consciousness-lineage in the next chapter.

Proto-Psychologies and Early Practices of Energy

Central to Esalen's enlightenment of the body is a kind of mystical psychoanalysis that is as comfortable with "sex" as it is with "peak experience," indeed that sees the peak spiritual experience as orgasmic and the orgasm as potentially spiritual. A mystically revisioned Freud may be counterintuitive with respect to Esalen's history, but in fact the historical origins of American psychology bear out these connections.

Over a century and a half ago now, America was all a rage with the Mesmerists, named after the Austrian charismatic healer, Franz Mesmer (1734–1815), who invented the technique. The method was first introduced to America in 1836, when the Frenchman Charles Poyen went on a Mesmerist speaking tour through New England. Early hypnotic healers and preachers like Poyen used something called *animal magnetism,* which they experienced as a mysterious fluid that permeated the entire universe. This animal magnetism, they claimed, could be transmitted from person to person in order to put people into trance states so that they could contact the other world and, more practically, heal themselves of an entire panoply of psychosomatic disorders. This was a kind of altered state of consciousness, a "waking" or "magnetic sleep" (first discovered and named by the Marquis de Puységur in 1784) in which the magnetized reported the movement of subtle energies, out of body experiences, thought transference, the supernormal ability to see into the body of the ill person, clairvoyance, and cure. Hence it was Mesmer who originally wrote, in 1781, of a "sixth sense." These same altered states were also often heavily eroticized, both by the technique's more honest proponents, who wrote about a certain "magnetic rapport" that often developed between the (male) magnetizer and the (female) magnetized, and its official detractors, who wrote about much more.

Baron Jules Du Petet de Sennevoy, for example, who believed that animal magnetism provided the true scientific base to the older magical and occult traditions, was especially explicit about how magnetic influences were generated in the brain and transmitted into material objects or other persons. He likened the empowerment of the magnetic will to the sexual arousal of a man who "is about to have a passionate outburst, although not yet letting it go." He burns. He trembles. His heart beats harder and harder, until "his volcano erupts over the human landscape in an outpouring of lava and a whirlwind of sulphur. Behold! This is how you must use your desires which are like a fire that glows and shines in you unseen. It is exactly like the basic act of reproduction, except that here the emitting organ is the brain."[4] Animal magnetism as a kind of sexual magic.

A bit earlier, an especially influential Swedish scientist turned religious writer by the name of Emmanuel Swedenborg (1688–1772) wrote volumes in Latin on what he considered to be the science of a mysterious *influx,* his term for a mystical energy that permeated the entire universe and descended into his own being in moments of inspiration in order to empower his visionary thought and writing practice. Swedenborg is the father of all later mysticism of science writers. Significantly, he understood the at once spiritual and scientific influx to be intimately connected to the sexual powers, whose numinous energies he attempted to sublimate into spiritual vision by meditating on the Hebrew letters as male and female bodies, by regulating his breath, by arousing himself to erection without ejaculation through the control of the male cremaster muscle, and by something he called "genital respiration." Such techniques led to a kind of erotic trance in which love itself (*amor ipse*) imploded into a nondual realization of itself and suffused the entire body with a palpable bliss closely akin to the pleasures of sexual intercourse. Here is how Swedenborg put it in his *Journal of Dreams:*

> In the spirit there was an inward and sensible gladness shed over the whole body; it seemed as it were shown in a consummate manner how it all issued and ended. It flew up in a manner, and hid itself in an infinite as a centre. There was love itself.... This love in a mortal body, whereof I then was full, was like the joy that a chaste man has at the very time when he is in actual love and in the very act with his mate; such extreme pleasantness was suffused over the whole of my body, and this for a long time.[5]

If this sounds like Tantra, that's because it probably is. As Marsha Keith Schuchard has argued, Swedenborg was most likely familiar with Asian Tantric cultures from Swedish soldier-scholars, relatives, and colleagues returning from the region of Tibet and Nepal and from Malabar Indians who were known to have visited the London Moravian communities he knew. Whatever the actual influence, Swedenborg became fascinated with the correspondences he saw in altered visionary states between spiritual union, sexual union, and the intellectual life. In his *The Delights of Wisdom Pertaining to Conjugal Love* (1768), for example, he wrote of how an angelic guide took him to a heaven where he met the "peoples of Asia" (*Populis in Asia*), one of whom spoke of how "the knowledge of correspondences connected the sensuals of our bodies with the perceptions of our minds and gained us intelligence." The same man then showed Swedenborg a room filled with works of art cast in silver, "pictures and forms representative of many of the qualities, attributes, and delights which come of conjugial love."[6] The Tantric transmission had already begun in the eighteenth century, even if it was in some very careful and nervous Latin.

There is a rather clear historical line of development from the European Mesmerists and Swedenborgians, through the Spiritualists of the 1850s and '60s (who were also religious rationalists who wanted to understand their experiences of spirit in terms of the science of the day), to the early psychology of religion and, a bit later, the American alternative religious scene of the 1960s and '70s.[7] Hypnotism, for example, was an early therapeutic technique developed from the magnetized sleep of the Mesmerists, first fully theorized in 1843 by the English physician James Braid. Rejecting the paranormal reports of the magnetized, Braid advanced instead a purely psychological model that spoke of "unconscious" and "conscious" levels of the mind and attributed all the curative and apparently supernormal perceptions of the magnetized state to the intense focusing of attention that could be artificially induced by hypnosis. It was only a short leap now from Braid to Freud, who practiced and then abandoned hypnotism for his own "psycho-analysis." Still, as Adam Crabtree, another Esalen regular, pointedly puts it with respect to this lineage from Mesmer to Freud, "all modern psychological systems that accept the notion of dynamic unconscious mental activity must trace their roots, not to Freud, but to those animal-magnetic-practitioners who preceded him by a century."[8]

Acknowledged or no, much of modern psychological thought—that modern "soul-talk" (*psyche-logos*)—is structured around what are essentially secularized versions of what were once esoteric practices and altered states of energy. Much of Esalen's history, particularly its rich psychological culture, is simply incomprehensible without a very clear awareness of this historical fact. This is especially true of Esalen's largely unacknowledged and largely unorthodox embrace of Freud.

The Freudian Left

It is an oft-noted truism that the Greek word *psyche*, which, of course, forms the basis for our modern English term "psychology," is probably best construed historically as "soul," not "mind."[9] Perhaps it should not surprise us, then, that modern psychological theories and practices have become the basis for much of modern American spirituality in both many of its traditional Christian forms (psychological training and analysis are now standard features of pastoral training and counseling in most mainline denominations) and almost all of its alternative or emergent forms.

Psychology was one of the three central pillars of Esalen announced in the earliest brochures, along with psychical research and drug-induced mysticism. And indeed, Esalen has been a profoundly psychological culture from day one. The common assumption is that this psychological culture—with its emphases on personal myth-making, synchronicity, and archetypes—has been primarily Jungian in orientation and content. There is considerable truth in this assumption, particularly with such figures as Frederic Spiegelberg, who knew Jung personally and traveled to Zurich with his family on a regular basis to lecture in Jung's Institute there; Joseph Campbell, whose understanding of myth is partially indebted to Jung's; and Stanislav Grof, who employs archetypal language in his writings.

But a Jungian framing of Esalen obscures more than it reveals. Campbell was not really a Jungian, as he himself repeatedly pointed out, and his writings are far more Freudian than is often realized.[10] Grof's system, moreover, as we shall also see, is a thoroughly psychoanalytic mysticism deeply rooted in both Freud's theorizing about mystical regression and Jungian archetypal psychology. Similarly, the psychologist most identified with Esalen, Fritz Perls, began his career as a committed Freudian and retained a profound psychoanalytic orientation throughout his career, as Esalen president Gordon Wheeler has recently reminded us.[11] Abraham Maslow, moreover, always insisted on the necessity of Freud's psychoanalysis as a firm foundation for any future humanistic or transpersonal psychology. Still again, much of the Somatics movement at Esalen is fundamentally psychoanalytic in orientation via the renegade speculations of Wilhelm Reich, who, as we shall see, was more Freudian than Freud. Finally, it seems worth mentioning that when I asked Michael Murphy explicitly about his own understanding of Jung, he replied that he was never particularly influenced by Jung, and that he finds himself always returning to Freud's thought as an invaluable guide on the spiritual path. Freud has become in effect another embodiment of what Murphy likes to call, with a grin, his "spiritual crap detector." Murphy, finally, is also quick to point to Freud's self-censored interests in parapsychology, telepathy, and the occult, which were indeed considerable if also conveniently forgotten.[12]

As a telling example of this "Esalen Freud," consider the following experiment. If one goes into the lodge, sits to the southwest of the salad bar and looks up as one munches, one will see a small wooden bookshelf carefully tucked away in one corner of the ceiling. There are two books in this affectionate nook, the two volumes of *A Course in Miracles*. Published in 1975 by Helen Shucman, this is one of the indisputable classics of modern American mystical literature. *A Course* is usually categorized in bookstores as "New Age." As Daren Kemp, however, points out, the text "was channeled through a professional [unwilling and baffled New York Jewish atheistic] psychologist (Helen Shucman), who was encouraged to accept and transcribe the material by another psychologist (Bill Thetford), and the text was edited by a third psychologist (Kenneth Wapnick)." Not only that, the foundation that controls the text actually petitioned the Library of Congress with the request that the text not be categorized under "New Age," partly on the grounds that "the *Course* draws on Freudian psychoanalysis and the Neoplatonic tradition."[13] Exactly like Esalen, what superficially looks "New Age" turns out to be a synthesis of psychoanalysis and mystical philosophy, in this case performed by elite professional intellectuals (both Shucman and Thetford were professors of Medical Psychology at Columbia University's College of Physicians and Surgeons) and *mediated in and through a text*. Indeed, *A Course*'s origins can be traced back to Shucman being overwhelmed by a series of highly symbolic dreams and finally submitting to a kind of inner-directed writing practice that she came to call the Voice. Freud, Neoplatonism, and Columbia University all coming together in a mystical writing practice: would one know *that*, though, by looking up in Esalen's lodge?

As Murphy's reference to an occult Freud and the foundation's invocation of Neoplatonism make clear, this Freudian lineage at Esalen is definitely not an orthodox one. We are hardly on the East Coast with the American Psychoanalytic Association. We are rather on the West Coast with a kind of psychoanalytic mysticism of energy whose central move— a thorough embrace of instinctual powers as essentially good and wise, even divine—can be traced back most immediately to Wilhelm Reich and a developing school of psychoanalytic thought that Paul Robinson has aptly named the Freudian Left.[14] The classicist turned poetic philosopher Norman O. Brown was probably the clearest and most widely read author of this Freudian Left in the late '60s and early '70s. Indeed, his *Love's Body* (1966)—which begins with Freud and ends with Buddhist Tantra— functioned as something of an intellectual Bible for the counterculture. The text is filled with passages like this one on what really unites mind and body:

> Knowledge is carnal knowledge. A subterranean passage between mind and body underlies all analogy; no word is metaphysical

without its first being physical; and the body that is the measure of all things is sexual. All metaphors are sexual; a penis in every convex object and a vagina in every concave one. Symbolism is polymorphous perversity. Orthodox psychoanalysis warns against the resexualization of thought and speech; orthodox psychoanalysis bows down before the reality-principle.... Nothing wrong, except the refusal to play: when our eyes are opened to the symbolic meaning, our only refuge is loss of shame, polymorphous perversity, pansexualism; penises everywhere. As in Tantric Yoga, in which any sexual act may become a form of mystic meditation, and any mystic state may be interpreted sexually.[15]

And so Brown shows the salient currents of the Freudian Left (and in turn, Esalen) were not just Freudian, but Tantric: the shameful fruit of the Garden of Eden can be redeemed by the shared gnosis of unorthodox psychoanalysis and Indian Tantra.

It should hardly surprise us, then, when this same Freudian Left will later provide the broad intellectual context through which the *shakti* (occult energy) of Asian Tantra will be transmitted *and transmuted* into American culture. When the Tantric guru Bhagwan Rajneesh observed that "Freud only got to the third *chakra*," he was saying at least two things, namely, that Freud's drive theory and Tantra's *kundalini* yoga are comparable models of occult energy and sublimation, and that Freud missed the "deeper" or "higher" bliss of the id beyond the first three centers of the anal, genital, and digestive systems (that is, the first three *chakras*). Freud, in other words, was not wrong; he simply did not go far enough. The language is Indian here, but the basic point is remarkably similar to some of the voices of the Freudian Left who out-Freud Freud by turning to explicitly religious or poetic languages in order to embrace and celebrate the id as a mystical force of orgasmic bliss, social revolution, and, as we will see, even bodily transfiguration. What we have in the Freudian Left, in other words, is a kind of left-handed psychoanalysis that always begins with Freud but often ends with a re-visioned Western Tantra.

Psychotherapy East and West

By the time Esalen arrived on the scene in the early 1960s, however, psychoanalysis had become thoroughly medicalized in the States. Psychoanalysis had come to represent not the radical intellectual circles it once did in Europe, much less the occult interests of Murphy, but a kind of normative conservatism whose thorough-going materialism was stifling to the broader humanistic and spiritual visions of Esalen. It was all largely about "adjustment" now, but what kind of health is it, some were beginning to ask, that adjusts itself to a sick, corrupt, or simply stifling society? This would no longer do. If Esalen was to embrace Freud's insights, then, it would have to do so through a different kind of history and practice. It would have to reject psychoanalytic orthodoxy, even as it embraced the psychoanalytic heterodoxy and turned to other figures—even Asian ones—to accomplish its own psychological, sexual, and spiritual goals.

Many at Esalen turned to a whole spectrum of Asian Tantric ideas that echoed and reflected psychoanalytic ones, but in a cultural key now that was neither reductive nor materialistic. And here they definitely did follow Jung. Though he always insisted on the unique nature and trajectories of the Western psyche, Jung had not hesitated to turn to Hindu Tantric yoga to catalyze his own theorizing; he even found there what he called "important parallels" to his depth psychology, "especially with *kundalini* yoga and the symbolism of tantric yoga."[16]

Probably the earliest major Esalen figure to envision a deep synthesis of Western psychology and Asian Tantra was Alan Watts in his *Psychotherapy East and West* (1961). Significantly, Watts framed his comparative reflections in a way that was particularly relevant to Esalen's own early psychological leanings, that is, in the insights of an emerging gestalt psychology that he believed was in sync with the metaphysical insights of contemporary physics and biology and, just as importantly, the nature of psychedelic experience. Interestingly, though, however much Watts turned to these gestalt psychologies of moment-to-moment awareness, a mystical language of energy returned again and again in his thought—consciousness and energy could not be separated.

Watts did not make the mistake of simply collapsing Western psychotherapy and Asian contemplative traditions into a single practice, as if they were the same thing. Rather, he chose to emphasize both their differences and their shared goals. Watts thought that the liberation of Asian contemplative traditions and the healing of Western psychotherapy—neither of which he saw as particularly sacrosanct or complete—are aimed primarily at the *transformation of consciousness.* He further believed that both Asian contemplation and Western psychotherapy accomplish this goal through similar means: the deconstruction of social conditioning, the collapse of the dualistic grammar of language (with a "subject" mysteriously acting upon some "object"), and the melting of the essentialist noun (as if anything were really a thing).

Put simply, language, words, and social identities dupe us into thinking that "things" or "individuals" exist independently from other "things" and "individuals." They do not. And liberation, healing, and enlightenment all consist in the realization that this is not so and in the subsequent events through which the organism can come to realize (that is, make fully conscious) its own radical relationality and effectively merge with the environment. Through this new Whole, a person can see that every "thing" implies and implicates every other "thing." Enlightenment and healing, in other words, are ultimately a function of becoming aware that one is *already, right now,* at one with the universe.

This release from the consensual trance of society and language into the gestalt or Whole of the world in turn produces a certain playful attitude in relation to what Watts likes to call "the skin-encapsulated ego." One certainly does not cease to have an ego, but now one can see that consciousness is not this ego, that is, that one truly *has* an ego. Subsequently, one can play at being a social self in the theatre of society and not take the game of life so terribly seriously. Paradoxically, this leads to both a greater individuality and a certain loneliness, for such an altered state can no longer find security in any crowd and can no longer believe "that the rules of the game are the rules of nature."[17] Such a form of awareness stands apart against society in a metaphysically grounded "counterculture."

Many of Watts's technical terms here are derived from Indian philosophy. He invokes *maya* as the "illusion" of the world and *lila* as the essential "play" of the divine in and as the universe, but he employs them in insightfully idiosyncratic ways toward his own ends. For Watts, the illusion of the world that Asian contemplative traditions attempt to be liberated from cannot be identified with the cosmic realm of nature, which Watts always insists (within a fundamentally Tantric move) is quite real and fundamentally divine. *Maya* rather must refer to the *social* world of culture, language, and even religion, all of which pretend to be real and authoritative but which are in fact so many games that people play quite unknowingly, that is, unconsciously.[18]

Up to this point, Watts appears to be suggesting that consciousness is everything. The body and its energies quickly return, however, and with considerable force. Watts, for example, insists that these two systems of liberation and healing also lead to a kind of resurrection of the body, that is, to a type of polymorphous eroticism for which he cites both Asian Tantra and Norman O. Brown's *Life Against Death*.[19] For Watts, writers like Brown are more Freudian than Freud to the extent that they embrace the id as fundamentally good (the central thesis of the Freudian Left).[20] We are not ill because of our illicit desires, as Freud is often understood to be saying. Rather, we are ill because our societies repress these energies in unhealthy and excessive ways. Sex doesn't make people sick; society does.

It is in this same spirit that Watts will reject the Asian call for life-long celibacy as "chronic prudery" and write that there is good reason to believe that a truly liberated sexuality "might be something like a mature form of what Freud so inappropriately called the 'polymorphous perverse' sexuality of the infant, that is, an erotic relationship of organism and environment that is not restricted to the genital system."[21] Here he turns to Chinese Taoist and Indian Tantric language to make his point: "for genital eroticism is simply a special canalization of the basic love which is the polarity of *yang* and *yin*," and liberated sexuality is something "completely genuine and spontaneous (*sahaja*)."[22] In this new Tantric light, Watts finds even Freud himself too prudish:

> In the stress upon the erotic and delightful character of this new feeling for the world, Westerners inclined to oriental mysticism will also demur out of the feeling that liberation is a purely "spiritual" condition. They join hands with Freud and the hard-boiled psychoanalysts in basic mistrust of the physical world, that is, in alienation from the organism, forgetting that when India and Tibet looked for the supreme symbol of the reconciliation of opposites they chose *shakta* and *shakti,* the god and the goddess, the figure and the ground, the Yes and the No, in eternal intercourse—using the most erotic image imaginable.[23]

In 1961, Watts thus aligns himself with the Freudian Left, which now morphs gradually but clearly into a kind of developing American Tantra. Here the id and libido are not "mere" energy. They are literally cosmic, for "what our social institutions repress is not just the sexual love, the mutuality of man and woman, but also the still deeper love of organism and environment, of Yes and No, and of all those so-called opposites representing the Taoist symbol of the *yang-yin,* the black and white fishes in eternal intercourse."[24] This eroticization of the cosmos is not supernatural. It is perfectly natural or, in Tantric language now, it is perfectly, spontaneously *sahaja* or innate. The natural universe is shot through with the divine. It is an erotic play of opposites.

In the end, then, Watts's reading of psychoanalysis is an ambivalent one. He may truly believe that "Freud's detection of the erotic in every-thing supposedly spiritual and sublime is really a marvelous revelation,"[25] but he is also insistent that the place of psychoanalysis in Western cul-ture remains incomplete. In essence, psychoanalysis is "a step in the right direction which has not gone nearly far enough." What would be far enough? Pretty damn far, it turns out. Indeed, Watts goes so far as to draw on Brown's radical notion that "eternity is the mode of unrepressed bodies" in order to argue that the "final aim of psychoanalysis must there-fore be a veritable Resurrection of the Body as distinct from some future reanimation of the corpse."[26] What Watts appears to mean here is more or less what Brown meant, that is, the appearance of the polymorphous perverse body, "which always retains the potentiality of a fully erotic rela-tionship with the world—not just through the genital system but through the whole sensory capacity."[27]

In this way, Watts transgresses the conditionings and norms of con-servative culture, divinizes the entire cosmos as an erotic play of opposites, and imagines an eternity of unrepressed flesh. If this is not an example of a Westernized Tantra, then nothing is.

Abe: Actualizing Huxley's Potentialities

It is easy enough, then, to read an Esalen figure like Alan Watts as a pro-ponent of a mysticism of energy on the Freudian Left. How, though, does such a thesis work out with respect to Abraham Maslow, a central psycho-logical and spiritual influence on Esalen? It is easier than one might think. We have already, of course, met Abe, but we have seen little of his thought.

Abraham Maslow did not begin his career talking about peak expe-riences and self-actualized human beings with Big Sur visionaries. He began with sex, monkey sex no less. His early doctoral work focused on the sexual behavior of primates, much of which—both heterosexual and homosexual—he noticed was clearly nonproductive but nevertheless so-cially significant: primates, he concluded, used sex to define dominance and submission within their social orders. Later, he would note paral-lels between the sexual behavior of primates and the sexual fantasies of psychoanalytic patients and explain how his first introduction to the analysis of Being was his exposure to the love-relations of self-actualizing individuals.[28] In other words, it was *eros* that initiated Abraham Maslow into Being. Only later did he explore the same peak experiences in theological, literary, and aesthetic literature.[29] Such sexual interests were certainly not ephemeral. While teaching at Brooklyn College, for example, Maslow would help a young Alfred Kinsey with his sex research in New York, even if he eventually had to conclude that Kinsey's statistics were skewed because he had recruited his subjects from populations that were more sexually active than the actual norm.

Perhaps it is no accident, then, that the famous "peaks" of Maslow's psychological theory often carry a certain orgasmic tone: *peak* and *climax* are very close, and Maslow was not the least bit hesitant about invoking the complete orgasm as an appropriate analogue to the peak experience.[30] A peak experience for Maslow was an extraordinary altered state of personal history that fundamentally alters the individual's worldview through an overwhelming explosion of meaning, creativity, love, and Being. Very much like an orgasm, the peak experience is temporary, essentially delightful, potentially creative, and imbued with profound metaphysical possibilities. One can hardly live on such peaks (just as a continual orgasm would make one's commute to work difficult at best), but a life without them is vulnerable to becoming sick, nihilistic, even violent.[31] It is certainly going too far, but it is still worth noting, then, that Maslow's self-actualization of Huxley's human potentialities resembles more than a little Wilhelm Reich's all-healing orgasms.[32] Energy is essentially divine here.

Maslow imagined the peak experience to sit, as its name suggests, on the top of a carefully built physiological and psychological foundation. Thus his first book, *Motivation and Personality* (1954), focused on what would become his famous hierarchy of needs. The idea was a simple one, but it had far-reaching implications. For Maslow, human beings have a universal set of needs (he explicitly rejected cultural relativism and social constructivism as exaggerated half-truths) that are hierarchically ordered in the sense that "lower" needs must be satisfied before the individual will pursue "higher" needs or values. The basic physiological needs of food, shelter, sleep, and sexuality thus form the broad base of an imagined triangle that includes—on the way up now—safety and security, love and belonging, self-esteem, and finally self-actualization at the very top or peak. Interestingly, the basic iconic symbol of this hierarchy of needs resembles an abstract mountain, which in turn suggests the image of the peak experience.

Maslow's hierarchy of needs have not been particularly salient at Esalen, but they can easily function as a working psychology for the place's sensual embrace of the body and the world and its general rejection of asceticism. Much of Esalen, after all, implicitly argues—as Maslow had explicitly theorized—that human development, including and especially spiritual development, requires the satisfaction of drives rather than their suppression or denial. It is worth noting here that such a psychology of accomplishment and satisfaction fits well with the socioeconomic facts of Esalen, which has always been dominated by a white upper-middle class base. The model suggests, after all, that the highest flights of spirituality will be found in those individuals who do not need to worry about their next meal, their social mobility, or their physical safety. Poverty is certainly not a sign of holiness here. It is a need not yet met on the way up the mountain toward the peak experience.

In *Toward a Psychology of Being,* the text he found the early Esalen community reading that dark night, Maslow turned from a general discussion of these needs and values toward the development of a psychology of the peak experience and the self-actualized person. He continued this project in a more radical and popular vein in his *Religions, Values, and Peak Experiences,* where he develops an idea that will have a long history in American alternative religion and is still very much with us today, that is, the distinction between organized "religion" and personal "spirituality."

Maslow never quite puts the distinction in just this way (he writes rather of "peakers" and "non-peakers" or of the "mystical" and "legalistic" dimensions of religion), but all his comments lean heavily toward a thoroughgoing critique of traditional religion as dysfunctional and as much too authoritarian for any modern democratic society.[33] If he did not then actually coin the phrase "spiritual but not religious" or originate the ideological move of identifying "experience" as the mystical core of religion (William James is probably the source of this), Maslow did as much as anyone in the modern era to lay the psychological foundations for the present prominence of these notions.

Maslow clearly wanted to imagine what he calls a "noninstitutionalized personal religion."[34] Such a nonreligious religion would obliterate the distinction between the sacred and the profane, rather like the meditation exercises of Zen monks, whom Maslow explicitly compares to humanistic and transpersonal psychologists (just as Spiegelberg had identified Zen as the closest analogue to the religion of no religion).[35]

Such a no-religion would also push the mystic beyond any kind of nationalism to a deep identification with the entire human species. Maslow's prime examples here are two Americans: William James and Walt Whitman. Indeed, this universalism is what "American" means for Maslow:

James and Whitman "were universal men not in *spite* of their being Americans, but just *because* they were such Americans."[36] Maslow's politics, in other words, were clearly liberal in orientation, and this American liberalism flows effortlessly into his models of the self-actualized person and the peak experience. For Maslow, self-actualization leads to a "more democratic character structure."[37]

As the above discussion makes clear, three forces in the psychological world were hardly enough for Abraham Maslow. He was constantly writing about altered states of consciousness and energy for which there simply were no adequate models or schools of psychological thought. As the '60s progressed, he was thus also talking and writing more and more about a Fourth Force, which focused on "transpersonal" states of consciousness especially prevalent in mystical literature.

The adjective "transpersonal" would come to have quite a history at Esalen and beyond. According to Stanislav Grof, Maslow got the term from him. Grof, a Czech psychiatrist who was specializing in LSD research at this time, was lecturing at Esalen in the mid- and late '60s. Paul Herbert, who handled all the tape recording at Esalen, approached Grof after one of his lectures: "Some of the stuff you're saying is just like Abe. The two of you should get together." Grof took him at his word and sent Maslow a kind of megamanuscript he was working on (it would eventually become five different books) and then followed it up with a visit to Maslow's Boston home.

Grof was greeted at the Maslows' door by a very stern and rude Bertha Maslow. Later she confessed to him why she was so unhappy with him that day: his huge manuscript had excited Abe so much that she feared he would have another heart attack. According to Grof, before Maslow had read his manuscript, Maslow was using the term "transhuman" or "transhumanistic" to describe this fourth realm of psychological thought. Now, following Grof's megamanuscript, he would adopt the term "transpersonal." And so the movement would be named.[38]

Maslow, however, would also retain the category of the transhuman for what he was soon calling a Fifth Force. In one of the very last texts he penned, for example, he wrote about how the adjective "humanistic" of humanistic psychology was already pulling at the metaphysical seams and generating from within what were essentially a set of mystical psychologies: "It's now being strained by its own inner dynamics, which are already generating a psychology and philosophy of the person-transcending (transpersonal) and of the humanness-transcending (transhuman). These newer developments come from within Humanistic Psychology, generated inexorably out of its own theoretical and empirical necessities."[39]

Murphy also remembers Maslow talking about such a Fifth Force toward the very end of his life: "You know what I mean," he would say. But Murphy didn't. Later, however, he would read Maslow's Fifth Force as an imagined future psychology that could join the self-actualization of the individual human being with a kind of cosmic actualization of the universe. In other words, very much like Carl Rogers, another Esalen seminar leader who moved closer and closer to an explicitly unitive worldview toward the end of his life, Abraham Maslow was migrating away from his life-long commitment to atheism toward a type of American nature mysticism that was "centered in the cosmos rather than in human needs and interest, going beyond humanness, identity, self-actualization, and the like."[40] For Maslow, such a Fourth or Fifth Force could only be naturalistic, empirical, democratic, and unchurched, very much in line with his American visionary heroes, themselves all self-actualized in his own mind: David Henry Thoreau, Walt Whitman, William James, and John Dewey.[41]

Abraham Maslow's final enlightenment, it turns out, was an American religion of no religion.

The Residential Programs and a Glimpse into the Community: Ed Maupin's Body Epiphany and Stuart Miller's Hot Springs (1971)

The late '60s and early '70s were, in many ways, the golden years of Esalen, at least for those who choose to idealize that countercultural era. Esalen stories abound about this or that memorable event or colorful personality during this time. Two sets of documents in particular are worth mentioning in this context: Stuart Miller's published memoirs, *Hot Springs* (1971), smartly summed up in the subtitle, "the true adventures of the first New York Jewish literary intellectual in the human potential movement," and John Heider's unpublished essays and Esalen journal.[42] Each author treats more or less the exact same time period (1967–71) from two very different perspectives. We will look at Miller's book here and Heider's writings below in subsequent chapters.

Stuart Miller grew up on Manhattan's Lower East Side. His academic credentials were impressive. A former Fulbright Scholar in Florence, Italy, and a Wilson Fellow at Yale, Miller did teaching stints at Berkeley and Rutgers before he took a more permanent position at an experimental college in Old Westbury, New York. There he managed to convince his administration that the future of education lay in the direction of Esalen (he had visited the institute the previous year), and that they should give him a sabbatical so that he could return to the educational mecca and bring back its wisdom to Old Westbury. They agreed.

What Miller was getting himself into was Esalen's second Residential Program, a kind of nine-month marathon of encounter groups, gestalt psychology, and body work that was put together in an attempt to systematize and realize the Esalen vision. The first had taken place in the fall of 1966 under the direction of the family therapist, Virginia Satir. Seventeen people signed up. Unfortunately, Satir decided to leave just a few weeks into the program. She just disappeared, without telling anyone. At that point, one of the seventeen, Ed Maupin, a young psychologist who had written his dissertation on the psychology of meditation at the University of Michigan, took over, and the first Residential Program stumbled along. They would try again the next year, with Will Schutz and Ed Maupin this time as leaders. The third year would see Maupin joined by Steve Stroud and John Heider.

Obviously, Ed Maupin was one of the key players here. Maupin had been invited into Esalen's Residential Program by Murphy in the spring of 1965, after Maupin's two essays on Zen meditation appeared in the *Journal of Consulting Psychology,* probably the first two essays on the subject of meditation ever to appear in an American psychological journal. Maupin remembers Murphy contacting him and then coming down to UCLA, where he was then teaching in the psychiatry department. Murphy told Maupin that he looked a lot like Ramakrishna.[43] Maupin remembers being deeply enthused by their lunch meeting, "probably," he points out, "in the original sense of that term" (literally, having "a god [*theos*] within [*en*]" one).

Much in line with my present readings, Maupin had first been awakened to the altered states of meditation through reading a book as he walked down Woodward Avenue in Detroit, probably in 1959. The book was *The Supreme Doctrine* by Hubert Benoit, a French psychoanalyst who was writing about meditation as a type of inner scanning. As Maupin walked and read, his consciousness suddenly shifted, then and there, and he found himself witnessing his own interior landscape. Emotions, thoughts, and social anxieties, even the physical pain of a dentist visit (for which he had refused Novocain), continued to emerge after that signal event, but he could stand back from it all now as a kind of pure Witness. This unusual ability continued for three full months, during which

Maupin came to a radically new relationship to his body and its energetic processes. Consciousness came to know Energy.

Hence what would become Maupin's key workshop at Esalen, Body Awareness and the Sense of Being, and his central notion of "the Body Epiphany." The latter was determined by Maupin's personal realization "that my body is an on-going process in the here-and-now; that it possessed an acute intelligence quite apart from my conscious thought; and that how my awareness was distributed in it determined my consciousness." Looking back on his Esalen workshop experiences in 1998, he wrote, "today I would say it was a kind of tantric experience," by which he means that it was about bodily energy, "feeling" a participant's energies through his own body, and monitoring group processes through this same flow of shared energy.[44]

Body epiphanies and Tantric energies aside, Fritz Perls was not entirely happy when Maupin became the director of the second Residential Program in 1967. Perls in turn announced to all that the most honest thing about Ed Maupin was his embarrassment. Maupin remembers how valuable and how on-target such a public declaration was (since at that point he was still a deeply closeted and shamed gay man), "but I kind of hated him, and I was terrified of him." Indeed, Maupin remembers to this day a dream he had just before his last workshop at Perls's house at Esalen. He dreamt of walking up to the house and passing a clothesline. On the line hung a row of jock-straps, with genitals hanging in each of them. Understandably, Maupin was too afraid to work with Perls about this particular castration-anxiety dream.

It was into this kind of emotional and sexual maelstrom that Stuart Miller willingly, if innocently, drove into the summer of 1967 in his flashy silver Corvette, picking up a young beautiful "California girl" in Berkeley on his way down to Big Sur. He was on his way to take part in Esalen's second Residential Program. Here is how he made his entrance, in his own words: "Enter Stuart. The blast can be heard on the road above Esalen. A high-powered engine shifts from fourth to third by the bridge, then down to second; without braking the car skids around the curve at the head of the driveway and plummets, at thirty or forty miles an hour, toward Camelot/Atlantis—the endlessly violated but seemingly serene ex-burial ground of the ex-Esalen Indians. Who is it? Steve McQueen? A motorist gone crazy? No. It is Stuart the Magnificent."[45]

Stuart the Magnificent wore a Swiss linen tie, leather English riding boots, and Brooks Brothers everything else. To say the least, he did not fit in. He remembers meeting "Old Abe" (Maslow), who was there to greet the Residential Program participants. Old Abe looked, well, old. He was. What Miller noticed most, though, was how badly everyone was dressed. His first perception of Will Schutz, for example, revolved entirely around sartorial issues (or the lack thereof): "Bill Schutz, the program leader, was also in short sleeves—Dacron, with a little button in the back of his collar that I supposed he thought fashionable, if he even knew what he was wearing. He was built like a football player, Yul Brynner in shaved head from the neck up, but relentlessly badly dressed below."[46]

But all was not for naught, as Miller also quickly noticed precisely what many other men immediately noticed—the breasts, that is, those "long-skirted waitresses without brassieres, their nipples peeping against jersey blouses." This was one of many reasons Stuart Miller considered Esalen to be the very "honey pot of eroticism," and why much of *Hot Springs* is in fact an elaborate description of Miller's sexual fantasies, exploits, and disappointments on the grounds.[47] The "hot" of Hot Springs, in other words, refers to more than just the water temperature.

Thus Miller tells the tale of one of his many Esalen girlfriends, who one day noticed another man staring at her breasts at mealtime (in his defense, she was wearing a crocheted blouse and no bra). She walked up to him, pulled up her blouse, and said to the astonished stranger: "Come on, Bebee; why just look? Get a good feel." She then grabbed his hand and pressed it up to her perfect breast, mostly to piss off Stuart. After a few seconds of this, she threw the man's hand off and blurted, "That's enough, buster; you've had yours. Come on, Stuart, let's go to the baths."[48] It was just another day in the lodge.

Breasts aside, Stuart Miller was first and foremost an intellectual, and so when he thought of developing the human potential, he thought of developing the intellect. He thought of people like Leonardo Da Vinci. It took him a full year to realize that this was not what these sartorially challenged Esalen characters had in mind: "the models these people were proposing to imitate, insofar as they knew what they were after, were not Western artists, engineers, and scientists, but rather the mystics. Their heroes, insofar as they had them, were not Mozart or Einstein but San Juan de la Cruz and Ramakrishna."[49] And then there was the enlightenment of the body, which was also a new idea for Miller: "I had never thought that accomplishments could be developments of the soul, of the heart, of the veins and arteries and the subtle messages and meanings of the blood."[50]

Most of *Hot Springs* is an honest description of Miller's own search for what he himself describes as "mystical experience" and of his struggles with the Esalen community, with his own womanizing, and with a series of serious bouts of depression and despair. Miller did not do well with his Residential Program confreres, and he quickly became convinced that Schutz and company were all crazy.

Miller drove up to San Francisco to plead with George Leonard and Michael Murphy to do something about the situation. They wouldn't. He returned to Esalen, left the Residential Program, returned to the East Coast, came back to Esalen, and eventually—toward the very end of the book— found his own spiritual breakthrough in a synchronistic experience with a Christian Bible and his subsequent reading of the New Testament.[51] It was finally service (making beds and cleaning toilets), a conscious decision to treat women as persons rather than as sexual objects, and the practiced virtue of humility that transformed Stuart Miller and provided him with a palpable sense of holiness that he treasured.

In the end, though, Miller chose to become neither Stuart the Rogue nor Stuart the Saint. He chose to descend into the nitty-gritty world of human relationships, emotion, life itself. On the very last page of the book, as he stands at the top of the high Esalen driveway, he looks out on the ocean and begins his literal and theological descent to the grounds below: "Just before I got half-way down the long hill, I closed my eyes and whispered a wish. I was glad to be going down and full of a sense of promise, but I silently prayed that what I was doing would lead me again, in whatever indirect way, to the Grace which I had had."[52]

$\mathcal{P}$erls to $\mathcal{P}$rice

CONSCIOUSNESS AND THE GESTALT LINEAGE

We used to joke about gestalt therapy being Jewish Buddhism or Zen Judaism. In this Fritz has his most significant and, hopefully, most enduring relationship to the initial idea of Esalen. Esalen began out of the founders' mutual involvement in Asian studies, coupled with Western social and psychological thought. If out of a chaos of events and programs Esalen strives for anything, it is in the development of a *sadhana* appropriate for the West.

"Fritz Perls and Esalen," Esalen catalog, Fall 1970

There is a marriage (in heaven) between psychoanalysis and the mystical tradition; combining to make us conscious of our unconscious participation in the creation of the phenomenal world.... Every perception is a creation—"when we see physical objects we are makers or poets."

NORMAN O. BROWN, *Love's Body*

Fritz Perls did not particularly like Abe Maslow or his brand of American enlightenment. Nor did he believe that there was such a thing as a hierarchy of instincts, or, for that matter, libidinal energies capable of metamorphosis and actualization.[1] Perls's was not a dynamic psychology of unconscious forces or occult energies. His was a psychology of pure consciousness, of pristine awareness in the here and now without a why. As for Abe, he was, in one of Fritz's many memorable quips, "a sugar-coated Nazi" who pandered to a happy world of optimism that did not in fact exist.

It was a cruel jab—and Perls could be very cruel—particularly since both men were Jewish intellectuals who had experienced prejudice and even persecution. Indeed, Perls actually had to flee Germany in 1933 when he appeared on the Führer's blacklist (along with Tillich and Spiegelberg), so the word "Nazi" was hardly an innocent one for him. Not that Maslow

FIGURE 12. Fritz Perls. Photo by Paul Fusco, printed with permission.

liked Perls much either, but his words were much more reserved and quiet: "He's not a nice man," as Maslow once put it to Murphy (Abe, as Gregory Bateson once observed, was simply "too nice" for his own tastes). This personal conflict between Perls and Maslow is more than anecdotal. It is one of many signs that the psychological culture of Esalen was a tensive and occasionally even a fractured one. No one may have been able to capture the flag, but many were certainly trying.

The Target Hits Its Arrow

And Fritz Perls came closer than anyone. How Perls and gestalt psychology got to Esalen and came to define much of its early culture is a complicated story. Perls asked the same question, but synchronistically reversed the line of causality: "How did the target Esalen hit my arrow, poised towards it years before I knew of the target's existence?"[2] Some of this at least can be pieced together through his autobiography, *In and Out the Garbage Pail,* a rambling narrative interspersed with bad poetry, bawdy jokes, philosophical reflection, and dozens of delightful line-drawings by Russ Youngreen that do as much as anything to capture the spirit that was Fritz. Perls composed this text over a three-month period on the grounds of Esalen itself, probably sometime in 1968. There are no page numbers in this book, perhaps an expression of its author's conviction that the secret of psychological insight was awareness in the here and now, not in the serial past or future.

Perls first appeared at Esalen around Christmas of 1963 as one of seven leaders in a symposium Gene Sagan (Carl's brother) and Frank Barron had originally organized for the University of California, Berkeley extension program. When the event did not draw enough participants in the Bay, the university cancelled it and Esalen agreed to host a smaller version of its own. Shortly after, Perls announced his intention to move in. Neither Price nor Murphy was terribly happy about this development, "having been more impressed by his rudeness than his skill," as a later Esalen catalog put it.³ He moved in anyway.

Perls gave his first workshop at Esalen in February of 1964. The first two lines of the pamphlet announcement summed up the seminar this way: "To expand the scope of awareness, to bring greater contact with the environment and to end the subject object split are the goals of Gestalt Therapy." The little paragraph went on to define gestalt therapy as concentrating "on *what* is rather than on *why* it is, in the present rather than in the past" and promised to relate this new psychology to both existentialism and Zen Buddhism. The registration fee was $15.

This first seminar was not well attended. But Fritz stayed on anyway and appeared again in the next pamphlet, the summer-fall program of 1964, right beside such figures as Joan Baez (The New Folk Music) and Alan Watts, who had just returned from a two-year fellowship at Harvard and was speaking in a session called An Exploration of the Self. The title of Fritz's seminar was the same as the first, Introduction to Gestalt Therapy, but now there were three separate weekend seminars listed, and the price had nearly quadrupled to $54 per weekend. Attendance also was now limited to fifty seminarians per weekend. Things would develop slowly but surely from here, until Fritz Perls became Esalen Institute's most famous celebrity. They even built him his own house, on the cliff overlooking the baths, from which he would drive down to the lodge for meals each day in his little car (a bad heart prevented him from walking up and down the cliff).

Perls had started out as a classical Freudian. He was analyzed in Berlin by Wilhelm Reich, and Freud's friend and biographer Ernest Jones supported him professionally. He first turned to psychoanalysis as a youth because he feared that he was ruining his memory through masturbation, and it seemed to him that psychoanalysis was all about sex and memory.⁴ Certainly there were plenty other reasons to turn to Freud and his brave realistic gaze on the family. According to biographer Martin Shephard, Fritz's home was not a happy one. His parents argued bitterly and often, and his father was not beyond physically abusing his mother. Nor was he beyond verbally abusing his son. He often called little Frederich a *stuck scheisse* (a piece of shit), and his mother beat him with whips and carpet beaters. Not surprisingly, the boy hated both his parents, and they called him "bad." He was expelled from school for bad grades and fired from an apprenticeship for bad behavior. He even had bad sex. His first sexual experience was at thirteen with a prostitute. It ended in both rejection and a deep sense of humiliation.[5]

Religion was another touchy subject. Perls said he became an atheist at an early age, so disgusted was he with the hypocrisy of his parents' assimilated Judaism. Psychoanalysis became his religion, his spiritual home. But doubts eventually crept in and Perls became "a nihilist—a negator of everything." He turned to Zen Buddhism for some time, that religion without a God, but even this soon failed him. "Then the enlightenment came: No more spiritual, moral, financial support from any source! All religions were man-made crudities, all philosophies were man-made intellectual fitting games. I had to take all responsibility for my existence myself."[6] If psychoanalysis and Buddhism had failed him, existentialism apparently had not. This was Fritz's religion of no religion, an oddly attractive synthesis of East and West that some playfully referred to as Fritz's Zen Judaism but that also strongly resembled a kind of psychologized Taoism. A tribute to Perls published in the Esalen catalog refers to all of this as Fritz's *sadhana*, a Sanskrit term with clear Tantric connotations meaning "spiritual striving" or "mystical practice."

But this would all come later in life. After his 1933 flight from Germany for Holland, he and his family moved on to South Africa in 1934, where Ernest Jones helped set Perls up as an analyst. There Perls flourished. He founded the South African Psychoanalytic Association and began writing his first book on the revision of Freud's notion of sexual orality, *Ego, Hunger and Aggression* (1942). Jan Smuts, the premier of South Africa and the author of a book called *Holism* (probably an early precursor of Perls's gestalt language), liked Fritz's book a great deal.

The psychoanalytic community, however, did not take so kindly to being revised. When he presented early versions of his ideas on "oral resistance" to the International Psychoanalytic Congress in 1936, Perls himself met great resistance. More disturbing still, when he showed up at Freud's door on that same trip, he was sorely disappointed that the master did not affirm his own sense of importance:

> I made an appointment, was received by an elderly woman (I believe his sister) and waited. Then a door opened about two and a half feet wide and there he was, before my eyes. It seemed strange that he would not leave the door frame, but at that time I knew nothing about his phobias.
>
> "I came from South Africa to give a paper and to see you."

"Well, and when are you going back?" he said. I don't remember the rest of the (perhaps four-minute long) conversation. I was shocked and disappointed.

In the end, all Perls got was a few minutes of polite conversation and a goose dinner with Freud's son. Perls would never forget this cold shoulder, and he was obviously still angry with Freud at the end of his life, still longing for "a man-to-man encounter" so that he could show the master his mistakes.[7]

Despite his constant attacks on Freud (a near obsession that was often noted by others), Perls remained very much indebted to Freud his entire life, particularly for his emphasis on the individual and for his remarkable ability to read sex into just about everything. To his great credit, he could also make fun of his Freudianism, noting its famous excesses through another classic Freudian medium—the joke. Dick Price's "Rorschach Institute" returns here, this time as a laugh:

> A psychiatrist invented a simplified Rorschach test. He used three basic figures. One day, examining a new patient he drew a triangle. What is this?
> "This is a tent. In this tent is a couple that's fucking."
> Then he drew a rectangle. What is this?
> "This is a big bed. Two couples are lying there fucking."
> Then he drew a circle. What is this?
> "That is an arena. There are a dozen fucking couples."
> You seem to have a lot of sex on your mind.
> "But doctor, you drew the pictures."[8]

It is difficult to be too hard on a man who could so heartily laugh at himself, describe himself in Freud's own terms as a polymorph pervert, and share with his readers his wife Laura's description of him as "a mixture of a prophet and a bum."[9] Laura was no doubt right.

Just as *Ego, Hunger and Aggression* appeared, Perls enlisted in the South African Army and became captain in the medical corps. He immigrated to New York City with his family in 1947, where he met other émigré intellectuals and two American psychological thinkers named Ralph Hefferline and Paul Goodman. The three of them penned what would become a classic text, *Gestalt Therapy: Excitement and Growth in the Human Personality* (1951).

What, then, was gestalt psychology? Most simply put, gestalt is an attempt to focus on a subject's conscious experience and construction of the here-and-now (instead of on the forgotten past and the unconscious dynamics that the past produces, as Freud attempted to do). Within this total field of social relations and perceptions, the self co-constructs both its own experienced reality "out there" and its own running narrative-of-who-I-am "in here." Once again, human experience works very much like the reading of a text—it is *interpreted into being*.

As a major force within this gestalt lineage, Esalen president Gordon Wheeler summarizes the basic principles this way:

> Gestalt, most succinctly stated, is the psychology of Constructivism. That is, the model grows out of the foundational insight that our experiential world is not and cannot be *given* to us, all prepackaged and organized in any direct, representational or camera-like way (the old assumption known in philosophy as "representational" or "naive" realism) without need of organization or interpretation. Rather, we *construct* that world–often on the fly, as it were, and in the pressures of the living moment–out of some dynamic synthesis of our own past experience and beliefs, attentional habits and capacities, expectations, present felt needs, future intentions, cultural and dispositional screens, *and* present conditions and stimuli (but even these are screened, selected, and pruned through our own neurological and experiential filters). In other words, there is no "pure data." Perception itself is an act of interpretation, rendering "sense data" (itself selected and interpreted) into useable whole units, or "gestalts," of imaginal pictures, narratives, and other sequences.[10]

There would also, of course, be humorous sound bites of the same. Seymour Carter, for example, would sometimes declare in more "theological" (and playfully sexual) terms, "There is no immaculate perception."

As we have already noted, it was *Gestalt Therapy* that Alan Watts would turn to in his 1961 *Psychotherapy East and West* as the only radical psychology capable of nondual thinking, that is, of challenging the imaginary boundary between organism and environment. Watts pointed out, for example, that one does not hear a sound, as if the sound were somehow separate from the hearer. Rather, "the sound is the hearing, apart from which it is simply a vibration in the air."[11] To the playful philosophical question, then, of whether a tree falling in a lonely forest makes a sound (as opposed to a vibration in the air), Watts and gestalt psychology gave a simple answer: no.

The Ego Act and the Hot Seat

Fritz Perls was seldom this philosophical. Actually, he hated philosophical discourse. He called it "mind-fucking" or "elephant shit," the latter for its purported size and importance (he was equitable enough to spread this kind of fecal talk around, dubbing small talk "chicken shit" and misleading rationalizations "bullshit").[12] His gestalt workshops, which became one of the main attractions at Esalen in the late 1960s, were full of theatrical gestures and dramatic techniques. Part of this was biographical: he had had acting aspirations as a young man, and he craved attention, perhaps because he received so little as a child.

Much of this Perlsian theatre, however, was also metaphysical, that is, the techniques themselves witnessed to his convictions that reality and fiction are more or less synonymous, that the ego is both an actor and an act, and that psychological maturity was all about individuals becoming aware of their own play scripts, refusing to live in someone else's script, and taking full responsibility for their own chosen performances. Just as Alan Watts (not to mention Shakespeare) had argued, life really *is* a stage. Fritz's goal was to get people to see this, and then to get them to take more control of their ego-acts—a kind of existentialism as stage performance, as it were.

There was, for example, the famous "hot seat." Any chair would do. People would gather around, and Perls would ask for volunteers to sit in the hot seat. He would then proceed to take the person apart by noticing and commenting on every defense mechanism, every body posture, every quiver of the voice or eyes. Or perhaps Perls would ask the volunteer to tell him about his or her dreams (which he insisted, as a constant jab at Freud, should not be interpreted). Often this would result in Fritz asking the person to enter a dialogue with the personas of the dream, which were always interpreted as aspects of the dreamer's own self, as if they were standing right there, or, better yet, sitting in the hot seat.

A kind of one-person psychodrama would ensue—the more crying and volume, the better. Fritz would encourage the individual to project the various personalities of his or her psyche into the room and deal with them verbally and emotionally in an attempt to reintegrate the fractured self and so create a new gestalt or whole. Dozens of books and hundreds of hours of audio recordings, films, and videos of Perls's gestalt sessions were written, recorded, and shot.[13] They witness again and again to how he was able to isolate a psychological block or complex almost instantly and then go after it, often with stunning results. "Miracle cure" stories abound in the Esalen lore. To take just one example, Sukie Miller notes that Perls had a wall in his room decorated with eyeglasses from clients who had recovered normal eyesight following a gestalt session.

Perls was not simply miraculous. He was also eminently quotable. Perls of wisdom abound in the Esalen memory. He had quips like "I am I. You are you. I do my thing. You do your thing. I am not in this world to live up to your expectations. You are not in this world to live up to my expectations." Or the more cartoonish version of the same: "I am who I am, I fuck when I can. I'm Popeye the Sailor Man." One of Fritz's most oft-quoted blurbs involves his memories of visiting Zen monasteries in Japan. This kind of meditation, Fritz insisted, was a form of constipation. It's like sitting on the pot: one just sits there, neither shitting nor getting off.

Perls's potty-humor jab at the Buddhists returns us to an important issue, that is, his cantankerous relationship to religion. Perls, like so many other intellectuals of his generation who had witnessed with horror the Nazis' effective use of religion, was a militant atheist dead set against what he liked to call "the black mud of occultism and mysticism" (a phrase he got from Freud, who used it to reject Jung). Given the historical context, this is certainly understandable. But Murphy insists that Fritz remained nonetheless something of a closet mystic himself, and that he occasionally even experienced "little *satoris*" or mini-enlightenments in Murphy's presence. Such language is certainly faithful to Perls's own self-understanding. Indeed, this Zen Buddhist term for enlightenment (*satori*) was a word both Perls and his followers used often to describe those sudden flashes of pure awareness that gestalt psychology attempts to catalyze. Interestingly, though, they usually qualified their Zen Buddhist *satori* talk with the prefix *mini-*, as if to distance themselves from any religious claims.

Murphy recalls another time in the late 1960s when he was talking to Perls about a philosophical issue regarding Aurobindo's thought. Something that was said caught Perls's attention. As Murphy remembers it, "Fritz looked at us and said, 'Yes, yes, gravity itself is love.'"

Certainly similar mystical currents can be detected in Perls's obvious appreciation for what he called "the zero-center of opposites," which he first encountered in Sigmund Friedlander's notion of creative indifference.

"Zero is naught, is nothing. A point of indifference, a point from which opposites are born," he wrote.[14] Or again: "What is, will differentiate into opposites. If you are caught by one of the opposing forces you are trapped, or at least lopsided. If you stay in the *nothing* of the zero center, you are balanced and in perspective." Eventually, Perls recognized that this was "the Western equivalent of the teaching of Lao-Tze," that is, that it was a philosophical form of Taoism.[15]

But Fritz could get even more metaphysical. In his autobiography *In and Out the Garbage Pail,* for example, he is quite clear that "everything is awareness," and that even matter and molecules have some quantum of consciousness.[16] "The cells know much more" than we think, he insisted in another bad poem, and, in his usual sexual register, "The ovum thus might not accept / The most ambitious suitor."[17]

He certainly believed that physical existence was all there is, but he did not understand this physicality to be of a mechanistic nature; on the contrary, he insisted that "you and I, and I and Thou / Are more than deadly matter," and that we all exist in "truly Buddha-nature."[18] That is, his materialism was a mystical materialism imbued with consciousness down to its deepest depths. Indeed, this is precisely what gestalt seems to be about for Fritz, that is, the realization that a certain form of experience, deeply rooted in the body, is possible beyond all religious or philosophical frames, a "way to see the world not through the bias of any concept, but where we understand the bias of conceptualizing."[19] This pure consciousness beyond all perspectives but embedded deeply in the wise consciousness of cells and molecules was both Fritz's religion of no religion and his own enlightenment of the body.

After his first seminar in February of 1964, Perls stayed on at Esalen as a more or less permanent fixture until the summer of 1969, when he founded a life-long dream of his, a gestalt kibbutz, at an old fishermen's motel he had purchased on Lake Cowichan in British Columbia. Actually, in his own mind, he was also fleeing the United States, which he feared was becoming fascist, as he had watched Europe do before. Whatever the specific motivations, as the Esalen catalog reported it, a number of Esalen disciples followed him up to the Gestalt Institute of Canada, and together they began to create a kind of Canadian Esalen.[20] A year later, Perls took a trip to Europe. On his way back, he stopped over in Chicago to make some appearances. There, weakened by a developing case of pancreatic cancer, his long-ailing heart finally gave out. He entered a clinic and died on March 14, 1970.

The Flying Circus: Will Schutz and the Encounter Group Movement

If Perls came closer than anyone to capturing Esalen's flag, Will Schutz came closer than anyone to taking it away from him. William C. Schutz (1925–2002) came to Esalen, like so many others, through the academy. He had earned a PhD in psychology from the University of California, Los Angeles, and he had taught in the psychology department of the University of Chicago, in Harvard's department of social relations, and at the University of California, Berkeley. It was here that he first began hearing about Esalen. He was leading T-group sessions there in the early 1960s (*T* stood for Training, an early name for the encounter group technique as it was pioneered by the National Training Laboratories in Washington D.C. and applied to organizational dynamics). Drawing on the work of Carl Rogers, Schutz created his own model of "open encounter," which basically involved bringing people together in a group where they could work through their psychological issues through role playing, emotional catharsis, and mutual truth telling about one another. One of his students told him about this funky place down in Big Sur where they were doing similar things. This caught his attention, but not yet his life.

It wasn't until a few years later that Schutz received a letter from Michael Murphy, inviting him down to this same funky place to lead encounter groups. Mike, he once recalled fondly for the Esalen community, had the unusual gift of happily inviting anyone who had something to offer, regardless of whether he happened to agree with it or not (this, I suspect, was Schutz's way of acknowledging the fact that Murphy had grown very disenchanted with the encounter group movement). Murphy was clear with Schutz that Esalen could not offer him any money, and that he may have to sleep on a floor in a sleeping bag. They could offer him one thing, though, with little trouble: a title. In fact, Murphy went on with his usual humorous charm, Esalen would be happy to give Will any title he liked. And so, Schutz recalls, "I became the first emperor of Esalen."

The emperor title was more than a joke. It was also a not-so-subtle challenge to Fritz and an implicit claim on the ground that had caught the media's attention as *the* cutting edge of American therapeutic practice. Abraham Maslow had baptized it as such. Fritz Perls had then taken it over and planted the gestalt flag. And now Will Schutz had arrived to take it from Fritz and plant his own flag of encounter.

Schutz appeared in his little kingdom in August of 1967. A month after he arrived, Schutz published *Joy: Expanding Human Awareness*, which was an immediate popular success.[21] Within a little over a year, it had gone through nine printings. The book begins and ends with Schutz's infant son, Ethan, and Schutz's observations about the innate pleasure Ethan took in the simplest forms of sensual experience. His thesis followed from comparing Ethan's joy to that of the typical American adult. All human beings are born with a surplus of a kind of full-body joy or innate pleasure. Life and society, however, inevitably distort, constrict, and repress this joy until we feel chronically depleted, depressed, sick. There are techniques available, however, to reignite this pleasure and open human awareness back up to the beauty we all saw and knew as infants. Thus Schutz writes in the prologue, "Perhaps we can recapture some joy, regain some of the body-pleasure, share again the joy with other people that once was possible."[22] As for joy itself, the author defined it as "the feeling that comes from the fulfillment of one's potential."[23] I suspect strongly that what Schutz actually had in mind here was the Sanskrit *ananda* or "bliss." So, for example, his More Joy workshop of January 1967 leads off with the assertion that "there is an ancient belief that the natural state of the human organism is joy."

Both the framework and the specifics for developing one's human potential and so re-experiencing this ancient bliss turned out to look a lot like the Esalen curriculum. Indeed, it *was* the Esalen curriculum as understood and "captured" by Schutz's encounter group movement. It was also the basis of the second Residential Program of 1967, where we met Stuart Miller's roaring corvette, sartorial disappointments, and personal struggles.

Fritz Perls had often referred to his gestalt workshops as his "circus." Schutz and his disciples now followed up on this and did him one better, calling their own group the Flying Circus. The phrase was meant to both attract attention and confess a certain dangerous playfulness, a kind of bold showmanship, perhaps even a level of trickery. The Flying Circus, which included John Heider and Stuart Miller, among others, took over the Residential Program that Murphy and Virginia Satir had pioneered the year before as a more stable form of transformative practice and morphed it into an all-out assault on the psychical frontier.[24] They became, in their own terms, "psychonauts" intent on exploring the deepest recesses of inner space. This essentially meant taking risks: psychedelics, yoga, meditation, massage, and, of course, the encounter group session itself.

The latter mirrored the boldness and occasional cruelty of the Flying Circus show. Heider, one of the principle players of the group (Heider and Steve Stroud were known as the Psychedelic Madmen), later summed up the method this way: "Under this Encounter Contract I say how I feel about you. My obligation to be polite, kind, or considerate is, for the time, set aside. This Encounter Contract replaces the familiar Social Contract."[25] Schutz added to this logic his own language about "making it real."[26] Honesty and transparency were everything. Civility and manners meant nothing.

And language was key. The group, for example, had an unusually intense relationship to the nature of metaphor and symbolism. If, for example, a man would confess to feeling "held down" by life, Schutz might instruct the men of the group to pile on him until he screamed under the pressure and was forced to fight his way out, not just from the dog-pile but from his emotional constriction as well. Another encounter experiment, cleverly entitled "Pandora's Box," involved the group working through the women's fears concerning their genitals. The women would expose their vaginas, the group would look at Pandora's Box, and then they would process the feelings, fears, and desires together, acting out the myth, as it were, in order to transcend its fundamental misogyny.[27]

The breakthroughs were often admittedly impressive. Heider, for example, wrote in his journals about an occasional "transcendent space" that would erupt through such dramatic encounters, that is, about "that supreme delight, the visceral sense of containment and timeless patience and objectivity."[28] But these transcendent moments were also short-lived. Heider compared the five-day group encounter to the traditional revival tent meetings. Five days of revival were certainly possible, but nine months? The second Residential Program of 1967 would be the last nine-month attempt. After that, they were toned down to four-month sessions and, finally, in 1971, eliminated altogether. It was not just that the encounters were too long. They could also be quite cruel, if not actually dangerous. Price summarized Schutz's approach with his own typical bluntness: Schutz's method was essentially "beat 'em up, fuck 'em at the first opportunity."[29]

Still, the Flying Circus became famous, and they were soon giving workshops around the country. The *New York Times Magazine, Time* magazine, and *Life* all did stories on Esalen around this same period. In the course of this media blitz, Heider writes, they were held in awe wherever they went as Esalen people.[30]

Like Price, Perls was not at all happy about such developments, but for different reasons. Although he and Schutz were on good terms for the first year, things quickly soured, and Fritz was soon making nasty jabs at "the instant joy boys." A war was brewing. Murphy was now living in San

Francisco, and Price was unwilling to take control. The man who would eventually have to step in and broker a peace, however brittle, didn't know it yet. Indeed, he hadn't even arrived.

Julian Silverman and Price's Revenge

Julian Silverman also came to Esalen through the academy. A clinical psychologist, he was working for the National Institute of Mental Health in Bethesda, Maryland, and was doing some consulting work in San Francisco when he ran into an old friend from graduate school, Ed Maupin. It was Maupin who first invited Silverman down to Esalen. Silverman first arrived early in 1967 at the height of the hippie movement. What he encountered there both stunned and delighted him: candlelight dinners in the lodge with beautiful braless women waiting on tables. "The atmosphere was very bawdy, and the scene was extraordinarily sensual."[31] Julian Silverman, in other words, immediately noticed exactly what Stuart Miller had noticed: the breasts.

In the shadows of the lodge, Silverman met Michael Murphy, who was more than impressed with his new acquaintance's research credentials. Murphy learned that Silverman held a senior research position at the National Institute of Mental Health, that he was interested in schizophrenia, that he was well versed in the literature on psychedelics (and had experimented with LSD), and that he had even published an essay on shamanism and schizophrenia in the *American Anthropologist,* a high-end academic journal. Murphy did what he usually did in such situations: he invited Silverman to give a seminar at Esalen. Silverman accepted the offer and returned in the summer of 1967 to lead a workshop entitled Shamanism, Psychedelics and the Schizophrenias.

Price, who was gone during Silverman's initial visit, attended the seminar. Always interested in the subjects of psychedelics, altered states, and psychosis, the two men hit it off immediately. Price saw the potential, and the two men began organizing a series of seminars that would take place the following summer entitled The Value of Psychotic Experience. Such a project was in perfect line with both the early traumatic inspirations of Price and the earliest brochures of Esalen.

As Erickson has pointed out, from its very beginning, Esalen sought to confront and address the issue of mental illness and how it was being treated in the United States. Indeed, the second Esalen seminar announced in the very first brochure was Gregory Bateson and Joe K. Adams's seminar Individual and Cultural Definitions of Reality (October 1962). The seminar's title was something of a transparent euphemism. What they were actually up to was an explicit comparison between the present state of the mental health profession and the Inquisition of the late medieval period. In other words, Esalen literally began "on a Dick note," that is, with a direct assault on the madness of "madness" and an implicit attack on both traditional religion and psychiatry as forms of torture and abuse. This was radical stuff. And it only increased with time. "By the mid 1960s," as Erickson points out, "an alternative view of severe mental illness was beginning to emerge in this country and Esalen Institute was one of the main forums supporting it."[32] As Murphy once put it, "Esalen is Price's revenge on the mental hospitals."[33]

For the 1962 seminar, Bateson and Adams had suggested Thomas Szasz's *The Myth of Mental Illness,* but by 1967 no one claimed more authority on this subject than R. D. Laing. Laing was a radical British psychiatrist who had become famous for his attacks on the establishment's reliance on drugs and shock therapies and, in response, had opened up his own alternative hospital, Kingsley Hall in London. "Ronnie," as the Esalen leaders called him, had been to Esalen the previous year at the invitation of Murphy and Price. The intimate connections between Laing's antipsychiatry and Dick's own psychotic-mystical experiences must have been apparent to everyone. Laing in fact was to be the main attraction for Dick and Julian's summer seminar series.

Many big names showed up—including Joe Adams, Stan Grof, and Allen Ginsburg, who led a symposium on The Poetry of Madness—but Ronnie Laing was not among them. He had become convinced that a civil war was about to break out in American society, and that he would be arrested or perhaps even killed if he landed on American soil. So he didn't.

Price's Second Psychotic Break and Gestalt Practice

Silverman was deeply impressed with Esalen. He left his post at Bethesda and took another one at Agnews Hospital in San Jose, no doubt partly to be closer to Big Sur. It was there that he and Price initiated a three-year, federally funded, double-blind study of Esalen-inspired treatments of schizophrenia with 127 young male patients. Just as this study was beginning, Price began entering another psychotic state that would last for a total of four months. Erickson has given us our fullest description and analysis of this event.[34] He isolates four precipitating events: Price's recent break-up with a woman he deeply loved, Jeanie McGowan, and his subsequent efforts to be celibate; some difficult psychological material in his work with Fritz; power struggles over Esalen itself as hundreds of hippies camped on the grounds; and, finally, his father's visit to Esalen.

Toward the end of 1968, Herman Price visited Dick. For the first time, the father shared with his son some horrifically violent memories from his Lithuanian childhood involving the murder and round up of Zionists or Zionist sympathizers. These affected Dick deeply. Soon after Herman Price left, Dick Price felt himself entering another psychotic episode. He knew it was coming on and so made arrangements with local friends to look after him while he was out.

They did their best, but in the end Price's psychosis proved to be too much even for Esalen. Heider tells the story in his journals: "Sunday May 5, 1969. Today Dick Price 86'd Baba Ram Dass. Dick said that BRD had killed him in an earlier incarnation.... Hot Springs Loony Bin. Hopefully Dick will regain a center before long." He didn't. Five days later Heider describes a particularly dangerous scene during which Price actually held a knife to a woman's side. "What kind of animal are you?" he asked. "A cat." "What color cat?" "A black cat." "Well, okay then."[35] Enough was enough. Jack Downing, a psychiatrist and friend of Price's, finally took responsibility for admitting him to Agnews Hospital. Even this quickly turned into a scene, however, when Price managed initially to convince the hospital staff that he was the psychiatrist and Downing was the patient. For a moment, Downing found himself being admitted.[36]

It was at Agnews that Price finally came down. He was released ten days later in late 1969. Silverman and Price then traveled to Canada to watch Perls work his new gestalt commune. Price had been working closely with Perls since 1965. Although initially suspicious of Perls when he arrived, Price decided to enter therapy with him, found the experience helpful, and soon embraced gestalt as one of his main spiritual practices (alongside sports, Buddhist meditation, and "voyaging" with psychedelics in the Ventana Wilderness just above Esalen).[37] This trip acknowledged both Perls's gestalt lineage, as well as the frail state of his heart. At this point, a meeting with Perls was also a potential goodbye.

Silverman recalls a number of psychiatrists observing a session Perls led with Price on the hot seat. Just as the session was ending, a beautiful Vancouver sun broke through the clouds and shone into the room. During the question session, a psychiatrist asked, "I can understand what you did with Dick, but how did you get the sun to come out?" Perls reached down to the floor near his chair, "I have a button right here."[38]

Solar button aside, this was a symbolic moment for the history of Esalen. At the end of this training session, Perls pronounced that it was time for Price to begin working with others. Price returned to Esalen and became the community's most consistent and beloved gestalt practitioner. Perls died the following year. In the synchronistically timed sunlight, the torch had passed from Perls to Price: a lineage had been recognized and preserved. Now Price would render Perls's methods more gentle and insert a certain Taoist and Buddhist sensibility into them. He would rename the hot seat "the open seat" and would institute his own central dictum as an antidote to the cultish gurus and psychotherapists: "maximum availability, minimum coercion." He would also repeatedly say, "I'm Dick, not Fritz." Perhaps most significantly, he would distinguish his own methods by referring to them not as a therapy, but as a "gestalt practice."

The later phrase is particularly important, as it carries definite connotations in the language of Esalen, where practice is understood to be *transformative practice*, a consistently used technique that can effect a real metamorphosis of consciousness and energy. Price came to gestalt psychology through Buddhist meditation. He systematically used psychedelics to further expand his consciousness and empower and deepen his gestalt practice. Those who knew Price best, including Chris Price, Eric Erickson, and Steve Harper, have all commented extensively on the incredible "space" or broad "field" that he seemed to inhabit while he worked with people. Erickson, himself no stranger to either meditation or altered states, has argued that Price "accessed a spiritual dimension of consciousness that was grounded in the experience of the basic interconnectedness of all existence." Erickson describes this spiritual dimension as consisting of two poles: the pole of "the experience of unity or interconnectedness," and the pole of "fundamental difference or alterity, which flows out of and is grounded in the first pole."[39] Again, a kind of psychological Taoism. Certainly such spiritual dimensions can be detected in many of the images that we have of Price working with people, including Julian Silverman.

Chris Price, who did so much with her husband Dick to develop a unique approach to gestalt, is equally clear that it is a serious mistake to limit his gestalt practice to a purely psychological realm. For Chris at least, Dick's propensity for experimenting with altered states brought a certain "shamanic dimension" to his gestalt practice that was layered over and deepened by the existential and psychoanalytic dimensions he had learned from Fritz.[40] There was also always something fundamentally *physical*

FIGURE 13. Dick Price working with Julian Silverman. Printed with permission of the Esalen Institute.

about Dick and his gestalt practice, a palpable strength and grittiness that everyone immediately recognized: the Illinois state wrestling star was still there.

The Tantric Shamanism of Claudio Naranjo

Along with Dick Price, Perls considered Claudio Naranjo to be one of his most gifted successors. Naranjo is a Chilean-born psychiatrist who made his first trip to the States in the early 1960s for family medical reasons (his mother needed an eye doctor). While in Boston, he met the psychologist

FIGURE 14. Claudio Naranjo as Shaman of Thanatos and Transformation. Painting by Antonella Cappuccio, 2004, with permission of Claudio Naranjo.

Frank Barron at Harvard. When Naranjo later won a Guggenheim fellowship, Barron invited him to Berkeley, where he was introduced to the anthropologist Michael Harner. Harner was working on the Jivaro Indians of the Amazon basin and their use of the yage vine as a psychotropic ritual substance. Harner in turn introduced Naranjo to a young graduate student at UCLA named Carlos Castaneda, who was working on similar subjects in Mexico, allegedly with a native shaman named Don Juan. Naranjo and Castaneda would become close friends. Castaneda even claimed that Don Juan had "smoked" Naranjo, that is, seen him in a vision.

One of Naranjo's first visits to Esalen involved a local television station (KRON), which had decided to film Murphy, Perls, Naranjo, Harner, and Castaneda discussing the subject of shamanism just after a seminar with a female Pomo Indian healer. Naranjo remembers arriving at Esalen and finally encountering one of his idols standing in the front door of the Big House, Fritz Perls. Having read *Gestalt Therapy,* Naranjo was somehow expecting a young man. Instead he met what he calls "an old sea wolf." This old sea wolf, moreover, was not just old. He was old and feisty. Specifically, he objected strenuously to the "occult mud" that he felt Harner and Castaneda were dishing out to a gullible audience. Indeed, when at one point Castaneda asked something like, "How do I know that consensual [socially constructed] reality is real?" Fritz reached over and slapped him, not out of anger, but as if to demonstrate how reality is not *that* consensual.

Reports differ, but most say Castaneda responded with some version of "Fuck you, old man!"

Old man or not, slap or not, fuck or not, Perls made a profound impression on Naranjo. In one conversation that Naranjo remembers especially well, Perls pointed out to him that he could do all the things the female Pomo Indian healer could do: if she was a shaman, well, then so was he. Observing first-hand Perls's uncanny psychological powers, Naranjo could only agree with him: "I came away feeling that he really was a genius, a shaman in another culture." Indeed, he agreed so much with Perls's personal assessment of his own shamanic powers that he left his original psychoanalytic orientation and became a gestalt therapist. By 1969, Claudio Naranjo was one of the second-generation gestaltists, along with Dick Price, Julian Silverman, Jack Downing, Bob Hall, and Jim Simkin. Esalen was quickly turning into a kind of gestalt mecca.

Certainly Esalen embraced Naranjo. Perls gave him a "free scholarship" to any of his gestalt sessions, and Price offered him a space on the floor anytime he wanted to come with a sleeping bag to Big Sur. Naranjo had effectively won a permanent invitation to Esalen. He was part of the inner circle. Naranjo remembers well what a tremendous impact the place's spirit of experimentation and sexual liberation had on him in turn. Born Jewish and having grown up in a sexually repressive Latin American Catholic environment in which "the flesh" was more or less a synonym for "sin," Naranjo found Esalen's metaphysical synthesis of sensuality and spirit especially powerful.

Like Price but in a somewhat different key, what Claudio Naranjo became known for was a creative synthesis of Asian meditation (again, with a pronounced Buddhist accent) and western psychotherapy. Alan Watts, of course, had written and talked about this a great deal, but it was Naranjo who perhaps did more than anyone to act on these remarkable resonances and come up with models and exercises to realize them.[41] He left Esalen in the early 1970s to found his own psychospiritual school along these same lines (SAT Institute, located first in Berkeley and now moved to Spain). Perhaps most interesting of all, however, is the fact that Naranjo's path through Esalen toward his own psychospiritual community displays in some frankly astonishing ways many of the central themes I am tracing here, from the esoteric roots of western psychotherapy, to the felt energetic states of a distinct Tantric transmission. The later Naranjo understands such a transmission not as some ethnocentric Asian privilege, but as an always available gnostic contagion, a universal human potential rooted in the physiology of the human body and its enlightenment.

Naranjo understands perfectly well that the original impulse for psychotherapy came from the altered states of Mesmer's magnetism and Freud's interest in hypnosis.[42] Accordingly, he insists that, "psychotherapy is always more than what it purports to be."[43] This is also no doubt why his mature teachings on psychotherapy—as a kind of "assisted liberation from the barriers of ego" through a yielding to the body's "organismic" spontaneity[44]—draws deeply, not only on Reich and Perls (the "organismic" part) but also on his own mystical experiences of Hindu Tantra and *kundalini* yoga, which he intuitively (and correctly) understands to be related to Tibetan Buddhism and Chinese Taoism.[45] It is hardly an accident, then, that the very first workshop Naranjo led at Esalen carried an explicitly Tantric title: Sadhana for the West. In short, he has received the Esalen gnosis. *Naranjo knows.*

How he came to know through what he himself calls his "tantric journey" is a story very much worth telling here.[46] It involves Naranjo's *kundalini* awakening, which he likens both to being possessed by a serpent and to an alchemical process that transfigured his flesh and bones, a kind of 'kundalinization' of the body from head to feet," as he puts it.[47] Interestingly, such an awakening was transmitted to him not by the touch of a Hindu guru in the Himalayas, but in a gestalt session with Jim Simkin at Esalen. Simkin told Naranjo that he needed to work on his breath, to pay attention to his breathing. This led Naranjo to hyperventilate, then to a new awareness of his ongoing experience, and finally to a "*satori* lasting some two hours as I drove back to Berkeley from Esalen." Naranjo felt he had received a kind of "wordless contagion" that allowed him to surrender to the spontaneous movements of his own body. This, he speculates, can happen through a formal initiation with a guru, spontaneously, or in groups conducted by a spiritual teacher who can inspire real surrender.

He is fairly certain such awakenings are *not* actual flowings of "subtle energies." In a fascinating move, Naranjo suggests instead that, "blasphemous as it may sound," the felt experiences of energy movements so common in so many types of psychospiritual experience (from Reichian therapy to the *shakti-pat* initiations of gurus) are in fact "an ever-shifting tonus dance that takes place in our muscle system in the situation of ego-dissolution." One might *feel* that there is a literal flow, but "the anatomical fact is one of coordinated volleys of nerve impulses that follow preestablished patterns (according to the organization of our nervous and muscle systems)." But the key is not the metaphysical status of the subtle energies. It is the very real spiritual state of which all of this is a bodily response, that is, the spiritual state of surrender and ego-dissolution.[48] In the end, then, there is no literal Tantric transmission. There is the enlightenment of the universal body through the surrender of the social self.

Having noted Naranjo's elaborate analysis of his own *kundalini* awakening, it would be a serious mistake to lock Naranjo's teaching into any single historical tradition, including Indian Tantra. Hence Naranjo actively resists any use of Hindu scripture or mention of the yogic *chakra*s to explain what happened to him, and he does not hesitate to turn to Taoist dragon or Mexican eagle and snake symbolism to explain his more mature shamanic experiences of his scapular bones as felt "wings" and his nasal region as a kind of experienced "beak" (and indeed, in his own mind, it is finally a nontraditional shamanism, not Asian Tantra, that best describes his mature spiritual life).[49] Twenty-seven years of meditation, psychotherapy, and altered states cannot be pigeon-holed into any "Hindu" frame for Naranjo. How could they be? The "inner serpent" of *kundalini* yoga is simply a South Asian construction of a universal neurobiology; it is "no other than our more archaic (reptilian) brain-mind." The serpent power "is 'us'—i.e., the integrity of our central nervous system when cleansed of karmic interference," the human body-mind restored to its own native spontaneity.[50]

Put a bit differently, Naranjo's "one quest" is a religion of no religion that has come to realize how "instinct" is really a kind of "organismic wisdom" and how libido is more deeply understood as a kind of divine Eros that can progressively mutate both spirit and flesh once it is truly freed from the ego.[51] This, of course, is yet another version of what we have learned to call the Freudian Left, an enlightenment of the body that has passed through both a Western psychotherapy (that is always somehow more) and an Asian meditative discipline (that is more often than not Tantric). Such was the Tantric journey of Claudio Naranjo to and through Esalen.

Oscar Ichazo and Arica

Naranjo's last major impact on Esalen was an indirect one. Oscar Ichazo was a charismatic teacher from the Chilean seaport city of Arica (pronounced a-*ree*-ka).[52] He claimed to be initiated into a legendary Sufi lineage called the Sarmouni or the School of the Bees. Naranjo helped Ichazo establish a community in Santiago, mostly by supplying him with many of his earliest disciples, who had earlier gathered around Naranjo himself. Subsequently, Naranjo returned to Esalen and brought back to

Santiago many of the place's central players (around fifteen, according to Naranjo) to apprentice with Ichazo. There was psychiatrist and pal of Price, Jack Downing. There was psychologist and human-dolphin interaction researcher John Lilly, who, among many other remarkable things, gave dolphins LSD and told the almost believable story of a dolphin named Dolly who seduced a man into making love with her in a holding tank.[53] There was also encounter-group leader Steve Stroud. All came with Naranjo back to Chile to study with Ichazo, whose influence on Esalen is now legendary. Heider's journals, for example, record that Steve Stroud sold his house for $5, quit his Esalen job, and "gave away all his stuff" to travel down to South America.[54] As for Heider himself, he didn't go. He felt that those who did go were "copping out" to an external authority. Cop-out or no, "Arica cleared our bench," as Price put it.[55]

It also enriched their catalog. The winter Esalen catalog of 1972 included its own section called Arica Training, a series of workshops with titles like Arica Awareness Training and The Human Biocomputer taught by Esalen regulars who had traveled to Chile to study with the new master.

This event would go both well and not so well for Naranjo. Ichazo, like so many other guru figures, turned out to be a highly authoritarian teacher. He also had a way of turning the tables on his original generous host. After secretly sending Naranjo out to the desert for a special forty-day retreat designed to rapidly spiritualize Naranjo's life, Ichazo gave the community the impression that Claudio was a megalomaniac who had disdained the community and was on a kind of Jesus trip. In actual fact, Ichazo had sent him out and Naranjo had experienced the desert retreat as "a kind of rebirth, a true beginning of a spiritual life." It would be the first of many lessons for Naranjo in the spiritual potentials, ethical dangers, and psychological limitations of charismatic teachers.

Even Dick Price would come to study with Ichazo, this time in New York, only to learn similar lessons. One day in the early months of 1971, Price came up to Silverman and said, "It's yours. Take it." And then he walked away and left for New York City to take part in a three-month-long Arica training session. Price's Esalen ethic of never coercing a student or seminarian were violated again and again during his own retreat. The final straw was an exercise in which the group members were asked to perform a *mudra* (a Tantric yogic term for a hand posture symbolizing a particular state of consciousness) that happened to be identical to the Nazi *Heil Hitler!* salute. There is no such *mudra* in Hindu or Buddhist yoga. Price, having grown up in postwar America in a Jewish family fearfully pretending not to be, was not impressed with such an exercise. He had

had enough and left eight days before the retreat was scheduled to end. Other Esalen figures, however, would stay, and still others would take up Arica in various ways over the next four decades, indeed until this very day.

Ed Maupin, for example, speaks warmly of how his own Arica training from 1972 to 1973 in New York began his "karma cleansing about sexuality." He believes that Arica's turn to such a focus was "a fundamentally new departure in alternative spirituality and in the human potential movement" and "had effects far beyond the borders of Arica." More personally, it helped him come to positive terms with his homosexuality. Such feelings could be adequately processed now. He thus ended an affectionate but somewhat troubled marriage and, in 1974, met his partner, with whom he has lived happily for the last thirty-three years.

When Price left Esalen for New York, Silverman became, instantly, the new director of Esalen. He quickly learned that he would now have to deal with Will Schutz, the emperor of Esalen, not to mention a whole bunch of hippies who had camped out on the famous grounds and were tripping on God-only-knows-what. Everyone may have been "tuning in," as Timothy Leary would have put it, but they were also driving poor Julian crazy. Silverman called a community meeting to try to take some control of things. He began by telling people what they were going to do. Richard Tarnas raised his hand and asked in his typically gentle fashion, "But isn't this a democracy?" Silverman erupted, "This is not a democracy! This is a damn business!"

Schutz's response to Silverman's business meeting was to organize "an experiment in democracy" with the kitchen staff. Essentially, this was an implicit form of mutiny (or, as some have it, a desperate attempt to improve the quality and diversity of the menu). Silverman went along with it anyway, to a point, and then declared the experiment over. In Silverman's words, the two men then "went at it" but ultimately survived each other. As did Esalen. In the end, though, it was gestalt psychology, not open encounter, that would come to dominate the Esalen catalogs well into the 1970s and beyond.

As for Julian, he stayed on for a full and fruitful seven years. Silverman finally stepped down as director in January of 1978, but only after he had penned with Wendy Ovaitt a manual on how to manage Esalen: *Notes from an Esalen Director's Handbook*.[56] This document, which was typeset and even illustrated but never professionally published, provides a clear window into the kinds of institutional changes Esalen underwent between 1971 and 1978, complete with salaries and budgets (Silverman's director's salary was \$1,100 per month in December of 1977). In 1971, Silverman points out, the place was staffed by "transient hippies," "male chauvinism" was the norm of the day, and Perls's dictum "lose your mind and come to your senses" had been translated into a dysfunctional and rampant "emotionalism." Not surprisingly, the institute was also a quarter of a million dollars in debt: "In all but legal declaration," Silverman sighs in his introductory remarks, "we were bankrupt." By 1978, however, the place was in excellent financial shape and the key managerial terms were now self-responsibility, co-operative processing, and nonhierarchical decision making. Things had changed quite a bit. Schutz was gone and Silverman was leaving too. But Esalen would go on, and it would continue to change.

Esalen Goes to the City

THE SAN FRANCISCO CENTER

So leap with joy, be blithe and gay,
Or weep, my friends, with sorrow.
What California is today,
The rest will be tomorrow.

RICHARD ARMOUR, *Look*, September 25, 1962

A sunny day. Faint mist on the hills. Dozens of white sails between here and Tiburon.
San Francisco is a new Tibet. The vitality of the quest grows each year. Disciplines for
everyone, new gurus every week. A psychic field is being built here—a culture to support
this exploration.... I walked for an hour through the city. Telegraph Hill was swarming
with beggars and dirty vagabonds, and I imagined Bon sorcerers cooking their brews in
old flats, their pants and serapes stained with wine and Tantric practice.

MICHAEL MURPHY, *Jacob Atabet*

San Francisco. It is a stunning city, especially for someone born on the
open plains of Nebraska, where flatness is a major river (the Platte, French
for "flat") and the Amerindian name of the state itself means "Land of the
Flat Water." But San Francisco is more than its famous steep neighborhoods, streetcars, golden bridge, and beautiful bay. Consider, for example,
Brad Newsham's encounter with what appears to be a Sikh gentleman
in front of the American Embassy in New Delhi. When the man learned
that Newsham was from San Francisco, he responded: "Oh, how lucky
you are!... Everyone knows that San Francisco is the spiritual center of
the world." Newsham expressed considerable surprise at this news. He
had, after all, come to India looking for, "well—something *better.*" The
gentleman went on to explain how "the earth's spiritual center shifts every
few hundred years or thousand, maybe. It used to be in India, but now it
is San Francisco. All our gurus are moving there to open ashrams."

Newsham scoffed, but a desk clerk at his hotel later that day "wiped the smirk right off my face." Newsham asked him to define what a stunning phrase like "spiritual center of the world" could possibly mean. "Oh," he casually responded, "that is simply the place where new ideas meet the least amount of resistance." This definition struck Newsham as immediately self-evident. As if to further establish the already obvious, he goes on to note that he has circled the planet four times now and has never encountered a place where new ideas meet less resistance than they do in that spiritual center of the world, San Francisco.[1]

This same spiritual center, sometimes sarcastically described as "forty-two square miles of prime real estate surrounded on all four sides by reality," would come to play an increasingly major role in the history of Esalen over the years. And indeed, to this day the city and the larger Bay area of which it is a part define much of that history and meaning as the present home of Esalen's cofounder, much of its board, and most of its past visionaries. And why not? For Esalen is a kind of mini–San Francisco, as it were, another spiritual center where Asian teachers find attentive hearts and new ideas encounter very little resistance.

A Bishop's Heresies

By 1966, Michael Murphy was spending more time in San Francisco and less in Big Sur. The talents and friendship of two men in particular drew him to the city: Bishop James Pike and George Leonard. Pike and Leonard both encouraged Murphy to open an urban branch of the institute. As Anderson points out, there were many good reasons to do this, including the numerous growth centers opening up in cities around the country that had been inspired by Esalen's success.

Perhaps more importantly, an urban environment promised to balance or even correct some of Esalen's shortcomings, including the prices it had to charge for room and board and its failure to reach outside the white middle-class for its central clientele.[2] Ron Brown, for example, who led racial encounter sessions in San Francisco under the Esalen banner, liked to refer to Big Sur as "the South."[3] Thus if Price Cobbs and George Leonard could pull off Racial Confrontation as Transcendental Experience, a marathon racial encounter workshop at Esalen in 1967, then the San Francisco Center could think bigger than its southern sister.[4] The San Francisco Center sponsored four consecutive racial encounter workshops that, all and all, ran from 1967 to 1970. The registration form for these events appeared in the summer of 1965, a little over two years after the chaos and destruction of the Watts Riots in Los Angeles:

> Open racial confrontation in this country is at last a reality, but it has brought bloodshed and death, terror and polarization. Rather than fear a confrontation, we must welcome and embrace it. For only in direct and honest encounter can white racism and black self-hatred be discarded. This series of Racial Confrontations is to allow for bloodless riots where the most dreaded thoughts and emotions may be expressed, where self-delusions that limit can be stripped away. Only when such confrontation has occurred can man expand his blackness and whiteness into creative humanness.[5]

San Francisco offered some rather astonishing talent living here, few perhaps as provocative as Bishop James Pike of the Grace Cathedral Episcopal Church up on Nob Hill. Pike was the fifth Episcopal bishop of California and a force in both the church of the time and the Bay area. In his previous career, he had been a successful lawyer, a path he left in midlife to study with Paul Tillich at Union Theological Seminary in New York. He then became dean of St. John the Divine in New York and later came out to San Francisco to assume the duties at Grace Cathedral. Pike had participated in seminars at Esalen in 1965 and was instrumental in bringing theological mavericks both to Esalen and to the city, including Bishop John Robinson of *Honest to God* fame.

Pike's chaplain, Robert Warren Cromey, had originally brought Pike to Esalen in 1965 and would later become famous for his fearless and passionate defense of gay rights both in the church and in the city. He had marched in Selma during the early civil rights movement, and then applied the same social logic to the civil rights of sexual orientation, becoming one of the founders of the Council on Religion and the Homosexual. At Esalen in the summer of 1966, Cromey and David J. Baar offered a seminar called The New Morality to match Pike and Robinson's "new theology."[6] Three years later, perhaps following in the footsteps of Leonard and Cobb and their racial encounter groups, he went so far as to offer Homosexual-Heterosexual Encounter with Donald Lucas.[7] By the late 1960s, in other words, Esalen, through Cromey, had helped open up a cultural space to address the intersections of sexual orientation, spirituality, and social justice.

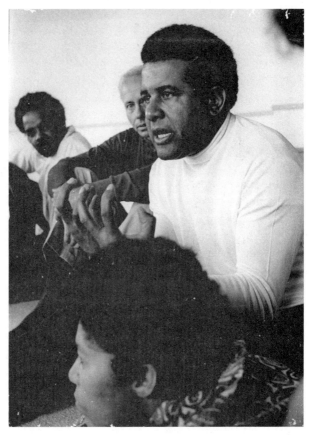

FIGURE 15. Price Cobbs and George Leonard leading a marathon racial encounter group, 1970. Photo by Paul Fusco, printed with permission.

Pike was also in touch with the Beats and Zen Buddhists, and was close to Alan Watts. Actually, James Pike was rather like Alan Watts. Both emerged from the Episcopalian tradition. Both experimented with psychedelics in a rather undisciplined way. Murphy fondly remembers how at St. John the Divine in New York, Pike had anointed himself with some sort of concoction that he claimed was a faithful reproduction of the ancient Israelite anointing oil. As he ascended the stairs to preach, whatever was in the oil took effect and put him in what Murphy describes as a "two-martini state of mind." Apparently, it was quite a sermon.

The story, like most such stories, is emblematic. Pike, like Watts, struggled throughout his life with alcoholism. The latter in fact would help end Watts's life on a night during which both Murphy and Leonard independently sensed something unusual. Leonard woke up in his home feeling the presence of death and became terrified that he himself was dying of a heart attack. While meditating that same evening in the Big House at Esalen, Murphy experienced a deep pain and a sense of confusion, which he had never felt before during meditation. Within hours, they both discovered that Watts had died that same evening.

While still alive, Pike, very much like Cromey, embraced any number of liberal social causes, from civil rights to the ordination of women. On this point, Anderson points out, he was probably even more radical than Watts. As subversive as Watts could be—his clergy career effectively ended with his public defense (and practice) of free love—his consistent embrace of nondualism, which essentially refused to see any ultimate distinction between good and evil, prevented him from embracing any real social program of change. In the end, Alan Watts saw the social world as the realm of purposeless play, certainly not the historical stage of real and lasting progress.

Pike was also the era's most famous theological renegade. The "new theology" he developed with Bishop John Robinson was explored in the Exploration into God seminar he brought to Esalen in 1966.[8] He publicly repudiated the Christian dogmas of the Virgin Birth and the Holy Trinity and saw the historical Jesus as a kind of political revolutionary or social critic (very much in line with some of the best historical criticism of today). Despite numerous warnings by church leadership, Pike refused to keep quiet and was actually put on trial in 1967 for heresy by his Episcopalian superiors in a nationally covered fiasco.[9] As a former Episcopalian himself, Michael Murphy fondly remembers the irony of a heresy trial in so liberal a tradition: "It's very hard to be a heretic in the Episcopal Church."

In 1967 Pike officially resigned his bishopric and took a fellowship at the Center for the Study of Democratic Institutions in Santa Barbara. He had, in effect, left the Church. So too would Cromey, although Cromey would return and Pike would not. Before he left, however, Pike did his best to support the early San Francisco ventures of Esalen. It was finally Pike's successor, Bishop Kim Myers, who lent the spaces of Grace Cathedral to Esalen for its initial city seminars.

Will Schutz was one of many holding encounter groups in the city now under these auspices, some of them in the basement under the nave of the cathedral. Late one night, the Virger, or head custodian, peered into this particular seminar room and saw twenty naked bodies. Legend has it, according to Murphy, that the Virger was so shocked by the sight that he fell back (rather ironically, into the arms of his male lover). The story got back to the conservative Board of Trustees of the cathedral, who were not at all amused. Murphy was furious with Schutz.

Similar to Abe Maslow, Pike was a fatherly figure to Murphy, and the two men shared not only a closeness, but also similar ideas. Both Murphy and Pike dreamed of a new kind of spirituality that could embrace all the bits and pieces of religious insight into a greater whole and take seriously the social revolutions that are implied in any true democracy. The two men also shared a firm conviction in psychical phenomena. When Pike's son Jim tragically committed suicide, the father communicated with his son through a medium and then wrote about the experience and his convictions at considerable length.[10] On February 3, 1966, the night before he died, Jim had actually tried to get ahold of Murphy in New York. Soon after this, a medium, who had apparently read about the suicide in the papers, contacted Murphy to tell him that Pike's son was trying to contact Bishop Pike through her. According to Murphy, the medium knew of Jim's suicide but had never met Pike and did not in fact know that Murphy and Pike knew each other.

Opening Night

Although the actual Esalen Center was not officially opened until the fall of 1967, the inaugural event in San Francisco was on February 6, 1966 (the Feast of the Epiphany) at Grace Cathedral. Abe Maslow was the featured speaker and delivered "The Farther Reaches of Human Nature," a lecture that later became part of his book by the same title. With very little advertising, the event attracted two thousand people. The church was packed. It was a stormy night, but the clouds broke and the moon began to shine through just as Murphy and Leonard approached the church. They had two bishop chairs waiting for them.

Because of his shyness, Murphy insisted that Leonard introduce the event. As Murphy paced back and forth at the back of the church, Leonard opened the lecture with his booming voice. Leonard well remembers the acoustics of the space and the seven-second reverberation as his voice traveled through the loudspeaker and bounced back to him, and how many in the audience thought he was delivering a prayer and so began to kneel. He went on anyway:

> We believe that all men somehow possess a divine potentiality; that ways may be worked out—specific, systematic ways—to help,

not the few, but the many toward a vastly expanded capacity to learn, to love, to feel deeply, to create. We reject the tired dualism that seeks God and human potentialities by denying the joys of the senses, the immediacy of unpostponed life.[11]

Leo Litwak would later quote these same lines in his piece on Esalen, which ran on the last day of 1967, "Joy Is the Prize," a widely read essay that would spark a media blitz in the early months of 1968.[12]

The center finally opened in September of 1967, in the powerful wake of the Summer of Love and at the height of the antiwar movement. Pike had already resigned his bishopric, largely because of his battles with a conservative Board of Trustees over the Vietnam War, which he strenuously opposed. The media naturally associated the new Esalen Center with the hippies. The list of speakers Esalen chose, however, to help open the center suggested otherwise: B. F. Skinner, the father of behaviorist psychology, for example, may have been many things, but he was hardly a hippie.

David Barr, who had been Pike's chaplain after Cromey at Grace Cathedral, was the center's first director. He did not last long, but the center managed to carry a certain Christian edge to it for some time, no doubt partly influenced by the charismatic and defining presence of Pike himself. By 1968, the Esalen catalog was featuring an impressive array of events sponsored by the San Francisco Center, many of them displaying a distinctly Christian bent. In the winter and spring of 1968 the center held a series of five five-day workshops called Theological Reflections on the Human Potential. These attracted the participation of a number of young theologians who would help define the contours of liberal Protestant theology, which was very much on the ascendant in the late 1960s: process theologian and Whitehead philosopher John Cobb, Harvard theologians Harvey Cox and Gordon Kaufman, Sam Keen, then of Louisville Presbyterian Theological Seminary, Michael Novak, and Bishop Pike were all among the ranks.

This was no strictly academic affair, however. What the seminars actually intended was an integration of Esalen experiential techniques (encounter groups, sensory awakening, gestalt psychology, and massage), in which the theologians actively participated, and sustained theological reflection in order "to ground theology and philosophy in human experience."[13] As in the theology of Harvey Cox, moreover, secularity here was not a curse, but a religious gift and promise.[14] The group thus echoed Spiegelberg's mystical "religion of no religion" beyond the boundaries of all dogma and tradition.

FIGURE 16. Joseph Campbell celebrating a birthday at Esalen, 1983. Printed with permission of the Esalen Institute.

Birthdays for Joe

Joseph Campbell died in 1987. Very early in his career, he played important roles behind the scenes in both the translation of European scholarship into the English-speaking academy (his editing of the Eranos papers for Bollingen) and the transmission of an important Shakta Tantric tradition into American culture (his work with Swami Nikhilananda on the latter's influential 1942 translation, *The Gospel of Sri Ramakrishna*). Campbell, however, did not really enter the cultural mainstream until the year after his death, that is, in 1988, when Bill Moyers aired his PBS six-part series, *Joseph Campbell and the Power of Myth*. For a full two decades before this, however, Campbell was giving seminars at Esalen, where he eventually became a quite literal perennial favorite: each year he would come to Esalen to celebrate his birthday with the community. Once again, Esalen preceded the culture, here by over two decades.

Campbell first came to Esalen in 1966 at the invitation of Michael Murphy. His first Esalen seminar was Mask, Myth and Dream.[15] It was Alan Watts who had encouraged Murphy to invite Campbell. Murphy and Stewart Brand, founder of *A Whole Earth Catalogue*, traveled to the San Francisco airport, where Campbell had a brief lay over, to meet with him and offer an invitation. Campbell accepted and returned again and again over the next two decades, often to lead seminars with theologian Sam Keen, Tai Chi teacher Al Huang, and Jungian psychologist John Weir Perry.[16] Both Campbell's written corpus and his charismatic presence were deeply influential on cultural phenomena ranging from the human potential movement and a popular New Age aphorism ("Follow your bliss"[17]) to George Lucas's *Star Wars* movies and the culture of Hollywood screenwriters.[18] Many individuals, moreover, have echoed the comments of Lucas, who, drawing on his own famous myth-making, observed that a certain "life force" seemed to pour out of Campbell in order to activate the spiritual adventures of those who were moved by his words and ideas. Indeed, at the 1985 National Arts Club awards banquet, Lucas went so far as to deliver a lecture in Campbell's presence called "You're My Yoda."[19] As the filmmaker Phil Cousineau put it, something other than reason and intellect was communicated through Campbell's books.[20]

Academic assessments of his work have been much more critical, noting, for example, that Campbell often forced the otherwise riotously various mythological material into his tidy theories and, more troubling, that he often displayed a rather obvious anti-Semitism in both his writings and his private comments. I certainly would not want to deny the latter point. Indeed, I have encountered real recognition of it in my interviewing. But Campbell's historical presence and influence at Esalen also intersect closely with our present exploration of Esalen's enlightenment of the body, specifically through the early and later presence of Asian Tantra in Campbell's thought; the central roles that the body, biology, and psychoanalysis all play in his system; the essentially mystical structure of his writings (if not his experiences); and, finally, his seldom noted but clearly critical assessments of Asian cultures. I want to make these points, moreover, in a way that is closely grounded in and at Esalen. This, it turns out, is easy to do, since, beginning in January of 1982, Campbell engaged in a series of conversations about his life and work on the grounds of Esalen. Phil Cousineau filmed these conversations and later transcribed them for the book *The Hero's Journey*.

Like many other Esalen figures, Campbell was a transmitter of Tantra-related ideas into American culture, transmuted and translated through a general psychoanalytic lens. With Campbell, this is hardly simply a creative interpretive projection, since, as I have already noted, Campbell helped translate a Bengali Shakta Tantric text into English. He also more or less wrote the Tantric summary and summation of Heinrich Zimmer's influential *Philosophies of India*.[21] I would argue that these were formative acts for Campbell, and that something of these two texts carry through Campbell's entire corpus as a constant guiding inspiration. From the hero figure itself (the *vira* or hero is a central theme in most Tantric systems), the hero's supernormal powers, and his mystical marriage with the Great (Mother) Goddess, to Campbell's provocative deconstructions of religious orthodoxies of all kinds, his consistent employment of *kundalini yoga,* and his unitive or nondual metaphysic, Tantric themes appear throughout his work.

The second major appearance of Campbell at Esalen involved a flurry of Tantric references. In October 1967, Campbell gave three separate seminars, two in San Francisco and one in Big Sur. The first in San Francisco, Freud, Jung and Kundalini Yoga, synthesized Western depth psychology and Hindu Tantra to explore "the relevance of Kundalini Yoga for modern psychological theory and the modern quest for meaning." Campbell was after a Western psychologized Tantra, hence his second seminar, The Lessons of Kundalini Yoga for Western Psychology. Indeed, even when he drove down to Big Sur after this last appearance for his seminar The Mystical Experience and the Hero's Journey, it was "Gnostic, Neoplatonic, Tantric, and modern psychological interpretations" that he was advertising, not some abstract "mysticism" or faceless "hero." Certainly, Campbell had no interest, at all, in mimicking what the Asian traditions had historically accomplished. Rather, he was interested in exploring how these "initiatory symbols" could take on relevance for what he called "the adventure of modern life."[22] This was pure Esalen.

Appropriately, then, *The Hero's Journey* ends as Zimmer's *Philosophies of India* once began, that is, with a Tantric parable from *The Gospel of Sri Ramakrishna.* Campbell tells the story of a vegetarian tiger cub raised in a flock of goats who has to be shocked into his own tiger-identity by another tiger, who forces him to transgress his own conditioned feelings of disgust and social propriety in order to eat meat. Campbell summarizes the moral of the parable as the secret of his entire lifework. The moral of the story is, "that we're all really tigers living here as goats. The function of sociology and most of our religious education is to teach us to be goats. But the function of the proper interpretation of mythological symbols and meditation discipline is to introduce you to your tiger face."[23] The Tantric tiger.

Within this same reading, it is perhaps not surprising to learn that Campbell's approach to comparative mythology traveled straight through the body—mythology as an expression of human biology.[24] Nor should it surprise us that for Campbell, the mythology of the hero's journey tends to follow the developmental paths of human sexuality. Hence it is Freud and Jung who provide the interpretive frame through which Campbell wrote his first and probably most influential book, *The Hero with a Thousand Faces.* Here Campbell can write of "the revelations that have emerged from the mental clinic," of the "bold and truly epoch-making writings of the psychoanalysts," and of the analyst as "an experienced initiate in the lore and language of dreams" who "enacts the role and character of the ancient mystagogue, or guide of souls."[25] Again, psychoanalysis as mysticism.

Psychoanalysis enabled Campbell to form his most central thesis: the monomyth of world mythology that retells in countless ways the hero's initial separation from society, his trials and supernatural aid, his initiatory encounters with the Goddess, and his eventual divinization and return back to society with a paradoxical wisdom that can embrace both the transcendent and immanent orders of being. Here is how he originally put it: "*A hero ventures forth from the world of common day into a region of supernatural wonder: fabulous forces are there encountered and a decisive victory is won: the hero comes back from his mysterious adventure with the power to bestow boons on his fellow man.*"[26] The hero may indeed have a thousand faces, but his journey looks very much like a creative fusion of Freud's oedipal complex and a reimagined Tantric *sadhana* or transformative practice. Thus the Campbellian hero departs society for adventure, meets and mystically marries the (Mother) Goddess, wins atonement with the Father, and returns to society as a divinized Master of the Two Worlds. It is this same metaphysical fusion of the Two Worlds, this constant affirmation that the human being and the cosmos are essentially one that gives Campbell's texts their deepest draw and energy.

It is a mistake, I think, to read Campbell as a professional scholar. He was a mystical writer who was particularly skilled at drawing his readers into both this fusion of the Two Worlds and a deep identification with a particular myth or image. Certainly, Campbell himself had a mystical understanding of artistic or textual encounter: "Now the trick for the artist is to present his material so that it doesn't put a ring around itself and stand there as separate from you, the observer. And that *Aha!* that you get when you see an artwork that really hits you is, 'I am that.' I am the radiance and the energy that is talking to me through this painting. In purely empirical terms it's called participation. But it's more than that. It's identification."[27] To claim that Campbell was primarily a modern mystical writer, however, is not to claim that he was a mystic. Sam Keen once described his old friend and mentor to me as "the world expert on a journey he himself never took." And indeed, Campbell commonly denied any real interest in actual spiritual experience or religious experimentation. He made it quite clear that his spiritual practice consisted of reading, reading, and more reading. He thus showed little real interest in many of the meditative, somatic, or explicitly religious practices in which Esalen had put so much hope. Or rather, he proposed deep and extensive reading as *the* transformative practice.

Huston Smith makes the same point in the Esalen catalog shortly after Campbell died. He tells how Campbell seemed to have more energy than the yogis, gurus, and psychics at a Menninger conference they both attended. When asked about his "yoga," Campbell denied that he had one, other than "reading books." He then thought for a moment: "Actually, I do have a yoga," he said. "It consists of rare roast beef, good Irish whiskey, and forty laps in the pool every day—in twenty minutes."[28] The Tantric tiger cub again.

The fact that Campbell the reader, drinker, and eater of beef was an archetypal Esalen figure only underscores Esalen's cultural role as a predominately intellectual one, and that its cultural influence has been disseminated primarily through books. Campbell's transformative practice of reading, reading, and more reading (and then writing, writing, and more writing) is closer to the spirit of Esalen than most have assumed.

Finally, it is worth mentioning that Campbell's critical reactions to Asian cultures reflect quite accurately many of the ethical and philosophical concerns that other Esalen figures were learning to recognize and work through in their own encounters with Asian teachers and ideas. Few popular writers ever cite Campbell's journals, *Baksheesh and Brahman* (on his often disillusioning travels in India) and *Sake and Satori* (on the same through Japan), but both of these texts are central to any full analysis of Campbell's views.[29] His critical assessments of Western monotheism, particularly in its Jewish forms, are well known and famously criticized.[30] Such criticisms are certainly well taken, but they also have to be contextualized in the larger frame of Campbell's rejection of *all* traditional religious systems that make any claim to absolute, exclusive, or literal truth. A conservative Hindu's belief in the actual existence of Krishna or an orthodox Christian's belief in a literal resurrection are just as misplaced and mistaken as an orthodox Jew's or Muslim's claim to an exclusive monotheism (or the land of Israel). They are *all* goats fooled by their social systems, not tigers awakened into their deeper human-divine natures through transgressive acts.

Campbell's hero's journey is yet another form of Esalen's religion of no religion. It is free to draw on mythical material from around the world and throughout all time, but in the end it refuses either to accept any religious claim at face value or to identify with any single tradition. Instead, it moves beyond them all into something essentially new, that is, a psychologically reflexive and "heroic" individualized modern mysticism. "If there is a path," Campbell observed, "it is someone else's path and you are not on the adventure."[31]

Esalen Goes to Europe (1970)

Stuart Miller and his new wife, Sara Unobskey "Sukie" Miller, played major roles at Esalen in the late 1960s and early '70s. Stuart became director of development and editor of the Esalen Publishing Program, initially with McGraw-Hill and then switched over to Viking. Sukie and Stuart would grow particularly close to Murphy. Together, they called themselves the Three Bears as they pursued various research interests, public relations parties, and fundraising adventures in the States and Europe.

Much of this was successful. The *New Yorker* covered a fundraiser in April of 1970 in Manhattan that drew over one thousand people.[32] In May and June of that same year the Three Bears took off again, this time to travel to England with a small crowd of Esalen notables, including Alan Watts, George Leonard, Will Schutz, and George and Judith Brown. In England they were interviewed by the BBC and socialized with one of their heroes, R. D. Laing, the radical antipsychiatrist. They also met with Douglas Harding, whom the Esalen catalog described as "the inventor of a new approach to enlightenment which, among other things, involves the perception that we have no head."[33] Harding, it turns out, was being perfectly serious. While hiking in the Himalayas, Harding came to the realization that consciousness is completely independent of the brain. He would later write about the experience in a beautiful essay, appropriately entitled "On Having No Head," in an influential book on the philosophy of mind.[34]

While in England, the Esalen group helped start the first growth center there and had, as Walt Anderson put it, "a hell of a lot of fun." As Anderson recounts the story, the British tabloid press announced the group's partying, preaching arrival with the headline, "Strange Cult Visits England."[35]

This "strange cult" then traveled through Europe and, eventually, to Italy, where they met another one of their favorite authors, Roberto Assagioli.[36] Assagioli had invented Psychosynthesis, an especially bold synthesis of various psychological schools and physical techniques that looked a lot like, well, Esalen. Assagioli was indeed an archetypal Esalen figure in both his psychology and politics. He had known both Freud and Jung as a young man. As a Jew, he had been imprisoned by the fascists and was more or less deaf from a bomb blast. When the Esalen crew finally caught up to him, he was an eighty-three-year-old man sitting behind a Victorian desk dressed in a smoking jacket. They apparently liked what they found. Stuart Miller's Esalen series would publish two of Assagioli's books, *Psychosynthesis* and *The Act of Will.* The Esalen catalogs of the early 1970s are filled with seminars and mini-essays on Psychosynthesis. For a time, particularly in the mind of Stuart Miller, it looked like Assagioli's system might even capture the flag. It never did.

A Glimpse into the Community: The Essays and Esalen *Journal of John Heider (1968–1971)*

The same Summer of Love Stuart Miller was racing westwards across America in his silver Corvette and designer clothes, John and Anne Heider were driving from New York to California by way of Mexico City on their BMW motorcycle. Born in 1936, John Heider had grown up a faculty brat. His parents, Fritz and Grace Heider, were both academic psychologists first at Smith College and then at the University of Kansas/Menninger Clinic. Heider followed in their footsteps. He graduated from Harvard College in 1960 and went on to pursue a PhD in psychology at Duke University. Despite a dominantly cerebral academic environment that was hostile to both his research interests in yoga and meditation, Heider managed to locate those aspects of the university that interested him the most. Put simply, what he wanted to do was join the best of the two worlds of the "community of scholars" and "mysticism."[37] Toward this end, he took LSD as part of a university hospital study, participated in ESP research with J. B. Rhine's parapsychological team, wrote his major area paper on the perceptual benefits of meditation, and finally finished a dissertation on creative states of awareness that drew on such nontraditional psychological sources as the poems of William Blake, Mircea Eliade's classic study of yoga, the Buddhist writings of Alan Watts, Huxley's *The Doors of Perception,* even the Beatles—not your typical behaviorist tract.[38]

Heider barely squeaked through the system. After all, he was not interested in the positivistic methods and statistical analyses of experimental psychology. He was interested in how human consciousness could be expanded, or, as he later put it, he wanted to ask questions like, "What is the life force?" "Is Energy real?" and "Do people have a god within themselves?"[39] Heider was an energy mystic. It struck him in an especially powerful way that libido remains a mere metaphor for orthodox Freudian psychology, and that Reich's central heresy lay in his insistence that the orgone is *real,* an objective fact of both the human body and the cosmos. No medical school or department of psychology in the country professes the physical and spiritual reality of the life force. He was interested, in other words, in the Freudian Left. A highly trained intellectual with existential and theoretical interests in the psychological, the psychedelic, the psychical, and the mystical—John Heider was Esalen incarnate. This is no doubt why Esalen was the first place he ever lived where he felt truly at home. Esalen, like no other place he knew, believed in the reality and power of Energy as a mystical and erotic force.

Practically speaking, John and Anne got to Esalen the same way many other people did. Ed Maupin invited them. Like Heider, Maupin had written his dissertation on meditation. When the Heiders met him in Los Angeles that summer, he invited them up to Esalen. Maupin remembers being enamored of John. He would struggle with that attraction. The Heiders later returned to Big Sur and stayed for almost four years. During this time, John would become one of the central players of the Flying Circus and would become known in the community, along with Steve Stroud and Seymour Carter (who now playfully describes himself as "a living artifact of the 1960s"), as among the wildest and most daring of the group leaders.

Heider's private journals and unpublished essays are some of the most insightful and entertaining things one can find on this period of Esalen's history. His psychological insights are acute, and his commentary often hilarious. He is also radically blunt about both the halos and the holes of what he witnessed first-hand and often helped effect. And he is as graphic and as fierce about his own neuroses, projections, desires, and bodily fluids as he is about anyone else's.

John Heider certainly knew all the big names, but he also loved all the little names, all the unknown X-Men and X-Women of the world who never made it into the catalogs or histories but who nevertheless made Esalen Esalen in the late 1960s. There was "the lady who showed us how to stroke auras," for example, and "the gold miner from Willow Creek." Then there was "the dishwasher who can read your palm; the group leader who was a chicken farmer in India where he studied magic rather than going to college; the baker who had been an addict, a huckster, a circus fire-eater, and,

FIGURE 17. Alan Watts performing a wedding with Steve Stroud, John Heider, and Will Schutz looking on (to Watts's right). Printed with permission of the Esalen Institute.

coming to Esalen, became a teacher of small-group process."[40] And that was just the beginning. "Doubtless," Heider observes, "I accepted many false teachings and enjoyed many illusions."[41] The emphasis was clearly on *enjoyed*.

The journals orbit around Heider's central role in the Flying Circus and the larger encounter group movement. Encounter, for Heider, involves the key notion of human *potential*, which he glosses as "power." Encounter is thus about the activation and integration of more and more energy or power into a human life. Physically speaking, it is about literally activating more and more cells of the body through action and acting out. Psychologically speaking, it is about the integration of the "inner man" and the "outer man," which leads to a kind of radical "integrity." Encounter group work is about truth telling and risk-taking toward what Heider calls an "enlargement of the Self." "Since," however, "what one might be is latent," encounter involves "techniques to make the latent manifest and the unconscious conscious."[42] Both the human potential and group encounter, in other words, display a distinctly psychoanalytic structure in Heider's journals.

Heider's writings also show that he grasps this psychoanalytic structure in theologically poetic language. Quoting the poet Rainer Maria Rilke, he writes "Jeder Engel ist schrechlich" (Every angel is terrifying). But this means that the converse is also true: "every terror we honestly face becomes an angel." Thus the Esalen motto, "go into the pain," until the pain becomes its opposite, until it becomes pleasure.[43] This, Heider points out, is a classically Freudian move: face the fear, stare down the emotion, go into the neurosis, and assert the nondual logic of the unconscious and the emotions, where love is also hate and where pain can morph into pleasure.

While he was still living at Esalen, Heider wrote an essay that explored Esalen's success. It had to do, he thought, with the intimate relationship between "chaos and creativity." Esalen's wisdom came from the freedom it granted individuals to experiment and so expand their range of consciousness and energy. As Ed Maupin declared, "Mother Esalen permits." Indeed, she did. Sociologically speaking, this goddess-like permissiveness was partly a function of the fact that Esalen inhabited a liminal position between the academy and the counterculture. The fact that there were no nay-sayers around meant that people were always doing things that were technically (or culturally) impossible: "no one at Esalen would seriously contend that the human aura does not exist. No one laughs at the young lady who came here hoping to learn to become a clairvoyant. No one here pretends to know the limits of the possible.... Today's skeptic risks being remembered as an idiot tomorrow; and tomorrow comes very soon at Esalen."[44]

Heider worried, however, much like Murphy still worries, that because Esalen is essentially an oral culture, there are no clear lines of transmission or memory, and so some of the most remarkable teachings are effectively lost the moment the visiting practitioner departs. And almost everyone departs. Murphy came to call this the problem of broken lineages. Heider dreamed of creating a kind of "research field station" at Esalen that could record much of what was happening without interfering in it. Nonintervention would be particularly important: "Certainly I didn't want to kill the goose that laid so many golden eggs, just for the pleasure of dissecting her reproductive system."[45] It was a wise dream, the outlines of which even made it into the Esalen catalog, complete with two proposed directors, Heider himself and John Lilly.[46] But nothing ever came of it, except of course John Heider's journals.

Heider began his journal on August 14, 1968, with an answer to George Leonard's question about what it was like to live at Hot Springs.

Heider's answer was disarming: "I wondered if it might not be akin to his WWII experience: wonderful, awful, wouldn't have missed it, would never wish to be there again."[47]

Heider records the wonderful and the awful, giving us a real picture of the place as it grew and changed. "The community has been in turmoil the past few weeks," Heider begins in an entry from April 1969. "Dick Price finally took his far-out trip and became a seer with a vision. Unfortunately this vision includes getting rid of Will Schutz and turning Esalen into a monastery." Rumors flew and a good deal of ill will took its toll. "The Flying Circus will probably die," Heider concludes. It did.

By February 5, 1971, Heider was even more down: "In September 1967, Esalen seemed a paradise of permission, opportunity, beauty and truth. By February 1971, both I and the institute seem older and weary, jaded by too many miracles too quickly digested." He seizes upon the inevitable paradox of Esalen: "filth amid natural beauty," the baths as both "meditation and massage in the sun," and "dreadful grime, old cinder blocks, body lice and staph." "Perhaps," Heider muses, "Esalen's power rests on this co-existence of good and evil."[48] The wisdom of Murphy and Miller's Hieronymus Bosch again.

By the early 1970s John Heider was increasingly critical of Esalen's high divorce rate, its high staff turnover, and especially its high suicide rate. He now counted four friends who had taken their own lives. That was more than enough. On September 2, 1971, Heider announces his departure in the journal and enters one final meditation on sex, drugs, and Esalen: "Incredibly, Esalen was never busted. We knew they knew, but they left us alone. In what other institute in the country would girls working in the garden expose their breasts freely without hostility or fear? Esalen is another world. A foreign land and culture. Probably the most beautiful place, the highest place, the freest place I'll ever live.... After Esalen 1967–1968, there really was no place to go, was there?"[49]

"Joy Comes on Thursday": The Harvard Crimson Essays (1969)

John Heider had a remarkable way of working with people. One of the strongest testimonies is a series of four serial essays that appeared in the *Harvard Crimson* during the week of Valentine's Day in 1969.[50] Written by a young Harvard undergrad named Nicholas Gagarin, these were essentially session reports of Gagarin's experience of a More Joy workshop that took place on January 26–31, 1969.

The Harvard essays are important for a number of reasons. They demonstrate once again that the connections between academia and Esalen have been intimate, and they are among the most insightful pieces one can read about the Esalen encounter experience. The essays also indirectly brought to the institute Richard Tarnas and Andrew Gagarin, each of whom would end up playing major roles in the community life of Esalen for the next decade or so. Tarnas, who read the essays while he was an undergrad at Harvard, would become a central member of the community and serve in several roles, from front gate guard to Esalen catalog editor. He lived on the grounds from 1974 to 1984, a period in Esalen's history that he recalls as a kind of magical equipoise that settled in between what he calls the crazy festival of the 1960s and the broad cultural clamping down of the '80s. Andrew Gagarin was Nicholas's father and a Yale-educated businessman. He would become one of Esalen's directors in the 1970s and eventually its primary financial administrator.

Numerous Esalen characters appear in the *Crimson* essays, including Stuart and Sukie Miller, Steve Stroud, and George Leonard. But it is a group leader we meet as simply "John" who focuses the narrative. Gagarin begins by telling us that he had traveled 3,000 miles from Cambridge with a friend, an older black man whom we meet as "Paul," in order to attend the workshop. We also learn that there are thirteen individuals in his group, among whom Gagarin is, by far, the youngest—hence, I gather, his self-description as "the boy."

Heider gets the group to feel comfortable with themselves through a simple exercise in which individuals tell the rest of the group what they fear. An older woman named Elizabeth, it turns out, is afraid to fart in front of the group. A dialogue about farting—and some actual farts—follow between Elizabeth and John. Later Elizabeth lies down and John puts his hand on her stomach.

"What do you feel?" he said gently.

"Your hand."

"And what do you feel now?"

"Warmth"

"And what do you feel now?" His hand remained in the same place. Elizabeth was crying. "Now let that feeling rise." She relaxed.

"And what do you feel now?" His hand was still on her stomach.

"More warmth."

"And what do you feel now?"

"A slight awakening in my vagina."

Gagarin then comments in the *Crimson:* "Things were indeed warming up, the boy thought to himself.... If [John] can bring Elizabeth's vagina to life, the boy thought, there should be a lot going on by lunch."[51]

Maybe not by lunch, but by Monday evening for sure. It was then anyway that a woman named Susie lies down on the group room floor. John puts his hand on her stomach, exactly like he did with Elizabeth. She almost immediately becomes nauseous and throws up violently into a paper bag that John, somehow, produces from behind her. She lies down again and begins a kind of open fantasy that quickly turns into a kind of Freudian parody. She opens her legs wide and has sex with "Papa." Then she gives birth to her son, whose testicles take a few minutes to descend from his newborn body. "Look at him, look at those balls of his, look at that cock. I'd like that cock inside of me." Gagarin, who professes not to know much about Freud, provides more comment, and some hint of concern: "So that was it, the boy thought to himself, the whole cycle. She had slept with her father, given birth to a son, and now she was sleeping with the child."[52] Did similar desires and fantasies lie hidden in *him?*

There is an encounter group saying, Gagarin tells his readers: "Joy comes on Thursday." For Gagarin's third installment and Thursday issue of the *Crimson,* he describes himself entering the circle. He is massaged by the entire group, learns to trust his breathing, and learns from John how he has cut off his body-sense at the neck ("Because you go to Harvard," John, himself a Harvard alum, teasingly claims). Finally, the boy feels a tremendous peace wash over him. On this same day, he also receives a sensuous massage from a beautiful naked masseuse named Gabrielle down at the baths (massages were commonly given in the nude then). There is a double bed in the room with the massage table, he notes wryly. Afterwards, Gabrielle and the boy talked about "commonplace things, and both laughed when she said she had married a Yale man. It was, the boy thought to himself, as though they were talking after making love. He was filled with joy. It was Thursday, after all."[53]

In the last Friday installment Gagarin notes that society and capitalism both teach individuals to put off pleasure more or less permanently, to deny their bodies for a future that never seems to come. In his confessedly non-Freudian mood, he calls this odd cultural phenomenon "castration." "What the people at Esalen have got, in the simplest terms, is the body. For 15,000 years civilization has repressed the body. Now, suddenly, it is coming awake."[54] Not just the body—the mystical body still beyond the present reach of science. When John asked the members of the group to move their hands together slowly to a point where they almost touched, writes Gagarin, "the boy had discovered that when his hands were about half an inch apart, he could bring them no further together. This was not a hypnotic trick; he was totally in control of himself. But it was as though there were very strong magnets in his hands which would not be forced together.... This energy current lies in all of us; we need only to become aware of it."[55]

Gagarin concludes that the "biggest thing" at Esalen is not the body but the future of education. He quotes George Leonard's *Ecstasy and Education* (to which we will return in the next chapter). Esalen, Gagarin finally suggests, may be where the practice and art of education should go after Harvard.

Rick Tarnas took Gagarin very seriously: he moved to Esalen after Harvard. Sadly, Nicholas Gagarin was not able to follow Rick. He did attend one of the four-month Residential Programs. It was not enough, though. He later shot himself on Friday, November 26, 1971, in his parents' home library, by most accounts because he was deeply conflicted over his homosexuality. His grieving father, Andrew, knew that his dead son loved Esalen and wanted to know more now. When he visited the institute he, like his son, fell in love with the place and the people. In the years that followed, Andy Gagarin would become Esalen's director and later its chief financial officer. He would also eventually buy property and a house near Esalen. It was there, in Big Sur, that he lived out the rest of his life, near the place his gay son had loved and written about with such affection and insight in the *Harvard Crimson.*

On Ecstasy, Education, and the End of Sex

GEORGE LEONARD AND THE HUMAN POTENTIAL MOVEMENT

What is the lexicology of ecstasy? There are no respectable words.

GEORGE LEONARD, Esalen catalog, January–March 1974

George Leonard was one of the greatest supporters of opening an Esalen branch in San Francisco. As the editor of *Look* magazine Leonard had opened a California office in 1956 to cover the world from what he called "this outpost on the edge of a continent" and "the California game."[1] In 1962, he was given control over the magazine's Los Angeles office as well. As things turned out, he was never as interested in movie stars as he was in human potential.

There are many different ways to think of Leonard's place in Esalen's history. Although some would disagree, it is difficult not to see George Leonard as a kind of "third founder," given his exceptionally close relationship to Michael Murphy and the long-term impact he has had on the place through forty years of writing, teaching, and leadership. In any case, Leonard quickly became a kind of spiritual brother to Murphy. While Price was now based full time at Esalen in Big Sur, Murphy found a kindred soul in George Leonard in the city of San Francisco.

Kindred, but not the same. These two men's differences, although often subtle and often unnoticed, are as important as their shared visions, particularly in the ways that these differences balance out their respective thoughts and worldviews. Leonard, for example, is generally much more critical of religion and its conservative influence in society than Murphy is. Granted, Murphy can be quietly radical when it comes to moving beyond religion to Spiegelberg's religion of no religion, and he can be wickedly funny in private about the stupidities of both traditional religious belief and some of the more recent New Age excesses, but he remains a gentle revolutionary at heart, "overly bred" by his Salinas family, as he sometimes put it, so as not to give too much offense to the polite public.

Not so with George Leonard. Having grown up in the racist South of the 1940s, flown low-level bombing and strafing missions in the Pacific front of World War II as a young man, and witnessed firsthand as a journalist many of the central figures and events of the civil rights movement, Leonard is significantly less reserved. Indeed, with his deep, booming voice and towering six-four frame, he often sounds like a fiery southern preacher or prophet of social justice. In essence, he still flies low. As a critic and gadfly, he is especially important to the history of Esalen, particularly when this history is often misrepresented as devoid of a sharp critical social consciousness or a keen awareness of the dark sides of religion. Certainly there are uncritical moments in this history, but those involving George Leonard are not among them.

So too with the erotic. Whereas Murphy is relatively reticent about emphasizing the erotic dimensions of the mystical life in his published texts (even as he privately acknowledges them), Leonard writes and speaks often of sexuality and even penned three separate books on the subject. His book *The End of Sex,* for example, advances the spiritual and physical eroticization of all of life in the wake of the sexual revolution. Here too Leonard balances Murphy, even as Murphy's intellectual and religious influences on Leonard are equally obvious (Murphy's love of evolutionary mysticism, East-West integralism, and the *siddhis* or superpowers are omnipresent in Leonard's corpus). Leonard's language is most often that of education reform, social transformation, grand paradigm shifts, and the martial art of aikido (an Asian "spirituality as sport" to balance Murphy's "mysticism of golf"), but the same patterns are all here: from the controversial title of *Education and Ecstasy* (1968), through the orgasmic rhythms of *The Silent Pulse* (1978), to the polymorphous eroticization of *The End of Sex* (1983), Leonard's voice is permeated by a certain ecstatic quality that understands the body not as a container of a disembodied soul, but as a holographic microcosm of the entire cosmos and its mysterious and ultimately free creative energies, energies that manifest most easily in the West within the mystery of sexuality and the altered states of sexual arousal and orgasm. The enlightenment of the body.

Murphy and Leonard originally met in San Francisco on February 2, 1965. The meeting was memorable and life-changing for both men

(Leonard, for example, always quotes the date to me when our conversation drifts in this direction). To appreciate fully what happened on this date, however, it is important to back up a bit first and meet the man who met Murphy that winter day.

Early Life, Early Esalen

George Leonard was born in Macon, Georgia in 1923.[2] Three years later his family moved to Atlanta. His first memory, signaling his own later flying career, was of Lindbergh's flight across the Atlantic. Particularly important to his early intellectual development were the three consecutive summers, from the ages of thirteen to fifteen, he spent with an older cousin, Ed Stephenson, who was in college and would later become a professor of English. Stephenson acted as Leonard's tutor, essentially teaching his charge in a single summer everything he had learned the previous year in the classroom. Together they read Wordsworth, Coleridge, Blake, Swinburne, Keats, Shelley, Shakespeare, Milton, Donne, Hemingway, Sinclair Lewis, and William James. Leonard still remembers these childhood summers as the most intense reading and learning experience of his life.

It was the experience of unimaginable racial injustice, however, that left the most indelible mark on George Leonard's soul. This realization made it impossible for him to look upon society or religion innocently. He knew how both subtle and gross the prejudice could be and how deep it ran through every social and religious institution of the land. Indeed, his autobiographical reflections on the 1960s, *Walking on the Edge of the World,* begin with the '40s and his experience of a racism he knew his own family supported. The turning point came for him at thirteen, when he looked into the eyes of a chained black man on the courthouse square of Monroe, Georgia: "What I experienced was a sense of utter horror, a sickness and despair that stayed with me for several days. I emerged with one unshakable certainty. They were all wrong—my father and my grandfather and all the ministers and doctors and teachers and politicians. My whole society was terribly, tragically wrong on a matter of immense importance."[3]

On December 7, 1941, Japan attacked Pearl Harbor. Leonard enlisted in the air corps as soon as he was old enough, and in March 1944 graduated first in his class of 310 cadets. The top six candidates of this class were kept on to teach new recruits until they managed to convince their superiors to send them into combat. All six were then trained to fly the A-20, a swift and low-level attack plane with six forward-facing machine guns and a gunner in the rear designed to support troops on the ground and "loosen up" resistance. In April of 1945, Leonard joined a combat squadron in the Philippines and flew twenty-two combat missions before he was sent to Okinawa in August to prepare to raid Japan itself. "I am one of those people the A-bomb might have saved, and I still don't think it was moral," Leonard admits. When the war ended with the holocausts of Hiroshima and Nagasaki, Leonard headed back home among those who would create the baby-boom generation and lay the social foundations for the 1950s, '60s, and '70s, that is, for the origin-era of Esalen and the American counterculture.

As a young man in the late 1940s, Leonard dreamed of becoming a novelist. He enrolled at Chapel Hill to study English literature and graduated in the summer of 1948. He worked for Sears and Roebuck just long enough to realize that the corporate world held little for his soul, and then re-enlisted in the air force, eventually landing a position as an intelligence analyst at the headquarters of Air Training Command at Scott Air Force Base. There he could make a living, support his wife and two young daughters, and finish his first novel, *Shoulder the Sky* (1959). He later started a glossy magazine for Air Training Command, producing sixteen issues before he landed a job at *Look* magazine in New York in 1953, when magazines were the major media, television was a little fuzzy screen, and something like the Internet could be imagined only in science fiction.

Leonard worked for *Look* for seventeen years until he resigned in 1970 to write and work within the human potential movement full-time. The magazine position, as he often describes it, was "the best job in the world." He was given long stretches of time to research and write feature stories and supervise special issues. He also had generous travel budgets and almost complete creative control of his projects, which included award-winning stories on the condition and reform of American education, the civil rights movement, the Iron Curtain, and, eventually, that ferment of American cultural experimentation and creativity—California.

When Leonard was assigned to open an office in San Francisco, he commuted from New York, logging twenty-four trips in 1961 alone as he memorized the American landscape below. Leonard's journalism was a kind of participant-observation, that is, he rejected distant objectivity and instead participated in whatever he was reporting on. When the desegregation riots broke out in Little Rock, for example, he returned to his native South and began covering the civil rights movement by meeting with Martin Luther King, Jr., and by joining the Selma demonstration march. Similarly, when he reported on the educational system, he sat with children in schools for weeks at a time to get some sense for how they felt and thought about the schools.[4]

On Magazines and Movies

This New Journalism came to define his research for a June 28, 1966 special *Look* issue on California as what he called in the issue's opening pages "a window into the future." The issue was filled with dramatic photos of both the heaven and hell of the new California scene: the "cars gone mad" of hot rod legend and Kustom Kar King George Barris; the new sky-diving craze; angry black men staring at the reader from within the burned-out district of Watts after the riots; topless waitresses serving coffee (very carefully, no doubt); and an entire photo section on what Leonard was calling "the turned-on people," those cultural entrepreneurs who embodied best Thomas Wolfe's hymn to the American soul as seeker: "Go seeker, if you will, throughout the land, and you will find us burning in the night."[5]

It was this California spirit of "the seeker" that Leonard was interested in tracking here: "The game is no longer to explore and conquer your physical environment, nor to build empires on the face of the earth, but to explore and expand yourself, your institutions and all of human possibilities, to seek ever-receding frontiers in the infinitely rich and varied common countryside of humanity."[6] A long photo-series called "The Turned-On People" began immediately after Leonard's opening editorial comments. The series in fact began with none other than Michael Murphy, announced here as "the prophet of joy" (years later, the *New Yorker* would change the title to the more accurate "mystic of joy").

The piece included a brief synopsis of the Esalen Institute at Big Sur Hot Springs and a large photo of an ecstatic Murphy in a bright red sweater, arms upraised, grinning into the sky. The photo captured well Murphy's famous exuberance, but it was hardly a spontaneous shot. Indeed, Murphy recounts with his usual grin how difficult it was to pose in such a way for shot after shot until the photographer was finally happy with what he got—spontaneity is hard work. But Esalen had in fact already appeared on a previous page of the same issue, this time within the gentle silhouette of a nude female bather in quiet contemplation at the baths.[7] These images of Esalen from the summer of 1966 were probably the earliest the general American public saw.

FIGURE 18. *Look* magazine feature photo of Michael Murphy (June 28, 1966). Photo by Paul Fusco, used with permission.

Historically speaking, however, this particular *Look* issue represented more than the liberal California dream that was sweeping the nation. More personally for Leonard, it embodied his new friendship with Murphy. It also expressed something of the American seeker's inner frontier that these two men had already named one evening in 1965 as the human potential movement.[8] It happened in a kind of brainstorming session that involved the two free associating with various ideas, jotting them down on little slips of paper, and then tossing the slips on the floor. At some point, surrounded by a kind of paper snow, Leonard kept coming back to a set of associations hovering around the civil rights movement. Certainly this set well with his own fierce memories of the South and the dramatic ways that the civil rights movement was able to change the legal landscape, almost overnight. There had been a civil rights movement and a free speech movement. Why not, then, also a human potential movement? Leonard jotted the phrase down and tossed it on the floor with all the others: "Neither Mike nor I had any idea I had just labeled a 'movement' that over the next five years would be interpreted and misinterpreted in hundreds of articles, that eventually, in one way or the other, would affect the lives of millions of people, and that ultimately would be taken for something that neither of us had intended."[9]

Historically speaking, the term encoded Murphy's abiding commitments to Huxley's human potentialities, psychical research, and meditative experience, as well as Leonard's fierce memories of Martin Luther King, Jr., the desegregation of the schools, and the Berkeley free speech movement's battle with censorship. The phrase coded, in other words, a literary influenced, profoundly ethical, socially engaged American mysticism. The dream would be misinterpreted in a hundred different ways. But the intentions of the original dreamers were certainly clear enough.

This same human potential vision was announced in the fall 1966 Esalen catalog as From Dream to Reality: A Call to Action: "The era of the human potential is already upon us. All of us—aware of it or not—have roles to play in a human drama involving basic shifts in the aims and expectations of life on this planet. The seminar leaders will celebrate the new era, make explicit the hopeful and ever-evolving goals of Esalen Institute and engage in dialogue with seminar participants about the part that each can play in changing the world."

Shortly before this workshop and just after the *Look* magazine issue had appeared, Esalen decided to introduce its new vision of the human potential to Hollywood. No one quite knew what the specific goal was, but it seemed worth trying anyway. Actually, the casual connections between Hollywood and Esalen were intimate ones from the beginning. When he left Big Sur in the early '60s, Dennis Murphy became a Hollywood screenwriter, and stars and pop singers routinely show up at the baths to this day. No one was quite this positive about the summer party of 1966, though. Indeed, the event turned out to be more humorous than meaningful. It became known, after all, not as "The Night Hollywood Embraced Esalen," but as "The Night Fritz Perls Spanked Natalie Wood."

On July 29, 1966, the Hollywood actress Jennifer Jones gave a party in her Hollywood home in an effort to bring Esalen figures and Hollywood personalities together. When Leonard arrived, Jones immediately introduced him to Rock Hudson, Glenn Ford, and Eddie Albert. Leonard noticed that Shirley MacLaine was charming Mike Murphy. Later, he would dine with Dennis Hopper and talk shop with James Coburn. The guest list was indeed impressive.

Fritz made his entrance later that night, dressed not in his usual jumpsuit (which is what he always wore at Esalen), nor in the more casual attire like the other guests, but in a formal tuxedo. After dinner and a viewing of an amateurish film on encounter groups, Carl Rogers offered to lead an encounter group. Midnight came, and the crowd became more and more boisterous. Leonard ventured outdoors and discovered that Fritz was leading a gestalt session near the pool. Natalie Wood was in the hot seat.

> It was another part for her to play, and she was enjoying herself immensely. Fritz tried to get her to admit she was acting. She skillfully slipped out of his verbal traps. Then Fritz let her have it.
>
> "You're nothing but a little spoiled brat," he said in a voice harsh enough to stop time, "who always wants to get her own way."
>
> She gasped and her mouth fell open. A moment later Fritz somehow had her over his knee, spanking her. It was a brief episode, hard for the senses to register or credit. Natalie flounced away, and her friend Roddy McDowell offered to fight Fritz. Fritz ignored this offer. About two minutes later, Natalie marched out of the party with no goodbyes, her nose angled sharply upward.
>
> Not long after that, Tuesday Weld sat in the hot seat, with approximately the same results, minus the spanking. She too stormed out, her long blond hair streaming.

Leonard finally left around 2:00 a.m. Dennis Murphy showed up at 3:00 a.m. and, with his brother Mike, helped charm the party to sunrise. Not much came of the event in terms of actual relationships between Hollywood and Esalen, except perhaps for two movies. *Bob and Carol and Ted and Alice* with Natalie Wood satirized something called "the Institute" (the directors wanted to do the filming on the grounds of Esalen but were turned down). Tuesday Weld would also later star in *The Serial,* which also poked fun at the human potential movement.[10] No one was spanked in either movie, though.

Education and Ecstasy *(1968)*

To this date, George Leonard has published over a dozen works of fiction and nonfiction and literally hundreds of magazine essays toward the actualization of this same human potential. A full study of this corpus would require a long trip through his journalism years with *Look* from 1953 to 1970 and on into his career as a freelance author within the human potential movement from the 1970s to the present. For the sake of space, I will approach Leonard's early vision through just four of his early books: *Education and Ecstasy, The Transformation, The Silent Pulse,* and *The*

End of Sex. It is certainly no accident that such a list begins with ecstasy and ends with sex. Such is the nature and spirit of Leonard's writing style, metaphysical sensibilities, and moral message.

He is very much present in these subjects. Once one has met him in person, one quickly realizes that the pages and the person express the same presence. A hint of jazz. An occasional war story. A method of argument that resembles the "blending" of an aikido throw. An ecstatic quality to the writing that turns to the body for its deepest intuitions and creative impulses. A fearless condemnation of social injustice in all its forms. And a careful suspicion of all things religious or dogmatic. These are the rhythms of George Leonard as text, as body, and as personal presence.

Leonard's assignment to report on public education for *Look* turned out to be life-changing. After months of in-depth reporting, Leonard produced an impressive sixteen-page feature for the February 1956 issue that was very well received. The National Education Association ordered a million and a half off-prints, numerous state education associations reprinted Leonard's "A Magna Carta for Teachers," and at the end of the year the piece was given the top award for education coverage from both the NEA and the Education Writers' Association. Over the next decade and a half, Leonard won a total of eleven awards on education reporting. It was this writing and experience that he summarized in his first major monograph, *Education and Ecstasy,* which was first published as a book in 1968 and then serialized in three consecutive issues of *Look.* The book went on to sell over 300,000 copies.

Leonard's popular but controversial thesis was as simple as it was radical. Modeling his education theory on the human potential movement, Leonard proposed that education as it was currently being practiced in the United States was largely about restricting or damning up the immense human potentials of the mind, spirit, and body, and that the true purpose of education should be about the removal of what William Blake had called the "mind-forg'd manacles" of society, so that America can work toward a more integral cultivation of ecstasy.

Leonard was quite serious about that word "ecstasy." He had to fight hard with his publisher to keep it in the title. Well within the Freudian Left, he also refused to surrender the word to the materialism of a purely mundane sexuality. Thus he did not hesitate to turn to mystical language to explicate its deepest meanings: such a term evoked for him at least, "not simply pleasure as in the equation of Bentham and Mill, not the libido pleasure of Freud, but ecstasy, *ananda,* the ultimate delight."[11]

The Sanskrit metaphysical reference was hardly accidental. After all, Leonard will later use another Sanskrit/Tantric term, *sadhana,* to describe Michael Murphy's spiritual practice.[12] Leonard, however, insisted that what was needed for real human flourishing was not more Asian spirituality per se, but rather a more integral understanding of cultural accomplishment that could move beyond the limited visions of both the West and the East, both of which have produced "massive human unhappiness" by focusing all of their best energies on only one aspect of the human being (the West on technological control, India on the attainment of ecstasy). In the freedom they give us from practical concerns and the day-to-day running of society, modern science and technology, and particularly what Leonard imagined as the telecommunications miracle of the computer, offered a way out of this impasse, that is, a place "where the successful control of practical matters and the attainment of ecstasy can safely coexist; where each reinforces the other; and quite possibly, where neither can long exist *without* the other."[13]

"The times," Leonard insisted, "demand that we choose delight."[14] Here he was certainly not writing simply about personal emotions. He was convinced rather that ontological delight had real social pay-offs, that it could offer humanity a positive vision of what cultures could be in the future rather than what they have been in the past. For Leonard, the cultivation of joy as the deepest secret of human nature was the only long-term solution to the engrossing interests and horrors of war that he understood firsthand.[15] He suspected, moreover, that any serious pursuit of a technology of ecstasy would eventually lead individuals to the human potential, that is, to what has traditionally been labeled the "psychic," the "mystical," even the "fantastic."[16] Noting the human ability to harness through technology what were previously undreamed of electromagnetic energies, he insists that education can now dream of harnessing the invisible energies of that "vast, unknown realm that we call (pending the time we learn to manipulate each of its specifics) the 'mystical.'"[17] There is, in other words, a future science of mysticism, a technology of ecstasy, that lies at the heart of the evolving human potential, and Leonard was out to propose it as the very heart of the future of American education.

In a chapter appropriately entitled "The Rogue as Teacher," Leonard offers three figures as heralds or models of this vision of the future: the radical technologist, the mystic, and the artist. Prometheus-like, the technologist represents that figure who knows that "*any radical change in the technology within an established order will surely bring that order down.*"[18] To establish his point, Leonard cites historical examples of cultures that feared innovation, all ultimately in vain: the Greek Daedalus warning Icarus not to fly too high, the Israelites fearful of the Babylonians' tower as somehow "against God," the traditional Arabic condemnation of *bid'a* or "novelty" as "heresy," and Mary Shelley's 1818 prophecy of modernity, *Frankenstein.* As for the mystic, perhaps "the most dangerous of all," Leonard is fully aware that his or her practices often perpetuates conservative and essentially oppressive social structures (India is his example here again),[19] but he also knows that such practices carry within themselves other fundamentally transgressive and deconstructive possibilities: *"But beware.* At any moment, the mystical impulse can bring the structure down. For mysticism admits no boundaries whatever, not even the minimal interface between self and other."[20]

So too with the artist, who "must destroy the forms and perceptions of his time" in order to "journey beyond the conscience of his race."[21] Great art, like great technology or mysticism, always goes beyond what is acceptable. It is in its deepest nature essentially new, heretical, offensive, that is, ecstatically creative. The world is now filled with such rogues by the hundreds of millions, ready, like Blake, like X-Men, to burst the shackles of the past and open minds to the future evolution of the human potential. And indeed, Leonard even claims to meet a psychically gifted young woman, an eroticized witch, in a high school classroom at the very beginning of *Education and Ecstasy.*

The Confluent Education Program (1967–1968)

Leonard's interests in "education and ecstasy" were hardly tangential to the social and intellectual life of Esalen, which was for Leonard a central exemplar of what education could be in America. Of course, some of the institute's earliest inspirations were derived from Aldous Huxley's call for a more rounded education and for something the writer called "the non-verbal humanities."

Beginning in 1967, Esalen attempted to institutionalize something of this vision through a joint program it undertook with Professor George I. Brown of the department of education at the University of California, Santa Barbara. Brown first came to Esalen to participate in its early workshops on creativity. There he and his wife Judith became involved with Perls's gestalt workshops. Impressed with her natural psychological abilities, Fritz asked Judith to be a cotherapist with him. From these creative and gestalt beginnings, the Browns helped initiate the Confluent Education Program. The project consisted of bringing elementary and high school teachers to Esalen over approximately a dozen weekends in order to introduce them to encounter group dynamics, to sensory awareness, and to various other emotional or affective modes of learning. The idea was a simple but effective one. Once introduced to these new confluent methods, the teachers could then take them back to their schools and integrate them, in their own ways, into their individual classrooms.

The program received two healthy grants from the Ford Foundation ($35,000 to Esalen in 1967, and $350,000 to Santa Barbara in 1968). Over the years, it helped produce over one hundred MAs and over thirty PhDs in Confluent Education through the university for over twenty countries, with Norway and Japan producing some of the most notable numbers.[22] This general Esalen concern over education also produced three books for the Esalen Viking series, including Janet Lederman's *Anger and the Rocking Chair,* which actually led off the series, and George Brown's *Human Teaching for Human Learning.*

Becoming Conscious of Culture: The Transformation *(1972)*

Leonard left *Look* two years after *Education and Ecstasy* appeared. He was becoming increasingly frustrated with the East Coast establishment's dismissal of the human potential movement and its almost complete inability to appreciate what was happening in California. In truth, however, Leonard's resignation was simply the final act of a long intellectual, emotional, and spiritual transformation that had been going on inside him for years. He was no longer an East Coast journalist. He was one of a handful of writers and leaders imagining the human potential into existence. Very much in pursuit of this developing vision, Leonard signed a contract with an advance of $50,000 to write his second monograph, *The Transformation.*

In *Education and Ecstasy,* Leonard had imagined a radically liberal education of the future that could assist the evolutionary process by liberating, nurturing, and developing the natural psychical mutations of gifted individuals. He had also speculated about how American society might learn to produce a new type of human being who could learn and mutate individually instead of having to wait for the much slower changes of society and conservative tradition.[23] *The Transformation* picks up on these same themes through two central categories: Civilization and Transformation. For Leonard, Civilization is "that mode of social organization marked in general by political states, markets, legal sanctions and social hierarchies, wherever in the world it occurs." Transformation stands for "both the process that spells the end of Civilization and the period during which the process takes place."[24]

Leonard's thesis was that we are now living through the most radical change in human social practices since the invention of agriculture (about five thousand years ago), and that to the extent that we are becoming conscious of how Civilization constructs and so limits our experience of the world and ourselves, we are effectively waking up from culture and so ending the long spell of Civilization. In other words, we can no longer be individually duped by *any* culture, mythology, or religion (especially our own), for we now know that all such systems are constructed by us and, as such, are expressions of human nature.

The downside of such an insight into the religion of no religion and the culture of no culture is the troubling realization that we are all being duped (and occasionally literally killed) by the literalisms and logic of our own creations. The upside is that, if we can accept this enlightenment, it is in our power now to deconstruct and reconstruct these visions toward greater and greater returns of delight, creativity, and transfiguration. Put simply, we now recognize myth for what it has been all along, that is, *myth.* And to the extent an individual or a culture becomes conscious of its own mythology, it has transcended that mythology for some future life or mode of being.

Fish are the last creatures one would expect to discover, analyze, and wake up from water, Leonard had already pointed out in *Education and Ecstasy.*[25] Similarly here, religious believers, politicians, and patriots are hardly our best hope to wake up from culture and Civilization, and we are only now beginning to emerge from our long watery existence: "We are evolutionary creatures. Like our ancestors in the late Devonian Period some 400 million years ago, we have just pulled ourselves out of the waters in which we have lived for millennia." And "the first thing we notice is the water itself, Civilization. While we were in it, we had no way of knowing how it shaped our existence. Now we are beginning to understand."[26]

There is something fundamentally Freudian about this Transformation. This becomes particularly obvious in "The Gift," a chapter that reflects on and critiques Freud's famous analysis of the impossibility of true happiness in his *Civilization and Its Discontents.* Leonard is obviously deeply appreciative of Freud's insights into the necessary repressions and inherent pathology of any stable society, but he ultimately rejects Freud's pessimism for the brighter hopes and future of the human potential. What if, Leonard asks, the human being was not "the born monster that Freud paints him?"[27] What if Civilization itself creates the aggression and frustration from which human beings suffer? "Freud's first great insight holds. Clear conscious awareness of how a particular dis-ease is inculcated is likely to make that particular dis-ease leave us."[28] So what if we were to now become consciously aware that our most basic dis-ease is caused not by some inborn original sin or genetic flaw but by Civilization, that is, by our very own societies and religions? Can we be healed from *them?* Can we become conscious of our own cultures and so wake up from their spells without sacrificing the gifts that they also so clearly bestow?

What Leonard is suggesting is that Freud's id, literally "the it," may not be the dark dangerous force of unconscious instinct that orthodox psychoanalysis holds it to be, and that it is repressive society, not human nature, that distorts and mangles life and so produces neurosis. Here, of course, Leonard writes solidly in the lineage of the Freudian Left that we have already identified as one of the central streams of Esalen.

There is something fundamentally sexual about the social and spiritual Transformation Leonard imagines. Within three particularly suggestive pages, for example, he moves from reflections on the sexual maturation of twelve- and thirteen-year-old girls in a southern church in the 1930s—"Lust rises and falls around them like the cicada's song while the minister's voice extracts only dust and dry bones from the bloodless body of Christ"[29]—to the seemingly impossible social transformations of the civil rights movement. With respect to race, "the greatest danger lies in the fact that the awakening doesn't happen to everyone at the same time. When some people begin to see things that other people don't see, the resulting crisis may strain at every stone in the social edifice." What he calls "the revelation of the secret" that the emperor of racist America is naked has infuriated many "who find security and identity only in the sleep of the senses."[30] Thus, the sexual ignorance and prudery of the churches and the structural violence of American racism are very much connected, and, as Leonard will develop the idea further in *The End of Sex*, society, erotic love, and the body are all related, so to change one is necessarily to change the others. Little wonder, then, that the greatest threat to a racist society is always and everywhere intermarriage, that is, sex and love toward the genetic fusion of "black" and "white."

In Tune with the Universe: The Silent Pulse *(1978)*

The Silent Pulse shows a significant shift in style and content from Leonard's earlier work. We move from the social concerns of race relations, education, and social change to the personal practices of an American mysticism that is at once scientific and artistic in its metaphors, democratic and individualist in its orientation, and socially conscious in its moral conclusions.

Leonard never really leaves social criticism behind, however. Indeed, much of *The Silent Pulse* is concerned explicitly with developing a worldview that can synthesize both the social or ethical and the personal or mystical dimensions of human reality into a greater integral whole. The text actually ends with practical instructions on how to get in tune with the silent pulse or "elemental vibrancy" of the universe, which Leonard draws from his teaching experience with over 20,000 students. By 1978, in other words, George Leonard himself has clearly experienced a rather dramatic transformation from a national journalist and educational theorist identified with (and rewarded by) the East Coast establishment to a popular international teacher of the human potential both at Esalen and in Mill Valley on the West Coast. And this pattern will only intensify over the next two decades. By 1978, Leonard had already developed Leonard Energy Training (LET) from his aikido and energy awareness training with the martial arts master, Robert Nadeau. He transformed this teaching practice again in the early 1990s, this time with Michael Murphy, to create something called Integral Transformative Practice (ITP). Leonard's three most practice-oriented books also appeared in that decade: *Mastery* (1991), *The Life We Are Given* (with Murphy) (1995), and *The Way of Aikido* (1999).

Practice, however, had always been a part of Leonard's life. His mastery of music as a young man and aikido later in life allowed him to access new levels of awareness and new forms of energy. In *The Silent Pulse,* Leonard's understanding of mastery through practice connect with the metaphorical patterns in science to create a new musical-mystical vision. And this underlying beat of all things takes him well beyond both practice and science into the elemental vibrancy, a metaphysical pulse that connects sexuality, mystical experience, and social reform.

Like all things, the text begins with sex: "The sperm cell swims with rhythmic strokes and joins the egg. Molecules of DNA dance together. Pulselike concentrations of fields interact, multiply, differentiate. A singular pattern emerges, something unique in the universe: a new being."[31]

He then moves immediately to state his central thesis: *"At the heart of each of us, whatever our imperfections, there exists a silent pulse of perfect rhythm, a complex of wave forms and resonances, which is absolutely individual and unique, and yet which connects us to everything in the universe. The act of getting in touch with this pulse can transform our personal experience and in some way alter the world around us."*[32] This is not a set of ancient beliefs to take on faith. It is a kind of modern gnosis based on the equally fantastic realms of biology and quantum physics. Science imitates mysticism, as with so many other texts that have flowed out of the Esalen orbit. Hence we are told that Pythagoras instructed his followers two and a half millennia ago "that a stone is frozen music, an intuition fully validated by modern science; we now know that every particle in the physical universe takes its characteristics from the pitch and pattern and overtones of its particular frequencies, its singing."[33] Modern science, then, does not simply imitate mysticism: it advances and deepens it.

As for the body, Leonard is fully aware of how sharply his views contrast with all those ascetic views of the body, found in both the West and Asia. He even names the rejection of the world and the body in its Indian guise, that of *samsara* (literally, the "round" of birth and death). But he hardly accepts the usual moral conclusions. Rather, he simply reads this round as a natural function of biology: "In the kingdom of the corpuscles, there is transfiguration and there is *samsara,* the endless round of birth and death. Every passing second, some two and a half million red cells are born; every second, the same number die." Moreover, there is something deeper and more mysterious at work "beneath" or "below" this *samsara* of the flesh. He imagines a microscope looking further and further into the mysteries:

> As the magnification increases, the flesh does begin to dissolve. Muscle fiber now takes on a fully crystalline aspect. We can see that it is made of long, spiral molecules in orderly array. And all these molecules are swaying like wheat in the wind, connected with one another and held in place by invisible waves that pulse many trillions of times a second. What are the molecules made of? As we move close we see atoms, tiny shadowy balls dancing around their fixed locations in the molecules, sometimes changing position with their partners in perfect rhythm.... We come closer, increasing the magnification. The shell dissolves and we go on inside to find ... *nothing.*[34]

Hence Leonard's final enlightenment and the answer to his original question: "Of what is the body made? It is made of emptiness and rhythm. At the ultimate heart of the body, at the heart of the world, there is no solidity. Once again, there is only the dance."[35]

So what, then, of the mind or soul? The individual is a series of energies and patterns that can be summed up as a single wave function or inner pulse, and that manifest simultaneously through fingerprint patterns, memory traces, the personality, even the mystical fields of the subtle or astral bodies: "Thus, separating mind and body is theoretically as well as practically impossible. Indeed, in terms of this speculation, it is the inner pulse that is stable and persistent at the most fundamental level: the unitary identity that explodes out into the world as a multiplicity of identifying characteristics."[36] Along similar lines, Leonard is clear that a person's identity should not be confused with the ego or with normal consciousness; such an identity rather resides in that deep and unique inner pulse that vibrates, for example, in the rhythm of words and thought of a good writer or in the deep intentionality, again often unconscious, of a person's life.[37]

Winged Thoughts toward an Explosion of Spirit: The End of Sex *(1983)*

In *Education and Ecstasy,* Leonard had described an ecstatic education in which the solving of a complex mathematical problem shares in the same delight-filled dynamics as sexual intercourse. *The Transformation* pointed to an "elemental vibrancy" or "ecstatic impulse" and had linked this life force to both the erotic and to new forms of social consciousness and hence to actual social and political reform.[38] In the very first chapter he recounts a mystical event he once knew with a lover "in the deepest hours before dawn, after a night of love, when consciousness itself began to change," here into a radical state of reciprocity: "But I must tell you that the moment did come when our own once separate and private emotions began to appear on each other's faces. Just that.... There was nothing metaphorical about this merging. In the faint light from another room, each of us could see our actual selves embodied in another—and we were terrified."[39]

Sex then contains within it the possibility for transformation. "Sex remains one of the most readily available ways of sampling the primal consciousness," Leonard writes, "the knowledge contained in the full orgasm is considerable."[40] At times, this orgasmic gnosis takes on a psychical form:

a similar erotic encounter in *The Silent Pulse,* for example, manifested itself in precognitive and synchronistic events in the external world.[41] To be "in tune" with the elemental vibrancy of sexuality is also, sometimes, to be in tune with the silent pulse of reality itself.

This radical claim is developed in much fuller fashion in *The End of Sex,* a text that attempts to complete or fulfill the sexual revolution of the 1960s and '70s by moving beyond all the cathartic releases and Kinsey-like obsessions with mechanics and number of orgasms to a more sublimated, all-encompassing eroticization of society and indeed the cosmos itself. "The end of sex," then, is not really the end of sex—it is the end of the gross materialism and common selfishness of the sexual revolution and the annunciation of a full-bodied and more relational erotic mysticism. It is both a refusal to reduce the erotic to the simply sexual and a call to raise the sexual to the mystical through a personal encounter with another human being as other and lover.

As with all of Leonard's books, there are clear biographical trajectories at work in *The End of Sex.* Indeed, the author tells us matter-of-factly that a great deal of this book is based on his own erotic experience.[42] Some of this, it turns out, dates back to Leonard's adolescence and the total repression and successful sublimation of his own budding sexuality. Schooled by the Victorian South and his own well-meaning father in the evils of "self-abuse" (that is, masturbation), Leonard's sexual repression was more or less total. It was not that he struggled against sexuality at puberty. It was that he felt no explicit or conscious sexuality at all. Subsequently, the entire natural world became erotic for the young boy. He could barely make out the boundaries between self and world. And he found himself passionately involved in an impressive array of hobbies, from snake-collecting (the Freudian can only smile here) to radio electronics and band music.

He also distinctly remembers a type of intense sublimated love—clearly erotic, even mystical,[43] but never quite sexual—for his slightly younger sister, who would bounce around in the hot southern house wearing as little as possible on her beautiful body, parts of which, Leonard writes, "drew my hands as if with a powerful magnet." In a chapter called "Familial Love," Leonard bravely explores his incestuous desires for his sister, his paradoxical realization that, "I would never be able to join with what was closest to me, what I most loved," and the complete disappearance of that illicit desire at age seventeen. Leonard, in other words, believed in the mysterious powers (and costs) of repression and sublimation, the sexual dynamics of the family, the power of *eros* to bind social groups together, and the potential beauties of a kind of mystical eroticism beyond any kind of simple genital sexuality. "I became aware of Eros early in life," he writes. "It was the mysterious force that was more powerful than my powerful father, that drew me toward my beloved sister, that imbued all of nature with an almost painful wonder."[44] No one could tell him Freud was wrong. Limited perhaps, but also dead-on.

What Leonard is really after here with what he calls "the end of sex," then, is analogous to what he was after with "the end of Civilization," that is, a kind of transfiguration of the world through a calling up of another kind of human potential and another kind of physical transformation, here expressed in the gorging and morphing of the sexual organs and the dramatic chemical, cellular, and even atomic transformations of the body during sexual arousal and orgasm. *This* is the enlightenment of the body for Leonard.

Little wonder, then, that the religious and mythical imagination from prehistoric shamanism to ancient India and medieval Europe has imagined the penis, in Leonard's phrase now, as a "winged thought,"[45] or that the narrative structure of every story, play, or tale (excitement, plateau, climax, resolution) follows "the primordial story" of erotic arousal and consummation.[46] Certainly, such bold extensions of sexual forces into every facet of life is not some simple Freudian fantasy or imaginary projection for Leonard. Rather, it is simply good metaphysics, for the universe itself is erotic through and through—*everything* is a silent pulse, a rhythm, a dance, a musical score, an orgasm. Leonard thus wants to re-conceive the erotic beyond genital sexuality and reunite it with creativity, with society, with nature, "and perhaps with the stars." Moreover, he wants a kind of full-bodied eroticism that can embody a radical democratic politics, much like that announced by Blake in his little humorous and irreverent ditty: "Embraces are Cominglings from the head even to the feet, / And not a pompous High Priest entering by a Secret Place."[47]

As with *The Transformation,* there is also a certain social radicalism in *The End of Sex,* for Leonard, like Reich, whom he draws on explicitly here, believes that society, sexual love, and the body are all intimately woven together, and so to tinker with or change any one of these is to change the others. What Leonard wants ultimately is a nonrepressive society that is bound together by the sublimated forces of sexuality and that can imagine erotic forms of being beyond the merely genital, a way of living that encourages and nurtures ecstasy and delight and so renders violence and war unnecessary and distracting. He also wants to heal the primordial split or "war" between the sexes. *Sexus,* we are told, is derived from the Latin *secare,* to separate or sever. The mystical life here, in other words, is fundamentally about the restoration of a primordial unity that is temporarily lost in the biology of sexual differentiation and the social injustices of gender construction and inequity.

Finally, Leonard is after a kind of sexual sacrament, a pure reciprocity imagined as a divine encounter. A world "in which your erotic partner is thought of or treated not as an object but as a *person,* a sacred being encompassing the universe." Thus in an early imaginative description of a sexual encounter with clear Tantric undertones in chapter 3—appropriately entitled "An Explosion of Spirit"—a man discovers in and through his lover's body that no discrimination is possible between body and spirit or between pain and pleasure, and that penetration and orgasm might propel them both into a dimension "beyond his body and hers, beyond the universe," into a kind of "ultimate, shining darkness."[48]

This encounter often bears within its furious ecstasy the "shining affirmation" of new human life; sexuality and procreation cannot ever be fully separated. For Leonard, there is violence and darkness in sexuality as well, and the spiritual forces of evolution are driven by the bumping, grinding hips of hard sex and real sexual desire and selection.

In this way, every mystical tendency toward unity must be balanced by the equally true and important truths of identity and individuality. Indeed, throughout his entire corpus, Leonard continually warns his readers to beware skewed preferences for pure transcendence or prudish spirituality. The world is not to be ascetically denied. It is to be erotically embraced and transformed through the pure reciprocity and delight most commonly known in full orgasm, that "explosion of spirit," that enlightenment of the body.

The Serpent Spine of Spirit and Sex

DON HANLON JOHNSON AND THE SOMATICS MOVEMENT

What else is to be found in psychoanalysis, by those determined to find, about the one body, the mystical body?

NORMAN BROWN, *Love's Body*

One more year of this, and then we go to Lourdes.

RICHARD PRICE and MICHAEL MURPHY

There are many ways into the body-practices and healing arts of Esalen. The most reliable and effective are through the practices themselves. Unfortunately, this is not something a book can do. Short of that, we are left with the thoughts of those who have spent their lives experiencing and practicing these methods and thinking about them on the public page for us. Although there are many impressive treatises here, perhaps no one has been more eloquent, prolific, and wisely critical within this specific enlightenment of the body than Don Hanlon Johnson. Johnson is doubly important for our story, since he also happens to be one of the present Members of Esalen, seven individuals elected to ensure that the Board of Trustees remains faithful to the original vision and mission of Esalen. In Don Hanlon Johnson, in other words, we have a central Esalen player who has been associated with the institute for almost all of its history, that is, since 1967.

Indeed, in my conversations with Murphy over the years, there are few names that have come up more often as a model of what Murphy imagines for Esalen than Don Hanlon Johnson. He has a deep familiarity with a broad range of body practitioners, a deep grasp of the human body

FIGURE 19. Don Hanlon Johnson (center) with Charlotte Selver and Charles Brooks.

as an object (and the subject) of philosophical reflection, and a sensitivity and openness to the body's mystical, even occult, potentials. He also does not hesitate to turn critical lenses on Esalen itself, often with uncomfortable, if incisive results. And perhaps most importantly for the long run, Johnson has produced a small library of beautifully produced texts that crystallize his life-work for future generations. He understands, in other words, the importance of texts, even and especially when they are all about bodies—a double *corpus,* if you will.

I must also confess a personal bias here, as Johnson's biographical trajectories through Roman Catholicism and his long exposure to the world religions converge with mine. We share certain convictions, especially the ethical position that it is the integrity of our human bodies that grants us our surest philosophical base from which *both* to appreciate and encourage the plurality of human cultural practices *and* to resist any amoral relativism that does not distinguish between cultural practices that nurture and those that harm these same bodies. In historical terms, it is the "universal body"—my body, their bodies, *your* body—that allows us to compare and understand other human beings across times and climes, even to access something of their altered states of consciousness and energy. It is also the welfare of this same body that allows us, that *calls* us to condemn cultural practices that endanger or harm this *corpus mysticum* in any way.

Secondly, there is our shared conviction that the vast majority of traditional religious systems fail this "body test" rather spectacularly. Nowhere is this more true than in the ways the religious stories understand and (mis)represent women from the religions' own allegedly divine (read: male) perspectives. Johnson understands human beings live by and find meaning in stories (or myths), and he knows the more stories we have the richer and safer human life is likely to be. But he is also aware that a few particular stories—usually those of the Western monotheisms—have claimed to speak for all human beings and so have not hesitated to silence the stories of other peoples. Moreover, he knows that the scriptures of the religions all emerged from within social systems that no sufficiently educated person deeply committed to democracy or social justice could possibly accept. In Johnson's own words, virtually all of the old stories "were created within a hierarchical context in which democratic values were not even a question." These same old stories "take for granted the subjection of women, children and slaves to men who were in positions of power" and are "rife with images of communities embattled by outsiders who are thought not to possess the Truth."[1]

We are approaching again a set of truths outside any established religion and any imagined past. We are approaching the religion of no religion. Johnson once made a simple observation: he is not familiar with a *single* body worker who has remained within his or her original church, synagogue, or religious community. Just as Spiegelberg imagined it on his walk through the wheat, the divine is located in the human body here, not in a building or single tradition.

Thirdly and finally, there is our shared psychosexual conviction that the dynamics of male Catholic asceticism and spirituality, or what Johnson quite correctly dubs "the monastic discipline of the penis," are not so much about repressing and eliminating sexual energies as they are about *exaggerating*, disciplining, analyzing, and sublimating them into more and more intense (homo)erotic forms.[2] Fundamental to Johnson's own approach to "the mystically erotic world of *spirit*" are the many years he spent as a Jesuit novice and priest in the Roman Catholic Church. It was in a Jesuit seminary, for example, that he first encountered the intensely physical and sensual nature of religious practices and realized that his religious superiors were generally "those with proclivities for lace, incense and theatrical gesture." It was also here that he realized that the secret forces of the mystical life are very much related to the hidden forces of the private parts: "The genitals," he writes, "are the devil's favorite playground, as well as the bower where one can achieve the greatest intimacy with the divine lover. This dual possibility accounts for two-thousand years of Catholic texts debating how to handle them."[3] Amen, I say.

Such handling for Johnson, it turns out, often involved ascetic disciplines that stemmed back to Ignatius of Loyola, the sixteenth-century founder of the Jesuits, but bore an uncanny resemblance to the sado-masochistic sexual rituals of some of the more radical strands of contemporary S and M culture:

> Father Healy taught us to cultivate what I would now call a homoerotic relation with the imagined naked body of Jesus hanging from the cross, imagining ourselves being embraced, even kissed by him. He gave me a reproduction of a crucifixion by Utrillo, with a voluptuously writhing muscular Jesus, naked save for a wisp of a cloth across his penis.... I would spend hours absorbing myself in that image, imagining the pain of the nails in my hands and feet, the pricks of the thorns in my head, the muscular strains in my body. I felt deliciously aroused.[4]

Indeed, during the weekly flagellation rituals in the seminary (for which, Johnson explains, a young seminarian named Jerry Brown, future governor of California and long-time Esalen friend, made the heavy cord whips), the novices would return to their rooms after night prayers, drop their pants and underwear, and ritually whip their naked buttocks. Johnson would sometimes get an erection. When he confessed such a confusing physiological response to Father Healy, the latter responded that, "Rodrigo, brother of St. Teresa of Avila and a missionary who died fighting natives in Brazil, wrote to her of a similar problem."[5] This last line is particularly representative of Johnson's writing style, blending as it does a keen psychosexual awareness and a fierce postcolonial critique of monotheistic violence.

It was not always so, however. As Johnson explains, the Ignatian ascetic disciplines completely repressed his awareness of sexuality for a full ten years until 1963, when these forces were released again by an encounter with that mystical sacrament we have already met above: LSD. Its bearer this time, however, was not a CIA agent (as we shall see in our next chapter) or a former Harvard psychologist turned Hindu guru and federal criminal. It was a very famous Jesuit theologian.

In the early 1950s, John Courteney Murray had argued, against considerable Catholic precedent, that the best political arrangement for the mature flourishing of the human spirit was not a monarchy, theocracy, or some other totalitarian regime but an American-style liberal democracy. Pope Pius XII quickly condemned Murray's writings, but Pope John XXIII eventually rehabilitated him. The Second Vatican Council (1962–65) embraced his ideas as fundamental to any truly modern and viable Catholicism, and a young John F. Kennedy invoked him again to calm his Protestant critics, who worried (not without some historical reason) that a Kennedy presidency might very well turn out to be a papal one.

Murray, it turns out, was also one among many Jesuits who, like many other elite American intellectuals, were experimenting with LSD in the early 1960s to catalyze their thought, meditation, and artistic endeavors. More specifically, Murray was taking LSD at a Jesuit house in Los Angeles between Vatican sessions; he was there participating in a program sponsored by the Fund for the Republic, a kind of think tank under the direction of Robert Hutchins, founder of the great books program at the University of Chicago. It was at the Jesuit house that Johnson met Murray and listened to other fellow Jesuits tell about similar experiments. Two of them, for example, were taking the substance at the UCLA medical center with the clinical psychologist, Ed Maupin.

More or less exactly as Leary would later claim in the *Playboy* interview, these sessions often released fantastic powers that would intensify and cosmicize the sexual energies. Leary had not yet given his *Playboy* interview in 1963, of course, but Johnson and his fellow Jesuits needed no such news. Johnson remembers one Jesuit brother returning from Maupin's sessions describing a trip that began as he laid face down on a hospital bed: "The bed suddenly became the universe and he, her lover; the two joined in cosmic bliss. He said the experience left him with a profound sense of the meaning of Christ's becoming embodied and how being a priest giving the sacraments was taking part in a ritual of mystical love."[6]

Johnson's own trip had a different, but equally erotic effect on him. The experience gave him back his sexuality. In torrents. As he put it to me years later, until Murray's introduction, he simply had experienced "no temptation" at all, so effectively repressed were his sexual energies by the Ignatian exercises. Then he took the LSD with Murray, came home with a huge erection, and began to witness psychedelic explosions and stars in his head.[7] That was the beginning of the end of his celibacy.

It also signaled the eventual transformation of Johnson's earlier attempts via repression and sublimation (not to mention the whips) "to become the Bride of Christ" into an active heterosexuality expressed with a flesh-and-blood woman and real orgasms. In this, Johnson was making the same mystico-erotic move Esalen had made earlier: he was moving from a sublimated homoerotic orthodoxy to an expressed heteroerotic (and so heterodox, if not actually heretical) mysticism.

Significantly, it was also LSD that first drew Johnson to Esalen in 1967. He had heard that psychedelics and mysticism were topics regularly discussed there. He had heard correctly. In his first visit, he listened to Huston Smith talk about his LSD trips at Harvard with Leary and Alpert and how such experiences were related to the mystical traditions of Asia. It was LSD again that helped Johnson begin to break down the division between the inner self and the outer world and experience firsthand layer upon layer of bodily desire, subtle impulse, and philosophical idea, all somehow coded in his body-spirit. Such altered states of consciousness and energy caused him to begin to wonder about the possibility of "a differently organized, less hierarchical world," that is, he began to ask why body and spirit could not be understood and actually experienced in radically different ways. Had he not? Democracy, he was beginning to see, was not just a powerful idea about representation and human equality; it was also, more fundamentally, *a physical state of being,* a very specific and, he would eventually realize, very rare and difficult enlightenment of the body seldom fully realized anywhere.

In 1969, Johnson was finishing his PhD in philosophy at Yale. He had also been assigned the duties of assistant pastor and chaplain of the graduate school. He had a small budget, and he used it to bring some Esalen practitioners to New Haven to introduce Yale students to sensory awareness, encounter groups, and psychodrama. In one particularly funny moment, this Yale group found themselves in a seminar led by an Esalen leader who, they later discovered, was in reality a cook from the Esalen kitchen posing as a teacher. After the cook's outing, the evening ended with Johnson's future wife and an African-American drummer leading everyone in an evening of nude body movement.[8]

It was an extremely aggressive form of Esalen "massage," however, that Johnson found particularly revelatory, and it was Ed Maupin again who acted as the initiator. In a series of one-hour sessions, Maupin dug his elbows and knuckles deep into Johnson's pectoral muscles, hips, soles, and spinal column, sending him into spasms of intense pain, absolute terror, and crystal-clear memory and emotion. The sessions confirmed for Johnson what he had already intuited in the LSD sessions, namely, "that matters of the spirit as well as memories, emotions and ideas are embedded in muscle, intestine and lungs. They are not separate *things,* but layers of the self, like the successive civilizations archaeologists unearth on a dig at an ancient mound."[9]

Johnson had been Rolfed.

Somatics at Early Esalen

We will get to what it means to be Rolfed in due time. To understand what happened to Don Johnson at Yale, and later at Esalen, we need to back up a bit and provide some historical background. Maupin's elbows, after all, carried a very specific altered history.

Philosophically speaking, the healing practices of Esalen developed within an integral worldview that centers on the spiritualization of the flesh and turns to the union of "body" and "soul" as the most reliable source of wholeness and health. Johnson summarizes the worldview this way: "*body* and *spirit* do not stand for identifiable objects; they are names which people use to indicate different aspects on the continuum of human experience."[10] For Johnson, a similar realization is historically encoded in Christian mysticism, particularly in its doctrine of the resurrection of the body. In its central ritual of the eucharist, the believer consumes the flesh and fluids of a god-man in order to be physically transfigured into the god, and—as we have already noted—does so in a series of esoteric (and, for a male, largely homoerotic) monastic and ascetic practices that function as "an elaborate set of technologies to transform bodies from what Saint Paul calls *sarx* ('hunks of meat') into *soma,* the quivering flesh of Christ."[11] The goal, put in theological terms, is *transfiguration* and *resurrection* not only in some future state, but also in the here and now, that is, in the glorified body of the Christian mystic.

Not every important religious influence that has passed through Esalen has been of Asian or Amerindian origin; traditional Christian doctrines such as the incarnation and the resurrection have played their own hidden roles. One could cite many examples here, including Murphy's consistent use of incarnational language to describe his own thought, as well as his special love of Corinthians 1:15, where Paul sets out the mysterious transformation of *sarx* into *soma.* Indeed, this biblical text even receives a special appendix in Murphy's occult novel on the transfigurations of the flesh, *Jacob Atabet,* entitled "Glorified Body."

Most of the body practices at Esalen for the last forty years do not, however, derive so directly from Christian mysticism. Rather, they derive from the German Gymnastik movement that began around 1900, primarily around Hede Kallmeyer of Berlin, Bess Mensendieck of Hamburg, and Elsa Gindler.[12] Although these women were all trained by men (Francois Delsarte, Leo Koffler, and Emile Jacques-Dalcroze), the Gymnastik movement at this point was a predominately female movement of private studios, only some of which were state-licensed, that offered an alternative to the macho military-like physical education of the traditional school system and the gymnasium. Gindler, for example, bravely refused to have her studio licensed by the Nazis. Whereas traditional physical education sought to mold every body into a common fit form or acceptable structure (consider the rigid body movements of the Nazi march and salute), Gymnastik encouraged difference, spontaneous movement, and a kind of moving meditation that prized awareness and consciousness above all else. The implicit political philosophy was as radical as it was simple: freedom is quite literally a bodily state, and if you cannot move your body however you wish, then you are not free.

World War II decimated free bodies, and the Gymnastik practitioners, many of whom were Jewish, were widely scattered. A number of them fled to the United States, where they settled in New York, Boston, and San Francisco. They taught and healed for years in the cities, usually without significant contact with other similar practitioners, until many of them finally found both a public showcase and a place of intellectual regathering at Esalen in the 1960s.[13] There teachers and disciples such as Alexander Lowen, Charlotte Selver, Moshe Feldenkreis, and Ida Rolf attracted large followings and generated considerable excitement.

As this was happening, a group of young intellectuals discovered these same practitioners at Esalen, submitted their bodies and minds to their healing arts, and began to use their intellectual training to systematize the various models into a coherent philosophical movement. Foremost among these new intellectuals were Thomas Hanna, who founded the journal *Somatics,* and Don Hanlon Johnson.

Having written his dissertation on Norman O. Brown's *Love's Body* (a mystical psychoanalysis from the Freudian Left, if ever there was one), Johnson, like Hanna, approached the body workers as a phenomenologist, that is, as a philosopher tuned into the subtlest movements of psychological and physical experience. Philosophers such as Edmund Husserl and Merleau-Ponty had laid great stress on the minute and careful observation of direct experience, the complexities of awareness and the central role of the body in doing philosophy. It was this same tradition that Johnson and

Hanna used to articulate what the body workers already knew but had never systematized into a public body of theory.

It was phenomenology again that resulted in the eventual naming of this broad collection of practice as "Somatics," a term coined by Hanna from the related term *psychosomatic* and from Husserl's notion of a *somatology* as a particular task of phenomenology that could integrate the mechanized body of medical science with the flowing or "lived" body of direct experience and consciousness. Briefly, Hanna intended Somatics to signal a field of practices that approaches the body as the entire person (as in the English "somebody"), that refuses the mechanistic and reductive understandings of orthodox medicine (the body as "machine"), and that can finally recover something of the spiritual luminosity of the earlier Christian notion of resurrected *soma* (the Christian mystical tradition again).[14] In the influential essay "What Is Somatics?" Hanna writes, "Somatics is the field which studies the *soma:* namely, the body as perceived from within by first-person perception. When a human being is observed from the outside—i.e., from a third-person viewpoint—the phenomenon of a human *body* is perceived. But when this same human being is observed from the first-person viewpoint of his own proprioceptive senses, a categorically different phenomenon is perceived: the human *soma.*"[15] Put in my own terms now, the *soma* of the Somatics movement is the human body enlightened by its own native consciousness, by a specific set of bodily practices, and by the professional discipline of philosophy.

Of course, Christian mysticism and Continental phenomenology by no means exhaust the conceptual models of body practitioners of Esalen. For example, Moshe Feldenkreis, who gave his first American seminar at Esalen, was inspired by the Japanese martial arts of judo and ju-jitsu and by the astonishing, and occasionally hilarious, psychic and healing abilities of a certain Dr. Noguchi. Noguchi could allegedly do things like transmit his vital "electricity" into a distant bud to make it blossom or, alternately, put his left- and right-brain to sleep so that he could work for two days and nights straight (with the unfortunate, if quite funny, side-effect that the two sides of his face would alternately collapse into sleep and so appear crooked).[16]

Whatever the particular language frame (and Somatics practitioners tend to think that language is incapable of expressing the subtle physical states of consciousness they are after), it is safe to say that central to most of these practices is the invocation of models of life-energy that bridge or, perhaps better, violate the usual boundaries between what we today call *religion* and *science* or, alternately, *spirituality* and *medicine.* Again, there are many historical precedents for naming such energies, but one of the most influential at Esalen was certainly Wilhelm Reich (1897–1957). Reich is one of those few figures—alongside William Blake, Sigmund Freud, William James, and C. G. Jung—who helped define some of the deepest currents of both Esalen and the American counterculture, primarily through his central erotic notion of the *orgone*. The orgone, for Reich, is a subtle cosmic energy that links the sentient and nonsentient worlds and expresses itself through the various mediums of the pulsing rhythms of simple-cell organisms, the intensely pleasurable contractions of the human orgasm, the healing charisma of Christ, and atmospheric weather patterns. Even when he is not explicitly invoked or perhaps even known about, Reich is—very much like his concept of the orgone—somehow everywhere at Esalen. And nowhere is this more true than in the rich array of body-work practices that have flowed through the institute and mingled with the Freudian Left and the Asian Tantra, turning the grounds into a place of healing.

Reich and the Orgone

It's hard to understand, much less appreciate, a man who managed to get himself kicked out of Freud's International Psychoanalytic Association, the Austrian Social Democratic Party, the German Communist Party, and *five* different countries. And this is all before he settled in the United States in 1939, where the FDA—catalyzed by Mildred Edie Brady's widely read article in the *New Republic*, "The Strange Case of Wilhelm Reich" (May 26, 1947)—would eventually proscribe his orgone energy accumulator in 1954, burn most of his books in 1956, and then send him to prison. It was there he died a few months later, of a coronary attack or, as his biographer Myron Sharaf puts it, of a broken heart.[17]

There were clearly many reasons for such events, from Reich's difficult, authoritarian, and occasionally paranoid personality, to his life-long addiction to cigarettes. But Reich always insisted that the deepest reasons for the dramatic resistance he encountered were the profound, almost primordial, fear people have of their own life-energy and the dramatic ways that his thought forces individuals to confront the pathological blockages these innate streamings meet in their own physical and social bodies.

According to Reich, people refuse to accept their sexuality because they refuse to accept their mortality. Sexuality and death are apiece: without death, there would be no need for sex. On a more immediate level, people fear their own cosmic sexualities (and sexuality is quite literally cosmic for Reich, since the same energy that constitutes the pleasure of the orgasm shimmers in the atmosphere and the stars) and so construct elaborate defenses against these universal energies in the form of neuroses and more or less sick societies and religions, which they then mistakenly identify with and defend as their deepest selves.

Reich had many names for this energy. As a very young disciple of Freud, he originally referred to this energy as *libido.* Soon, however, he moved on to speak and write of *vegetative energy, bio-electricity,* and energetic *streamings (Strömung)* in the body. These he often described in quasi-religious terms that bear unmistakable similarities to earlier es-oteric notions of magnetic influence (Paracelsus), influx (Swedenborg), animal magnetism (Mesmer), causal energies (Theosophy), aura phenom-ena (parapsychology), and any number of Asian yogic and Tantric terms (*prana, shakti,* and *kundalini*).[18] By the summer of 1974, the Esalen cata-log was quoting Reich's own conviction that it was this "bioelectric nature of sexuality and anxiety" that constituted both "the simplicity" and "the secret which some people sense in my work." Certainly there were many such people sensing such a Reichian secret at Esalen.

This same secret got Reich into trouble with Freud. The most basic disagreement was over Freud's notion that human nature contains an immutable movement toward both Eros and Thanatos, that is, toward both Life and Death. Reich, very much at this point under the sway of Marx's thought, argued that Thanatos was a function of social and political conditioning and was not necessarily an aspect of human nature. In other words, Reich essentially held a more positive and hopeful view of human nature than Freud did—the drive toward death was a function of social pathology, not of human nature.

Reich also insisted on the literal existence of the libidinal energies, whereas Freud, and certainly much of later psychoanalysis, moved to a more metaphorical understanding of the libido. Reich always felt that it was the psychoanalysts who had abandoned psychoanalysis, and that it was he, not they, who remained faithful to the original energetic vision. Af-ter Reich was effectively excluded from the International Psychoanalytic Association, the first paper he delivered to his former colleagues, now as a heretical "guest" at the Lucerne Congress of 1934, was one dedicated to these same mysterious streamings. In the '50s this same streaming energy, now called orgone, focused the FDA's wrath and subsequent banning and burning of Reich's books. The FDA in fact explicitly identified any mention of the term orgone as *the* criterion for banning and burning a particular Reichian text, and to this day Reichians generally avoid the same term, no doubt partly to avoid further government persecution.

Reich's awareness of these streamings originated in his own personal sexual experience in 1916 in the arms of an Italian village girl with whom he had intercourse as a soldier.[19] This was hardly his first experience of sexual intercourse, but it was the first time he knew something "other," something so astonishing that he would spend the rest of his life fighting for its full physical and intellectual expression. He struggled against each obstacle set up against this natural bliss, from the most subtle of Freud's theoretical convictions about how civilization requires libidinal repression and sublimation, to the grossest evils of Nazi prudery, censorship, and violence. Wilhelm Reich had received a revelation in the arms and body of an Italian village girl.

It was not, however, until he moved to America in 1939 that he hit on the full force of what he felt had been revealed to him. It was there that he began constructing his famous orgone energy accumulator or "orgone box," a relatively simple wooden and metal structure just big enough to sit in and designed to concentrate an individual's energies for study and healing purposes. Actually, the orgone box was a development of an earlier structure Reich had used to try to isolate bions (units of the presumed energy) in biological cultures, in this case heated ocean sand. When such material was stored in a dark basement, he claimed to see a bluish light emanating in the room. He constructed the earliest boxes to isolate and study this same phenomenon more efficiently.

There was just one problem. Reich was puzzled that he could detect bions in the boxes even when no biological culture was present. His confidence waned, and he began to doubt. Then in 1940 he rented a small vacation cabin on Mooselookmeguntic Lake near Rangely, Maine, to take a break from his labors. As he sat up one night, he began to observe the night sky. To his astonishment, he began noticing vivid flickerings in the darkness between the stars, flashes of energy that looked exactly like what he had observed in his basement cultures and boxes. He suddenly realized why he had kept detecting bions in his empty boxes—the energy is not restricted to living organisms; it is everywhere, including and especially in the atmosphere. In other words, he now understood that the nonordinary energy he was studying was cosmic and not simply biological.[20] He could now break with subjective terminology while maintaining both his original psychoanalytic conviction in the essential sexual nature of this energy and his later biological researches into cultures and bions. Hence his American coining of the term "orgone," a Reichian neologism derived from "orgasm" and "organism."[21]

It is important to point out that the orgone for Reich was no theory or metaphor. It is the logical extension of what Freud had correctly identified as the libido but then failed to pursue to its empirical biological and cosmic end. For Reich, the orgone is a quantifiable force that future psychology, physics, and biology will someday confirm and understand. It is also the very secret of life whose subtle streamings through the orgastically potent body constitute the surest signs of health and happiness.

But if it is a secret, it is a secret that people fear. They armor themselves against it with muscular rigidities, emotional complexes, neuroses, pathological social practices, and alienating religious beliefs, all of which work together to effectively block the free flow of orgone in the body. It was these muscular blockages that had focused Reich's earliest psychoanalytic work and resulted in his conviction about how the bodies of his patients mapped in their tensions and distortions the neuroses and even memories of their emotional histories. What Reich called character analysis was a specific combination of traditional psychoanalytic technique (the "talking cure") and Reich's own insights into first locating these physical locks in the body and the breathing styles of his patients and then physically releasing or relaxing them through various pinches, pokes, and psychological probes.

Reich always insisted that he was not doing simple massage; he was rather working on muscles as the physical expression of emotions. Reich believed that because the emotional complexes are literally stored in the body structure, simply talking about them is not enough; they also have to be worked out *in the body.* He thus found himself violating one of the firmest of psychoanalytic taboos, that against touching the patient. And eventually he went even further, asking his patients to strip down to their underwear and bras so that he could observe their muscles and skin more directly.

Reich eventually located and identified seven segments or "rings" of the body armor, all arranged perpendicular to the central axis or spinal column of the body through which the energetic streamings, which he now understood to be cosmic orgone, ideally flowed. Reich began at the uppermost ring, the ocular ring of the eyes and forehead and worked down, through the oral, neck, chest, diaphragm, and lower abdominal regions, until he could finally work on the pelvic ring of the hips and genital region.

It is here that the Indologist finds it difficult not to speak up. A streaming, intensely blissful cosmic energy residing in the body that needs to be released through various physical manipulations, the loosening of seven rings or circles located along the central spinal column, and the intimate relationship between breath and bioenergy: all of this reproduces in a Western psychological register the central categories of many Asian Tantric yogic systems, including the *shakti* or "occult energy" that streams through the aspirant's body during initiation and spiritual ecstasy, the serpentine energy called *kundalini* that normally "sleeps" in the body but can be awakened through various physical postures and meditative techniques, the seven *chakra*s or "energy circles" located perpendicularly along the central spinal channel (their actual number varies in different systems), and the ancient yogic concept of *prana* as "breath" or "life-energy." There are, of course, also important differences and qualifications to note, particularly surrounding Reich's deep suspicion of the whole category of "mysticism." But these would take us far afield. In the end, the analogies remain dramatic enough to warrant W. Edward Mann's conclusion that, "the orgone theory may be a Western scientist's rationalistic attempt to capture, unconsciously, certain Eastern insights for Western man."[22]

Reich's secularized divinization of erotic energy constitutes *the* central move of the Freudian Left that later sparked and then arced through Esalen. One should also note here the central salience of body armor and its therapeutic dissolution at early Esalen, and, perhaps most significantly, Esalen's turn to touch, massage, and the physical manipulation of the human body as the most effective practices of healing. It is to these that we now turn.

Ida Rolf and the Tantrik Yog in Nyack

Ida Rolf (1896–1979) was one of the central players at Esalen in the late 1960s and early 1970s. Her path to Esalen was a long one. As a young woman, newly graduated from Barnard College, Rolf was kicked by a horse on a camping trip in 1916. She quickly developed pneumonia and soon could barely breathe. A fever soared. She was taken to a small town in Montana, where an osteopath manipulated her spine. To her astonishment, the fever immediately lessened and her breathing returned. She had been introduced to the central principle of osteopathic medicine, first developed by the Missouri doctor, Andrew Still, that *structure determines function,* that is, that the alignment or misalignment of the body along the central spinal axis dramatically affects one's physical health.

This experience of being healed by an osteopath was definitive for the young Ida Rolf. She would go on to get a PhD in biochemistry from Columbia University in 1920 and spend the rest of her life learning from osteopaths and chiropractors until she eventually developed her own unique form of bodily alignment through the manipulation of deep tissue and skeletal form. Technically, she would call her method "structural integration," but her charisma and personality overwhelmed such technicalities and the method became known more popularly as "Rolfing."

Rosemary Feitis recalls the story of Rolf's early training influences in the 1920s. Feitis and a friend were publishing a piece on Rolf and decided to make up a "plausible lie" about her earliest beginnings with the hope that Rolf herself, as editor, would correct the mistake before it went to print. So Feitis and her friend claimed in the article that Ida Rolf had begun her quest in an ashram in Bombay. But when Rolf edited the piece, the claim hardly fazed her; she simply crossed out "Bombay" and inserted "the Bronx."[23]

Rolf had in fact spent the decade of the 1920s associated with "an ashram in the Bronx," studying with an American Tantric yogi named Pierre Bernard (1875–1955).[24] Bernard was a remarkable figure whom Rolf referred to as "the Tantrik yog in Nyack." We know little about his early life, except that he was born in 1875 (or 1876) in Iowa. At the age of thirteen, he met a Syrian-Indian by the name of Sylvais Hamati in Lincoln, Nebraska (Hamati's father was Syrian, his mother Bengali). Hamati, it turns out, was an accomplished Tantric yogi. From the late 1880s to just past the turn of the century, Hamati traveled with Bernard, perhaps as entertainers in a circus. Bernard first appears into clear historical view on January 29, 1898, on the front-page of the *New York Times,* and under the symbolic banner of the Hindu goddess Kali no less. Ironically, he appears, well, dead. He had given a public demonstration of his *Kali-mudra* or "death trance" to a group of physicians in San Francisco, during which he seems to have successfully slowed his vital functions sufficiently to mimic death.[25]

Catalyzed by such publicity and psychophysical abilities, Bernard now morphed into "The Hypnotist Dr. Bernard" and became a famous (or infamous) personality in the Bay area. He left San Francisco sometime around the great earthquake in 1906. Around this same time, he also founded the first Tantric Order in America and published a single issue of what must be the first Tantric publication in the United States, the *International Journal of the Tantrik Order.* By 1909, we find him in New York, where, after various legal and criminal fiascos involving his sexual practices, Bernard eventually emerged as a successful teacher of yoga and opened a series of institutions. From one of these, the local press, which had now rather cruelly dubbed him the "Omnipotent Oom," reported such things as "wild Oriental music and women's cries, but not those of distress."[26] By 1919, Bernard had moved his teaching practices to a lush seventy-three acre estate in Upper Nyack, where he was teaching some of New York's elite, including Mrs. William K. Vanderbilt and her two daughters, and making a great deal of money in the process (the next year he bought another Nyack estate of thirty-nine acres and later in life he would settle down as president of the State Bank of Pearl River and collect expensive automobiles). Nyack is where Ida Rolf met and trained with him in the 1920s.

Pierre Bernard is a key historical figure for our narrative here, as he is the first in a long line of Tantric gurus in America whose combination of charisma and controversy carries through his later successors, from Bhagwan Rajneesh (who also loved to collect expensive cars) and Swami Muktananda, to Chogyam Trungpa and Adi Da. Bernard also plays a minor but humorous role in pre-Esalen. Michael Murphy remembers his father worrying about his early Hindu interests and warning him not to become one of those gurus, "like Oom the Omnipotent."

The grain of truth here is that the moniker suggests that a kind of Tantric transmission has run through Esalen's history, mostly through Murphy himself. The fuller truth, of course, is that Murphy did not become like Oom the Omnipotent. He has, after all, consistently rejected the antinomian and sexual methods of the Tantra and of the American counterculture (which he has often described to me as a kind of left-handed Tantra) and has opted instead for the more stable "right-handed" metaphysics of meditation and Sri Aurobindo's writings. He, in other words, seems to have listened to his father's advice.

As for Ida Rolf, it is not entirely clear how involved she was with Bernard's Tantric community. We know that there were both exoteric and esoteric features of his teaching (the *International Journal of the Tantrik Order,* for example, makes it clear that it was an "external issue for public use"), and that the esoteric dimensions almost certainly involved actual sexual practices. We also know that Bernard taught a doctrine that was essentially a religious version of Reich's later and more rationalized system. In Bernard's language now, "love, a manifestation of sexual instinct, is the animating spirit of the world."[27] It seems almost certain that

Rolf would have heard similar things from him. Don Hanlon Johnson, for example, remembers Rolf often speaking about the evolution of the human body toward greater and greater consciousness. She would then crystallize what she was trying to say by quoting Bernard: "Worship the body."[28]

Rolf did not share in the sexual-emotional excesses of Bernard, though she most certainly appreciated the centrality of the body and made it her own. As Feitis and Johnson both point out, the young Rolf carried Bernard's teachings about the alignment and activation of the spinal *chakras* over into her own later system, now synthesized with her os- teopathic and chiropractic training. "In those years of practicing yoga and discussing its principles," Feitis writes, "she was establishing the basis of all her future work; that bodies need to lengthen and be balanced, and that a balanced body will give rise to a better human being."[29] This was Ida Rolf, not Pierre Bernard.

Rolf's methods, however, did sometimes take on explicitly erotic forms in the hands and bodies of others. Relevant here is Johnson's convic- tion that one of the secrets of Rolfing is the dramatic manner in which the spinal manipulations can sometimes effect a deep and delicious release of sexual energies. This in fact may go back to Bernard's teaching, as it is clear that he was after something very similar. It also, I must point out, makes a good deal of anatomical sense, since, neurologically speaking, the spine is a serpent-like channel of bioelectric energy and tiny arcing light- ening bolts that connect the genitals and the brain: open *that* up (that is, awaken the snake) and all sorts of things can happen, many of which, of course, will be simultaneously mystical and erotic. Consciousness and en- ergy, brain and genitals meet and communicate—literally—up and down this hissing serpent spine of spirit and sex.

Rolf "Kills" and Heals Fritz

The Tantric yogi from Nyack, however, was hardly Rolf's only influence. She also studied with F. Matthias Alexander and imbibed the esoteric teachings of the "rascal" mystic Gurdjieff with a small group in London. In New York she met Greta Garbo and Georgia O'Keeffe, both of whom she would later take on as clients. But it was Fritz Perls who finally got her to Esalen.

By the 1950s, Rolfing was an established discipline on the edges of osteopathy with a very small cohort of practitioners, including Rolf's son,

Dick, and a woman named Dorothy Nolte. Nolte went to hear Fritz lecture on gestalt psychology sometime in 1965. She noticed that he was in obvious physical pain and offered to help him. Fritz felt much better but soon returned to his normal misery. He asked Nolte again, but Nolte, worried about Fritz's serious heart condition, refused. She suggested instead that Perls invite Rolf herself out to California to work on him. He did.

Rolf arrived on a Friday afternoon and worked on Perls for an entire week, one hour at a time. In the meantime, she sat in on his sessions, to the significant annoyance of the Esalen regulars: "they thought it a damn shame that here was this woman sitting in his class and she wasn't part of his class, and she wasn't partaking in the class, and who the hell was she anyway?"[30]

In her "seventh hour" with him, that is, during the seventh Rolfing session on the following Friday, Fritz went completely unconscious. This is how Rolf remembered it: "I had a *very* bad two minutes, and I said to myself, 'You bloody fool, taking a man who is dying of a heart failure, putting him through Rolfing, you deserve what you've got. See, the man's dead." But he wasn't dead. Rolf decided to wait and see what happened next, "and pray to God he doesn't know where he's been." Her prayer went unanswered. "But God was out to lunch. When Fritz came around, the first thing he said was something that indicated he knew perfectly well that he'd been unconscious. He said that he had once been injured by an anesthetist in surgery.... So you see, when I got into his neck, I began to raise that whole trip."[31]

Though Fritz would eventually die of a heart attack, for now Ida Rolf had effectively healed him, if not of his heart condition, then certainly of the debilitating pain it caused him. For the next few years, Rolf and Perls would play a kind of tag-team Esalen game, with Perls noting potential patients and sending them down to the baths to get Rolfed with Rolf, and Rolf encouraging people to work with Perls, who came to appreciate more and more the benefits of combining psychological and physical work. Fritz, now especially grateful for Rolf's role in healing his ailing heart, affectionately called her "Mrs. Elbow."

Much later, in 1983, Dick Price would suggest in the Esalen catalog that there were two major streams of practice that came together at Esalen in the 1960s: Fritz Perls on the plasticity of the character structure; and Ida Rolf on the plasticity of the physical structure.[32] Psyche and body joined and transfigured again.

With respect to Rolf, however, it is important to point out that structural integration for Ida Rolf was not primarily about healing or even about the "miraculous" cures that often went with her work. She insisted, for example, on working with "clients," not "patients," and she saw herself as an educator, as Dr. Rolf. Her work, moreover, was about a kind of "cosmic mysticism" (my terms, not hers) that involved aligning the posture and body with the gravitational field of the earth. She was, in Johnson's words now, fundamentally about "initiating people into harmonious spiritual consciousness, which in her view coincides with having vertically aligned body segments."[33] Moreover, she understood the body and spirit not as separate metaphysical substances or things, but, in Johnson's terms again, as "something like different layers of energy or refinement." Hence to touch and manipulate the bodily tissues was to touch and release the human spirit.

Johnson's Doubts

Don Hanlon Johnson suffers from a congenital condition that fuses the vertebrae and causes intense and chronic back pain. Getting Rolfed at Yale, then, was hardly a minor event for him. Indeed, he was so moved by the experience that he later sought Ida Rolf out in New York to see whether she would take him as a student. He later began training with her in the summer of 1971 in a house near Esalen. In 1972, he was a director on the board of her organization and was instrumental in establishing the Rolf Institute in Boulder, Colorado. Five years later, Rolf finally published her book on the practice.[34]

Johnson, however, was beginning to have reservations. It pained him greatly to see the same kinds of orthodoxy and rigidity he had witnessed in Roman Catholicism now taking over the Rolf community. Johnson remembers, with a kind of searing humiliation, for example, how Rolf once ridiculed his posture in front of fifty other students. "I can't see this," he admitted in reference to some point she was teaching at the time. "How could you?" she snapped back, "where your third cervical vertebra is!"[35] In his mind, this was a strange and inexplicable response to something that he was born with and has no control over. This event led him to compose a potent little essay first for the journal *Somatics,* then for the Esalen catalog entitled "Somatic Platonism," his term for any view that "perceives, evaluates, and works with the individual body by comparison to some idealized design," in other words, what Ida Rolf had done to him.[36] The essay has become one of the most well-known and oft-cited essays in the Somatics community.

Although Rolf had great appreciation for those realms of experience we might call *body* and *spirit,* she had little patience with what we might call *mind* (that "luminescent experience... [that] develops into the kind of inquisitive spirit that raises the uncomfortable questions which true believers try to ignore") or *psyche* ("the murky region of emotions and unconscious processes revealed in dreams, tics, fantasies, hallucinations and slips of the tongue"). Johnson sadly notes that Rolf's rejection of this latter region, which of course is essentially the psychoanalytic domain, reminded him of how his Jesuit superiors had tried to ignore and discredit it as well. This, in his mind, was clearly a serious mistake.[37]

Johnson also recounts how as Rolf neared death, she began to make quite dogmatic statements about what she was calling the Template, the Rolf Line, and the Recipe, all metaphors for the alignment of the body and consciousness she sought in her clients. She was also beginning to make odd and disturbing statements about the creation of a superior race through imposing the Template on a small elite. In one of her final letters to the Rolf Institute, for example, she wrote: "It is possible that we are seeing here the first conscious attempt at evolution made by any species in modern times."[38]

Similar statements had been made by the Mother in the Aurobindo ashram when Murphy was living there in 1956 and 1957. These had worried Murphy, and now they were worrying Johnson. Murphy left the ashram and eventually founded Esalen as a place where "no one captures the flag." As Murphy left the Aurobindo ashram, Johnson would leave Rolfing and become one of the Somatics movement's most accomplished intellectuals, spanning the entire movement not for a single dogmatic truth or a straight line (as *ortho*-doxy or a properly aligned spine), but as a pluralistic collection of witnesses to the spiritualization of the flesh (*sarx*) into the luminous experience of an enlightened body (*soma*). The quivering flesh of the resurrected Christ now had its own spiritual spine, which resembled more than a little both the shimmering Tantric *chakras* of Pierre Bernard and the streaming body segments of Wilhelm Reich.

The Program in Humanistic Medicine (1972–1975)

Such altered states multiplied into the hundreds, then thousands, throughout the 1960s and '70s until something of a critical mass of vision was reached. This was the experiential context in which Esalen began to play an important role in the early development of alternative and complementary medical practices in the United States.[39]

Complimentary and Alternative Medicine (CAM) is now a relative commonplace in research-oriented medical schools. As a cultural mark of its success, best-selling alternative health authors like Dr. Andrew Weil are now household names and routinely appear in the pages, even on the cover, of magazines like *Time* (October 17, 2005). In the early 1970s, however, this was new and quite radical stuff. Andrew Weil was certainly not on a magazine cover, but he was at Esalen.

Weil first visited the institute in 1971 and then in 1973 gave his first workshop there on the subject of altered states of consciousness (based on his book, *The Natural Mind*). Well into the 1980s, he participated in various workshops, first on altered states and psychedelics, then on mind-body interactions (especially psychoneuroimmunology), and then on the larger subject of alternative medicine. Weil also took a gestalt workshop with Chris Price and commonly spoke on psychoactive plants.[40] In the summer of 1982, he moved to Big Sur's Sycamore Canyon for four months, where he began to develop his own philosophy of integrative medicine. It was during these same formative, Esalen-connected years that he conceived and wrote the first half of his bestselling book, *Health and Healing,* which laid out the theory from which his later best-selling volumes would draw.

Weil was by no means alone in his Esalen ventures. He was joined by a whole host of other forward-looking health professionals, a list of whose names reads like a Who's Who of the contemporary alternative and complementary medicine scene: Ken Dychtwald, Wayne Jonas, Dean Ornish, Ken Pelletier, and Rachael Naomi Remen, to name a few. Remen, for example, widely recognized in the field of CAM, was also one of the first twelve medical practitioners invited by Stuart and Sukie Miller to initiate the Program in Humanistic Medicine at Esalen in 1972. Remen describes those meetings as "life-changing."[41] Jonas first came to Esalen four years later, in 1976 for a month-long workshop led by Al Drucker.[42] Jonas would go on to become the second director of the Office of Alternative Medicine at the National Institutes of Health.

Mind-body issues, of course, went back to the very beginning of Esalen's history. In the spring of 1970, however, the focus turned to the practice of medicine itself with a seminar on the dynamics of the doctor/patient relationship in dentistry led by Jack Rosenberg, DDS, and George Brolaski, MD. A year later, Rosenberger expanded his scope to include professionals in the other health fields, along with their assistants and spouses. His concern here was the spiritual health and wellbeing of the practitioners and their social networks.

Out of such earlier experiments, Stuart and Sukie Miller initiated Esalen's Program in Humanistic Medicine in 1972. Humanistic medicine—an expression clearly intended to evoke Maslow's humanistic psychology—was defined thus: "Our intent is to humanize the medical situation by helping medical personnel to be more sensitive to the full human needs of their patients and themselves. Esalen techniques such as encounter, gestalt therapy, sensory awareness, psychodrama, fantasy and others would be used to teach personnel to be more fully aware of the personal and interpersonal dynamics of the medical situation."

The leaders, of course, had no illusions about Esalen becoming a medical school. What they wanted to do with the health professionals was what they had earlier done with the educators in the Confluent Education Program: bring them to Big Sur, catalyze their enthusiasms, introduce them to new ideas, and then send them out to seed their own professional cultures. There was more in this seed, though, than just a collection of new and exotic techniques. As Sukie Miller pointed out to me with some passion, for the Esalen organizers at least, these early alternative medicine ventures were first and foremost about the metaphysical, that is, about the astonishing nature of the human being that the alternative techniques implied and empirically dramatized. Hence the Esalen organizers included in the program's curriculum not just workshops on acupuncture and bio-feedback, but also truly daring subjects like the work of the American psychic Edgar Cayce, the mind-body intricacies of Tibetan medicine, and the recent findings of parapsychology. In effect, the Program in Humanistic Medicine was another way into the enlightenment of the body.

These seed groups met at Esalen more or less monthly for about three years. As was the norm, the project quickly developed its own momentum and spun out of its original Esalen orbit. In 1974, after receiving a $1.2 million grant from the Department of Health, Education and Welfare, Esalen's Program in Humanistic Medicine became its own independent organization and was renamed the Institute for Study of Humanistic Medicine. Both this program and its new source of funding were subsequently moved to Mt. Zion Hospital in San Francisco.

There were also more political ventures. In 1976, many of the personalities who had been meeting at Esalen delivered papers at a conference in Washington D.C. These caught the ear of an assistant of Senator Jacob Javits. Stuart Miller subsequently worked with Senator Javits that year to pass the "Health Professions Education Assistance Act" (PL-94–434).

According to Bill Benda, the most important achievement of this bill, probably the first of its kind, "was the insertion of the term 'humanistic medicine' into a document of federal legislation, thus lending legitimacy to the concept."[43]

What had begun in Big Sur in 1972 was now, in 1976, passing through the Senate. There would be many other accomplishments along these medical and medicinal lines, and many false starts, along the way. But another seed had been planted. It would take decades to grow into the public consciousness.

Healers among Us

Many healers have shaped Esalen, including F. Matthias Alexander, Bonnie Bainbridge Cohen, Eimilie Conrad Da'oud, Moshe Feldenkreis, Alexander Lowen, and John Upledger.[44] Two in particular, though—Charlotte Selver and Bernard Gunther—deserve our final consideration, as they played important roles in the founding of what is perhaps *the* central Esalen healing practice: full-body contemplative massage.

If the hot baths are the central ritual space of Esalen, massage is its central body-practice. Hence it is no accident that massage traditionally takes place at the baths themselves (although it is practiced elsewhere on the ground as well, for example, near the swimming pool on the front lawn).

The baths preceded Esalen, but massage did not. It was probably from Charlotte Selver's sensory awareness work, mediated in turn through Bernard Gunther's "sensory awakening," that the practice of Esalen massage first developed. The shift in terminology from "sensory awareness" to "sensory awakening" encoded some disagreements Selver had with Gunther's understanding of her work. Regardless, it was Bernie Gunther who became a resident staff member at Esalen from around 1964 into the early 1970s. It was also Gunther who probably did more than anyone to establish what he called "massage meditation" at Esalen.

Charlotte Selver (1901–2003) was a teacher of the Gindler method of awareness and exercise. She came to the United States in 1938 as a refugee to New York, where she taught her methods to such notables as Fritz Perls, Alan Watts, and Erich Fromm. Her method of sensory awareness revolved around a basic distinction between *sensation* and *emotion*. She respected but was not interested in psychological issues (that is, in the complexities of emotion); she was interested in the senses and the ways that they mediated moment-to-moment experience. One can easily imagine how such methods would have fused seamlessly with the methods of Esalen's early gestalt practitioners, who were similarly interested in the experience of immediate contact with the environment.

Bernard Gunther took Selver's methods and developed them for his own purposes. One, and only one, of these was massage. There were in fact dozens, if not hundreds—from finger head massages and the "Gunther hero sandwich" (whole groups "spooning" one another), to contemplative coffee drinking, hand or body salt rubs, and mutual hair shampooing. Regardless of the specific sensory awakening exercises, all were designed toward the same goal, that is, to awaken the senses and allow the individual to live more fully in the here and now. Something of the range and feel of such exercises can be gleaned from Gunther's two early books, both heavily indebted to Esalen: *Sense Relaxation* (1968) and *What To Do Till the Messiah Comes* (1971). These same volumes also contain a wealth of Paul Fusco photos of early Esalen figures as naked of clothes as the early Esalen grounds were denuded of trees. Any modern visitor to the place, now so thick with trees, flowers, and bushes, can only marvel at how *bare* these same grounds were back in the 1960s.

As for the specifics of the Esalen massage technique itself, these developed gradually over time and are now practiced in highly developed, professional, sublimated, and systematized forms.[45] Like many things Esalenesque, however, the technique's origins possessed some rather clear erotic dimensions. Seymour Carter, for example, who trained some of the massage practitioners who are still working at Esalen today, is clear why he and John and Anne Heider turned to Gunther's approach in order to develop the art of the Esalen massage: to become better lovers. The historical fact that early Esalen massage was often done in the nude only added to this original eros.

It is futile to communicate in words the experience of an Esalen massage, then or now. I will simply observe this. Part of the power of the practice resides, like so much else about Esalen, in the primacy of the universal human body. White bodies, black bodies, brown bodies, male bodies, female bodies, young bodies, old bodies, skinny bodies, fat bodies, heterosexual bodies, homosexual bodies, bisexual bodies all get the exact same nurturance, touch, and care. All meet and merge in a kind of physical meditation that is all about *removing* things (clothes, stress points, thoughts, anxieties) in order to reveal a more fundamental and natural state of relaxation and wellbeing. Certainly there are no absolutes to argue about here, no religious doctrines to debate, no petty intolerances to suffer. There are only two human beings enacting a largely silent and deeply sensuous ritual of the enlightenment of the body over the ocean. Like democracy in Don Johnson's vision of things, peace here is not an abstract idea or an aggressive doctrine. It is a bodily state covered only by a white cotton towel.

v

The Occult Imaginal and Cold War Activism (1970-1985)

The Cosmic Womb

STANISLAV AND CHRISTINA GROF AND THE COUNSELS OF SPIRITUAL EMERGENCE

Finally, as the time of his death approaches he sees a bright light, and being unaccustomed to it at the time of his death he is perplexed and confused. He sees all sorts of things such as are seen in dreams, because his mind is confused. He sees his (future) father and mother making love, and seeing them a thought crosses his mind, a perversity (*viparyasa*) arises in him. If he is going to be reborn as a man he sees himself making love with his mother and being hindered by his father; or if he is going to be reborn as a woman, he sees himself making love with his father and being hindered by his mother. It is at that moment that the Intermediate Existence is destroyed and life and consciousness arise and causality begins once more to work. It is like the imprint made by a die; the die is then destroyed but the pattern has been imprinted.

Saddharma-smrityupasthana Sutra 34

Buddhatvan yoshidyonisansritan
Buddhahood lives in the vagina of a woman.

Sanskrit saying quoted in Aldous Huxley's *Island*

By 1970 Esalen had turned a corner and ended an era. James Pike, Fritz Perls, and Abe Maslow all died in 1969 or 1970. Both Dick Price's and Mike Murphy's fathers, moreover, both passed away in 1969 as well. A year later, both founders turned forty. The institutional impact of all of this was quite real. "The deaths of these various mentors," Anderson observes, "had the effect of sealing off the previous decade into the irrecoverable past."[1]

Indeed, it did. But there were other teachers, and there would be other Esalens. Few, if any, were more important to the seminar and intellectual life of Esalen in the 1970s and early '80s than Stanislav Grof, the Czech psychiatrist who has worked for almost fifty years now, fourteen of them on the grounds of Esalen, to integrate the altered states catalyzed by psychedelics into our modern psychological maps of the mind. How he went about doing this, it turns out, again involved Tantric Asia.

In a move clearly designed to protect other cultures from psychological analysis, cultural critics of psychoanalytic thought often claim that its insights are applicable only to Western culture, where, or so they assume, all of its insights were first born and developed most fully. Only Westerners, such critics claim, have something like an unconscious, an oedipal complex, or omnipresent and constantly morphing libidinal drives.

Ancient Asian texts such as our first epigraph make a mockery of such a position.[2] In this Buddhist near-death experience (which is really more of a near-birth experience), translated into the Chinese from the Sanskrit around 542 CE, the author advances a theory of what we today call gender identity that is remarkably congruent with the Freudian one. Freud, of course, would locate these processes in the psychosexual stage of late infancy and childhood, whereas the Buddhist text "out-Freuds Freud" and locates them much further back in the Intermediate Existence, that is, in that marginal realm after the soul has died in its previous life but before it has taken on another body in its future life. But the classical oedipal structure of this process (with the child loving one parent and feeling hindered by the other) is nevertheless as obvious to the reader as it is confounding to the cultural relativist.

The soul's witnessing of the primal scene is not some accident—on the contrary, its primordial "imprinting" is permanent for the course of a life, *even if* its source or "die" has been destroyed or, as we would say today, has become unconscious. Moreover, it is precisely this voyeuristic event and these sexual and aggressive drives that set the very wheels of causality and existence into motion again. They, in effect, create the personal reality of this particular human life. Obviously, this was not a culture that took sexual desire (even that of a prefetal soul!) and the interfamilial dynamics of what Freud would later call "the family romance" lightly.

As it turns out, these same cross-cultural patterns were also noticed by those who were taking psychedelics while they read Buddhist and Hindu scriptures in the early counterculture. Leary, Metzner, and Alpert, for example, comment on the uncanny correspondences between Freud's oedipal theory and ancient Buddhist descriptions of this same *bardo* or "intermediate state" in their psychedelic manual based on *The Tibetan Book of the Dead*. Indeed, they quote Jung to the effect that Freud's psychoanalysis constitutes the first Western theory to map out the psychic territory that was much earlier explored by Tantric Buddhism.[3]

Similar psychoanalytic-Tantric correspondences, of course, have been central to Esalen as well. One of the most striking embodiments of this pattern is Stanislav Grof. In Grof, Tantric Asia, psychedelics, and psychoanalysis all meet within thousands of clinically regulated psychedelic sessions to form a corpus of writing and a body of therapeutic work that constitute some of the most intellectually developed, emotionally provocative, and aesthetically stunning displays of Esalen's altered states of history.

Albert's Bike Ride, the CIA, and Stan's Freudian Crisis

This particular story actually begins not in Big Sur in the early 1960s, but in prewar Europe in the '30s. There, a thirty-seven-year-old chemist named Albert Hofmann working at the Sandoz Pharmaceutical Laboratory on the Rhine in Basel, Switzerland, was in the business of synthesizing ergot analogs, that is, creating human-made compounds that bore strong chemical similarities to the alkaloids naturally occurring in ergot, a tiny mushroom that grows on different types of grain. Many of these compounds turned out to have useful medicinal properties, and—in a small but fascinating detail that will become more significant below—there was interest in exploring these compounds for their circulatory and contractual effects on the uterus, that spasming female organ of ecstatic orgasm, pregnancy, and childbirth. The twenty-fifth compound in this laboratory series was synthesized in 1938 and was lab coded—not very imaginatively— LSD-25. It caused test animals to become restless and created "strong uterine-constricting effects." But that was about it. Or so it seemed.

Accordingly, the compound was set aside until 1943, when Hofmann received what he later called "a peculiar presentiment." In essence, he felt that LSD-25 was worth looking at again. So on the Friday afternoon of April 16, 1943 (delightfully christened "Better Friday" by Peter Stafford), Hofmann resynthesized the compound in his lab with the intention of submitting its chemical portfolio to Sandoz again. During this work, however, it seems he accidentally ingested a minute amount of the substance. He noted some slight, unexplained effects and decided on the next Monday to submit himself to what he considered to be a ridiculously safe amount of the substance: 250 micrograms (that is, 250 millionths of a gram). He became "strangely inebriated," the shape of time became distorted, and fantastic colors and shapes began to appear before his eyes. His psychedelic bike-ride home is now the stuff of legend. Later, researchers would learn that 100 micrograms is a full dose for humans. Hofmann, in other words, even in his excessive pharmacological care, had given himself a double dose, and then some. In the process, he had discovered one of the most powerful molecules in human history.[4]

Once it came on the research market, LSD-25 was used extensively in the 1950s and '60s for both psychotherapy and research, often with the initial assumption that it could evoke a "model psychosis" and so provide psychiatrists with a unique opportunity to get at the chemical origins and mechanisms of mental disease. In a bizarre twist of events in the late 1940s and early '50s, the CIA discovered the drug, partly through a rumor that the Soviets had purchased a massive amount of the stuff and were planning to use it as a weapon of war. The rumor was completely false (no such stockpiles existed), but now the CIA itself became acutely interested in exploring LSD's mind-control potentials and began to generously fund research projects at various American university research hospitals.

A series of quite remarkable cultural events, criminal activities, and human follies followed, from the use of hypnosis and drugs to elicit information from CIA operatives, students, mental patients, and prisoners, to the setting up of a house of prostitution to test LSD on its patrons and the tragic suicide of a top scientist who had been given the drug (he ran through a tenth-story window). Many of these events were later documented by former U.S. State Department employee and later Esalen associate, John Marks, in his best-selling *The Search for the "Manchurian Candidate."*[5] After considerable effort and money, the CIA eventually concluded that LSD was useless for such ends. In the meantime, however, the control-obsessed secret organization had, quite ironically, helped fuel what would quickly become a very public American counterculture.

LSD-25 was slipping fast into the broader culture, primarily through CIA-funded psychiatrists like Dr. Harold Abramson, who seemed to revel in sharing the stuff with university intellectuals. Along with artists and religious explorers, academics were both constitutionally suited and culturally poised to make the most of this still secret substance and the esoteric society that was quickly forming around it. Michael Hollingshead was more influential than most here. According to Peter Stafford, he distributed the substance to, among others, Paul McCartney, Keith Richards, Frank Barron, Huston Smith, Timothy Leary (who "took a tablespoon and a half from Hollingshead's mayonnaise jar of LSD cut with sugar-icing—and didn't talk for five days"),[6] Richard Alpert, Ralph Metzner, and Alan Watts. Thus the chemistry of the counterculture began.

Stanislav Grof, however, did not enter the field through the mayonnaise jar of Michael Hollingshead. Turned on by Freud's *Introductory*

Lectures on Psycho-analysis in college, the young Grof entered medical school and became an orthodox Freudian analyst. In 1956, just a few months after graduating from medical school, he volunteered for an experiment with LSD in the Psychiatric Department of the School of Medicine in Prague under the direction of Dr. George Roubicek. The experience permanently shattered his Freudian materialism. Later work with thousands of LSD sessions would consistently and dramatically confirm the psychological processes Freud had so famously mapped, but they now took their own place, for Grof anyway, within an immeasurably richer and deeper consciousness. Grof would dedicate the rest of his life to understanding the altered states of "mind manifest."

His first response was a purely professional one. He traveled to London in 1964 for a conference on LSD, where he met an American psychologist, family therapist, and Esalen seminar leader by the name of Virginia Satir. In 1965 Satir invited him to the West Coast and introduced him to the community at Esalen. There he gave an impromptu workshop and felt a strong and immediate connection to Michael Murphy. When he returned to the United States again in 1967, it was at the invitation of Dr. Joel Elkes for a fellowship at Johns Hopkins University School of Medicine in psychedelic research.

Grof's plans, however, would change. A week before his arrival in Baltimore, Maimon Cohen published an article on the effect of LSD on the chromosome, a piece that started a national hysteria about the potential deleterious effects of the substance on heredity. Elkes decided to scrap his plan. As luck would have it, however, the last surviving psychedelic research program in the country happened to be conducted in Baltimore's Spring Grove Hospital. Instead of launching a new program at Johns Hopkins, Grof joined the staff at Spring Grove. It was during these two years (1967–69) that Grof began to draft his first book on his LSD research, *Realms of the Human Unconscious.*[7]

Here in Baltimore he also underwent a shattering of the space-time continuum within a high-dose psychedelic session at the Maryland Psychiatric Research Center. Grof considers this event to be one of the most extraordinary and important of his own inner life. "It appeared to me" said Grof, "rather obvious that there are no limits whatsoever in the realm of spirit and that time and space are arbitrary constructs of the psyche."[8]

Grof decided to test his newfound conviction and travel to his parents' Prague apartment in the session. He imagined himself flying through space in the proper direction. He sensed that he was moving at an incredible speed, but he was in fact going nowhere. He realized that such imagined flight was still bound by a spatial mindset and that it might be better to simply imagine that Baltimore and Prague were the same place. At once he found himself inside his parents' television set! This he recognized as a symbolic spoof on his still unconquered assumptions about what was possible (a television satellite signal, after all, can travel these sorts of distances easily).

Once he could renounce this second dysfunctional frame of mind, the television set turned inside out and he found himself standing in his parents' apartment. He walked around, found his parents sleeping, and noticed a clock on the wall that correctly registered the six-hour time difference. But suddenly he became very anxious, as he felt no drug effect and he couldn't tell, at all, if he was really in Prague and his Baltimore existence was a dream, or whether he was actually in Baltimore and this was a hallucination produced by the LSD. He thought immediately of Chuang-Tzu, the Chinese philosopher who once famously asked whether he was a man imagining that he was a butterfly or a butterfly imagining that he was a man.

Grof decided to perform a simple experiment. He would take a picture off the wall and then ask his parents in a letter whether anything unusual happened that night. As he reached for the picture, however, he felt great anxiety. Images of black magicians, gambling casinos, and high-level government and military meetings flashed before his mind's eye. He realized the terror of what he was about to do: after all, if he could transcend space and time so easily, so could others, and then what? And where would this stop? He could make millions in the casinos and psychically spy on government officials around the world (as we shall see in a later chapter, he would not be the last to entertain the latter idea). But Grof in 1967 was not so sure: "If I could get confirmation that it was possible to manipulate the physical environment at a distance of several thousand miles, my whole universe would collapse as a result of this one experiment, and I would find myself in a state of utter metaphysical confusion. The world as I had known it would not exist any more."[9] In the end, with the world itself at stake, he decided against the experiment. To this day, he is not certain whether he had truly transcended the space-time continuum, or whether he had simply had a very interesting drug trip.

In 1968, the Soviets invaded Czechoslovakia. Grof was ordered by the authorities to return to Prague. He made a fateful decision to disobey the order and stay in the States. He lived in exile for almost twenty years until the liberation of Eastern Europe. When he did finally return to his home country, it was to search for a proper venue for an international conference on transpersonal psychology to be held in 1993 under the aegis of his friend and then president of Czechoslovakia, Vaclav Havel. Vaclav's brother, Ivan Havel, had helped nurture an underground interest in things transpersonal and mystical throughout the Soviet era.[10]

In 1969, when his Spring Grove fellowship ended, Grof was offered the positions of assistant professor of psychiatry at Johns Hopkins and chief of psychiatric research at the Maryland Psychiatric Research Center. He held both positions until 1973. That same year, he went to New York City to sign a contract to publish *Realms of the Human Unconscious* in the Esalen book series that Stuart Miller had arranged with Viking Press.

While in New York, he was invited to a party, where he met Michael Murphy again. Murphy offered him a place at Esalen, where he could be a resident scholar and finish his book. Grof had given a formal Esalen workshop on his work as far back as 1967 in Berkeley.[11] Now, moreover, he was publishing his first book under the Esalen banner. Murphy's invitation must have struck him as a natural one. He accepted the offer and left the East Coast for the West Coast, as Leonard had done before him.

Freud on LSD (and Cocaine)

"If I am the father of LSD then Stan is the godfather," Hofmann once noted. "Nobody has contributed as much as Stan for the development of my problem child."[12] Certainly the cartography of consciousness that Grof developed with the help of over 4,000 clinical sessions or "trips" on LSD, psilocybine, mescaline, dipropyl-tryptamine (DPT), and methylene-dioxy-amphetamine (MDA) is an impressive one.[13] Later, he would add to this fund of experience over 30,000 sessions of Holotropic Breathwork.[14] Grof's publications are many and diverse, and he continues to publish. His work, however, has remained astonishingly consistent over the years. A reader of his first book, for example, will recognize many of the patterns of one of his recent texts, *The Psychology of Being.* Given Grof's metaphysical commitments, this makes some sense. It is almost as if Grof's initial mystical collapse of space and time in his early LSD initiation constituted a kind of full and complete revelation that he has since spent his decades expressing in linear logic and temporal words, always somehow grounded in that initial altered state of consciousness and energy beyond the four dimensions of space and time.

For our own purposes here, however, we will attempt to enter this state of consciousness and energy through Grof's most developed, if also profoundly ill-timed, statement, his *LSD Psychotherapy* (1980). This book appeared, as Grof himself notes, just as widespread drug abuse, a sensationalizing media, and an increasingly hostile political environment threatened to sink the entire subject into oblivion. The counterculture was over. The Reagan years were about to begin. One might as well have been writing high school workbooks on Darwinian evolution and biblical criticism for a fundamentalist-controlled textbook board.

Grof begins *LSD Psychotherapy* as William James once began his *Varieties of Religious Experience,* that is, with a methodological principle of excess. James had argued that mystical forms of consciousness exaggerate normal psychological processes and so can act like a mental microscope for psychological study. Similarly, Grof points out that LSD research began and developed with the conviction that LSD is to psychiatry what the telescope is to astronomy and the microscope to biology: psychic processes initiated under its influence make possible the observation of dynamisms and levels of psychic functioning that are not normally available for analysis. In Grof's own words, "LSD psychotherapy seems to intensify all the mechanisms operating in drug-free psychotherapies and involves, in addition, some new and powerful mechanisms of psychological change as yet unacknowledged and unexplained by mainstream psychiatry."[15] LSD, for example, catalyzes and magnifies the recall of repressed memories, transference phenomena between therapist and client, and the emergence of unconscious material. In one particularly controversial mode of LSD therapy known as *anaclitic therapy,* characterized by a fusion technique of full body contact between client and therapist, LSD has effected dramatic age regression.[16] What we are dealing with here, then, is a kind of radicalized psychology, a psychoanalysis as Western mystical technology, if you will.

In the mid 1960s, R. E. L. Masters and Jean Houston had already identified four levels of psychic functioning within psychedelic experience: the sensory, the recollective-analytic, the symbolic, and the integral or mystical.[17] Grof seems to have picked up on this and identified what he called the abstract or aesthetic, the psychodynamic, the perinatal, and the transpersonal. Both systems recognize an early and rather superficial level of abstract geometric patterns that are commonly seen in the early stages of psychedelic states (the sensory or aesthetic). Both also recognize the general fit between their second levels and the processes described by depth psychology (the recollective-analytic or psychodynamic). The third and fourth levels (the symbolic/integral and perinatal/transpersonal) are where both models begin to diverge from—they would say transcend— the standard psychoanalytic maps.

It is crucial to repeat, however, that Grof's work with LSD powerfully resonates with the earlier discoveries of Freud, which some have argued were catalyzed by Freud's own use of another drug that he himself actually helped "discover" (to both positive and personally tragic effect), that is, cocaine.[18] It appears that both drugs allowed these respective psychiatrists to access otherwise completely unconscious levels of the mind and then map them out for the public in their analytic writings. In other words, Grof's work with LSD, although moving in transpersonal directions that can only be described as post-Jungian, also had deep historical and theoretical roots in Freud's psychoanalysis, which may have been linked to cocaine revelations. Grof thus embodied for Esalen *both* of the great Western masters.

Even Freud was not as opposed to the mystical as is often thought. Edged on by his "oceanic friend," Romain Rolland, Freud speculated that mystical experiences of oneness stem back to fusion experiences between the newborn infant and the mother: "An infant at the breast does not as yet distinguish his ego from the external world as the source of the sensations flowing in upon him," Freud writes. "Originally the ego includes everything, later it separates off an external world from itself."[19]

> Our present ego-feeling is, therefore, only a shrunken residue of a much more inclusive—indeed, an all-embracing—feeling which corresponded to a more intimate bond between the ego and the world about it. If we may assume that there are many people in whose mental life this primary ego-feeling has persisted to a greater or less degree, it would exist in them side by side with the narrower and more sharply demarcated ego-feeling of maturity, like a counterpart to it. In that case, the ideational contents appropriate to it would be precisely those of limitlessness and of a bond with the universe—the same ideas with which my friend [Romain Rolland] elucidated the "oceanic feeling."[20]

Later theorists radicalized this idea by extending it from Freud's focus on the nursing breast back to the womb of natal existence, a kind of *regressus ad uterum* or "return to the womb." Otto Rank, moreover, speculated that many psychological patterns and problems could be traced back to the trauma of childbirth and the infant's dramatic passage through the vaginal channel.[21]

Grof synthesizes and develops these ideas even further, locating a whole series of what he calls basic perinatal matrices (BPM) around the clinical experience of birth and the intrauterine life of the infant, all creatively relived (and no doubt reinterpreted) within the LSD experience. There are four such basic perinatal matrices: BPM I, II, III, and IV, described respectively as "Primal Union with Mother," "Antagonism with Mother," "Synergism with Mother," and "Separation from Mother." All of this flows out of Grof's Rankian conviction that there exist "astonishing parallels" between the patterns seen under LSD and the clinical stages of delivery.[22]

BPM I is related to the infant's primal union with the mother and manifests itself under psychedelic conditions as undisturbed states of cosmic unity. Here the erotogenic zones of the body are free from tension and the libidinal drives are satisfied.

Soon, however, powerful chemical signals and muscular contractions will signal the early stages of delivery, which in turn will produce an experience of cosmic engulfment or restriction for the infant. Hence are initiated the cluster of experiences around BPM II, characterized by alienation, helplessness, guilt, constriction, and destruction. The erotogenic zones are now highly tensive, related (in the adult) to feelings of hunger, thirst, retention, sexual tension, and early delivery pains.

BPM III accentuates these processes, even as it opens up (quite literally in biological birth) a way out. In terms of actual delivery, the infant may come into intimate contact with blood, urine, even feces, hence the scatological motifs of some types of religious experience (including some types of Tantric ritual, by the way). Symbolically, an agonistic struggle or fight ensues that constitutes a classic death-rebirth experience. Within this struggle, powerful energies, many of them sexually related, can flood the organism, resulting in intense pain and pleasure and a whole series of pornographic and violent visions, a kind of "volcanic ecstasy," as Grof describes it.[23] Sudden release and relaxation define the erotogenic zones here, as we find most classically in sexual orgasm and delivery (itself sometimes accompanied by overwhelming sexual spasms).

Finally, BPM IV revolves around the expulsion through the vaginal canal and the sudden relief of birth and spiritual renewal. The erotogenic zones are defined by that kind of satisfaction and peace that constitute the satiation of basic drives.

Under the right conditions, such perinatal experiences can mediate access to what Grof refers to as the transpersonal realm, those levels of consciousness where the individual and the cosmos are intimately connected, where all sorts of parapsychological experiences may occur, and "orgiastic feelings of cosmic proportions, spiritual liberation and enlightenment" can appear alongside "mystical union with the creative principle in the universe."[24] Ultimately, the individual may be ushered into absolute reality or what Grof calls the Supracosmic and Metacosmic Void.

Significantly, the Hindu Tantric goddess Kali is consistently named by Grof as one of those archetypal patterns that constitute the perinatal matrices (particularly in BPM III and IV), usually as an example of the Jungian archetypes of the Great Mother and the Terrible Mother. Moreover, like much of Tantric culture in India, Grof's entire basic perinatal matrix model is centered on the infant's experience of the Mother and her body—it is a maternal mysticism focused on what the Tantric traditions know as the "cosmic womb" (*yoni*), that is, the female genitals and womb as the transmitter and creative source of cosmic life and divine energy. Add to this the essentially Hindu-perennialist nature of Grof's worldview evident in books like *The Cosmic Game* as well as his dialectical nondual metaphysics, and one begins to sense that there is something profoundly Tantric about all of this.[25] When we encounter explicitly Tantric *yantras*, authors, and deities in his texts and recall the central place that sexuality plays in his conclusions, such a Tantric transmission becomes even more obvious.

And that Western Tantrika, Sigmund Freud, is always just around the corner. Grof again: "This paradigm demonstrates, among other things, the close parallels between the stages of biological delivery and the pattern of sexual orgasm. The similarity between these two biological patterns is a fact of fundamental theoretical importance. It makes it possible to shift the etiological emphasis in the psychogenesis of emotional disorders from sexual dynamics to perinatal matrices, without denying or negating the significance and validity of the basic Freudian principles for understanding the psychodynamic phenomena and their mutual interrelations."[26]

For Grof, the triad of "birth, sex, and death" are physically and spiritually related, and the religious traditions are simply wrong to suppress or deny this connection: "Because of their intimate link with spirituality, birth, sex, and death also show a significant experiential overlap with each other. For many women, an uncomplicated delivery under favorable conditions can be the strongest sexual experience of their lives. Conversely, a powerful sexual orgasm in women, as well as men, can occasionally take the form of psychospiritual rebirth. The orgasm can also be so overpowering that it can be subjectively experienced as dying."[27] Here also he points out that the classic near-death experience—with the soul traveling through a tunnel to an ecstatic Light—looks a lot like a transformed memory of birth through the vaginal canal. This is not to suggest that one can be reduced to the other. It is to reiterate the metaphysical point that birth, death, sex, and spirit are all apiece throughout the entire human lifecycle (and, possibly, beyond that lifecycle).

Beyond Freud to the Tantra

Grof's system, however, should not be confused with Freud's or Jung's. It certainly incorporates both, but it also goes way beyond them, particularly in its metaphysical conclusions. Grof draws a number of these from his years of research with both LSD and Holotropic Breathwork, which we might summarize as follows:

- "Consciousness is not a product of the brain, but a primary principle of existence," and "it plays a critical role in the creation of the phenomenal world."
- "The psyche of each of us is essentially commensurate with all of existence and ultimately identical with the cosmic creative principle itself."
- The material universe is "a virtual reality created by Absolute Consciousness through an infinitely complex orchestration of experiences."
- As a virtual reality, akin to a kind of cosmic movie or theatre, the universe is "a cosmic game" that we should delight in playing in the spirit of the Tantric branches of Jainism, Hinduism, and Buddhism, all of which have "a distinctly life-affirming and life-celebrating orientation."
- As these same ancient Tantric texts suggest, "the human body literally is a microcosm that reflects and contains the entire macrocosm," thus "if one could thoroughly explore one's own body and psyche, this would bring the knowledge of all the phenomenal worlds."
- Finally, the universe is not moral in any normal social sense of that term; rather, it is, to use a Nietzschean phrase (itself reflective of the Indian Upanishads), "beyond good and evil," hence "aggression is woven into the natural order and...it is not possible to be alive except at the expense of other living creatures"; this in turn forces us to acknowledge that "the creative cosmic principle...is directly responsible for all the suffering and horrors of existence."[28]

For the sake of space and economy, I have listed these metaphysical conclusions in a brief and overly abstract way here, but it is important to point out that Grof also embodies them in his person. I realized this myself with some force during a lunch conversation with him. For some reason, we were talking about the popular Evangelical fascination with end-of-the-world scenarios. Stan became reflective, looked up from his clams and cappuccino, and said something to the effect that the archetypal reality of the apocalypse first became meaningful to him in a fascinating MDMA (Ecstasy) session in which he realized for the first time that all we see around us and assume to be real is in fact a kind of virtual illusion, that in actual fact *it does not exist* in any real way: at that moment the world literally ended for him. Now this was hardly news to me, as I had encountered this belief a thousand times before in my reading of the world's mystical literature, particularly that of India and its famous doctrine of *maya* or "illusion." But I had never heard anyone say the same with such conviction and in such an obvious matter-of-fact way. It wasn't what Stan said; it was *how* he said it. Put differently, Stan Grof was not telling me that he believed this. He was telling me that he *knew* this.

Tantric Energies and Spiritual Emergence: The Life and Work of Christina Grof

Central to this story is Stan's co-worker, soul mate, and wife, Christina.[29] As a teenager, Christina Goodale remembers various spiritual experiences involving Jesus around Easter, but she also remembers having no real context in which to understand these. Her education at Sarah Lawrence College certainly helped, particularly through the lectures and friendship of a certain professor there whom she knew simply as "Mr. Campbell." Joseph Campbell's lectures on the mythologies of death and rebirth, the hero's journey, and the (Tantric) themes of the *chakras* and the *kundalini* moved her in an especially deep way. Christina "had no idea at the time that these themes were to become experiential realities in my life."[30] That is, she could not quite shake the sense that such things only really happen to "them," that is, to people living in other countries, like India. She, of course, was hardly alone in this conviction. We might recall an exceptionally well-read Huston Smith taking more or less the same position at MIT before he was initiated into the mystical by Leary's mescaline one New Years Day.

Christina graduated from college in 1964. She then married, moved to Honolulu with her new husband, and soon became pregnant. To help her through the pregnancy, she practiced yoga and did Lamaze training, focusing on how to relax and breathe deeply. The birth, however, was not to be a simple one. The cosmic womb (*yoni*) showed itself to Christina here in dramatic and traumatic form. During the birth of her first child, Christina experienced an eruption of what the Indian Tantric traditions call the *kundalini*, the "coiled" serpent power of Tantra said to lie dormant at the base of the spine awaiting awakening through various intentional yogic postures or spontaneous life experiences. All kinds of altered states of consciousness and energy flowed out of her. The doctors were baffled and did not know what to do. As Christina experienced white light and ecstatic energies shoot up her spine and as her body began to manifest various spontaneous movements (what the yoga traditions call *kriyas*), the medical staff gave her medications to control and subdue her in a manner that eerily, and depressingly, recalls for us Dick Price's experiences of similar energies awakened and medicated.

Two years later, she had a similar experience in the birth of her second child. Christina definitely thought that something was wrong now. She became depressed. She was, however, still practicing hatha yoga, now at a fairly advanced level. Around 1973, she heard that an Indian saint named Swami Muktananda, who taught in a Tantric lineage often referred to as Kashmir Shaivism, was coming to town with Ram Dass (the Hindu-American guru previously know as Richard Alpert, the former psychologist and colleague of Timothy Leary) and Werner Erhardt, charismatic inventor of EST. Later she took a four-day retreat with Muktananda or Baba (literally Papa), as he was affectionately called by his devotees.

Christina took *darshan* with the guru and asked him questions about her now failing marriage. Later, in the context of a group meditation, she received the initiation of *shakti-pat* (literally "energy-descent," a kind of initiatory transmission event in which the guru transmits his energy and consciousness directly into the disciple). She did not understand what was happening. Baba simply touched her with a peacock feather. Later, when she opened her eyes and saw him looking at her, the *shakti* took effect: "Everything I had tried to hold down came rocketing up my spine, spontaneous tremors, much stronger than childbirth episodes; it all just developed from there." Unfortunately, in some ways, this only made things worse, as she was now living in two seemingly incompatible worlds: "I was a very good girl, and I was a housewife with two small children; I was doing yoga simply for exercise. I saw no connection between it, Joe [Campbell], and these *kundalini*-like experiences. I was scared and magnetized at the same time."

She was also separated from her husband. Soon after, she was in a serious automobile accident. On the way home from yoga class one day, the brakes of her Volkswagen bus failed. She was speeding down an eight-lane highway at the time. Her bus careened across all four lanes, hit a retaining wall, bounced back, and slammed into a large construction truck sitting on the side of the highway. While all of this happened, Christina could see what she describes as "a continuum of spirit or consciousness beyond death." "I could see the curtain of death, then myself going through that opaque curtain and seeing that I was part of everything. It was blissful, and it all happened before the impact and the injury. I remembered looking down and seeing blood, and that I had lost a toe, but I was in this other place. I was watching it all from some other place." Unfortunately, she had no knowledge about what researchers were beginning to identify as the NDE or the near-death experience. For Christina at least, such ecstatic experiences of a transcendent consciousness were just more evidence that she was "nuts."

She left the islands as soon as she could, went back to New York, called up Campbell, and sat down with him over dinner together in a small Italian restaurant to tell him about her birth (and death) experiences. She remembers being scared. Campbell told her that he had never been through such things. He liked to keep his feet on the ground. But he knew someone who could help her from both the experiential and intellectual planes. His name was Stan Grof, and he was living at a place on the West Coast called Esalen. Campbell offered to call him for Christina. He introduced them over the phone. A few weeks later in the summer of 1975, Christina asked her former husband to take care of the children, got on a plane, and visited Grof and his wife Joan Halifax in their Big Sur home. During this visit, she decided to attend a six-week seminar on Buddhism and Western psychology co-led by Grof, Halifax, and Jack Kornfield. In the meantime, she had also decided to stay on the mainland, primarily to be around Swami Muktananda.

By the time Christina arrived at Esalen in the summer of 1975, it was becoming increasingly clear to both Grof and Halifax that their marriage was nearly over. It ended three years later, and both Grof and Halifax moved on to new lives. In the meantime, Christina had moved in with Stan, in November of 1975. They were living in the house just off the Esalen property where Ida Rolf had lived. Neither thought of themselves as Rolf's successors, but the two of them would live there for the next twelve years and help define the Esalen culture of the 1970s and early

'80s. Halifax would go on to become a well-known Zen Buddhist abbot or Roshi.

In the spring of 1976, Christina had what she calls her first "spiritual emergency." A friend of theirs known for his psychedelic research sat with her for five full days. Visions, past lives, and spontaneous bodily movements were "all over the place." The *kundalini* experiences also intensified, and she began to realize that they were somehow connected to her original *shakti-pat* initiation with Muktananda. Looking back after years of work on the spiritual emergencies of others, Christina also realizes now that such events are often triggered by an experience of deep loss. Her own emergency began when she had just learned she would lose custody of her children.

In order to get some intellectual handle on this spiritual crisis, she began to read in the growing literature on *kundalini*. She had already read Muktananda's autobiography, *The Play of Consciousness,* in which he recounts his own awakening to these mystical energies, occasionally in some rather graphic sexual terms: his own awakening was accompanied by an extended erection that burrowed into his belly.[31] Now she was reading Gopi Krishna's autobiography, *Kundalini: The Evolutionary Energy in Man* (significantly, with an elaborate Jungian commentary written by James Hillman).[32] Both texts would have been classic reads within the California counterculture of the 1970s. But neither really helped her. In her own words, she needed "to hear it from a Westerner," that is, she needed Western psychological categories to make sense of it all and to integrate these Tantric energies into her own American life. Lee Sannella's *Kundalini: Psychosis or Transcendence?* turned out to be the turning point.[33] It was Western psychology, not Asian yoga, that ultimately did the trick, or, more accurately, it was Western psychology put into intimate dialogue with Hindu Tantrism that ultimately gave Christina what she needed: an integral understanding of what she had been experiencing in her cosmic womb and in (and outside) her own body for years.

About this same time, Stan and Christina began to work closely together on a shared religious calling. "Stan opened his whole life to me," said Christina, "including his heart and work. He very much wanted a partner in the work, and I was very honored." It helped that Christina was teaching yoga at the time. Their backgrounds in LSD research and *kundalini* and *hatha* yoga began to meld. Christina took Stan up to Oakland to meet Swami Muktananda. Stan never became a devotee, but the guru's Kashmir Shaivism matched to an astonishing degree both what Christina had been experiencing in her inner world and what Stan had

FIGURE 20. Christina and Stanislav Grof, with apparent chakras. Printed with permission of Stanislav Grof.

been mapping in the minds of his LSD participants. As if to express this psychedelic-psychoanalytic-Tantric confluence further, they jointly organized in cooperation with the Siddha Yoga ashram in Ganeshpuri a large international transpersonal conference called Ancient Wisdom and Modern Science at the Oberoi Hotel in Bombay in February of 1982. The event resulted in another book.[34] Muktananda and Mother Teresa both spoke at the conference, as did a whole host of Esalen personalities, including Claudio Naranjo, Rupert Sheldrake, Frances Vaughan, and Fritjof Capra.

The Grofs were also extremely active in the social and seminar life of Esalen at Big Sur. Indeed, "the Grof groups," as they came to be called, dominate the Esalen catalogs of the late 1970s and early '80s.[35] These constituted major commitments—spiritually and financially—on the part of both the participants and the Esalen staff. Often there were whole teams of instructors involved. The groups usually met for four to six weeks in the Big House. Richard Tarnas, an Esalen community member who lived and worked on the grounds between 1974 and 1984, played a major role in organizing, envisioning, and teaching the topics. Seminars ranged widely but orbited faithfully around classical Grof themes: Interrelations between Consciousness, Energy and Matter; Energy: Physical, Emotional and Spiritual; East and West: Ancient Wisdom and Modern Science (with Fritjof Capra); Mind and Body; Tantric Art and Ritual (with Ajit Mooker-jee); and Alternative Futures. And there were still others, like Birth, Sex and Death, which met in May of 1977. These last four weeks involved thirty faculty mentors, including Gregory Bateson and the famous researcher of death and dying, Elizabeth Kübler-Ross.[36]

The Spiritual Emergency Network (1980–1989)

Dick Price had begun his religious career in a state of psychosis or mystical trauma imbued with transcendent possibilities, almost all of them shut down by the brutality of insulin, electroshock, and institutionalization. He had cofounded Esalen to help build a place and a space in which people who had been through similar experiences could come and be healed. This mission fit beautifully the life experiences of Christina Grof. She too, after all, had been through "spiritual emergencies" that she did not understand at the time and that she learned to interpret only with considerable study and support. She too had come to know *both* the traumas *and* the "extraordinary healing potential of nonordinary states of consciousness."[37] It was only a matter of time, then, before her life-experiences, Stan's therapeutic training, and Dick's vision for Esalen came together in some concrete form.

In 1980, with the moral support and financial assistance of Price, who often funded projects from his own personal resources, Christina and Stan Grof started the Spiritual Emergency Network (or SEN) at Esalen. Dick offered Stan and Christina one of the Esalen houses and enough financial backing to bring in two work scholars every month to work with them. Robert Forte, who had left a graduate career at the University of Chicago Divinity School to come to Esalen and study with Stan Grof, was SEN's second coordinator and helped get the project off the ground. They began putting together contact lists, that is, names of individuals across the country in every major city to whom they could then refer individuals who called their hot-line for help. They also sponsored week-long workshops to look at the notion of spiritual emergency in a more systematic way. Later they would organize a four-week seminar with, among others, the Jungian psychiatrist John Perry, the Buddhist teacher and meditator Jack Kornfield, opthalmologist and *kundalini* theorist Lee Sannella, Esalen psychologist Julian Silverman, and two of Muktananda's devotees.

By 1989, SEN had grown to become an international organization with 1,100 helpers and a mailing list of over 10,000 names. At this point, moreover, it was handling approximately 150 calls a month. An analysis of 501 calls and 117 letters from November of 1986 through July of 1987 revealed that the typical caller was a forty-year-old female (69 percent) experiencing some type of *kundalini* awakening (24 percent).[38] Christina Grof was on to something.

The real crisis, it turned out, was often primarily a hermeneutical or cultural one, that is, Westerners were undergoing intense spiritual experiences that could not be understood, much less appreciated, within their own cultural frames. They were thus experiencing tremendous cognitive, religious, and emotional dissonance. In colloquial language, they felt that they were going mad when in reality, according to the Grofs, they were often undergoing a kind of spiritual rebirth that was best understood within the vocabulary and categories of the Asian traditions (inevitably in one of their Tantric forms). There were also, of course, real cases of psychotic suffering that needed to be handled professionally, but they were careful to try to distinguish between the psychotic and the transcendent, even if, as numerous writers from R. D. Laing and Thomas Szasz to John Perry and Lee Sannella had shown, the line between these two realms was a very thin and wavy one. Joseph Campbell put the matter as well as anyone: "The mystic, endowed with native talents . . . and following . . . the instruction of a master, enters the waters and finds he can swim; whereas the schizophrenic, unprepared, unguided, and ungifted, has fallen or has intentionally plunged and is drowning."[39]

SEN is no longer active, but Christina Grof continued to pursue various types of therapeutic and healing work, particularly in the realm of addiction and alcoholism, from which she herself suffered and recovered. Her most recent book, *The Thirst for Wholeness,* argues that physical, sexual, and emotional abuse are very much related in people with addictive problems, and that addiction itself often displays powerful spiritual currents.[40]

A Yoni-Tantra for Our Times

Thus, another altered state of history emerged, another enlightenment of the body shone through the lives of Stan and Christina Grof. Stan's psychoanalysis and LSD research, Christina's *kundalini*-laced childbirth experiences and Tantric transmissions from a modern Hindu Tantric saint, and two lifetimes of Holotropic Breathwork, spiritual counseling, and public writing have produced a psychology of religion that dramatizes the findings of classical psychoanalysis (even as it also relativizes them) and sexualizes mystical states in an explicitly Tantric fashion. The same mystical psychoanalysis struggles openly with issues ranging from the spiritual needs of terminal cancer patients to the addictive behaviors of alcoholism and drug abuse and concludes, after thousands of experiments with tens of thousands of participants and patients, with what is essentially an American-Tantric worldview. And why not? Christina knew early on from her own spasming mystical womb what Stan was mapping, from the other side as it were, in his LSD researches: subject and object met and united here. The couple's later meeting through the arrangement of the era's most famous mythologist (Joe Campbell), marriage, and life-long partnership constitute a kind of archetypal union of Western psychology and Indian Tantra for our times. Psychoanalysis, in both its Freudian and Jungian streams, has morphed into an American Tantra, and in the process the Indian Tantric traditions have been enriched by an encounter with both Western psychology and one of the most potent of all Western mystical technologies, LSD-25.

The result, in the end, is a decades-long meditation on the human experience of the female body, a kind of Western *Yoni-Tantra* or "Mystical Treatise on the Cosmic Womb" that incorporates the ecstatic and visionary experiences of thousands of individuals in order to explore and then map out the *yoni* (as mystical uterus and vagina) in all of its sexual, traumatic, mythological, and transcendent complexities. Such an eccentric reading may appear stretched or odd to the uninformed or uninitiated, but it makes more than a little sense. Stan Grof's constant reference to what he calls the "cosmic creative principle" is in fact a very traditional translation of the Sanskrit (and very anatomical) *yoni.* It was this same ecstatic *yoni,* moreover, that initiated Christina into a spiritual path and took her directly into the heart of a modern-day Tantric system in the person of Swami Muktananda. Just as significantly, it also made her especially sensitive to the therapeutic vision of Dick Price, who knew his own spiritual emergenc(e)y and found the mystery of his own sexuality awaken in a state of enlightened psychosis. Less consciously and less directly, the Grofs' life-affirming Tantric spirituality would also echo many of the themes of Michael Murphy's reading of Sri Aurobindo and Murphy's own life-affirming Tantric vision.

Given this double resonance with both founders, it should probably not surprise us that Stan and Christina Grof lived on the grounds as Esalen guides, teachers, and popular seminar leaders for fourteen years. With the important exception of Dick Price, no Esalen visionary was there longer, and few have done as much to define what the place would and could be. Nor should it surprise us that Stan and Christina Grof's work on the cosmic womb and the counsels of spiritual emergence constitute some of the most provocative and clearest examples of Tantric thought and practice at Esalen. The place and the vision were very much at one here, at least for a time.

Golf in the Kingdom

PLATO AND RAMAKRISHNA FOR REPUBLICANS

After Freud, we tend to presume a space within the head, a sealed chamber within which the poem gestates, partitioned from the world outside. But such an account is based on a metaphor: one can no more locate the unconscious impulse to a poem among the synapses of the brain than one could uncover the source of Helicon's springs. We might as well declare that poems drop from the sky. In the last fifty years, there have been American poets who have claimed as much. For them, the occult has involved not so much a question of belief but a cloud of unknowing that settles over the writing desk, unsettling metaphorical relations, as well as those between reading and writing. Despite its association with bad faith and chicanery, the occult has for poets constituted part of a restless intellectual investigation that moves beyond our commonly accepted paradigms for authorship and consciousness.

DEVIN JOHNSTON, *Precipitations: Contemporary American Poetry as Occult Practice*

The modality of spiritual existence is often none other than that mode of existence where imagination has become empowered.

JESS BYRON HOLLENBACK, *Mysticism*

Since his car accident in 1962, Murphy had found it difficult to return to his center. It wasn't, of course, simply the accident. It was what the 1960s came to represent for him. No longer celibate, his energies for meditation waned at the end of the decade, just as he found himself drawn into countless astonishing interests and necessary duties with the young institute. He felt himself both immensely energized and somehow scattered.

Then there was his personal life, which stumbled. He entered and then exited a first marriage to Patricia Felix, a woman he had met at an Esalen seminar who moved to the grounds in 1966 to be with Murphy during the first Residential Program. After a two-year affair, they married one May night in 1968 after seeing *Zorba the Greek* and driving up to the famous marriage mills of Sparks, Nevada. There the formalities were performed by a man who, oddly, looked like Buckminster Fuller. The marriage was over by May of the next year. In the summer of 1969, Murphy, now living in a small one-bedroom apartment in the North Beach district of San Francisco, gathered his energies, recentered himself, and found a voice to express the secrets of his inner life. That voice, it turned out, was no longer simply meditation. It was meditation and writing.

One of the more intriguing aspects of Esalen's history—and the working method of the next four chapters—is that a good share of its intellectual and social life has been defined by a writer of fiction, Michael Murphy, whose occult novels have guided, responded to, and occasionally even prefigured the legend and lore that is Esalen. This should not surprise us. "Art is our only salvation," insisted Frederic Spiegelberg, who summoned the spirit of Oscar Wilde in his conviction that, "life imitates art far more than art imitates life."[1] Certainly the fiction of Michael Murphy and its effects "in the real world," as we say in our lazier intellectual moments, more than live up to such a salvation, where life is an art and art possesses its own secret life.

The literary critic Daniel Noel once observed that whether or not Carlos Castaneda's stories faithfully reflect his peyote rituals, whether or not his teacher Don Juan even existed, what we have, in the end, are not sacred plants or Indian sorcerers, but Castaneda's *texts,* which are themselves a kind of mind-altering substance. "Words," Noel observes, "are the only psychotropic agents Castaneda gives us."[2]

We are in a very similar situation with Murphy's occult novels, and particularly with his first, *Golf in the Kingdom.* After all, the novel's central figure, the mysterious Scottish golf pro Shivas Irons, took on a mythological force in the professional sports world of the 1980s and '90s similar to that which Castaneda's Don Juan took on in the psychedelic counterculture of the late 1960s and '70s. Although Shivas is almost certainly a fictional character, one is never entirely sure. Murphy himself leaves us guessing with one-liners like that in the fall Esalen catalog of 1974, which described Shivas Irons as "a philosopher athlete I met by chance in Scotland during the summer of 1956." Not your typical fictional character. In the end, though, what finally links the golf swing of a reader and the mysterious "true gravity" of Shivas Irons, is not Shivas as a historical person, but Shivas *as a text.* Words are the only golf swings Murphy gives us.

Here reading is a transformative practice, an altered state of self-hypnosis and creative trance. We saw this phenomenon at work with the Tantric transmission that occurred between a young Michael Murphy and Aurobindo's *The Life Divine,* and again with respect to Joseph

Campbell's yoga of reading, reading, and more reading. We will see it again in the remarkable reception history of *Golf in the Kingdom,* whose reading events constitute a series of playfully encoded Platonic and Tantric transmissions. Within his own mystical art, Murphy expresses both his deepest convictions and his most haunting doubts about the occult potentials of the human body, and has a good-hearted laugh at the whole subject in the process. He has also encoded a set of deeply personal mystical experiences in a way that renders it well nigh impossible to distinguish between what is "real" and what is "fictional." He has hidden himself in his own text. He has occulted the occult, secreted the secret. The transmission thus now lies in potential in the text, waiting to be activated, awakened by a reader ready for its revelation.

Helpful here is Murphy's own understanding of how he writes and how what he writes should be read. In conversations with Clint Eastwood about making a movie based on *Golf in the Kingdom,* Murphy drew a four-part distinction between fantasy, science fiction, magical realism, and his own occult or mystical realism. Whereas *fantasy* is that genre of literature that is purely fictional and is meant solely for the entertainment of the imagination (think *Lord of the Rings*), *science fiction* is roughly based on reality, that is, on the future possibilities of technology and science (think *Star Trek*). Often, moreover, the latter is intended to be predictive of what will someday be. For Murphy, though, a novel like *Golf in the Kingdom* or *Jacob Atabet* is not quite any of these things. These rather are expressions of what he calls *occult* or *mystical realism,* which he defines as an imaginative elaboration of human experiences that have actually occurred to numerous individuals (and distinguishes from *magical realism* in its avoidance of completely impossible physical happenings, like goldfish raining from the sky or men flying up waterfalls).

The case of Castaneda is again especially instructive. Murphy points out that he had heard back in 1964 (from Castaneda himself) the stories Castaneda told in 1968 in his classic *The Teachings of Don Juan.* He thus believes some of the stories reflect real experiences Castaneda had had in the field. For Murphy, however, as Castaneda published book after book, this original mystical realism morphed into a wild magical realism (where men now literally flew up waterfalls). An unfortunate blurring of genres, truths, and falsehoods was the result.

Such literary and moral distinctions are very important to Murphy, and they bear directly on the nature and function of Esalen. After all, much that wants to come to Esalen is, in his mind, essentially a wishful form of magical realism (which can never happen), rather than a sophisticated expression of mystical realism (which happens all the time). He wants to resist the former illusions and nurture the latter potentials. In comparison, every experience described in his own occult novels, he points out, has been reported numerous times by reliable sources. No one, though, levitates in these pages. His texts thus reflect what he would like Esalen to be: a place where the human potential can be actualized, a place where the mystical can become real. A profoundly future-oriented soul, Murphy also believes that such a novel place, like science fiction, can be predictive. He thus opens *Jacob Atabet:* "It is hard to tell whether the strangely formed narrative that follows is a record of actual events or an imaginative probe of the future." It is, of course, both for him.

The central issue here is a classical Esalen theme that goes back to the very first seminars, that is, the psychology of creativity and inspiration, those mysterious psychic wellsprings from which the poem, the art, or the big idea bubbles up, as if out of nowhere—as if from Helicon's mythical springs. For these early Esalen participants, and certainly for Murphy himself, the human imagination is not some weaver of fantasy or fiction without connection to the real world. Under the right conditions, it is also an empowered organ of gnosis capable of making contact with other dimensions and truths, if always through the medium of the symbol, the vision, the dream, and the myth (or the novel). The art of the imaginal, the art of the mystical realist novel, is thus something both fundamentally subjective (mystical) but also empirical and objective (realism). Such an art participates in that altered realm of being that F. W. H. Myers called the subliminal and that Johnston refers to above as the occult. This is the paradoxical both-and realm of the unconscious, creative inspiration, automatic writing (another textual expression of the mystical), genius, synchronicity, possession, trance, ecstasy, and spiritual union.

And, oddly enough, the game of golf . . .

An Indecently Alluring Novel

Dennis Murphy could not have been more prescient when he called his brother, who was rapt in his meditative approach to the sport, a golfing yogi. Nor could he have possibly known how richly future history would unpack his off-hand fraternal remark.

In 1972, at the age of forty-one, Michael Murphy published his first book, *Golf in the Kingdom.* In terms of both sales and public reception, it has been, by far, his most successful publishing venture. The book has sold well over one million copies and has become something of a cult classic among both amateur and professional golfers. Other than a few instructional manuals, no book on the subject of golf has sold more copies than *Golf in the Kingdom.* The title routinely shows up on various published lists of the most influential books written on the game; Murphy was once the featured speaker at a national meeting of the PGA; and the party scene from the novel has been dramatized on stage at Pebble Beach.

The novel's influence, however, extends well beyond the PGA. Phil Jackson, the most successful coach in NBA history, is an enthusiastic reader of *Golf in the Kingdom* and gave it (along with Murphy's *The Future of the Body*) to Michael Jordan and other members of the Chicago Bulls when he was coaching them toward their six titles.[3] Jackson, moreover, would later follow Murphy's lead and write his own book on a similar athletic-mystical theme, that is, the Zen of basketball or *Sacred Hoops.*

As further cultural signs of the book's importance, a fan club has formed around the book, its lore, the ambiguous existence of its central character (Shivas Irons)—the society has even playfully split into two schools over the central doctrinal issue of whether or not Shivas really exists—and what is called the "as-yet-unknown pleasures to be gained from this indecently alluring game." The reader thus stumbles upon the Shivas Irons Society at the very back of the book. The society is described on its own advertising page as "a nonprofit corporation organized to further the pleasure of golf and explore its many mysteries." Fittingly, its logo is artistically rendered by the abstract symbol of a putting green drawn in the shape of a figure-eight infinity sign.[4]

The society has members in more than twenty countries and at one time or another has boasted members in every single state (South Dakota was the last to be added). It even has its own high-end, beautifully produced journal on golf, literature, and art, *The Journal of the Shivas Irons Society.* The first issue, for example, includes such wonders as three separate pieces on or by Bernard Darwin, one of the most famous golf writers of all time who also happened to be the grandson of Charles Darwin. Evolution and golf are deeply and humorously intertwined in *Golf in the Kingdom,* so this link between evolutionary theory and golf writing is not without meaning for Murphy—another piece of smiling synchronicity.

The little book also has its own Hollywood story. Movie rights have been sold to different producers nineteen times now, if still without cinematographic result. Comedians Bill Murray and Tommy Smothers are fans. As is Men's Wearhouse CEO, George Zimmer, who built his own nine-hole golf course in Hawaii after a map of the novel's sequel, *The Kingdom of Shivas Irons.*

How to begin to explain all of this? How to make at least some sense of the phenomenon that is *Golf in the Kingdom* and, with it, that frustrating and yet seductive game that Murphy likes to refer to as "a mystery school for Republicans"?

Story and Structure

The story is a remarkably simple one. The novel encodes a grand, if never quite fully developed, philosophical vision within a single twenty-four-hour period, which occurred, we are told, in June of 1956.[5] Murphy writes autobiographically here, that is, as himself traveling to Pondicherry to live in Aurobindo's ashram. And this no doubt adds a certain realism to the story; he did, after all, travel to India in this same year, and he did stop over in Scotland to play a round of golf at St. Andrews, the Vatican of the golf world, as it were. So too in the novel, he stops over in Scotland, in the Kingdom of Fife (or "the Kingdom," as it is called, no doubt as an allusion to Jesus's teaching about the kingdom of God), and plays a round of golf on Burningbush Links (clearly a fictional and humorously Mosaic stand-in for St. Andrews) with Shivas Irons, a local, lanky, buck-toothed golf pro, and his present student, Mr. Balie MacIver.

After the game, Murphy joins Shivas and his friends for an evening dinner and drinking party and then, after the party, follows him into a ravine off the thirteenth fairway to look for Shivas's mysterious and legendary teacher, Seamus MacDuff. After failing to find the master (only his ancient club and balls seem to be down there, although Murphy swears he saw someone peering at him from the cliffs), the duo returns to Shivas's apartment. Later Murphy observes with some horror an unconscious (or superconscious) Shivas rigid in a meditative trance as the sun comes up. Eventually the men converse and the odd golf pro shares his metaphysical theories and the numerous "dangerous connections" that he purports to detect in human history and the advances of science and technology.

Finally, Murphy, conscientiously bound to his travel plans and proper schedule, leaves the next afternoon for London and then Paris, all to Shivas's great disappointment and Murphy's considerable guilt. An epilogue finds Murphy in the Cathedral of Rheims with a young woman named Dulce, struggling with the competing lures of asceticism and eroticism and, again, with a possible vision of Seamus, whom he thinks he sees in the dark reaches of the church's upper nave. There too an old lady opens his heart and ears to divine voices: "Come home. Come home." As he is on his way to India, even this divine voice remains ambiguous, however. Is his true home India via some past-life memory? Or is he being asked to go back to California to start some new adventure there? Or is this perhaps a call back to the Plotinian Mystical One as primal home? All of these readings seem reasonable as the novel ends, simultaneously in both 1956 and 1972.

Structurally speaking, the book is divided into two parts. Part 1 relates the events just summarized. Part 2 then expounds on the teachings Murphy received from Shivas, at least as he claims to remember them sixteen years later, that is, in 1972. By this time, however, the author has tried and failed to locate Shivas, who is either now dead or long gone (like any number of figures in the history of Western esotericism, we are never quite sure). There have been many "sightings" over the years, of course. In the summer of 2005, rumors even circulated through the Shivas Irons Society that Murphy was about to release an old film of Shivas. Our best guides here, though, are clearly an appreciation of Irish humor, a grin, and another beer. I certainly wouldn't put any bets, not large ones anyway, on the existence of the rare film clip.

Platonic Golf

We need not detail the entire story here. Two scenes, however, are especially pertinent to my own developing tale about Esalen: the party scene just after the round of golf, and the night Murphy spent with Shivas in his apartment. These two scenes, it turns out, are structured around two classics of mystical literature, one Western, one Indian: Plato's *Symposium* and *The Gospel of Sri Ramakrishna*.

The dinner party took place at the home of Shivas's friends, Peter and Agatha McNaughton. Murphy comments explicitly on the latter's shapely figure and the fact that she "wore a light brown woolen blouse that showed the contour of her breasts."[6] These sexual details set the scene, as this chapter, "Singing the Praises of Golf," is playfully but closely modeled after that ancient Greek banquet where Socrates and others make their speeches on the mythological, philosophical, and mystical natures of love or *eros*.

Agatha, for example, stands in for the original Agathon, while Shivas fills the role of Socrates. Exactly like Socrates in the *Symposium*, Shivas shows up late for dinner after becoming lost in a trance state outside. Murphy even has Shivas's golf disciple Evan Tyree show up late and wax eloquently about Shivas's teachings on self-control on the golf course, much as Alcibiades shows up late in the *Symposium* and speaks admirably of Socrates' sexual control and his refusal of Alcibiades' sexual advances. By replacing the original subject of love with that of golf and structuring the McNaughton party scene around the Platonic dialogue, Murphy has effectively eroticized both the game of golf and its "indecently alluring" mysteries. Agatha's blouse and breasts are indeed beautifully relevant here.

Also attending are an old eccentric psychiatrist and doctor named Julian Laing (who stands in for the original Eryximachus, with certain echoes perhaps of Esalen's own Julian Silverman), Adam Greene and his wife Eve (echoes of Genesis 2–3 are evident here), and Peter McNaughton's sixteen-year-old son, Kelly. Each takes a turn singing the praises of golf and exploring its many symbolic, psychological, historical, and occult dimensions.

But it is the sexual readings that sparkle the brightest in the early speeches, at least for awhile, until they are eclipsed by the more encompassing metaphysical theories of Adam and Shivas. Peter, for example, observes that he endures the same troubles with golf that he does in his relationship with lovely Agatha: "Like marriage it is, like marriage!"[7] Agatha seems to agree on the sexual component of the game, although she differs on the specific direction these classically male desires take. Toward the very end of the speeches, she speaks in her Scottish brogue about the homoerotic bonds that define the game, that is, "about golf and about the love men have for one another": "All those gentlemanly rools, why, they're the proper rools of affection—all the waitin and oohin' and ahin' o'er yer shots, all the talk o' this one's drive and that one's putt and the other one's gorgeous swing—what is it all but love? Men lovin' men, that's what golf is."[8]

Sexual dimensions are never fully replaced or denied in the narrative (and they are only strengthened by the Hindu Tantric connotations of a later chapter), but they are more or less eclipsed by the metaphysical theories that come to dominate the later speeches. This too, of course, is faithful to the doctrinal development of the *Symposium,* where the energies of *eros* are eventually revealed, especially in Diotima's teaching as reported by Socrates, to be a fundamental metaphysical force that, properly sublimated, provides the catalyst for the intellectual vision of Beauty and its ultimate bliss.

Agatha hints at such a Platonic vision, but it is Adam Greene and Shivas who come to elaborate it most fully. Adam's theories are the most eccentric, a hilarious (self-)parody on the pleasures and dangers of excessive metaphysics. As a kind of Scottish Aurobindonian, Adam alternately claims, for example, that "Golf is the new yoga of the supermind,"[9] and "Golf recapitulates evolution."[10] He even invokes the great Neoplatonic philosopher Plotinus in order to describe the parabolic path of the golf ball as "the flight of the alone to the alone" and intones the mystical phrase "hole-in-one," "as if it were the holy of holies."[11] But this is too much for Julian. He scolds Adam for comparing "the average gowfer wi' Plotinus": "It's a dim connection, Adam." "But it's so *real*," Mr. Greene snaps back.[12]

For his part, Shivas turns to the teachings of his master, Seamus Mac-Duff, as they are written in his unpublished Pythagorean manuscript, *The Logarithms of the Just*, "bein' first notes for a physics o' the spirit."[13] Thus Shivas introduces to the party his central doctrine, the mysterious subject of true gravity, "something as far as I could make out," Murphy had earlier noted on the golf course, "that involved an awareness of 'energy-dimensions' and the relations of things." Now Shivas spoke of true gravity and its relationship to "the subtle forces of the human soul."[14] More specifically, he spoke of the true gravity of fascination.

Julian had earlier claimed that most people are lost in a kind of mass public hypnosis, and that only a few remarkable individuals like Shivas and Seamus can see through the illusions by which the rest of us are deluded. Shivas does not counter this conviction, but he is not so quick to dismiss the powers of hypnosis and the human imagination: "But we must remember that hypnosis is first cousin to fascination . . . and all art and love depend on fascination." He then relates a theory of fascination that Seamus had taught him: "Accordin' to him, life is nothin' but a series of fascinations, an odyssey from world to world. . . . Fascination holds us there, makes us believe 'tis all-important. . . . fascination has a gravity of its own. It can draw upon the subtle forces, draw them round us li' a cloak, and create new worlds."

The imagination, in other words, can call on subtle energies and forces and, through them, grant human beings access to dimensions of the world that are otherwise closed off by the senses and the analytic mind. The imagination as fascination is an essentially mystical organ, for with it, "we can begin to look around and ken these many worlds, what they are and what they make us." It frees us from our socialized assumptions and "opens the doors to where we want to go." "In this," Shivas finally confesses, "I think we're like the great God, who lost Himself in this dark unconscious universe and wends His way back toward light and fullest knowin'.

Forgettin' and rememberin', losin' and findin' our original face—the great
God and all of us are in the game together. We're all o' us joined to the
growin' world, with God we're wakin' up."[15]

Tantric Golf

If Shivas and his fellow speechmakers were Platonic figures at the dinner
party, in the fifth and last full chapter the symbolic references shift to two
Indian figures, Ramakrishna and Aurobindo. The average reader would
certainly not expect as much. Nor, it turns out, did the author always realize
just how close he was. Murphy, for example, was not aware that the title
of this chapter, "We Are All Kites in That Wind," is strongly reminiscent
of a famous Tantric song that Ramakrishna liked to sing (it is very likely
that Murphy had earlier encountered the same song in *The Gospel of Sri
Ramakrishna,* which he read as a young man). In the original Bengali
context, the line referred to the kite competitions that Bengali children
love to play, pitting their little paper kites against one another in the
wind as they try to cut each other's lines with their own. The Tantric poet
had taken the game and used it as a metaphor to express the manner
in which all human souls are like little kites in the wind of suffering
existence, and how the Goddess chooses, for her own mysterious reasons,
to cut the strings of only a few and so release them into the *moksha* of
freedom and spiritual liberation. Here in Murphy's novel, of course, the
meanings have all shifted, and the original Tantric line refers now to the
"true gravity" of Shivas and Seamus, that energetic emptiness in which
we all float and whose mysterious powers the golfer can tap into with the
proper imaginative techniques and teachings.[16]

Such initial symbolic connections between Shivas's golf game and
Tantrism are speculative at best and need not be read into the novel. But
the Tantric echoes of the later scenes are everywhere for the knowing,
resonating subtly with the erotic harmonies of the earlier dinner. It is as
if Plato's *eros* meets Ramakrishna's *shakti* here within the same infinite
void of Seamus's true gravity.

After the party, Murphy and Shivas venture down into a ravine off
the thirteenth fairway looking for Seamus. Around 2:00 or 3:00 in the
morning, Murphy realizes that Seamus is not going to show up. So the
two of them make their way back to Shivas's apartment. Shivas then
relaxes in his "meditation chair" as Murphy eyes a banner tacked to the

wall listing philosophers and inventions under the heading "DANGEROUS CONNECTIONS." He tiptoes over to the library when he thinks Shivas is asleep. Thomas Carlyle, Coleridge, Max Müller's *Sacred Books of the East*, the *Enneads* of Plotinus, the Koran, and *The Gospel of Sri Ramakrishna*: "it was almost the library I would like to have."[17] He then picks up a volume that was particularly familiar to him, *The Gospel of Sri Ramakrishna*, and notices something strange about the sleeping Shivas:

> I read a page or two of Ramakrishna's sayings, marvelous passages I had read before, and looked at the pictures [which include a famous photo of Ramakrishna in *samadhi* or ecstatic absorption]. I reached down for the tea and looked at Shivas again; he was still sitting erect as he stared across the room. He was absolutely motionless. I cleared my throat to catch his attention but he did not respond. There was something odd about his posture; I could feel it, something had happened. I stood up and tiptoed around in front of him—and suddenly felt faint. His eyeballs were rolled back leaving nothing but white. He was totally unconscious.[18]

Murphy fears an epileptic seizure, a heart attack, or a stroke and calls the emergency number: 999. As he is fumbling around with the operator, however, Shivas awakes: "At that moment I could have sworn I saw an aura around him. For a moment he was sitting in a pool of turquoise light—just for a second—then I could feel some quick shutter close in my brain." "I almost disappeared," Shivas said softly. "Almost disappeared." Then he stared into Murphy's eyes and uttered the Tantric saying of the chapter title: "'Do ye' na' ken ye're flyin' heer like a kite—wi nae mair than a threid holdin' ye? . . . We're all kites in that wind,' he said. And off he went into trance again." Another half hour or so would pass as Murphy moved through various conflicting emotional states—fear, anger, wonder. He then makes explicit the scene's connection to the Hindu text he had been reading: "In the Ramakrishna book there is a picture of the saint's disciples staring up at him with bulging eyes as he stands in ecstatic trance. I must have looked like that as I watched the incredible corpse in front of me."[19] He also wonders whether or not *he* could brave these same strange states. Was this not, after all, the reason he was traveling to India?

Synchronicities, both unconscious and conscious, crystallize in this same chapter. We are told, for example, that the eighteenth green of Burningbush Links was built on the remains of a graveyard, and that such an ending might signal the great round of birth and death that is the course of a life.[20] Years after he had written the novel, Murphy learned, to his great astonishment, that the eighteenth hole of St. Andrews is actually built on a graveyard, exactly as he had imagined the eighteenth hole of Burningbush (so too, by the way, is Esalen).

And then there is Shivas's name: Shiva(s). In an opening essay, Murphy denies that the name has any historical or proper etymological connection to the Hindu God Shiva, a fact which disappoints him. But he also wisely (and no doubt suggestively) tells us that "direct etymologies are not the only sign of inner connection."[21] Indeed they are not, and so when Murphy goes on to describe the ecstatic Shivas as a corpse, it is worth knowing that in Tantric art Shiva is routinely represented lying prone beneath the Goddess Kali and is similarly described as a *shava,* that is, as a corpse.

If such a Tantric reading seems stretched, consider that Shivas himself appears to enjoy a word-play on Shivas/Shiva; that Shivas had earlier stated at the party that he wanted to play golf in Tibet; that Murphy notes that some of Shivas's exercises reminded him of "Tantric disciplines which used the natural impulses as pathways to enlightenment"; and that when Murphy is allowed into Shivas's secret library, he synchronistically opens a book and immediately, as if guided by some unknown *daimon* or genius, his eyes fall upon what turns out to be a classic Tantric saying on the lifeless, corpselike nature of Shiva without his divine lover, Shakti: "*Shiva* without *Shakti* is *Shava,*" that is, "God without the Goddess is a corpse."[22]

But it is not all Ramakrishna here. There is also a fair bit of Aurobindo. Murphy thus notes the titles of some of the long brown scrolls on the wall: "DANGEROUS CONNECTIONS," "GOD IS WAKING UP," and "HISTORY OF THE BODY." The first title could describe the comparative vision of Shivas (and Murphy), the logic of synchronicity, or the ancient magical principle of like affecting like. The second title is an Aurobindonian reference. And the third is perhaps an early version of what will become (twenty years later) Murphy's magnum opus, *The Future of the Body* (1992). The "real-life Murphy," in other words, has put his own metaphysical project up on Shivas's apartment wall.

As the morning advances, Murphy realizes that Shivas is looking for a biographer who can effectively link him to the outside world, a translator of sorts. For the meantime, Murphy will let him down badly. As the day advances and his afternoon schedule looms, he decides to honor that schedule and departs for London on his way to Pondicherry through Paris.

In the Zone: The Esalen Sports Center (1973–1975)

Shortly after *Golf in the Kingdom* appeared, Murphy was flooded with fan letters, many from individuals who had undergone psychical events on the golf course or in some other athletic context more or less just as Murphy had described them in his "fictional" book. Murphy remembers how about fifty such reports were coming in each week by the end of 1972. One of them, paraphrased in the fall Esalen catalog of 1974, was from a skydiver who wrote Murphy how "the book reminded her of a time she rode a thermal up-wind on her parachute for over an hour while a company of dazzling figures danced around her—figures with human shapes made of nothing more substantial than light." The same issue also quoted John Brodie, the star NFL quarterback for the San Francisco '49ers: "Often in the heat of excitement of a game, a player's perception and coordination will improve dramatically. At times, and with increasing frequency now, I experience a kind of clarity that I've never seen adequately described in a football story. Sometimes, for example, time seems to slow way down, in an uncanny way, as if everyone were moving in slow motion. It's beautiful."[23] Brodie had recognized something of both that clarity and that alteration of space-time in *Golf in the Kingdom.*

There is a funny story here. Robert Ornstein, the psychologist who would become well known for his work on the bilateral or right-left functioning of the human brain, asked Murphy to give golf lessons to an acquaintance of his. When Murphy showed up at Ornstein's house in Palo Alto, Ornstein and Dulce Murphy, Michael's new wife, were hiding in the bushes, waiting mischievously for John Brodie, the man who needed the golf lessons. Murphy, who had followed Brodie's career since his All-American days at Stanford, was ecstatic when the football star appeared. Indeed, there is some light-hearted debate about whether or not Murphy actually got down on one knee when he saw Brodie. Knee or no knee, Brodie expressed real appreciation for *Golf in the Kingdom,* and invited Murphy to the '49ers training camp.[24]

When he got to the '49ers camp, Murphy was stunned to learn that the synchronicities and altered states that he had written about in *Golf in the Kingdom* were the Sunday stuff of professional football players as well. As more and more fan mail poured in, moreover, it began to dawn on him that out-of-body experiences, altered perceptions of space and time, extraordinary elevations of physical and psychical energy, even precognitive dreams and telekinetic-like phenomena appear throughout the amateur and professional sports worlds with a remarkable consistency:

"talent," "luck," and "psychical powers" all seemed to be more or less inter-changeable in this arena. This anyway was what his correspondents were telling him in no uncertain terms.

And he believed them. Murphy began to collect a personal archive of this spontaneous material and with the parapsychologist Rhea White, who had been filling the spaces of her own house with an immense library of psychical material and technical studies, published *The Psychic Side of Sports* in 1978, which was later retitled *In the Zone: Transcendent Experience in Sports.*

In the Zone draws on over 6,500 sources (its bibliography of published sources alone runs to over 1,500 titles) and spans dozens of sports, from mountain climbing and skydiving to baseball and basketball. It makes the provocative case that there is a kind of spiritual underground in the sports world, and that the psychodynamics of athletics (extreme disci-pline, physical suffering, risk-taking, scripted trauma) bear some rather striking resemblances to the earlier cultural patterns of shamanism and mysticism. As Murphy put it in another context, "there are deep structural similarities between these two worlds of experience, yogic and athletic."[25] More particularly, the authors concluded that the high-risk or "extreme" sports are especially capable here (no doubt for their ability to induce or mimic trauma states), but that even low-risk games (such as tennis and golf) can become veritable "theaters of the occult."[26]

Murphy and White were not quite arguing that athletes are mystics, much less saints or shamans. They were arguing, however, that sport is an arena with a particular genius for shifting consciousness and energy and spontaneously inducing states that are well known in the history of religions. By making such a case, they were doing what Murphy had done earlier in *Golf in the Kingdom,* that is, they were engaging in a grand act of comparison that explicitly connected a supposedly "secular" pursuit with a traditionally "sacred" one. They were reuniting the world again. They were also often returning to an explicitly Asian model, in this case an East Asian one, where "athletics" and "mysticism" have long been fused within the martial arts traditions.

The language of nonordinary energies structures much of the book, and this from the very opening pages. White, for example, dedicates the volume to "the Energy that moves us all," and Murphy begins by point-ing out that William James published *The Energies of Man* alongside his more well-known *The Varieties of Religious Experience* (the polarity of energy and consciousness again). There are also elaborate descriptions, based on first-hand athletic testimonies, of any number of altered energy

or "flow states." Drawing on Asian contemplative and martial arts traditions, and especially Japanese aikido, the authors create a typology that
locates athletics along a hierarchy of energy-realizations: "The first stage,
which is the one most relevant to current athletics, involves individual coordination and centralization of *ki*. In the second stage, the influence of *ki*
extends beyond the individual and touches others. The final stage—rarely
tapped—puts the athlete in touch with the center of life itself."[27]

The invocation of the Japanese term for energy or *ki* was hardly
accidental. Behind this term stood Murphy's best friend George Leonard,
who by this time had become a fifth-degree black belt in aikido under
Robert Nadeau. Actually, four years before the Murphy and White volume,
Leonard had published his own book on the mystical dimensions of sport,
The Ultimate Athlete, based largely on his aikido training with Nadeau.
By this time, he was also already teaching his own form of nonordinary
energy, Leonard Energy Training (or LET), both at Esalen and in the Bay
area. In 1974, with foreshadowings of *The Silent Pulse* (which would not
appear until 1978, the same year as *The Psychic Side of Sports*), Leonard
set out one version of the theory in *The Ultimate Athlete* this way: "The
human individual is viewed as an *energy being,* a center of vibrancy,
emanating waves that radiate out through space and time, waves that
respond to and interact with myriad other waves. The physical body is
seen as one manifestation of the total being, coexisting with the Energy
Body. . . . In some mysterious way that we can't yet fully understand, the
Energy Body also seems to transcend space and time, connecting each
human consciousness to all of existence."[28] Murphy and White quoted
the same passage to explain how the fundamental unity of mind and
body, consciousness and energy, might be revealed in the altered states
of sport. Shivas and Seamus were back, but now they were doing more
than playing golf. They were jumping out of airplanes, climbing mountain
faces, and playing professional football.

Behind all of these textual events—from *Golf in the Kingdom* to
The Ultimate Athlete and *In the Zone*—sat yet another Esalen experiment (after the Confluent Education Program and alongside the Program
in Humanistic Medicine), that is, the Esalen Sports Center, which was
hatched out of Esalen's San Francisco Center. Its historical roots, however,
stretched in many directions. One of these led back to Charlie Tart, the
parapsychologist who first suggested to Murphy that they meet Robert
Nadeau. (On a humorous and synchronistic side-note, Tart once told me
the story of how a golf ball bounced into his living room as he pondered
how he could write a review of *Golf in the Kingdom;* he, after all, never

golfed.)[29] Murphy agreed to Tart's suggestion and convinced Leonard to join them. Nadeau became a regular teacher at the San Francisco Center. While Murphy remembers practicing on the mat for about one year (George insists Mike is exaggerating here), Leonard would practice for life and would eventually become an aikido master himself and one of the sports most well-known authors. The Sports Center was kicked off in 1973 with a major two-day sports symposium in San Bruno, California.

The symposium was a huge hit. David Meggyesy, a former NFL linebacker for the St. Louis Cardinals and cultural critic of the sport, was there as the new codirector of the Sports Center, along with fellow codirector Bob Kriegel. Meggyesy's commitments to the subject were more than administrative. Indeed, he claimed that while he was playing professional football he could sometimes see auras around other players and could anticipate the moves of his opponents in a kind of "precognitive playing trance."[30] Other professional athletes, coaches, and Esalen personalities mixed on the marquis: John Brodie, Will Schutz, Stanley Keleman, George Leonard, and Al Huang were all listed. All in all, four hundred teachers, coaches, athletes, and fans showed up. The press was extremely positive. The *New York Times* went so far as to identify the event as a possible turning-point in American sports history, akin to the central event of the French Revolution: "Such is the clout generated by Esalen," William Wallace wrote, "that the occasion may be to a change in sports what the storming of the Bastille was to the French Revolution."[31]

Alongside these official public events, the Sports Center also worked through a kind of inner esoteric circle, that is, a loosely knit group of friends and students who formed around Murphy and a specific training-meditation routine. In 1973, at the age of forty-three, Murphy had turned to running as his principal athletic yoga (by 1983, he would place third in the 1500 meter race for fifty-year-olds at the Masters National Championship at Rice University in Houston). The same discipline quickly also became a way of gathering students around him. Mike Spino, whom Murphy describes affectionately as "the great wild man," coached and trained them.[32] Among these runners were a number of individuals who would soon become central players in Esalen's history: Jim Hickman, Mary Payne, Keith Thompson, Steve Donovan, Ed Ferry, Bruce Nelson, and Dulce Murphy. A typical training day up in Sonoma Country saw some version of this group engaged in a full-day ritual of meditation, walking meditation, jogging, Feldenkreis exercises, swimming, and sharing the lore of running with Coach Spino. At the end of the day, they would enjoy dinner, beer, wine, and philosophy together. By 1977, the Esalen catalog referred to this group as the Esalen Athletic Club and advertised a two-month long, nonresidential program in San Francisco. The cost was $200.[33]

Despite such public success and private discipline, the Esalen Sports Center was ending by mid-decade, along with the San Francisco Center itself, which was at this time directed by Dulce Murphy. By the end of 1976, the San Francisco Center would close.[34] There were two basic reasons for this. First, the center had essentially put itself out of business by spawning an explosion of similar courses in the extension programs, churches, and colleges: it simply was no longer the cutting edge. Secondly, Dick Price and Andy Gagarin, Esalen's financial officer, felt the San Francisco operations were excessive and were draining Esalen of precious resources. The cultural gravity of the place would now return to Big Sur. Murphy was upset by the decision to shut down the San Francisco Center, but he finally accepted the inevitable. A year later, in 1976, much of the Sports Center running club would morph into the Transformation Project, to which we will return soon enough.

Criticisms from the Right and Left: Sam Keen and the Spiritual Tyranny Conference (1973)

It was in the late 1960s and early '70s that Esalen began attracting some rather severe critiques from both the right and left. We have already seen the Nixon administration's attempt to bring the institute down by falsely linking Esalen and the Manson murders. This was an old take on Big Sur, going back at least as far as Mildred Brady's 1947 rant in *Harper's* against "sex and anarchy" and her attempt, a year later, to bring Wilhelm Reich to justice in the *New Republic*.

It would not be long before the political left tried its own hand at Esalen's demise, if in some decidedly more civil and thoughtful means. *Harper's* would again play a central role. Ironically, one of the more important and vocal forces of objection came out of an Esalen symposium that tried to address the very issues many liberal thinkers were rightly concerned about: spiritual authoritarianism.

When Dick Price returned disillusioned from his Arica training with Oscar Ichazo, he was convinced even more of the authoritarian dangers of charismatic teachers. Murphy shared these concerns from his experiences in the Aurobindo ashram. In December of 1973, Esalen hosted a conference in the city to explore the issue—Spiritual and Therapeutic Tyranny: The Willingness to Submit. Though it was a particularly contentious and angry gathering, it further established Esalen's willingness to take on the problem of religious authority, even the authority of the teachers it invited to attend.

The confrontations, it turned out, began before anyone actually arrived. Despite the fact that the conference had been organized by a committee of mostly women, there were no women on any of the panels. This infuriated the female contingent of the Esalen San Francisco community, who proceeded to picket the event.[35] It was not an auspicious beginning.

There were other obvious gaps. Chogyam Trungpa, a Tibetan Tantric teacher considered "a foremost exponent of the 'crazy wisdom'" (code for radical and often abusive teaching techniques), neglected to show up. Most of the other invitees did show, however, including Werner Erhard of EST, Will Schutz, and Jerry Rubin of the Berkeley Free Speech movement and future son-in-law of George Leonard. But the highlight was Sam Keen, a young Harvard-trained theologian and friend of Michael Murphy who enacted a dramatic assault on the whole psychology of spiritual submission through his keynote address, "The Tyranny Game, or, How to Play Follow the Leader." Sam Keen was not about to follow or submit to anyone.

Keen was a gifted and well-known writer by this time. He had been long mentored—"brooded over," as he put it in a dedication—by Howard Thurman, the African-American theologian and mystical writer.[36] Keen's autobiography, *To a Dancing God,* had chronicled his spiritual recovery from southern fundamentalism, his theological training at Harvard Divinity School, and the birth of a new kind of mythopoetic theology that could find beauty and truth in world mythology, including and especially in the Greek figure of Dionysus, that dancing god. It was in this same book's depiction of Dionysus that Claudio Naranjo first recognized what he was trying to say with his Apollonian/Dionysian reading of Esalen's culture in the 1960s. Keen's relationship to Esalen, however, hardly ended there. By 1973, he was already quite close to both Michael Murphy and Joseph Campbell, and he had interviewed most of the major players of the alternative religion scene, including Norman O. Brown, Herbert Marcuse, John Lilly, Carlos Castaneda, and Oscar Ichazo.[37] When he stepped up to the podium to speak of "the tyranny game," then, he knew well of what he was speaking, and to whom he was speaking.

Keen, it turns out, had long been critical of what was then called Eastern religion, which he frankly suspected of "a retreat from history." "I have observed," Keen wrote in *Voices and Visions,* "that people who get heavily committed to meditation often lose both their outrage and their compassion. Peace of mind can be gained by withdrawal from the world.... But how much inner peace is appropriate in a world that contains Attica, Vietnam, Johannesburg, Biafra, Pakistan, and sub-Sahara Africa?"[38] What we need, Keen concluded, is a kind of Janus-face, that is, a double vision that can look both "in" via meditation and mysticism and "out" via social consciousness and radical criticism. In the "anti-tyranny kit" of his plenary, he invoked a classical Tantric phrase to capture the same double truth: "*I believe in permanent imperfection....* Samsara is nirvana."

This was a crucial point. And a hard lesson. The human potential movement, through figures like Keen, was beginning to realize by the early 1970s that the mystical is not the ethical, that spiritual authority is often more or less identical to moral tyranny, and that the Asian systems, embedded as they are in ancient hierarchical and highly authoritarian social systems, can only deliver so much to a modern liberal democracy.

The Esalen symposium on spiritual tyranny enacted many of these same critiques. Oddly, however, the most enduring result of the symposium was a highly influential attack on the whole Esalen scene that effectively branded it as "narcissistic." This was Peter Marin's *Harper's* essay, "The New Narcissism." As Anderson notes, from Marin, future liberal critics, from Alan Wolfe to Christopher Lasch, would pick up on this label of "narcissism" and run with it, often to great effect.[39]

These critics had a point, even if it was also a somewhat myopic one. They all seemed to lack what Keen had in spades, that is, a double vision that could appreciate both meditation and Marxism. Their vision was singular. Marin's basic point was that to claim, as many in fact were claiming, that we are all responsible for our fates—that the poor are poor because they somehow wished to be, that the Jews must have wanted (or worst, deserved) to be burned by the Nazis, and so on—is a reprehensible moral error rooted in a kind of gross solipsism of the self. It is the community, not the self, that was fundamental for Marin. He was thus particularly disgusted with any high-minded notions that "smother the tug of conscience" and hide gross social injustice beyond "the assurance that it all accords with cosmic law." Such ideas, he pointed out, effectively hide the social structures of socioeconomic inequality that are the real roots of evil and human suffering. People are not poor because of their *karma*, because they somehow deserve to be. They are poor because global capitalism (or the caste system) needs their labor and their poverty to make other people rich and comfortable. Period.

It is difficult to argue with any of this. I won't anyway. Indeed, I have spent much of my career being pilloried by hysterical religious voices for pointing out the relationship between sexual abuse and mystical states, and I have argued extensively, to largely deaf audiences, about how the mystical is not the ethical and never can be. No, Sam Keen and Peter Marin were dead-on.

What is more difficult to see, however, is how Marin and his editors could so easily implicate Esalen in all of this moral blindness. Had the institute not just held a public symposium to highlight and confront these very problems? Granted, the condemnation of Esalen was carried mostly by the pictures. The images published alongside the text—of an Esalen group hug, of Werner Erhard and EST, of an Arica meeting, of Ron L. Hubbard and Scientology, of Reverend Sun Myung Moon, of the Hare Krishnas, and of the Esalen Institute (in that order)—quietly and cleverly left the reader with the impression that the Esalen Institute was the "frame," the beginning and the end, in which all of these authoritarian movements found their justification and meaning. At the very least, the article implied that going to Esalen was more or else equivalent to becoming a Scientologist or submitting to Werner Erhard, Oscar Ichazo, or Krishna.

At best, this is difficult to see; at worst, it borders on pure nonsense. In historical fact, Esalen functioned in the 1960s and '70s as a kind of "guru detox center" for countless souls abused and manipulated by a whole stream of charismatic teachers and totalizing systems. At Esalen, no one captured the flag.

The same message, of course, could have been easily heard in Sam Keen's plenary address (which Marin completely ignored in his *Harper's* essay). "We enjoy the luxury of speaking openly about tyranny because we have so little of it," Keen began. "We are free to shout about repression because we are not repressed." He then went on to address the less violent but nonetheless real tyranny of teachers and gurus and the race, class, and gender dynamics of their "tyranny game": "Should we mention in passing that the leaders are usually male, privileged, articulate, more comely than average, up-tight, and are often more successful in public than private? No. Let's not mention that."

And then, of course, there was sex. Here Keen turned the lens on himself: "When I was thirteen with one wild hair I knew beyond a shadow of a doubt that Jesus would come gain and usher in the Millennium. I longed for the age beyond ambiguity. But I prayed that Jesus would wait until I lost my virginity. My prayers were answered and since that day it has been hard for me to believe in the second coming." Such honesty continued in the address with a Freudian meditation on how everyone wants a Master-Father-Guru-God, who, of course, never quite delivers what he promises. Religion, salvation, and perfect enlightenment are so many illusions that go back to the dependencies of childhood:

> So the search begins for a new Father.
> Let's pretend you are wise and strong
>> and I am your little child.
> But for most of us the game gets old.
> The best therapist turns out to have
> a clay heart.
> And Fritz was a nasty old man
> And Maharaji has ulcers
> And Freud couldn't give up cigars
> And Bill Schutz doesn't jump for joy
> And Ida needs rolfing
> And Tillich was a swinger
> And John Lilly has migraines in his tape loops.
> And the President was a criminal
> And Sam Keen can't dance
> And it is probable that
> Mike Murphy plays only average golf.... [40]

It is time, Keen believed, to say Goodbye to this "Big Daddy in the Sky." Few, of course, were ready to listen to such a tough Freudian message. And those who were ready—that is, the intellectual left—knew nothing about the deeper dynamics of Esalen's culture and preferred to tag it with the opposite message. It was in this way, Anderson wrote, that "the Spiritual Tyranny conference... brought into being the strongest indictment of the movement as a whole; it was like a mythic allegory in which the hero forges the weapon that is later used against him."[41]

Joseph Campbell would have understood that. So too did his student, Sam Keen.

Jacob Atabet and the Tantra of Physics

Science itself is in its own way an occultism...a vast system of physical magic....All insistence on the sole or the fundamental validity of the objective real takes its stand on the sense of the basic reality of Matter. But it is now evident that Matter is by no means fundamentally real; it is a structure of Energy; it is becoming even a little doubtful whether the acts and creations of this Energy itself are explicable except as the motions of power of a secret Mind or Consciousness of which its processes and steps of structure are the formulas.

SRI AUROBINDO, *The Life Divine*

Michael Murphy published his second occult novel in 1977, five years after *Golf in the Kingdom.* Although *Jacob Atabet* would never match the literary success of its predecessor, the book is in many ways a very similar production. Like the first, it focuses on the *siddhis* or supernormal powers of a mystically and athletically gifted teacher, in this case a metaphysical painter who also happens to be an extraordinary amateur marathon runner.

Jacob Atabet is a more philosophically developed text than *Golf in the Kingdom.* In his second novel, Murphy further theorizes his own occult experiences and begins to dream of a kind of magnum opus, a book to end all books on both the reality and evolutionary encoding of supernormal phenomena throughout human history. Consequently, there are at least two magical centers of *Jacob Atabet:* the morphing body of Jacob Atabet, and Darwin Fall's 1,723 page manuscript that keeps appearing in the story as a guide to Jacob and as the obsessive goal of all of Darwin's reading, meditative experiences, and discussions. A body and a book, then, or, if we like, two bodies, for as Darwin sees in a dream and notes in his secret diaries, even a book may be thought of as a kind of subtle body—the text again as *corpus mysticum*.[1]

What's in a Name?

Darwin Fall, the narrator, is working on an immense manuscript on the evolutionary relationships between mind and body. Jacob Atabet, a metaphysical painter living in North Beach, San Francisco, who has physically suffered through a series of three major mystical events in his life, is now turning to Darwin and his masterwork for help on how to best understand and so further his occult life. A cast of supporting characters round out this basic plot, including: Corinne Wilde, Jacob's supportive companion and spiritual lover (loosely based, I gather, on Dulce Murphy); Kazi Dama, a Tibetan lama and close friend of Jacob's who helps guide Jacob's unprecedented spiritual gifts with the meditative wisdom of the Vajrayana or Tibetan Tantric Buddhism; Casey Stills, chief editor at Greenwich Press, which Fall partly owns and through which he plans to publish his big book; and Armen Cross, a local writer who had once tried to write an essay on Jacob and now is a bitter skeptic.

Having once met a character named Shivas Irons in a story infused with Hindu meanings and suggestions, the reader is ready to see more than the accident of birth in the two central names Murphy has picked for this second novel, "Darwin Fall" and "Jacob Atabet." And so one does.

Sort of. As it turns out, we are told a good deal about the first name, and almost nothing about the second, except that it is Basque. Darwin, for example, tells us that he was named after Charles Darwin, the great evolutionary theorist, and that his great grandfather, Charles Fall, was a close friend of the elder Henry James (father of Henry, Jr., the novelist, and William, the Harvard psychologist and philosopher). Later we are told that Henry Sr. had arrived at a vision of cosmic involution and evolution that is eerily similar to that of Sri Aurobindo's *The Life Divine* (with the divine embodying itself as this universe and then progressively, spontaneously manifesting more and more of its latent divinity).[2]

Darwin Fall, in other words, is a condensation of three of Michael Murphy's heroes: Charles Darwin, William James, and Sri Aurobindo. On another level, what we have in the family history and name of "Darwin Fall" is a symbol suggesting the downward-arc of Darwin('s) Fall, (that is, Darwinian evolution as a reduction of humanity to the animal world), but also prefiguring the upward-arc of the evolutionary vision of Henry James Sr. and Sri Aurobindo. It is precisely this involution-evolution mysticism that Darwin Fall will discover is dramatically embodied in the physical transfigurations and suffering symptoms of Jacob Atabet.

The name "Jacob Atabet" is another secret cipher, but one not decoded for us in the novel. Murphy's mother, it turns out, was of French Basque descent (one of Murphy's fondest childhood memories is waking up to French crepes every morning), and at the time of the writing of the novel (in the mid-1970s) he was living in the North Beach district of San Francisco, which is populated with more than a few Basque hotels. In fact, the many descriptions of Jacob's roof apartment and view of the city and Bay are based on Murphy's own North Beach apartment during this period of his life.

With the character of Jacob Atabet, Murphy intended to create an American figure analogous to the Indian one of Ramakrishna, whom he here sought to translate into an athletic frame and toward an alchemical bodily transformation (a perfect "fictional" example of my thesis about how the epicenter of the West's encounter with India and the Tantra shifts from Calcutta in the nineteenth century to San Francisco in the twentieth). This literary translation of Ramakrishna into Jacob Atabet, however, is not some simple mimicry or faithful reproduction. It is also a kind of "correction" or "evolutionary advance." Hence Jacob himself confesses in the novel to a recurring dream in which he sees the flaws of three famous Indian saints (Aurobindo, Ramana Maharshi, and Ramakrishna) humorously exaggerated, "as if my unconscious had decided to dramatize the fact that they weren't perfect."[3]

The surname "Atabet" is an Anglicized version of Murphy's maternal grandmother's maiden name. His great uncle, Jacques Atabet, suffered from a kind of manic mood disorder, not unlike Dick Price. Jacques and Dick, then, are also somehow woven into the figure of Jacob Atabet. As is the biblical patriarch Jacob, who wrestled with the angel and saw a ladder connecting heaven and earth—an appropriate biblical analogue to what Jacob and Darwin try to do in the novel, that is, unite the two worlds of being and becoming, spirit and evolution.

After the novel appeared and in one of those moments of synchronicity that have punctured Murphy's writing life, Angeles Arrien, an Esalen regular of Basque descent, shared with Murphy her own mystical etymology of the name. Arrien claimed that *ata* can mean "cosmic or personal soul" and *bet* "body" or "small point." In other words, the name encoded a kind of Basque shamanism of which he was previously unaware and one, more strangely still, that seems to encode the paranormal focus of the novel itself, that is, the soul's *animan siddhi,* or "superpower [to see things or become] very small."

The Story

The story itself begins in a Catholic church. Darwin is attending mass at Sts. Peter and Paul in the North Beach district, when he begins to recall a dream he had had about something significant happening to him at 12:30 p.m. He looks at his watch. It's 12:29: "I glanced around me. In the dream the place had looked like this, now I could remember. A light had erupted from the chalice and a figure hurtled toward the sun. Then the light from the chalice had cut through me like a sword." A cold sweat breaks out on his body. "There was an explosion of light on the sanctuary steps and the priest fell back on the floor. The communicants at the front stood transfixed, while a man knelt alone in front of the over-turned priest. I started back. A light from the kneeling man's body broke into a rainbow of color, and for an instant it flooded the church."[4]

Darwin questions various onlookers. The priest, Father Zimbardo, refuses to talk to him, and everyone else seems to be rationalizing what they actually saw. Frustrated and still somewhat dazed, Darwin stumbles out of the church and lies down on the grass in the park across the street. So begins his own visionary experiences:

> There was a tunnel to another world now, at the axis of a turning wheel. My body turned slowly above me. I looked up at the church for support. But the church was turning too, and slowly undulating.... Then there were forms in the air—seahorses bobbing, jelly-fish a foot from my nose, and strands of human cells around them. For weeks they had flickered at the edges of awareness like this and it had taken all my strength to suppress them. "What holds them?" asked a tiny voice. "What is the membrane you see through?"[5]

Somehow the man in the church had transmitted his vision of things to Darwin in the exploding rainbow, and what Darwin now saw in his own altered state he later sees on the same man's canvasses. After learning Atabet's name and general whereabouts, Darwin finally tracks Jacob down and meets him in his apartment studio. There he ponders bizarre paintings that both upset and fascinate him as somehow familiar: "The canvas was a pageant of sealife—of octopi, fish, and seaweed intertwined with one another. And in the midst of these were human organs. Hearts, livers and lungs were wrapped in the arms of a squid."[6]

The story develops from there, with Darwin's relationship with Jacob deepening through extensive metaphysical discussions and various adventures, such as a dangerous swim into the Bay, a marathon, and some very raucous scenes with the San Francisco '49ers, all based closely on events in Murphy's own life. George Leonard, for example, appears briefly in the novel in a bar near the stadium, standing on a chair and shouting, *"The Super Bowl is the Supermind!"* The same Aurobindonian cheer would later appear in real life as a sign heralding Murphy's Super Bowl party of 1982, when the '49ers finally made it to the big game.

Darwin, moreover, begins to experience his own physical transfigurations, particularly through his dreams. One night he dreams of being dismembered by a giant black bird: "I lay trembling on the bed, released into wide open spaces. The walls of the room might serve as my body, or I might stretch to the edge of the Bay. This freedom had been trying to happen for as long as I could remember. I knew my body would not be the same. The waves of pleasure passing through it told me that."[7] On the next page, he finds a passage in his own manuscript that speaks directly to the night vision, a passage on Siberian shamanism and the motif of dismemberment: "I shook my head with wonder as I read it."[8] These synchronistic moments between life and text, between corpus as body and corpus as text, in fact define much of the narrative and form the very basis for Jacob and Darwin's relationship. Darwin's manuscript has become a kind of road map or synchronistic guide for Jacob's mysterious transformations. Reading and writing have become, once again, transformative practices.

But there are surprises on the way, particularly at the very end of the narrative, when Jacob is attempting something he calls "the Descent to the First Day." This is the culmination of the *animan siddhi,* Darwin's Sanskrit term for Jacob's psychic ability to peer into his own physical body, its cellular structure, even the blinding spins and jumps of its quantum processes. As Jacob imagines a return to the First Day of creation, Darwin invokes Freud to make some sense of it (and unknowingly recreates a classical Tantric creation myth in the process). Such a feat, he speculates, would be equivalent to remembering the great cosmic orgasm, the ultimate Primal Scene, and "our first and ultimate trauma," the Big Bang itself. Here he dreams of a kind of mystical psychoanalysis aimed at "making the unconscious conscious right down to the original Quantum." If we could only remember that, Darwin notes, we could "win a new freedom and mastery in this form of spirit we call matter."[9] Such a thing is possible at all, moreover, because "all time is remembered in the body." The claim might sound immediately outrageous, but it is only "an extension of the idea that ontogeny recapitulates phylogeny—but down to the level of molecules, atoms and fundamental physical forces."[10]

In short, Jacob thinks that "we can enter the place where matter is rising from mind," and that, moreover, we can achieve such a level while still in the body. "There's an ocean of fire down there," admittedly, but the risks are worth taking since the possible transfigurations promise so much: "With this deeper access to the secrets of matter, it is possible we can assume the powers it holds—powers conceivably that will change our relationship to some of the world's basic laws."[11] Jacob is on his way to just such a Descent to the First Day. He has already known the reality of Brahman (in 1947), had his first glimpse into the *animan siddhi* (in 1962), and experienced something called "cellular *samadhi*" reading Darwin's manuscript (these three moments sound like a fictional elaboration of Murphy's own mystical life). He is now ready for the ultimate descent into the body and its primeval memories. Were not these very atoms once born in the ancient cosmos? Then why not remember with, in, and *as* them?

Everything comes to a dramatic climax on November 20, 1971. As Jacob attempts his descent, he appears to Darwin's vision as a vertical bar of silver light that soon rotates ninety degrees until it is hovering horizontally and expands into a vista of ravishing beauty and light. And then it is all over. Nausea overtakes Darwin, as Jacob just seems to sit there like a corpse, very much like Ramakrishna in *samadhi,* we are told (and here we are reminded immediately of Shivas Irons's own corpse-like position). But Jacob, like Shivas, is not really dead. He whispers to Darwin: "You have seen what the world might look like."

Later that same day, even while away from Jacob, Darwin gets drunk on more symbolic visions, as if he were somehow participating in Jacob's own secret experiment. Then about 7:00 p.m. Corinne calls to inform Darwin that the Descent has ended, and this with a rather surprising twist: "Jacob said his voyage to the First Day had turned into a vision of the planet's possible future!" The circle of involution and evolution has been completed. The Descent to the First Day has morphed into a vision of the Future Day: beginning and end are now connected within a kind of eternal circle joined by the arcing evolution of time. Accordingly, a certain radical wisdom sets in upon Darwin. He realizes that he no longer needs to try so hard, for everything is *already* perfect, already realized: "A whole level of striving has dropped away, for I know more deeply than before that the world is completed."[12]

Darwin's Theory

Such a story is, obviously, fantastic, but it bears a quite serious purpose, that is, Murphy's own developing theory about evolution, psychical research, and the occult future of the human body. In 1992, these will be presented in analytic form as *The Future of the Body*. Here in 1977, they appear in the more confessional form of Darwin Fall's secret diaries.

Stated most succinctly, Darwin's theory is that full enlightenment involves the transfiguration of the body as well as the transcendence of the spirit, and that the religious traditions have generally missed this integral goal. In one passage, for example, he writes how the religions seem depressingly stuck on their knees or in the lotus posture; he wonders out loud what happened to the legs and arms of the mystical life. Ida Rolf had made the same criticism of the lotus posture: it effectively cuts the line of the human form off at the waist.

Darwin also insists that the scientific theory of evolution is our best framework for understanding and furthering this embodiment. Evolution, in other words, is the key, the magical philosopher's stone that puts together all the previously random pieces and parts of the history of religions. If this evolutionary gnosis could be joined to an adequate transformative practice, who knows what might happen? The fall Esalen catalog of 1979 at least suggests that, "a coming stage of human evolution may involve purposeful bodily transformation through an integration of spiritual and physical disciplines."[13] This is clearly Murphy speaking.

And Darwin Fall:

> to put it briefly—I think there's an immense frontier hidden in these things. A frontier that's hardly been explored. The kind of things that happened to Bernardine Neri—the stigmata and luminosity, "her marks of the risen Christ"—point toward it. I've collected thousands of examples like hers, from the contemplative literature, psychiatric histories, sport, hypnosis, spiritual healing and other places, to show that there are possibilities in us for an evolutionary transformation, if you will. . . . By collecting these examples I want to show how widespread the phenomenon is and discover something about its essential dynamics.

Darwin's project, in other words, is one of the comparative imagination, here guided by his study of the history of religions and empowered by his own and Jacob's altered states.

Darwin's project is also very much a religion of no religion. How could it be otherwise? The religions, after all, have seriously missed the mark: "The Scriptures don't tell us everything. The more research I do the more I'm convinced that the contemplative traditions have misperceived part of the process, especially in regard to the body."[14] Certainly what were once rejected as distractions (the *siddhis*) now need to be integrated as jewels in the crown of illumination. "In the religious traditions, the goal of life was generally conceived in terms of release rather than embodiment," Darwin goes on in Hindu (and soon Christian) terms:

> "*Moksha* before *siddhi*, liberation before powers. Things like Bernardine Neri's physical light were seen as distractions from the path into God. Part of what I'm doing is simply to show what a frontier there is in the *simultaneous* transformation of consciousness and the body, what an adventure there is in embodied existence."
>
> "So you don't see the body as an impediment to realization?" He stood and went to the window. "Is that what you're saying?"
>
> "I'm saying more than that. I'm saying that the body is *meant to manifest the glories*."[15]

Jacob's Tantra

There are many ways to approach a text like *Jacob Atabet*. According to Murphy, for example, the metaphysical painter Alex Grey has embraced the book as a manifesto of the intimate links between creativity and mystical experience. Appropriately, one of Grey's paintings, of the subtle energies and inner-body of an athlete, appears on the cover of a recent edition of *In the Zone*. Indeed, the novel is very much about the altered states of artistic, literary, and religious creativity. Jacob, after all, is a painter who believes that the process of painting helped catalyze his physical transfiguration. He communicates his ideas through his art and visionary experiences, themselves a kind of psychical painting. So strong is this link between the mystical and the artistic that at one point Darwin sees a blue sheet of fire pass from Jacob's hand directly into one of his paintings. No wonder, then, that some of his paintings are even said to move and come alive when one looks at them: like mystical texts, they somehow have the power to activate in the viewer states analogous to those that originally produced them.[16] They are alive. They *transmit*.

The transformative practice of the golf game has been replaced by the transfiguring art of painting. In both cases, however, the vision communicated is fundamentally a Tantric one. In *Golf in the Kingdom,* this Tantra was implicit in the figure of Shivas-as-Ramakrishna. Here in *Jacob Atabet,* this Tantra is implicit again in the figure of Jacob-as-Ramakrishna. The same Tantric subtext is announced when Murphy introduces Jacob in his introduction as an example of the *dehasiddhas* of the yogic tradition, "a master of bodily transformation who was achieving an unprecedented conquest of matter."[17] The *dehasiddha* (he whose body is perfected) is a figure of Indian Tantric lore who is believed to have perfected the arts of alchemy and so achieved some type of physical immortality. On this same page, Murphy announces the central Tantric doctrine: salvation is a matter of full embodiment and not just spiritual transcendence.[18] Later, Darwin will suggest that the scriptures will offer up new meanings when they are read again "from the incarnational point of view," and he will openly criticize the ascetic impulse of the religions as "a seduction from our larger possibilities."[19] Hence Darwin can write of Jacob in his diary entry of August 14, 1970: "Agrees with me completely that Being and Becoming, nirvana and evolution, are compatible truths."[20]

I have already commented on how the development and use of the *siddhis* or superpowers are central to the Asian Tantric cultures. It is no accident, then, that the central topic of *Jacob Atabet* is such a *siddhi* (morphed here through Western science), the *animan siddhi* of being able to see down into the cellular, molecular, and even subatomic levels of the human body. This focus on the Tantric superpowers was inspired partly by a long list of Sanskrit terms for such *siddhis* Haridas Chaudhuri had sent Murphy in 1975. Murphy was working on *Jacob Atabet* at this time and had asked Chaudhuri for some help with the Sanskrit and Bengali lore. As if to seal its symbolic importance, Chaudhuri died on the very day Murphy received the letter-list in the mail.

"Yogic Potentials and Capacities, or *siddhis,* in Hindu-Buddhist Psychology" is a fascinating document whose synthesis of humanistic psychology, psychical research, quantum physics, and Bengali Tantric lore both looks back to earlier Esalen figures and prefigures much that will come later at Esalen with its mysticism of science literature. Chaudhuri can translate the Sanskrit *brahmasiddhi* (literally, the "power of the Brahman") as "Transpersonal Being-cognitions" (Maslow wrote of Being-cognitions). Following Western parapsychology, he could also write of "extrasensory perceptions" and "psychic powers" to explain Sanskrit terms. Moreover, in a creative synthesis of science and Tantra, he could gloss the awakening of the "psychonuclear" energy (*kundalini*) as a form of "the greatness of Kali" (*Kalimahima*) and poetically describe this force again as the "most powerful cerebrospinal energy, dark yet luminous, like flashes of lightning in dark clouds." Being-cognitions, psychonuclear and cerebrospinal energies, psychic *siddhis*—*all* of these are creative American-Tantric fusions.

But it is not simply Tantra that explains Jacob's physical transfigurations. It is also depth psychology and quantum physics, a truth already signaled by the original cover. On the second page of the novel, Murphy writes, "That such a person [as Jacob] actually exists (or existed) seems plausible to me, increasingly so as the discoveries of psychology and physics continue to reveal the intertwinings of mind and the physical world. It is inevitable, I think, that pioneers like this will appear in our midst, that the modern West will produce its own kind of religious genius."[21] In a similar science-spirit synthesis, Kazi, Darwin, and Jacob are all insistent that the West and its science have something very important to add to the spiritual quest, something never before available. "Crazy as it seems," Jacob says to Darwin, things like Bell's Theorem, Einstein-Rosen bridges, wormholes, and extreme warps in space-time "provide some of the most suggestive metaphors I've encountered in any tradition to describe the turns I take."[22]

By 1977, in other words, quantum physics was well on its way to becoming one of the privileged mystical languages of the human potential movement in general, and once again Esalen was ahead of the curve. In 1974, the institute had already highlighted these mystical-quantum correspondences with the ninth book in its Viking Esalen series, Lawrence Le Shan's *The Medium, the Mystic, and the Physicist: Toward a General Theory of the Paranormal.* There were, of course, numerous important precedents for this. The science writer Corey S. Powell, for example, has argued that Einstein's spiritualization of matter ($E = MC^2$) actually represents a turning point in human spirituality akin to the earlier revolutions sparked by Jesus, Buddha, and Muhammad, and that Einstein is the "prophet" of this new developing synthesis of science and religion, of this "sci/religion," as Powell dubs it.[23] I would prefer rather to speak of a new *mysticism of science,* that is, of specifically religious uses of scientific theory that venture well beyond the science for the sake of bold metaphysical speculation.

Einstein, of course, famously resisted quantum physics, largely for aesthetic reasons ("God does not play dice").[24] Other physicists, however,

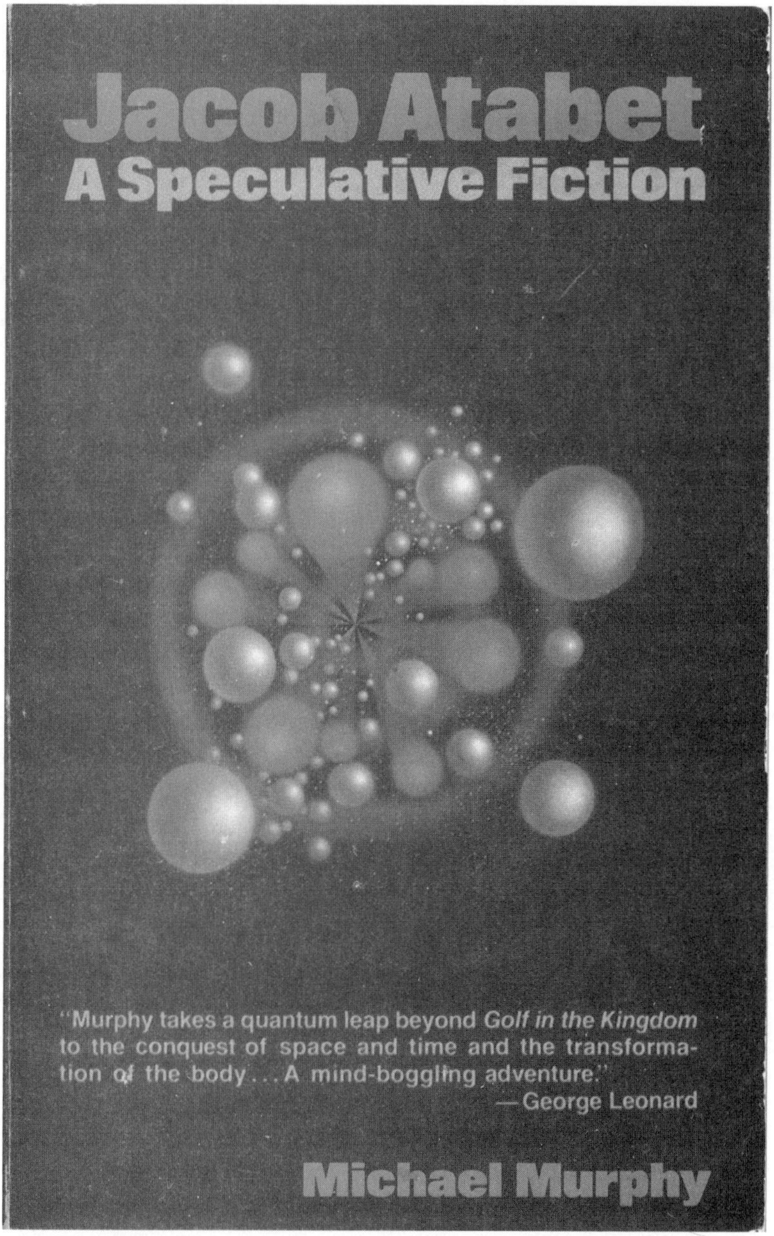

FIGURE 21. Original "quantum" cover of *Jacob Atabet*, 1977. Printed with permission of Michael Murphy.

did not share Einstein's theology and embraced what they saw as the rather obvious mystical implications of quantum theory. With respect to our own story, much of this excitement was generated by a single artful book, Fritjof Capra's *The Tao of Physics* (1975). A few years later, Gary Zukav would follow Capra's success with *The Dancing Wu Li Masters* (1979), which literally begins at a conference on the physics of consciousness in the Big House.[25] Nick Herbert's *Quantum Reality: Beyond the New Physics* (1987) was similarly inspired by his participation at Esalen. As an enthusiastic member of the California counterculture and a practitioner of Tai Chi, Capra would turn to a Hindu god (Shiva) and Chinese Taoism for his best conversation partners with particle physics. Gary Zukav, inspired by Chungliang Al Huang in the lodge during his "Big Week at Big Sur"— and, more specifically, by what Alan Watts had written about Huang in a foreword to Huang's *Embrace Tiger, Return to Mountain*—would similarly opt for a general Chinese or Taoist frame of reference. Nurtured by texts like *The Gospel of Sri Ramakrishna* and Aurobindo's *The Life Divine,* Murphy had already turned to specifically Tantric forms of Hinduism for his own quantum inspirations.

But the point remains: Jacob needed a science to support and explain his astonishing physical transfigurations, and that science was quantum physics. How this "fictional" event of Jacob's quantum transfiguration was related to the "historical" events of Esalen is very much worth telling. It is certainly no accident that as Murphy wrote *Jacob Atabet,* he was being tutored by the physicist Saul-Paul Sirag. It is also no accident that Esalen initiated in 1976, just one year before *Jacob Atabet* appeared, one of its longest running symposia series, on the physics of consciousness. What came to be known as the Bell's Theorem Group met for ten full years, from 1976 to 1985.

Before we get to these gatherings, however, it is necessary to back up just a bit and begin with another important Esalen figure, Fritjof Capra, a particle physicist who was not a part of the Bell's Theorem Group but who has had a major impact on both Esalen and the human potential movement through his many books, seminars, and lectures.

The Dance of Shiva: Fritjof Capra and The Tao of Physics *(1975)*[26]

Born in Vienna, Fritjof Capra found himself in California in the 1960s, working as a particle physicist at the University of California, Santa Cruz.

FIGURE 22. The original Dancing Wu Li Master, Chungliang Al Huang. Printed with permission of the Esalen Institute.

Powerfully drawn to the various mystical strands of the American counterculture, Capra did his scientific work at the university during the day and engaged in extensive reading, meditation, and religious experimentation in his free time. At the age of thirty, in 1969, these two worlds came together within an altered state of consciousness and energy that would radically change Capra's life and, through his writing, alter the way many individuals would think and talk about their own religious experiences. Once again, an altered state produced *a text*.

Capra's description of what happened on that single summer afternoon appeared on the first page of the preface to the first edition of his first
book. As such an experience fits beautifully into both the altered states of
history and the consciousness/energy paradigms I am developing here, it
is well worth quoting at length:

> Five years ago, I had a beautiful experience which set me on a
> road that has led to the writing of this book. I was sitting by the
> ocean one late summer afternoon, watching the waves rolling in
> and feeling the rhythm of my breathing, when I suddenly became
> aware of my whole environment as being engaged in a gigantic
> cosmic dance.... All this was familiar to me from my research in
> high-energy physics, but until that moment I had only experienced
> it through graphs, diagrams and mathematical theories. As I sat
> on the beach my former experiences came to life; I 'saw' cascades
> of energy coming down from outer space, in which particles were
> created and destroyed in rhythmic pulses; I 'saw' the atoms of
> the elements and those of my body participating in this cosmic
> dance of energy; I felt its rhythm and I 'heard' its sound, and at
> that moment I *knew* that this was the Dance of Shiva, the Lord of
> Dancers worshipped by the Hindus.[27]

Capra was familiar with basic aspects of yoga and Hinduism, hence his
awareness of his breathing and his invocation of the Hindu icon Shiva
Nataraja or Shiva Lord of the Dance. I asked Capra how much he knew
about Asian religions before this event. He shared with me that he had in
fact been reading Alan Watts—he recalls in particular *The Way of Zen*—
and had met Watts when the latter came to his university to lecture. All
of this, of course, was very much in the air, as it were, and Watts himself
had drawn some fairly elaborate parallels between physics and Eastern
mysticism as far back as 1962 in *The Joyous Cosmology*, as we have
already seen.

Shortly after the event on the beach and in the midst of a marital crisis,
Capra resigned from his position at Santa Cruz in December of 1970 and
moved to London, where he managed to convince a fellow physicist at
Imperial College to give him some office space for the next four years.
It was there in London that he decided to pursue the parallels between
particle physics and Eastern mysticism. The decision was inspired by a
photomontage Capra had designed in California. It showed the classical
dancing Shiva superimposed on an image of colliding subatomic particles

in a bubble chamber, expressing the same basic intuition of his mystical experience on the beach. Capra hired a London hippie-artist to produce a large poster of this dual image. The result was striking. "One day I sat in my tiny room near Imperial College and looked at this beautiful picture, and suddenly I had a very clear realization. I knew with absolute certainty that the parallels between physics and mysticism, which I had just begun to discover, would someday be common knowledge; I also knew that I was best placed to explore these parallels thoroughly and to write a book about them."[28]

Unfortunately, not everyone was so convinced. The idea was rejected by press after press. Finally, however, Capra found a brave publisher, collected a modest advance to live on, and sat down to write. He tested the material in two brief essays and shared the manuscript with the legendary physicist Werner Heisenberg, who affirmed the basic substance of the manuscript's ideas.[29]

The Tao of Physics appeared in its British edition in 1975. Its basic theories are three: wholism, dynamism, and parallelism. Capra argues that the world is an indivisible whole whose functioning cannot be accounted for without consciousness. Second, he argues that, contrary to the Cartesian model or the common-sense notion of "objects" and permanence, reality is in fact in radical flux and is fundamentally dynamic. There are no substances or things anywhere in the world; there are only processes and relationships. Third, he argues that there is a strange, even uncanny, parallel between the findings of particle physics and Eastern mysticism, particularly as the latter is displayed in Hindu Tantra, Buddhist Mahayana, Chinese Taoism, and Japanese Zen (that is, in the supertradition of Tantra, which he does not name as such because it had not been identified as such by scholars yet). The Asian (Tantric) mystics had arrived at the same metaphysical truths through intuition and mystical experience that modern physics had arrived at through more rational and mathematical means. Psychologically speaking, he was no doubt employing his mystical experience of Shiva's Dance on the beach as his hermeneutical key here.

It was the latter thesis that won him the most fans in the counterculture and the most critics in the physics community. The latter reviewers could not see how a collection of odd Zen riddles and extremely vague poetic utterances from the Hindu and Buddhist scriptures could come even close in explanatory and predictive power to the mathematical precision and technological feats of modern quantum physics and the high-energy particle collider. They had a point.

Looking back now, there are many things that could be said about Capra's enthusiastic embrace of Asian religions, about his commitment to a model of physics (Geoffrey Chew's boot-strap theory) that would soon be abandoned, and about his implicit reductionism. Gregory Bateson, for example, once said of his good friend, "Capra? The man is crazy! He thinks we are all electrons."[30] Ken Wilber would also later famously advance a similar critique, insisting that, because the levels of reality are essentially hierarchical and holonic (with each level encompassing and transcending the lower levels while being itself encompassed by levels above it), what holds true on a quantum level does not hold true on a higher level of consciousness or the spirit. Hence the former quantum realm can hardly be parallel or similar to the latter realm of higher consciousness.[31]

All well enough. But these criticisms have missed Capra's deeper philosophical intuitions about wholism and the intimate embrace of consciousness and energy within reality, each of which still appears to be quite plausible, even within the physics community.[32] Had not the great Danish physicist, Niels Bohr, seen more or less the same parallelism between physics and Taoism? And had he not actually put the Taoist *yin-yang* symbol on his coat of arms, accompanied by the Latin line *contraria sunt complementa* (contraries are complements), to express the nonduality of his own quantum theories back in 1947?[33] Although it is undoubtedly true that one does not need Asia to make these points (Bohr, after all, had done it in Latin too), it does appear that some form of mystical thought is a natural and nearly irresistible conversation partner, hence Shimon Malin's recent invocation of Plotinus and Whitehead to make very similar scientific-mystical connections.[34] If this always growing quantum-mystical literature means anything, *something* is going on here, and the first author to do this something in a systematic and aesthetically engaging way was Fritjof Capra.

What the critics of Capra have missed, almost entirely, are the beautiful ways that he was able to communicate his own mystical experiences through the words and art of his text. The *yin-yang* icon on the front cover (refigured as a Buddha face and a mathematical equation), the iconic juxtaposition of physics equations and Sanskrit texts (both equally mysterious, if not meaningless, to the uninitiated), Bohr's coat of arms, and the fusion of the Dance of Shiva and the dancing particles of the bubble chamber: all of these images, most created by Capra himself, are brilliant aesthetic moves that make his argument eminently accessible and attractive to the ordinary reader, whether or not such a reader critically understands the math or the Asian religions (and, of course, almost no one would have been qualified to do either, much less both).

Finally, it is also worth defending Fritjof against Gregory's friendly jibe: after all, we all, as bodies, really *are* dancing, spinning electrons, starstuff, as Carl Sagan so beautifully put it in his own cosmic register. Unless we want to escape our physicality (and many, of course, want to do precisely this), I personally see little to object to in Capra's mystical reductionism. In other words, I read *The Tao of Physics,* not as a physics textbook (which is what he originally set out to write before his revelation), but as a modern mystical text empowered by his own altered states of consciousness and energy that in turn has had a profound influence on alternative American religious thought. Once again, it is the text—like Jacob's paintings—that lives, that transmits the Tantra.

Meeting and Saying Goodbye to Gregory (1978–1980)

Capra arrived at Esalen in 1976, the same year the American edition of his new book hit the bookstores. He remembers meeting Joseph Campbell on the deck of the lodge, visiting with Michael Murphy about Sri Aurobindo, and becoming friends with Dick Price. A few years later, the anthropologist, naturalist, and philosopher Gregory Bateson (1904–1980) would come to play a major role in Capra's intellectual development. Bateson would help Fritjof move away from his privileging of physics to a broader systems view of life and ecology.

Although Bateson's time at Esalen was relatively brief, his relationship to the place and the founders went back to the very beginning. When Price was admitted into the air force hospital, he had approached Bateson for advice. By 1961, Bateson had a place in Big Sur and had met Murphy as well. Indeed, he and Joe Adams led one of the very first seminars at Esalen that first fall.[35]

Bateson was married for fourteen years to one of the most famous anthropologists of his generation, Margaret Mead (who, interestingly, was especially supportive of psychical research throughout her distinguished career). Together, the two did fieldwork in the South Pacific. Bateson went on to work in mental hospitals in the United States, where he developed his double-bind theory of schizophrenia in which individuals "resolve" early contradictory experiences of love and rejection through schizophrenic states. Later, he would also work with marine mammals. In 1976, he was named Regent of the University of California system, a position he used to press (in vain) for the university system's withdrawal from nuclear weapon research.

After nearly dying from cancer in 1978, Gregory was invited to live on the grounds of Esalen. It was a natural fit. Both Bateson's antinuclear stand and his insistence on what he called "the patterns which connect" set out in such books as *Mind and Nature* (1979), which he finished while living at Esalen, reflected and contributed to Esalen's deep commitment to ecological matters. Bateson died on July 4, 1980. A funeral ceremony with his ashes was held on the grounds. Zen teacher Richard Baker Roshi presided. Governor George Brown read the twenty-third Psalm. Fritjof Capra delivered a eulogy.[36]

Fritjof fondly remembers Gregory showing him his working manuscript for the book that would become *Mind and Nature* and explaining to him how mind is not restricted to a skull or a set of neurons but is a product of any complex living system.[37] Bateson's thought was radically holistic here; there were no such things as fingers or trees or lobsters in his world, only evolved parts of a human body or ecosystem that functioned within a larger natural mind or integral whole. He also rejected all supernaturalism as grossly dualistic and deeply offensive to this same wholism.

Which is not to say that Bateson did not have his own spiritual sensibilities. Like so many other countercultural and Esalen figures, he especially loved William Blake. In an Esalen seminar that Capra remembers particularly well, Bateson quoted from memory his favorite lines from the poet's *The Marriage of Heaven and Hell:*

> Dualistic religions hold that man has two real existing principles, a body and a soul; that energy is alone from the body, while reason is alone from the soul; and that God will torment man in eternity for following his energies. The truth is that man has no body distinct from his soul, the so-called body being a portion of soul discerned by the five senses; that energy is the only life and is from the body; that reason is the outward bound or circumference of energy; and that energy is eternal delight.[38]

The same words could have been uttered by Michael Murphy. Indeed, Murphy opens his *The Future of the Body* with a line from this same page. The psychologists' gestalt, Bateson's natural mind as the manifestation of a complex system, Capra's mystical-quantum wholism, Murphy's soul-body integralism—we are approaching, and very quickly, a consensual world-view here. We are approaching the Esalen body, which is also Jacob's body.

A Science for Jacob: Henry Stapp and the Bell's Theorem Group (1976–1985)

Fritjof Capra was not a part of the Bell's Theorem Group that met at Esalen between 1976 and 1985. With the important exception of Gary Zukav, this was not a group of thinkers strongly disposed to Asian spirituality. Whitehead certainly; the Buddha or Shiva, no way. Perhaps this was partly because the group had its origins not at Esalen, but at the Lawrence Berkeley Laboratory at the University of California, Berkeley. Zukav makes this quite explicit in his acknowledgments, where he thanks Jack Sarfatti, director of the Physics/Consciousness Research Group, and Elizabeth Rauscher, who founded the Fundamental Physics Group and encouraged nonphysicists to attend. Among those attending the latter group (at Berkeley), Zukav lists Fritjof Capra, John Clauser, who would later help to establish experimentally the truth of Bell's Theorem, and Fred Wolfe, who would go on to write a number of popular books on the mysticism of physics.

In short, this was a small group of intellectuals who first gathered in the early 1970s at Berkeley to explore how consciousness and energy might be related and then met annually at Esalen in the late '70s and early '80s to continue their conversations. What they said, and particularly what some of them wrote, would have a major impact on the American alternative religious scene.

But it was Henry P. Stapp of the Lawrence Berkeley Laboratory who probably had the most influence on this group of technical and popular thinkers, if often behind the scenes. Stapp is a theoretical physicist who has dedicated most of his professional life to the theorization of Bell's Theorem and some of the mathematical and conceptual problems surrounding the foundations of quantum theory. In his youth, he worked with both Wolfgang Pauli and Werner Heisenberg, two giants in the field. He now publishes on the philosophy of quantum theory and, most recently, on mind-brain interactions.

Stapp appears throughout Zukav's *The Dancing Wu Li Masters* as *the* authority on Bell's Theorem.[39] Very generally, the theorem states that because two electrons that once collide appear to be able to communicate instantaneously thereafter, wherever they happen to be in the universe, deep reality must be *nonlocal.* The secrets of matter appear to transcend space-time.[40] Stapp put it this way: "Everything we know about Nature is in accord with the idea that the fundamental process of Nature lies outside space-time...but generates events that can be located in space-time."[41] Such a bizarre claim (in religious terms, the paradox of simultaneous transcendence and immanence) would be easy to ignore, except for the troubling fact that in 1972 Bell's Theorem was experimentally established by John Clauser and Stuart Freedman in the Lawrence Berkeley Laboratory. So much for simple materialism.

It was Stapp who delivered an early lecture at the laboratory, probably around 1970, that first set out the radical philosophical implications of Bell's Theorem that so excited Capra, Zukav, Wolfe, and Herbert, all of whom would go on to write books on the subject for a lay audience. Stapp himself remembers how, "those talks that I gave initially caused a good deal of excitement in the Bay area," and he speculates that it was probably those same lectures that initially inspired most of the popular authors. The physicist Saul Paul Sirag, Murphy's physics tutor, was also at those meetings. Henry Stapp, in other words, is not simply the professional theoretician behind most of the early popular books on the physics of consciousness. Conceivably, he is also the physicist behind Jacob's quantum body mysticism.

Having noted that, it must also be said that Stapp, like almost all professional physicists, is profoundly uncomfortable with the popularizers, and particularly with their penchant for Asian spiritualities and their tendency to draw elaborate metaphysical conclusions from the much more humble suggestions of the physics. Stapp is clear that quantum mechanics is about high-order mathematics and laboratory predictability, not dancing with Shiva or becoming a Wu Li Master, and he cautions against the kind of countercultural or hippie enthusiasms that originally drove so much of the popular literature. Still, he does not deny that a real wholism is implied by quantum mechanics, and much of his own philosophical work is precisely about reintroducing mind, consciousness, and free will back into the scientific picture through an ontology he describes as a *quantum interactive dualism.*

For Stapp at least, the philosophical implications of quantum mechanical theory are clear: reality is psychophysical *all the way down.* I have neither the mathematics nor the space to explain the physics, but suffice it to say that, for Stapp, for quantum theory to work at all, mind and matter must be accepted as *both* different ontological orders *and* as intimately, inseparably connected. This is what Stapp means by quantum interactive dualism, which "postulates the existence of two entirely different kinds of realities, mental and physical, that interact."[42]

According to Stapp, the key weakness of both classical physics and philosophical dualism is that they keep these two orders separate or distinct, and so they cannot explain how something like conscious effort affects, say, a neural event in my brain or the moving of my left arm (much less the largely unconscious moving symphony of my rapidly typing fingers). Something as simple as moving my left arm has all the mystery of an occult telekinetic event in both classical physics and our present dualistic scientific worldview. No one can really explain how it happens, because mind and matter are not supposed to have any real connection. Or rather, mind is supposed to be only an epiphenomenon or surface product of matter. The "explanation" of the experiential fact of volition and subsequent physical effect is that conscious intention and free will are illusory. My arm is moving, but I'm not really willing it to move. This, obviously, is not a terribly satisfying resolution of the problem.

Stapp points out that this problem goes back to Descartes and the beginning of modern science, which split up reality into two seemingly unrelated dimensions, the mental or subjective (*res cogitans*) and the physical or objective (*res extensa*), and then ignored the mental as nonexistent or as causally ineffective in order to study the objective physical world as a series of mathematical processes that could be mapped and manipulated without any reference to human consciousness. For Stapp, what quantum mechanics does is make the latter move impossible, that is, "orthodox quantum mechanics brings into the dynamics certain conscious choices that are not determined by the currently known laws of physics but have important causal effects in the physical world." What this means is that the outcome of a quantum physics experiment depends upon the conscious choices of the human experimenter. As weird as it sounds, quantum reality as measured in the laboratory actually behaves differently depending on how the experiment is set up. Put differently, the human brain is part of the experiment, and its cognitive processes and volitional powers appear to affect (if not actually effect) quantum reality.

In an interview largely about a new book he is working on for a broader audience, Stapp glossed his own technical philosophical thought: "The essential point I am making is that in quantum mechanics (as opposed to classical physics) reality is not determined. The uncertainty principle wrecks that. You have to add these conscious choices, which are important and are not determined by laws. Hence the title of the book,

The Mindful Universe. That's the message in a nutshell. It puts us back into the world, which we have been excluded from for three hundred years." Stapp knows that he will have his critics, particularly from neuroscientists, psychologists, and philosophers of mind, almost all of whom are "determined that materialism is correct and that dualism is the enemy. They all think that physics supports monistic materialism. But it does not. They are simply wrong about this." Not only are they wrong about the physics. Their bad physics leads indirectly to bad ethics and a spiritually empty culture. Stapp again: "This [materialist monistic] attitude then filters out into whole culture, which is built upon respect for science. Everyone starts believing that we're not responsible. How could we be, if we are just robots? It's very corrosive."

In Praise of Beauty

Three other corollaries, I believe, follow closely behind. The first is that the same three-century Cartesian split between the mental and the physical that produced modern "science" also produced modern "religion." It did this by bracketing out religious doctrine as something essentially mental and so without any necessary connection to the physical world as we know it. In essence, faith was given a "free pass" to go its own merry way, whether or not it completely contradicted what we know about the history and structure of the universe. One of the things that made early and later Esalen so distinctive was its firm refusal to participate any longer in this split. Any adequate spirituality now, at the very least, should not contradict the science. Hence the earliest brochures, which featured mathematical equations, line drawings of the lotus, and photos of a Buddha bust.

The second corollary that follows from Stapp's quantum interactive dualism is that, if we are really now interested in healing the three-century split, "the blind acceptance of which," Stapp writes in a moment of poetic exasperation, "has rendered our lives unintelligible,"[43] we must admit to ourselves that some traditional religious systems fit the new scientific picture much better than others. Moreover, precisely as Darwin and Jacob (and Capra and Zukav) intuited, it seems entirely reasonable to observe that it is the mystical and nondual traditions that generally do the better job. Certainly, for example, there is nothing in the basic outlines of Stapps's interactive dualism that contradicts the Tantric model of consciousness and energy and the enlightenment of the body that I have been developing all along as the modal Esalen worldview. Indeed, the two fit beautifully together.

Which is not to say that they are the same. Stapps's quantum interactive dualism is the theorization of a disciplined scientific model that relies on the ordinary ego-state of human consciousness, the predictive power of mathematics, and the general rigors of the laboratory. The enlightenment of the body is a poetic expression whose intuitive truths can be directly accessed only through the wildly unpredictable, more or less unrepeatable, entirely unfalsifiable, and quite extraordinary states of consciousness and energy that constitute the history of religious experience. Put negatively, Stapp's philosophy of quantum mechanics and mind assumes the relative completeness and reliability of egoic awareness as an accurate barometer of reality. This, of course, is necessary for the performance of professional science. It seems unlikely, however, that such a method can represent the full human experience of reality. To put the matter in the language of Esalen, the methods of physics are *state-specific,* that is, specific to the ego and its forms of awareness.[44] With other forms of consciousness, however, likely come other forms of reality. Whether a traditional "science" is possible at all with these is an open question.

Finally, there is an important third corollary. It involves the claim that the quantum relationship between consciousness and energy is restricted to the subatomic level. Such a claim is often made by those who seek to reject the mystical uses of quantum language as inappropriate to the spiritual realm, which allegedly cannot have anything to do with the secrets of matter. The claim certainly doesn't mesh with Stapp's quantum mechanics (not to mention Jacob Atabet). Stapp, after all, argues quite explicitly that quantum effects go all the way up to the neurology of the human brain (where mental intention seems to increase the probability of neurotransmitter activity) and to the very mechanics of the laboratory experiment. Within this same conception of consciousness and the brain, we might think of the unconscious as a kind of quantum cloud or smear of neural probabilities before the intentional intervention of the conscious ego collapses it into a specific form of experienced reality, that is, into a specific state of consciousness.[45]

More radically still, Stapp goes so far as to suggest that quantum mechanics has effectively replaced material substances with potentialities. This, I would suggest, has immense implications for a place like Esalen. After all, what it implies is that—to redescribe the human potential language of the early Esalen brochures now—reality itself, including the reality of the human being, truly is *potential*. Add to this the quantum principles of nonlocality (that the secret of matter transcends space), complementarity (that an electron can be measured as a particle or a wave), and mind-matter parallelism (that consciousness cannot be reduced to anything other than itself, even as it always remains intimately connected to matter) and one begins to see why quantum physics has become one of the privileged mystical languages of Esalen, with or without the physicists. This is not simply understandable. It is inevitable.

There is a great deal of confusion still on this point, primarily because most keep insisting on reading this mysticism of physics literature literally, that is, as physics. This is a mistake, as it misses the deeper influence and cultural importance of this literature. Whatever they themselves thought at the time, I think it is fair to say now that authors like Capra, Zukav, and Wolfe were not writing physics. They were writing modern mystical literature. They were attempting—and with considerable success—to remythologize and rehumanize a cosmos that the dualisms of science had previously demythologized and rendered inhuman, objective, and cold.

They were also advancing another form of the religion of no religion, for science, as Theodore Roszak has noted, "is the infidel to all gods in behalf of none."[46] Here, after all, is a set of truths beyond all culture and clime, yet rooted in the deepest nature of matter itself, everywhere and always.

Put simply and truly, then, these Esalen-related writers turned to the language of quantum physics not to become professional physicists, but to become modern mystics. Like the young Michael Murphy, they were deeply moved by a set of truths that suggested to them that the depths of human subjectivity (the *atman*) and the deepest energies of the objective universe (the *brahman*) are in some sense one, and yet also two. Their own enlightenment of the body thus worked very much like both the common Esalen experience of synchronicity and Murphy's literary technique of occult realism. It participated in both the world "out there" and the world "in here." It was both. And it was neither. Admittedly, this is a difficult, paradoxical gnosis, and one all too easily literalized as pure fact or dismissed as pure fiction. In this, it is much more akin to a painting or a novel than an equation or a laboratory.

Jacob, at least, would have understood that.

Superpowers

COLD WAR PSYCHICS AND CITIZEN DIPLOMATS

A few days after we left Prague, the Soviet Union invaded. . . . Helmeted Soviet soldiers were squatting on the castle heights overlooking the city where we'd seen long-haired hippies painting Art Nouveau designs on the sidewalk: curlicues of LOVE and the injunction "Make Love Not War" . . . And now? The new energy may disappear under a new iron curtain. The Czechs told us there were isolated people in Europe and America working quietly on this "vital energy."

SHEILA OSTRANDER and LYNN SCHROEDER, *Psychic Discoveries Behind the Iron Curtain*

It is a common observation among historians of religion and cultural critics that when the human potential movement of the 1960s and '70s (originally modeled, we might recall, after the civil rights movement) morphed into the New Age movement of the '80s and '90s, it lost much of its original radicalism and became increasingly apolitical and corporate. Essentially, it was assimilated.

There is much truth in this. One of the most striking features of Esalen's history, however, is that its institutional life during this same period contradicts this pattern: the late 1970s, the entire decade of the '80s, and the early '90s were the most politically active and socially engaged chapters of Esalen's history. It was during these decades, after all, that Esalen's extensive experience with encounter groups and its signature trademark interest in the human potential came together to help address *the* political crisis of the day—the cold war and its terrifying threat of nuclear annihilation.

It may be hard to believe, but it is true. Through a catalyzing passion for the occult, a long-term commitment to the administrative, fundraising, and political work necessary for exchange programs, and a kind of eccentric diplomatic genius, Esalen played its own part in the collapse of Soviet Communism, the softening of American militarism, and the ending of the cold war. It was Esalen, for example, that sponsored, organized, and directed Boris Yeltsin's 1989 trip to the United States, where he was converted in a Houston megagrocery store from the Marxist ideology of Soviet Communism to the efficiency of American capitalism. Yeltsin would leave that grocery store furious at the lies of Soviet propaganda, return to Moscow, quit the Party, and help lead a revolution that would eventually help topple Soviet Communism. The rest, as we say, is history.

But we are getting ahead of ourselves here. As with most things involving Esalen, the political and public details of this story are intertwined with both the altered states of history and the deeply human ways that Esalen was able to build warm relationships of trust between top Soviet officials, economists, artists, and intellectuals and their counterparts in America within a cold war environment dominated by distrust, distorted propaganda, and, of course, espionage.

The James Bond analogy has been made before: rumors of power, something playfully called ESPionage (but seriously funded by millions of U.S. dollars and Soviet rubles), NASA, the CIA, and the KGB—all were part of a world as weird as anything seen on the silver screen. But this is about Esalen's diplomatic role in the cold war, not Hollywood's simplistic morality play rhetoric. And if there is one defining characteristic of this Esalen chapter, it is the obvious warmth and friendship between the Americans and the Russians. Friendship was *the* method here.

In the end, then, this is not so much a story about occult powers and psychic espionage (although it is that too); it is a story about a shared humanity known and cherished over a glass of wine and a bellowing laugh in the Big House, about an amateur softball game played in Moscow, about a political system that was quickly imploding under the force and farce of its own lies, and about the men and women in both countries who tried in their own unique ways to make a real difference.

It turns out they did.

Psychic Discoveries Behind the Iron Curtain *(1970)*

Michael Murphy had always been interested in parapsychology. He read about William James's experiments with the Boston psychic, Mrs. Piper. He cherished Freud's papers on telepathy. And he was long inspired by F. W. H. Myers and the London Society for Psychical Research. Indeed, we might recall that "psychical research" was one of the three pillars of the early brochures. But things hardly ended there. Gardner Murphy, an American psychologist who moved in Esalen circles and was interested in similar things, had visited the Soviet Union as early as 1960.[1] In the late '60s, Michael Murphy began to hear rumors about various forms of scientific research on psychical abilities that were allegedly going on in the Soviet Union. He wrote letters to Czechoslovakian scientists. He read. And he wondered.

About this same time, Sukie Miller brought a new book to Murphy's attention. Sheila Ostrander and Lynn Schroeder's *Psychic Discoveries Behind the Iron Curtain* was making something of a public splash.[2] In the summer of 1968, the authors had attended the first annual International Parapsychology Conference in Moscow. Trekking through the Russian Republic and Eastern Europe, particularly Czechoslovakia and Bulgaria, they interviewed and photographed a number of researchers and practicing psychics. Most importantly, however, they possessed a flare for getting people's attention. Everyone had heard about the "space race" and the "arms race." Ostrander and Schroeder now proclaimed a new "inner space race" surrounding the espionage potentials of ESP research, a race they claimed the Russians were clearly winning. Their story had enough grounding in Soviet research to make it engaging and more than enough tales about fantastic superpowers to make it exciting.

Ostrander and Schroeder wrote with a type of energy language that explicitly linked the astonishing scientific breakthroughs of the atomic age, the apocalyptic weapons of the arms race, and the philosophical implications of psi as a mysterious "x-force" (the X-Men again). In this same spirit, they reported that in 1968 a group of Czech scientists had issued a kind of public manifesto, which was later presented at the 1968 International Parapsychology Conference in Moscow. In it they suggested that the nature of matter is not dual (matter or wave), but triadic. Essentially, they postulated a new third form of energy—clumsily named "psychotronic energy"—that can be derived from certain extraordinary manifestations of the human psyche.[3] Such an energy, they claimed, cannot be explained by contemporary physical or biological models, but it is common among "religious mystics" and particularly creative writers like Franz Kafka, who, we are told, believed in a third form of energy that was present in all living beings and could be transferred from one living being to another.[4] A kind of Russian Mesmerism.

Significantly, the language of the book also displays some rather obvious influences from the human potential movement and its original Esalen orbit. Ostrander and Schroeder, for example, asked rhetorical questions about whether humanity possessed "unused, undreamed of potentials," and whether parapsychology could "melt the barriers and create the supernormal human being."[5] Indeed, they even defined parapsychology—an ugly and controversial word—with an expression that could have come off the pens of F. W. H. Myers, Sri Aurobindo, or Michael Murphy, that is, as "the study of the supernormal."[6] Such borrowings, of course, may have been simply coincidental, but sometimes they were patently obvious, as when, for example, Ostrander and Schroeder quoted Bishop Pike on how "this whole psi field has opened up a much bigger view of human potential for me."[7] This was pure Esalen, at least as it was developing up in the Bay area around the Esalen San Francisco Center in the late 1960s.

Ostrander and Schroeder also told fantastic stories about the psychics they heard about or actually met. There was Karl Nikolaiev, for example, who taught himself yoga through books and allegedly received telepathic transmissions in Leningrad from a controlled sender in Moscow. There was Dzhuna Davitashvili, the personal faith healer of Leonid Brezhnev. There was also Wolf Messing, the Polish Jewish immigrant who had to flee Poland when Hitler put a price on his head for prophesizing the Führer's death. Messing had met both Einstein and Freud (in Einstein's apartment no less) and happily submitted to a psychic experiment they arranged for the meeting. At another time, he had successfully passed Stalin's test of his psychic abilities and made so much money with his superpowers in Russia that within two years after his flight there he was able to buy two fighter planes and present them as gifts to the Soviet Air Force! And that was only the beginning.

Ostrander and Schroeder were certainly giving the material a sensationalistic spin, and that is probably an understatement. But they were not making it up. Nor did they or their subjects miss the philosophical and essentially religious implications of what they were studying. A certain Dr. Kuchynka, for example, thought that, "the importance of parapsychology for us lies precisely in its possibilities of elucidating by its discoveries the true nature of man and of showing that man is linked to the cosmos more closely than he'd ever supposed."[8] In other words, the Soviet military machine may have thought it was funding an experimental espionage technology, but what it in fact was doing was helping to further a new mystical anthropology, and this in the very heart of the Communist system. The results were, to say the least, somewhat ironic.

And expensive. Ostrander and Schroeder claim that by 1970 the Soviets had at least twenty centers dedicated to the study of the paranormal with an annual budget somewhere between thirteen and twenty-one million dollars. Similar investments were later made by the Americans for their own psychic projects. Humorously enough, the Russian project was reportedly first catalyzed by rumors published in 1959 in French newspapers that the Americans were using ESP on their *Nautilus* sub to communicate with the shore.[9] Whether the rumor was true or not (probably not), the Soviets allegedly took this startling news as both a threat and challenge, and proceeded to pursue ESP research.[10] As the story goes, they were nudged into a highly unusual path, very much as the Americans had earlier been led into the intelligence potentials of LSD by the (false) rumors of Soviets purchasing immense amounts of the substance from the Swiss Sandoz lab. The CIA had tripped on LSD, and now the KGB was psyching out on ESP.

The First Trip and the Elephant (1971)

Murphy was fascinated with the psychical research, rumored or real, and he wanted to connect with people who shared this passion. He had been corresponding with Russians on the topic since 1966. Esalen, moreover, had been aware of the Soviet interest in such things early on from the travels of both Fritz Perls and Stanislav Grof. But it was the Ostrander and Schroeder book that really made the difference here. Sukie Miller remembers the book's effect on her. Unlike J. B. Rhine's parapsychology research coming out of Duke, the Ostrander and Schroeder approach was neither statistical nor abstract. It was not about guessing abstract shapes on cards or determining bloodless probabilities. It was about *people,* about real human beings. Moreover, it was about an all-too familiar Eastern Europe and Russia, not a romanticized or orientalized Tibet. Here was something, Sukie felt, Esalen could also do. This was, after all, one of the things she felt they did best, that is, make real connections with real human beings. What they were finally experts at was *friendship.*

And so Sukie convinced Stuart and Michael to travel to the Soviet Union by way of Western Europe in 1971 to explore the cultures there within a kind of occult pilgrimage—the Three Bears again. Sukie may have been the real instigator here, but all three of them were convinced, like many in the Esalen orbit, that the human potential movement was not just another California quirk. In Murphy's memory now, it was more of a global breakthrough. Hence they were off to Russia. On their way, they stopped over in Florence to visit an elderly wisdom figure they had met for the first time the previous year, Roberto Assagioli. From Assagioli's Florence the trio went on to Prague, where they met with what Murphy calls "a very colorful cast of characters," many of whom would later find fictional forms in his occult novel, *An End to Ordinary History*. When they finally got to Moscow, they stayed in the grand National Hotel. Russians were not allowed into the hotel, except with very special permission. The Americans were fairly certain they were being bugged.

Over the next few weeks, they met numerous Soviet researchers who were experimenting with everything from clairvoyance to past-life memories—the same cast of figures Ostrander and Schroeder had described. On the one hand, the Esalen group concluded that the authors had exaggerated the extent of psychical research behind the Iron Curtain.[11] On the other hand, the spiritual landscape they encountered there went far beyond the scientistic categories of Marxist-oriented psychical research. They found everything from yoga and Theosophy to shamanism and Christian mysticism. Murphy remembers one séance they visited in which the participants were attempting to commune with the spirit of the great sixteenth-century Spanish mystic, St. John of the Cross. He also recalls being deeply moved by Russian Orthodox theologians (particularly Vladimir Solovyov) who insisted that their Christianity was not so much a matter of the immortality of the soul as it was a "resurrection of the flesh." A type of esoteric Christianity with its own unique enlightenment of the body, in other words, was an intimate part of the cultural landscape.

It was this same (heterodox) Orthodox theology that would eventually inspire Esalen to cosponsor a small library of Russian philosophical and theological works with the Lindisfarne Press, with telling titles like *Lectures on Divine Humanity, Sophia: The Wisdom of God,* and *The Meaning of Love.*[12] In other words, incarnation, the feminine aspect (or even Goddess) of the Godhead, and the rich spiritual dimensions of *eros* were all selected out and celebrated again, if in a very different theological frame. In an (unsigned) afterword to these volumes, Murphy describes this Russian philosophical tradition by a set of defining characteristics: "*epistemological realism; integral knowledge* (knowledge as an organic, all-embracing unity that includes sensuous, intellectual, and mystical intuition); the celebration of *integral personality* (*tselnaya lichnost*), which is at once mystical, rational, and sensuous; and an emphasis upon the *resurrection* or *transformability* of the flesh." With its Russian venture, Esalen was no longer inhabiting the symbolic universe of, say, Aurobindo's India or Huxley's California. Still, the specific themes (and even words) it chose remained remarkably consistent.

But these philosophical reflections would come later. For now, all was not well on their travels. Things were getting just plain weird. More specifically, the group began to worry that their presence was endangering those whom they were meeting. Interviewees began to say things like, "Next time you meet me, pretend like you don't know me and that it's the first time." Or their young female translator—who, according to Sukie, had fallen for Mike—would insist that the long Russian ramble of a particular scientist was best translated as "puppy." "*Puppy?*" Sukie would ask in exasperation. "Do you mean the little furry animal, as in Bark! Bark!?" as she herself then barked like a rather big puppy. "Yes, puppy." Between translated one-liners like "pretend like you don't know me" and "puppy," Sukie, Stuart, and Mike were beginning to get the message. Granted, it was an exceptionally confusing message, but it was a message nonetheless.

They took the hint and decided to cut their trip a week short. But first, Sukie insisted, they should do what they did best, that is, host a dinner party for their new friends. They certainly had the right place. Their suite in the National, although sparsely finished in typical Soviet style, was immense. The room also had a fantastic view of the Kremlin, whose tower silhouettes and flapping flags could be seen outside their window across the street in the beautiful light of a full moon.

The meal itself Sukie describes as "horrid" and "simply heartbreaking." The chickens they served, for example, were painfully thin. At some point, however, someone suggested that they liven things up a bit by doing an experiment. Karl Nikolaiev, the famous psychic whose exploits Ostrander and Schroeder had featured, showed the group how to set up a psychic experiment between a "sender" and a "receiver." Yuri Kamensky (a biophysicist by training who often acted as Karl's sender) and Murphy went to the Millers' room, which adjoined the dining room, while Sukie, Stuart, Karl, and the other guests remained in the dining room. Yuri began digging around the Millers' bedroom for some object to send Karl. What he finally chose was a container of popular moisturizer available at the time from a company called Love Cosmetics. In Sukie's own words, "it was phallic, shaped like a bullet, and it was very *au courant* in San Francisco at that time." It had a shiny, chrome-like cap or corona on the end. Not surprisingly, it also had something of a reputation among the three American travelers. They called it Sukie's love-stick.

Yuri's methods were rather unique. He believed that to properly send an image or object to a receiver, one had to use all five senses. He would thus look at, listen to, touch, smell, taste, even kiss whatever he was about to send. All this he did to Sukie's love-stick. In the dining room, something was coming through. Karl described the object in words approximating these: "It's a hard object, but it's strange. It has a mirror on one end, but when I see myself in it the image is distorted. It's smooth. There is a liquid. It's a third full. It smells sweet. It's cloudy." After the experiment, when Yuri and Mike brought Karl five objects, he immediately reached out for the love-stick.

Sukie's reading of the experiment is interesting. She notes in particular the problem of cultural context. After all, Nikolaiev "nailed every single property, but he didn't have the cultural context for it, so he couldn't really identify it." Until he saw it, that is. Then he immediately recognized it. Mike was so impressed with the performance that he kept Sukie's love-stick as a kind of definitive relic of their little Moscow miracle (Dulce Murphy recently rediscovered the long-lost relic in a box). The group left the next day, with suitcases stuffed with documents that numerous researchers had insisted they take back with them but whose contents the trio knew nothing about. They could not, after all, read Russian.

When the group got back, they decided to try the experiment again in the fall, this time between San Francisco and Moscow. Charles Tart, a professional parapsychologist and Esalen friend, set up the experiment. Nikolaiev, as usual, would act as the receiver, and Michael would act as the sender. Tart picked five or so objects at random with the help of a dictionary and butter knife—an old parapsychology trick to generate a random object for an experiment. Essentially, what this involved was Tart putting the dictionary behind his back and then sticking the knife into its pages; wherever it landed, he would pick the word on that page that was accompanied by a picture. The first picture page happened to be that of an elephant. For convenience sake, they chose a small wooden toy elephant with a moveable trunk.

It was noon San Francisco time, midnight Moscow time. They were, quite literally, sitting on opposite sides of the globe as they tried to connect with one another as friends and psychics. Karl began by describing the room in which Mike was sitting in his North Beach apartment. Nikolaiev began. "He is sitting in a red chair." Michael was. "With a lamp over his shoulder." Right on again. Karl went on, again in more or less these words: "It's wooden. It's round at one end. And it has something like a moveable nosedropper." As the toy elephant was wooden, had a round rump, and featured a moveable trunk, the group considered this a direct "hit." Sukie, however, points out again that Nikolaiev lacked the cultural context for such a toy elephant. He thus did exactly what he did with her love-stick in Moscow—he described all of its properties with an uncanny accuracy

FIGURE 23. James Hickman (left) and Joseph Montville (right), c. 1981. Printed with permission of the Esalen Institute.

but missed its general or overall cultural function. The remaining objects failed, however, to be so impressively transmitted.

Legalizing the Unconscious (1979)

James Hickman was a major force behind Esalen's Russian projects in the late 1970s and early '80s.[13] Like many in this movement, he attributes his inspiration for these Esalen Russian adventures to Michael Murphy, who taught him "how to sit," that is, how to meditate and access that "deeper nature" from which arise new human possibilities and, through a kind of engaged synchronicity with the cultural environment, new political opportunities. Hickman took his first trip to the Soviet Union in 1972 to attend a conference on the extended abilities of the human being. For the following six years, he continued this same research, traveling in Eastern Europe to learn as much as he could about the Soviet advances.[14] In 1975, he joined Murphy to pursue something the two men called the Transformation Project. This would become a seventeen-year archival project that was based closely on *Jacob Atabet* and would eventually take form as Murphy's 1992 magnum opus, *The Future of the Body*.

It was Dulce Murphy who first encouraged Mike and Jim to turn the fictional archive on supernormal functioning that had appeared in *Jacob Atabet* into an actualized one. Dulce's idea, it turns out, would prove to be a very fruitful one, as it was this same Transformation Project that would lead to Hickman traveling to Central Asia in 1979, partly to research mystical currents there for Murphy's third occult novel, *An End to Ordinary History,* partly to attend a conference on Freud and the unconscious. This same trip would in turn play an important role in catalyzing Esalen's later

Soviet dialogues in the 1980s. In effect, the Transformation Project of *Jacob Atabet* and Murphy's occult novels helped spark a long-range Esalen adventure that began as a metaphysical quest and then morphed, through innumerable other individuals and events, into a unique Esalen activism. The political had become a synchronistic expression of the metaphysical: the inner and the outer had merged. It was precisely this mystical art, this contemplative practice of altering public life, that Jim Hickman learned from Mike Murphy.

And Jim was hardly alone. Anya Kucharev, a Russian-American who in 1979 had just quit teaching Russian in Monterey, was taking a holistic healing course and meditating with a yogi. While in a local bookstore, Murphy's *Jacob Atabet* simply "dropped off the shelf," as she puts it. She stayed up all one August night reading the book, excited by its ideas but struggling with their expression and implications. The next day, the phone rang. Kucharev was stunned. It was Michael Murphy, seeking advice for an upcoming trip to the Soviet Union. This was more than a coincidence for Kucharev. It was a deeply meaningful synchronicity and a new way to begin healing the painful experience of growing up in a Russophobic America. Kucharev soon joined the research staff of the Esalen Soviet-American Exchange Project to translate Russian scientific articles about the paranormal and to help Murphy with his novel about Russia, *An End to Ordinary History*.

The trip about which Murphy called Kucharev occurred in the fall of 1979, when Hickman spent seven weeks traveling through the country again, this time with his partner Mary Payne and, for at least part of the trip, an accomplished American parapsychologist by the name of Stanley Krippner. Krippner was an old friend and mentor of Hickman's. Indeed, in 1968, at the age of twenty-one, Hickman was working with Krippner as his research assistant. He had also been part of Krippner's storied telepathic dream research at Maimonides Dream Laboratory in Brooklyn.[15] It was this research that first attracted the attention of the Soviets and brought Krippner to Moscow.[16]

Krippner's involvement with anomalous states of consciousness hardly ended there, however. He had visited Timothy Leary's Castalia Foundation in Millbrook and the psychotronics laboratories in Prague. Moreover, he had attended a parapsychology conference in Moscow in 1970 and gave the first lecture on parapsychology ever delivered to the Academy of Pedagogical Sciences in the summer of 1971, again in Moscow.[17] For the latter occasion, Krippner brought along copies of *Psychic Discoveries Behind the Iron Curtain* (joking with his slightly offended hosts that they could title their own *Psychic Discoveries in Imperial America*). He lectured for two hours on, among other things, astronaut Edgar Mitchell's ESP experiment on Apollo XIV and a particularly colorful (and especially Tantric) telepathic dream experiment he arranged on February 19, 1971. For the latter experiment, two thousand people attending a Grateful Dead rock concert were shown a painting entitled *The Seven Spiral Chakras* and were asked to "send" it to a named sleeping subject forty-five miles away in the Maimonides Dream Laboratory. That night the subject dreamt of natural and solar energy, a man suspended in mid-air, rocket ships, an energy box, and a spinal column.[18]

The present trip, however, was not about the study of Teletantric dreams. It was about the International Symposium on the Problem of the Unconscious. Held in 1979 in Tbilisi, Georgia, the conference was sponsored by the Georgian Academy of Sciences of the USSR. It sought to address the problematic status of Freud's psychoanalysis in Russian history and culture, a form of thought that before this official conference was essentially illegal and politically repressed.

It is worth remembering that Freud's thought has often functioned as a kind of barometer of freedom and democratic reform in the modern world. It is hardly an accident that his books were burned by the Nazis, and that he ended his life in London, in exile from his beloved Vienna, then overrun with fascist armies. When he learned of the book burnings while still living in Vienna, Freud famously joked about civilization's "progress": in a previous age they would have burned him. What he did not know at the time was that this same regime would soon be burning millions of human beings, among them his own sister.

The Nazis saw (quite correctly) that Freud was a real threat to their fascism, that his thought affirms the individual against all external authorities. This is no doubt one reason why Freud's psychoanalysis has been most successful in the liberal open societies of the West, particularly the United States, Britain, and France, while it has been actively forbidden and systematically suppressed in one authoritarian regime after another. Its "barometer function" has been particularly obvious in Latin America, where "the downfall of each successive dictatorship invariably has been accompanied by a flowering of psychoanalysis."[19] There appears to be an inverse correlation, then, between totalitarianism and psychoanalysis (much as there appears to be a positive one between totalitarianism and Marxism).

The Russians, of course, hated the Nazi regime as much as anyone. But they too would reject Freud for their own authoritarian reasons. These, it turns out, were also metaphysical. Marxist doctrine was explicitly materialistic, that is, it recognized no extramaterial forces or influences on human behavior. Accordingly, it was deeply suspicious of Freud's unconscious and indeed saw this central psychological notion as an essentially spiritual or immaterial fiction. After an initial flowering in the first decades of the twentieth century among cosmopolitan Russian philosophers, artists, and creative writers, psychoanalysis was officially suppressed in the Soviet Union.

Until 1979. Actually, the conference on "the problem of the unconscious" had been scheduled and cancelled three times. There had been two top Soviet officials who objected strongly to the subject matter and who simply would not let the event take place. But they were now both dead, and so the conference could finally be held. As it turned out, the conference was not entirely devoted to Freud but rather functioned as a kind of cultural cover for any number of other alternative interests. As Hickman put it: "As soon as the Academy says let's look at a broader range of experiences in this area [of the unconscious], everybody comes out of the closet and it turns out that for twenty years they've been looking at para-psychology."[20] "Scratch a Russian," as the saying went, "and you will find a mystic."

Several psychic healers attended the conference and demonstrated their powers and methods. Also attending was a delightfully eccentric figure who would come to play an important role in Esalen's future history, Joseph Goldin. Goldin was a manically magical figure. Hickman at least was so impressed with him that he convinced Murphy to put Goldin on the Esalen Board before the two had even met, indeed before Goldin ever sat foot in the country.

Joseph Goldin was a biochemist by training who was now producing television programs and doing screenwriting. Joseph was a huggable Russian bear who just seemed to "appear" on the Esalen scene in order to propose a whole series of outrageous (and often truly brilliant) metapolitical projects. His English was excellent, if also somewhat eccentric. He would say things like, "We are all mutants!" and, now pounding a fist into an open hand, "We will *flatten* them!" (Political activist Harriett Crosby does the best Joseph Goldin imitations.) Some of Joseph's ideas, though, were just plain crazy, like one of his last proposals that involved shooting an intercontinental missile filled with Russian products and gifts into the bay of Seattle as a gesture of peace. Just not a good idea.

Officially (that is, in those long Russian titles), Joseph Goldin was scientific secretary of the Commission for the Complex Study of Man. What this actually meant was that he helped lead an eclectic commission that

FIGURE 24. Joseph Goldin seated on the floor with Richard Baker Roshi on the Volga, summer 1982. From the archives of Jim Hickman, printed with permission.

studied what he had dubbed "hidden human reserves," which included such things as the psychology of creativity, cybernetics, sexology, architecture, film, music, nontraditional healing, parapsychology, and sports performance. With their conference on the problem of the unconscious, in other words, the Soviets were seeing and now saying what their European and American counterparts had been seeing and saying for decades, namely, that Freud and his unconscious helps explain *a lot.*

After the Tbilisi congress, Hickman and Payne went on a kind of tour of Soviet science looking into similar matters, not unlike the earlier visit of Ostrander and Schroeder. They visited scientists in Alma Ata, Kazakhstan, in Novosibersk, Siberia, and in Moscow to discuss Soviet research on psychoenergetics, information transfer over long distances, interactions between separated cell cultures, telepathy, electromagnetic models that sought to explain both the communicating cells and the telepathic humans, and something called "anthropomaximology." The latter monstrosity was coined by Dr. V. V. Kuznetsov, chairman of the Department of Theory of Top Competition Sports in the All-Union Research Institute of Physical Culture. By it, he meant the study of maximum human capacities displayed in such fields as sport: "In his model," Hickman and Murphy write, "normal people are underdeveloped but can progress toward optimal

FIGURE 25. Hidden Human Reserves logo created by Joseph Goldin, summer 1982. From the archives of Jim Hickman, printed with permission.

functioning through appropriate training. He believes that Olympic athletes are examples of the development which is possible for all of us."[21]

While meeting with Kuznetsov, Hickman was asked to cochair a section called "Sport and Maximum Human Performance" for another upcoming Soviet conference, the International Conference on Sports and Modern Society. They invited Michael Murphy to be a featured speaker. The event was to be held in conjunction with the 1980 summer Olympics in Moscow.

The Matter of Sport: The 1980 Olympics

The Soviets invaded Afghanistan in December of 1979. One of President Carter's responses was to boycott the 1980 summer Olympics in Moscow. Dulce Murphy was with Carter when he announced this. Present or not, though, this was not good news for the Esalen contingent. They had been invited to a major international conference that seemed to fit beautifully with their own vision of things, both athletic and potential. They would not be easily frustrated.

Jim Hickman approached one of their contacts in Washington D.C., Soviet expert Marshall Brement. They received unofficial permission to violate the boycott and attend the conference. This they did in the summer of 1980. Michael and Dulce Murphy, Jim Hickman, and Mary Payne traveled together. Mike and Jim would speak. Mary came as a trustee of Esalen and Dulce as a representative of the California Governor's Council on Physical Fitness and Wellness.

In July 1980 the Soviet congress convened in Tbilisi with 1500 participants from forty-two countries attending. The session Sports in Modern Society was opened by Joseph Goldin, whose jolly manners often infuriated his more proper Soviet colleagues. Goldin wore his shirts much too tight and short for his plump frame, so when he spoke excitedly or laughed (which he did often), his big belly would pop out of his shirt and bounce up and down. It was Joseph Goldin, bouncing belly and all, who opened Section 2.8.

Murphy's paper, "The Future Evolution of the Body: Possibilities for Human Transformation Revealed by Sport and Other Disciplines," was a kind of channeling of Darwin Fall speaking about Jacob Atabet in hushed reserved tones. It was also something of a summary of *In the Zone*, now rendered more sober for what Murphy knew might be a tough crowd. The paper was also as much a diplomatic speech as a scientific or visionary document:

> After reviewing the sweep and novelty of our program this week, no one could accuse the sponsors of timidity! Their boldness and sense of adventure should encourage us all. Indeed, the conference could lead us toward some magnificent projects for the development of the human potential. Ever since we received our invitations to participate, my colleagues and I have thought that scientists from the Soviet Union, the United States and other nations could come away from Tbilisi with a mandate for new international ventures to explore the hidden reserves, the vast untapped potentials this meeting points us toward.[22]

The human potential movement, in other words, was realizing its own potentials, not simply as a psychology, but as both a diplomatic strategy and a fundamental ontology to ground international relations, a kind of mystical humanism for the future. And sport had become its universal language.

There was still no question, however, about what Murphy was primarily interested in: the supernormal, the transfigured body, and Jacob's *animan siddhi*. He thus spoke of sport as "a kind of laboratory in which supernormal possibilities are being tested—however inadvertently—for the human race in general." He mentioned his work with Rhea White on the parapsychology of athletes and questioned whether our social scientific models are adequate. He quoted his friend John Brodie on a certain mysterious clarity the latter claimed to experience on the football field. And, very much in his Jacob Atabet mode, he asked rhetorical questions about a certain "inner seeing": "Maybe we possess a rudimentary scanning device—something like a built-in microscope complete with zoom lens and television screen for easy readout!—by which we can zero-in on whatever ails us or on whatever body part we want to change." "In that case," he went on, "body builders and runners who have glimpsed their own muscles and capillaries might be learning how to use a hidden capacity. Perhaps they have unknowingly discovered a latent human power."[23] He may have been speaking in careful subjunctive moods ("maybe . . . might be . . . perhaps . . . "), but there was little doubt for those who could read between the lines: Michael Murphy believed in superpowers, in hidden human reserves. Jacob lived.

The two couples had opportunities to meet with numerous Soviet scientists who had come to the conference explicitly to meet with them and learn more about American ventures into alternative medicine, psychology, and psychical research. They also met with a number of practicing psychics, often in their homes over dinner. Here in particular the Americans noticed a real frustration with the Soviet system and a certain new willingness to criticize it. This was something that they had not noticed on their earlier trips.

What the Esalen associates discovered on their trips in 1979 and 1980 was certainly less grandiose than what Ostrander and Schroeder had claimed to find in the late 1960s, but they found something real nonetheless. They found that the Russians were steeped in the supernormal, and that these interests often pushed them to combine their Marxist materialist doctrines and their mystical convictions in strange, and often humorous, ways. If the scientists could coin words like "psychotronic energy" and "bioplasma," others could go even further. Murphy, for example, remembers meeting a certain Proton Nikolayev, who had a brother named Neutron and a sister named Electron. When speaking about Electron,

Proton could say with a completely straight face, "She is very small and light."

Bound by strict Marxist doctrines that allowed for no spiritual or extramaterial forces, the Soviets had in effect invented a whole new vocabulary, but one that the Esalen associates recognized immediately to be analogous to what they were calling "the human potential." Hickman and Murphy described the situation this way shortly after their travels in 1980:

> There is a remarkable symmetry between Soviet and American interests in this field. The Soviet term "hidden human reserves," for example, is almost identical to the American "human potential" as a guiding idea. Soviet concern with "maximum performance" resembles American investigations of "peak experience." Soviet studies of "bioplasma," "biophysical effects," and "distant bioinformation interactions" resemble American studies of "energy fields," "dowsing," and "remote viewing." Training in "psychical self-regulation" techniques is the Soviet equivalent of "biofeedback" and "stress management" programs in the U.S. In both countries these ideas have stimulated new approaches to education, health-care, and sports.[24]

Esalen, in other words, had effectively located an entire "Soviet Esalen" (and a government-sponsored one at that) and accompanying vocabulary by 1980, and it was now eager to pursue these comparisons in the interests of both the human potential and the global peace.

The Soviet-American Exchange Program and Track-Two Diplomacy

When the Esalen contingent got back to the States after their 1980 trip, it was clear to them that something needed to be and *could* be done. They had essentially found a deep spiritual vein in Russia, and they were convinced that it could form the basis for real cross-cultural dialogue between the two cultures. Esalen also, however, had close friends in Washington who were telling them that things were more likely to get worse than better on the public diplomatic front over the next decade, and that if they wanted to make a difference, it would have to be through unofficial, nongovernment channels. These same friends in high places also assured them that their own Esalen exchanges with the Soviets had no national security implications.

In essence, they had been given a green light, in Hickman's words, "to take the high ground together to explore the further reaches of the human spirit, to explore the spiritual dimension of the human being which was clearly being explored in a different language but in a similar way in the USSR at that time."[25] Obviously, however, there were real dangers here as well, for this was all pursued at the very nadir of the cold war at a time when the specter of a nuclear holocaust hung over American public culture like a haunting ghost.

Esalen called together a symposium in the fall of 1980 that effectively initiated, now formally, its Russian-American ventures. At first, they wanted to call their new project The Institute for Theoretical Studies, but George Leonard offered them some sage advice: "Come on folks, you can't name this thing TITS."[26] George had a point. The name was quickly changed to the Esalen Soviet-American Exchange Program. It would run for sixteen years, eventually changing its name to The Russian-American Center (or TRAC) and, very recently, to Track Two: An Institute for Citizen Diplomacy.

Around this same time, Hickman and Murphy were introduced by Harriett Crosby to Arthur Hartman, a U.S. diplomat who would soon become the ambassador to Moscow under President Reagan. Crosby had been to Esalen in the early 1970s for workshops with Joe Campbell, Sam Keen, and Stan Grof and later trained as a psychoanalyst at the C. G. Jung Institute in Switzerland. She was a close friend of Donna Hartman, Arthur's wife, and lived in the Hartmans' home in Washington, D.C., while Arthur was the ambassador to France.

Ambassador Hartman would learn a good deal about Esalen through both Crosby and Hickman. He apparently liked what he heard. After he was appointed by President Reagan, he began hosting the Esalen troupe and their Russian friends at Spaso House, the private ambassador's residence in Moscow. These gatherings generated a great deal of cultural and diplomatic exchange. Russians were encouraged to engage the Americans (this was, after all, Spaso House, the home of Reagan's key representative in Moscow), and news of the citizen diplomacy efforts got back to the White House. Murphy also remembers having a direct line to Hartman's office in Moscow whenever he needed help or advice or thought he was being bugged or followed (which was often). He also remembers sitting within Hartman's "safe-room" in the embassy, a specially designed space that was supposed to be immune to Soviet intelligence. Esalen had come a long ways since the Nixon days.

Crosby tells a number of humorous stories about this period. There was the time, for example, she and Donna told Arthur during breakfast that they should build a hot tub in their D.C. backyard, where they could "warm" Soviet-American relations and "melt" the cold war by inviting Soviets to disarm and undress, "just like they do at Esalen." The idea (and its language) actually had originated earlier in an Esalen hot tub conversation between Crosby and Hickman in an attempt to distinguish their own Russian efforts from the "ping-pong diplomacy" with the Chinese via goodwill tournaments. Crosby was now trying it out on the Hartmans. As Donna and Harriett did the dishes after breakfast, the two women were startled to hear a chainsaw suddenly roar into gear. They looked out the window: there was Arthur Hartman, cutting down a beautiful dogwood tree to make room for a redwood hot tub.

The fallen tree would not die in vain. Many Russians and Americans would be entertained in the new hot tub, including Senator Claiborne Pell and folk singer John Denver, who was briefed there before his own trip to the USSR. Denver would later travel to Moscow with Jim Hickman, where he performed with Jim Henson and Kermit the Frog (yes, Kermit the Frog) for the U.S. Embassy children. On that same trip Denver composed a song ("Let Us Begin"), which he sung as a duet with Russian pop star Alexander Gradsky as a gesture of peace and goodwill.[27]

Then there were all those Russian psychics. When Crosby found herself calling on psychic healers for interviews, she found it necessary to walk the streets of Moscow and make her calls from public pay phones so that the calls would not be coming from the U.S. embassy. She quickly discovered that there were two quasi-magical phrases that opened almost every Russian door for her: "Esalen" and "Jim Hickman."

Once Crosby took the Hartmans to a Russian healer, despite Arthur's skepticism. The healer passed her hands over Arthur's body and proceeded to tell him how he had broken his arm as a boy, how they had put a metal plate in his upper arm, and why, by the way, didn't they ever take it out? Hartman was flabbergasted. All of this was perfectly true, and no one (not even his wife) knew anything about it until that moment.

As with the Esalen healings that eventually resulted in the public forays into Humanistic Medicine in the early 1970s, one need only multiply these eccentric Russian moments of the '80s into the hundreds, and then the thousands, in order to begin to get a sense of the real human base—Joseph's "hidden human reserves"—from which much of the Esalen activism was actually accomplished. The skeptic may scoff at Ambassador

Hartman's hidden metal plate, but there is little to scoff at in the twenty-five-year public record of TRAC and Esalen in Russia. Consider the following, grossly partial, list.

In 1982, working with Stephen Wozniak, cofounder of Apple Computers, TRAC and Esalen employed satellite communication technology to pioneer the first spacebridge communications between Americans and Soviets. The occasion, on Labor Day weekend, was what Keith Thompson described in the Esalen catalog as a "Satellite Rock-and-Roll Fest." American and Russian bands and ecstatic youth in San Bernardino, California, and Moscow screamed, grinned, and danced to each other's music as they watched one another on large screens.[28] To the astonishment of everyone, Soviet television showed clips of the event on the evening news, partly no doubt because Hickman and crew had cleverly billed the band "Men at Work" to fit the Labor Day theme and the official Russian sensibilities. Things were dodgy on the American side, though, as one of the organizers of the event, Bill Graham (promoter of the Grateful Dead), literally pulled the plug half way through the concert. Graham was convinced that the whole thing was a KGB trick, and that none of it was actually coming from Moscow.

A second Russian-American concert was organized on Memorial Day Weekend in 1983, and other musical diplomacies quickly followed, including one Jim Hickman helped organize with Billy Joel in Moscow. Among other memorable moments, Joel brought in thousands of hot-dogs and hamburgers from Frankfurt, Germany, in order to help celebrate the end of the concert with their new Russian friends and fans. He was, after all, just as his remake of the old Beatles song celebrated, "Back in the USSR."

In the summer of 1982, Apollo IX astronaut and space walker Russell "Rusty" Schweickart traveled to the Soviet Union with Hickman and the Murphys, where he met, among many other Russian marvels, the healer and national psychic star, Dzhuna Davitashvili. About this same time, he began working with Hickman to form the Association of Space Explorers (ASE). From space, Schweickart had literally seen the earth not as a collection of divisive nation-states or competing religions, but as a single planet, as a Global Gestalt to invoke an Esalen language, and he thought that this "space perspective" gave astronauts and cosmonauts a particularly powerful position from which to encourage their countries to protect and nurture the planet. The ASE was officially formed in 1985. It meets to this day and now counts among its members 90 percent of those who have traveled in space.

In 1983, Esalen worked with diplomat Joseph Montville and psychologists Joan and Erik Erikson to inaugurate the Joan and Erik Erikson

FIGURE 26. Apollo IX astronaut Rusty Schweickart and Russian psychic healer Dzhuna Davitashvili, summer 1982. Photo by A. A. Zadikian, from the archives of Jim Hickman, printed with permission.

Symposia on the political psychology of Soviet-American relations. Central here was what Sam Keen had so eloquently called "the faces of the enemy," whose projections he uncovered and analyzed in political cartoons, nationalist propaganda, and religious imagery.[29] The idea for the Erikson symposia was both simple and profound. Psychopathologies, they concluded, are seldom simply personal; they are also cultural and political. In order to address effectively diplomatic impasses and political crises like the cold war, organizations must eventually engage the depth psychologies of the cultures involved and the unconscious roots of the violence they perpetuate.[30] By 1987, they had organized four of these symposia on the psychoanalysis of political life.[31]

On September 11, 1986, Esalen returned to the spacebridge idea to cohost another on "Chernobyl and Three Mile Island" with the American Association for the Advancement of Science, the USSR Academy of Sciences, the USSR Ministry of Television and Radio, and Internews. Esalen president Steve Donovan welcomed the panelists communicating through the orbiting satellites, Carl Sagan participated, and Esalen activist James Garrison offered closing remarks. And these events were complex. This single symposium required the cooperation of twenty-one foundations and individual donors, ten advisors, over twenty-three volunteers, the co-operation of three major universities (Harvard University, University of Colorado, and University of South Carolina), and an Internews production staff of twenty-nine professionals.

In 1989, the institute enlisted the support of Susan Sontag and Nor-man Mailer to help bring the Soviet Writers Union into the International Pen Club. Dulce Murphy was particularly influential here, as was Paul Pozner. Writer Kurt Vonnegut and actress Lauren Bacall also played sup-porting, if more minor, roles. This was an especially powerful political act, since before the Glasnost of the Gorbachev era, Russian writers suffered from almost constant censorship, often simply because they belonged to their own writers' union. It was Esalen's Soviet-American Exchange Program that helped put an end to this suppression of intellectual and creative freedom. Nor has this literary accent ended. The former dissident writer Victor Erofeyev, author of *Russian Beauty, Life with an Idiot,* and *The Good Stalin,* is a good example. Erofeyev's 1979 activity with the Metropol group resulted in a national ban on his books until it was lifted in the Gorbachev era. He continues to be involved with Esalen and Track Two. Now an established voice in American letters, he writes for the *New Yorker,* the *New York Times,* and occasionally offers his American friends wry one-liners like, "It is possible to be a dissident writer in America now" and "We're all finally equal now; we're all in the same shit."

Throughout the 1980s and '90s, Esalen and TRAC facilitated confer-ences, exchanges that both propelled the human potential movement (at a time when it was supposedly sunk in a state of asocial stupor) furthered a cross-cultural warming of relations between the United States and the USSR as it transformed back into Russia. The topics the groups have ad-dressed vary wildly, from psychoneuroimmunology to international trade, from the problem of neo-Bolshevism to the art of ballet, from translations of Russian philosophical texts to sports psychology, from the disaster of 9/11 to ethnic conflict and Islamic terrorism. The list goes on and on, spanning three decades and reaching into the new millennium.

Track Two now operates out of its own office in San Francisco under the leadership of Dulce Murphy and has expanded its mission to other cultures and more contemporary problems, including the challenge of fundamentalism to our open liberal societies. Much of its most recent work with Esalen, for example, has involved meetings and projects with forward-looking Muslim intellectuals and leaders, very much in the model of the earlier Soviet-American meetings. Indeed, the Muslim journalist

Anisa Mehdi now sits on Esalen's board—a direct outcome of these latest Esalen symposia on the challenges of fundamentalism.

Many activist organizations were first inspired at or around Esalen programs. John Marks, the former U.S. State Department employee and author of *The Search for the "Manchurian Candidate,"* was first invited to Esalen for the 1980 meeting to advise Murphy on how to deal with the intelligence agencies the Esalen group would encounter in the Soviet Union. "Be transparent," said Marks. After that meeting, he found his life changed forever by Esalen. Marks went on to found Search for Common Ground, the world's largest conflict resolution NGO that specializes in political reconciliation and creative public policy initiatives. He and his wife, Susan Collin Marks, now come to Esalen once a year to give a workshop on social entrepreneurship. Both explicitly cite Esalen and the Murphys as their mentors and key inspiration. Indeed, Susan once went so far as to call Michael Murphy "our shaman."

Harriet Crosby went on to found the Institute for Soviet American Relations (ISAR) in 1983, this time in order to bring the various citizen diplomacy groups into closer conversation and collaboration. As Ambassador Hartman had pointed out to the activists, the wheel did not need to be reinvented every time. Better communication was needed. A newsletter, "Surviving Together," was started and ran for twenty years. Over the years, ISAR would award grants to NGOs in all fifteen republics of the Soviet Union. After the Soviet Union collapsed, it worked in nine different cities in order to provide computers, copiers, consulting, and conference organization for literally hundreds of environmental, women's, and health education groups.

The media (rather like the contemporary academy) was predictably fixated on the baths and generally preferred either to ignore all of this wide-ranging political activity and activist influence, or to collapse it into what *Newsweek* called "hot-tub diplomacy."[32] This language, of course, had an Esalen history. Still, it predictably offended many Soviet officials, who thought that they were involved in something far more serious than hot tubs and feared that such presentations might jeopardize their work and positions back home. More importantly, those who actually pursued such ventures (as opposed to superficially reporting on them) much preferred to refer to their lifework as "citizen diplomacy" or "track two diplomacy."

The phrase "track two diplomacy" was coined by career diplomat and public intellectual Joseph Montville at that first defining meeting at Esalen in 1980 that resulted in the creation of the Soviet-American Exchange Program. By track-two diplomacy, Montville intended to evoke all those "unofficial" cultural, scientific, and personal exchanges between nations that seldom make the news but nevertheless have their own effects. In the essay "Foreign Policy according to Freud" he coauthored in 1982 with William Davidson in *Foreign Policy,* Davidson and Montville defined track-two diplomacy as "unofficial, non-structured interaction. It is always open minded, often altruistic, and . . . strategically optimistic, based on best case analysis. Its underlying assumption is that actual or potential conflict can be resolved or eased by appealing to common human capabilities to respond to good will and reasonableness."[33] Although certainly no substitute for traditional track-one diplomacy with its very real "carrots and sticks," track-two diplomacy has its own genius and role to play in international relations, and Esalen's efforts were a perfect example of this.

Even by official government standards, such lay diplomacy worked and played an important role in helping to end the cold war and initiate political reform within the Soviet Union. To take a single measure of this real-world accomplishment, consider the witness of Stephen Rhinesmith. When Rhinesmith was appointed by President Reagan in 1986 to facilitate Russian-American exchanges, he was told immediately that he needed to go to Esalen, as that was where the real action was. President Reagan knew about Esalen and was supportive of their track-two initiatives, often over the loud objections of some of his own more hawkish cabinet members.[34]

It would certainly be going too far to attribute any direct causality to these Esalen projects, as if Esalen somehow caused the collapse of the Soviet Union. But it would also be unfair, and historically irresponsible, to ignore the indirect roles institutions like Esalen played in these reform movements. In the words of Robert Pickus of the World without War Council, "It was the imagers, futurists and New Agers who tried to get other currents of thought moving."[35]

It would not, of course, be difficult to find examples of Esalen seminars and figures who confirm for the cynic the common image of Esalen as a New Age center of navel-gazing narcissists devoid of any social consciousness (at least as long as one ignores the economic fact that it is precisely all those "narcissistic" seminars that help underwrite all that social activism). Such major Esalen stories as the Russian adventure and the institute's quarter century of systematic political, literary, economic, and environmental activism, however, should warn the careful historian against any such simplistic readings.

Sex with the Angels

NONLOCAL MIND, UFOS, AND *AN END TO ORDINARY HISTORY*

Recent experiments in remote viewing and other studies in parapsychology suggest that there is an "interconnectedness" of the human mind and other minds and with matter.... The implications of these results is that the human mind may be able to obtain information independent of geography and time.

Committee on Science and Technology, U.S. House of Representatives, June 1981

I often say that I worked as a psychic spy for the CIA and found God.

RUSSELL TARG

If we were to read the Russian chapter of Esalen's history through the Flatland of a purely historical or political lens, we would miss much. Indeed, we would miss just about everything. Most importantly, we would overlook what Esalen likes to call human potential and what the Russians were calling hidden human reserves. We would also fail to intuit those events and meanings that constitute the altered states of Esalen's history. The Esalen activists, after all, were after more than political diplomacy with the Soviets. They wanted a global breakthrough into a new spiritual dimension. They wanted to live in a world in which Russians and Americans, then alleged "enemies," could commune with one another across *and beyond* space and time. It is thus difficult not to read their psychical experiments, which they believed connected them supernormally across the globe, as a cold war mystical narrative that enacted a deeply felt desire to be one or, at the very least, not to be so dangerously two. Whether or not they could link San Francisco and Moscow through the x-power of their minds, they certainly helped unite the two cities through their friendships.

Nonlocal Mind: The Secret of the Spy, the Psychic, and the Mystic

A major player in these ventures whom we have not yet met was the laser physicist, turned CIA psychic spy, turned American mystic, Russell Targ. Targ once marveled at the fact that as a trained physicist he has somehow managed to write five books with the word "mind" in their titles.[1] Through such books and a host of technical essays, Targ has recounted to both lay and scientific audiences some of the "remote viewing" experiments he helped oversee. His story, many details of which only recently became declassified by the CIA under the Freedom of Information Act,[2] is deeply intertwined with Esalen's story and embodies the kinds of scientific-spiritual transformations Esalen had been pushing for from the beginning. Targ's life-work also happens to ground much of the narrative of Murphy's third occult novel, *An End to Ordinary History,* in some real-world cold war events and government-funded research. Fiction and reality, spirit and science morph into and out of one another here in ways that can only be called fantastic.

Russell Targ actually credits Michael Murphy for setting up the events that would indirectly lead to much of this. Not that Targ himself didn't have his own psychical interests. While working as a laser physicist, he had started the Parapsychology Research Group (PRG) in Palo Alto in 1965. He also had taken gestalt and encounter workshops at Esalen with Perls, Schutz, and Gunther in the 1960s.[3] But it was not until early in 1972 that Targ himself began giving workshops at Esalen, this time around an ESP teaching machine that he had invented and was trying to test market. That same spring, Murphy called up Targ and asked if he could fill in for him at one of the Esalen-sponsored Grace Cathedral lecture events in the city. Murphy was scheduled to speak but could not make it. Targ agreed and delivered a lecture on Soviet and American parapsychology in March of 1972.

In the Cathedral audience that evening was a man named George Pezdirtz. Pezdirtz was NASA's New Projects administrator. He was intrigued enough by what Targ had to say to invite him to an upcoming NASA conference that he was organizing on speculative technology. Also attending were NASA director James Fletcher, science fiction writer Arthur C. Clark, pioneering rocket scientist Werner von Braun, and Apollo astronaut Edgar Mitchell. Mitchell had had a life-changing mystical experience in space that inspired him to found (that same year, in 1972) the Institute of Noetic Sciences dedicated primarily to the pursuit of rigorous psychical research.[4] Esalen and Mitchell's Noetics Institute, it turns out, would go on to form numerous institutional and close personal connections that continue to this day. Marilyn Schlitz, for example, the Noetics Director of Education and Research, sits on Esalen's Board of Trustees.

Targ accepted Pezdirtz's offer and used the occasion to pitch his ESP teaching machine as a way of helping astronauts get in touch with their own psychic powers, skills that would be highly beneficial in the dangerous work of space flight, where the astronauts could use all the help they could get.[5] The stakes were extraordinarily high, and so the thought had to be exceptionally bold. In a later public lecture, Targ recalls that, despite the fact that his ESP project was the only one of those presented at the conference to be finally chosen for funding, NASA refused to print his presence or his project in the conference brochure: Russell Targ had literally become a government secret (and a funded one at that).

He also remembers some of the humorous details of how he actually got the NASA grant. Targ and some conference participants were standing on a pier at St. Simon's Island just off the Georgia coast (Targ refers to this as their "psychic pier group") when Werner von Braun turned to Jim Fletcher and said something like, "Oh, give him the money, Jim. We all know that this stuff is real. My grandmother always knew when the trains would crash or when someone was about to die."[6] These may have been accomplished scientists, but their experience of the world was much deeper than their current science would allow. Apparently, Fletcher was listening to his psychic pier group. NASA subsequently awarded Targ his first major grant. With this money, Targ cofounded a program at the Stanford Research Institute (later simply SRI) with Hal Puthoff and helped direct it for ten years, from 1972 to 1982. (The program itself actually lasted until 1995, well after the cold war had melted away.)

When I asked Targ about Esalen's connection to all of this, he immediately commented on how generous Murphy was to the parapsychological community. Murphy hosted several five-day conferences on parapsychology in the Big House from 1981 to 1985, focusing on such topics as the effects of distant mental influence on healing and the implications of precognition on the philosophy of time and the physics of causality.[7] Targ remembers many happy weeks with Charlie Tart, Marilyn Schlitz, and others in the Big House, in the baths, and over the lodge dining table. He recalls how they would use these weeks as off-site retreat sessions to figure out what they wanted to do the next year at their respective research institutes. Stimulated by the discussion and refreshed by the grounds of Esalen, they would then go back to their offices and labs, do the actual research, and publish their results in professional journals.[8]

What Targ, Puthoff, and their associates became most famous for, however, was something called remote viewing (or ESPionage), which essentially involved the use of gifted psychics to locate and describe targets in the Soviet Union that were otherwise hidden or secret (very much like police departments today allegedly use psychics to help crack particularly difficult cases, locate bodies, etc.). In Targ's memory, it was he and Puthoff who actually coined the term "remote viewing" sometime in 1973, but it was the artist-psychic Ingo Swann who first developed the actual protocol, which often involved the remote viewer spontaneously drawing on a piece of paper what he or she was "seeing" after a preliminary period of meditative stillness. A number of writers in fact trace the origins of remote viewing back to the mysterious and essentially occult processes of artistic creativity and, in particular, to the art of telepathic drawing as it was explored in a 1946 Paris lecture at the Sorbonne, or, a bit further back, to Upton Sinclair's *Mental Radio* (1930), which describes Sinclair's telepathic drawing experiments with his wife, Mary Craig.[9]

The CIA, the Defense Intelligence Agency, the army, and the navy would all follow NASA, investing a total of over twenty million dollars in remote viewing programs, drawings and all. The SRI unit was hardly the only one in operation. In fact, the money was distributed through numerous channels and for a variety of programs, including Project Stargate out of Fort Meade, Maryland, where a man named Joseph McMoneagle worked as a particularly successful remote viewer for years after a dramatic near-death experience convinced him that his consciousness was not restricted to the biological boundaries of his skin and skull.[10] Dale E. Graff, the founder and director of Stargate, went on to pursue his own psychical research on intuition, remote viewing, and precognitive dreaming, which he believes are connected to the phenomenon of synchronicity.[11]

The Soviets got wind of these activities through a 1976 paper Puthoff and Targ wrote describing their clairvoyant experiments for the influential journal of the Institute of Electrical and Electronics Engineers (IEEE). They subsequently invited Targ to demonstrate their work for the Soviet Academy of Sciences in 1983.[12] This was the same year that Murphy's *An End to Ordinary History* appeared, telling the tale of an American psychical researcher named Lester Boone dealing with the Soviets.

Why so much money and international interest? According to many involved in these programs, such experiments consistently produced results that either met or far exceeded the expectations of the agencies doing the secret investing. To take just one of many examples, one of the group's most accomplished remote viewers, Pat Price, successfully and minutely described a secret Soviet weapons factory in Semipalatinsk, Siberia, with only the longitude and latitude coordinates given to him.[13] Targ's books, tapes, and papers are filled with dozens of similar examples, many of them accompanied by the original and now declassified drawings and actual photographs of the sites, for anyone who cares to look.[14] Many do not care to look, of course, I suspect because this material comes with a very heavy metaphysical price. Such results, after all, imply that the present materialistic picture of the universe is woefully, ridiculously inadequate.

Targ presents different mathematical models to explain psychical events, but he acknowledges that "every theory of being is perishable," and that future theories will no doubt arise to explain the same facts in a fuller fashion. Still, he is confident that psychic abilities are entirely natural functions of the geometry of space-time, that future physics will embrace them as once anomalous facts that signaled a major paradigm shift, and that any such future model will reveal at least two truths: (1) that such psychic events are not the product of any kind of energetic or electromagnetic transmission (if this were the case, they would erode quickly with distance); and (2) that these same psychic events are in some sense "an interaction of our awareness with nonlocal, hyperdimensional space-time in which we live."[15]

According to Targ, much of this depends heavily on the quantum interconnectedness of contemporary physics and the notion of "an instantaneous spanning of space and time"[16] derived from the famous 1935 paper of Einstein, Podolsky, and Rosen (or EPR) and later mathematically proven by J. S. Bell. For Targ, both the interconnectedness of Bell's Theorem and the "remote" of "remote viewing" do not simply apply to space, that is, to tracking quanta of light in a controlled laboratory or finding bomb sites in a winter Russian landscape. They also, most bizarrely, apply to *time,* that is, to precognition, even perhaps to seeing events and objects that exist only in the past or the future. Targ sees such precognitive (or, I suppose, postcognitive) events to be correlates of the space-time model of Einstein, who is on record as stating that time is a stubborn illusion. He also believes that they are implicit in Kant's famous notion that space and time are *a priori* modes of perception, that is, "powerful filters of our own invention"[17] that structure our ordinary phenomenal experience but are not necessarily accurate attributes of the noumenal world "out there."

As a striking example of just how filtered our ordinary perceptions of a very nonordinary universe might actually be, Targ tells the story of testing Pat Price's psychic superpowers at SRI. Price was asked to describe the location of a CIA agent who had traveled to a random location within the Bay area, this time a particular swimming pool in Palo Alto. Price accurately described the location of the agent, even getting the precise shape and measurements of the pool 90 percent correct. There was one significant error, however: Price insisted that there were two large upright water tanks established on the site. There were not. Targ chalked this up to some kind of simple error or mental interference. Until, that is, 1997, when he received in the mail a brochure for an historical celebration of Palo Alto's centennial celebration. In this brochure was a historical photo of the same site that they had used in the earlier test experiment. Targ found himself staring at the 1947 photo in disbelief; at this same site was a water purification plant at that point in space-time, and its central features were two upright water tanks that were the tallest structures of Palo Alto. Somehow, Targ was forced to conclude, Pat Price had "seen" not only across space but *back* into time.[18]

There were other such moments, some of them with a precognitive punch-line: metaphysics and mirth are always changing places here. Indeed, Targ confesses that the clearest precognitive events of his own life have been consistently more funny than meaningful. One afternoon, Targ had decided to perform a personal experiment with precognition. "I bought a racing form," he confesses, "and I am mildly embarrassed to say that I proceeded to do my meditation on the eighth race at Bay Meadows the next day."[19] Without looking at the race program, Targ sat down with a candle to meditate. Almost immediately the bust of Michael Murphy appeared, hovering in front of him just a few inches from his face (Targ is legally blind, hence the closeness and, Targ often jokes, his life-long interest in "remote viewing").

After his meditation, Targ eagerly sought out the race program to look for any possible correspondences. One of the horses was named "Friend Murph." Targ bet on the Murphy-like horse, which promptly came in first at five to one, winning the blind psychic physicist twenty-five dollars that day. Other more serious precognitive experiments won Targ and associates real success on the silver future market in the fall of 1982 (nine forecasts, all correct, earned them $100,000), a place on the front-page of the *Wall Street Journal,* and a program by NOVA titled *A Case of ESP.* The latter was partially inspired by a 1982 Esalen symposium on "Time and Psi."[20]

Targ eventually came to the conviction that his espionage activities (and gambling ventures) hid profound metaphysical truths, mounting evidence of what he likes to call "nonlocal mind." Nonlocal mind is a form of consciousness "that connects us to each other and to the world at large" and "allows us to describe, experience, and influence activities occurring anywhere in space and time."[21] Targ's work for the CIA was gradually pointing toward the mystical, what the history of religions knows as *mustikos* (literally "hidden" or "secret"). Psychic, spy, and mystic all met here for Targ—in the nonlocal mind beyond space and time.

In line with Esalen's history and influence, Targ's nonlocal mysticism would eventually take on a distinctly Tantric form. Over the years, Targ has passed through laser physics, psychical research, and Advaita Vedanta to Dzogchen Buddhism, the latter through the influence and filial love of his late colleague, Russian translator, and beloved daughter, Elizabeth. In every measure of the contemporary study of Buddhism, Dzogchen is a distinctly Tantric form of Tibetan Buddhism that emphasizes sudden enlightenment and the pristine nature of pure awareness beyond all conditionings and assumptions.[22] In Targ's own understanding, Dzogchen is a path uniquely suited to the modern American, as it constitutes a kind of fast-track to enlightenment (a traditional claim of most Tantric traditions) and does not ask you to believe anything.[23]

Frederic Spiegelberg had said more or less the same thing about Zen Buddhism; indeed, the similarities and perhaps even historical connections between Dzogchen and Zen are often commented on in the scholarly literature. In his spiritual journey, then, Targ has walked what I hope is by now an Esalen path familiar to the reader, that is, one that brings together (without equating) Western science, the psychical, and the practice of Asian contemplation within a religion of no religion, the latter with close ontological and historical connections to the pan-Asian Tantra.[24]

Secrecy, Spies, and Sufism: An End to Ordinary History *(1983)*

As *Jacob Atabet* opens, Darwin Fall has just disappeared on a trip to Russia and Eastern Europe "to investigate research there on 'the clairvoyant perception of atomic structure.'"[25] In the introduction, Michael Murphy reports that he would never see Fall again, even if he himself, both in real life and in the novel's narrative frame, would travel to Russia to investigate these very same psychical and mystical matters.

Murphy's third occult novel, *An End to Ordinary History*, follows-up on the second. Darwin Fall and Jacob Atabet both figure prominently in the story. Indeed, the novel is largely about Darwin's search for the legendary Russian scientist Vladimir Kirov, who, it turns out, has come upon one of Darwin's press catalogs in whose subject content and book cover images he sees numerous synchronistic connections with the teachings of his own secret Sufi school in Samarkand. The school's radical teachings have landed it in trouble with both the Soviet officials, who are suspicious of anything religious, and conservative Muslim groups, who fear that the brotherhood's promotion of ethnic harmony will have a corrosive effect on Islamic fundamentals.

Kirov himself feels conflicted, primarily because of the two central father figures of his superego: his grandfather, Ali Shirazi, who believed that his own mystical form of Sufism promised a transfiguration of both the body and the earth within a hyperdimensional reality called Hurqalya (Persian for "heaven"), and his father, a firm Soviet ideologue who believed that salvation could only be had in the worldly social and political transformations that Marxism heralded with such messianic zeal. Sufism and Communism thus battled in Kirov's soul for who would define "the end to ordinary history." Would that end be a mystical vision of earth within a larger heaven, or a withering away of the state within an entirely materialistic order of being?

While trying to synthesize these two inherited visions of the world, Kirov becomes struck by one of Jacob's paintings, this one of a San Francisco sunrise. Jacob's painting, we learn, is virtually identical to a Bronze Age icon hidden in an underground chamber below the Samarkand mosque that Kirov's brotherhood believes holds the key to their own ancient tradition. As the story develops, we see how both images come to suggest to Kirov, Darwin, and Jacob the inner cellular structures of the human body and its evolutionary transformation, the omen of the atom bomb as a perversion of the body's own atomic transfiguration, and something enigmatically described—often simultaneously—in apocalyptic, Marxist, and mystical tones as "the end of ordinary history."

But this narrative about the cross-cultural synchronicities of Jacob's painting and the ancient Sufi icon is in fact embedded in a second one about the crash of a Soviet space capsule and the disaster's connection to the Soviets' secret parapsychology research program, Project Elefant. Some of this project's practices are fictional elaborations of two separate psychic experiments Murphy himself participated in, that is, the sending of the toy wooden elephant mentioned in the previous chapter, and a random event generator that Murphy seemed to be unusually adept at influencing.

The random event generator experiment, invented by Helmut Schmidt, was a classical one in parapsychological labs. A subject is put in front of a random event generator and told to try to influence the machine's outcome in some ordered or nonrandom direction. The subject then spends a certain amount of time trying to "will" the machine's outcome around his or her own desires: a circle of lights on its black metal face registers whether the machine is generating random (clockwise) or nonrandom (counterclockwise) events. What was so unusual about Murphy's experience with the generator was that he felt erotic overtones in the encounter. "We were in love with each other," he told me. In any case, it was responding with ordered outcomes that far exceeded the expectations of chance.

In Murphy's novel, these experiments take the fictional form of a telepathic experiment between Darwin Fall and a famous Russian clairvoyant, Nikolai Gorski (a fictional reversal of the real-life name, Karl Nikolaiv), both of whom saw the experiment as a symbolic gesture of peace. Darwin and Nikolai also conduct telepathic experiments with an Argentinian boy named Ramon, whom the American weapons dealer, Lester Boone, loaned to the Soviets for their own parapsychological researches. Ramon was particularly effective with the random event machines, partly because the researchers knew how to get him excited. Indeed, Ramon would even get an erection. Darwin Fall remembers "the handsome boy from Buenos Aires stroking and kissing these metal boxes as if they were lovers."[26] It was "a grotesque sight" that left Darwin uneasy for days. Still, it worked.

Sort of. While Ramon attempts to contact the two Soviet cosmonauts in space and the latter try to reciprocate, something both profoundly mystical and disastrously erotic happens. Ramon displays an erection and tries to sexually assault a man during his visionary possession. At this very point, the cosmonauts begin having visions of another dimension that wants to pull them in through a "hole" or "gate." One of them, cosmonaut Marichuk, keeps screaming about an emerald space that is both very near and far and describing a being of some sort who wants to embrace him. The other, cosmonaut Doroshenko, frames his visions as an encounter with a saucer-shaped ship, that is, with a UFO. The cosmonauts eventually lose control of their space capsule, crash into the atmosphere, and burn up.

The Soviets form a special committee to investigate the matter and assign a certain Ivan Strelnikov, a pioneer of laser research (hints of Russell Targ?). Strelnikov reluctantly takes the job only to find himself, in the very last pages of the novel, being transformed in his dreams and theories, themselves infused with a certain erotic anxiety.

The Hyperdimensional World of Hurqalya

It is of some significance that *An End to Ordinary History* is partly inspired by a classical work of the history of religions, Henry Corbin's study of Ismaili Sufism, *Spiritual Body and Celestial Earth*. The connections are numerous, including one minor and indirect appearance of Corbin himself in the plot of the novel.[27] However, within all of these connections glows one central claim, namely, Corbin's radical denial of the usual dichotomy between "history" and "myth," or what we might better call here "reality" and "fiction."

Corbin accomplishes this through what he calls *the imaginal,* a neologism he employs in order to distance this dimension of human cognition from the French and English connotations of "the imaginary" (the false or make-believe) or even "the imagination" (in the sense of "not really true"). Through the imaginal, Corbin hopes to capture the paradoxical sense of the Persian mystical writers and their conviction that what we call the imagination and mistake as mundane is in fact a kind of psychical mode of cognition that, under the right circumstances and with the proper training, possesses the ability to mediate communication between the divine order and the human mind, mostly through coded symbols, visionary or dream phenomena, mythical material, and richly paradoxical doctrines.[28] The imaginal is "the world of visions, the world through which resurrection comes to pass, the world in which real spiritual events 'take place.'"[29]

As the reference to the resurrection as an imaginal event suggests, Corbin tends to deny the reality of the flesh for the sake of the spirit. The body here is a "seeming" or a "sort of" that is finally subsumed within the deeper reality of the spiritual world. The imaginal "is the place where spirit and body are one, the place where spirit, taking on a body, becomes the *caro spiritualis,* 'spiritual corporeity.'"[30] This is what the Persian mystics called the Hurqalya, heaven, that "interworld" where rational abstraction cannot penetrate but "our symbols are, so to speak, taken literally."[31]

Murphy both relies on and moves beyond Corbin in *An End to Ordinary History.* Hurqalya plays a central role in the novel as that spiritual space necessary for the development of the enlightened body. But this hyperdimension for Murphy is that space "in which the human body becomes a luminous form of the soul,"[32] not a heavenly transcendence in which the soul temporarily takes on a body (as we have it in Corbin). Murphy, in other words, takes Heaven in directions that neither Corbin nor his Persian mystics would have dared: he insists that Heaven is most fully known in and through the occult evolution of the flesh.

Kirov, at least, becomes convinced that his strange American friends were in fact "seeking a mutation of human flesh into the Earth of Hurqalya." He also insists that this mutated flesh requires a larger earth in which to evolve and display itself. This, he claims, is the secret space of the Earth of Hurqalya, "the larger Earth that contains this planet, connecting us to the larger life of the universe." Only such a hyperdimensional space, we are told, "can support the power of the angels," who appear both to inhabit it and to possess the power to move back and forth from it, very much like the UFO.[33]

Vladimir Kirov's conviction in the reality of this hyperdimension comes from his own mystical experiences, which he recounts to Darwin. He describes in the third person a man from his secret school who came to Moscow to work, only to become very depressed. He prayed for a vision and was granted a terrifying spectacle of Moscow crumbling as God told him to climb a ray of light from the sky. As he did, he found himself in a city with buildings, streets, parks, and people very much like our own, "but the space that contained it was a marvelous elixir!" This hyperdimension was Hurqalya. When he opened his eyes he understood that the vision had delivered him into his own familiar world, his own Moscow, now made radiant in the light of Hurqalya. This was the "first gate" of the larger Earth, one that he would never forget, but there was also a "second gate." Whereas the first gate involved an intellectual vision, this second gate would embrace the body as well. Kirov identifies the first gate as the traditional way of the saints and the second as the way of Darwin Fall and his friends.

Sex with the Angels

However the reader chooses to interpret the hyperdimension of Hurqalya, it is difficult to miss the fact that the central event of the novel is an "alien" encounter suffused with sexual energies and fears. A bit of comparative history is in order here.

One would not know it from the guardian angel lore of popular Catholicism or the sweet childish art of Evangelical Christianity, but the history of the angel in both Jewish and Christian history is rife with sexuality, power, and violence. Indeed, the first appearance of angel-like beings in the Bible, the mysterious *nephilim* of Genesis 6, involves a dramatic sexual transgression. These four little lines tell the story of a host of horny "sons of God" seeking out and having sex with the "daughters of men," an act which in turn produces a new race of hybrid heroes or divine-human beings. The erotic angel appears again in the New Testament, in such places as the infancy narrative in Luke, where an angel announces Mary's illegitimate pregnancy as "of the holy spirit," that is, as another divine-human sexual encounter.

Such "sex with the angels" found elaborate expression in some of the early Christian gnostic churches. It later took a darker turn in the medieval *succubi* and *incubi* traditions (perhaps first mentioned by Augustine in his fifth century text, *The City of God*), involving male and female demons that come at night to seduce and have sex with humans while they sleep (the medieval explanation for the "wet dream").[34] Here also we can place the late medieval witchcraft traditions of having sex with Satan, and, much later, modern UFO lore about alien abductions and bizarre sexual experiments involving ovum extraction, forced insemination, and the creation of a hybrid human-alien race on hovering space craft. In other words, in the modern alien abduction, we are back to Genesis 6, even if the symbolic frame has shifted from an ancient mythological code to a modern technological one. Such mythologies, of course, are negative transformations of repressed instinctual energies. Hence the classical "Devil" in the Christian imagination—cloven feet, pitchfork in hand, horny head—is clearly a mythical transformation of the half-goat shepherd Pan, the Greek god of fertility. What a culture represses returns to haunt it.

These are hardly irrelevant details. *An End to Ordinary History,* after all, appeared between two Esalen symposia on the subject of UFOs. Both were attended by astronomers, officials from NASA, and, most importantly, philosophically inclined Esalen intellectuals who easily recognized the UFO phenomenon within a larger comparative pattern of the history of religions, that is, as a modern religious or imaginal experience. The guest list of the first conference in 1975 was so secret that they had to hold the proceedings off the grounds at a private ranch in Sonoma County. The second, The Further Reaches of UFO Research, took place in 1986.[35] NASA was there, as were a number of Ivy League scientists and Peter Surrock, a Stanford astronomer.

This second symposium helped Keith Thompson produce *Aliens and Angels,* an eloquent analysis that represents the best of what I would call the standard Esalen reading of UFOs.[36] Thompson firmly resists "the bucket of bolts landing on the White House lawn" scenario, that is, any literalist or simple technological reading. Instead he engages an explicitly hermeneutical approach that understands UFO encounters as modern mystical experiences requiring our active translation and interpretation (thus the best ancient analogue of the UFO for Thompson is the Greek trickster god Hermes, after which the transactional art of interpretation is literally named).

Once so hermeneutically or Hermes-like engaged, Thompson interprets UFO encounters as modern synchronistic experiences of some hyperdimensional reality that participates in *both* the physical *and* the mental but is likely reducible to neither (affirming, once again, the deeper paradoxical unity of energy and consciousness). Here, of course, that reality is filtered through the imaginations of technologically oriented moderns for whom a spinning space-ship zipping down from the stars makes a good deal more sense than the standard god or savior-figure descending from the heavens. Put simply, aliens are our modern angels who appear precisely to confound all either-or thinking about the cosmos and our paradoxical place in it. In a different mythological code, they function very much like Michael Murphy's mystical realism, that is, they come down to trick, to shock us out of our mundane metaphysics, and, above all, to open up a channel of communication, however confusing, between the empirical and the mystical.

Kirov is very much aware of this same history. Indeed, he has even performed, very much like Keith Thompson, his own study comparing "Islamic, Buddhist, and Christian angelic lore with UFO sightings."[37] He notes such comparative patterns hardly prove the objective reality of UFOs, but he also sees they are suggestive that "we are dealing with . . . something intrinsic to human nature, something that transcends cultural conditioning and common sense."[38] What is particularly interesting about the accounts of cosmonauts Marichuk and Doroshenko is that they differ, and together offer both a traditional mystical reading (Marichuk's terrifying vision of Hurqalya) and a science-fiction reading (Doreshenko's vision of a silver saucer that he could locate in space and time).[39] Once again, together they confound all either-or thought.

Kirov has no doubt that Marichuk's vision speaks of his grandfather's Persian mysticism, of the Hurqalya, and of his own ecstatic experience during an earthquake (not to mention thousands of modern near-death experiences): "Like the folding of space in certain ecstasies the thing made a tunnel in the sky. If you fastened your attention on it you felt yourself sucked into its wake."[40] Just before their capsule burned up, Marichuk experienced the encounter as vaguely erotic and explicitly terrifying as it exerted an inextricable pull: "The thing is talking now, embracing me! It wants to take us through that hole!" The transmission leads Kirov to believe that these "alien" beings are like fishermen, hooking us humans from the water of space-time into another nonordinary dimension above the surface of the water, as it were.[41]

The Soviet researchers read the mystical experience through their familiar Marxist materialism, focusing instead on the homoerotic dimensions of Marichuk's sexual encounter. Had Marichuk's mother not been hospitalized for a nervous condition? Had not Marichuk once confessed to sexual feelings toward a fellow pilot? "The profile was perfect. The man had hysteria in his genes—and homosexual tendencies. The angel that wanted to embrace him was a projection of his feelings for the other cosmonaut, and the surrealistic form it took was the result of his latent instability.... Both feared losing control, not only of their capsule, but of their sexual urges."[42] One of the researcher's final diagnosis was as simple as it was reductive: "It appears that the man was homosexual. His 'angel' was Doroshenko."[43]

"Angels Are Mirrors"

There are many other mystically erotic scenes in the novel, and all of them point away from the sexual reductionism of the Soviet researchers to something much deeper: an erotic occult opening to another dimension, a mystical revelation of the quantum connectedness of the cosmos. Some of these are quite simple, as when Jacob's remote viewing experiment in San Francisco reveals "breasts" on the Soviet landscape that turn out to be actual radar domes: even remote viewing, it turns out, can have its sexual fantasies.[44] Other more explicit features, however, inform the major events of the novel and bring the narrative's plot to a final concealing climax.

As the story proceeds, we learn that the space capsule crash was not simply homosexual in a reductive sense; it was also homoerotic in a mystical or psychical sense. After all, when the two Cosmonoauts encountered the emerald presence that wanted to embrace them, Marichuk and Doroshenko were trying to telepathically connect up with Project Elefant on the ground, where Ramon had entered an erotic possession state (clearly signaled by his visible erection) while he attempted to contact the cosmonaut crew.[45]

Ramon cannot crash on the ground, but he does lose control. He goes into a frenzy, tackles Kirov, and embraces him (exactly as the space presence wanted to do). As the boy sexually attacks him, Kirov immediately and mysteriously begins to lose consciousness but manages to hold on to a shred of awareness by focusing on his heart. By such a means, a meditative stillness breaks through and a "vast serenity" allows the voices encoded in Ramon's transmitted energies to speak to Kirov. He sees a sun rise out of the darkness, then a band of fire—a flame shaped like a hand that wants to plant something deep in his heart. When the flaming hand reaches out, Kirov enters an ecstatic swoon.

The assistants jump on Ramon and strap him down while Kirov witnesses a series of internal visions pass before his inner eye. "Two shadowy figures fringed with light circled around each other, and then began to embrace. Kirov wiped cold sweat from his face as another image formed. Two drops of water, vividly etched against an emerald wall, slid into one another." He was being given a revelation, whose meaning is suggested by a subsequent fantasy of two cartoon figures of his father (the Soviet ideologue) and grandfather (the Sufi mystic), each uncomprehending of the other's point of view. The merging water drops on the emerald wall were densely meaningful and consistently homoerotic: they dripped down the wall to join Ramon and Kirov, Ramon and the cosmonauts, the cosmonauts and the emerald space presence, even Kirov's grandfather and father, within a single phallic line of psychical transmissions.

"That was a sexual attack," one of the assistants says with a smirk. "Ramon still has an erection." "He is possessed," Kirov whispers. "Treat him gently." Kirov then wonders whether this is what the cosmonauts had feared, that is, the erotic element of their apparitions. "The only way to receive an angel, Kirov thought, was to be undivided. For the least fear could turn into panic as you were drawn toward a pleasure like death."[46] The only way to encounter an angel, in other words, is to accept the occult presence as fundamentally erotic, to not repress the same energies down into the unconscious but to integrate them into consciousness. This is what it meant to be "undivided," to not transform the "pleasure like death" that is the erotic into yet another "evil" projection.

Kirov, at least, had his vocation seminally planted in him by another man: "And now, the seed planted in his brain by a boy he had brought from the United States for a hideous project of psychic research was telling him something important about the entire process. His whole life, it seemed, was a project to find common ground," that is, between the visions of his Sufi grandfather and Soviet father.[47] Kirov finally concludes that Ramon awakened some type of disembodied being through his erotic-occult fits.[48]

Ivan Strelnikov, the Soviets' top official and laser scientist assigned to study the capsule crash, would come to a similar conclusion and revelation, but he would choose to bury it all again, that is, to repress it both psychologically and politically. Strelnikov has a dream of pleasurably riding Kirov, who had turned into a panther.[49] In the dream, Kirov intuits that the dreaming Strelnikov is entering a mystical state and may be open to a parable, so he tells him a Sufi story of a net of reflecting precious stones. "Angels are mirrors," we are told in another place (another homoerotic image to the extent that mirrors reflect back, even as they unite, a same-sex image).[50] The dream-vision suggests "that each of us reflects the other, to the end of space and time. It refers to mystic states in which one sees their essential unity with all others." "That each of us reflects the other," Strelnikov murmured, "to the end of space and time. Yes, I could see how one might struggle against that." He then remembers riding a panther through the streets, a panther like this Kirov. And he recalls how in the dream he hovered between pleasure and panic.[51]

In the end, though, the angelic-erotic net of jewels was more than poor Strelnikov could take. He removed all the documents Kirov had used for his own research: the UFO report, Darwin Falls's book, the tapes of the capsule accident. By late afternoon, nothing remained of the investigation. "All this was accomplished," we are told, "while Strelnikov's dreams sealed over." The secret was concealed again.

Almost. In the author's note at the end of the book, Murphy leaves the door (or "gate") open for those who are willing to read on in another future decade: "But we can be hopeful. Sometime in the next few years, Darwin Fall may write a book about these matters. With their Soviet friends, he says, he and Jacob Atabet are finding unexpected vistas beyond the labyrinths of ordinary history."[52]

The Marriage of Heaven and Hell

An End to Ordinary History is at once a cold war warning, a Freudian morality play, and a bodily hope. Much of it, moreover, revolves around the Russians' inability to fully integrate both the occult and the erotic into their Marxist materialist worldview, which, oddly enough, remains potently mystical in its insistence on the material implications of all human experience. Murphy explained the situation this way in an interview: "Sri Aurobindo said that from one view, matter is the densest form of spirit, and from another view, spirit is the most subtle form of matter. I believe that both cultures, Western and Soviet, have a secret love of the mysteries of matter and a destiny to understand these mysteries before seeking some kind of disembodied beyond." Murphy, in other words, had approached Russia as a third kind of culture that might avoid both the superficial materialism of the West and the disengaged and often frankly dualistic mysticism of the East.

It was this same enlightenment of the body, moreover, that he sought to communicate through Kirov's hyperworld of Hurqalya. "I've come to believe that when you radically alter the body," related Murphy, "you alter the structure of space-time around you.... The molecules in our cells are spinning or oscillating billions of times a second, in a quantum light show that would be altered in any radical bodily transformation. So I have imagined an opening into a larger space, a freer, more complex earth, which can be experienced through the body we are growing into."[53]

Cultures, however, can block or stunt this evolutionary growth. Just as individuals deny their own instinctual drives, the Russians officially repressed their own occult and psychical treasures, and so they had no stable practice or adequate vocabulary with which to integrate these universal human potentials. Moreover, when they did access the superpowers of telepathy and clairvoyance, they employed them for the wrong ends. Just as Targ himself would eventually learn in his own conversion from spy to mystic, Murphy insists this occult tale is not about espionage or national security. It is about the human potential, the need for a practice, and the real metaphysical truths of the mystic, the psychic, and the spy: "My theory is that the Soviet Union has more people gifted in the expression of occult powers like telekinesis than any other nation. The stupendous Russian energy for the mysteries is bound to find expression, in a return of the repressed."[54]

The Freudian reference—"a return of the repressed"—is significant. A good share of Murphy's narrative, after all, is encoded in sexual terms. The mystical can certainly not be equated with the sexual here, but the two are nevertheless inseparable, very much like the spirit and the body in Murphy's incarnational thought (or mind and matter in Stapp's quantum interactive dualism). Expressed and integrated, the body evolves into its own psychic powers and grows into the angelic joy and light that is the hyperdimension of Hurqalya and the precious net of jewels of the Sufi parable. Denied and repressed, however, the same body results in terrifying visions of demons, of socially dysfunctional forms of transcendence, and of "alien abductions." It is certainly relevant here that Murphy considers the UFO lore about alien abductions and sexual experiments on spacecraft to be often traceable back to the sexual repression of those reporting these events. In other words, the psychic mechanisms of repression and sublimation can take on modern technological forms as easily as they once took on medieval theological and demonic forms.

Of the cast of characters in *An End to Ordinary History*, only Kirov is able to accept the mystery of his sexuality and sublimate it into a rich spirituality of the body and the earth. Only he still dreams of uniting the moral and mystical visions of his Soviet father and Sufi grandfather. Only Kirov can accept the erotic seed planted in his heart by another man. Only he possesses a heart big enough to not give in to the panic and pleasure that feels so much like death. Vladimir Kirov, in other words, represents the mystical figure who can imagine enjoying "sex with the angels." Such beautiful apparitions appear to the unrepressed, not as demons to deny and project outside oneself as somehow Alien, but as angelic mirrors in which to see and love the divine human in every face, in every Other.

The Tao of Esalen

THE SPIRITUAL ART AND INTUITIVE BUSINESS
OF MANAGING EMPTINESS

Tao
   follows the Way
   of
   the
   Watercourse
   as the
   Heart/Mind
      through meditation
   Returns
   to the
   Sea.

public memorial to Dick Price by AL HUANG
on the Round House near the stream

The late 1970s and early '80s was a time of maturation for the Esalen community. The outlaw era of the 1960s and early '70s was more or less over, and things seemed to be settling down, a bit anyway. One would never think of bringing, much less raising, children here in the '60s (although there was one by the name of Orion). But by 1975, two children, Jenny Price and Christopher Flash Tarnas, had been born into the community, and soon others would begin appearing alongside their seminar-attending parents. When Jenny and Christopher Flash turned two, Janet Lederman stepped in and addressed the issue head-on with the creation of the Gazebo School.

Janet Lederman (1930–1992) had come to Esalen from a background in educational philosophy and reform. She had been a member of the Los Angeles Board of Education from 1956 to 1967, after which she helped

Fritz Perls open up his Gestalt Institute of Canada from 1969 to 1971. Her *Anger and the Rocking Chair* had appeared in the Esalen Viking Press series, in 1973. During the 1970s and '80s, Lederman served in various leadership roles at Esalen, including vice president, director, and general manager. Most who remember her remember a woman who wielded tremendous power throughout the Esalen community in a variety of administrative roles. But perhaps her most symbolic contribution was the Gazebo School. Founded in 1977, the outdoor preschool sports a small farm, an old boat converted into a classroom, a parked motorcycle gang of children's Big Wheels, and a *really* outdoor toilet (no walls, no door) designed to make the children feel comfortable with their most basic biological functions. Today, the school serves as a preschool for both Esalen staff children and those of local Big Sur residents.

In the 1970s and early '80s, the Murphys and Prices settled into complimentary vocations. While Mike now had a well-established writing and research career in the Bay area, with his various projects usually connected to Esalen in some way, Dulce administered and led much of the Russian outreach. Dick, on the other hand, had never left the immediate Esalen orbit. He was the definitive, if often backstage axis around which the daily life of Esalen revolved, while Chris worked as both an effective gestalt practitioner and as a central figure in the social life of Esalen.

It would be a serious mistake to paint this period as normalizing or comfortably institutionalized. It was often anything but normal, and "institutionalization" was a word Dick Price detested, and for very good reasons. Moreover, the community would meet its greatest challenge in the fall of 1985, when Price was killed in a freak hiking accident. Still, for now at least, Esalen had achieved a certain internal dynamic stability, a Tao or Way. Things were running more or less smoothly, even if it was often difficult to say exactly how. Murphy, schooled in the thought of Aurobindo, was well on his way to articulating his own metaphysical vision, and Price, skilled in Buddhist meditation and the *Tao Te Ching*, had learned the spiritual art of managing emptiness.

The Tao of Esalen

Since Perl's death in 1970, Price had become the person most consistently connected with gestalt groups at Esalen. By all accounts, he had a way of sitting with people, of being present to them. Eric Erickson, who was more than familiar with Hinduism, Buddhism, and Taoism when he came to

FIGURE 27. Michael Murphy, Richard Price, Christine Price, and Dulce Murphy, 1973. Printed with permission of the Esalen Institute.

Esalen, encountered in Price a practice of presence that reminded him of the meditation traditions of the Asian religions he had been studying: "It was very clear to me (and to many others), from the first time I saw Dick work, that his gestalt work was also a vital part of an ongoing personal, spiritual practice bearing a strong affinity with meditation."[1]

Chris Price's experience of Dick reflected Erickson's, but it was finally of a different order. She fell in love with Dick. Christine Stewart grew up in College Park, Maryland, where she attended an experimental high school. When she was sixteen, she read Perls's *Gestalt Therapy Verbatim* and experienced what she calls an "epiphany" through it. She remembers walking around at 10:00 p.m. one evening, sobbing with a kind of recognition that this is what she also wanted to do with her own life—yet another powerful textual transmission in Esalen's history.

It was a dramatic time. One of the young women killed at Kent State on May 4, 1970, was from Chris's high school. Such events affected her deeply. She graduated early, lived in a commune for a brief period, and decided not to go to college. She moved out to San Francisco to spend some time with her sister, Gail. One day, Gail took Chris to Esalen's San

Francisco office to pick up a catalog. Her parents agreed to put her college money toward some Esalen courses, if that is what Chris wanted to do. She enrolled in a seminar led by Dick Price called Gestalt and Structural Integration, a combination of gestalt work and Rolfing that worked on the principle that any deep psychological work would also have to be deep physical work, and vice versa.

Price's work was embedded in the body as strongly as he himself was embodied. Chris Price often speaks of "the Reichian aspects" he brought to his work and to how he held forth his own energetic presence. Price spoke of Reich often: the energy of Reich and the awareness of Buddhism came together in him. Both systems, moreover, spoke of an inner goodness or trust, of a human nature that was, in the end, eminently positive. Price was deeply moved by the contrast between the Reichian and the Freudian anthropologies, that is, the basic Reichian notion that at the core of the human being is wellness, wholeness, and heath, not a seething cauldron of instincts that needed to be contained by civilization. The human being was a self-regulating organism for both Wilhelm Reich and Dick Price. What gestalt work was about was coming to understand how society, families, and individuals twist and distort that basic self-regulation into sickness and dis-ease, and then working to remove, reverse, or dissolve those distortions.

"How deeply grateful I am for how he saw me," said Chris Price in an interview. "He had an inner gyroscope that I haven't found in people. He just had it. He was one of those souls who, however you get it, came in with one. He could really see that thread of truth that could come through different paths, as in Reich and Buddhism. In his own way, Fritz had that vision too, though not the integrity. They both had 'bullshit detectors' in that unofficial language of my [gestalt] lineage."

Toward the end of my visit with Chris, she reflected on how he is remembered, as a person and as a practitioner: "I wish that people would write more about [Dick's] practice than his life. I sometimes feel like the mythology is a little bit distracting." Perhaps, speculated Chris, this is about a connection between patriarchal or male-centered theology and the need or desire to divinize a mythical person, usually, of course, a man. But this same mythologization process works against "the formlessness of the big picture," she said. Dick was always clear that the teacher is not the teaching, that teachers come and go, but that the Way remains.

This is deliberate Taoist language. Dick Price, after all, used the classic scriptural text of Taoism, Lao Tzu's *Tao Te Ching,* to guide him in his administrative decisions and managerial style.[2] Chris would also later assign the same text to her gestalt workshops, alongside Perls's *Gestalt Therapy Verbatim*.[3] For the Prices, gestalt was the Way of Esalen.

Life on the Group Room Floor: The Human Potential Essays of John Heider (1976)

John Heider, who had left Esalen in 1971 to pursue his own career in leading group encounters in Kansas, California, and Florida, came to some very similar conclusions in his turn toward Taoism and the Way of Esalen. Heider's unpublished essays and novel, *Life in Paradox* (an exploration of what Esalen would be like in "Paradox, Kansas"), give us some insight into the Taoist currents of Esalen's history.[4]

Significantly, Heider's written work is reflective of the worldview of Dick Price and of much of early Esalen. Handled with enough care, Heider's texts can thus be approached as a kind of written commentary (and development) of the Esalen oral tradition that Dick Price embodied but never put to paper. In other words, we can use John Heider, who did write, to explicate Dick Price, who did not. Just as significantly, these same writings represent a rather astonishing confirmation of my own Tantric thesis. By 1976, John Heider had described group encounter and much of his own Esalen experience as explicitly Tantric in structure and meaning. Put simply, Heider realized, over thirty years ago, that the Tao of Esalen was Tantra.

This Tantric structure is already apparent in Heider's Esalen journals, where he writes of both the "Tao of Encounter" and "Encounter Tantra," thus implicitly (and probably correctly) uniting the Indian Tantric and Chinese Taoist historical streams.[5] He can also distinguish between being "Tantrically related" to a woman and being "karmically related" to his wife. The former he defines as a sharing of "vibration lust not ego entanglement."[6] Tantric sex, in other words, is about arousing, channeling, and sublimating energy, not developing a personal relationship. "Tantra" had not yet become interpersonal in the late 1960s. Toward the very end of the journals, Heider states his own concluding conviction: "The key to the secret of life [is] sex. Freud was right and far more so Wilhelm Reich." A question remains, however, this time as a warning: "Yet the power of sex is so great as to ruin lives and spoil nations so what right minded man or woman would not fear it?"[7]

This is more or less where John Heider left things when he left Esalen. His thought hardly ended there and then, however. Within five years, by

1976, he had produced over two dozen brief but potent essays on the dynamics of group encounter, which he collected into *Life on the Group Room Floor: An Introduction to Human Potential Theory and Practice.*

These essays represent a real shift for Heider. Seasoned by years of encounter group work at Esalen with Bill Schutz, not all of it successful (some of it, as I've mentioned, quite dangerous and irresponsible), Heider had already abandoned the confrontational group style of the Flying Circus and had evolved toward the subtler ways of what he was now calling the Tao of Encounter. He turned to the traditional Taoist image of flowing water to explain how his new methods differed from his older ways: "The word 'encounter' means 'to meet.' More narrowly it means a forceful meeting or confrontation. But I also use it to mean a far gentler coming to-gether or 'confluence,' as when two rivers meet or flow into one another."[8]

Among this collection of essays is Heider's "Electric Sex and Magnetic Sex," probably the clearest statement we have from a major Esalen figure on the psychology and mechanics of a contemplative sexual practice. The essay begins with the obvious: "More people experience energy sensations during sexual intercourse than during any other experience." Heider then proceeds to explain how these energy fields can be expanded, deepened, and developed through a contemplative approach to sexual foreplay and intercourse. Crucial here is Heider's distinction between *electric sex* and *magnetic sex.* "Electric sex is male sex, yang sex. Electric sex works when a body specifically stimulates sexual trigger points such as the head of the man's penis or the woman's clitoris."[9] This in effect "zaps" the body into arousal and eventually sparks an electric circuit through which the sexual energies can arc and discharge, leaving the body in a state of relaxation (or exhaustion).

Magnetic sex is different. Historically rare in the West but known throughout Tantric Asia, "magnetic sex is female sex, yin sex. Magnetic sex works when the fields of two people awaken and make contact. Magnetic sexual arousal is diffuse and felt more or less equally all over the body and in the space surrounding the body."[10] It need not lead to a traditional orgasm and the pleasurable discharge of the energies. Energies can build and build here and be sublimated into deeper and deeper states of bodily bliss and contemplative consciousness—an electro-magnetic sex life, if you will.

"Sex and Sin" pursues similar themes again, this time through the uses and abuses of sexuality. Heider is not particularly impressed with the sexual solutions of his own generation, which he frankly admits have not led to sexual bliss but to "a floating world in which many people, relentlessly aging, drift from pseudo-spouse to pseudo-spouse."[11] What Heider hopes for, then, is not a return to the sexual revolution of the 1960s, but a "new covenant," "a new Law" derived not from Paul or Christianity, which has always more or less "regretted that we [have] bodies with carnal impulses," but from the Asian Tantric traditions and their use of sex "to help people become increasingly married to one another and to the cosmic whole." Heider points out that this Tantric turn was anticipated in the West by Reich, who "specifically said that when sexual union is free from blocks, the energy fields of the two partners become one unified energy field."[12]

Heider's homiletic conclusion is well worth quoting in full here, as it beautifully incorporates so many of the themes I have identified here as Esalen's enlightenment of the body. Even Paul gets embraced, if also outshined:

> If we have been, as a culture, irrevocably sexualized, perhaps we are offered an opportunity to grow in awareness of ourselves and our part in the whole not by avoiding the difficulties that accompany sexuality but by becoming aware of our sexual natures and transcending the powerful attachments sex involves. In this way, we may possibly see more and more sexual experimentation leading to more and more sexual meditation and finally, as Paul would have it, more and more celibacy on the part of those who have climbed the sexual ladder to the point where everyday life outshines the brightest orgasm.[13]

Tantric Resurgence

As Heider's language suggests, Chinese Taoism includes some rather profound Tantric strands, including a basic sexual symbolism (the famous *yin* and *yang* icon) and an ancient sexual yoga tradition whose psychological sophistication and graphic discussion of sexual fluids and energies make many of our modern discourses on human sexuality seem boring at best. Some scholars have even speculated that Tantra originated in China and diffused from there into ancient India. The more abstract and philosophical Taoism of the *Tao Te Ching* and of Dick's management style, of course, was not quite this. If my Tantric transmission thesis about Esalen and my general claim that Indian Tantrism and Chinese Taoism are related in the American counterculture carry any plausibility, we might expect, then, that explicitly Indian Tantric patterns would surface somewhere in the spiritual life of Dick Price. They do.

In 1977, Dick announced, much to the confusion of his closest friends and colleagues, that he and Chris had become devotees of Bhagwan Shree Rajneesh, a charismatic Indian guru who was at that time synthesizing Tantric philosophy and Western psychology in a particularly potent mix.[14] The guru's devotees wore bright orange robes (the traditional color of renunciation in Hinduism) and a sacred *mala* (a kind of necklace made out of large red round seeds) around their necks, often with a picture of Rajneesh attached to it. Rajneesh's ashram in Poona, India, which offered everything from meditation and yoga to gestalt therapy and encounter groups, more than resembled what *Time* magazine called "Esalen East," as did the guru's talks, which could somehow relate the Buddha to Chuang Tzu to Wilhelm Reich to Jesus to Rajneesh himself, often all in the same hour.

Dick received the name Geet Govind from the guru (through the mail) and began planning what would become a month-long trip to Poona. This was big news at Esalen, as it seemed to suggest that one of the basic ground rules was about to be broken, or at least seriously tested. "No one captures the flag." No gurus. But now there was a guru, and one of the founders of Esalen appeared to be submitting to his teachings. Even the East Coast establishment saw what was at stake. *Time,* for example, ran a story on Rajneesh in January of 1978, which featured Dick's decision to travel to Poona: "Now the guru is instructing his best-connected disciple yet: Richard Price, cofounder and director of the Esalen Institute, the very fount of the encounter craze. Price will return to the Big Sur, Calif. center in mid-January to apply the teachings of his new master."[15] As Anderson makes clear, the subtext of the *Time* article was transparent: Poona may have been Esalen East, but Esalen was about to become Poona West.

That didn't happen. Dick spent the first two weeks in the ashram's meditation facility, where things went reasonably well. Then he moved into the encounter group sessions and participated in a session with an English psychotherapist who had studied with Will Schutz in London. Still well enough. Then in a session next door, a woman got her leg broken in a fight, apparently generated by the group session. This upset Dick deeply. What sealed his rage, however, was a second scene involving Rajneesh himself. Shortly after the broken bone, a woman stood up in the question-and-answer session and asked the guru about the violence. She questioned whether this was really necessary. According to Dick, Rajneesh not only did not respond to the question; he turned on the woman and tried to intimidate and shame her into silence.[16] That was it for Dick. Disgusted, he left the ashram in Poona, much as he had earlier left Ichazo's Arica retreat in New York.

Later, he wrote *Time* to correct any notion that Esalen East was Esalen at all, or that Esalen itself was about to become Poona West. *Time* never published that letter, but Anderson reproduces it for us in *The Upstart Spring*. It reads:

> Rajneesh is well worth reading.... He can speak brilliantly of the transformative possibility of human life. His "meditations" I find worth practicing. However, the ashram "encounter" group is an abomination—authoritarian, intimidating, violent—used to enforce conformity to an emerging orange new order rather than to facilitate growth. Broken bones are common, bruises and abrasions beyond counting. As such it owes more to the S.S. than to Esalen. Until the compassion Rajneesh speaks about with such eloquence is reflecting in his groups, I am content to be known as "Richard Price" rather than as "Geet Govind."[17]

Price's assessment is remarkably balanced, particularly in the light of what he had experienced in the ashram and his own psychological processes of disillusionment and deidealization. He praises Rajneesh's obvious genius, but he refuses the devotee pact. In the end, the guru's authoritarianism simply was not compatible with Price's belief in the need to privilege the individual. Something had to go, and that was the guru. Dick had met a modern form of left-handed Indian Tantra face to face, and he found it mystically brilliant but morally appalling.

And Dick had the last word. A passage from Rajneesh's writings appeared in the Esalen April-June catalog a few months after Dick's disillusionment in Poona. Its content? A sermon on the abuses of charisma.[18]

Jenny and the Nine

Price, however, used more than Taoist wisdom or Tantric enthusiasm to manage Esalen. In January and February of 1979, he also began using nine immaterial beings channeled through the automatic writing of a British psychic named Jenny O'Connor. This rather unusual administrative strategy, which went on for years, is easily one of the most infamous events of this period. Even the alternative press couldn't quite deal with it. *Mother Jones,* for example, commented on these events with the telling headline, "Esalen Slides off the Cliff."[19]

Jenny and the Nine, as they came to be called, were also quite controversial within the Esalen community, not because of O'Connor's alleged psychic powers or because the Nine happened to be from the star Sirius (that was all fairly normal fare), but because Dick decided to ask Jenny and the Nine to help him make tough administrative decisions, which included firing and hiring individuals. In Erickson's memory, around Esalen at least "the Nine were much better known for performing the role of extraterrestrial hatchet men than for giving psychic insight into how Esalen might actually improve its operations."[20]

There is, of course, some debate about what Price was really doing here. Did he really believe that the Nine existed? Or was he simply using this kind of occult theatre to justify (or humorously undercut?) decisions that were essentially his? John Heider, who was very close to Dick, was put off by this whole episode, and it was a well-known fact that Murphy thought very little of the Nine as well (to put it mildly). Price joked with Walter Truett Anderson about the differences between Murphy and himself and their own agreement to disagree about certain things: "He puts up with my ETI and I put up with his KGB."[21] In a similar spirit, he would also sometimes tease Murphy about his Three R's: running, writing and Russians.[22]

Rick Tarnas, who was living at Esalen during this period, knew O'Connor and witnessed much of this. He observes that before these events most of the administrative decisions were being made by Julian Silverman, Janet Lederman, and Andy Gagarin, but that after and probably through these events Dick began to take more and more control. Tarnas believes that Dick was genuinely interested in the Nine, but that he was hardly a true believer. His relationship with the entities was essentially an ironic and humorous one. "It was just something that clicked for him," Tarnas comments. "He used them as a creative touchstone to do certain things. They also reflected that part of him that was farther out there than Mike."

By the grace of some archival gods (acting through Frank Poletti and Steve Donovan), I have a copy of a typed transcript of one of these sessions, dated April 28, 1982. Jenny, the Nine, Dick, and another woman are discussing several things. Their conversations capture beautifully that combination of genuine interest, psychic intuition, creative interpretation, and playful humor that defines this whole episode. The transcript, for example, begins with Dick asking the Nine for book reviews. In particular, he wants to know about *The Upstart Spring,* Walter Truett Anderson's history of Esalen that was just about to come out, and Michael Murphy's *An End to Ordinary History.* The Nine find Anderson's history "incomplete." "Do you mean you've been left out of it?" Dick asks. "No." (And indeed, Anderson does discuss Jenny and the Nine.) "OK, what's missing?" Dick asks again. The Nine respond that they wanted to hear more about the author's own "investigation and production style," that is, they wanted to know more about Anderson's creative processes. Dick then asks what effect the book will have on Esalen itself. They refuse to respond. Price then asks for another review, this time of Murphy's *An End to Ordinary History.* "Good," the Nine reply, "We would have preferred an 'X' in front of ordinary." "They must mean 'extra-ordinary,'" Jenny chimes in. "An end to extraordinary history, or a beginning of extraordinary history?" Dick wants to know. The Nine respond: "Good pattern, and articulate."

The conversation then turns to advice on how to run the work-scholar program and a psychological reflection on the Nine themselves. Reflecting on the fact that the Nine do not respond well to any question involving "should" (nor, by the way, did Fritz Perls), the other woman comments that, "The Nine are gestaltists." Dick agrees: "They even use the same word I use for my role in gestalt—reflector. They are reflectors. So instead of asking about future predictions, use them more in terms of filling in a gestalt of what is presently." So the woman then puts to the Nine the question of how she can best use her time when she returns home from Esalen. She offers any number of admirable social projects as examples. The Nine respond with a rather unusual line of work that the woman had not mentioned: "To work in mime psychodrama with the deaf." Dick comments dryly: "That wasn't on your list, was it?" "Out of left field!" Somewhere the Nine were chuckling.

The conversation then turns to sports, in particular the Super Bowl, the San Francisco '49ers (the Nine correctly predicted the two Super Bowl teams and the final score within two points), and the 1982 Nebraska-Clemson college championship game, which Clemson won by 7 (22 to 15) as (sort of) predicted by the Nine ("Third team down on the right by 7"). For our own purposes here, though, perhaps the key moment in the transcript occurs at the point where Dick is asking the Nine about his own dreams. "And how do you see the place you hold in my dream?" he asks them. "In transition to await the next move," they answer back. "And how do you see my role in that transition?" he goes on. "As always, dear worker, facilitator."

Dear worker, facilitator—that, it seems to me, is as good a reading of Dick *or* Jenny and the Nine as any. However one judges the metaphysical status of these happenings (as alien contact, psychological probe, or conscious farce), it is difficult to ignore the fact that real-life work was being done, and that, more specifically, Jenny and the Nine helped Dick Price manage Esalen, his own dreams, and occasionally even his reading and sports interests in the late 1970s and early '80s.

As Anderson points out, the Nine were the only nonhuman beings ever to make an appearance in an Esalen catalog, where they were listed as program leaders. "They were also listed, elsewhere in the catalog, as members of the Esalen gestalt staff. Had Fritz not died already," Anderson observed with his usual wit, "surely that would have killed him."[23] Years later, Dick would add another nonhuman being to the Esalen catalog. He joked about making Aurora, his dog, chairman of the board.[24] At least everyone could see Aurora.

Alien Gnosis

One might imagine that Dick as a Rajneeshi or the Nine as program leaders were about as strange as things got at Esalen during this period. And one would be wrong. The theme of the extraterrestrial or the UFO experience was not unusual, and it was treated both with a certain ironic playfulness, and a very real scientific and epistemological sophistication, as we saw with the Esalen UFO symposia and *An End to Ordinary History*.

But these were not the only Esalen readings of the extraterrestrial. In December of 1983, Terence McKenna appeared on the grounds of Esalen to speak at the conference Consciousness and Quantum Physics, part of the long-standing series that had merged with Murphy's Atabetian speculations on the quantum transfiguration of the body in the late 1970s. As an amateur ethnobotanist specializing in the psychedelic properties of South American sacred plants used by indigenous shamans, McKenna actually had very little to say about quantum physics, but what he had to say about the nature of consciousness was as astonishing as it was almost completely unbelievable. Fortunately, we know more or less exactly what he said, because he later published the talk as "Tryptamine Hallucinogens and Consciousness."[25]

Not that the Esalen community did not already know about the connections between shamanism and psychedelic plants. That was old news. Indeed, the first seminar on the topic went all the way back to April 1963, when anthropologist Michael Harner, Jungian analyst Joseph Henderson, and psychoanalyst Charles Savage led the three-day seminar Shamanism, Supernaturalism and Hallucinogenic Drugs. McKenna knew more than a little about Harner, since much of Harner's work in the 1960s was, like McKenna's, centered in the Amazon Basin and focused on ayahuasca, a visionary vine whose psychedelic properties are usually assimilated through drinking a type of vomit-producing tea.

Terence McKenna (1946–2000) is one of the most uncanny minds ever to appear at Esalen. A colleague once described him as, "Dense. Technical. Fascinating. Infuriating. Marvelously weird."[26] That is an understatement. This was a man who could seriously entertain the idea that the original awakening and early primordial evolution of human consciousness was the result of the brains of our primate ancestors entering a symbiotic relationship with tryptamine-laced alien mushrooms, whose spores had literally floated in from the deep freeze of interstellar space to colonize the planet by taking refuge in the fertile microenvironments of cow pies that "followed" early human communities wherever they went. Obviously, without a few dozen pages of explanation (it's not quite as crazy as it sounds), we are not going to get very far into this mind. Not at least without the mushrooms.

We need to try anyway, and for three simple reasons. First, McKenna was a truly gifted writer; there are few more entertaining reads around, at least for those whose reality orientations are not, in Tom Robbins's jibe at the materialist, "lower than a snowman's blood pressure."[27] The ontologically timid need not bother.

Secondly, a surprising number of the central Esalen themes that we have encountered so far appear again in McKenna's thought, if often in spectacularly exaggerated forms: a deep appreciation for Amerindian cultures; an evolutionary mysticism; a kind of *animan siddhi* into the molecular structures of the body; a linking of quantum physics and mysticism; an understanding of synchronicity as a type of "alternative physics" that signals the essentially linguistic and imaginal nature of reality; a quite literal end to ordinary history through a hyperdimensional vision of the past, present, and future; an integral epistemology that can embrace both the truths of religious revelation and the critical methods of modern psychology and the natural sciences; a planetary ecological ethics involving the celebration of love, community, and sexuality; a linking of orgasm and mystical chemistry; UFOs and alien sex; and, perhaps most of all, a metaphysical blending, if not actual fusion, of the imaginal and the real. I know of no author in whose texts reality and the imagination, fact and fiction, merge more completely. Perhaps this is because McKenna thought that reality *is* a kind of mystical or occult fiction.

Thirdly, McKenna deserves our attention because the Esalen community loved Terence McKenna, and Terence McKenna loved the Esalen community. Steve Donovan first invited him to do a workshop and to become a teacher-in-residence around 1987. When McKenna was undergoing brain surgery for a cancerous tumor, he stayed in Donovan's home. He gave his last public lecture "Always Coming Home" to the Esalen community on October 20, 1999, shortly after his craniotomy. It was a beautiful, heart-rending talk punctured with weak coughing spells and remarkable moral and intellectual flourishes. Terence, for example, mused openly on the irony of him, of all people, dying from what was essentially a mushroom-like growth spreading through his frontal lobe.

McKenna had a very distinct and developed theory of the altered states of history that strongly resembles the synchronistic model with which we began our own journey. But before we get to this end—and it really *is* an end for McKenna—it is first necessary to explain how McKenna got there himself. Terence McKenna began his path to Esalen like many, that is, he came of age in the 1960s counterculture in Berkeley. He grew up, however, in the '50s in what he himself describes as a more or less fundamentalist town in Colorado—Paonia. His father was a traveling salesman. His mother was a housewife. At the age of fourteen, young Terence happened upon Aldous Huxley's *The Doors of Perception:* "I remember following my mother around our kitchen," he recalls, "telling her that if one-tenth of what this guy was saying was true, then this was what I wanted to do with my life."[28] He had his first LSD trip in Berkeley, where he studied art history and was an activist in both the antiwar and free speech movements. In 1969, he traveled to Nepal and spent the spring and summer there studying the Tibetan language and Buddhist *thangkas* (traditional sacred paintings that guide meditation practices). His working theory, which he derived from Leary and Metzner's popular psychedelic manual *The Tibetan Book of the Dead,* was that these iconic images could be instructively integrated into the LSD trip.

He discovered that they could not be. He knew, however, that Tibet had its own form of indigenous shamanism, Bön, the practitioners of which, according to McKenna, the Buddhists generally despised and considered heretical. He also knew that this tradition used psychoactive drugs, in particular hashish and datura, to alter consciousness. It was McKenna's hypothesis that the fierce protective deities and flaming auras of the

Tibetan Buddhist *thangkas* had their ultimate origins in these plant-induced states.

These Tantric beginnings are particularly evident in a chapter of *True Hallucinations*, "Kathmandu Interlude," which McKenna glosses with one of his amazing subtitles: "In which a flashback to Tantric excesses in the head nests of hippie Asia illuminates strange mushroom experiences at La Chorrera." In the course of this chapter, McKenna relates a trip he took with LSD and DMT on the winter solstice of 1969. It began the usual way: "I heard a high-pitched whine and the sound of cellophane ripping as I was transformed into the ultra-high-frequency orgasmic goblin that is a human being in DMT ecstasy." Later, he made love to a female acquaintance who had joined him on the roof. "Or rather we had an experience that vaguely related to making love but was a thing unto itself." Basically, his friend was transformed into a Jungian Tantric goddess. She became "pure anima, Kali, Leucothea, something erotic but not human, something addressed to the species and not to the individual, glittering with the possibility of cannibalism, madness, space, and extinction. She seemed on the edge of devouring me." Within this "fucking... at the very limit of what is possible," everything was transformed into "orgasm and visible, chattering oceans of elf language." Where their genitals met, moreover, there flowed out of the Tantric goddess and over McKenna and everything else "some sort of obsidian liquid, something dark and glittering, with color and lights within it." This, McKenna speculates, was the magical substance that would focus so many of his later speculations, the "translinguistic matter, the living opalescent excrescence of the alchemical abyss of hyperspace," perhaps generated by the sex act itself.[29]

Like many others, McKenna began his spiritual journey with a kind of psychedelic orientalism and a distinctly Tantric form of Buddhism. He would abandon both as mistaken and inadequate, however, and this is precisely what makes him so interesting. After traveling through India and much of Southeast Asia, he came to the conclusion that the guru-scene in India was very much a "shell game," a con game, and that Asian religion did not possess the answers he was looking for. What did have his answers was South American or paleolithic shamanism, which he defines, following the subtitle of Mircea Eliade's classic work on the subject, as "archaic techniques of ecstasy."[30]

In 1970, McKenna traveled to the Amazon Basin. He returned the next year with his brother Dennis, who would go on to earn a PhD in psychopharmacology. The McKenna brothers learned that the South

American tropics appear to have a virtual global monopoly on hallu-cinogenic plants, and that many of these are mushrooms or fungi that share the common molecular structure of tryptamine. The two brothers also experimented with ayahuasca and the tryptamine-laced snuffs of the Waika and Yanomamo people.

According to Terence, they were expecting a kind of LSD trip in which elaborate colors and geometric patterns would appear, along with a kind of psychedelic probing of unconscious processes, or perhaps, fol-lowing Jung (and Grof), of the collective unconscious—a kind of "instant psychoanalysis."[31] Instead, to their utter astonishment, they encountered an "invisible landscape" or "world of gnosis" that could not be mapped onto any cultural or religious tradition. They came to realize that what they were encountering in their trance states was a completely alien Other, an insectoid or elf-like presence that spoke to them within elaborate con-versations in an effort to reveal an entire hyperdimensional reality that overlaps with or suffuses our own. In religious language, they were re-ceiving a revelation.

This, McKenna eventually concluded, was the ultimate source of the UFO phenomena. Since mushroom spores could chemically survive space travel, he concluded, the mushrooms may in fact *be* aliens. Later, he would back down a bit from this claim, but never quite completely. He could never make up his mind whether (a) the mushrooms actually are aliens, or (b) their tryptamine nectar somehow allows our brains to puncture space-time and attain access into a cosmic channel of communication that is always both present and open to every other place in the universe. Often, he confessed, he felt like the little child who asks whether there are little people in the radio set. Like the radio, the mushroom was tuning him in to unimaginable marvels that appeared to be "in" the mushroom but probably in fact were elsewhere (or everywhere).

This, in any case, is what he spoke of to the small crowd of physicists and philosophers during his first visit to the Big House in December of 1983. He claimed "the major quantum mechanical phenomena that we all experience, aside from waking consciousness itself, are dreams and hal-lucinations." These visions for McKenna are a kind of electroscopic laser through which "we see interior images and interior processes that are psy-chophysical" and that "definitely arise at the quantum mechanical level."[32]

The mushroom forced him into contact with "self-transforming ma-chine elves" or "fractal elves" that communicated to him some sort of super assembly language or alien information system "that cannot be Englished."

McKenna glosses this linguistic revelation by comparing it to "a Kabbalistic language of the sort that is described in the *Zohar,* a primal *ur sprach* [primordial language] that comes out of oneself."[33] This all happened within twenty seconds after smoking DMT one day in 1966, he told his Esalen listeners. He came down from that experience and said to himself:

> "I cannot believe this; this is impossible, this is completely impossible." There was a declension of gnosis that proved to me in a moment that right here and now, one quanta away, there is raging a universe of active intelligence that is transhuman, hyperdimensional, and extremely alien. I call it the Logos, and I make no judgments about it. I constantly engage it in dialogue, saying, "Well, what are you? Are you some kind of diffuse consciousness that is in the ecosystem of the earth? Are you a god or an extraterrestrial? Show me what you know."[34]

The Logos apparently knew quite a bit. It taught McKenna that there seems to be "some latent ability of the human brain/body that has yet to be discovered; yet, once discovered, it will be so obvious that it will fall right into the mainstream of cultural evolution." McKenna believes that "either language is the shadow of this ability" or "this ability will be a further extension of language."[35] For my own part, I cannot but help wonder whether this Logos is precisely what made McKenna such an exceptional writer. On this level at least, I'm a believer—again, the mystical text as transmissive of something beyond itself.

By his 1983 address at Esalen, he had come to believe that "the human soul is so alienated from us in our present culture that we treat it as an extraterrestrial."[36] The UFO, in other words, is the human soul exteriorized into three-dimensional space as a religious experience. We will only overcome our own alienation when we realize that we ourselves are the alien, and that there is nothing more marvelous and bizarre in the entire known cosmos than what is going on in our upper cortex, right now, right here, quite beyond the three extended dimensions of space and the fourth of time, that of mere ordinary history.

For now, however, we can begin to connect all the dots with this new gnosis. We can enact a radical comparison between dream, psychedelic trance, quantum physics, mystical rapture, even death: "The mushroom consciousness is the consciousness of the Other in hyperspace, which means in dream and in the psilocybin trance, at the quantum foundation of being, in the human future, and after death. All of these places that were thought to be discrete and separate are seen to be part of a single continuum." And what we call history? It is nothing but a "dash over ten to fifteen thousand years from nomadism to flying saucer, hopefully without ripping the envelope of the planet so badly that the birth is aborted and fails, and we remain brutish prisoners of matter." History is "the shock wave of eschatology." Something at the end of time is acting as an attractor, drawing us all toward its final galactic wisdom and our "ingression of the novel into the plenum of being."[37] Using the ancient Chinese divinatory text the *I Ching* (the mushroom told the McKenna brothers to employ this text), a Mayan sacred calendar, and some mathematical equations, the McKenna brothers calculated that the end of time as we know it will occur in the year 2012.

In other contexts, McKenna will claim that reality is linguistic and imaginal, that is, that it is composed of a secret language which can be manipulated by focused imaginative acts (recall his first experience of this within his Tantric trip in Nepal). Magic is thus very much still alive, and its deepest gnosis comes from plants.

And, it turns out, from us. As McKenna points out, the fact that DMT is neutralized so rapidly by the human brain means that our neurochemistry is very much at home with this compound (and why not? in McKenna's system at least, we were long ago colonized by the tryptamine-based mushroom aliens). In fact, as clinical researcher Rick Strassman has speculated, the brain may actually produce tryptamine through the pineal gland, particularly in especially traumatic or dangerous situations, like death, in order to aid the soul's transit from the body.[38] Put simply, *the human body is itself a psychedelic plant,* a magical mushroom promising galactic gnosis, certainly at death and, with the right techniques and the right plants, *right now.*

McKenna would return to Esalen again in 1984 to speak to a gathering of ARUPA, the Association for the Responsible Use of Psychedelics (the acronym is a Sanskrit noun meaning "formless"). This was a loose gathering of psychedelic mystics, chemists, psychologists, and activists who met from 1983 to 1986 under the sponsorship and leadership (until 1985, at least) of Dick Price.

It is difficult to know what to do with McKenna today. Certainly there is what many Esalen figures would call a "woo-woo" factor in his numerology—it's just too much for them. Perhaps the year 2012 will change their minds. I seriously doubt it. Robert Forte, who knew McKenna and knows as much as anyone about this entire psychedelic culture, believes that Terence's fascination with the year 2012 was an intuition of his own imminent end (which came twelve years early). Along different critical lines, McKenna's vision of the Eschaton resembles a kind of cosmic determinism that essentially robs human beings of any real self-determination and, indeed, of freedom itself. This sort of thing does not sit well with other, much more open-ended aspects of Esalen's visionary culture. It also seems important to note that both Terence and Dennis McKenna have expressed reservations about their own youthful speculations. To his credit, Terence never actually claimed he was doing science. He knew better. He consistently claimed only that he was an "explorer," a "phenomenologist" of the invisible landscapes. He knew that it was much too early to make any firm conclusions. Later, he would describe his own ideas, in Wittgenstein's apt phrase, as "true enough" or, as the title to one of his books puts it, as "true hallucinations."[39]

Few other modern mystical texts are as provocative, funny, and intellectually stimulating as the books of Terence McKenna. But I would not quite end there. After all, Terence's texts (themselves a kind of literal plant product) force on us a potential encounter, if not with literal aliens, then at least with a kind of alien eloquence, translinguistic gnosis, or metaphysical trauma speaking through McKenna's words. We would do well, I think, not to reduce or metaphorize away his claims too quickly.

Consider, for example, the more recent work of Rick Strassman, another Esalen seminar participant who first came to Esalen in 1985 to speak about the pineal gland and its relationship to consciousness. Later Strassman acquired a permit from the Drug Enforcement Agency and Food and Drug Administration to experiment with DMT within a major research project at the University of New Mexico. From 1990 to 1995, Strassman administered approximately four hundred doses of DMT to sixty volunteers in a controlled lab setting. Strassman's results are certainly more staid than McKenna's (whose *wouldn't* be?), and he notes some discomfort with McKenna's popularizing presence.[40] Nevertheless, much that he has to say is uncannily in line with McKenna's "true enough" hallucinations.

Strassman argues that the pineal gland, which he (following Descartes) calls the seat of the soul,[41] secretes DMT in traumatic and ecstatic contexts, and that this "spirit molecule" is the secret catalyst of dreaming, schizophrenia, mystical experience, near-death experiences, and the alien abduction phenomenon (which is not to reduce any of these states to the chemical compound *per se*).[42] Strassman also thinks that a similar chemistry lies within the psychedelic-like phenomenology of sexuality and orgasm, hence both the common link of eroticism and mysticism that his subjects reported and Tantra's potent combination of meditation and sexual activity.[43]

Most interestingly of all, however, is the fact that Strassman willingly shut down his own research program in 1995, partly because his volunteers were routinely encountering insect-like or elfin "aliens," some of whom were devouring, probing, sexually engaging, or even occasionally raping them. Strassman became convinced that these were not simple projections (in McKenna's phrase, we might say that they were "true hallucinations"). Strassman speculates that DMT acts as a kind of "reality barometer," or, to use another metaphor, that the spirit molecule is somehow able to change the channels on the television set of the brain, thus giving us almost immediate access to parallel universes and the dark matter that surrounds us at all times. In other words, he had arrived at a transmission theory of consciousness, similar to that which Myers, James, Huxley, and Grof had advanced. To his own astonishment, Strassman had to conclude that this dark parallel universe may in fact be inhabited, and that his own university research might have been giving these beings an actual entry point into the imaginal worlds of his subjects. He ended his own five-year, government-approved research on a decidedly metaphysical note. Fact and fiction, reality and fantasy, science and mysticism had merged yet again.[44]

The Intuitive Business of the Esalen Catalog

My brief discussions of O'Connor, McKenna, and Strassman raise the larger issue of just how specific teachers get to Esalen. There are just two physical gates to Esalen (a back and a front to the north and south, respectively), but there are many cultural gate-keepers. One in particular, however, has had an especially central role in Esalen's programming for the last twenty-five years: Nancy Lunney-Wheeler. It would be difficult to measure and even harder to overestimate Nancy's influence on the overall vision and specific composition of the public programs at Esalen, which draw some ten thousand seminarians to the campus each year, decade after decade, and host over four hundred seminars on the ground annually. It is Nancy who decides who will run a seminar and who will not, and what the topics and program emphases will be. She is Esalen's talent scout.

"What I'm always looking for is the 'cutting edge,' the thing that isn't known and popular yet, the innovative pairing, the new approach to an old problem, the small-scale exploration or experiment, for students

FIGURE 28. Gordon Wheeler and Nancy Lunney-Wheeler.

and teachers alike. And it's not easy—because by definition, these things are not a guaranteed draw." Thus she is continually caught between two competing concerns: what represents true excellence measured against Esalen's own mission and understanding of itself, and what will draw enough tuition-paying seminarians. If anyone in America understands the history, business, politics, and personalities of what historians of American religion have called the "spiritual marketplace," it is Nancy Lunney-Wheeler.

Nancy Lunney took her first workshop at Esalen in 1972, a gestalt workshop taught by Dick Price. She had never been in any kind of group work. She was terrified. And it worked. "It was an epiphany in a certain way. Everything shifted somehow from that point on." Shortly after this experience, Lunney took another trip to Big Sur to meet privately with Beverly and Julian Silverman, the directors of Esalen at that time. Janet Lederman was also around, hence Lunney came to know most of the major players almost immediately. In 1973, she became one of the first work-scholars. For the next four years, until 1977, she was coming in and out of Esalen with her two children, a move that was unheard of at this time. She was also pursuing a masters in marriage and family counseling and working as a vocal coach. For the latter, she used her gestalt training to give singing lessons to Hollywood figures like Anne Bancroft, Dom Deloise, and Leslie Ann Warren, who needed to learn how to sing for a new role.

In the summer of 1977, Dick asked Nancy what she wanted. She told him that her marriage was ending, that she needed a place to live and work where she could also make a life for her young daughters, and that she wanted to do all that at Esalen. Dick invited her to do just that, and so she returned to Los Angeles to finalize her marital separation, collect her girls, and move to Esalen. Within a year and a half, Lunney was working in programs with Rick Tarnas. Tarnas had been living at Esalen since 1974. He would stay on until 1984. For the first five years, he worked primarily as a gate guard. For the last five years, he worked as Esalen's program manager. Tarnas, in other words, was Esalen's "gate-keeper" in both the literal and intellectual senses of the term.

By the summer of 1982, Lunney had taken over most of Tarnas's duties. Lunney also began to get to know Michael Murphy, who was generally not involved in the running of Esalen during this period. "Now understand," she observes, "up to that time nobody had ever asked Michael's opinion of the programs. I had barely met Michael, but as soon as I was hired I called him and asked if I could come to Michael and Dulce's home in Mill valley with the upcoming catalog and go over it with him." Nancy stayed with the Murphys for three days. They laughed at the same things. They groaned over the same absurdities, at Esalen and elsewhere—in particular, certain "New Age gurus" they considered to be self-important or otherwise risible. In her view, Murphy was also impressed with her "New York smarts" and her show business connections. In effect, they discovered that their sensibilities were more or less identical, and that they shared a complete understanding of one another. Nancy believes that Mike began a slow journey back to Esalen at this point, partly through her and the catalog.

Lunney tried hard to get Murphy's advice and recommendations for the programming and catalog. She has never been what she calls a "New Agey person." Indeed, she has never allowed the phrase into the Esalen catalog. Ever. She wanted what they did to be of a certain quality and excellence, and she wanted to retain the place's loyalties to particular teachers via the two founders' visions. She marvels now at how different the Esalen catalogs are from what they were in the early years. The first brochures contained only a few workshops. The biannual catalogs now contain literally hundreds. To bring in the new, however, Lunney has had to chip away at the old. Moreover, some things she knows will not draw the students she keeps anyway for the sake of excellence. "It's a funny sort of balance, and a good deal of it is intuitive on my part," she observes. Lunney still feels that her work in programming acts "like a conduit for these two men." She also realizes that she stands virtually alone in aligning herself with both founders.

Death in the Mountains

November 25, 1985 was a Monday. Dick was eager to do what he often did on Mondays: hike up into the mountains. This time it was to check "the source," the catch-basin that functions as the origin-point of Esalen's water supply about one mile up Hot Springs Canyon. No one knew he had left, which was not unusual. He had a 4:00 p.m. appointment with Esalen president Steve Donovan.

He never made it. At 8:30 p.m. Chris called Brian Lyke, Esalen's general manager, in order to tell him that Dick had not yet returned. They talked about what to do. It was not unheard of for Dick to wander in the mountains, even over night, so Chris suggested that they wait until morning and see if he showed up. Brian was not so sure. Neither was Chris. The moon, after all, was close to full, and Dick could have easily used its light to find his way back. Brian also worried that if Dick was injured, a night in the cold mountains without help could mean the difference between life and death. He asked Steve Beck if he would join him on a late-night hike up Hot Springs Canyon. Armed with flashlights, some medical supplies, warm blankets, coffee and cookies, the two men started up the mountain creek bed at about 9:30 in the evening.

They found Dick:

> He was just a few feet from the catch-basin, half sitting, half lying in the water. There was a large wound on his forehead, probably from the huge rock that had crushed part of the basin. We couldn't tell the extent of his injuries, and at that point it didn't seem important to know because he was clearly dead, his muscles already quite stiff. . . . We knew in that moment that our world was irrevocably changed, and our hearts ached, especially for Chris, Jenny, and David.

The two men knew that the coroner would want to examine carefully the scene, so they left the body where it was and walked back, thinking about how they were going to break the news to the family and the community. They entered the Little House at 11:30 p.m. Chris was waiting for them with two other women. "It's not good," Lyke began, "we found him at the source. He's gone."

It quickly became obvious to the men that they had to retrieve the body that same night. Whatever the professional needs of the coroner may have been, Chris needed to hold her beloved husband. She needed to touch him, and to say goodbye. A team of seven men headed out into the dark again and returned at 3:15 a.m. with the cold stiff body. Seven women were waiting to receive Dick. "They cut off his clothes and washed his body with an herbal solution and wrapped him in a clean sheet and blanket."[45]

Four days later, a memorial gathering was held on the front lawn.

VI

Crisis and the Religion of No Religion (1985–1993)

The Religion of No Religion

THE DONOVAN ERA

With one church you have tyranny; with two, civil war; but with a hundred, peace.

VOLTAIRE

It seems that capitalism is not rotting way, as we were told, but it seems to be prospering.... The Statue of Liberty is not some sort of a witch, but a very attractive lady.

BORIS YELTSIN in the *Washington Post* on September 11, 1989 on his Esalen-sponsored tour of the United States

Dick was killed, probably instantly, by a boulder. Edged loose from the previous summer's forest fire and finally released by the heavy rains that fateful day, it tumbled down the mountain and exploded like a bomb in the basin. A chunk struck Dick while he tended to repairs on the catch basin or sat in meditation.

Theories and legends quickly developed. Murphy commented on the incredible odds of being struck by a boulder bouncing down the mountain and through the trees: "It partook of the occult."[1] Max Sucharov, a psychological theorist, commented to Eric Erickson on the weird synchronicity that seemed to exist between how Bobby, Dick's childhood twin, had been killed by toxins exploding inside him, and how Dick had been killed by a boulder exploding outside him.[2] And then there was the community legend. Erickson explains: "The symbolism of being killed at 'the source' was embellished into a story in which he was killed while he sat in meditation (the source was a place Dick often stopped to rest on his hikes, and he sometimes did meditate there). Many looked at his death as a way for

Dick, as an evolved spiritual being, to gain a kind of transcendent departure from the difficult times he was known to have been experiencing."[3]

It is true that Price had been going through some difficult struggles, particularly with Murphy over the future of Esalen. But these had been resolved, and both Chris Price and Erickson believe that he was in a very good place when he died. John Heider, on the other hand, is not so sure. In his mind and memory, Dick was in the "slough of despondence." In Erickson's mind anyway, it was the rain and a loose boulder that took the life of an already actualized human being, not some transcendent script.

> My last memory of Dick is looking at his body, lying in state on his bed, framed by a background of bushes in the window behind him, bushes that were all bearing bright red fruit. I remember feeling that I was in trouble, many of my friends were in trouble, Esalen was in trouble, and especially Dick's wife Chris and his daughter Jenny were in trouble, but I did not have the sense that Dick was in any trouble at all. There was a profound feeling tone of peace and completion in the room that morning. It was as if Dick's lifework had been completed, and all was well in the world. It was a feeling I will always remember.[4]

The world may have been all well, but Erickson was right: the Esalen community was in real trouble. When Dick died, Esalen immediately entered a crisis mode. The founder who had lived on the grounds and guided the Way of the place for twenty-three years was gone. The other founder, moreover, had been living in the Bay area for twenty years and had no plans to return to Big Sur. Something had to be done.

Something, however, had already been done. Before Dick died, Steven Donovan had been appointed the new president of Esalen by both Price and Murphy. The idea was that Price, Murphy, and Donovan would manage the place together, each bringing their own specific talents and interests to the task. Dick had just begun to mentor Steve before his fateful hiking trip.

Steven Donovan was born in 1941 in Chicago and grew up in Short Hills, New Jersey. His paternal grandfather, Robert L. Donovan, was born in County Cork, Ireland, where the Donovan clan traces its lineage back to the twelfth century and to some striking ruins of what once was Castle Donovan. Steve remembers fondly how his grandfather liked to be called the Mystery Man and how he tempted his young grandson into a magical world where the mysteries reigned (to the great irritation of Steve's

FIGURE 29. Steve Donovan reading Aldous Huxley in Mikonos, Greece, June 1988. Photo by Anita Eubank, printed with permission.

Episcopalian mother, who later in life would become an Esalen enthusiast). Robert Donovan was in fact the Grand High Priest of the New York State's Royal Arch Masons.

Steve Donovan's mother, Vera, was a classical musician who taught students in her home studio. His father, Robert, was a Texaco executive and air force colonel. In 1951 the family moved to Hofheim, Germany, a beautiful medieval village in the Taunus Mountains, not far from Wiesbaden, where his father was stationed. Germany had a resounding effect on the young boy. Donovan remembers discovering a trap door and secret stash of Nazi flags, uniforms, and medals in the attic of a requisitioned house they lived in for a time (in 1995, this same house still stood abandoned, as if its haunting Nazi past has made it unlivable). He also remembers recurring dreams suggestive of concentration camps and recalls playing in the rubble of bombed-out neighborhoods, where he would find bloody rags and smashed toys. These memories would stick with Donovan and guide his future endeavors, all of which—from his work with Esalen and American-Russian diplomacy, to his fundraising for the preservation of indigenous Pacific Rim cultures—were inspired by a deep desire to contribute to a world that would not be anything like Nazi Germany.[5]

Donovan is a businessman. He completed his MBA at Columbia in 1967. In 1973, he was hired as a consultant and board director by the three founders of a little coffee, tea, and spice shop that had just opened up in Seattle's Pike Place Market. The three early partners called it Starbucks, after the first mate in Melville's *Moby Dick*. Donovan became the founders' only external board member. For the next fourteen years, the four men would meet, sometimes on Donovan's sailboat (where he lived), and Donovan would try to convince them, at first with little success, to expand outside of Seattle. Eventually, the first such Starbucks opened in 1984, in the Marina District of San Francisco not far from Donovan's own apartment.

It was Donovan again who interviewed and helped hire Howard Schultz, the man widely credited with transforming the little company into a transnational business empire. Schultz describes Donovan as the young company's "silent partner" and as a "tall, blonde, classically handsome man" interested in many things, including meditation research.[6] Donovan left Starbucks in 1988, this time to become a board member and board chair of Peet's Coffee and Tea. He stayed with Peet's from 1988 to 1994, helping again to transition a local retail operation into a national brand name. During much of this time, he also had his own consulting and head-hunting firm, Donovan Associates, which served large corporations, principally Cummins Engine Company.

Early in his career, though, Donovan was going through something of a personal spiritual crisis, catalyzed partly by a divorce in 1972. He was living on his sailboat, a thirty-six-foot sloop he had named the Ilinx. The name is as significant as it is unusual. When Donovan was working as the director of planning for K-2, a skiing equipment company, he read a dissertation on why people ski, surf, and sail. Athletes engage in high risk sports, he learned, to annihilate their limited consciousness in an intense sense of gliding and ecstatic danger. He decided to name his boat the Ilinx, defined on the boat's brass name plate as "an attempt to momentarily destroy the stability of perception and inflict a kind of voluptuous panic on an otherwise lucid mind." Donovan still keeps that defining name plate in his study.

Donovan too wished for some kind of altered state of transcendence, some voluptuous panic. Certainly he was suffering considerably. One evening in March of 1973, he did something he had never done before: he got up in the middle of the night to pray. Towards morning, something remarkable happened, and this in an instant. His pain was instantly healed, and the ocean dawn saw Steven Donovan a new man, reborn on a sailboat rocking in a beautiful bay.

It was this rebirth experience that opened Donovan up to more self-exploration and inspired him to join a local psychosynthesis group in Seattle. He also met a gestalt therapist, Jeanette Rainwater, who had been trained by Fritz Perls. She told him about Esalen. So in May of 1975, he traveled to Big Sur and participated in his first gestalt workshop with

Beverly and Julian Silverman, then directors of Esalen. He would later train with other Esalen notables, including both Dick and Chris Price and Jim Simkin. He immediately fell in love with the place and the people. It was, as he puts it, "beyond anything I had ever imagined." He returned home but continued to track and participate in a whole range of psychophysical practices offered through the Esalen catalogs.

In the winter of 1976, Donovan was on a plane from New York to San Francisco flipping through the January issue of the *New Yorker,* which included a long profile piece on Michael Murphy by Calvin Tomkins. Donovan read the essay and knew, "This is what I want to do." Murphy's interest in bodily transformation somehow spoke to his own deepest interests and that night on the sailboat. When he landed in San Francisco, he went straight to the Esalen office on Union Street. They told him that the first physics of consciousness symposium was taking place, but that there were no available rooms left. Donovan rented a station wagon to sleep in and drove down anyway. When he walked into the Big House, he encountered the physicist Saul Paul Sirag and Michael Murphy. He was impressed with Sirag, but he was stunned by Murphy. There was something about Murphy that he immediately recognized as oddly familiar, as if he had known him before. This feeling has never left him, not even thirty years later.

Donovan has thought a great deal about this sense of familiarity, and he now speculates that it is something ancestral. In our interview, Donovan pulled out a document he had clearly been working on for a very long time and read me a long list of Irish surnames that have played important roles at Esalen and in the broader human potential movement: Steven Donovan, Stephen Dinan (former director of Esalen's Center for Theory and Research), Tom Driscoll (major donor), Al Dugan (major donor), Don Hanlon Johnson, Timothy Leary, Terence McKenna, Michael Murphy, Brendan O'Regan (former vice president of research at Institute of Noetic Sciences), Alan Watts. He went on and on, twenty-six names in all. He also showed me on an ancestral map of Ireland how most of these names originated in the very same county of Ireland, County Cork (or, in the case of McKenna, just west of there in County Kerry). "What my colleagues in these [human potential] circles don't often realize," he told me, "is that a hundred years ago many of our grandfathers and great-grandfathers were all rubbing elbows on a parcel of land no bigger than Marin County in southern Ireland. It's uncanny, really."[7]

After his encounter with Murphy in the Big House, Donovan decided to move down to San Francisco. He rented an apartment on Marina

Boulevard overlooking the Golden Gate Bridge, Sausalito, and Alcatraz. He would live here for the next fifteen years, until he moved down to Esalen in 1989.

In September of 1977, Donovan heard about *Jacob Atabet*. He went to Celestial Arts, the publisher of the first 1977 edition, and pled for an advance copy. He immediately read it straight through. It became a kind of personal bible to him, the most influential book he had ever read. He was particularly moved by Darwin's book outline set out in "Evolutionary Relationships between Mind and Body." Indeed, until this day, *Jacob Atabet* continues to influence Donovan, who believes in the possibility of being able to alter the body at will. Many years of experience have humbled his expectations, but this basic of Atabetian convictions has never left him. The influences are indeed dramatic. In 1979, he took over from Jim Hickman the archival and organizational duties of the Transformation Project that flowed out of this same novel (much more on this in the next chapter). Donovan remained with the Transformation Project, which he directed out of his Marina Boulevard apartment, until 1988. During this time, he would also coauthor with Murphy *The Physical and Psychological Effects of Meditation,* become a trustee of Esalen from 1978 until 1993, and manage the place as president from 1985 to 1993.

Moving In

From 1985 to 1989, Donovan commuted back and forth between San Francisco and Big Sur to run Esalen. It was a "fierce place to manage," Donovan admits. His original agreement with Murphy and Price was to work half time, focusing primarily on the organizational structure and financial situation (within a year he was working full-time). The place had slipped back into the kinds of financial woes that Silverman had encountered in 1971. In 1985, Esalen was in a fairly serious financial crisis and was losing money again. By the time Donovan left in 1992, it was $500,000 in the black and was being referred to as a "cash machine." This, however, would take seven years of intense, and often painful, organizational change. In the meantime, Donovan continued his consulting practice, kept abreast of the rapidly unfolding Starbucks situation, and continued working with Murphy on their meditation monograph. This was a difficult juggle, particularly since his most significant consulting client (Cummins Engine Company in Indiana) and his associates on the board at Starbucks were essentially allergic to the word "meditation," not to mention "psychedelic," which was simply unutterable. Donovan was pressed from all sides now.

The financial situation was bad enough. The personal or communal side of things was much worse. Although Dick could certainly make some unpopular decisions and knew his own authoritarian moments, and although his administrative style occasionally bordered on the bizarre (recall Jenny and the Nine), the simple truth of the matter was that Dick was a founder and the undisputed beloved leader of the Esalen community for twenty years. His death left the community orphaned. Consequently, anyone who followed Dick Price, no matter what he or she did, was going to look very much like a stepparent. The times more or less guaranteed this.

Donovan, of course, was very much aware that he worked in the long shadow of Dick Price. It was also a personal shadow for Donovan himself, since Dick had been his mentor as well for a full nine years. In an attempted response, a little over three years after Dick's death, Donovan created the Teacher in Residence Program (in 1989) to help fill this sense of loss. In Donovan's plan, the Teachers in Residence would rotate through Esalen and live in the Little House, the former home of Dick and Chris Price. After Dick's death, Chris lived in the house for two years and grieved the loss of her husband. When she left, Donovan had the house remodeled. It was a deeply symbolic move. It was also a very unpopular move among those who saw the Little House as a kind of sacred shrine to Dick's memory. Donovan felt that the community needed to look forward. The community, however, was still looking back and grieving.

The future, however, was quite uncertain, particularly since so many people claimed so many rights to the place and its resources. Price, it seems, had made personal, unwritten contractual agreements with hundreds of people (or so they claimed) on issues ranging from financial support and future programming to living space on the grounds. All of these agreements, whether apocryphal or actual, had to be renegotiated now. Most of the discussions began with some version of "Dick said..." Working closely with general manager Brian Lyke, Donovan began the negotiations. They would continue for three years. Astonishingly, only one required legal intervention.

To get a sense of just how complicated the situation on the ground was, consider a monthly tally Lyke kept that he called "People on the Property." According to Donovan, these always numbered well over three hundred. There were approximately 110 seminarians at any given time, 35 core staff, 35 body workers, 25 contract staff, 20 "zeroes" (people who performed odd jobs for property and meal privileges, but no pay), and

60 work-scholars. Then there was the Big Sur community, who also felt entitled to the place, and the "Old Timers," close to a hundred former workshop leaders and staff members who were allowed access to the property at any time. How to manage *this?*

There were three keys or guiding principles to Donovan's eight-year tenure as Esalen president. First, there was the central notion of inclusion: Esalen would be a spiritual community that embraced as many paths and practices as possible. This, of course, was simply an extension of the original game-rule that, "No one captures the flag."

Secondly, and very much related to the first, there was Spiegelberg's notion of the religion of no religion, which Donovan now adopted as his guiding administrative principle, much as Dick had earlier administered the place through the empty Tao or "Way" of the *Tao Te Ching.* Indeed, Donovan actually writes of Dick's "Taoistic management techniques" and how these informed his own.[8]

The 1995 film *Frederic Spiegelberg and the Religion of No Religion,* which was made by Katrina Munthe and partially financed by Donovan, sets out Donovan's adopted philosophy. The film begins with a panorama of a Pacific Ocean sunset, no doubt shot from Esalen's cliff and perhaps intended as a kind of symbol of Spiegelberg's death, which had just taken place the year before. Over this seascape is superimposed an epigraph from one of Spiegelberg's favorite philosophers, his old colleague Martin Heidegger: "When man is drawing into what withdraws, he points into what withdraws. As we are drawing that way we are a sign, a pointer. But we are pointing then at something which has not, not yet, been transposed into the language of our speech. We are a sign that is not read."

A sign that is not read: this is another expression of the religion of no religion, a way of being in the world that points toward but does not yet signify or mean anything that is acceptable in speech. This is a difficult idea. Michael Murphy appears in the film in order to gloss his mentor's philosophy. No one was quicker to respect traditions than Frederic Spiegelberg, he points out, and no one was quicker to reject them. There was a freedom in Spiegelberg, a freedom to live life on his own terms, and this without resentment toward the religions. The key, Murphy points out, is not to be trapped in particular dogmas, to see it all as emergent, as developing, and as all-inclusive. He also pointed out that Spiegelberg had a unique ability to integrate the rational and the mystical. He was whole.

The third guiding principle that Donovan used was his decision to model his presidency on the Transformation Project and Murphy's *The*

Future of the Body, with which he had been intimately involved already for six years when he took over the presidency. Essentially, what Donovan decided to do as president was take what he knew best—Dick's managerial Taoism, Spiegelberg's religion of no religion, and Murphy's and his Transformation Project—and use them to guide Esalen. The result was a kind of administrative paradox: the religion of no religion would function now as a kind of Taoist administering without dictating, and the developing manuscript of *The Future of the Body* would function as the ideal map for the seminar planning and intellectual life of the place. There would be direction, and yet there should be no direction. Sometimes it worked beautifully. And sometimes it definitely did not. It all depends upon whom one asks. Donovan had both his severe critics and his real fans.

By all measures, though, it was an exceptionally tough time to be president of Esalen. The general culture of the 1960s and early '70s was famously conducive to the place's commitment to radical experimentation, but that of the '80s and '90s was not. Liberalism was now on the wane, while political conservatism, the Religious Right, and global fundamentalism were all on the rise. The Donovan era was often caught in this larger cultural shift, which felt very much like a retreat in Big Sur. Interestingly, though, there were no suicides during Donovan's presidency.

The Wild Rabbits versus the Teapots

It was also during Donovan's presidency that Esalen's Russian adventures came to something of a climax. Actually, there were two separate diplomatic highpoints during this period: one comedic and one political.

In Moose's, an upscale restaurant in the Italian district of San Francisco, there hangs an easily missed framed photo of a softball game that took place in Moscow on May 14, 1989. If the photo were all we had, we would have very little indeed. One can make out the back of Dulce Murphy's head (if one happened to know that that was her head) and a few fans in the bleachers, but that's about it. Fortunately, Ron Firmite managed to record the story of what is happening in the photo for posterity in a hilarious essay that appeared in *Sports Illustrated* in the early summer of 1989.[9]

Firmite explains that one of the local San Francisco saloons (the Washington Square Bar and Grill) boasted a rather illustrious slo-pitch softball team. This in fact was true. Murphy recalls that nightly news anchor Tom Brokaw sometimes played with them when he was in town, as did newspaper columnist and Bay area personality Herb Caen, former New York politician Mario Cuomo, and famous *Cheers* bar-fly George Wendt ("Norm"). Firmite explains that the bar had a tradition of taking this team to some faraway place every year "to give the team some legitimacy in the sports world." Since they first chose Paris (of course), they decided they should sound a bit cosmopolitan, so they named themselves Les Lapins Sauvages, "mistakenly convinced that this translated to 'the Wild Hares.' Alas, we have been the Wild Rabbits ever since."

In 1987, Vladimir Pozner, a Soviet television personality equivalent to a Russian Dan Rather or Peter Jennings, attended a Giants baseball game in Candlestick Park with Michael Murphy. Murphy took Pozner to the Washington Square Bar and Grill afterwards, the brandy did its work, and soon Les Laupins Sauvages were on their way to Moscow. As she was doing for so many of these Russian ventures, Dulce Murphy organized the trip, whose all-star cast also included Bill Walsh, the coach of the San Francisco 49ers, a friend of the Murphys.

The game itself was played at Young Pioneers Stadium. Firmite comments dryly that the stadium "seats about 95,000 fewer spectators than Lenin [Stadium], but it seemed more than adequate to our needs." Actually, about a thousand people did come to the game, almost all of them to root for the Soviets, who were actually athletes (their right-fielder, a Olympic gold medalist gymnast, even did cartwheels in pursuit of a fly ball).

The Russians had named themselves the Teapots, "that being not only the best-known receptacle in the land but also, in Russian slang, the equivalent of 'wild hares.'" The slo-pitch softball game between the Wild Rabbits and the Teapots was covered, believe it or not (I'm not sure I do), by both Soviet television and CNN. Moreover, George Wendt happened to be filming a movie in Moscow at the time and so showed up to help his old team. Moose corralled Wendt into playing an inning in right field (where, no doubt, he could do the least harm), and soon Norm was appearing in *Sports Illustrated* (on page 54), wearing a Washington Bar and Grill baseball shirt and running (somewhere, it's not at all clear where).

In the end, the final score was Wild Rabbits 18, Teapots 4. A member of the Wild Rabbits presented Pozner with a softball signed by President Bush. Pozner, who had diplomatically dressed in Los Angeles Dodgers *and* New York Giants paraphernalia for the game, in turn saluted his comrades from across the sea and declared that there were no losers that day, only winners. "We all drank to that," Firmite concludes. "And in our mutually expansive mood, the world seemed somehow smaller. And brighter."

Groceries for Yeltsin (1989)

It was not all softball and famous barflies, though. There were also more serious plans afoot. Shortly after this, for example, Esalen was chosen (out of fifteen eager organizations, including the Rockefeller and Ford Foundations and the Council on Foreign Relations) to host Boris Yeltsin's 1989 trip to the United States. Yeltsin's aides had approached a young Russian activist named Gennady Alfarenko and informed him that Yeltsin wanted to come to the United States with a private sponsorship. This, he believed, would give him more freedom. Alfarenko called Jim Garrison, the executive director of Esalen's Soviet-American Exchange Program, and asked if Esalen wanted to host the trip. Garrison flew over to Moscow and met with Yeltsin in his mayor's office to discuss the matter. In the end, Alfarenko and Garrison were able to convince Yeltsin that Esalen was the right host. Garrison flew back and immediately began a six-week preparation for the upcoming trip.

This trip, which took place on September 9–17, was widely covered in the American media, including in all the major newspapers and on *Good Morning America! Face the Nation, CBS News with Dan Rather,* and *The McNeil/Lehrer News Hour.*[10] Certainly this was a story that had real flare. To begin with, Yeltsin had decided to use all the money he earned for his speaking engagements on disposable hypodermic needles to be used back home in order to help prevent the spread of AIDS (six Soviet children had just been recently infected with the HIV virus from blood transfusions involving improperly sanitized needles). Indeed, the Memorandum of Intent he signed with Esalen stated that "all net proceeds shall be dedicated exclusively and specifically to stopping the spread of AIDS in the USSR," and that "Esalen intends to deliver $100,000 worth of supplies to the USSR, in particular disposable syringes with needles." The arrangement effectively protected Yeltsin from any political attacks on his personal motivations for the trip back home.

The man who won Yeltsin's confidence to handle the details of his trip was Jim Garrison. Garrison's path to Esalen was a long and winding one. He had met Dulce and Michael Murphy, Jim Hickman, and Steve Donovan in 1982 in Cambridge, England, where he was finishing a doctorate in theology and they were attending a centennial conference on the London Society for Psychical Research. Garrison's dissertation, *The Darkness of God: Theology after Hiroshima,* is a bold text, akin to Jung's *Answer to Job.* He argues that a completely good God can make no sense of human history, the cosmos or, especially, the Bible. Any honest reading of the biblical texts, he argues, must force the conclusion that there is a dark side of God, just as there is a light side. More radically put, there is an evil impulse present in the depth of the Godhead that any human community ignores or denies at its own real peril. Divinity for Garrison is an "antinomial polarity," a paradoxical coincidence of good *and* evil (this is a very ancient idea, developed in a particularly sophisticated way in medieval Kabbalah or Jewish mysticism and later readapted within Jungian depth psychology).

Through his continuing interactions with Esalen, Garrison became convinced that Jim Hickman and Esalen were the best things happening in the world of citizen diplomacy. He signed up in 1985 as administrator director of the Soviet-American Exchange Program. A year later, when Hickman left, Garrison became executive director, a position which he held until June of 1991, when he decided that Esalen's mission was primarily a metaphysical or mystical one, and that his own calling was more explicitly political.

But Jim Garrison had his own metaphysical moments. Indeed, it was his theology of an antinomial divine totality that empowered his work with the Soviet Union. Oddly, this same theology fit in rather weirdly with Ronald Reagan's famous *Star Wars* image of the USSR as an "Evil Empire" ("the Force" in George Lucas's films possesses both a light and a dark side, much like the Taoist *yin* and *yang* upon which it seems to be based). Garrison certainly did not think that the Soviet Union was evil, but he did recognize the reality of evil in both the world and God. He thought and acted, that is, in terms of complementarity and paradox: whatever was framed as dark he knew must also possess a light side (and vice versa). This is what it meant to live in the world and struggle with the good-and-evil God of the Bible. This is what it meant to be a Christian, from the cross to Hiroshima.

This is also how Garrison read Boris Yeltsin, that is, as a dark chthonic figure who needed to be taken seriously in any real democracy capable of embracing both sides of reality. Garrison described Yeltsin's Esalen-sponsored trip to the United States to me, for example, as "an epic of very turbulent proportions." The politics were especially complicated here, and there were some in the Esalen fold, including Michael and Dulce Murphy according to Garrison, who originally doubted the wisdom of sponsoring Yeltsin. The reasons were complex, but many of them boiled down to the simple fact that Yeltsin was, in Garrison's words, "completely consumed with a dark passion for overthrowing Gorbachev." But it was Mikhail Gorbachev who had done more than anyone to open up the Soviet Union to the West through his *glasnost* vision. Esalen in particular was very fond of Gorbachev and much that he stood for. Understandably then, many doubted whether it was now a good idea to sponsor a man who was essentially the political enemy of Gorbachev.

Then there was the further complicating issue of Yeltsin's alcoholism. According to Garrison, who accompanied the politician on the trip, Yeltsin was consistently drinking and was publicly drunk on several important occasions. He was drunk, for example, going into the White House, and there was a particularly infamous scene at Johns Hopkins University, which then president of the university Steven Muller described as "at best a mitigated disaster."[11] The *Washington Post* had a more alliterative take the next morning: "Boris's Borscht Belting: Yeltsin's Boozy Bearhug for the Capitalists." The official Soviet newspaper, *Pravda,* was crueler still in its attempt to paint the entire trip in lurid colors. Citing the Italian newspaper *La Republica, Pravda* slandered Yeltsin's America as "a feast, a theater stage, a bar 5,000 kilometers long." The latter reports were a mixture of historical truth and shoddy reporting. *La Republica* cited an entirely fictional Esalen accountant ("Alfred Ross") to tell stories about Yeltsin spending wildly in department stores. There was no such person, and no such department store visits. Garrison suspected that the story was planted on the Italian reporter, who admitted the mistake, by Soviet intelligence agents.[12] A few days later, *Pravda* apologized for its own story.

Possible plants, journalistic mistakes, completely fictional Esalen figures, and Soviet apologies aside, the alcoholism was quite real. Leon Aron, one of Yeltsin's most recent biographers, plays down this aspect of the American trip and in fact questions the accuracy of some of the charges, but Garrison was clear with me that the alcoholism was very destructive. For his part, Garrison simply lied to the press about Yeltsin's alcoholism because he felt an obligation to protect his guest. Moreover, he of course desperately wanted the trip to be a success, not a media fiasco or referendum on Yeltsin's personal problems. He also recognized something powerful in the man. Indeed, he sent a memo to Gorbachev more or less begging him to take Yeltsin seriously and predicting that Yeltsin "would bring this house down."

Still, much, if not most, of the visit was successful, even occasionally delightful and profound. From his first two mornings in New York, when he took a walking tour of the city with the homeless and then viewed the Statue of Liberty from a helicopter (the *New York Times* observed that the leader and the lady seemed to "have a special thing going"), to his visit to a

Houston megagrocery, the trip was for Yeltsin an "endless row of collapsed stereotypes and clichés." He had been taught that Lady Liberty looked like a witch. She was beautiful. He had expected Manhattan to be a collection of "piles of giant gravestones" and depressing slums haunted by roving murderers. Instead he found Fifth Avenue, safe late-night restaurants serving delicious food, impressive skyscrapers, and scores of friendly people eager to meet him. As for the real slums, he commented that some of them "would pass for decent housing in the Soviet Union."[13]

He also got to close the New York Stock Exchange, with Dulce Murphy standing at his side on the evening news. Finally, in a particularly brilliant move, he insisted on visiting President Reagan in his Rochester hospital room. Roses in hand, he entered the hospital room late in the morning of September 14. The two men engaged in what was by all accounts a warm, humorous, and friendly exchange. Later, he met with farmers, whose language he spoke, and marveled at $150,000 combines and computers on their desks. When an Indiana farmer asked him if he wanted to see his pigs, he replied, "Generally, I prefer to see Americans, but I guess pigs would do."[14] Alcoholism and language barriers aside, Boris Yeltsin could be absolutely charming.

The event that most deeply affected Yeltsin was his visit to a Randall's grocery store on his way to the airport from visiting the Lyndon B. Johnson Space Center in Clear Lake, Texas, just outside of Houston. Yeltsin had heard plenty back home about the evils of capitalism and the illusions of wealth that America pretended through a few fake grocery stores—props, as it were, in its "imperialistic" war against the glories of Soviet Communism. Deeply suspicious now of every other Party trope, Yeltsin apparently wanted to test this one too. Garrison remembers Yeltsin being in a "weird mood" when he asked the entourage to make the scheduled 1:30 p.m. stop at the grocery store.

It was a fateful stop. The Soviet visitors were immediately puzzled, as they found no long lines outside the store—the usual sight at a Soviet grocery store. Inside, however, things were even more bizarre. They were flabbergasted by a profusion of carefully arranged and beautifully lit fruits, vegetables, meats, cheeses, frozen entrees, and canned goods too numerous to count. They asked for a number. Around 30,000 items, they were told. Yeltsin stopped a woman shopping in the aisles, apologized for his intrusion, and then asked her two things: how much money her family earned per month, and how much she spent on groceries during the same period. Her answers ($3,600 and $170) stunned him, as he knew that Soviet citizens of that time spent around 59 percent of their budget on groceries (the American ratio came to about 6 percent), and this was only if they could find enough groceries, which was always doubtful.[15] Yeltsin was in shock.

According to Garrison, Yeltsin then went up to the manager of the store and asked him how many such stores there were like this. When he was told "thousands," Yeltsin became visibly angry and upset. According to his close aide, Lev Sukhanov, who accompanied his boss in those aisles and later sat next to him on the plane to his last stop in Miami, it was in that Houston grocery store that "the last vestige of Bolshevism collapsed" inside Boris Yeltsin. Later, in an interview for *Ogonyok,* Yeltsin described "this madness of colours, smells, boxes, packs, sausages, cheeses was—impossible to bear. Only in that supermarket it became clear to me why Stalinism so painstakingly erected the 'iron curtain.'"[16] Soon after this experience, Yeltsin would officially quit the Party and find himself standing on a tank in front of the Russian parliament before an international media. The rest, as we say, is history.

Gorbachev in the Presidio

Esalen's continuing influence in Soviet-American relations by no means ended with Boris Yeltsin's visit to America in 1989. Mikhail Gorbachev also came within Esalen's orbit, although indirectly now through the citizen diplomacy of Jim Garrison. After Garrison left his Esalen post in the summer of 1991, he went on to work with Soviet foreign minister Eduard Shevardnadze and U.S. secretary of state George Shultz to form the International Foreign Policy Association, whose mission involved things like mobilizing large shipments of aid to the children of the Soviet Union. It was in his capacity as director of the IFPA that Garrison visited Moscow in December of 1991, four months after the Yeltsin-led August coupe and literally days before Gorbachev's still secret resignation.

Jim Garrison was the last foreigner to visit Gorbachev in his Kremlin office. Alexander Yakovlev, an old associate of both Gorbachev and Shevardnadze, arranged the meeting for December 18, 1991. As Jim got up from the table, Yakovlev put his arm around him and told him that they would be resigning within one week. Garrison was stunned. "What?! Is there anything I can do?" he blurted out in shock. "Yes," Gorbachev responded, "you can get meat to Moscow. The children don't have enough food here." Garrison made a call to Donald Kendall, the former chairman of Pepsico, and arranged for a planeload of canned beef to be flown into

Moscow in the new year. But not before Yakovlev's secret became international news. Gorbachev resigned as president of the USSR at midnight on December 24.

Garrison returned with another planeload of meat during the third week of January. Again Yakovlev welcomed him, and again he arranged a meeting with Gorbachev, this time in the new headquarters of the Gorbachev Foundation. After realizing that Gorbachev and his associates understood their final historical mission to be one of promoting nonviolence and global peacemaking, Garrison managed to convince Gorbachev to come to the United States, be hosted by Ronald Reagan and George Shultz, and set up a Gorbachev Foundation/USA.

As a start, Garrison arranged a two-week American tour for the Gorbachevs on Steven Forbes's private jet, the latter playfully dubbed the *Capitalist Tool*. The American tour took place May 2–15, 1992, and was widely covered by the media, much as Yeltsin's tour had been. Reagan greeted Gorbachev at his new presidential library in Simi Valley, California, and Garrison arranged for Gorbachev to give a speech at Fulton, Missouri, on the occasion of the fiftieth anniversary of Winston Churchill's famous Iron Curtain speech. In many ways, Churchill's speech had inaugurated the rhetoric and dynamics of the cold war; Gorbachev now proclaimed its ending.

Less than a year later, in April of 1993, Gorbachev was standing on American soil again, this time below the Golden Gate Bridge in the Presidio alongside Mayor Frank Jordan, George Shultz, and Senator Alan Cranston, to accept the key to his new San Francisco based center, the Gorbachev Foundation/USA. With Garrison as president and Cranston and Shultz as chairmen, it was the first civilian organization to reside in what once was a military base. Fort Scott had originally been built in the nineteenth century, ironically to help stop the encroachments of the Russians coming down from Alaska. The symbolism of the Gorbachev event was apparent to everyone.

There were other, more familiar touches too. Billy Joel, facilitated again by Jim Hickman (who had also helped Garrison organize the Gorbachev trips), made another appearance. Appearing by satellite TV alongside his wife, Christie Brinkley, Joel announced another goodwill rock tour, this time to raise money for immunizations. Graham Nash, Bonnie Raitt, and Nirvana had also signed up, he told Mr. Gorbachev and the crowd. The rock stars were playing their role again.

Finally, in 1995, Garrison and Cranston went on to cofound the State of the World Forum, with Gorbachev serving as convening chairman.

This new venture was designed as a think tank and activist organization closely aligned to the Gorbachev Foundation. Indeed, the two organizations still reside in the same Presidio house.

It is never, of course, easy to determine the causal factors of history, and major Esalen actors disagree on the precise historical role Esalen played during this era. Garrison, for example, is guarded about some of the bolder claims often made here, although he fully acknowledges that, "it is not an overstatement [to say] that Esalen played an indirect but critical role in American-Soviet relations as well as in both *glasnost* and *perestroika* in the Soviet Union." Ever the theologian, he is also insistent that the theology of Esalen is essentially a heretical and so a culturally creative one. In times of transition, heresies need to be honored, since they will often become the orthodoxies of tomorrow. The theological role of Esalen, then, was one of essential heresy, transgression, and cultural ferment. Like the gospel image of the yeast, its purpose was to encourage growth and movement, to push the culture beyond what it felt comfortable imagining.

There are, however, bolder interpretations of Esalen's political role. As the meetings with the Soviets developed in the Big House in the late 1980s, Esalen figure and career diplomat Joe Montville became increasingly convinced that the Gorbachev administration was actually taking some of its ideological cues from that very room and its allegedly confidential conversations (the Russians would often ask that the tape recorder be turned off). He couldn't help but notice how they would explore a particular theme at a gathering, and then a few weeks later Gorbachev would be saying more or less the same thing in his public speeches.[17] At the first symposium held at the Gorbachev Foundation (on Bolshevism), Montville decided to ask Gorbachev about his theory. Gorbachev simply smiled, as he pointed to the ceiling in the traditional Russian sign of "you were bugged."

The Religion of No Religion and the American Spiritual Marketplace

Both Yeltsin's conversion to Western-style democracy and open-market capitalism in a Houston grocery store and Gorbachev's tour in the *Capitalist Tool* raise for us the important question about how democracy, capitalism, and religion have been intertwined in Esalen's history and, more to the point, how democratic capitalism provides the socioeconomic base for Esalen's religion of no religion. Related here as well are the issues of race, class, and wealth and the oft-noted observation that Esalen's clientele has been overwhelmingly white and upper-middle class.

Certainly Esalen leaders have been aware of this for decades. In the summer of 1974, for example, Esalen president Richard Farson worried that, "one of the more frequent and telling critiques of Esalen, a critique we staff members often make ourselves, is that our programs are necessarily limited to those people with enough time and money to come to California to attend workshops at Big Sur or San Francisco."[18] In fact, the prices for attending Esalen events ranged widely, from $2.50 (or free) for a San Francisco event, to $1,800 or more for a Grof month-long workshop in Big Sur. Still, Farson had a point.

The critical literature on the alternative religious scene as a kind of "spiritual marketplace" is considerable, and much of it applies quite accurately to Esalen's forty-five-year run.[19] The general point here is that modern capitalism tends to transform traditional religious beliefs and practices, which were originally based in tight-knit communities, into free-floating products available for purchase and consumption by individual consumers. This deracination process has understandably worried a great many analysts. It has also led to a growing critical literature on the socioeconomic dimensions of the alternative religious scene, little of which many scholars can bring themselves to appreciate from their own, often Marxist-oriented, perspectives. Individualism, religious freedom, and free markets—all of which appear to be historically related—become questionable values in this literature, primarily for their negative effects on traditional worldviews and communities, much of which (we are seldom told) are based precisely on the suppression of individualism, women, choice, and social freedom for the sake of an allegedly superior social coherence or sacred stability.

The latter effects can hardly be doubted: capitalism, democracy, universal education, and global communication are all indeed corrosive to traditional cultures, even if these globalizing forces also bring benefits that many cultural actors (like women) from these same traditional societies very much desire. If we add to this moral complexity a dark history of Western colonialism, which physically and ideologically ravaged ancient and indigenous civilizations around the world for three centuries (especially here in America), we can begin to appreciate just how difficult such questions quickly become. What should be preserved and protected? And what should be rightly criticized and let go? And, most importantly, who should decide which is which? The religion of no religion, it turns out, is fraught with economic and political implications.

At first glance, Esalen might appear to be a perfect example of the commodification and deracination of the sacred and the business of selling it to a general public. An institute named after an extinct Amerindian tribe, run by a former cocreator of Starbucks and Peet's, and celebrating the powers of Asian contemplative practices, shamanism, and sweat lodges for a clientele that is overwhelmingly white and middle-class can easily become fodder for any number of critical perspectives. Such criticisms, moreover, have hardly been restricted to professional intellectuals. Donovan, for example, recalls some graffiti painted on Esalen's entry sign in 1990: "Jive shit for rich white folk." In a similar spirit, the hippies referred to Esalen in the Summer of Love as "the country club," which, of course, they then happily visited in droves. Graffiti and hippies, however, seldom tell the full story, and even wealthy white folk can have rich spiritual lives. Any adequate trip through Esalen's history, then, can well have the same effect on the Marxist theorist that Yeltsin's trip through America had on his Soviet Communism, that is, it can function as an "endless row of collapsed stereotypes and clichés."

What are we to do, for example, with the fact that Steve Donovan helped raise two million dollars for the preservation of indigenous Pacific cultures? This is a rather odd response from a culture that allegedly does not care about traditional community or cultural pluralism. More to the point, it is important to remember that Esalen is *itself* a community, and that all of its seminar and outreach programs are grounded in and rely on that community base. Also relevant here is the fact that Esalen is a nonprofit organization that provides a decent but quite humble livelihood for this same community of about 150 individuals. Four hundred seminars a year do not happen by themselves. They depend on the physical and intellectual labor of gardeners, grounds keepers, fundraisers, plumbers, electricians, kitchen staff, accountants, work-scholars, and administrators.

It is also important to point out both the gendered and conservative aspects of the criticisms directed against the spiritual marketplace and the New Age. The fact is that most of these alternative religious movements are dominated by women, sometimes by as much as two to one. Once such an individual moves out of the belief system of an established tradition, he or she (usually she) can no longer rely on the usual means of financial and social support that the religions offer their own (usually male) specialists. Traditional systems, after all, are dominated by powerful men and intricate webs of wealth and prestige built up over centuries, usually within hierarchical social systems that have systematically silenced and suppressed female voices. Little wonder, then, that spiritual creativity, utopian individualism, and a certain economic entrepreneurship all be-come central features of a place like Esalen. One wonders how else these alternative voices are supposed to make a living as religious specialists without a religion.

One also wonders just whose interests are being defended and pre-served in the critiques directed against these same religious creatives. I am reminded here of Grace Jantzen's potent observations about medieval female mystics who had little access to the institutional and intellec-tual preserves of the male Church. When such women sought their own community forms in new lay organizations and expressed themselves in original visions and boldly sensuous ecstatic states, many of them were effectively labeled heretical, prideful, selfish, and so on by the orthodox tradition.[20] Medieval narcissists, no doubt. Alex Owen and Ann Braude have made very similar cases with respect to nineteenth-century Spiritu-alism in both England and America: inevitably, the spiritualist mediums were women with radically progressive political values who were seen, by both their husbands and the religious authorities, as a threat to the patriarchal order of tradition and right value.[21] Self-obsessed Victorians, obviously. Finally, David J. Hess has made a virtually identical argument with respect to the gendered structure of contemporary polemics against psychics and parapsychologists: it is difficult to miss the gendered fact that this discourse also takes on "the polarities of empowered men versus disempowered (and self-empowering) women."[22] I hear strong echoes in all these historical attempts to disempower female voices in the contem-porary critiques of the spiritual marketplace and the New Age.

None of this, however, is meant to deny the very legitimate con-cerns about the environmental and cultural dangers of capitalism and consumerism or the corporate erasure of cultural diversity, much less the tragedy of the Esselen people or the call for social justice and compassion that so admirably and obviously animates the cultural critics. It is simply to locate their important critiques in a more nuanced social context and problematize their sometimes simplistic readings.

Finally, there is an even deeper issue here, which we might call metaphysical. After all, the free exchange of religious beliefs and practices within free markets for the alteration of consciousness and energy can also be read as an inevitable outcome of the religion of no religion, particularly within a democratic social polity that values and protects religious free-dom. To speak in the philosophical terms of a Spiegelberg, once one recog-nizes that *all* religious beliefs and practices are approximations of a deeper source of Being (or Nonbeing), it becomes difficult, if not impossible, to essentialize any particular belief or practice as somehow inviolable or ultimate. To complete the circle, however, such a realization also renders obvious the fact that religious and cultural pluralism is fundamental to the full expression of the human species, that different traditions encode and catalyze different dimensions of the human potential, and that—as in biology so too in culture—diversity is the key to adaptation and survival. How, though, to keep these two truths in balance? How to honor and preserve both our fundamental biological sameness and our real cultural differences?

Certainly Esalen is not the first to struggle with this both-and. The Indian poet Kabir openly scorned any notion that his God could be bound by a Hindu or Muslim identity, even as he composed hymns in a particular language at a particular place and time. Ramakrishna struggled similarly. He concluded that all religions are paths to the same goal, but only after he actively experimented, very much like an Esalen seminarian, with any number of "foreign" religious beliefs and images, all of them "appropriated" very much out of context and against the wishes of those religions' representatives (any orthodox Muslim or Christian, for example, would have been horrified by his anthropomorphic vision of God and physical absorption of Jesus, respectively). If, then, the religion of no religion is constituted, as Spiegelberg wrote, by a "a psychological inversion of former ideas of some objective reality," that is, if an individual or community comes to realize that all religious systems are expressions of some deeper human potential, then something like America's spiritual marketplace or Ramakrishna's experiments follows quite logically.

These are difficult and perhaps academically incorrect truths. But they are truths nonetheless. America's spiritual marketplace is an expression of capitalism, democracy, and the religion of no religion.

Realizing Darwin's Dream

THE TRANSFORMATION PROJECT AND
THE FUTURE OF THE BODY

The present chapter aims at illustrating the difficulty of assigning precise limits to the range of those natural but unusual manifestations of man's spiritual being which science now takes account of under the name of abnormal psychology. Two centuries ago such phenomena were summarily dismissed, by Catholics and Protestants alike, as witchcraft, sorcery, or, in brief, the work of the devil. But this was before the reality of the hypnotic trance was recognized, and before attention was thus directed to possibilities of which earlier ages had no conception. We are somewhat wiser now . . .

      HERBERT THURSTON, S.J., *The Physical Phenomena of Mysticism*

"Darwin, you must finish your book."

      JACOB ATABET to Darwin Fall in *Jacob Atabet*

From the bold historical-comparative charts on Shivas Irons's apartment wall that the narrator encounters in *Golf in the Kingdom* (1972), to the constant journal and narrative references to Darwin Fall's developing tome on the future evolution of the body in *Jacob Atabet* (1977), to the very last lines of *An End to Ordinary History* (1983) on how, "in the next few years, Darwin Fall may write a book about these matters," the careful reader of Michael Murphy's occult novels cannot help but notice a developing subtext of his mystical realism that will eventually become *The Future of the Body* (1992).

This "future" text, it turns out, actually appears numerous times in *Jacob Atabet* as a fictional 1,723 page manuscript entitled *Evolutionary Relationships Between Mind and Body*, whose summary looks very much like the table of contents of *The Future of the Body.* Its content parallels Jacob's bodily transformations and, most importantly, helps him to make sense of these otherwise strange events within an evolutionary framework. Murphy's *The Future of the Body,* in other words, as both present 1977 fiction and 1992 reality, provides the model that makes the best sense of Jacob's occult experiences. It is the effective center and secret of the novel that works like one of Jacob's visions as interpreted through Darwin's worm-holes and extreme space-time warps, that is, as "a signal from the future."[1]

The Future of the Body represented for Murphy the intellectual summation of all that had preceded it in imaginal form. This indeed was not just a text about the future of the body; this was the text that constituted the future of Murphy's own corpus, a kind of attractor from the future that seemed to reach back into time to guide the plots and characters of the individual novels. Indeed, so strong does the "backward influence" of *The Future of the Body* appear to be on its novelistic predecessors that I am tempted here to recall Russell Targ's claim that "the data from precognition research strongly suggest that an experiment could, in principle, be affected by a signal sent from the future!"[2] If I can transform Targ's metaphysical exclamation into a literary method, I might say that *The Future of the Body* functions in the corpus of Michael Murphy very much like this psychic "signal sent from the future." It is almost as if we need to read Murphy's corpus or textual body *backwards* to understand it properly, as if we need to see literary and intellectual inspiration not simply as a set of ideas and desires that are systematically acted upon to produce some future effect (a book, poem, or philosophy), but also as a future reality that is already in existence further down some path of the space-time grid and whose shape can be gradually intuited and realized over time until that dream to perfect in the future becomes a perfected dream in the present.

There are numerous precursors of Murphy's *magnum opus* on the emerging human potentials of the evolutionary process. Four stand out as fundamental: the British psychical researcher F. W. H. Myers; the American psychologist, philosopher, and psychical researcher William James; Sri Aurobindo; and the Jesuit historian of Catholic sanctity Father Herbert Thurston. We have already had occasion to meet the American psychologist and the Indian philosopher. It is now time to introduce the British psychical researcher and the Jesuit before we turn to *The Future of the Body* itself and the extensive archival process that helped produce it.

The Supernormal and the Subliminal: F. W. H. Myers and
the London Society for Psychical Research (1882–1903)

Murphy was first introduced to F. W. H. Myers by Willis Harman in 1962, just as Esalen was getting off the ground. The immediate "lock-in" Murphy experienced with Myers's *magnum opus* was one of many reasons he asked Harman to lead the very first seminar, The Expanding Vision. Although never mentioned in the early brochures, then, Myers goes back to the exact beginning of Esalen.

Frederic William Henry Myers (1843–1901) was trained as a classicist at Trinity College, Cambridge. From the age of seventeen, the year he entered Cambridge, to twenty-three, his worldview and interests were all more or less defined by classical Greek culture and literature. He then returned to Christianity for a time, but only to be disillusioned after a fuller exposure to the study of science and history rendered these traditional beliefs cognitively impossible (recall Murphy's own journey through the same disillusionment). To complicate things further, in 1873 Myers fell deeply in love with a married woman, Annie Hill Marshall, the wife of his cousin no less, Walter James Marshall. Perhaps not accidentally, the fall of this same year Myers experienced for the first time what he later called "forces unknown to science."[3]

The next year, on May 9, 1874, Myers and his friend Edmund Gurney met the famous medium and preacher Stainton Moses, an event that Myers describes as "epoch-making" for both his and Gurney's lives. Two years later, on August 29, 1876, tragedy struck: Annie Hill Marshall died suddenly, leaving Myers grief-stricken. Later he would communicate with her through a medium. In 1882, a now existentially perplexed and suffering Myers was wondering whether the study of psychical phenomena might resolve his crisis. At the encouragement of his teacher Henry Sidgwick, an eminent professor of moral philosophy at Cambridge, he helped found the London Society for Psychical Research (SPR) with Gurney, Mr. and Mrs. Sidgwick, and others in 1882.

Myers dedicated most of his remaining years to the systematic study of psychical phenomena, often by placing ads in newspapers and other periodicals, following these up with further correspondence, interviews, and corroborating documents (there were 10,000 letters written in 1883 alone, mostly by Myers and Gurney).[4] Myers also became a close friend of William James, the most eminent member of the American Society for

Psychical Research. Myers died in Rome in 1901, fully convinced that the human spirit does indeed survive the disintegration of the body and that, moreover, what he liked to call the subliminal self was the secret of genius, dream, hypnotism, automatic writing, ghostly apparitions, telepathic communication with the living and dead, trance, possession, and ecstasy.

Myers, in other words, had left the world the basic elements of an entire mystical psychology of religion. Two years later, in 1903, his colleagues Richard Hodgson and Miss Alice Johnson completed and published his greatest work, *Human Personality and Its Survival of Bodily Death,* a two-volume, 1,360-page work that stands to this day as a remarkable testament to Myers's ability to combine a unique sensibility for religious phenomena with an unwavering, unflinching insistence on exposing these experiences to both critical psychological analysis and a comparative method. Through such a dual method, truth is progressively advanced not through traditional authority or revelation, but through the careful collection of case studies, systematic classification of patterns that emerge from this evidence, consideration of a wide range of naturalistic and religious explanations, and finally theory building, itself always recognized as necessarily tentative and open to further qualification, development, or rejection.

Murphy adopted a similar double method for *The Future of the Body* as a kind of "natural history of the supernormal." He saw Myers's and his own work as similar to Darwin's, who came to his insights into biological evolution through what were also essentially collecting and comparative means: Why is this beak different than that one? Why do these particular species only exist on these particular islands? Why do the skeletal structures of mammals all look more or less alike? How do we define and explain the biological development of both this more and this less? And so on. So too with the religious material. Why is this apparition different than that one? Why do we find these particular religious experiences to be common in this particular culture and time? Why do reports of psychical powers or bodily transfigurations appear more or less alike and line up as extensions of the natural sensory and motor apparatuses of the human being wherever we find them? And so on.

Almost all of Myers's final conclusions mirror the early brochures of Esalen. Basic to the entire system, for example, is his complete rejection of what he calls "the wall between science and superstition." He insisted that any modern inquiry into postmortem survival required that the earlier evidence of folklore, religion, mysticism, occultism, and Spiritualism be submitted to the discipline of "science." This included three tests: all anecdotal accounts should be checked and confirmed for authenticity; natural causal factors, particularly psychological ones (suggestion, projection, chance, etc.), should be considered before any supernatural or extramaterial forces are entertained; and as many cases as possible should be collected before constructing any conclusion.

Myers realized with some embarrassment that his conclusions about the survival of the soul and the possibility of spirit communication mirrored the earlier evidence of shamanism, "Stone Age religion," medieval witchcraft, Mesmerism, and of work of people like Emmanuel Swedenborg. He still treated all of this earlier material, however, with a combination of skepticism and psychological appreciation: "For my own part I regard Swedenborg,—not, assuredly, as an inspired teacher, nor even as a trustworthy interpreter of his own experiences,—but yet as a true and early precursor of that great inquiry which it is our present object to advance."[5] Myers practiced both a hermeneutics of trust, which was willing to listen seriously and sympathetically to the voices of religious experience, and a hermeneutics of suspicion, which was equally willing to expose those voices to the critical lenses of modern theory.

Little wonder, then, that Myers considered much of what passed as spirit communication or automatic writing to be in fact subliminal phenomena issuing ultimately from the minds of the living mediums. Little wonder also that he was the first to introduce the writings of Freud to the British public, and that Stainton Moses eventually left the SPR in protest over the researchers' insistence that all reported experiences be submitted to the discipline of critical scholarship and that no religious claim be taken at face value. Myers knew how to think toward his own religion of no religion.

He also knew how to fashion new words that could embody such a vision. It was Myers, after all, who first coined the word "telepathy" (in 1882) for "the transference of ideas and sensations from one mind to another without the agency of the recognised organs of sense."[6] Myers believed that telepathy represents a clear evolutionary advance on human sensory capabilities.[7] In *The Future of the Body,* Murphy would later opt for a similar reading of human potentials as buds of evolving metanormal capacities and as evidence for a human supernature.[8]

The phrases "metanormal capacities" and "human supernature" are Murphy's, but they speak through the spirits of both Myers and Aurobindo. Myers had coined the key adjective "supernormal" in 1885 "on the analogy of abnormal," to refer to "phenomena which are *beyond what usually happens—beyond,* that is, in the sense of suggesting unknown psychic laws." Myers explains:

> When we speak of an of abnormal phenomenon we do not mean one which *contravenes* natural laws, but one which exhibits them in an unusual or inexplicable form. Similarly by a supernormal phenomenon I mean, not one which *overrides* natural laws, for I believe no such phenomenon to exist, but one which exhibits the action of laws higher, in a psychical aspect, than are discerned in action in everyday life. By *higher* (either in a psychical or a physiological sense) I mean 'apparently belonging to a more advanced stage of evolution.'[9]

Both "metanormal" and "supernormal" insist on naturalizing the supernatural and collapsing any boundaries between the sacred and the profane. Murphy would thus see the supposedly supernatural or miraculous psychical powers as entirely natural expressions of evolution and its latent cosmic forces. This was a gnosis already embedded in those first two Sanskrit words that he heard Spiegelberg utter in that Stanford classroom back in 1950—*brahman* and *atman,* the universal essence and the self that are one. Similarly, Myers ended his masterpiece insisting on the essential unity of the human spirit and the universe: "That which lies at the root of each of us lies at the root of the Cosmos too."[10] Both systems are defined by a thoroughgoing super naturalism, which we might also frame as a kind of cosmic humanism, hence the much later phrase, *the human potential* (and not the divine potential).

Myers also helped introduce another key term, the "subliminal," which Aurobindo would later adopt (or recreate) for his own *The Life Divine.* Long before Aurobindo, the expression entered Western psychology and helped effect its radical shift in how we view religious, and especially mystical, phenomena. Myers saw that many of the visions and apparitions earlier thinkers had read as external realities were in fact projections from below (*sub*) the threshhold (*limen*) of their own psyches, even if he also suggested the possibility of a certain "phantasmogenetic efficacy." The latter was essentially the idea that something of a (living or deceased) psyche's subliminal substance can exist in space in some real, if nonmaterial, way and interact with another human psyche.

So too with the material of dream, of much psychosis, of ecstasy and possession, and of genius. All of it for Myers manifested a relationship to the subliminal realm and the latter's connection to the supernormal powers of telepathy, inspiration, and spirit communication. In other words, Myers's subliminal Self was more like Jung's unconscious than Freud's, even if he insisted, with Freud, that "hidden in the depths of our being is a rubbish-heap as well as a treasure-house."[11] Indeed, Myers even recognized something very much like synchronicity.[12]

Like Freud, moreover, Myers considered the phenomena of genius and artistic creativity to be some of the clearest, most accessible, and yet most mysterious manifestations of this subliminal or unconscious realm. Genius for Myers was "an uprush of the subliminal" into the supraliminal or conscious self, "a fulfillment of the true norm of man, with suggestions, it may be, of something supernormal." The difference between a genius and a normal human being thus resides not in any obvious physical or intellectual difference, but "in an increased control over subliminal mentations."[13] In other words, it is the subliminal as the realm of the supernormal that creates true genius, and those who can open their psyches up to this subliminal region will be far more likely to receive inspiration than those who cannot.

As Ann Taves points out, such a model of human consciousness as "multiplex" or "fissiparous," even in normal or healthy individuals, had profound consequences for the interpretation of religious experience. Supernatural or pathological explanations were no longer entirely believable or necessarily sufficient. Myers, for example, had effectively demonstrated that what the Spiritualists had explained by the supposition of actual spirit communication and the clinical psychologists had reduced to pathological dissociation could just as easily be understood as perfectly natural but no less amazing "supernormal" manifestations of the subliminal depths of consciousness itself.[14] Moreover, foreshadowing later trauma theory (but also moving well beyond it), Myers and his colleagues had also shown that these psychic hyperdimensions normally reveal themselves only in traumatic contexts that break down or bypass entirely the normal workings of the conscious self. Hence the society's "crisis apparition," a telepathic message sent from the psyche of a dying loved one. As Taves has shown, it was this same psychology of mystical trauma (death being the ultimate trauma or dissociative state) that James adopted to construct his own psychological model of mysticism in *The Varieties*, which came to play such a central role in the modern study of religion.[15] The London and American Societies for Psychical Research, in other words, lie behind both the modern study of mysticism and Esalen's psychological culture.

Myers finally arrived at a system that sees three degrees or stages in the subliminal life of humanity: (1) the inspiration of dream, genius, and psychosis in which the subliminal doors are opened by sleep, skill, or psychological disintegration; (2) the psychic phenomena of telepathic communications with a departed or still living mind that give witness to the supernormal potentials of us all; and (3) the complete "take-over" of the conscious self in trance, possession, and ecstasy.

Myers was particularly impressed with ecstasy, seeing it as something "neither subjective nor objective" that constituted "the highest form which the various religions known to us have assumed in the past."[16] He also considered some of the automatic products of possession states—particularly texts and poetic or mystical utterances—to be "among the most important phenomena yet observed by man."[17] In the end, he arrived at a kind of mind-body dualism, fully convinced that *a mind uses a brain,* and that the "human brain is in its last analysis an arrangement of matter expressly adapted to being acted upon by a spirit."[18] Evolution, in other words, is guided by spiritual forces that have, over the course of millions of years, evolved their own bodily receptors.

The evolutionary language is more than metaphor. Myers is quite clear that the history of spirit communication gives witness to "the evolution of human personality," and that his work speaks "of faculties newly dawning, and of a destiny greater than we know."[19] He even suggests that humanity may be able to hasten its own evolution, "a cosmic moral evolution," and openly encourages his readers to see that their greatest duty is to increase the intensity of their spiritual lives and so come to recognize that "their own spirits are co-operative elements in the cosmic evolution, are part and parcel of the ultimate vitalizing Power" common to all religions.[20]

Jacob Atabet could hardly have asked for more.

On the Holiness of the Body: Father Thurston's The Physical Phenomena of Mysticism *(1952)*

Michael Murphy first encountered *The Physical Phenomena of Mysticism* in 1958 or 1959, after he returned from India. The work of Herbert Thurston, S. J. (1856–1939) was not as influential as Myers's *Human Personality,* but it was nevertheless important, and this for at least three reasons.[21] First, Thurston was almost alone in his focus on the specifically *physical* effects of mystical experience as recorded in the annals of Catholic sanctity and in the broader history of religions. Secondly, he pointed out that the Church, through its beatification and canonization processes and its legal institution of the *Promotor Fidei* (the Promoter of the Faith, more popularly known as "the Devil's Advocate"), has always approached such phenomena with doubt and a presumption of pious exaggeration or even fraud. Thirdly, and perhaps most radically, Thurston bravely turned to Spiritualist, psychical, secular, and psychiatric material as a comparative base to understand the hagiographical material. Indeed, he insisted that our present psychiatric knowledge about hypnotic trance, hysterical suggestibility, and dissociative states can be used to correct the misreadings of the religious past (and, by implication, some of the horrible moral judgments, physical tortures, and even executions that were inflicted on these poor souls for their nonordinary gifts and graces).[22] Thurston was clearly reading Myers, and quite carefully. He references *Human Personality* and actually joined, with some professional and religious risk, the London Society for Psychical Research.

Thurston examines any number of physical phenomena, including levitation, stigmata, telekinesis (particularly as manifested by floating or flying eucharistic wafers), luminous bodies (another "enlightenment of the body"), incombustibility or resistance to burning (the "human salamander" phenomenon), bodily elongation, the experience of the *incendium amoris* or "fire of love," the odor of sanctity, incorrupt corpses, blood prodigies (blood that flows for months or even years after death), seeing without eyes, *inedia* (living without eating), and the multiplication of food. It is difficult to finish the book without a rather uncanny sense that both the human body and the physical universe are not quite (or at all) what they appear to be.

The Physical Phenomena of Mysticism is a collection of separate essays that Thurston wrote over a nineteen-year period (1919–1938). Thurston's major intellectual breakthrough came in 1933 when a German doctor demonstrated conclusively that stigmata could be produced by suggestion in a hysterical patient.[23] Thurston had expected just such a link but never had this kind of dramatic confirmation. Now he did. His long treatment of the history and psychology of stigmatics in both the medieval and modern worlds demonstrates a familiarity with early psychiatric models of multiple personality disorder, dissociation, and hysteria (whose very terminology, he notes, designates a female—and I would add, sexual— origin).[24] He also notes but does not follow up on the dramatic gender pattern of this phenomenon: virtually all complete stigmatics have been women (Francis of Assisi and Padre Pio are important exceptions). Not a single male stigmatic has demonstrated the periodic bleeding that defines so many of the female cases. The psychosexual dimensions of an ascetic, sexually inactive female body that is penetrated—sometimes in five or six different places—and who bleeds periodically within intense states of devotion, love, and physical suffering seem obvious enough, even if what it all means is hardly clear.

Thurston also describes "tokens of espousal," the phenomena of magical or flesh-raised wedding rings appearing on the fingers of celibate nuns and holy women. Another later chapter focuses on the palpable heat or even burning fire that constitutes the well-known *incendium amoris* or "fire of love," which, unlike the stigmata or the magical rings, is common in both female and male figures. Clearly, the mystical body we are speaking of here is also an erotic body, a body on fire.

The Transformation Project (1976–1992)

In one of those many fusions of fiction and reality that define the history of Esalen, while Murphy was writing *Jacob Atabet* in the early to mid-1970s, Dulce Murphy suggested to Michael that he actually pursue the bibliography and sources upon which Darwin Fall had claimed to have based his masterwork manuscript, *Evolutionary Relationships Between Mind and Body*. Just as Corinne supported Jacob, Dulce was now encouraging her husband to take on the persona and project of his own "fictional" character and "become Darwin Fall."

And this is what he did. In fact, Dulce was simply encouraging Michael to own up to and act on something he had already decided to be in the novel. In effect, he was imagining himself into a new kind of existence in the occult text, and now he was deciding to turn this imaginal identity into an historical and public one.

This is fascinating enough, but it becomes even more so when we realize this had major effects on the future of Esalen. Murphy's efforts with Jim Hickman, and later Steve Donovan, to establish the Transformation Project would soon play right into Esalen's Russian ventures and the eventual founding of its Soviet-American Exchange Program. It would also help mentor a future trustee and president of Esalen, Steve Donovan, and lead to Murphy's and George Leonard's work with ITP (Integral Transformative Practice).[25]

Murphy had long been interested in cataloging the data of supernormal functioning. In 1967–68, Esalen had sponsored a comprehensive cataloging of the available psychophysical disciplines designed to expand human energy and awareness. This resulted in Severin Peterson's 1971 book, *A Catalog of the Ways People Grow*. The Transformation Project was part of this same initial drive to create a "natural history" of the human potential. It was officially founded in 1976 (right as Murphy was finishing *Jacob Atabet* and the San Francisco Center was closing) as "a research program to study extraordinary human functioning and the mental and physical strategies that accompany it, in part by compiling, analyzing, and computerizing the relevant literature."[26] In other words, this was Darwin Fall come alive and walking right into the world.

Hickman directed the project for almost three years, providing much of its original Russian direction and energy. He also laid its archival foundation by traveling to the Menninger Clinic in Topeka, Kansas, which was at that time known for its work in such medically anomalous fields as parapsychology, biofeedback, and hypnosis, all subjects boiling down to a basic metaphysical interest in the mind's influence on the body. Hickman traveled to Topeka, worked through their archives, and came back with a few hundred articles that became the basis for the Archive of Bodily Transformation.

Hickman, however, was much more of an activist than an archivist, and so he quickly lost interest in this work. The boxes of Menninger materials were moved into Donovan's San Francisco apartment in 1978, and by 1979 Donovan had become both the second director of the project and an Esalen trustee. He began working with the librarians at the University of California, Berkeley with huge computer print-outs of materials he wanted to locate and copy. For the next five years, Donovan collected, carded, and filed away thousands of different essays and books, all arranged according to the visionary categories of *Jacob Atabet*.

Donovan also hired three college interns from Brown, Harvard, and Yale, who worked under him for two consecutive summers. This trio would be given titles of books or essays, which they then had to go out and find. Through such methods, Donovan was able to create what they called the Archive of Exceptional Functioning. The archive consisted of ten five-drawer black filing cabinets in his living room filled with 10,000 technical essays, books, and reference materials. To help them further, they hired a full-time research associate, Margaret Livingston, with a budget of $24,000 for the 1984 fiscal year.[27] By that same year, Murphy and Donovan had completed *Contemporary Meditation Research*, a compendium of some 1,700 studies on meditation and its physiological and psychological effects that can be read as a kind of forerunner of what would eventually become *The Future of the Body*.

Mythically speaking, the Transformation Project was a social and intellectual incarnation of Jacob Atabet: a collection of historical and empirical evidence suggesting "that evolutionary transformation of the human body can be effected by appropriate psycho-physical discipline."[28] In his efforts to publish *Contemporary Meditation Research*, Donovan outlined the project's, indeed, Jacob and Murphy's vision of human development:

> The Project's archive... contains 9,000 studies.... Its working hypothesis is that man is intended to live a life that is richer and more physiologically, behaviorally, and experientially than has ever, outside of mystical literature, been imagined. We believe that a reframing of current scientific information, in a way that demonstrates correspondences with anecdotal and speculative information, will provide powerful and unrecognized hints of such a life. For it is conceivable that an evolutionary continuum exists from the depths of disease to what one might metaphorically call the luminous or glorified body, and within certain limits, man is able to have an influence on where he is on that continuum.... No one has systematically put these diverse practices into an evolutionistic framework. We believe we might open up the culture to the evolutionary advances our research suggests the way Charles Darwin did with his theory of natural selection.[29]

What Murphy had mystically encountered in Aurobindo's *The Life Divine* and reimagined in this own occult novels was now taking a much more analytic and empirical form. His altered states were evolving into altered ideas.

The Spiegelberg Apartment Lectures

These intellectual efforts were also bolstered by the lectures Frederic Spiegelberg gave at Donovan's Marina Boulevard apartment between November 1978 and January 1983. Murphy had introduced Donovan to Spiegelberg. The two quickly developed a close friendship. About once a month from 1978 to 1990, Donovan would pick Spiegelberg up at his San Francisco apartment and the two of them would go off to an art gallery or museum that Spiegelberg had chosen from the Arts sections of the newspapers. Spiegelberg would give Donovan a running commentary on the art as they walked for no more than an hour (the elderly man's limit). Spiegelberg occasionally offered eccentric commentary as well, like his suggestion that women's high heels symbolized a distant cultural memory of the religious theme of levitation. After the art, the two men would dine at the best restaurant they could find, always with a bottle of fine wine. Donovan would then take Spiegelberg back home, where he would nap for two hours. Apparently, such rituals were more than a little effective. Spiegelberg died in 1994, at the age of 98.

For the lectures, Spiegelberg would make a list of topics he wanted to discuss, work on one or two for weeks at a time, and then announce he was ready to go. The group never consisted of more than thirty people at a time. Spiegelberg would sit at a chair in front of a window overlooking the marina and hold forth in his typical style. For four years, the group moved through dualism, karma and reincarnation, priestess to prostitute, Zarathustra, body and soul, Plotinus, Tibetan ghost stories, the faces of enlightenment, alchemy, Qabalah (Kabbalah), ancient Indian dream doctrines, *The Bhagavad Gita*, self and nothingness, polytheism to monotheism, and finally (and no doubt most important) the religion of no religion.

A friend of Donovan's named Anne Page recorded these lectures for posterity in thirty-eight cassette tapes. The lectures constitute the study of comparative religion in the grand style. Spiegelberg picks some particular theme or pattern and then moves through the history of religions looking for its various manifestations. Finally, he reflects on what it all might mean for the contemporary listener or reader. Space prevents me from an analysis of these lectures, but two brief points are in order.

First, Spiegelberg's apartment lectures culminated on January 24, 1983 in his final reflections on the religion of no religion. It was a final return to the subject of his first book, *The Religion of No-Religion*. Here Spiegelberg revealed the mythobiographical roots of this concept in his walk through the wheat in Holland as a young seminary student, in his natural mystical experience of cosmic unity, and in his subsequent disgust with the gray church that lay just beyond the bend in the road on that same beautiful spring day. Donovan has told me that he always sensed that it was the religion of no religion that anchored his mentor's worldview, that, in the end, this was his final philosophy. I suspect that Donovan is right about this. I also suspect that this is the final philosophy of Esalen—a learned panentheism or nature mysticism.

Spiegelberg, however, did not actually share many of the ideas that drove the Transformation Project. This is my second point. He took a skeptical view of most spiritual practices and thought little of most gurus.

He was deeply skeptical of reincarnation. And he had little use for any talk of the mystical potential of psychedelics or of Tantra. Perhaps most humorously, he thought the practice of running or jogging (much less as a spiritual practice) was one of the silliest things he had ever seen. Donovan, an avid runner, fondly remembers his old friend perched in his upper-floor apartment and watching the hundreds of people running along the bay: "What a stupid thing to be doing with one's time," he would gruff. "That is the stupidest thing I think I have ever seen."[30]

The Magnum Corpus

After a decade and a half of archival work, lectures, and reflection, Darwin's dream was finally being realized. Murphy was finishing *The Future of the Body*.[31] In 1992, the book appeared. It was nearly eight hundred pages and contained no less than twenty-one appendices. Earlier manuscript versions were almost twice as long.

The book has three parts: "Possibilities for Extraordinary Life" sets out a visionary theory; "Evidence for Human Transformative Capacity" presents a comparative history of extraordinary experience; and "Transformative Practices" offers how-to suggestions on how to act on this vision and realize aspects of human potential individually or within a community. All three parts—theory, history, and practice—recall and are nicely encoded in *Jacob Atabet*:

> We are certain that a surprising transformation of the human form is possible through the agency of spirit and that in some sense evolution intends this. It is clear to us, however, that the great contemplative disciplines have generally missed the mark in this regard because the traditions in which they were embedded aimed at a release from embodiment, at a liberation from the wheel of death and rebirth or the world of the flesh and the devil [Theory]. . . . Yet there is much evidence that the body can manifest the glories of spirit— evidence from myths and legends all over the world, from hypnosis and psychical research, from the lore of spiritual healing, from the stigmatic prodigies described in the religious and psychiatric literatures, from sport and Tantra, etc., etc. There is no denying the constant witness to it once you perceive the main pattern [History]. The problem of course is in forming the discipline to give it birth [Practice].[32]

The same is true of *The Future of the Body*. Although most of the book is dedicated to setting out the visionary theory of bodily transformation through evolution, demonstrating this through mysticism, psychical research, folklore, hagiography, psychiatry, and sport, it is in fact the project of "forming the discipline to give it birth" that is the volume's final goal. This was the heart of Murphy's vision for Esalen. *The Future of the Body* is, if you will, what Murphy imagined for Esalen all along, what he always wished it to see and to become. It is his magnum corpus, his *The Life Divine.*

In laying the theoretical groundwork of his vision, Murphy limns four evolutionary domains or eras of cosmic life: (1) the astrophysical development from the Big Bang to the creation of galaxies, stars. and planets; (2) the biological evolution on this planet driven by sexual reproduction, natural selection, and genetic mutation; (3) the psychosocial human development shaped by social organization, language acquisition, education, childrearing practices, ritual, and technology; and finally (4) the metanormal development evoked by "self-discipline, supporting institutions, and conceivably by processes beyond those involved in ordinary human functioning."[33]

Drawing on the work of evolutionary theorists Theodosius Dobzhansky and Francisco Ayala, Murphy names the two leaps from a previous evolutionary domain to a subsequent one *evolutionary transcendence.* "Inorganic evolution went beyond the bounds of [its] previous physical and chemical patternings when it gave rise to life," Murphy writes quoting Ayala. "In the same sense, biological evolution transcended itself when it gave rise to man."[34] Dobzhansky and Ayala recognize only three evolutionary domains and two moments of evolutionary transcendence (from inanimate matter to life, and from life to human consciousness and culture). Murphy offers a third moment of evolutionary transcendence into a fourth domain, the domain of a broadly conceived history of mysticism and the supernormal transformations of the human form. In Murphy's words now: "certain types of extraordinary human development, I believe, herald a third evolutionary transcendence. With them, a new level of existence has begun to appear on earth, one whose patterns cannot be adequately specified by physics, biology, or mainstream social science."[35]

For Murphy, then, the human animal is a transitional being evolving into a supernature with its own supernatural powers or *siddhis.* Murphy calls them the "budding faculties of our greater humanity."[36] These powers line up along the sensory, somatic, and mental capacities that evolution has already endowed us with and is now developing further through the irruption of nonordinary energies—what are traditionally called in Christian theological language graces or charisms (telepathic abilities are an extension of our mental capacity to communicate verbally, clairvoyance is an extension of our sensory capacity to see, and so on).

Although he does not claim to fully understand all the details or causal mechanisms and remains patently agnostic about many of the more extreme claims of the literature, Murphy believes that the patterns of evolution possess meaning, that they constitute a kind of cosmic code hidden right under our noses that, if properly deciphered, can reveal something of our own evolving destiny, our own "future of the body." Paraphrasing the physicist Joseph Ford, he writes, "if the randomness evident in all evolution to date is characterized as a kind of dice-rolling, the extraordinary advances described here suggest that the dice are loaded."[37] For Murphy, a quantum mystic, the God of cosmic evolution not only plays dice; he also cheats.

This is not to say that Murphy is advancing a type of theistic creationism or a naïve theology of intelligent design (he reads the latter movement for what it is: fundamentalism in disguise or, as an evolutionary biologist and Esalen regular once put it to me, "lipstick on the creationist pig"). He does not want to force the science into a particular theology. He rather seeks to derive an adequate theology from the science, broadly conceived here to include the empirical data of the history of mysticism. What he finally ends up with through such a method is an *evolutionary panentheism,* that is, a philosophical system in which God's transcendence and immanence are simultaneously affirmed (*pan-en-theism,* literally "all-in-God-ism") and both find expression through the very process of cosmic evolution, randomness and all.[38] Drawing on Neoplatonism, J. B. Fichte, F. W. J. von Schelling, G. W. F. Hegel, Henry James Sr., and Sri Aurobindo, Murphy suggests that the historical evidence supports the idea "that this world's unfoldment is based upon the implicit action, descent, or involution of a Supreme Principle or Divinity," and that, in the words of Aurobindo, "apparent Nature is secret God."[39]

In other words, what is traditionally called "God" is woven into the very chemical, atomic, and quantum fabric of existence, and it is the long process of evolution, catalyzed now by human intention and transformative practice within a fourth evolutionary domain, that gradually, every so gradually, will reveal this always present Divinity. God is the secret unconscious of Nature, if you will, and evolution is the long cosmic process through which this God awakens into superhuman consciousness and takes flesh. Involution and evolution are thus two sides of the same enlightenment of the body, of the same incarnational process.

Murphy broaches the historical evidence to show neither the sciences nor the traditional religions are capable of seeing this grand vision, primarily because they are restricted by their own philosophical assumptions. They are both too small. Whereas the sciences possess the key of evolution but generally lack any real metaphysical depth, the religions possess the metaphysical depth but generally lack (or refuse) the evolutionary key. In a classical Esalen mode that goes back to the very first brochures, Murphy combines science and spirituality into an integral vision that wants to subsume both into a higher plane of truth.

Take, for example, the superpowers. Whereas traditional science denies their existence, the traditional religions acknowledge their reality but generally shun them as dangerous distractions on the path. But the religious traditions, Murphy observes, lacked the facts of evolution and so had no way of understanding their central roles in human development. They had no larger model or theory to "plug" the powers into and so make comparative sense of their apparent anomalous appearances in history. But we do. Here Murphy follows closely his original Indian guru, Sri Aurobindo, who once wrote: "We need not shun the siddhis and cannot shun them. . . . [The yogin] can no more avoid the use of the siddhis of power and knowledge than an ordinary man can avoid eating and breathing; for these things are the natural action of the consciousness to which he is rising, just as mental activity and physical motion are the natural action of man's ordinary life."[40] Later authors, including the political scientist Fred M. Frohock, have suggested that psychical, and particularly telepathic, abilities may very well be operative, largely unconsciously, in the experience of "luck" and in the uncanny ways some individuals manage to negotiate so successfully through life.[41] In evolutionary terms now, such abilities are highly beneficial and so may have been naturally selected out by millions of years of human evolution.

There are many things that could be said about Murphy's comparative history. His incorporation of modern American sport seems especially original (and jarring for the pious or those fond of rigid cultural categories). Professional quarterback John Brodie and body-builders Arnold Schwarzenegger and Frank Zane, for example, all make personal appearances.[42] Murphy had met each of them. I am also particularly struck by the central role that Catholicism and Christian mysticism play in *The Future of the Body*. Mostly due to his reading of Thurston, Murphy was especially impressed with the archival and critical processes of the

Catholic canonization process and the manner in which these procedures wisely recognized that occult phenomena and ethical behavior need not meet.[43] The traditional Christian doctrines of the transfiguration, the glorified body, and the resurrection seem to lay behind much of Murphy's theorizing on the enlightenment and future of the body. On one level at least, admittedly a heretical one, *The Future of the Body* can be read as a Christian mystical text.

It is also interesting to ask what is missing from Murphy's elaborate histories of the body's transformations. Donovan tells the story of presenting the published volume to Laurance Rockefeller, who had helped fund the project and whom Murphy thanks in his acknowledgments (Rockefeller once told Murphy that there were three people he was watching closely: Governor Jerry Brown, Woody Allen, and Murphy). According to Donovan, Rockefeller immediately noticed that two important subjects had been left out: sex and psychedelics.

Sort of. It is true that there is no mention of psychedelics in the text, and this despite their central role in both Esalen's history and the general history of religions. Rockefeller's observation is entirely accurate here. It is not true, however, that Murphy completely avoids the subject of sex. He does treat the psychosexual dimensions of the stigmata phenomena.[44] He also describes the experiences of a husband who saw around his wife "a nimbus of greenish-blue light that radiated from her whole body" during intercourse.[45] He also quotes at some length the mysticoerotic experiences of George Leonard and cites, among other accounts, a woman's experience of Tantric intercourse.[46]

It is true, though, that Murphy does not treat in any extended fashion the well-known eroticism of mystical literature or the ritual uses of orgasm and sexual arousal as effective techniques of altering consciousness and invoking occult energies. Rockefeller appears to have felt that this was a missed opportunity. He had a point. After all, by neglecting the erotic here in the context of an evolutionary mysticism, Murphy neglects what is perhaps *the* supernormal power of both biological evolution and the history of mystical experience: human sexuality very broadly conceived, that is, as a finally mysterious force, at once spiritual and physical, capable of virtually infinite transmutations, sublimations, repressions, pathologies, ecstasies, and—let us never forget—actual births. Deprived of the erotic dimensions of evolutionary transcendence and the very literal embodiment of pounding sex passing on hidden genetic codes, one is finally left wondering how exactly the evolutionary buds intuited in transformative practice are finally transmitted from one generation to the next and allowed to blossom into stable physical form and cultural practice. It would be tempting to suggest that Murphy is simply concerned about cultural evolution here. But he is not. He is very much about the future *of the body,* not simply the future of society or culture. In the end, he seems to have in mind—although he never specifies it as such in this text—some sort of mystical or occult mechanism of spiritual-physical evolution, similar but not identical to what we find in Aurobindo's *The Life Divine.*[47]

In many ways, practice is the central theme of both *The Future of the Body* and of Esalen. This is the notion that, although these types of nonordinary experiences can and often do happen spontaneously, what is needed are new and more integral practices that can stablilize and develop these forms of consciousness and energy into public social life. Murphy is clear that natural selection is no longer at work. Human beings long ago switched to quicker forms of psychophysical transformation, particularly culture and the fourth domain of meditation, prayer, and various forms of physical discipline, such as the martial arts and Western sport. Transformative practice so conceived thus works very much like evolution itself, only quicker—both act to "progressively embody our latent supernature."[48] And if particular supernormal capacities (like telepathy) and profound experiences of mind-over-matter (like mental healing) or even extreme states of cosmic consciousness (like mystical union) sometimes result, that is because these forms of consciousness and energy were always latent in supernature, because everything is *already* connected, entangled, One.[49] Involution-evolution. Through the long, slow processes of evolution and now the quicker and more conscious processes of transformative practice, we thus become manifestly what we already are secretly— *super.*

The evolutionary or developmental model that Murphy is proposing, however, forces certain judgments upon previous transformative practices. For example, hypnosis, psychotherapy, and sport by themselves will not be enough, since they lack a deep metaphysical sensibility and are not designed to awaken supernormal energies. Nor, however, are most traditional religious practices that are designed to awaken these energies, since their ascetic teachings generally condemn or limit embodiment. What Murphy is ultimately after, then, is a "coevolution of our various attributes with illumined consciousness."

Murphy encourages his readers to "think big." That is, he encourages them to abandon methods and philosophies that constrict the human potential. Instead, he writes, we should be working toward transformative practices that are truly integral: "Only practices that enhance our psychological and somatic functioning while making special 'drafts upon the Unseen' are likely to facilitate a balanced growth of our greater capacities."[50] It is not merely a matter of personal or social effort "from below." The Divine responds to effort and answers "from above," even if in the end this below and this above turn out to be different moments in the same circle of involution and evolution that constitutes the deepest supernature of both the cosmos and its most magnificent expression, the human being.

Realizing Darwin's Dream

After Darwin's *The Origin of Species* appeared in 1859 and set the Western world all abuzz, numerous scholars of religion began to apply various Darwinian models to the history of humanity's religious life, inevitably with dubious ethical results. "Primitive religions," more or less defined by some form of animism (the worship of nature as en-souled), were commonly said to evolve into some form of polytheism, which was said to evolve into different types of monotheism, which inevitably found their most developed form within a worldview that looked remarkably like the Lutheranism, Catholicism, or modernism of the scholar doing the comparing. We have rightly learned to be suspicious of such developmental models as coded forms of ethnocentrism and cultural hubris.

It seems difficult to accuse Murphy of this type of self-serving comparativism. His main inspiration, after all, was Sri Aurobindo, a Bengali revolutionary turned saint who was more or less imprisoned in his own Pondicherry ashram by the British secret service for most of his life—hardly your typical colonial apologist. More importantly, numerous recent developments in the last two decades are beginning to teach us to be suspicious of our own suspicion and return to more reflexive and sophisticated forms of the evolutionary hypothesis. This is particularly evident in the new fields of sociobiology, evolutionary psychology, and in some of the bolder reaches of astrophysics and complexity theory. Writers such as Steven Pinker, Robert Wright, and Pascal Boyer, for example, have demonstrated that a remarkable range of otherwise puzzling human behaviors, from sexual habits and moral behavior to religious beliefs, make very good sense once they are set in an evolutionary frame of reference.[51] Similar evolutionary patterns can be seen in the humanities and social sciences.

Psychologist of religion Kelly Bulkeley, for example, has recently penned a convincing plea for the relevance of cognitive science and evolutionary psychology to the study of religion.[52] Political scientist and historian of the alternative medicine movement Fred Frohock has suggested that "ESP may be a simple extension of existing powers, while precognition would require a dismissal of time's arrow (and perhaps lead to a dramatic expansion of quantum phenomena to the macro events of conventional human experience)."[53] This sounds remarkably like Michael Murphy (or Darwin Fall).

I mention all of this not to claim Pinker's, Wright's, or Bulkeley's visions as my own (Frohock's is astonishingly close), nor to declare a particular final truth, but simply to point out that Michael Murphy's evolutionary panentheism as set out in *The Future of the Body* is well within the range of speculation within some of the bolder reaches of the sciences, social sciences, and humanities. Still, I do not finally read Murphy as an academic writer. I read him as a mystical writer, or better, I read him as a mystical writer who wants to incarnate and integrate his experiences into the very heart of the modern world, that is, into its most disciplined forms of knowledge.

In the end, this is not Charles Darwin sailing on the Beagle. This is Darwin Fall falling into the Hurqalya as he walks into the physics labs of Berkeley. Indeed, if the reader pays close attention and knows something of the larger imaginal corpus in which *The Future of the Body* is embedded, one can distinctly hear the voices of those old friends, Jacob Atabet, Darwin Fall, and Vladimir Kirov. Listen:

> Some mathematicians and physicists have speculated that theories aiming to unify the fundamental forces in a space-time with more than four dimensions (sometimes called Kaluza-Klein theories) might account for paranormal phenomena. Physicist Saul-Paul Sirag has written, for example, that "we may view the body as a projection from the total hyperspace. Plato apparently had such a scheme in mind when he proposed in his cave allegory that we tend to identify ourselves with our three-dimensional bodies, just as chained slaves identified themselves with their two-dimensional shadows." In any case, hyperdimensional models of the universe ... have a resonance with esoteric accounts of extraspatial worlds in which our familiar existence is embedded, and from which phantom figures, luminosities, odors of sanctity, and other extrasomatic phenomena materialize, and through which highly

developed spirit-bodies move. Might our present movement abilities be analogous to those of early amphibians that had not learned to breathe or move freely on land?[54]

Jacob, Darwin, and Vladimir have hardly left us here. They have become a mathematical equation, a hyperdimension, and a conviction posing as a question.

VII

Before and After
the Storm
(1993-2006)

After the Storm

REASSESSMENT, DISASTER, AND RENEWAL

To such facts we now appeal. We look, not backward to fading tradition, but onward to dawning experience.

F. W. H. MYERS

Take the hit as a gift.

Aikido instruction of SENSEI GEORGE LEONARD

The staff of Esalen traditionally takes a retreat together in December, usually the week before Christmas. In 1991, the staff invited an old friend and veteran group facilitator, John Heider, to help them process their reflections and frustrations. Heider, as we have already seen, lived at Esalen from 1967 to 1971, during what was perhaps Esalen's most well-known and celebrated period. Since then, Heider had gone on to work at the Menninger Clinic in Topeka, Kansas; he had helped found a human potential center in Mendocino, California; he had become a successful encounter group leader and author; and, finally, he had nursed his parents through the portals of old age and death in his hometown of Lawrence, Kansas, where he resides now. John Heider knew more than a little about Esalen's history, and his years there are still fondly remembered by the Esalen community members.

On the last day of the retreat, Heider delivered a talk entitled "Olden Times and New: Sex and Drugs at Esalen."[1] It's a remarkable document, certainly for its historical content, but also for how it marks a particular moment of the community's history, that is, a kind of post-Price period of nostalgia and resentment. Heider is quintessentially himself here, that is, in turn funny, shocking, irreverent, chiding, and loving. He at once affirms the value of the transgressions of the Outlaw Era and gently encourages the community to stop romanticizing a past that was at best deeply ambiguous (and occasionally deadly) and move into a renewed vision of what Esalen can be in what is, by all measures, a radically different present.

Technically, Heider's address lies slightly outside of the historical period I am treating here (1993 to the present), but it deals with themes that were crucial throughout the 1990s and are in many ways still with the community today. It makes some sense, then, to begin this final chapter with Heider's historical reflections on the '60s and '70s and his challenges to the Esalen community to embrace their own present and future, in this case, that of the '90s.

Reassessment: John Heider's "Sex and Drugs" Staff Week Seminar (1991)

As Heider introduces the talk to his readers and contextualizes its original delivery, he recalls how much of the December 1991 retreat discussions revolved around a single issue, the issue of freedom of self-expression. "A great deal of energy went into saying, well, it wasn't like this in the old days. Or—if Dick Price were only here . . . " Heider signals what he is about to say in the text of the talk by reminding his readers that not everyone in the 1960s condoned the excesses of the counterculture, that these excesses did not represent the culture of Esalen San Francisco, "which I barely knew," and that many individuals who came to Esalen Big Sur "were disturbed by what they found, and left." "In the end," Heider points out, "exhausted, I left too." Interestingly, Heider's long-hand notes to himself at this point in the manuscript read: "[Aleister] Crowley Do what thou wilt antinomian heresy" and "Svecchacara [a Sanskrit term meaning roughly 'the practice of following one's own will']: Tantra idiotae: self-gods." Heider, in other words, connects the power, promise, and problems of this era with Western sexual magic and Indian Tantra, very much along the lines I have been suggesting all along. He knows.

The actual retreat talk begins with Heider observing that the community seems relatively peaceful now at the end of 1991, "more harmonious in most respects than it has in all its history." He also observes that "Esalen is blessed and burdened with a myth of the total freedom of olden times," and that, like many myths, "this one has a measure of truth." He remembers, for example, two Esalen sayings that he heard when he arrived on these grounds in 1967: "You can do whatever you have the balls to do in Big Sur," and Ed Maupin's famous, "Mother Esalen gives permission."

"But this is 1991," Heider insists. "No community leader would say that today.... Times have changed." The transgressions of the 1960s made good sense, as they functioned as a meaningful response to a repressive, frightened, and stunted culture. Much of that repression and transgression, moreover, revolved around sexuality. "Sex was Topic A," and the men at least "assumed that men and women wanted the same thing: more." There were certainly few serious sexually transmitted diseases to worry about. Antibiotics were effective. The pill was nearly universal. Esalen even had its own VD clinic provided by Monterey County, which provided services down at the baths every few weeks. Granted, female sexuality was still a mystery, but that was changing too. The *mysterium* of the Tantric *yoni*, for example, was not simply a matter of psychedelic vision, psychoanalytic speculation, or Tantric iconography. It was also a matter of actual empirical observation:

> It was Lenore, the county crotch doctor's nurse, who brought us our first plastic speculums on August 27, 1968. These gynecological instruments were to Esalen as Galileo's telescope or Leeuwenhoek's microscope had been to pioneers of an earlier time. The plastic speculum let us see, see what had never been seen before: the *mysterium altum,* the inside of a vagina. No one I knew had looked into that darkness before. Not into a vagina, not at a penis. No one I knew had ever sat and meditated on a *lingam* or a *yoni.* No one had seen menstrual blood ooze out of a cervix.[2]

And it wasn't just sex that was everywhere. Danger too lurked around every corner, or more accurately, along every cliff-edge: "The paths were unlighted, the cliffs unfenced. Esalen was not a safe place. People came for the danger, the risk, the freedom." But this freedom, Heider chides, meant far more than doing what one wanted to do. It also meant doing precisely what one did *not* want to do at all, that is, what one most feared. "Remember the Freudian belief that resistance is a sure sign of work to be done; think of the body worker's attitude toward chronic muscle tension." Push and press there. Make the unconscious conscious. The principle was a simple (psychoanalytic) one: "The greater the fear, the more energy is bound up in it, the more potential for liberation." The human potential, in other words, was not simply about joy and light; it was also about *fear* and the psychoanalytic attempt to release often terrifying amounts of bound-up energy and power.

And then there were the drugs. As we have already seen, for the most part, this was not about casual drug use at all. Rather, drugs were what Heider calls "the Royal Road to higher consciousness." "Our goal," Heider insisted, "the goal of Esalen and of much of the counterculture, was simple: enlightenment." But there were casualties on this royal road to enlightenment and its transgressive ways. Occasionally, too occasionally, there were even real deaths. In his journals, Heider had listed four: Marcia, who shot herself in a pick-up truck; Diane, who hung herself from the loft in Staff 1; Art, who had been thrown through a window during an encounter group only to kill himself within the year;[3] and Sunshine, who shot himself in the head at the craft barn. Such memories were personally crushing for Heider.[4] Now he remembers for the community what his father had said to him about these terrible deaths: "Yes, but you'll never know how many people went to Esalen already on the edge and decided *not* to kill themselves because of what happened there." Heider also remembers what his teacher, Will Schutz, called Esalen: "the court of last resort."

Heider ends his retreat talk by noting that every counterculture is eventually itself countered. The pendulum swings back. If the 1960s were a reaction to the McCarthyism of the '50s, the '80s would be a reaction to the '60s and '70s. In the '80s, the Outlaw Area shrank. The baths were cleaned, the paths were paved and lit, and fences were installed on the cliff. Heider then utters the thought many were thinking. "Put a date on the day the music finally stopped." The day? Dick's death. "Dick's death ended Esalen's role as blow-out center."

Almost. Heider finally pushes his listeners to wake up to their own historical moment and renew the spirit of Esalen, not in the then and there, but in the here and now:

> But has the Outlaw Area really shrunk or have individuals shrunk from the burden of being outlaws? Do you still await the return of the '60s, the Second Coming of Dick Price? I hope not. Your task is harder. You do not have the support of a culture in revolt.... You must be your own Fritz Perls, Will Schutz, Dick Price. If that won't do, then wait and the unfolding gestalten [wholes] of time will soon enough deliver us into another revolutionary era, a new and unimaginable cultural shift.... I ask you, in the light of the 1990s, to take stock: What are your beliefs, your customs today? Where do you stand on sex, drugs, and acting out your repressed

selves?... What matters, what excites you, where are your frontiers? What are your freedoms and the limits to your freedoms? Why are you here? What are you doing at Esalen, what is Esalen's mission now?

Heider's tough but loving questions, if not his actual words, would ring through the next decade like an annoying but essential meditation bell.

Finding the Beat Again

The *yoni* returned again six months later, this time on a book tour. As president of Esalen, Steve Donovan helped Murphy promote *The Future of the Body* and raise money for the institute on a national book tour in May of 1992. While they were in Seattle, Donovan was looking to buy a sailboat (recall that he had had his first transformative experience on the Ilinx in March of 1973). While in the harbor at Seattle he found one in particular that seemed perfect. When he looked over the transom, it seemed even more perfect: painted on the back of the sloop was the name Yoni. Donovan describes this lucky find as a "cosmic joke." And one well worth telling. After having Spiegelberg draw "Yoni" in Sanskrit to be painted on the transom, Donovan sailed the Yoni the thousand sea miles south to Sausalito with his wife and two professional sailors on rough seas, much of it filled with playing dolphins, threatening great white sharks, and huge forty-foot swells. The Tantra resurged and returned again, this time as a vaginal sailboat from the sea.

In December of that same year, Donovan went on a seven-day Zen retreat with Richard Baker Roshi in Crestone, Colorado. On the last night of the retreat, he received a powerful energized dream that he would name "The Mongrel Dog." He interpreted the dream as a sign that he should resign as president of Esalen. This is precisely what he did when he returned from Colorado. On the last day of 1992, he handed in his resignation. There were many reasons for this decision. For a start, having to live on the grounds in Big Sur was creating marital tensions. There were also financial considerations and disagreements with Murphy over the directions Esalen should take now. In the end, though, "It was simply time to leave." His last day on the grounds in his official role was March 22, 1993. Like John Heider before him, he left exhausted.

After Donovan's departure, Murphy decided to take the reins himself. This, it turns out, was a mistake. In his own words, "It was not a pretty

FIGURE 30. Steve Donovan's former sloop named Yoni, 1992. Photograph by Steven Donovan, Seattle, Washington, printed with permission.

sight." He lasted about a year. A woman by the name of Sharon Thom was then hired as president. Thom would last about two. One of Thom's most lasting legacies were two individuals she hired to run the Esalen business office: Pat Lewine and David Price (Dick's son). Lewine and Price would do a great deal over the next ten years to run the business office and bring it into greater focus and efficiency.

As always, the programming and seminars ran apace of the administrative drama, and charismatic teachers continued to arrive at Esalen throughout the 1990s. In the fall of 1992, Donovan brought Brother David Steindl-Rast, a Trappist monk and popular spiritual writer, to Esalen and gave him one of the middle-point houses. Steindl-Rast lived there for about two years. His presence added a strong Christian spirituality to the place, even as it tended to strengthen Esalen's symbolic links with the Carthusian monastery just up the road, to which Steindl-Rast also had connections. Donovan cites Brother David as the man who first encouraged him to practice Zen Buddhism. Steindl-Rast was the last teaching figure to reside on the grounds for an extended period of time.

In the 1990s, Esalen also renewed one of its most long-standing and deepest ethical commitments, that is, its association with the ecological movement. The catalyzing event was the 1993 appearance of Theodore Roszak's *The Voice of the Earth*. Murphy invited Roszak to lead a 1994 symposium on the principles and future of what Roszak and others were now calling an ecopsychology, yet another system of Esalen-related thought that attempts to reunite mind with matter, here framed as the human psyche and the total natural ecosystem. With Mary Gomes and Allen Kanner, Roszak gathered twenty-seven participants to Esalen. To help frame their project, they drew on classical Esalen thinkers and themes, in particular Abraham Maslow and Sigmund Freud. Maslow, after all, had called for "a still higher Fourth Psychology, transpersonal, transhuman, centered in the cosmos rather than in human needs and interest, going beyond humanness, identity, self-actualization, and the like."[5] Roszack saw his ecopsychology in this same stream of thought: "By defining mind and sanity in the context of a living planet, ecopsychologists are redefining human consciousness and health in terms of the wisdom of the id and the ecological unconscious."[6]

Roszack bows to Freud here, even if he bows, like so many others, in the direction of the Freudian Left. The id, for Roszack, is not some infantile or dangerous force to be controlled by the socialized ego. Rather, it is "the protohuman psychic core that our environment has spent millions of years moulding to fit the planetary environment."[7] It is our innate wisdom, our mystical link with the cosmos. The goal of ecopsychology is not so much to conquer more and more of the id for the ego, as Freud understood his own psychological project, as it is to unite the natural id with the social ego in order to propel the species toward "greater evolutionary adventures" and "a psyche the size of the Earth."[8] By now, these are familiar Esalen themes, in whatever theoretical language they are expressed.

Another significant Esalen figure of the 1990s was Babatunde Olatunji, a Nigerian-born drummer who played a major role in the '60s and '70s introducing indigenous African music to American audiences. Olatunji spent the last years of his life going back and forth between two American alternative communities, Esalen Institute in Big Sur and the Omega Institute in Rhinebeck, New York, giving multiple concerts at each to adoring crowds. Esalen eventually provided Olatunji a house to live in when he was ill. It was there that he died.[9]

El Niño and the Collapse of the Baths

The 1990s rolled, or perhaps closer to our present discussion, beat on. Then, in the winter of 1998, disaster struck. An El Niño appeared in the Pacific. The winter storms that it whipped up over months of rain, wind, and cold eventually soaked and finally collapsed the cliff over the baths in February of 1998. The force of the rock and dirt seriously damaged the structure's integrity. The community tried to salvage their famous cliff-side institution, but to no avail. At midnight, on Tuesday, April 28, 1998, the baths were officially closed.

As natural disasters go, this was a relatively minor one. No lives were lost. No cities lay in ruins. No mountaintops were blasted into smithereens and spread over an entire continent in clouds of dust and dark. Still, the forced closing of the hot springs took on immense symbolic resonances for the community and its leaders. Everyone saw that they had arrived at a fork in the road. The leadership was particularly somber. They knew that the place had been running in the black for years, particularly since Donovan's business-savvy reforms. Still, they quickly realized that they had no endowment and so no extra resources. There was discussion about throwing the proverbial towel in and calling it quits. Esalen had run its course, and the storm had now given them a reason finally to admit this.

Acting as president, Leonard drew on his aikido training and encouraged the community to "take the hit as a gift." In effect, Leonard said to them: "Let's roll with the punch (or in this case the storm) and use its energy toward our own ends. Let's use this as an *opportunity* to test our mettle and our skill at dealing with whatever life gives us." What this meant practically was that the leadership of Esalen decided to recommit themselves to the long-term stability of the place and rebuild the baths, not as they were in their simple cinder-blocks, but in a kind of renewed aesthetic glory.

Architect Micky Muennig was hired to create a design. The structure itself was constructed primarily of board-formed concrete, sandstone, and clearstory windows. The design emphasizes elegance, simplicity, and a certain vague but distinct Japanese accent. As one walks down into the shower rooms, the visitor is first greeted by water flowing over a tiled mosaic image crafted by artist Elle Leonard and based on a Japanese print by Hokusai entitled *Amida Waterfall on the Kiso Road.* The design, the Esalen website points out, "was chosen to represent a peaceful recollection along a journey."

There was more to the project, however, than simply the baths. The baths, after all, were never the real problem. The cliff was. The planners took a very bold step. Learning a thing or two from the California crews that had built Highway 1 through some of the most treacherous landslides and cliffs in the world, they decided to cover the entire cliff with a metal net and then secure it with dozens of twenty-five- to forty-foot pylons driven deep into the cliff. They then planted natural indigenous flowers and shrubbery on the cliff side, which soon covered the net and rendered the entire artifice virtually invisible.

Stability, strength, and long-range commitment appear to be the defining metaphors of the entire project. In 2000, for example, I walked down to the foot of the baths as the work crew laid the foundation. They were drilling immense holes forty feet straight down into the Big Sur rock to ground the structure. "Forget El Nino," Murphy joked, "Hell, a nuclear submarine could hit this structure and it wouldn't budge." An exaggeration perhaps, but the point was entirely justified. What I saw that day was the foundation of a deeply symbolic structure built to last. The baths now stand as a symbol of commitment, no longer to a temporary experiment built in cheap cinder-blocks, rotting wood, and countless ecstasies, but to a twenty-first century establishment embodied now in rock, concrete, glass, and sculpted metals.

These also, I think, are the defining metaphors of Esalen during the late 1990s and at the turn of the present century: long-range stability, long-term commitment, and what Murphy calls, in his usual theological language, a decision to incarnate in the world. Three men have determined these commitments over the last ten years: Andy Nusbaum, Gordon Wheeler, and Michael Murphy.

During his tenure, Nusbaum dedicated much of his time and energy to helping the institute develop and pursue a long-range developmental plan that is both ecologically and economically sound, as is evident in the impressive 2000 planning manual he guided through production.[10] Gordon Wheeler, as president, has reformed the governing structure of the institute and brought it back to some of its original gestalt origins, this time revisioned by Wheeler's own extensive theoretical writings and therapeutic experience as a gestalt training analyst. And Murphy finally has brought the institute back to its original intellectual and visionary origins through the formal establishment of the Center for Theory and Research.

From Iconoclast to President: Gordon Wheeler and the Renewal of Community

Gordon Wheeler's spiritual life first took a definite shape in the 1970s within a devotional relationship to Swami Muktananda, the charismatic Tantric Hindu guru we met above with Christina Grof. Wheeler lived with his first wife and children in Muktananda's ashram in Fallsburg, New

York for some time. Before this formative experience, the only contact he had with altered states of consciousness was through his own relational sexuality. It was Muktananda who gave him a language of transcendence to describe what he already had intuited within the erotic and the relational but could not quite name or develop.

From the Hindu Tantra, Wheeler turned to gestalt psychology and became an accomplished therapist and theorist. Indeed, he made a considerable name for himself among the gestalt psychology community for his many books and, in particular, for his critical insistence that the exaggerated individualism advocated by figures like Fritz Perls needs to be balanced by a deeper sense of community and connection. Perls may have had a crucial and necessary historical role in catalyzing the field, Wheeler acknowledges, but his individualism also sits in serious tension with gestalt philosophy's radical insights into the centrality of relationship, figure-ground context, and, of course, the gestalt or whole.[11] Perls's relationship to his own family was, at best, disturbing. One would never know he had children by reading his books. Moreover, there were only two sorts of individuals he banned from his Canadian gestalt kibbutz late in his life: dogs and children. In Wheeler's reading, Perls could only see family commitments and children as barriers to his own personal freedom. Children were not gifts or graces to embrace and nourish; they were nails in the coffin of a murdered individualism.

This did not go over very well in many sectors of the gestalt community, and Wheeler became something of an *enfant terrible* in that world. But many others were also listening and taking note, among them Eric Erickson of Esalen. Erickson decided to invite Wheeler to Esalen to balance out what many in the Esalen community were beginning to realize was an unhealthy emphasis on the self at the expense of relationship and community. Wheeler was scheduled to be in the Carmel area in 1996, so they contacted him and invited him down to Big Sur for the day. Nancy Lunney met him for the first time then. She called him again a year later and convinced him to offer a seminar. It was a two-week workshop on gestalt therapy in February of 1997. Lunny agreed with Erickson that it would be good to get Wheeler to Esalen on a more permanent basis to "wholize" gestalt at Esalen.

Erickson liked Wheeler and his message a great deal. But Nancy Lunney actually loved him. The feeling, it turned out, was mutual. In Lunney's memory, "Gordon kept coming back for me. It was totally *eros*—he wouldn't have come back without me." Out of this initial passion developed a long-term commitment and eventually a marriage. Gordon would move to Esalen to live with Nancy. George Leonard formally handed over the presidency during a board meeting the end of July in 2004. Nancy Lunney is now Nancy Lunney-Wheeler, and the program director and the president of Esalen live and work out of the same tiny house on a cliff overlooking the sea.

The Center for Theory and Research and the Renewal of Vision

In Wheeler's mind, the Esalen of today rests on four central pillars: the magic of the physical place; the global community of Esalen's seminarians, readers, and supporters; the programming and seminars; and the think tank of active research and scholarship.[12] The latter pillar, although clearly stemming back to Esalen's origins and the earliest brochures (indeed, this pillar *was* Esalen's origins), was not actually formalized until 1998, when it was named the Center for Theory and Research. The CTR is, as Murphy puts it, the research and development arm of Esalen. The CTR, as I would prefer to put it (that is, mythologically), also happens to be the direct heir of Darwin Fall, Jacob Atabet, and the earlier Transformation Project that led to *The Future of the Body*.

The central practice of CTR is the five-day invitational seminar. Such invitational symposia have long been the centerpiece of Esalen. The first seminars were symposia of sorts, in that they routinely featured two or three speakers on a particular topic. But they were hardly invitational conferences. They were entirely open to any interested person willing to pay the attendance fee, and they generally lasted only one, two, or three days. The more extended invitational, private, five-day model took time to develop. Murphy considers the America and China conference the first real Esalen invitational, a three-day gathering held in January of 1965.The event was open to the public and advertised as a "critique of American policy toward Red China." It featured six speakers, including Nobel-prize winner Linus Pauling from the Center for the Study of Democratic Institutions in Santa Barbara and Dennis Doolin of the Hoover Institute at Stanford.

Things developed gradually from there. A standard five-day format developed over the next decade and was solidly in place by the mid-1970s, when the practice hit something of a peak with almost twenty invitational seminars taking place each year. Although expenses have limited these to around eight or ten per year, the format has remained more or less the same. Twenty or so individuals are invited to discuss a specific topic. Participants show up on Sunday afternoon and are welcomed in the Big

FIGURE 31. The Big House, 2006. Photo by Daniel Bianchetta. Printed with permission of the Esalen Institute.

House, where most of them will also be staying. Sunday night is dedicated to social ice-breaking. Morning, afternoon, and evening sessions then follow Monday through Thursday. All the meals are taken in the lodge, and participants are given time to enjoy the baths, arrange for a massage, or enjoy the grounds. Traditionally, Thursday dinner functions as a kind of capping event and is served more formally in the Big House's main meeting room, usually by Esalen's chefs.

It isn't unusual for Esalen to commit to a topic for four or five years that may involve the participation of between seventy-five and one hundred individuals, many of whom have advanced degrees and work in academia. The PhD is as common in the Big House as water.

The topics of the invitational conference events range widely, but they usually revolve around a particular theme whose integral nature (at once rational and mystical) has rendered the idea too anomalous and too technical for either the traditional halls of the academy or the popularizing bookstores. The first five series of the CTR, for example, were (1) subtle energies (that is, the nonordinary energies of *chi, prana, psi,* etc.); (2) postmortem survival research; (3) the philosophical implications of evolutionary theory, led by the philosopher Jay Ogilvy and molecular biologist David Deamer; (4) transformative practice; and (5) the ethical urgency of ecological and sustainability issues.

As the years ticked by, the postmortem survival series was the only one to, well, survive. Two other topics were eventually added: (1) the history of Western esotericism, an explicitly joint American-European venture I direct with Wouter Hanegraaff of the University of Amsterdam; and (2) contemporary fundamentalist challenges to scholarship on religion, which has now morphed into the psychodynamics of global fundamentalism and is led by the career diplomat and political psychology theorist Joseph Montville.

The series Beyond Fundamentalism was initially conceived and led by Dulce Murphy, Paul Courtright, and me to address with our Indian colleagues the political threats to critical scholarship on Indian religion and culture that many of us have experienced since the late 1990s, mostly from groups involved with the Hindu essentialist movement (Hindutva). Understanding the Nature of Our Offense took place in December of 2004. Over the next two years, the Murphys and Montville followed this initial gathering with symposia on Islamic, Christian, and Jewish fundamentalism.[13] In many minds, the Muslim gathering in particular had "all the feel of the early American-Soviet meetings." That is, it is a topic of immense political relevance that can be creatively approached through Esalen's classical methods of citizen diplomacy, personal friendship, and partnering with liberal religious and mystical voices.

In December of 2005, Esalen sponsored a symposium on epistemology, that is, on the vexing question of how one knows. I mention it here because it was an attempted updating, revisioning, and critique of the original Esalen notion of the integral that had been announced forty-three years earlier in the first brochures by the contemplative lotus and the calculus equation. We thus come full circle.

By the 1990s, and certainly by the turn of the millennium, most major Esalen intellectuals had abandoned the Huxley-like perennialism with which they began in the '60s. They certainly still held to a kind of deep human universalism grounded in the body, but few still believed that the major religions were saying more or less the same thing, or ever would (or ever should). They thus loved what anthropologist Richard Shweder had to say about what he calls Confusionism, that is, his own take on the dilemmas of cultural pluralism: "The knowable world is incomplete if seen from any one point of view, incoherent if seen from all points of view at once, and empty if seen from 'nowhere in particular.'"[14] Certainly such a conclusion can be read as an apt description of forty-five years of Esalen cultural and religious experimentation, even perhaps as a kind of rationalist version of the religion of no religion.[15] A completely unified system of human knowledge, a total integralism, it turns out, may very well be both intellectually impossible and morally undesirable. The world is irreducibly plural.

Murphy has shared with me many times since these discussions how liberating he found Shweder's Confusionism. In particular, it helped him remember and understand a very early Esalen debate (the second seminar of the second brochure, to be exact) between Bill Harman, who was expounding the all-encompassing metaphysical system of Sri Aurobindo, and Joe Adams, who found all such systems quasi-fascist and politically dangerous. Oddly, Murphy found himself viscerally aligned with Adams against Harman, and this despite his own Aurobindonian convictions. Now he knew why.

As such examples make clear, the invitational conferences tend strongly to go after "the big picture." The minutiae of research are highly valued and deeply admired in such gatherings, but it is implicitly understood that the gatherings are not about these otherwise crucial stages of human learning. This is different. This is about building and nurturing a kind of gnostic community, that is, an intimate group of individuals who are committed to some form of deep and deeply humane experiential knowledge that is at once rigorously intellectual, socially and politically engaged, and religiously nuanced. In this way, Esalen has provided real institutional support for an emerging worldview not provided by either the universities, with their *reason,* or the churches, with their *faith.* It is finally a place of *gnosis.*

Survival: The Final Question Concerning Consciousness and Energy

Given its implications for the central theme of this present volume, that is, the nature and relationship of consciousness and energy, as well as its status as the longest standing running series of the CTR, it is perhaps appropriate to end both the present chapter and the book as a whole with a discussion of the postmortem survival symposia. For the last nine years (1998–2006), the CTR has sponsored an annual Survival of Bodily Death conference on its grounds, affectionately known to its participants simply as Sursem (survival seminar). The list of attendees includes near-death researcher Bruce Greyson, neuroscientist Ed Kelly and psychologist Emily Williams Kelly of the University of Virginia, psychical researcher Marilyn Schlitz of the Institute of Noetic Sciences, transpersonal psychologist Charles Tart, analyst and historian of psychology Adam Crabtree, and quantum physicist Henry Stapp of the Lawrence Laboratory in Berkeley. There are also some delightful surprises here, including the Esalen aficionado and comedian John Cleese of Monty Python fame, whose philosophical and mystical interests run deep.

The series was initiated in December of 1998 by Murphy, who has long been impressed with such figures as the British psychical researcher F. W. H. Myers and the American psychologist William James, each of whom had dedicated much of his life to the subject of psychical research and, by implication, the question of postmortem survival. Murphy's question was, in many ways, the most basic of all religious and philosophical questions: Do we survive the obvious biological destruction of our bodies?

The series participants chose not to attack this question quite so directly. Instead, they chose to address an even more basic issue: What is the relationship between mind and matter or, in our own terms, consciousness and energy? Their reasoning was simple. If mind is *produced* by matter, as in most present neurological models, then mind necessarily ends when the brain stops functioning, and none of us will survive bodily death in any form. If, however, mind is *transmitted* by the brain, as a kind of biological TV or radio, then it is quite possible that mind does not end when the brain stops; in Myers terms, human personality, or at least some aspects of it, may actually survive bodily death. A further corollary possibility follows. If scientifically controlled evidence can be collected that suggests living individuals receive reliable and accurate information from deceased personalities, then this would more or less seal the case for both the survival of bodily death and the relative independence of mind over matter.

And so they began to arrive in December of 1998. At the top of Murphy's list of invited guests was Ian Stevenson of the University of Virginia, probably the most impressive researcher in the survival studies field. For the last forty years, Stevenson has produced book after book, documenting cases drawn from his collection of hundreds, then thousands of case studies of past-life memories, particularly in Hindu and Buddhist South and East Asia (India, Sri Lanka, Thailand, and Burma), Shiite Lebanon and Turkey, West Africa, and Northwest America.[16] As of 1997, Stevenson had collected 2,600 reported cases of past-life memories and had published 65 detailed reports on individual cases, including a massive and eerily suggestive study of 225 cases of what he calls "the biology of reincarnation," that is, the phenomenon of birth-marks or birth-defects as physical "marks" from a previous life's violent ending by knife, rope, or bullet wound—yet more evidence for what Murphy would call the mind's power to influence and transform, quite literally, the future of the body.[17]

Stevenson, however, could not come to the conference, so he sent his colleague, Emily Williams Kelly, in his place. Kelly was a natural pick for the series, since she had written her dissertation at the University of Edinburgh on Myers.[18] She chose Edinburgh because no one in the States was willing to work with her on this subject. Edinburgh was also emerging as a global center for parapsychology since the writer Arthur Koestler had endowed the university toward this same end. Emily's husband, Ed, tagged along to the first conference in 1998, "to carry the bags," as he puts it. Actually, however, he too had considerable experience in the field. After completing his PhD at Harvard in psycholinguistics, Ed had done a stint at J. B. Rhine's parapsychology lab in Durham, North Carolina, before getting involved in EEG research in the electrical engineering department at Duke University and then moving into neurophysiological studies at the University of North Carolina, Chapel Hill. By carrying his wife's bags into the Big House, he was effectively reentering the field of his first intellectual love: psychical research, as broadly conceived by Myers, James, and modern figures such as Ian Stevenson and Michael Murphy.

Within a few years, the man carrying the bags was appointed series leader and eventually led the effort in editing, with Adam Crabtree, Sursem's most lasting testament to the first seven years of its proceedings, a volume entitled *Irreducible Mind*.[19] The launching point for this book is Myers's *Human Personality*, which Sursem members believe is representative of a synoptic—that is, at once empirical and theoretical—approach to the study of consciousness that was all but lost in the narrower behaviorist and neurological approaches of the twentieth century. Among the latter, they often cite J. B. Rhine's parapsychology, which, with its restrictive reliance on artificial laboratory settings and statistical methods (Zener cards, random number generators, bored or tired undergraduate volunteers), ends up missing entirely the strongest empirical evidence, that is, the dramatic real-world appearances of psychical phenomena that seem to be invoked as responses to traumas, challenges, and inspirations. Staring at abstract shapes on playing cards and suffering the physical terrors of a car accident are simply two different things, and it is the latter, not the former, that most effectively calls forth the psychical (hence the virtual impossibility of studying robust psychical phenomena in a controlled and moral laboratory). Significantly, the book is dedicated to two iconic figures: Ian Stevenson and Michael Murphy. The Kellys understand Stevenson and Murphy to be among the few true descendants of Myers, James, and other nineteenth-century founders of psychical research who took a similarly broad empirical and theoretical approach to important human questions.

They also point out that, again like Myers, Murphy has lived his entire professional life outside academia, even as he has embodied the best of that world, that is, a combination of an intellectual openness and a critical rigor that will not allow him to accept any cheap solutions. Murphy's dual mind, for the Kellys at least, is also reflective of Esalen's history, which, they point out, has often swung rather wildly between these two playful-imaginative and critical-analytic poles. Ed in particular points to some of the "New Age bullshit" that he sees represented at Esalen and notes that he believes Murphy has grown impatient with much of this and is now looking for a more solid and lasting accomplishment. "The CTR is his vehicle for this," Ed observes, "and *Irreducible Mind* is meant to be a part of this legacy." "We are going to make a lot of people uncomfortable with that book, like Myers, Gurney, and company did at the turn of the last century," Kelly observes. "We want scientific psychology to return to its original challenges and insights, after wandering in the desert for its first century."

It is certainly true that Murphy has grown impatient, although "impatient" is probably not the best word after forty-five years of almost preternatural tolerance and millions of spent Esalen dollars. With the survival question in particular, Murphy has grown increasingly frustrated with what we might call faith and belief, neither of which the group are particularly interested in affirming. As Murphy once put it to me: "The older I get, the more impatient I get with organized religion." Certainly Sursem does not want yet another religious model of the afterlife. Like Myers, they operate with the conviction that the question of the afterlife is not simply a conceptual or metaphysical question; it is also an *empirical* one. This is what Ed Kelly meant when he commented on their "uncomfortable" challenge to both the academic and religious establishments. The group thus operates with the conviction that the survival of the human personality after death is simply the most extreme case of the question of mind and matter (or consciousness and energy), and that this question can and should be explored empirically as well as philosophically and speculatively.

The first eight years of Sursem were dedicated not so much to the survival of bodily death as to the (irreducible) nature of mind itself. The volume argues that the best model available to us at this moment to explain *all* the empirical evidence is not the epiphenomenon thesis (mind is a surface product of the brain) but the transmission thesis developed by Myers and named by James (consciousness is best imagined as transmitted through the brain). I would only add here that this Myers-James transmission thesis fits very well with Aurobindo's understanding of consciousness and seamlessly with the Bergsonian filter thesis of Albert Hofmann, Aldous Huxley, Huston Smith, and Stanislav Grof with respect to the psychedelic revelations, and Arthur Koestler with respect to *psi* phenomena (in which psychedelics or *psi* events are understood to remove or suppress the brain's filtering mechanism). Indeed, Albert Hofmann had even delivered a public lecture called "The Transmitter-Receiver Concept of Reality" in 1983 as the real lesson he had learned from his forty-year career with the chemical sacrament.[20] If one is looking for a kind of "Esalen orthodoxy" with respect to the nature of consciousness, then, Sursem's transmission thesis is a very good place to start.

The Sursem group is now moving into a second stage of questioning, one that involves more the speculative construction of actual psychophysical causal mechanisms and possible postmortem scenarios. The question is this: given the empirical evidence we now have, what would a reasonable model of the afterlife look like? Most basically, are we talking about something that resembles the single-life model of Western religions (single birth, single life, single death, judgment, followed by some sort of eternal state), or perhaps something more along the lines of what the Asian religions have imagined (multiple births, lives, and deaths toward some sort of liberation or enlightenment)?

The Sursem group has yet to come to any consensus on this. When I pressed Murphy on the differences between the one-life models of the Western near-death experience and the multiple life models of the Asian religions, however, he pointed out that the modal Western near-death experience does not seem to be a true death experience. It is a *near*-death experience. The researchers are consistent in their consensus that the person does not actually die in these events. The past-life memories, on the other hand, represent a death that was carried through. The easiest way to synthesize the Western and the Asian models for Murphy, in other words, may be to adopt an evolutionary model of reincarnation and assume that the Western near-death experiences are just that—*near*-death experiences, which, if carried through, would have led to a next-life scenario, very much as we find them in Stevenson's literature, where they have been freed by a comparative method from the traditional boundaries of culture and recentered in a single species.

Obviously, such a broad global perspective untethered from any local culture does not constitute a ringing endorsement of the religions, Asian or otherwise, for Murphy. Quite the contrary, as we have already seen, his fiction and analytical works are filled with serious criticisms of these traditions' common antiworld and antibody attitudes, all of which flow into their postmortem models as well. Moreover, he is intriguingly insistent that the soul is never without a body of some sort, and that both *evolve*. For Murphy, in other words, the possibility that the always embodied human personality lives on again and evolves into another form of life, here in another birth or on some other plane or dimension, is a possibility that finally escapes *all* previous religious models and explanations.

"That which lies at the root of each of us lies at the root of the Cosmos too," Myers had written at the very end of his two-volume masterpiece. Frank Poletti used the same quote to lead off his summary of the 2004 gathering of Sursem, and appropriately so. The little phrase, after all, brings us back full circle to the very beginning of our long narrative. Myers's cosmic-human identification is strongly reminiscent of the *brahman-atman* doctrine that first moved Murphy so in that Stanford lecture hall back in 1950. It is the same truth in another language.

And yet it is not the same truth at all, for now this most basic of all mystical intuitions has become "unhitched" from any and all religious traditions and sacred languages. In other words, even and especially when it came to *the* religious question, the subject of death and the survival of the soul, Murphy and his Esalen visionaries arrived once again at a kind of religion of no religion.

Whither Now?

So what now? What of John Heider's challenge to the Esalen staff to stop looking backwards, to stop waiting for "the second coming of Dick Price" and instead take stock of the challenges of the immediate present and the coming future? What of Gordon Wheeler's challenge that the radical individualism of Esalen's gestalt lineage should now be balanced by a greater sense of community and connection? What of Michael Murphy's CTR and its implicit reminder that everything stems back finally to the original founding visions, and that, without a solid intellectual base, Esalen becomes just another Big Sur resort, a mere spa?[21] Or, finally, put in the terms of the Sursem group, will "Esalen" survive and evolve, like the subtle body-soul of Murphy's speculative vision? Or will it just eventually fade away, like virtually every other new religious movement or countercultural moment, with the inevitable deaths of its founders?

At first glance, the cultural contexts Esalen now finds itself in could not be more different than those it first encountered and countered in the early 1960s. But first glances are often deceptive ones. Esalen, we must remember, did not arise out of the excesses of the counterculture, with which it is always (mistakenly) conflated. Rather, it arose out of the conservatism of the 1950s *before* the counterculture in an attempt to free itself from the stifling conformity—the "air-conditioned nightmare," as Henry Miller once put it—of the baby-booming '50s. Some of the primary manifestations of this conservatism were a censoring McCarthyism, a thoroughgoing militarism, a conservative academy, a nuclear terror, and a hypocritical sexual prudery on screen and in print. The hysterical polemics of a Mildred Brady and the phobic politics of a Joseph McCarthy were the order of the day, not the exceptions.

Esalen figures fought every one of these cultural wars in some way or another and, with the broader forces of history and the individual choices of millions of other social actors, won for a time almost every single battle they fought. The last twenty-five years, however, exactly as Heider observed, have seen a gradual but consistent swing back to conservatism, if not to an outright fundamentalism, in American culture and religion. The Bradys and McCarthys of the world are very much in power again. We have also, of course, seen a dramatic return to terror, if not to the apocalyptic variety expressed so dramatically by a Soviet-American Armageddon (one of those "rapturous" scenarios so sadistically beloved of the Christian Right), then certainly to the Islamist suicidal version of the human bomb. In many ways (certainly not all), we are back to the '50s, as it were.

One wonders where the countercultural actors, erotic mystics, psychedelic visionaries, ecstatic educators, esoteric athletes, psychic spies, gnostic diplomats, and cultural visionaries are now. Or perhaps more accurately, one wonders why those who are around are not more active in shaping the public culture. The challenges are certainly different these days, but they are not *that* different. In any case, it has become again a matter of reassessment, disaster, and renewal. In the end, the question is not who has the biggest or most bombs, as any stupid bomb (including a human one) will effectively shred the evolved beauty of the enlightened body. The question is rather whose ideas manifest the greatest human potential.

And that, that is a very different question indeed.

The Future of the Past and the Mystical Idea of "America"

We are the present-day inheritors of that collective longing, still in search of its grail . . . This theme, the liberation of vital energy, is one of the major motifs of our intellectual heritage. Freedom is our goal, and natural life is our justification. [But] Blake and Reich warn us that the project is a political one, capable at any time of attracting reactionary attack. It is important that our students have an historical understanding of this conflict and are able to recognize the traditional religious and political positions which they may threaten.

   EDWARD MAUPIN, "Somatic Education: Its Origins, Ancestors, and Prospects"

Democracy breaks the chain and severs every link of it.

   ALEXIS DE TOCQUEVILLE

Next world, *please!*

   Russian enthusiast JOSEPH GOLDIN
   to his Esalen friends on the next scheduled event

How, then, to conclude a narrative that is still narrating? I am tempted to conclude by simply quoting Darwin Fall, and completely out of context at that. Darwin once reflected in his journals on his friend Jacob Atabet, who, we might recall, functions in the novel as a kind of avatar or incarnation of Murphy's Esalen ideal. Puzzling through the mysteries of Jacob's psychophysical transfigurations and how these might be contextualized in the broader history of religion and science, Darwin finally falls into a kind of vulgar despair: "'Oh Jesus,' I sighed. 'I don't know. I just don't know. The whole thing is so fucking complex.'"[1]

449

The same could be said of Esalen. The whole thing is so fucking complex. At the very least, such a swearing honesty could free us from the simple stereotypes and superficial journalistic accounts that have dominated discussion of this movement and community for the last forty years, with precious few exceptions. In the end, though, it is much more helpful to point out what is probably already obvious, namely, that much of this history can be understood through the tensions and complementarities of the two founders.

Dick Price, working out of his own spiritual trauma and subsequent struggle with the psychiatric community, sought to create a place where people could come and encounter one another in their full humanity, act out their conflicts, express their emotions, and perhaps even come to some sense of healing. He was by nature a boundary-crosser who, by his very presence and person, gave permission to others to experiment, as long as this did not endanger or impinge on the integrity and freedom of others: "maximum availability, minimum coercion" was his mantra. Psychoactive drugs, emotional catharsis, psychological breakdown, the baths, nude volleyball on the oval lawn, the notion of a more or less permanent community—Price was comfortable, quite literally at home, with all of this in a way that Murphy was not and never would be. But Price was never entirely supportive of many of Murphy's own deepest passions: the San Francisco Center and the Russian adventures, for example, won little more than toleration from Price, and even that often wore thin. Dick also never wrote, and, perhaps most importantly for Esalen's later history, Dick died.

From the very beginning, Murphy's vision of the place was different, although not so different that the two men could not work together and forge a common enterprise. For Murphy, Esalen was always about an East-West integralism, about an evolutionary mysticism inspired by Sri Aurobindo that looked ahead to new advances in scientific and religious thought that could in turn reach toward a new global gnosis. Empowered by a series of personal meditative, occult, and athletic experiences that remain still unidentifiable and finally mysterious, he has also displayed a life-long fascination with the empirically real supernormal powers that the Tantric traditions have long called *siddhis,* the modern West now calls psychic, and he and Leonard reframed in 1965 as the human potential.

Within this vision, it would be a serious mistake to locate the deepest meanings of Esalen anywhere in the past, particularly in some imagined golden age or origin myth of the counterculture, a culture Murphy never fully embraced. For Murphy, any truth worth dedicating one's life to, including the truth of Esalen, can only lie in the future. The past, in other words, is a kind of *foreclosure* for Murphy, and he refuses, adamantly, to foreclose. He is also much more comfortable with the intellectual and explicitly political projects that have defined part of Esalen's history. Thus it is the symposia of the Center for Theory and Research, not the community or the advertised seminars, that constitute the secret core of the place for him. It is here, after all, that Darwin Fall and Jacob Atabet are always meeting again.

Obviously, there are real tensions between these two visions of Esalen. As Nancy Lunney-Wheeler once put it to me, there are essentially two different models at work in the day-to-day operations of the place, and each is rooted in the vision of one of the founders. In one, Esalen is first and foremost a village, and the CTR visits Esalen occasionally. In the other, Esalen is more of a corporation or a think tank, the CTR is its proper heart and mind, and the public seminars are a kind of outreach and money-making venture to support the esoteric vision.

The total history of Esalen has been defined by a tensive and creative movement back and forth between these two poles. In the beginning, the poles seemed to work almost seamlessly together: there was one integral vision. Then the American counterculture appeared and more or less overwhelmed Murphy's earlier vision of things (even as it gave a distinctive left-handed energy to his right-handed Tantric vision) and pushed Esalen ever closer to Price's personality and gifts. Esalen thus became a "blowout center." It was this same general countercultural funkiness that determined both Esalen's public image in the media and much of its internal culture until 1985.

Price's sudden death spelled the end of the primacy of his vision and the beginning of a gradual swing toward Murphy's. The next two decades were difficult, as the past attempted to negotiate with the present, the present attempted to negotiate with the past, and everyone began to worry about the future. Esalen, it is safe to say, is still very much in the midst of those negotiations, and much depends upon how its leaders and community comes to terms with the now central question of transmission. Can the charisma and visions of both Dick Price and Mike Murphy be carried over into future generations? Or will one trump the other? Or will both eventually fade and grow stale, like so many other nascent communities of the past?

One fruitful way to begin thinking about these tensions is to invoke the anthropological distinction between written and oral cultures, and, analogously, between written and oral histories. Oral cultures tend to value strongly intimate person-to-person interactions. They emphasize the importance of oral lore and memory. And they understand religion as essentially locative, that is, they tend to define themselves as local traditions intimately bound up with a particular landscape or sacred place. Written cultures, on the other hand, are more mobile and do not rely as closely on person-to-person interactions or on a specifically locative understanding of religion. Generally speaking, land is not the primary locus of the sacred for written traditions. Texts, doctrines, and sacred scriptures are, and these are all easily transportable through language, image, and ritual.

As with all things, there are advantages and disadvantages to either approach, and it is one of the many integral features of Esalen that it has developed complementary (if often competing) oral and written versions of itself. Numerous exceptions aside, it is certainly not too far from the truth to observe that Dick Price, and with him the gestalt and encounter methods, was the axis around which much of the on-the-ground oral traditions of Esalen revolved, just as Mike Murphy has functioned as the institute's most successful and well-known writer and public personality. Thus just as Price's gestalt practice relied heavily on oral face-to-face communications, Murphy's writing practice and mystical fiction rely just as heavily on texts, footnotes, archives, and bibliographies.

Obviously, through my sustained exegesis of Murphy's occult novels and evolutionary panentheism, I have spun my narrative toward Murphy's vision of things and towards the written tradition. And why not? I am, after all, a writer, not a gestalt therapist or encounter group leader. But it needs to be repeated: a different book could have been written with Dick Price's vision as primary and with a much greater attention to the oral tradition and to the community. And this too would be Esalen. Indeed, many would argue, and with more than a little justification, that this would be the "real Esalen." Such a book, however, was not given to me.

How, then, to reconcile or at least integrate these two visions, one of which, by virtue of the visionary's death, lies primarily in the past, the other, by virtue of the visionary's evolutionary vision, lies primarily in the future? Put personally, how might we conclude as we began, with both founders very much together again in the present?

The Future of the Past

As a means of crystallizing my thought, I have written the present text around four paradoxical poetic allusions: *the religion of no religion, the altered states of history, the Tantric transmission, and the enlightenment of the body.* In order to answer the present question and conclude, I want to introduce two more: *the future of the past* and *America* as a mystical idea.

By *the future of the past,* I intend to communicate at least three different processes. First, I intend to advance a specific hermeneutical conviction that a later interpretive method can sometimes detect meanings in a particular historical moment that the original historical actors could not quite see or perhaps only vaguely intuited. To take a simple example, any reasonably nuanced gender analysis of a historical culture can quite easily detect sexual patterns in myth, ritual, belief, and social institution, many of which the cultural actors of that particular historical moment almost certainly would not have recognized as such and perhaps would have vociferously denied. Similarly, I have read much of Esalen's history, not exactly as the figures themselves would have understood it at the time, but rather as a kind of encoded Tantric transmission, the latter defined from the perspective of forty years of scholarship that simply did not exist in the early 1960s. In doing so, it was my conviction—which was really more of a hope—that otherwise unrecognized meanings could be brought to the surface and revealed, that is, that the future of our present could throw new light on the past and bring it to some measure of focus.

Very much related to this first sense of the future of the past is the second, perhaps even more radical notion that any profound engagement with the past will inevitably help effect one's own *and one's subject's* future. Very much like an experiment in quantum mechanics, one's conscious choices actually determine the outcome of the experiment and, consequently (and perhaps most bizarrely), the future of some small aspect of the "objective" universe. The historical future, in other words, can actually crystallize through one's study of the historical past, very much like a probability wave-function "collapses" into an actual event in the quantum physical model at the moment of human observation. Such epistemological matters necessarily complicate, if they do not actually shatter, any naïve notion of objectivity or similar simplicity about "the insider" and "the outsider" in the study of a religion (as if an "inside" can exist without an "outside"—another useful but ultimately unbelievable dualism). Certainly I have claimed no such dualism here. This was no objective history, no faithful photograph of some perfect past, no predictable mechanical clock ticking away for the rationally certain. This was a journey at once subjective and objective, a synchronicity, an occult novel that has written my life as much as I have written it.

Henry Corbin, the historian of religions who influenced Murphy's *An End to Ordinary History,* intuited something of this when he was studying the medieval Persian mystical writers. Corbin believed that a medieval Persian mystic actually initiated him into his study—a "future of the past," if ever there was one! Perhaps it is this he had in mind when he wrote:

> as a rule, when discussing past events, we fix them in the dimension of the past and are unable to agree on their nature or their significance. Our authors suggest that if the past were really what we believe it to be, that is, completed and closed, it would not be the grounds of such vehement discussions. They suggest that all our *acts of understanding* are so many recommencements, re-*iterations* of events still unconcluded. Each one of us, willy-nilly, is the initiator of events in "Hurqalya," whether they abort in its hell or bear fruit in its paradise. While we believe that we are looking at what is past and unchangeable, we are in fact consummating our own future.[2]

Something similar became obvious to me as I worked on the oral histories for the present text, particularly in the different ways many individuals embraced my historical project as crucial to their own interests and struggles. They may or may not have agreed with everything I happened to think about their stories, but they also knew on some very deep level that this retelling, if done with enough nuance, would help them rethink both their own lives and the future of Esalen. They knew perfectly well that, when "we are looking at what is past and unchangeable, we are in fact consummating our own future."

There is a real danger here, of course. To return to the physics metaphor again, my biggest fear in writing this book was (and remains) that readers will take me too seriously and mistake the ways that the probability function collapsed in my particular hermeneutical experiment for the full wave function of Esalen's total history. This would be a serious mistake.

But also a very common one, given what we know about the paradoxical function of religious language as a mode of human expression that simultaneously reveals and conceals that of which it speaks. As a trained theologian, Spiegelberg saw this clearly: "The paradox of the religion of no-religion," he wrote, "is produced by the fact that the human mind cannot grasp and realize any feeling or any fact without giving it a name.

Names are the miraculous key to every possibility of understanding and $\longleftarrow$ of remembrance. On the other hand, names are dangerous instruments because they spoil so much of real life by tying it to one single meaning."[3] $\longleftarrow$ Names reveal. And names conceal. Poet and social critic Ronald Gross put the same dialectical insight in countercultural terms in 1967, when he offered the Esalen workshop Language as Psychedelic Experience. Gross noted that words often blind us "to the full nonverbal realities of living," but that they also can "open our eyes to new experience." Language, Gross suggested, "can turn us on as well as off."[4]

Murphy has said more or less the same thing to me over the years. At some points, he has obviously taken great joy, for example, in Haridas Chaudhuri's Sanskrit list of *siddhis* or in an unpublished technical glossary of Sri Aurobindo's *Record of Yoga*: for him, such words are at once crystallized states of consciousness and quasi-magical invocations capable of invoking similar states in their sensitive and properly prepared readers. At other times, however, he has recalled how he and Leonard once invented both a "hospital" and a "cemetery" for sick or dying words that have long spent their meaning. Even as he complained of the banal superficiality and commercialization of expressions like "the human potential" and "the New Age," he actively encouraged me to *name* the altered states of history I saw.

I have done that. I can only hope that my words, my attempts to capture "Esalen," that is, to name the unnamable, will function more as Spiegelberg's miraculous key to understanding, or as Chaudhuri's list of supernormal potentials than it will Murphy and Leonard's hospital and cemetery for spent words. In any case, the attentive reader will note, perhaps with some frustration, that I have refrained from defining Esalen in any way. I hope the reason for this is clear by now. I do not believe that Esalen *can* or *should* be defined. Its genius resides precisely in that empty space of nondefinition, in that refusal to be pinned down to any final position. To the extent that Esalen seeks a place at the table of established religions, it has ceased to be what it is—that is, the religion of no religion—and has begun its own burial. The deepest meanings of Esalen, in other words, reside precisely in a constant deferral, in a refusal of closure, and in a sacralization of the future as a constantly receding horizon of unimaginable *potential.*

Which leads us to the third and perhaps most paradoxical sense of the future of the past, that is, to the notion that one can be simultaneously respectful and critical of tradition, that one must often *go back to move forward.* This was certainly Spiegelberg's position. As many in his midst $\longleftarrow$

often commented, no one was more respectful of religious tradition, and no one was more critical. This in turn, of course, produces the logical structure of the religion of no religion, a kind of postreligious position that engages the religious past, but only to move beyond it.

Within this triply defined future of the past, consider again the two respective visions of Dick Price and Mike Murphy. Even if much of the immediate future will likely be defined by the spirit of Murphy, most of Esalen's communal past was in historical fact shaped by the spirit of Price. The present institutional turn to Murphy's vision need not be read, then, as an especially dramatic change; it could just as well work as a balancing, that is, as a return to dual origins and a kind of double vision that grants depth. After all, without the specific differences of the two founders, without their specific ontological accents and fascinations, Esalen would never have been Esalen. To the extent, then, that the movement wishes to remain faithful to its original founding inspiration, it will honor both visions. It will affirm both its right-handed and its left-handed memories and myths, even as it tries constantly to keep Dionysus and Apollo in some integral dance. It will settle down into a stable community, into a *we,* but not too far. It will also finally recognize the future of the past, that is, it will come to understand that the future can reveal new truths about the past, that the study of the past can help define the future, and that to engage the past creatively is also to move beyond it.

The Enlightenment of the Body

Hence we come finally to the enlightenment of the body, a shining forth or making conscious of the matter of the occult flesh that draws deeply from the pasts of both Tantric Asia and the European Enlightenment but also moves beyond these into something more integral, something both "beyond belief" and "beyond reason," something fundamentally gnostic. The enlightenment of the body certainly does not come all at once or in any single form. Nor is its appearance always theorized as such, that is, made conscious or "enlightened" in just this way. At Esalen at least, it has always come in fits and starts, developing both gradually over weeks, months, or even years of elaborate discussion, and quite suddenly within a thousand mini-*satoris* in the baths, lodge, or Big House. As John Heider saw already back in the late 1960s and Murphy has worried a thousand times since, this same enlightenment has always been in danger of being repressed, censored, or simply forgotten. It is a work in process, a lineage constantly broken and so in need of re-membering.

In the end, it must also be admitted that this enlightenment of the body is difficult to see clearly without the benefit of the altered states of critical theory, mystical experience, and historical knowledge; it always and everywhere relies on *interpretation* for its full revelation (which is not, at all, to reduce this appearance to "just an interpretation"). The enlightenment of the body is a paradoxical reality that participates in both the subjective and objective realms simultaneously, rather like one of Murphy's mystical realist novels or the experience of synchronicity. It is certainly not like, say, a rocking chair or a rock, but neither is it an illusion or a fantasy.

Here, then, is my own vision of Esalen, that is, what I have interpreted (and been interpreted by). I have seen a constant tacking back and forth between systems of thought and practice that emphasize consciousness, awareness, or spirit, and others that emphasize energy, emotion, or the body. We saw this pattern early in Esalen's history between those psychologies that emphasized metaphors of invisible energy (like those of Mesmer, Swedenborg, Freud, and Reich), and those that turned to a language of pure consciousness (like the Perlsian gestalt tradition or Price's Theravada Buddhist practice). Most, of course, fall somewhere between these two hypothetical extremes, employing both languages of consciousness and energy simultaneously or alternately.

In this model at least, a "full" or "ideal" Esalen worldview would embrace both consciousness and energy without either reducing one to the other (or trying to separate them). In my own readings, then, I have refused any kind of monism, be it idealistically defined (as *brahman,* God, or some other metaphysical absolute) or materialistically and reductively understood (as in many forms of contemporary neuroscience and philosophy of consciousness). Nor, however, have I proposed a dualism, as if consciousness were really separate from matter and energy, as if spirit and sex were not always and everywhere enfolded into one another. I have rather suggested a paradoxical nondualism, a dynamic *both-and* whose precise relationships I do not pretend to understand rationally, much less scientifically, but which I do claim to intuit as the driving force of Esalen's altered states of history. That is my claim anyway, my Esalen gnosis, such as it is.

As a simple (and I hope not simplistic) example of how such a gnosis might throw light on the total history of Esalen, consider once more the writings of just three Esalen figures: Russell Targ, Wilhelm Reich, and

Michael Murphy. For Targ, what comes out of his research on remote viewing is a scientific body of evidence that strongly suggests that "we are not a body, but rather *limitless, nonlocal awareness* animating or residing as a body."[5] Energy fares little better than the body in Targ's system. Targ, for example, employs the same model of nonlocal mind to explain the common Tantric phenomena of *shakti-pat* or "the descent of power," which he understands to be a kind of nonlocal or direct mind-to-mind transmission. Many of the metaphors used to describe these experiences— like that of *shakti* itself as a kind of "occult energy"—may imply a kind of electromagnetic phenomenon. Haridas Chaudhuri, for example, defined *skakti-pat* in his list of *siddhis* for Murphy as "the ability to transmit spiritual energy or the power of illumined existence to others," and indeed some of the initiatory rituals, which often rely on actual physical touch, seem to support this model further. But Targ points out (quite correctly) that numerous reported cases of *shakti-pat* have occurred in dreams or spontaneously thousands of miles away from the initiating gurus, who in some cases may even be long "dead" (another dramatic example of the future of the past). Put simply, Russell Targ is suspicious of energy as a marker of spiritual experience and affirms the primacy of pure nonlocal consciousness.

On the other end of this consciousness-energy spectrum, we can comfortably place a figure like Wilhelm Reich. Reich focused his work on notions of the libido, vegetative energy, and the orgone. He developed a psychoanalysis that was very much a bodily practice that sought to remove the muscular and emotional armor of the body that blocks the free orgasmic flow of the orgone. Indeed, so literal were his notions of energy, he even built wooden and metal boxes to detect, collect, and increase these energies in the human body and a "cloud-buster" to increase them in the atmosphere. Consciousness as consciousness was not something that particularly concerned Wilhelm Reich, at all. It was all about energy and the body.

Michael Murphy's model participates in both of these two poles but moves beyond them in an attempt to complete or transcend their specific limitations. He fully acknowledges the depths and riches of consciousness and has practiced meditation his entire adult life, but he also insists that the body and its evolving transfigurations should play an integral, if indeed not a central, role in the contemplative life and the future of the species. And again, Murphy's writings on this unity of consciousness and energy are rich in explicit and implicit Tantric language, figures, and doctrines. It is almost as if the one requires the other for its full expression.

The Future of the Past and the Mystical Idea of "America"

If Russell Targ is the physicist-psychic of the Nonlocal Mind and Wilhelm Reich is the renegade psychoanalyst of the Erotic Body, then Michael Murphy is the occult novelist and evolutionary metaphysician of the Enlightenment of the Body. And *together,* along with the hundreds of other figures we could line up along this same polarized spectrum, they all form what we might call the Esalen Tantra of Consciousness and Energy. None alone, however, is quite complete. Targ tends to dismiss the body, and Reich more or less ignores the contemplative heights of consciousness. Murphy comes closest to the full picture, even if he shies away from some of the more transgressive, Reichian, or "left-handed" techniques of this history. In his own terms, his life has been a constant struggle to balance the contemplative heights of *brahman* or pure consciousness and the "world game" of *shakti* or occult energy. Each visionary mode thus requires something like the other two to form the woven whole of consciousness and energy I am imagining here.

The Future of the Body

But the traditional Asian reference of "Tantra" is, in the end, a kind of naming. And, like all names, as Spiegelberg taught us so well, it both reveals and conceals. It is both true and false. I have said enough about what I think the name of Tantra reveals about the altered states of Esalen's history. It is time now to explain what I think it conceals, what it cannot say, and how we might say it differently.

The issue, in effect, is not whether there is something like an enlightenment of the body, but rather *whose* body can be enlightened. Is this enlightenment just another male privilege, another patriarchal penis, father-god, purity code, or white body posing as absolute truth? Must consciousness and its *ananda* or bliss always be male, always be phallic? What of the vagina or *yoni* and its specific forms of consciousness and bliss, its own orgasmic *jouissance,* as the French feminists say so well? Certainly the religious traditions have generally understood consciousness, spirit, and transcendence to be male and energy, body, nature, and immanence to be female (and the Tantric traditions are often no better here). This metaphysic, as common in the West as it is in Asia, has been thoroughly deconstructed and roundly rejected by feminist theologians, historians of religions, and biblical critics for almost forty years now as a socially constructed fiction and as fundamentally oppressive to at least half the species. What does the story of Esalen have to say about this?

The history of Esalen gives only implicit answers to such questions.[6] That is, Esalen has not yet adequately theorized its own enlightenment of the body along these lines. Should it choose to do so, it will likely find that its own answers are very different than those of the historical religions. Most traditional forms of mysticism, after all, not only frame spirit or God as male; they are also structured along male homoerotic lines. From Plato's *Symposium* and *Phaedrus,* which explicitly employ pederastic infatuation to wing the philosophical soul and spark visions of the divine realm of Ideas; to the Gospel of John's beloved disciple trope (with Jesus as an unmarried lover of a younger man); to the medieval Christian male mystic's desire to become the "bride of Christ" and experience a "mystical marriage" with the Godman; to the male Sufi's passionate love of (a male) God; to the Jewish mystic's interest in the phallus as circumcised sign of the covenant, spiritual crown, and object of mystical union; to the most recent controversies surrounding the American gay priest—the pattern repeats itself over and over (and over) again throughout monotheistic history. Hence early Esalen workshop leader Ed Maupin's (unpublished) book manuscript on *The Gods and Other Men,* in which he parses out the various types of male attraction in Western religion and myth: Apollonian homosexuality, Zeus and his boy lover Ganymede, the homoerotic mentor in the Odyssey, and, his personal favorite, the gentle biblical lovers of David and Jonathan.

Structurally speaking, it hardly takes a Freud or Foucault to see that monotheism can do no other, for if there is only one God, and if that God is imagined as male, human males who represent the tradition and who passionately love this God are involved in an implicit (or explicit) homoerotic relationship. I have formulated such a comparative pattern this way: "*Whereas male heteroerotic forms of the mystical generally become heterodox or heretical, sublimated male homoerotic forms generally become orthodox.*" Similar patterns can easily be located throughout Buddhist, Hindu, and Jain Asia, where monasteries (male same-sex communities), the institutional privileging of male celibacy (non-heterosexuality), and elaborate theories about the spiritual potency of semen (repression and sublimation) create similar, if by no means identical, homoerotic patterns.

The Asian Tantric traditions are heterodox *precisely* to the extent that they attempt to transgress these orthodox homoerotic structures and affirm an explicitly heterosexual spiritual life, that is, to the extent that they encourage the male to take up a heterosexual position vis-à-vis the divine as She. Aurobindo certainly understood this, but his Tantra appears to have been an entirely right-handed, sublimated approach to the Goddess.

There is no evidence that he acted physically on his mature system's sexual structure and implications.

And this is *precisely* what constitutes Esalen's left-handed radicalism: it did. It acted. Esalen "did it." It abandoned the sexual prudery Murphy had uncomfortably witnessed in the ashram of the 1950s and enthusiastically embraced the excesses of the sexual revolution, the psychedelic revelation, and the American counterculture in the '60s. It moved from the Apollonian to the Dionysian, from the right hand to the left. It became an American heterosexual mystical tradition. Hence Esalen's origin-myth of the Night of the Dobermans, in which the rowdy homosexual men were kicked out of the baths, after which a kissing heterosexual couple appeared synchronistically on the highway. Hence also Esalen's central ritual space of *mixed* nude bathing and general rejection of celibacy as a positive sign of sanctity. And hence Esalen's essential heresy with respect to the churches and its "anti-Christ" status with respect to the Evangelicals. To affirm a male heterosexual approach to the divine, at least in the West, is always and everywhere to become a heresy.

Now, obviously, there are both promises and problems in all of this. On the promise side, such a heretical move produces a much more positive assessment of women, the body, and nature, all of which are related in both traditional male psychology and the history of religions. Male dominated homoerotic systems (that is, most orthodox religions) have little need of women (except to reproduce more males) and have in fact produced a stunning array of misogynistic metaphysical systems and institutional practices to exclude, control, hyper-clothe, and generally oppress them (often with their pious cooperation and socially constructed assent). But male heteroerotic systems, at least ideally, both physically desire and really love women.

But that "at least ideally" must be stressed with respect to Esalen's sexual history. Early Esalen was no model of gender equity or of female empowerment. Julian Silverman saw this clearly with his critical observations of the "male chauvinism" that defined Esalen in the early 1970s. Similarly, Ed Maupin tells the story of a conversation he had with Betty Friedan, who more than anyone helped initiate the American women's movement with the publication of her *The Feminine Mystique* (1963). Early Esalen struck Friedan as positively retrograde with respect to gender. "The prevailing ethos at Esalen," Maupin explains, "was mountain man macho man." The supposedly liberated hippies were no better. "They kept their women barefoot and pregnant up in the mountains." The real liberator of sexuality at early Esalen, according to Maupin, was something much more mundane and simple: the relative lack of bedrooms. "So any-one who had a bedroom had plenty of access to sex, and the best way to get in was to be willing to share a bedroom."

This would all change at Esalen, but only gradually. In time, strong female voices, real institutional empowerment, and, above all, more re-ciprocal child-rearing practices would appear. Men would rear and raise children. Women would lead, teach, and administer. The majority of work-shop participants would be women (and still are). Women would sit on the Board (and still do). Nancy Lunney-Wheeler would look over the intel-lectual and spiritual "gates" of the institute for over a quarter of a century. Dulce Murphy would help lead high-level political and cultural exchanges for the same decades in a citizen diplomacy movement, itself filled with powerful and influential women. And so on.

On the problem side, there is the glaring issue of gay and lesbian bod-ies that do not wish to take the only traditional path offered to them (the attempted repressions and sublimations of celibacy). The heterosexual symbolism can hardly work for them. Historically speaking, something like the Night of the Dobermans could have easily resulted in a further narrative of exclusion. It did not. Janet Lederman, who wielded tremen-dous power over Esalen in the 1970s, was a lesbian, and the grounds have remained friendly to a broad range of sexualities for decades. Indeed, as early as 1972 and 1973, the topics of homosexuality, feminism and gay consciousness, third-world women, masturbation, lesbianism, bisexual-ity, and child sexuality were all being discussed at Esalen symposia.[7] And heaven only knows what has been expressed in the baths.

But again, we must be careful here. Maupin points out that the Esalen of the 1960s was not particularly friendly to homosexuality. It certainly allowed such people on the grounds, even into the community, but it also kept them "in a sort of cocoon of isolation." He remembers writing about his own homosexuality in his private journals as HE, his own secret code for homoeroticism, which he understood, with Plato and the many male mystics of the history of religions, as something much deeper and much broader than simple "sexuality."

Thus, although it must be admitted that Esalen's general history is predominately a masculine one and that its clientele is overwhelmingly upper middle class, heterosexual, and white, it is also safe to conclude that Esalen's ideal answer to the question, whose body is to be enlightened? appears to be the same ideal answer it gives to the question, whose body can be massaged? That answer is *every body*. Corporately and ideally speaking, then, the religion of no religion promises a sexual orientation of no sexual orientation, a gender of no gender, that is, a polyamorous eroticism, a culture "beyond gender" that refuses to be dogmatic about desire. And this is an enlightenment of the body that goes well beyond anything that ever existed in Asia or the West. This is an enlightenment that depends directly on Western history and critical theory, on Freud, Foucault, and feminism, that is, on the enlightenment of reason, liberty and equality.

Such an egalitarianism, of course, is never perfect, never complete. Gender imbalances, socioeconomic injustices, and essentialist assumptions of all sorts remain. Men and women in this history disagree, fight, and divorce. Women are abused and taken advantage of by powerful charismatic men. Women picket and debunk symposia featuring only men. Race and class remain troubling categories. Colored bodies are not well represented on the grounds, and most bodies simply cannot afford an Esalen massage or a trip to Big Sur. Looking back, there were probably no events more damaging to the institute's potential ability to reach a much wider socioeconomic base than the decision to close the San Francisco Center. Economically, that decision made good sense, as the center was always losing money. Socially speaking, however, this closing more or less guaranteed that Esalen's clientele would remain upper middle class and overwhelmingly white. And so it has.

Obviously, these are historical human beings and fallible communities, not holy cards and fictional saints. Still, the ideal remains, and ideals matter: the enlightenment of the body is the enlightenment of every body, regardless of gender, sexual orientation, race, class, or religion. Such anyway is the nature of Esalen's utopian ideal, its own vision of the human potential.

America as a Mystical Idea(l)

What we have in the end, then, is a development of that with which we began—a democratic mysticism, a religion of no religion. Although Esalen's religion of no religion was clearly indebted to any number of previous Asian and Western experiments, this was an experiment whose success depended (and still depends) most profoundly on a uniquely American political arrangement, the constitutional separation of church and state. It is this "mighty great wall" that in turn nurtures the human potential through an ever greater freedom *for* religion but also, simultaneously and paradoxically, *from* religion, particularly when the latter grows intolerant, bigoted, and exclusive. The result is, if you will, a kind of mystical space that is at once profoundly secular and deeply spiritual (but not religious, as the saying goes). "We hold our dogmas lightly." "No one captures the flag."

We have seen this religion of no religion appear again and again in our historical narrative. Still, it bears repeating, such a vision, much like Esalen's embodied egalitarianism, is always in the making. Its radical promise always lies in the future of the past, not in the past or present. Perhaps no one has expressed this same mystical humanism more clearly and more passionately than Don Hanlon Johnson, when he wrote about his trip to Rome and the emotional responses the center of his own native Roman Catholicism had on him: "I was flooded by images and feelings of the unity among the caesars, the popes, metropolitans, ayatollahs, generals and party chairmen, all blurring into one another: old men and their sycophants, detached from sensuous life and fascinated by power which was rationalized by complex abstract ideas, contemptuous of the earth-based spiritual practices of native peoples, served by tamed women."[8]

As I close these pages, I can only marvel with Johnson at how rare a fully embodied, truly democratic-erotic spirituality is, how such a hope or dream still lies very much in the future. No major religious tradition of which I am aware has ever been able to develop religious ideas and practices that affirm the radical integrity and freedom of each and every individual without then immediately compromising that integrity and freedom with any number of hierarchical beliefs about the authority of tradition, about the subordination of women, about the literal truth of scripture, about the impurity of sex and food and blood, about (male) omnipotence, (male) judgment, (male) mercy, about salvation from, devotion toward, and obedience to the divine (male).

I can also not help but recall something Jim Garrison, the Esalen citizen diplomat, said in the Big House in the spring of 2006, just as I was finishing this book (literally in that room, on a laptop, as he spoke). *The global problem*, he suggested, is no longer American-Soviet relations, or American-Iranian relations, or any other kind of relation. The problem is *America itself*. Nothing, he insisted, is more urgent now than to reimagine this "America" and so return the ideal to its originary genius in those universal ideals of human freedom and dignity that were once so admired around the globe but have now been largely lost.

But can we reclaim that which we have lost? More specifically, can we revision "America" not as a globally hated imperial superpower, not as a "Christian nation" obsessed with mad and arrogant apocalyptic fantasies abroad and discriminatory "family values" at home, not as a monster consumer of the world's ever-dwindling resources, but as a universal human ideal yet to be fully realized, as a potentiality yet to be actualized, as an empty and so creative space *far* more radical and free than the most patriotic or religiously right among us have dared imagine? Can we see that such a vision will nurture almost any religious community, as long as none attempt to impose beliefs on the rest, as long as no one is allowed to "capture the flag"? (Tellingly, our fastest growing churches are now wrapped in the flag.) Can we also see that this same democratic vision of the religion of no religion will inevitably result in a free combination and recombination of ideas and beliefs that some might decry as a form of spiritual capitalism or as a debasement of religion itself but that others will recognize as the familiar and necessary evolutionary pattern of every new religious creation? "I am spiritual, but not religious." Are we really ready for such an affirming denial, for a radically American mysticism, for an "America" *as* mysticism?

There are many possible ways into such an America, including the two dozen biographies of America's founding fathers that Michael Murphy has spent the last decade reading religiously, as if to realize the fundamentally American secret of his own vision and life. These were individuals who did things like join secret Masonic lodges (ever look at a dollar bill?) or take scissors and glue to the New Testament until all the miracles were cut out and the text looked more like the heretical Gospel of Thomas than any recognizable form of Christian belief.[9] These were men who spoke not of "tolerance" or some "Christian nation," but of "liberty," "diversity," and an "eternal hostility against every form of tyranny over the mind of man," including and especially the tyranny of religion.[10]

But it is a poet, not a political thinker, who comes to mind here as especially emblematic of this America-as-mysticism, the poet with whom we began our long journey through Esalen's religion of no religion: Walt Whitman. There are many reasons to invoke Whitman here at the end, from the simple fact that Aurobindo admired him, to the more complicated fact that the twentieth century's first explicit evolutionary mysticism (1901) came from the pen of Richard Maurice Bucke, a Canadian doctor who knew Whitman personally and whose spontaneous enlightenment in 1872 was catalyzed by a reading of Whitman's poetry earlier that same night. Bucke would later express this "Cosmic Consciousness" in a highly influential book through Upanishadic language strikingly similar to that of Spiegelberg and Murphy: "Into his brain streamed one momentary lightning-flash of the Brahmic Splendor which ever since lightened his life," he wrote in the third person. "Upon his heart fell one drop of the Brahmic Bliss, leaving thenceforward for always an after-taste of Heaven."[11]

Bucke aside, Whitman's *Leaves of Grass* stands as one of the unquestioned classics of American literature on its own terms. It also happens to be a central celebratory scripture of what the literary critic Harold Bloom has called the American Religion, a religion whose fundamental gnosticism and individualism look very much like those of Esalen.[12] And indeed, the poet's greatest work often sounds like so many prefigurations of the Esalen gnosis:

> I have said that the soul is not more than the body,
> And I have said that the body is not more than the soul,
> And nothing, not God, is greater to one than one's-self is.[13]

> I believe a leaf of grass is no less than the journeywork of the
>   stars.[14]

> I bequeath myself to the dirt to grow from the grass I love,
> If you want me again look for me under your bootsoles.[15]

Or again, with respect to the doors of tradition and their removal before "the sign of democracy":

> Unscrew the locks from the doors!
> Unscrew the doors themselves from their jambs!

> Whoever degrades another degrades me.... and whatever is done
>   or said returns at last to me,
> And whatever I do or say I also return.
> . . . .
> I speak the password primeval.... I give the sign of democracy;
> By God! I will accept nothing which all cannot have their
>   counterpart of on the same terms.[16]

Certainly Whitman's panerotic revelations and sublimations—at once heterosexual and homosexual—also fit beautifully into the general spirit of Esalen:

> Through me forbidden voices,
> Voices of sexes and lusts.... voices veiled, and I remove the veil,
> Voices indecent by me clarified and transfigured.[17]

As does what Bloom calls the poet's "masturbatory Muse," that is, Whitman's explicit insistence that he was inspired by an autoerotic arousal that was also an enlightenment of the body suffused with real knowledge: "A touch now reads me a library of knowledge in an instant," the poet claimed.[18] Bloom at least is clear that the Whitmanian "headland" is both an apt metaphor for autoerotic arousal and the originary sign of America's literary genius: "'I went myself first to the headland' is Whitman's crucial beginning as the New World's bard, however uncomfortable this may render some among us."[19]

Indeed, who is really ready to know that the ecstatic origins of one of America's greatest poems lie as much in Whitman's (left?) hand as they do in his claims to a transcendent eternal Witness consciousness that can identify with everyone everywhere as the "Song of Myself"? Who is ready for the breathless, spasming touch of Whitman's "body electric" and its inspirational, life-giving release of what the poet called, no doubt with an arched grin, "the fatherstuff"?

Wilhelm Reich and Henry Miller were ready. So too were George Leonard, Stanislav and Christina Grof, and John Heider. Did Leonard not write ecstatically of an "explosion of Spirit"? Did not the Grofs insist on relating the highest reaches of spiritual experience to the blood, ecstasy, and spasms of the cosmic womb? Did not Heider write of electromagnetic sex as a path to contemplation and the eventual outshining of the orgasm? If then, as Bloom claims, "Emerson invented the American Religion," and "Whitman incarnated it,"[20] I think it is entirely fair to say that Esalen took it further still, that Esalen is a clear heir of the progressive Transcendentalism of Emerson and Thoreau, and of Whitman's "Song of Myself" (and, behind them all, of a distant Tantric Asia). It is precisely in this Whitmanian sense, I think, that Esalen's enlightenment of the body can truly and finally be called "American."

In any case, I can think of no better way to end my own reflections on Esalen's America than with Whitman's Song of Myself and Body Electric, that is, with the fundamental nonduality of Consciousness and Energy, that final mystery that is constantly irrupting in and as the altered states of history and so transforming the world into an occult novel or ecstatic poem that we ourselves compose, that we ourselves are. *There,* in this Song of Myself that is also and always a Body Electric, lies Whitman's book-filled gnosis. There too lies Henry Miller's Big Sur Garden of Earthly Delights, at once erotic and mystical. There lies Michael Murphy's unity of *brahman* and *atman* and all those supernormal powers, graced to the species through billions of years of cosmic, terrestrial, and now psychocultural evolution. There lies Dick Price's Tao, the *yin* and the *yang*, the Way of the Whole, the Gestalt. There too lies every Tantric transmission, every body, every serpent spine of spirit and sex connecting the "headland" of the genitals to the thoughts and texts of the brain. There finally lies the human potential, always capable—who knows when?—of actualizing something more of the future of the past, the enlightenment of the body, and the religion of no religion that still lies hidden in "America."

Abbreviations

Notes

Acknowledgments

1. Robert C. Gordon, *Gospel of the Open Road: According to Emerson, Whitman, and Thoreau* (Lincoln, NE: iUniverse Press, 2001).

Introduction

1. A few initial key definitions are in order here. In Murphy's corpus, the adjective *mystical* refers to any altered state of consciousness, traditional or contemporary, that is revelatory of some deeper truth or reality. The adjective "occult" is best thought of as related to the exalted contemplative states of the mystical life, but with a heavy accent on what Murphy calls the *supernormal powers* (Sanskrit: *siddhis*), that is, the psychical and physical phenomena of mysticism (precognition, clairvoyance, bodily transfiguration, reported levitation, and so on) that are usually dismissed by both the religious traditions and traditional scholarship but nevertheless seem to be an integral part of what these altered states intend "in the direction of evolution" (HP, 1.xxii), and here he follows Aurobindo quite closely (LD, 680). The *supernormal* must in turn be distinguished from the *paranormal*. For Murphy, what Western cultures refer to as paranormal is in fact perfectly normal, that is, following Freud (and again Aurobindo), he believes that these are largely unconscious abilities that appear supernatural or "beyond the normal" (*paranormal*) because they are not yet under conscious control. The supernormal, then, is the paranormal that has come under conscious control (FOB, 587).

2. For the definitive study of Eranos, see Hans Thomas Hakl, *Eranos: An Alternative Intellectual History of the 20th Century* (Equinox, forthcoming).

3. The expression *altered states*, although possessing clear precedents in William James's notion of consciousness as multiple, finds its more immediate origins in the classic volume of psychical researcher and Esalen regular, Charles Tart, *Altered States of Consciousness: A Book of Readings* (New York: John

Wiley and Sons, 1969). Here Tart defined an altered state of consciousness (ASC) as one in which the individual "clearly feels a *qualitative* shift in [the] pattern of mental functioning" in that "some quality or qualities" of the "mental processes are *different*." This same text anthologized any number of Esalen figures (Edward Maupin, James Fadiman, Willis Harman, etc.), included a fascinating essay by Milton Erickson on the altered state of Deep Reflection out of which Aldous Huxley composed his novels, and explicitly names the Esalen Institute as one of the few places taking the positive force of ASCs seriously. Three years later, Tart applied this same line of thought to the methodology of science in another important publication that would flow into the thought and history of Esalen, his "States of Consciousness and State-Specific Sciences," *Science* 176 (1972): 1203–10.

4. I fully recognize that my narrative does not do justice to the oral histories and present life of the Esalen community, those few hundred or so individuals who have actually lived on the grounds (or very near them), given their life-work to the Esalen vision, and so made the place work on a day-to-day basis over the last four decades. Very much related to this is the fact that my narrative does not always accurately represent the interests and life mission of Richard Price, Murphy's cofounder who understood Esalen very differently, eventually turned to a form of gestalt practice and the spiritual art of psychological healing as the central core of the place and its spirit, and lived on the grounds as the community's charismatic and administrative axis for nearly a quarter of a century.

5. Frederic Spiegelberg, *The Religion of No-Religion* (Stanford: James Ladd Delkin, 1953).

6. Walt Whitman, *Leaves of Grass, The First Edition 1855*, edited with an introduction by Malcolm Cowley (New York: Barnes and Noble, 1997), "Leaves of Grass," line 1092.

7. Ibid., "A Song for Occupations," lines 77–82.

8. Cowley, introduction to *Leaves of Grass*, xxii–xxv.

9. Jeffrey J. Kripal, *Roads of Excess, Palaces of Wisdom: Eroticism and Reflexivity in the Study of Mysticism* (Chicago: University of Chicago Press, 2001).

10. Jeffrey J. Kripal, *Roads of Excess*; and *The Serpent's Gift: Gnostic Reflections on the Study of Religion* (Chicago: University of Chicago Press, 2006).

11. HP, 2.279.

12. John Heider, "Olden Times and New: Sex and Drugs at Esalen" (1991), unpublished essay.

13. It is, I think, this fundamental nondual structure that renders the "wild facts" of psychic phenomena of all sorts so difficult to render in traditional scientific methodologies, which of course presuppose a rather firm distinction between "subjective" and "objective." It is this same nonduality that makes them so threatening to people committed to strictly materialistic or dualistic worldviews,

be they scientifically or spiritually framed. Having said that, the scientific evidence for such phenomena is much greater than people commonly assume. See especially Dean Radin, *The Conscious Universe: The Scientific Truth of Psychic Phenomena* (New York: HarperEdge, 1997).

14. Cowley, introduction to *Leaves of Grass*, xxiii.

15. I have described and psychoanalyzed this initiatory event in *Roads of Excess*, 199–206. I will use it again below in two "secret notes," to interpret Emmanuel Swedenborg's *influx* and Rick Strassman's tryptamine states, respectively.

16. See especially Hugh Urban, *Tantra: Sex, Secrecy, Politics, and Power in the Study of Religion* (Berkeley: University of California Press, 2003).

17. For the modern attractions of Tantra, see Geoffrey Samuel, *Tantric Revisionings: New Understandings of Tibetan Buddhism and Indian Religion* (London: Ashgate, 2005). For California becomes Kalifornia (and so much more), see Erik Davis and Michael Ravner, *The Visionary State: A Journey through California's Spiritual Landscape* (San Francisco: Chronicle Books, 2006).

18. David Gordon White, Introduction to *The Practice of Tantra: A Reader* (Princeton: Princeton University Press, 2000), 8.

19. Ibid., 9.

20. Quoted by White in ibid., 8. In the background of White and Padoux's definitions is that of Madeleine Biardeau, *Hinduism: An Anthropology of a Civilization* (Delhi: Oxford University Press, 1994).

21. There are, of course, numerous exceptions to note here as well. For further treatments of this metapattern, including a discussion of its recent attempted censorship by ultraconservative Hindu groups, see my "Western Popular Culture, Hindu Influences On" in D. Cush, C. Robinson, and M. York, eds., *The Encyclopedia of Hinduism* (London: Routledge/Curzon, 2007); and "Remembering Ourselves: Some Notes on the Counterculture of Contemporary Tantric Studies," in *Religions of South Asia* (forthcoming).

22. Similar left-right connotations, of course, also exist in Western religious traditions and language, where the Latin for *left* is *sinister*, *right* means *correct*, and anything "on the left," from a political opinion to a religious belief, is easily demonized as inimical to conserving the proper order of things.

23. This phrase displays obvious resonances with the teachings of Bubba Free John (born Franklin Jones, now Adi Da) in *The Enlightenment of the Whole Body* (Middletown, Calif.: Dawn Horse Press, 1978). Although what I will develop here as Esalen's enlightenment of the body is derived from a very different textual corpus, I want to acknowledge here Adi Da's teaching as one inspiration of my own thought.

24. Emily Williams Kelly, "The Contributions of F. W. H. Myers to Psychology," *Journal of the Society for Psychical Research* 65.2, no. 863 (2001): 78–79.

25. I am indebted for this way of framing the dialectic of universalism and constructivism to George Leonard, who wrote in his *The Silent Pulse* that, "each of us is, in essence, a context, a weaving together of universal information from a particular point of view" (*The Silent Pulse: A Soviet for the Perfect Rhythm That Exists in Each of Us* [New York: Arkana, 1978], 166; cf. 139).

Chapter 1

1. OHB, 4.

2. US, 6.

3. Don Lattin, *Following Our Bliss: How the Spiritual Ideals of the Sixties Shape Our Lives Today* (New York: HarperSanFrancisco, 2003).

4. Virtually all of the major players of Esalen detest the expression "New Age," primarily because of its connotations of superficiality, flakiness, anti-intellectualism, and social disengagement.

5. *Friends of Esalen Newsletter*, Fall/Winter 2004, vol. 16, no. 3, p. 5.

6. Tomi Kay Lussier, *Big Sur: A Complete History & Guide* (Big Sur, Calif.: Big Sur Publications, 2003), 41.

7. Guy S. Breshcini and Trudy Haversat, *The Esselen Indians of the Big Sur Country* (Salinas: Coyote Press, 2004), 189–205.

8. See ibid., 141–67.

9. See ibid., 152, for a photograph of what the authors call "Hands Rock."

10. Thomas Roy Hester, "Esselen," in *Handbook of North American Indians* (Washington, D.C.: Smithsonian Institution, 1978), 497.

11. Video, "Tour of the Big and Little House."

12. Hester, "Esselen," 499.

13. Ibid.

14. Quoted in Breshcini and Haversat, *The Esselen Indians*, 41; italics in original.

15. Ibid., 42; italics in original.

16. Ibid., 87.

17. Ibid., 175.

18. Alfred L. Kroeber, *Basic Report on California Indian Land Holdings*, in *California Indians IV* (New York: Garland Publishing, 1974), 16.

19. "Ohlone/Costanoan Esselen Nation," http://www.esselennation.com (accessed August 27, 2004).

20. "Ohlone/Costonoan Esselen Nation," 2.

21. William Everson, *Archetype West: The Pacific Coast as a Literary Region* (Berkeley: Oyez, 1976), 4–5.

22. Most of this history is based on *Pacific Coast Highway,* aired on the History Channel, 13 July 2004.

23. See, for example, his *Zen and the Beat Way* (Boston: Charles E. Tuttle Co, 1997).

24. Michael Schumacher, *Dharma Lion: A Biography of Allen Ginsberg* (New York: St. Martin's Press, 1992), 95.

25. Everson, *Archetype West,* xiii.

26. Ibid., 108.

27. Ibid., 135.

28. OHB, 3.

29. OHB, 244.

30. OHB, 391.

31. OHB, 12.

32. E. R. Hutchinson, *Tropic of Cancer: A Case History of Censorship* (New York: Grove Press, 1968).

33. Charles Rembar, *The End of Obscenity: The Trials of* Lady Chatterley, Tropic of Cancer, *and* Fanny Hill (New York: Simon and Schuster, 1968).

34. OHB, ix–x.

35. Mildred Edie Brady, "The New Cult of Sex and Anarchy," *Harper's Magazine* (April 1947), 318.

36. OHB, 31–32.

37. Contemporary scholarship insists Fränger was mistaken about this. Regardless, the probable fact that the painting is not connected to the Free Brethren only strengthens my thesis about the initial erotic inspirations of Big Sur literary culture and, later, Esalen. What we have here is another "Rorschach test" in which Esalen actors (Miller, Murphy, and Gerald Heard, whom we will meet later) saw their own mystical images accurately reflected in a highly idiosyncratic reading of a late medieval painting. Even if, then, they are not accurately seeing Bosch's original intentions, they are most certainly seeing something of their own, and quite clearly so. Such projections speak volumes.

38. Wilhelm Fränger, *The Millennium of Hieronymus Bosch* (Chicago: University of Chicago Press, 1951), 104; quoted in OHB, 22.

39. OHB, 23.

40. OHB, 29.

41. OHB, 34.

42. Quoted in Elayne Wareing Fitzpatrick, *Doing It with the Cosmos: Henry Miller's Big Sur Struggle for Love Beyond Sex* (Xlibris Corporation, 2001), 147. See also OHB, 244.

43. Brady, "The New Cult of Sex," 314.

44. Ibid., 316.

45. Wilhelm Reich, *The Mass Psychology of Fascism* (New York: Farrar, Straus and Giroux, 1970).

46. Reich reproduces the Gestapo order in footnote 1 of the preface to the third edition in ibid., xviii.

47. Quoted in Barry Miles, *Hippie* (New York: Sterling, 2004), 13.

48. *New Republic,* May 26, 1947.

49. US, 20. The orgone accumulator was a kind of sitting box for preserving and collecting "orgone," Reich's term for the sexualized energy that constitutes the lifeenergy of the cosmos.

50. Everson, *Archetype West*, 108–9, 113, 115.

51. Fitzpatrick, *Doing It with the Cosmos*, 72–73.

52. American writers have long been attracted to the occult, particularly as a means to create poetry. For an excellent discussion of this, see Devin Johnston, *Precipitations: Contemporary American Poetry as Occult Practice* (Middletown: Wesleyan University Press, 2002).

53. Fitzpatrick, *Doing It with the Cosmos*, 77.

54. OHB, 126.

55. OHB, 129.

56. OHB, 130.

57. OHB, 401.

Chapter 2

1. Katriona Munthe and Ted Helminski, *Frederic Spiegelberg and the Religion of No Religion* (video, 1995).

2. Frederic Spiegelberg, *The Religion of No-Religion* (Stanford: James Ladd Delkin, 1953), 18–19.

3. Thus, according to Spiegelberg, the origins of Buddhism lie in the religion of no religion of ancient Hinduism, and the origins of Christianity can be read as the religion of no religion of ancient Judaism. In my own terms now, "mysticism" and "the comparative study of religion" can similarly be read as the religion of no religion of all the religions.

4. Ibid., 17.

5. Ibid., 21–22.

6. Ibid., 29, 40.

7. See Spiegelberg, *The Religion of No-Religion*, 19, 39–40, 83, 108, 122.

8. Frederic Spiegelberg, *Spiritual Practices of India* (New York: Citadel Press, 1962); italics added.

9. Interview with Katriona Munthe-Lindgren (March 2006) in response to the present work. My deepest thanks to Katriona and Antonella for all their help and insights here.

10. Spiegelberg, *Spiritual Practices of India*, xx.

11. Munthe and Helminski, "Frederic Spiegelberg and the Religion of No Religion." The film makes no mention of the book inscription. For more on Spiegelberg's *darshan* with Aurobindo, see "German Savant in India: An Interview with Dr. Frederic Spiegelberg," *Mother India*, April 30, 1949, p. 5. My thanks to Peter Heehs for kindly sending me this article.

12. Quoted in Keith Thompson, "The Astonishment of Being," EC September 1993–February 1994, 7. "Hindi" should be "Hindu" or, better, "Sanskrit" here.

13. US, 28.

14. Alan Watts, *In My Own Way* (New York: Vintage, 1972), 285.

15. This was not the case for every reader. George Leonard humorously responded to this line of mine with the quip: "I wish the hell it would have read me."

16. I have also discussed this text in OTE, 99–131.

17. The text was originally published as fifty-four installments in Aurobindo's journal *Arya* between August 1914 and January 1919 and later revised for book-publication in 1939 and 1940. India won independence on August 15, 1947, on Aurobindo's seventy-fifth birthday.

18. I am not the first to note the Tantric elements of Aurobindo's thought. Kees Bolle wrote the same the very month Esalen began in "Tantric Elements in Sri Aurobindo," *Numen* 9, no. 2 (September 1962): 123–42.

19. *Sri Aurobindo on the Tantra* (Pondicherry: Sri Aurobindo Ashram, 1972), 39.

20. Ibid., 12. Like many later Esalen writers, Aurobindo insists that the brain is "only a channel" of consciousness and not its material producer (ibid., 22).

21. Ibid., 13. Although Aurobindo does not mention Myers as the source of this category, it is almost certain that he was familiar with Myers's work. Hence in LD, 524, he more or less uses the title of Myers's greatest work (*Human Personality and Its Survival of Bodily Death*) to open a sentence: "Survival of the body by the human personality..." See also LD, 769, 780, 831.

22. *Sri Aurobindo on the Tantra,* 14.

23. One of the few places where Aurobindo explicitly employed Tantric language was in his private correspondence with his revolutionary brethren. In these documents, he uses Tantric expressions as a code language to refer, for example, to revolvers they were attempting to transport through the French postal system or to specific revolutionary actions (see Peter Heehs, *The Lives of*

Sri Aurobindo [New York: Columbia University Press, forthcoming], ch. 26, MS pp. 17–18).

24. LD, 209.

25. Sri Aurobindo, *Record of Yoga* (Pondicherry: Sri Aurobindo Ashram, 2001), 484.

26. Ibid., 204.

27. Sri Aurobindo, *Essays Divine and Human*, vol. 12 of *Complete Works of Sri Aurobindo* (Pondicherry: Sri Aurobindo Ashram, 1995), 483.

28. *Sri Aurobindo on the Tantra*, 1–2.

29. As Patrick Olivelle has demonstrated, there is an "explicit and unambiguous connection between *ānanda* as orgasmic rapture and *ānanda* as the experience of *brahman/ātman*." Olivelle demonstrates, moreover, that this orgasmic bliss was understood to be a function of the penis: just as the ear is the organ of hearing and the eye the organ of sight, the penis was said to be the organ of *ānanda*. See Patrick Olivelle, "Orgasmic Rapture and Divine Ecstasy: The Semantic History of '*ānanda*,'" *Journal of Indian Philosophy* 25 (1997): 153–80. See also LD, 950, where Aurobindo clearly relates Ananda and sexuality in a sophisticated dialectical fashion. He knew.

30. Heehs, *The Lives of Sri Aurobindo*, ch. 27, MS p. 11.

31. LD, 126, 84. See especially LD, 126.

32. LD, 1005, 1011, 1007.

33. Talk partly published in *Sri Aurobindo Circle* 9 (1953), 207.

34. *Sri Aurobindo on the Tantra*, 44.

35. LD, 684. It is important to keep in mind here that "the body" in Aurobindo's thought, as in much South Asian thought (and in Michael Murphy's later thought), is a hyperdimensional reality that exists on many planes, from the observable physiology of the physical body to the more and more subtle dimensions of occult, visionary, and spiritual experience. It is thus not always entirely clear what "body" Aurobindo claims is mutating.

36. LD, 266, 269.

37. LD, 241. I strongly suspect that "supernormal" is another Aurobindonian borrowing from Myers.

38. LD, 216.

39. LD, 23.

40. Put differently, mythology has overtaken phenomenology, that is, Aurobindo's doctrine of the descent of the Supermind appears to be a mythologization of the phenomenology of *shakti-pata* or "descent of the power," a common mysticism of energy whereby a palpable occult (and often erotic) force is felt to "descend" into the devotee's body through the touch, gaze, or even dream appearance of the guru.

Chapter 3

1. Interview with Eric Erickson, October 26, 2003.

2. For more on David Price and his memories, see Lattin, *Following Our Bliss*, chapter 1.

3. PRP, 65.

4. PRP, 68.

5. PRP, 68.

6. PRP, 69.

7. PRP, 140.

8. PRP, 72.

9. US, 34.

10. PRP, 101.

11. For a taste of this "Beat Way," see the Pacifica Radio Network talks Watts gave on August 6, 11, and 15, 1959, as transcribed in Alan Watts, *Zen and the Beat Way* (Boston: Charles E. Tuttle, 1997).

12. PRP, 101.

13. Nyanaponika Thera, *The Heart of Buddhist Meditation: A Handbook of Mental Training Based on the Buddha's Way of Mindfulness* (Boston: Weiser Books, 1965/1954).

14. PRP, 133.

15. PRP, 102.

16. PRP, 102.

17. PRP, 103.

18. Quoted in ibid.

19. PRP, 105.

20. US, 38.

21. Murphy is reluctant to describe Aurobindo's system as Hindu, since Aurobindo generally avoids such a designation himself. Later, of course, it will be appropriated as such.

22. R. B. Blakney, *The Way of Life: Lao Tzu, A New Translation of the* Tao Té Ching (New York: New American Library, 1983/1955), 63.

23. Ibid., 109.

24. Ibid., 116.

25. "Remembering Richard Price (October 12, 1930–November 25, 1985)," Esalen catalog, May–October 1986, 5.

26. Alan Watts, *Psychotherapy East and West* (New York: Ballantine, 1961), 56.

27. Douglas Wile, *Art of the Bedchamber: The Chinese Sexual Yoga Classics Including Women's Solo Meditation Texts* (Albany: SUNY, 1992), 11.

28. US, 104.

29. PRP, 105.

30. US, 39. The mystical experience of "fire" appears to be a common theme in the empowerments of both founders. Murphy has made constant reference to being "totally on fire" at this same time.

31. PRP, 106.

32. PRP, 107.

33. PRP, 110.

34. PRP, 108.

35. PRP, 110, 111.

36. PRP, 113.

37. PRP, 118, 117.

38. PRP, 123.

39. PRP, 307.

40. For the latter, see especially Haridas Chaudhuri, *Integral Yoga* (London: Unwin Paperbacks, 1990 [1965]).

41. Although Chaudhuri was not a major influence on either Murphy or Price, it is interesting to note that his philosophical system, like Esalen's, was an artful synthesis of Aurobindo's Tantric yoga, evolutionary biology, the Western practice of social reform, and psychoanalysis. His *Integral Yoga* is thus filled with statements about the occult power of sexuality and its sublimations, the Shakta Tantric polarity of Shiva as Consciousness and Shakti as Energy, the neuroses of sexual repression and celibacy, the authoritarian dangers of the guru and devotion, and the spiritual potentials of an East-West integralism. It is perhaps no accident, then, that the two Esalen founders first met in Chaudhuri's meditation house, that is, in the doctrinal space of an Americanized Bengali Tantra.

42. PRP, 166.

Chapter 4

1. Huxley appears to have given the same lecture a year later at MIT, a recorded version of which appears in the bibliography. He did not invent the expression "human potentialities," however. That honor probably belongs to the Menninger Foundation psychologist and psychical researcher Gardner Murphy, who published his *Human Potentialities* in 1958, two years before Huxley's lecture. The first recorded appearance of the expression *the human potential* was probably George Leonard's *Look* essay, "Pursuit of the Human Potential Could Become a National Goal," 1966, 116. My thanks to John Heider for both of these references.

2. Quoted in US, 10–11.

3. Alan Watts, *In My Own Way* (New York: Vintage, 1973), 208.

4. The *philosophia perennis* or "perennial philosophy" was probably first clearly articulated in 1540 by a Vatican librarian named Agostino Steuco in order to capture the Renaissance philosophy of Marsilio Ficino, who believed, in the words of Mark Sedgwick, that "all religions shared a common origin in a single perennial (or primeval or primordial) religion that had subsequently taken a variety of forms, including the Zoroastrian, Pharaonic, Platonic, and Christian" (Mark Sedgwick, *Against the Modern World: Traditionalism and the Secret Intellectual History of the Twentieth Century* [New York: Oxford University Press, 2004], 24). Similar ideas can also be found in Nicholas of Cusa (c. 1401–1464). Quote taken from Aldous Huxley, *The Perennial Philosophy* (Cleveland: Meridian Books, 1962), iv.

5. Ibid., 36.

6. Ibid., v–vi.

7. Aldous Huxley, *Island* (New York: Bantam, 1971), 52–53. Hence the figures of the pious Queen Mother Rani, that "clutching and devouring mother" (ibid., 54), and her homosexual son, Murugan, who was especially fond of a military dictator (Colonel Dipa), the Sears catalog, and weaponry. The novel, however, has no trouble embracing unrepressed bisexual and homosexual expressions as perfectly legitimate and entirely natural (ibid., 73).

8. Ibid., 169. See 73–79 for Huxley's fullest treatment of this central theme.

9. Ibid., 149, 37.

10. Ibid., 205.

11. Ibid., 199. See the epigram to chapter 2 for this passage.

12. US, 12.

13. See Timothy Miller, "Notes on the Prehistory of the Human Potential Movement: The Vedanta Society and Gerald Heard's Trabuco College," OTE 80–98.

14. Gerald Heard, *Pain, Sex and Time: A New Outlook on Evolution and the Future of Man* (New York: Harper and Brothers, 1939).

15. Ibid., 72.

16. Ibid., 75, xxi.

17. Christopher Isherwood, *My Guru and His Disciple* (New York: Penguin Books, 1981), 247–49.

18. Gerald Heard, *The Five Ages of Man: The Psychology of Human History* (New York: Julian Press, 1963), 362.

19. KCMAC, Sprott papers, Gerald Heard to W. J. H. Sprott, S. 140 (undated), King's College Library, Cambridge, WJHS/1/44. My thanks to Alison Falby for sharing this archival document with me.

20. See *One: The Homosexual Magazine,* 1/11 (November 1953) and 3/3 (March 1955), and *Homophile Studies: One Institute Quarterly* 1/2 (summer 1958). My thanks to Michael Murphy for bringing these essays to my attention and supplying me with D. B. Vest's actual identity.

21. US, 47.

22. US, 47.

23. *Rogue* (July 1961). See US, 52–53 for extracts and a discussion.

24. US, 53.

25. Jack Kerouac, *Big Sur* (New York: Penguin, 1962), 106.

26. OHB, 239.

27. US, 52. There are minor differences between the accounts of Anderson and Murphy. I have followed Murphy's memories.

28. US, 50.

29. PRP, 166.

30. US, 4.

31. For more on Adams, see US, 59–62. For more on Thomas Welton Stanford and his psychical gifts to the new university, which included transcripts from séances at his home and "Welton apports," that is, objects reportedly materialized at these séances (such as a live tortoise), see Theresa Johnston, "Mrs. Stanford and the Netherworld," *Stanford Magazine,* May–June 2000.

32. William Irwin Thompson, "Going Beyond It at Big Sur," chapter 2, *At the Edge of History* (New York: Harper and Row, 1970), 39.

33. Spiegelberg would later repeat the substance of this seminar on October 22, 1980 in Steve Donovan's apartment, for which we have an audio recording (see audiography below).

34. Theodore Roszak, *The Making of a Counter Culture: Reflections on the Technocratic Society and Its Youthful Opposition* (New York: Anchor Books, 1969), 135–36. Roszak did not quite initiate the idea. It was probably J. Milton Singer who first used a similar term ("contraculture," which he adapted from Talcott Parsons's "counter-culture") in 1960 as a marker of moral opposition to dominant culture forms. See Peter Braunstein and Michael William Doyle, "Historicizing the American Counterculture of the 1960s and '70s" in Braunstein and Doyle, eds., *Imagine Nation: The American Counterculture of the 1960s and '70s* (New York: Routledge, 2002), 6–7. As for the phrase "the tantric tradition," Roszak almost certainly borrowed it from the Austrian anthropologist, Hindu monk and American Tantric mystic, Agehananda Bharati (born Leopold Fisher), who published *The Tantric Tradition* in 1965 with the same press that would later publish Roszak's *The Making of a Counter Culture* (another textual link between "counterculture" and "tantric"). Bharati was, by far, the most knowledgeable and

sophisticated countercultural voice in these decades concerning the Asian origins of "Tantra."

35. US, 283.

36. Heard, *Pain, Sex and Time*, 41.

37. Ibid., 184.

38. This homoerotic hermeneutic is one of the basic theses of my three previous books: *Kali's Child, Roads of Excess,* and *The Serpent's Gift.* I will not defend it here. I will perform it.

Chapter 5

1. Robert C. Fuller, *Stairways to Heaven: Drugs in American Religious History* (Boulder: Westview Press, 2000).

2. This is a common opinion among my Esalen sources, one of whom referred to Castaneda simply as "that liar."

3. I am indebted for this line of thought to Robert Forte, who also showed me copies of the actual photographs taken on this night and described the details of the event.

4. R. Gordon Wasson, "Seeking the Magic Mushroom," *Life* (May 27, 1957).

5. O'Flaherty was convinced that Wasson was right about *soma* being some type of psychedelic substance, although she has remained agnostic about whether this substance can be identified as the *Amanita muscaria.* For a brief discussion of this story, see Wendy Doniger O'Flaherty, "Epilogue," in R. Gordon Wasson, Stella Kramrisch, Jonathan Ott, Carl A. P. Ruck, *Persephone's Quest: Entheogens and the Origins of Religion* (New Haven: Yale University Press, 1986), 138–39.

6. R. Gordon Wasson, Albert Hofmann, and Carl A. P. Ruck, *The Road to Eleusis: Unveiling the Secret of the Mysteries,* (Los Angeles: William Dailey Rare Books Ltd, 1998/1978).

7. For more on this and Wasson, see especially Robert Forte, "A Conversation with R. Gordon Wasson," in Robert Forte, ed., *Entheogens and the Future of Religion* (San Francisco: Council on Spiritual Practices, 1997), 67–94.

8. Wasson, et al., *Persephone's Quest,* 35–36.

9. Paul Schimmel, "'Live in Your Head'—Ecstasy: In and About Altered States," in Paul Schimmel, ed., *Ecstasy* (Cambridge, MA: MIT Press, 2005), 30.

10. Diedrich Diederichsen, "Divided Ecstasy: The Politics of Hallucinogens," in Shimmel, ed., *Ecstasy,* 189.

11. This is not exactly true, but it is true enough. Murphy first took LSD with Laura Huxley as his guide on December 7, 1962, in Rancho La Puerto, Mexico, where it was still a legal substance. This was five days after the final session of

the first brochure. His first trip with a natural psychedelic substance (peyote) took place the summer before, in the Big House (US, 76–78).

12. US, 72.

13. Aldous Huxley, *The Doors of Perception and Heaven and Hell* (New York: Harper and Row, 1963), 13–14. See also Michael Horowitz and Cynthia Palmer, eds., *Moksha: Aldous Huxley's Classic Writings on Psychedelics and the Visionary Experience* (Rochester: Park Street Press, 1999).

14. Huxley, *The Doors of Perception*, 16.

15. Ibid., 17–18.

16. Ibid., 18–19.

17. Ibid., 26.

18. Ibid., 35, 40–41.

19. Ibid., 41.

20. Ibid., 79.

21. R. C. Zaehner, *Mysticism Sacred and Profane* (Oxford: Clarendon Press, 1957), xi.

22. Ibid., xiv.

23. Ibid., 13.

24. Watts, *In My Own Way* (New York: Vintage, 1973), 396.

25. Ibid., x.

26. Ibid., ix.

27. Alan Watts, *The Joyous Cosmology: Adventures in the Chemistry of Consciousness* (New York: Pantheon, 1962), 12.

28. For Leary's memory of this event, see his *High Priest* (New York: College Notes and Texts, 1968), 289–90. For Smith's session report, see his "Empirical Metaphysics," in *Cleansing the Doors of Perception: The Religious Significance of Entheogenic Plants and Chemicals* (New York: Jeremy P. Tarcher/Putnam, 2000), 9–13.

29. Ibid., 80.

30. Watts, *The Joyous Cosmology*, 3.

31. Ibid.

32. Ibid., 58.

33. This category is usually associated with the thought of the Romanian American historian of religions, Mircea Eliade, but it is also central to the corpus of Watts; indeed, it is so central that Watts wanted to title his autobiography *Coincidence of Opposites,* but the editors vetoed this as too highbrow.

34. Ibid., 71–72.

35. Ibid. 40.

36. Ibid. 48.

37. Ibid., 78.

38. See especially ibid., 34 and 58.

39. Watts, *In My Own Way*, 399.

40. See especially Jack Kornfield and Robert Forte, "Psychedelic Experience ad Spiritual Practice," in Forte, ed., *Entheogens and the Future of Religion*; and Allan Hunt Badiner and Alex Grey, eds., *Zig Zag Zen: Buddhism and Psychedelics* (San Francisco: Chronicle Books, 2002).

41. Baba Ram Dass, *Be Here Now* (Albuquerque, New Mexico: Lama Foundation, 1971), n.p.

42. EC, May 15, 1969.

43. Robert Forte, "The Esalen Institute, Sacred Mushrooms, and the Game of Golf: An Interview with Michael Murphy," in Forte, ed., *Timothy Leary: Outside Looking In* (Rochester: Park Street Press, 1999).

44. Forte, "The Esalen Institute," 199.

45. One of these Tantric paintings reappears in Leary's *High Priest*, right in the middle of his discussion of how he discovered his primordial Hindu-ness in the Boston ashram (Leary, *High Priest*, 299).

46. Timothy Leary, *Psychedelic Prayers and Other Meditations* (Berkeley: Ronin Publishing, 1997); originally published as *Psychedelic Monograph II* in 1966.

47. Timothy Leary, Ralph Metzner, and Richard Alpert, *The Psychedelic Experience: A Manual Based on the Tibetan Book of the Dead* (New York: Citadel Press, 1992).

48. Leary, *High Priest*, 154–55.

49. Quoted in Forte, ed., *Timothy Leary*, 108–9.

50. This entire scene is based on Leary, *High Priest*, 296–300.

51. The German talk show took place on July 16, 1993. Albert Hofmann, "My Meetings with Timothy Leary," in Forte, ed., *Timothy Leary*, 91.

52. Timothy Leary, *The Politics of Ecstasy* (Berkeley: Ronin, 1998), 127, 128, 129.

53. Leary, *High Priest*, 288.

54. Quoted in Forte, "A Conversation with R. Gordon Wasson," in Forte, ed., *Entheogens*, 84.

55. HJ, 2.

56. Forte, "The Esalen Institute," 200.

57. Ibid.

58. US, 239–40. Anderson names White House aid Charles Colson and the Springer News Service, but Murphy thinks we do not and cannot know.

59. US, 108.

60. Forte, "The Esalen Institute," 200–201.

61. US, 269.

Chapter 6

1. As far as I can tell, Maslow's first published piece on the notion of Eupsychia appeared in 1961, just before he was introduced to early Esalen: "Eupsychia—the Good Society," *Journal of Humanistic Psychology* 1 (1961): 1–11.

2. Abraham H. Maslow, *Toward a Psychology of Being* (New York: D. Van Nostrand Company, 1968), 4.

3. Both lineages can also be traced back to Freud's original psychoanalysis, whose "mixed discourse" of energy metaphors and interpreted meaning Paul Ricouer identified as one of the deepest sources of Freud's genius.

4. Quoted in Adam Crabtree, *From Mesmer to Freud: Magnetic Sleep and the Roots of Psychological Healing* (New Haven: Yale University Press, 1993), 196.

5. Emmanuel Swedenborg, *Journal of Dreams*, nos. 87–88, quoted in Marsha Keith Shuchard, *Why Mrs. Blake Cried: William Blake and the Sexual Basis of Spiritual Vision* (London: Century, 2006), 80. A bit of "secret talk" is in order here: I find myself struck dumb by such a passage, as I could easily use this journal entry as my own, that is, as a *perfect* phenomenological description of the waking or magnetic sleep of "that Night" or Tantric transmission in Calcutta through which I wrote *Kali's Child*, and now, through the recognizing reception of Michael Murphy, this history of Esalen.

6. Emanuel Swedenborg, *The Delights of Wisdom Pertaining to Conjugal Love,* translated by Samuel M. Warren and revised by Louis H. Tavel (New York: Swedenborg Foundation, 1954), 86–87.

7. Ann Taves, *Fits, Trances and Visions: Explaining Religion and Explaining Experience from Wesley to James* (Princeton: Princeton University Press, 1999). See also See Robert C. Fuller, *Mesmerism and the American Cure of Souls* (Philadelphia: University of Pennsylvania Press, 1982).

8. Crabtree, *From Mesmer to Freud*, vii. See also *Animal Magnetism, Early Hypnotism, and Psychical Research, 1766–1925* (White Planes, NY: Kraus International Publications, 1988). Crabtree's luminous work is a deepening and development of Henri Ellenberger's classic, *The Discovery of the Unconscious: The History and Evolution of Dynamic Psychiatry* (New York: Basic Books, 1970).

9. This point was most famously made by Bruno Bettelheim, *Freud and Man's Soul* (New York: Vintage, 1982).

10. Robert A. Segal, *Joseph Campbell: An Introduction* (New York: Penguin, 1990). Campbell's Freudian influences will be discussed at greater length in a later chapter.

11. Gordon Wheeler, "Spirit and Shadow: Esalen and the Gestalt Model," in OTE, 165–96.

12. Ernest Jones, *The Life and Work of Sigmund Freud*, 3 vols. (New York: Basic Books, 1957). See vol. 2, ch. 14, "Occultism." See also George Devereux, ed., *Psychoanalysis and the Occult* (New York: International Universities Press, 1953); and J. Eisenbud, *Psi and Psychoanalysis* (New York: Grune and Stratton, 1970).

13. Daren Kemp, *New Age: A Guide* (Edinburgh: Edinburgh University Press, 2004), 25, 28.

14. Paul Robinson, *The Freudian Left: Wilhelm Reich, Geza Roheim, Herbert Marcuse* (Ithaca: Cornell University Press, 1990).

15. Norman O. Brown, *Love's Body* (Berkeley: University of California Press, 1966), 249–50.

16. C. G. Jung, "Yoga and the West," in *The Collected Works of C. G. Jung*, 11:537.

17. Alan W. Watts, *Psychotherapy East and West* (New York: Ballantine, 1961), 146.

18. Ibid., 60–66, 77.

19. Norman O. Brown, *Life Against Death: The Psychoanalytical Meaning of History* (Middletown, Connecticut: Wesleyan University Press, 1959).

20. Watts, *Psychotherapy East and West*, 125. cf. 189–90.

21. Ibid., 102; 103–4.

22. Ibid., 104; cf. 207. *Sahaja*, literally "born with" or "innate," is a technical Tantric category found in both Hindu and Buddhist forms of Tantra in India, Nepal, and Tibet.

23. Watts, *Psychotherapy East and West*, 169.

24. Ibid., 56.

25. Ibid., 206.

26. Ibid., 192.

27. Ibid., 199.

28. A. Maslow, H. Rand, and S. Newman, "Some Parallels between the Dominance and Sexual Behavior of Monkeys and the Fantasies of Psychoanalytic Patients," *Journal of Nervous and Mental Disease* 131 (1960): 202–12.

29. Maslow, *The Psychology of Being*, 72–73.

30. Ibid., 111.

31. Ibid., 81–82. Echoing the Neoplatonic tradition, evil for Maslow is a function of ignorance and frustrated potential, not of some fallen or corrupt human nature.

32. "All peak-experiences may be fruitfully understood . . . on the paradigm of the Reichian type of complete orgasm, or as a total discharge, catharsis, culmination, climax, consummation, emptying or finishing" (ibid., 111).

33. Abraham H. Maslow, *Religions, Values, and Peak Experiences* (New York: Viking, 1970), 29, 25.

34. A. H. Maslow, *The Farther Reaches of Human Nature* (New York: Penguin, 1971), 211.

35. Maslow, *Religions, Values, and Peak Experiences*, x.

36. Maslow, *Toward a Psychology of Being*, 181.

37. Ibid., 26.

38. Stan Grof Interview, Mill Valley (July 17, 2003).

39. Foreword to Frank Goble's *The Third Force: The Psychology of Abraham Maslow* (New York: Grossman Publishers, 1970), viii.

40. Maslow, *Toward a Psychology of Being*, iv. For Rogers's late migration to his own personal mysticism in conversation with Esalen, see Robert C. Fuller, "Esalen and the Cultural Boundaries of Meta-Language," in OTE.

41. Maslow, *Toward a Psychology of Being*, iv.

42. Another text that could be treated here is Rasa Gustaitis, *Turning On* (New York: Signet, 1969).

43. It is not lost on Maupin, now, that he "looked like Ramakrishna in more ways than one," that is, that he was a closeted gay man at this point in his life. More on Maupin's homosexuality below.

44. Edward W. Maupin, "Somatic Education: Its Origins, Ancestors, and Prospects," no page.

45. Stuart Miller, *Hot Springs: The True Adventures of the first New York Jewish Literary Intellectual in the Human Potential Movement* (New York: Viking, 1971), 3–4.

46. Ibid., 5.

47. Ibid., 91, 15.

48. Ibid. 313.

49. It is significant that the two saints Miller chooses to name here were almost certainly homoerotic mystics (for that matter, perhaps Leonardo da Vinci also was). For the knowing and unafraid (admittedly a small crowd), this raises the question of how we are to understand the panerotic space of Esalen vis-à-vis these traditional homoerotic mystical systems. More on this in my (In)-Conclusion.

50. Ibid., 44.

51. Miller captures beautifully the phenomenology of synchronicity in ibid., 261–62, where he relates it to the mystical systems of pantheism, Plotinus, and Advaita Vedanta.

52. Ibid., 341. Although the scriptural character of such a synchronistic experience is classic (as noted in the introduction), its explicitly Christian nature for a Jewish man at Esalen is curious. Miller is fully aware of the dissonance and comments on it at some length.

Chapter 7

1. Frederick S. Perls, *In and Out the Garbage Pail* (Lafayette, CA: Real People Press, 1969), 88–89. As noted below, there is no pagination in this text. I have located references by supplying my own.

2. Ibid., 100, 117, 139.

3. EC, May–October, 1983, 5.

4. Perls, *In and Out*, 136.

5. I am relying here on Erickson's summary (PRP, 234) of Martin Shepard's biography, *Fritz: An Intimate Portrait of Fritz Perls and Gestalt Therapy* (New York: E. P. Dutton, 1975).

6. Perls, *In and Out*, 59.

7. Ibid. 56.

8. Ibid., 234.

9. Ibid., 95, 43.

10. Wheeler, "Spirit and Shadow," in OTE, 172. This radically constructivist gestalt lineage renders any attempt to read Esalen as a purely perennialist institution difficult, if not actually impossible.

11. Alan Watts, *Psychotherapy East and West* (New York: Ballantine Books, 1974), 179, 97.

12. Perls, *In and Out*, 199–200.

13. For a marvelous bibliography of primary and secondary sources on Perls, including a list of films, tapes, and oral interviews, see Jack Gaines, *Fritz Perls, Here and Now* (Integrated Press, n.d.), 427–40.

14. Perls, *In and Out*, 76.

15. Ibid., 74.

16. Ibid., 60, 27–28

17. Ibid., 18.

18. Ibid., 27.

19. Ibid., 60.

20. EC, Fall 1971, 4.

21. William C. Schutz, *Joy: Expanding Human Awareness* (New York: Grove Press, 1967).

22. Ibid., 10.

23. Ibid., 15.

24. As the Esalen catalog described it, the Flying Circus team was John Heider, Stephen A. Stroud, Betty Fuller, Stuart Miller, Sara Unobskey Miller ("Sukie"), and Seymour Carter. These circus players were in turn assisted by Pamela Portugal (yoga), Anne Heider (Tai Chi Chuan), and Linda Cross (massage). *Esalen Programs* 8, no. 3 (1969).

25. John Heider, *Human Potential Papers*, 19.

26. Ibid., 21.

27. HJ, 5, 9.

28. HJ, 25.

29. Quoted in PRP, 194.

30. HJ, 53.

31. US, 215.

32. PRP, 186.

33. Calvin Tomkins, "New Paradigms," *New Yorker*, January 5, 1976, 35.

34. PRP, 193–213.

35. HJ, 65.

36. This story is told in a number of places, including HJ, 65.

37. Erickson does an excellent job of describing Price's consistent use of psychedelics throughout his life and of analyzing how they helped him negotiate and prepare for the altered states of psychosis that he also knew so well (PRP, 182–85).

38. Silverman tells this story in Will Schutz and Julian Silverman, *An Evening of Esalen History* (private video, January 24, 1996).

39. PRP, 308–9.

40. PRP, 309–10.

41. Hence his first book, published in Esalen's Viking Series: Claudio Naranjo and Robert Ornstein, *Psychology and Meditation* (New York: Viking Press, 1971).

42. Claudio Naranjo, *The Way of Silence and the Talking Cure: On Meditation and Psychotherapy* (Nevada City: Calif.: Blue Dolphin, 2006), 73.

43. Ibid., 69.

44. Ibid., 73.

45. Ibid., 38. Actually, Naranjo takes this pan-Asian Tantra even further, to ancient Greece, by noting that there is some reason to believe that the Greek Dionysus and the Indian Shiva are cultural manifestations of the same underlying Indo-European mythology (ibid., 40). In this context, then, even Naranjo's

Apollonian/Dionysian typology of early Esalen possesses a rather clear Tantric subtext or secret: Dionysian Esalen is Tantric Esalen.

46. Ibid., 60.

47. Ibid., 43.

48. Ibid., 57–58.

49. Naranjo's Esalen-realted "tantric journey" to a nontraditional shamanism strongly echoes that of Terence McKenna, discussed below, in ch. 17.

50. Ibid., 51.

51. Claudio Naranjo, *The One Quest* (New York: Viking Press, 1972), published in Esalen's Viking Press series. According to Seymour Carter, this was an especially important book for the Esalen community, as it gave the community an early "map" or frame through which to understand itself (52–53).

52. For further discussion of Arica and its pass through Esalen, see US, 223–29, 241–43, 262.

53. For Lilly's personal reflections on life, including his experiences with LSD, sensory deprivation tanks, Arica and Esalen, see John C. Lilly, *The Center of the Cyclone: An Autobiography of Inner Space* (New York: Julian Press, 1972).

54. HJ, 74.

55. US, 227.

56. My sincere thanks to Steve Harper for sharing a copy of this document with me. There are no pages and no publisher listed, only a copyright date: 1978.

Chapter 8

1. Brad Newsham, "The Spiritual Center of the Earth," *San Francisco Chronicle*, November 23, 1999.

2. US, 148.

3. US, 197.

4. The workshop's title, writes Leonard, "came more from my reckless enthusiasm than from [Cobb's] considered judgment." George Leonard, *Walking on the Edge of the World: A Memoir of the Sixties and Beyond* (Boston: Houghton Mifflin, 1988), 267.

5. "Esalen Encounter Groups, Summer Series 1968: Four Racial Confrontation Workshops," registration form. See US, 195–99, for a discussion of these racial encounter groups and their final unraveling.

6. EC, July 29, 1966.

7. EC, July 28, 1969.

8. EC, January 11 and February 3, 1966.

9. See James A. Pike, *If This Be Heresy* (New York: Harper and Row, 1967), and William Stringfellow and Anthony Towne, *The Bishop Pike Affair* (New York: Harper and Row, 1967).

10. Bishop James Pike, with Diane Kennedy, *The Other Side: An Account of My Experiences with Psychic Phenomena* (Garden City, NY: Doubleday, 1968).

11. This speech became known as "The Statement."

12. Leo Litwak, "A Trip to Esalen Institute—Joy Is the Prize," *New York Times Magazine*, December 31, 1967. Leonard considers this one of the finest single essays ever written about Esalen.

13. See especially Harvey Cox's description of receiving an Esalen massage in Jon Alexander, ed., *American Personal Religious Accounts, 1600–1980: Toward an Inner History of America's Faiths* (New York: Edwin Mellen Press, 1983), 428–29. Significantly, Cox relates his massage experience to the erotic mystical traditions of the West and Asia, very much as I have done with Esalen as a whole.

14. Esalen Programs, 1968, 4.

15. EC, October 14, 1966.

16. Joseph Campbell, *The Hero's Journey: Joseph Campbell on His Life and Work*, edited by Phil Cousineau (Novatao, CA: New World Library, 2003), 142–43.

17. Campbell comments on this proverb (ibid., 63–64). Its history and Sanskrit background ("bliss" as *ananda*) fit seamlessly into my Tantric transmission thesis.

18. For Campbell's influence on screenwriters, see Christopher Vogler, *The Writer's Journey: Mythic Structure for Writers*, 2nd ed. (Studio City, CA: Michael Wiese Productions, 1998).

19. EC May–October 1988, 8.

20. Campbell, *The Hero's Journey*, viii.

21. Heinrich Zimmer, *Philosophies of India,* ed. Joseph Campbell (New York: Bollingen Foundation, 1951), ch. 5, "Tantra."

22. EC, October 13, 1967.

23. Campbell, *The Hero's Journey*, 232.

24. For one, Esalen-related, text to this effect, see Stanley Keleman, *Myth and the Body: A Colloquy with Joseph Campbell* (Berkeley, CA: Center Press, 1999). See also Campbell, *The Hero's Journey*, 138.

25. Joseph Campbell, *The Hero with a Thousand Faces* (Princeton, NJ: Princeton University Press, 2003), 4, 8.

26. Ibid., 28; italics in original.

27. Campbell, *The Hero's Journey*, 38. There is another Indic echo here. Campbell is almost certainly taking the phrase "I am that" directly from the Upanishads, where it appears as, "You are that" (*tattvamasi*).

28. EC May–October 1988, 6.

29. Joseph Campbell, *Baksheesh and Brahman: Asian Journals—India*; and *Sake and Satori: Asian Journals—Japan* (Novato, CA: New World Library, 2002).

30. For a clear example of Campbell's rejection of Jewish exceptionalism, see *The Hero's Journey*, 166: "The whole idea of a chosen people, for example, is pathology. *Every* people is a chosen people." See also Campbell's reported exchange with Martin Buber, who objected to Campbell's observation that Hindus experience God all the time, in ibid., 136.

31. Quoted in Campbell, *The Hero's Journey*, vii.

32. US, 219.

33. EC, Winter 1971, 10.

34. D. E. Harding, "On Having No Head," in Douglas R. Hofstadter and Daniel C. Dennett, eds., *The Mind's I: Fantasies and Reflections on Self and Soul* (New York: Basic Books, 1981).

35. US, 220.

36. I am basing this on EC, May–June 1970.

37. HJ, 88.

38. John Heider, "The Enhancement of Perceptual Acuity as a Result of Meditation," Duke University, 1965; "The Flexibility and Rigidity of Perceptual/Cognitive Constructs: A Study of Creative States of Awareness," PhD dissertation, Duke University, 1968.

39. John Heider, *Human Potential Papers: 1968–1997*, 1.

40. Ibid., 7–8.

41. Ibid., 9.

42. HJ, 78–79.

43. HJ, 3.

44. Heider, *Human Potential Papers*, 12.

45. Ibid., 6.

46. EC, vol. 8, no. 3, 1969, 19.

47. Heider, *Human Potential Papers*, 17.

48. Ibid., 42.

49. Ibid., 50.

50. Nicholas Gagarin, "Big Sur, California: Tripping Out at Esalen," "In the New Pastures of Heaven," "Into the Center of the Circle," and "Esalen and Harvard: Looking at Life from Both Sides Now," *Harvard Crimson*, February 10, 12, 13, 14, 1969.

51. Gagarin, "Big Sur," 3.

52. Gagarin, "In the New Pastures," 3.

53. Gagarin, "Into the Center of the Circle," 4.

54. Gagarin, "Esalen and Harvard," 4.

55. Ibid., 4–5.

Chapter 9

1. George Leonard, "Where the California Game Is Taking Us," *Look*, June 28, 1966.

2. This section is based on Leonard's *Walking on the Edge of the World: A Memoir of the Sixties and Beyond* (Boston: Houghton Mifflin Company, 1988); my visits with Leonard; and Megan McFeely's "'Renaissance Man' Redux."

3. Leonard, *Walking on the Edge*, 110.

4. For this observation, I am indebted to Jeremy Tarcher, the unnamed author of the publisher's note for the second edition of Leonard's *The Transformation: A Guide to the Inevitable Changes in Humankind* (Los Angeles: J. P. Tarcher, 1978), xii–xiii.

5. Quoted by George B. Leonard in *Look*, June 28, 1966, 30.

6. Ibid., 32.

7. Ibid., 31.

8. It was in late February or early March. Leonard's memoirs are not entirely clear on this point (Leonard, *Walking on the Edge*, 168–79).

9. Ibid., 179.

10. Ibid., 251–55.

11. George Leonard, *Education and Ecstasy* (New York: Delta, 1968), 17.

12. Ibid., 210.

13. Ibid., 17.

14. Ibid. See also 130 and 230.

15. Ibid., 130.

16. Ibid., 49.

17. Ibid., 59.

18. Ibid., 92; italics in original.

19. Leonard, as always, refuses to make the gross mistake of conflating ecstasy and ethics or mysticism and morality. As he himself puts it, "*Ecstasy is neither immoral nor moral in itself*" (ibid., 231; italics in original). This, I think, is what sets human potential writers like Leonard apart from some of the more popular New Age writers. The latter do in fact often lack this crucial insight.

20. Ibid., 96.

21. Ibid., 97.

22. EC, September 1983–February 1984, 8.

23. Leonard, *Education and Ecstasy*, 67, 71, 78.

24. Leonard, *The Transformation*, 2.

25. Leonard, *Education and Ecstasy*, 52.

26. Leonard, *The Transformation*, 162.

27. Ibid., 80, 81.

28. Ibid., 99.

29. Ibid., 109.

30. Ibid., 109–12.

31. Leonard, *The Silent Pulse: A Search for the Perfect Rhythm That Exists in Each of Us* (New York: Arkana, 1978), xi.

32. Ibid., xii; emphasis in original.

33. Ibid., 76, 3, 9.

34. Ibid., 32, 33.

35. Ibid., 34.

36. Ibid., 63.

37. Ibid., 113, 137

38. Leonard, *The Transformation*, 10, 11, 14, 20–22, 99, 137, 197–99, 202, 232.

39. Ibid., 21.

40. Ibid., 20.

41. Leonard, *The Silent Pulse*, 104–11.

42. George Leonard, *The End of Sex: Erotic Love After the Sexual Revolution* (Los Angeles: J. P. Tarcher, 1983), 14.

43. Leonard actually uses the term: "the two of us were connected in a way that was somehow both visceral and mystical" (ibid., 55).

44. Ibid., 60, 69.

45. Ibid., 120–21.

46. Ibid., 24.

47. Quoted in ibid., 168.

48. Ibid., 137, 38.

Chapter 10

1. Don Hanlon Johnson, *Body, Spirit and Democracy* (Berkeley, CA: North Atlantic Books, 1994), 14.

2. Ibid., 57. I suggest the homoerotic dynamics of male Catholic asceticism and spirituality extend to most any male ascetic system.

3. Ibid., 41, 37, 38.

4. Ibid., 55.

5. Ibid., 56.

6. Ibid., 72. One wonders whether the man's physical position, "on top" in the traditional missionary position vis-à-vis the "female" table, did not partly determine the gender structure of this experience, with a male mystic making love to a female cosmos. Certainly such a heteroerotic structure would have been heretical within any traditional Catholic spirituality, where the beloved is always male. In any case, it took LSD to catalyze such an unorthodox *eros*.

7. Cf. ibid., 59, 175.

8. Ibid., 78.

9. Ibid., 69. Freud, by the way, spoke of the layers of the unconscious in identical terms.

10. Ibid., 6.

11. Ibid., 9.

12. Thomas Hanna, interview with Carola Speads, *Somatics* (Spring/Summer 1981): 10–13; reprinted in Don Hanlon Johnson, ed., *Bone, Breath and Gesture: Practices of Embodiment* (Berkeley: CA: North Atlantic Books, 1995), 25–28. Don Hanlon Johnson traces the movement a bit further back to around the middle of the nineteenth century in "From Sarx to Soma: Esalen's Role in Recovering the Body for Spiritual Development," in OTE, 250–67.

13. Johnson, *Body, Spirit and Democracy*, 16–17.

14. Johnson, *Bone, Breath and Gesture*, xv.

15. Thomas Hanna, *Somatics* 5, no. 4 (Spring/Summer 1986), 4; quoted in Johnson, *Body, Spirit and Democracy*, 223n2.

16. Thomas Hanna, interview with Mia Segal, *Somatics* (Autumn/Winter 1985–86): 8–20; reprinted in Johnson, *Bone, Breath and Gesture*, 131, 129.

17. Myron Sharaf, *Fury on Earth: A Biography of Wilhelm Reich* (New York: St. Martin's Press/Marek, 1983), 177.

18. W. Edward Mann, *Orgone, Reich and Eros: Wilhelm Reich's Theory of Life Energy* (New York: Simon and Schuster, 1973).

19. Sharaf, *Fury on Earth*, 52.

20. The charge that Reich was simply confusing ocular activity in his eyeballs for objective processes in his biological cultures and the atmosphere is an old and understandable one. Reich was adamant that he was seeing something objective.

21. Sharaf, *Fury on Earth*, 280.

22. Mann, *Orgone, Reich and Eros*, 142. Reich "did refer to Hindu yogic practices on several occasions and was apparently fairly well acquainted with them" (W. Edward Mann and Edward Hoffman, *The Man Who Dreamed of Tomorrow: The Life and Thought of Wilhelm Reich* [Los Angeles: J. P. Tarcher, 1980], 161).

23. Rosemary Feitis, "Ida Rolf Talks about Rolfing and Physical Reality, introduction to Johnson's *Bone, Breath and Gesture*, 152.

24. Nyack, the site of Bernard's Tantric lodge, is not in the Bronx, though I suspect that Rolf was simply playing alliteratively with words here: Bombay, Bronx. My treatment of Bernard is indebted to conversations with Robert Love of Columbia University's Graduate School of Journalism and an editor-at-large for *Playboy*. Love decided to write a biography of Bernard after he discovered that

the house he bought in Nyack was decorated with carvings of esoteric symbols from Bernard's original Tantric community. See his forthcoming *The Great Oom* (Viking Press).

25. This appears to be Bernard's very loose and creative translation of *Kali-mudra*, which literally translates as "posture or gesture of Kali." Kali is often associated with death and destruction.

26. Nik Douglas, *Spiritual Sex: Secrets of Tantra from the Ice Age to the New Millennium* (New York: Pocket Books, 1977), 195; quoted in Hugh B. Urban, "The Omnipotent Oom: Tantra and Its Impact on Modern Western Esotericism," http://www.esoteric.msu.edu/VolumeIII/HTML/Oom.html.

27. Pierre Bernard, "Tantrik Worship: The Basis of Religion," *International Journal [of the] Tantric Order* 5, no. 1 (1906): 71.

28. Don Hanlon Johnson, personal communication, April 2003. See also *Body, Spirit and Democracy*, 84.

29. Feitis, "Ida Rolf Talks," 157.

30. Ibid., 165.

31. Ibid.

32. EC, May–October 1983, 5.

33. Johnson, *Body, Spirit and Democracy*, 87.

34. Ida P. Rolf, *Rolfing: Reestablishing the Natural Alignment and Structural Integration of the Human Body for Vitality and Well-Being* (Rochester, VT: Healing Arts Press, 1989).

35. Don Hanlon Johnson, personal communication, April 2003.

36. EC, May–October 1981, 8.

37. Johnson, *Body, Spirit and Democracy*, 94.

38. Quoted in ibid., 91.

39. This section relies heavily on the research of Bill Benda, MD, and Rondi Lightmark, particularly their unpublished paper "The Lost Years." My sincere thanks to both for sharing this information with me.

40. See, for example, Andrew Weil's audiocassette, *Psychoactive Drugs through Human History*, University of California, Santa Barbara, May 1983.

41. www.hippocrates.com/archive/June2000/06features/06featphy_satis.html.

42. I am relying here on Steve Harper.

43. Benda, "The Lost Years," 11.

44. For first-person descriptions of these figures, see Don Hanlon Johnson, *Groundworks: Narratives of Embodiment* (Berkeley, CA: North Atlantic Books, 1997).

45. For a visual representation and a brief discussion of the philosophy, see *Esalen Massage* (Looking Glass Home Video, 1997).

Chapter 11

1. US, 212.

2. Translation by Arthur Waley in Edward Conze et al., *Buddhist Texts through the Ages* (Oxford: Bruno Cassirer Ltd., 1954), as quoted in Mircea Eliade, *Essential Sacred Writings from Around the World* (New York: HarperSanFrancisco, 1977), 336.

3. Timothy Leary, Ralph Metzner, and Richard Alpert, *The Psychedelic Experience: A Manual Based on the Tibetan Book of the Dead* (New York: Citadel Press, 1992), 89.

4. I am relying here on Peter Stafford, *Psychedelics* (Oakland: Ronin, 2003). For Hofmann's reflections on this story, see his *LSD: My Problem Child: Reflections on Sacred Drugs, Mysticism, and Science* (Jeremy P. Tarcher, 1983).

5. John Marks, *The Search for the "Manchurian Candidate": The CIA and Mind Control* (New York: Times Books, 1979). John Marks would later come to Esalen, have a series of life-changing experiences there, and dedicate his life to peace-making. For more on this, see chapter 14, 337.

6. Stafford, *Psychedelics*, 48, 50–51.

7. Stanislav Grof, *Realms of the Human Unconscious: Observations from LSD Research* (New York: Viking Press, 1975).

8. Stanislav Grof, *The Cosmic Game: Explorations of the Frontiers of Human Consciousness* (New York: SUNY Press, 1998), 89. The full account of this trip appears on pp. 89–91 and 194–96.

9. Ibid., 195–96.

10. Ibid., 92–93.

11. EC, September 21, 1967.

12. Quoted with a 1999 photo of the two researchers in Grof, *LSD Psychotherapy* (Sarasota: Multidisciplinary Association for Psychedelic Studies, 2001), 80h.

13. Grof, *The Cosmic Game*, 9.

14. Holotropic Breathwork is a type of group breathing meditation spontaneously developed by Stan and Christina Grof in the late 1970s at Esalen when Stan threw his back out gardening and couldn't run a scheduled seminar as usual. "Holotropic" is a word coined by Grof from the Greek that means, literally, "seeking or following (*tropos*) the Whole (*holos*)." Grof uses it to refer to the psyche's natural tendency to strive toward an integral wholeness that involves both egoic and transpersonal dimensions.

15. Ibid., 28.

16. Ibid., 33, 54, 40.

17. R. E. L. Masters and Jean Houston, *The Varieties of Psychedelic Experience* (New York: Holt, Rinehart and Winston, 1966). See Robert C. Fuller, *Stairways to Heaven: Drugs in American Religious History* (Boulder: Westview Press, 2000), 74–75, for a summary of these two models and their place in American religious experimentation.

18. See, for example: Robert Byck, ed., *Cocaine Papers: Sigmund Freud*, notes by Anna Freud (New York: New American Library, 1974); and Robert C. Fuller, "Biographical Origins of Psychological Ideas: Freud's Cocaine Studies," *Journal of Humanistic Psychology* 83, no. 3 (summer 1992): 67–86.

19. Sigmund Freud, *Civilization and Its Discontents*, S.E., vol. 21 (London: Hogarth Press, 1975), 66–67.

20. Ibid., 68. I am indebted for this line of thought to William Parsons.

21. Otto Rank, *The Trauma of Birth* (New York: Harcourt Brace, 1929).

22. Grof, *LSD Psychotherapy*, 71.

23. Ibid., 82.

24. Ibid., 72.

25. Grof, *The Cosmic Game*.

26. Grof, *LSD Psychotherapy*, 71.

27. Grof, *The Cosmic Game*, 136.

28. Ibid., 3, 211, 212, 58, 110, 113; Grof relates a series of LSD visions highly reminiscent of Kali to explicate this difficult nondual ethical position (ibid., 123).

29. This section is based on a phone conversation with Christina Grof, January 28, 2004.

30. EC, May–October 1988, 9.

31. Swami Muktananda, *The Play of Consciousness: A Spiritual Autobiography* (South Fallsburg, NY: SYDA Foundation, 2000), chs. 14–15.

32. Gopi Krishna, *Kundalini: The Evolutionary Energy in Man* (Berkeley: Shambalah, 1971/1967).

33. Lee Sannella, *The Kundalini Experience: Psychosis or Transcendence?* (Lower Lake, CA: Integral Publishing, 1987); originally 1976. Sannella was an early Esalen seminar leader (EC, November 17, 1967).

34. Stanislav Grof, *Ancient Wisdom and Modern Science* (Albany: SUNY, 1984). The cover of this book features a version of Fritjof Capra's quantum dancing Shiva, which had become something of an archetypal symbol for the mysticism of science movement by this time (see chapter 13).

35. See EC, September 1988–February 1989 for a retrospective essay on the Grofs' work at Esalen.

36. EC, January–April 1977, 23.

37. EC, September 1984–February 1985, 4–5.

38. Stanislav and Christina Grof, eds., *Spiritual Emergency: When Personal Transformation Becomes a Crisis* (New York: Jeremy P. Tarcher 1989), 227.

39. Ibid., 1.

40. Christina Grof, *The Thirst for Wholeness: Attachment, Addiction, and the Spiritual Path* (New York: HarperSanFrancisco, 1993).

Chapter 12

1. As quoted by Frederic Spiegelberg, *The Religion of No-Religion* (Stanford: James Ladd Delkin, 1953), 81.

2. Daniel Noel, "Taking Castaneda Seriously: Paths of Explanation," in Noel, ed., *Seeing Castaneda: Reactions to the "Don Juan" Writings of Carlos Castaneda* (New York: Perigee Books, 1976), 22.

3. Bill Bradley told this story to Murphy before he interviewed him on his Sirius Satellite Radio show, "American Voices," broadcast on October 30, 2005 (Show 1-22).

4. GK, 223.

5. Murphy has followed here the literary example of James Joyce's *Ulysses*, which similarly sets out a grand mythological vision within a seemingly mundane twenty-four hour period. To support such an interpretation, it is perhaps worth pointing out that Murphy actually invokes the character of Ulysses in the novel with reference to the powers of fascination and their ability to reveal the plural nature of reality. "Now this happens all the time, every day," Shivas proclaims, "and we go like Ulysses from place to place, hardly knowin' what we're about" (GK, 65).

6. GK, 40.

7. GK, 45.

8. GK, 63–64. According to Murphy, at public events dedicated to the novel, this is the most oft-quoted and acted out speech of the book.

9. GK, 52.

10. GK, 53. Such a claim finds a humorous synchronicity in the previously mentioned genetic relation of Bernard Darwin, the famous golf writer, and Charles Darwin, the famous naturalist.

11. GK, 54–55.

12. GK, 55.

13. GK, 60. Such a fictional description prefigures the physics of consciousness conferences that will later dominate much of the Esalen discussion in the late 1970s and early '80s (see below, chapter 13).

14. GK, 31, 61.

15. GK, 65, 66.

16. The same image of the (Tantric) kite appears on the cover of the novel's sequel, *The Kingdom of Shivas Irons* (New York: Broadway Books, 1997).

17. GK, 99. This, by the way, *is* the library Murphy has.

18. GK, 99–100.

19. GK, 101.

20. GK, 111.

21. GK, 11.

22. GK, 155, 180, 123. Along similar lines, Murphy makes a connection between the radical "left-handed paths" of Hindu and Buddhist Tantra and contemplative techniques that appear to be designed "for getting around the left lobe of the brain [which controls the right side of the body]" (GK, 203). To practice "from the left," in other words, is a Tantric-neurological move designed to redress the balance of a right-handed, right-eous world.

23. EC, Fall 1974, x.

24. For a discussion between Brodie and Murphy, see *Intellectual Digest*, January, 1973.

25. Michael Murphy, "The Esalen Institute Transformation Project: A Preliminary Report," *Journal of Transpersonal Psychology* 12, no. 2 (1980), 3. See also Murphy, "Sport as Yoga," *Journal of Humanistic Psychology* 17, no. 4 (fall 1977).

26. Michael Murphy and Rhea A. White, *In the Zone: Transcendent Experience in Sports* (New York: Penguin, 1995), 3.

27. Ibid., 77.

28. George Leonard, *The Ultimate Athlete* (Berkeley: North Atlantic Books, 2001), 279.

29. As I walked around my hometown pondering how to rewrite this very section, I stumbled upon, yes, a golf ball, lying in a gutter.

30. EC, Fall 1974, 4.

31. "New Esalen Center Spurs a Sports Revolution," *New York Times*, Sunday, April 15, 1973.

32. See the bibliography of *In the Zone* for some of Spino's writings on sport and meditation.

33. EC, April–June 1977, 5.

34. US, 279.

35. US, 267.

36. Sam Keen, *Beginnings without End* (San Francisco: Harper and Row, 1975).

37. Sam Keen, *Voices and Visions* (New York: Harper & Row, 1970).

38. Ibid., 16.

39. See Tom Wolfe, "The 'Me' Decade and the Third Great Awakening," *New York*, August 23, 1976; and Christopher Lasch, *The Culture of Narcissism* (New York: W. W. Norton, 1978).

40. The entire address can be found in *Beginnings without End*, 25–42.

41. US, 265–66.

Chapter 13

1. JA, 189.

2. JA, 118. Murphy also likes to cite here F. W. J. von Schelling's *deus implicitus* becoming the *deus explicitus*, that is, the "God implicit" in the natural universe becoming the "God made explicit" in a now consciously divine cosmos.

3. JA, 67.

4. JA, 5. The rainbow light evokes the "rainbow-body" of Tibetan Tantric Buddhism.

5. JA, 7. This initial vision of Darwin's is likely based on one of Murphy's own mystical experiences. He had just finished working out and was unusually exhausted and nauseous. He in fact thought he was having a heart attack. He laid down in the grass and began to see a vision in the sky of bursting capillaries, like snakes: "Instantly I knew I was seeing my own capillaries; and the instant it occurred to me that this is what it was, a healing balm spread through my chest—the *animan siddhi* at work" (personal conversation, August 6, 2002).

6. JA, 26.

7. JA, 42.

8. JA, 43.

9. JA, 129.

10. JA, 162.

11. JA, 152.

12. JA, 201–3.

13. EC Fall 1979, 10.

14. JA, 21.

15. JA, 23–24.

16. JA, 48. Darwin advances this theory in two enigmatic diary entries: "Great art captures living entities, fixes them. Then the viewer brings them back to life" (JA, 178); and, "Every artwork is transactional, a passageway for forms and energies high and low" (198).

17. JA, 2; cf. 120, 124.

18. JA, 2. See JA, 120, 124, and 199 for other references to Jacob as a *de-hasiddha*.

19. JA, 210, 66.

20. JA, 72.

21. JA, 2.

22. JA, 144.

23. Corey S. Powell, *God in the Equation: How Einstein Became the Prophet of the New Religious Era* (New York: Free Press, 2002).

24. Later thinkers, including Murphy, will meet Einstein halfway by embracing the randomness of quantum physics and evolution while observing that "the dice appear to be loaded."

25. Gary Zukav, *The Dancing Wu Li Masters: An Overview of the New Physics* (New York: Bantam, 1979).

26. This section is based partly on an interview I did with Capra on March, 5, 2004 in Berkeley.

27. Fritjof Capra, *The Tao of Physics: An Exploration of the Parallels between Modern Physics and Eastern Mysticism* (Boston: Shambala, 2000; fourth edition), 11. There appear to be psychedelic dimensions to Capra's narrative. He writes, for example, of "power plants" being especially helpful at the beginning of his journey (12).

28. Fritjof Capra, *Uncommon Wisdom: Conversations with Remarkable People* (New York: Bantam Books, 1988), 35.

29. Fritjof Capra, "The Dance of Shiva," *Main Currents in Modern Thought* (Sept.–Oct. 1972); "Bootstrap and Buddhism," *American Journal of Physics* 42, no. 1 (January 1974): 15–19; Capra, *Uncommon Wisdom*, 49.

30. Ibid., 73.

31. Ken Wilber, ed., *Quantum Questions: Mystical Writings of the World's Greatest Physicists* (Boulder: Shambalah, 2001).

32. I also worry about a certain lingering dualism that seems implicit in such criticisms, as if it would somehow be a bad thing if matter turned out to be intimately related to spirit, as if the quantum body (which is also the physical and sexual body) still needs to be resisted.

33. For a photo of this coat of arms, see Capra, *The Tao of Physics,* 144.

34. Shimon Malin, *Nature Loves to Hide: Quantum Physics and the Nature of Reality, a Western Perspective* (New York: Oxford University Press, 2001).

35. EC, October 6–7, 1962.

36. For a synopsis of Bateson's life, see EC, January 1981–June 1981, 3–15.

37. Gregory Bateston, *Mind and Nature: A Necessary Unity* (New York: Bantam, 1979).

38. Quoted by Capra in *Uncommon Wisdom,* 82.

39. Capra also acknowledges the influence of Stapp (*The Tao of Physics,* 132).

40. See also EC, Fall 1979, 29.

41. Henry Stapp, "Are Superliminal Connections Necessary?" *Nuovo Cimento* 40, 1977, 191, as quoted in Zukav, *Dancing Wu Masters*, 295.

42. Henry Stapp, "Quantum Mechanical Theories of Consciousness," *Blackwell Reader in the Philosophy of Mind* (forthcoming).

43. Stapp, "Appendix G: Comments on Searles' New Book," *Mindful Universe* (unpublished manuscript), 13.

44. The Esalen catalog borrowed this language from Charles Tart in describing the physics of consciousness series.

45. Cf. Stapp, *Mindful Universe*, 26–27.

46. Theodore Roszak, *The Making of a Counter Culture* (New York: Anchor Books, 1969), 211.

Chapter 14

1. Stanley Krippner, *Human Possibilities: Mind Exploration in the USSR and Eastern Europe* (Garden City: Anchor Press/Doubleday, 1980), 9.

2. Sheila Ostrander and Lynn Schroeder, *Psychic Discoveries behind the Iron Curtain* (Englewood Cliffs, NJ: Prentice Hall, 1970).

3. Ibid., 418. The Czech Manifesto is reproduced as appendix C of ibid.

4. Ibid., 330; see also ibid., 157 for a discussion of the paranormal dimensions of literary creativity.

5. Ibid., xix.

6. Ibid., 3.

7. Ibid., 9.

8. Ibid., 320.

9. Ibid., 6–7.

10. One of the Russian scientists they interviewed, Edward K. Naumov, later told Jim Hickman that the authors had grossly distorted and exaggerated what he had said to them about a Soviet experiment performed, supposedly in reaction to this rumor (see Krippner, *Human Possibilities*, 15–16).

11. EC, Fall 1971.

12. For a list of this Esalen-Lindisfarne Library of Russian Philosophy, see the bibliography.

13. This and the following section are based largely on a single unpublished document: James Hickman and Michael Murphy, "Human Potential Interest in the Soviet Union and the Esalen Institute Soviet-American Exchange Program" (Mill Valley, CA: Esalen Institute Center for Theoretical Studies, 1980).

14. Hickman, "Citizen Diplomacy," *Simply Living* (archival photocopy, n.p., n.d.): 15–16, 84–85, 104, 106.

15. See Stanley Krippner, M. Ullman, and A. Vaughan, *Dream Telepathy* (Baltimore: Penguin, 1974).

16. Krippner, *Human Possibilities*, 3.

17. For Krippner's life and research adventures up to 1975, see his autobiography, *Song of the Siren: A Parapsychological Odyssey* (New York: Harper and Sons, 1975). For a more up-to-date and mainstream summary of this field of study, see Etzel Cardeña, Steven Jay Lynn, and Stanley Krippner, eds., *Varieties of Anomalous Experience: Examining the Scientific Evidence* (Washington, D.C.: American Psychological Association, 2000).

18. Krippner, *Human Possibilities*, 10–11.

19. Alexander Etkind, *Eros of the Impossible: The History of Psychoanalysis in Russia*, trans. by Noah and Maria Rubins (New York: Westview Press, 1997), 347.

20. Hickman, "Citizen Diplomacy," 16.

21. Hickman and Murphy, "Human Potential Interest," 4.

22. Michael Murphy, "The Future Evolution of the Body: Possibilities for Human Transformation Revealed by Sport and Other Disciplines" (Mill Valley, CA: Esalen Institute Center for Theoretical Studies, 1980), 2.

23. Ibid., 6.

24. Hickman and Murphy, "Human Potential Interest," 2.

25. Hickman, "Citizen Diplomacy," 16.

26. I'm relying here on a personal communication with Roger McDonald, April 9, 2006.

27. For a video of this event, see *Let Us Begin Again,* Windstar Productions, 1986.

28. See Keith Thompson, "Satellite Rock-and-Roll Fest Beams U.S.-Soviet Band," EC May–October 1983, 8–9. There is also a quite moving chapter on this event in Gale Warner and Michael Shuman, *Citizen Diplomats: Pathfinders in Soviet-American Relations and How You Can Join Them* (New York: Continuum, 1987).

29. Sam Keen, *Faces of the Enemy: Reflections of the Hostile Imagination* (New York: Harper and Row, 1986).

30. See EC, September 1984–February 1985, 9.

31. EC, May–October 1988, 12.

32. "Esalen's Hot-Tub Diplomacy," *Newsweek*, January 10, 1983, 32.

33. William D. Davidson and Joseph V. Montville, "Foreign Policy According to Freud," *Foreign Policy* 45 (winter 1981–82): 145–57.

34. Rhinesmith described these events at an Esalen Reunion of Russian and American activists, April 9–14 2006.

35. Lawrence Wright, "Peace," *Rolling Stone*, November 16, 1989, 158.

Chapter 15

1. Russell Targ, *Limitless Mind: A Guide to Remote Viewing and Transformation of Consciousness* (Novato, CA: New World Library, 2004).

2. Russell Targ and Jane Katra, *Miracles of Mind: Exploring Nonlocal Consciousness and Spiritual Healing* (Novato, CA: New World Library, 1999), 2. Targ includes a copy of the letter from Edmund Cohen, chairman of the Agency Release Panel, on p. 62.

3. Much of what follows is based on a phone conversation with Targ on September 22, 2004.

4. See Edgar Mitchell, *The Way of the Explorer: An Apollo Astronaut's Journey through the Material and Mystical Worlds* (New York: Putnum, 1996).

5. This was by no means an unreasonable assumption. From the earliest days of F. W. H Myers, researchers have long known that psychic potentials are often activated in dangerous, life-threatening, or traumatic life situations. Murphy and White's *In the Zone* demonstrates the same pattern in the realm of extreme sports.

6. Russell Targ, "The Spiritual Implications of Psychic Ability," November 17, 1999 (Institute of Noetic Sciences), tape 1 of 2.

7. EC, January–June, 1985, 13.

8. For one of their more visible publications, see Russell Targ and Harold Puthoff, "Information Transfer under Conditions of Sensory Shielding," *Nature* 251 (1974): 602–7.

9. The lecture on telepathic drawing is discussed in René Warcollier, *Mind to Mind* (New York: Creative Age Press, 1948). For another account of this history, see Jim Schnabel, *Remote Viewers: The Secret History of America's Psychic Spies* (New York: Dell Books, 1997). See also Upton Sinclair, *Mental Radio* (New York: Collier, 1971). Telepathic drawing certainly goes further back than this, however. F. W. H. Myers, for example, includes a set of ten such drawings in his chapter on sensory automatisms in *Human Personality and Its Survival of Bodily Death* (1903).

10. See Paul H. Smith, *Reading the Enemy's Mind: Inside Star Gate, America's Psychic Espionage Program* (New York: Forge, 2005). See also Targ and Katra, *Miracles of Mind*, 55.

11. Dale E. Graff, *Tracks in the Psychic Wilderness: An Exploration of ESP, Remote Viewing, Precognitive Dreaming and Synchronicity* (Shaftesbury, Great Britain: Element Books Limited, 1998).

12. Harold Puthoff and Russell Targ, "A Perceptual Channel for Information Transfer over Kilometer Distances: Historical Perspective and Recent Research," *Proceedings of IEEE* 64, no. 3 (March 1976): 329–54.

13. For a discussion of this event and Price's drawings of the site and a special crane used there, see Targ and Katra, *Miracles of Mind*, 45–51.

14. See ibid., 24, 34, 43, 46, 48, 50, 58, 60, 71.

15. Ibid., 9. Or again: "the description of the mechanism of psychic abilities will be found in the geometry of space-time, and not in the electromagnetic fields" (12).

16. Ibid., xxviii.

17. Ibid., 7.

18. Ibid., 42–44. Myers encountered the same supernormal phenomenon in his work. He even gave it an official name—*retrocognition* (HP, 1:xxi).

19. Ibid., 15.

20. Erik Larson, "Did Psychic Powers Give Firm a Killing in the Silver Market?" *Wall Street Journal*, October 22, 1984; Targ, *Limitless Mind*, 90–91; EC, January–June, 1985, 13.

21. Targ and Katra, *Miracles of Mind*, 27.

22. Hence the recent Princeton reader includes at least two chapters on Dzogchen, including one on Targ's favorite author, Longchenpa (1308–1363), empowering a group of men and women into esoteric Tantric practices. See David Gordon White, *Tantra in Practice* (Princeton: Princeton University Press, 2000), chs. 14 and 32.

23. Echoing something Margaret Mead once told Targ about Giordano Bruno (who was burned at the stake for his writings), I would suggest that Targ is mistaken about this aspect of his thought, that is, about his own religion of no religion. Buddhism is in fact rife with doctrines to believe, and the nondual shape of Targ's thought is a radical philosophical challenge to all forms of Western monotheism.

24. Targ himself is very uncomfortable with the category of Tantra and wants to distance himself from the term's superficial sexual connotations. "If you are going to use the word like 'Tantric,'" he warned me, "you will have to spend a great deal of time carefully qualifying your terms. Otherwise, readers will simply associate the expression with a romantic weekend seminar with their lovers." Hence my introduction.

25. Michael Murphy, *Jacob Atabet*, editor's introduction.

26. EOH, 27.

27. EOH, 138.

28. See especially Corbin's prelude to the second edition of *Spiritual Body and Celestial Earth: From Mazdean Iran to Shī'ite Iran* (Princeton: Princeton University Press, 1997), "Towards a Chart of the Imaginal." Myers, by the way, had employed the exact same term in a very similar transcendental sense (HP, 1.xviii).

29. Corbin, *Spiritual Body*, xxvi.

30. Ibid., xxvii.

31. Ibid., xxix.

32. Ibid., 8.

33. Ibid., 18, 56.

34. Paul Deane, *Sex and the Paranormal: Human Sexual Encounters with the Supernatural* (London: Vega, 2003), 32. The Latin terms *succubus* and *incubus* refer respectively to the female and male forms of these demons and appear to be based on cultural assumptions about the proper sexual positions of the male and female in sexual intercourse: *succubus* is derived from *succubare* or "to lie under" (i.e., where the woman belongs) and *incubus* is derived from *incubare* or "to lie upon" (i.e., where the man belongs).

35. EC, September 86–February 1987, 5.

36. Keith Thompson, *Angels and Aliens: UFOs and the Mythic Imagination* (New York: Addison Wesley, 1991).

37. EOH, 78.

38. EOH, 172–73.

39. EOH, 70–71.

40. EOH, 77.

41. EOH, 133.

42. EOH, 149–50.

43. EOH, 179.

44. EOH, 159.

45. EOH, 152, 166, 171.

46. EOH, 145–46.

47. EOH, 148.

48. EOH, 173.

49. EOH, 181.

50. EOH, 82.

51. EOH, 193–94.

52. EOH, 213.

53. Michael Murphy in Keith Thompson, "Soviet Adventures in Consciousness," *New Age* (March 1982), 38.

54. Ibid., 36.

Chapter 16

1. PRP, 159.

2. Dick, Chris, and Steve Donovan all used R. B. Blakney, *The Way of Life: Lao Tzu, A new translation of the* Tao Té Ching (New York: New American

Library, 1983). Donovan has shared with me a copy Chris Price gave him, complete with a re-creation of the underlining and marginalia from Dick's original copy.

3. EC, January–June 1980, 36.

4. For more on this Tantric utopian novel, see my "From Paradise to Paradox: The Psychospiritual Journey of John Heider" (forthcoming).

5. HJ, 89. This quiet identification of Taoism and Tantrism appears again in Heider's *The Tao of Daily Living* (Palm Bay, FL: Process Publishing Company, 2000), whose delightful child-like drawings and simple text draw heavily on the Hindu Tantric *chakras* and the Taoist *yin-yang* symbolism, relating them in turn to Western figures like Walt Whitman and William Blake.

6. HJ, 90.

7. HJ, 140.

8. This line is actually taken from a second collection of essays, which Heider self-published as *Human Potential Papers: 1968–1997*, 39.

9. "Electric Sex and Magnetic Sex," ibid., 1.

10. Ibid., 2.

11. Ibid., 8.

12. Ibid., 9.

13. Ibid., 10.

14. My discussion of these events is based on both a conversation with Chris Price and Anderson's summary in US, 299–302. The Esalen influence on Rajneesh is worth underlining. The guru acknowledged Claudio Naranjo as one of his three Western influences, and a seasoned follower of Rajneesh told Naranjo that his interpersonal meditation technique was "daily bread" at the Poona ashram. See Claudio Naranjo, *The Way of Silence and the Talking Cure: On Meditation and Psychotherapy* (Nevada City, CA: Blue Dolphin Publishers, 2006), 95–96.

15. "'God Sir' at Esalen East," *Time*, January 16, 1978, 59.

16. I am basing this scene on the account of Chris Price, personal communication, September 12, 2005.

17. US, 302.

18. EC, April–June 1978, 6.

19. J. Klien, "Esalen Slides off the Cliff," *Mother Jones* 4 (December 1979): 26–33.

20. PRP, 297–98.

21. PRP, 298. ETI for extra terrestrial intelligence.

22. US, 305.

23. US, 304.

24. EC January–June 1985, 10.

25. Terence McKenna, *The Archaic Revival: Speculations on Psychedelic Mushrooms, the Amazon, Virtual Reality, UFOs, Evolution, Shamanism, the Rebirth of the Goddess, and the End of History* (New York: HarperSanFrancisco, 1991).

26. Foreword to the 1994 edition of Terence McKenna and Dennis McKenna, *The Invisible Landscape: Mind, Hallucinogens and the I Ching* (New York: HarperSanFrancisco, 1993), xi. See also Terence McKenna, *Food of the Gods: The Search for the Original Tree of Knowledge* (New York: Bantam Books, 1992); and *True Hallucinations: Being an Account of the Author's Extraordinary Adventures in the Devil's Paradise* (New York: HarperSanFrancisco, 1993).

27. Tom Robbins, foreword to *The Archaic Revival*, xiv.

28. McKenna, *The Archaic Revival*, 7.

29. McKenna, *True Hallucinations*, 60–61.

30. McKenna, *The Archaic Revival,* 67, 93, 96, 144. The book McKenna is referring to here is Mircea Eliade, *Shamanism: Archaic Techniques of Ecstasy* (Princeton: Princeton University Press, 1972).

31. McKenna, *The Archaic Revival,* 240.

32. Ibid., 34.

33. Ibid., 38. For McKenna's imitation of this alien speech, see (and hear) the recorded rave session, *Alien Dreamtime* (Rose X Media House, 1993), which was performed on February 26, 27, 1993.

34. McKenna, *The Archaic Revival,* 38.

35. Ibid., 39.

36. Ibid., 40.

37. Ibid., 41.

38. Rick Strassman, *DMT: The Spirit Molecule* (Rochester, VT: Park Street Press, 2001).

39. McKenna and McKenna, *The Invisible Landscape*, xxv.

40. Strassman, *DMT*, 349, 358, but cf. 21, 187.

41. He also points out parallels here with the *keter* or "crown" of Kabbalah and the thousand-petalled lotus *chakra* of Tantric yoga (ibid., 58).

42. Strassman also reports a kind of *animan siddhi* and the experience of bodily transfiguration. Some of his subjects, for example, "saw" the interior of cells and DNA-like spirals (ibid., 177). Others reported that the "aliens" reprogrammed their brains or restructured their bodies (ibid., 321). One also reported a McKenna-like Logos experience that constituted "the blue-yellow core of meaning and semantics" (ibid., 179).

43. Ibid., 79, 80–82, 197, 206, 208, 218.

44. I should come clean here through another bit of "secret talk." Although I have never taken a psychedelic substance, I did experience a mystical state while

living in Calcutta that bears all the hallmarks of a tryptamine-catalyzed ecstasy as studied by Strassman, including an overwhelming vibratory energy that was patently erotic, a weird sense that my body was being transfigured on a molecular or even atomic level, a feeling that a massive intuitive but as yet unarticulated gnosis was being transmitted into me, a frightening experience of floating off the bed, and an imaginal presence that wanted to engage me sexually. I interpreted all of these features through the Tantric doctrines I was then studying, but they could just as easily be read through Strassman's speculative categories (or, perhaps better, through the thesis that the sexual rituals and traumatic imagery of Tantra are designed to release tryptamine). In any case, I am certain that it is this single event that makes me critically sympathetic to the tryptamine thesis, even in some of its wildest forms.

45. Brian Lyke, "Remembering Dick Price," Esalen catalog, May–October 1986. Lyke's brief but powerful piece is, in my opinion, one of the most moving things ever written about Price. A subtle but unmistakable resurrection motif pervades the essay, particularly with the women preparing the body and in the implied enlightenment of Dick's corpse in the very last line.

Chapter 17

1. Alice Kahn, "Esalen at 25: How California's Legendary Human-Potential Mecca Has Changed, and Why the Magic Remains," *Los Angeles Times Magazine*, December 6, 1987, 40.

2. PRP, 306.

3. PRP, 301.

4. PRP, 306.

5. Virginia Vaughan Saldich, "Starbucks Early Contributor: Steve Donovan," *Overseas Brats*, May 2004, 14.

6. Howard Schultz and Dori Jones Yang, *Pour Your Heart Into It: How Starbucks Built a Company One Cup at a Time* (New York: Hyperion, 1997), 40–41.

7. As further evidence for this genetic-spiritual lineage, Donovan points to Diarmuid O'Murchadha, *Family Names of County Cork* (Cork: Collins Press, 1996).

8. Steven Donovan, biographical statement for the 1997 Fetzer Symposium on Spiritual Intelligence, unpublished document.

9. Ron Firmite, "The Day We Blasted Moscow," *Sports Illustrated*, June 19, 1989: 46–54.

10. See the bibliography, under "Newspaper and Periodical Pieces" for a representative sampling.

11. Quoted in Leon Aron, *Yeltsin: A Revolutionary Life* (New York: St. Martin's Press, 2000), 341–42.

12. Pete Carey, "Critic Who Called Yeltsin a Lush Was a Fake, Author Admits," *San Jose Mercury News*, Thursday, September 21, 1989.

13. Aron, *Yeltsin*, 325.

14. Ibid., 339.

15. See ibid., 328–29, for a fuller discussion of the numbers and analysis.

16. Quoted in ibid., 328.

17. For some indirect evidence of Montville's hunch, see Mikhail Gorbachev, *The Search for a New Beginning: Developing a New Civilization* (New York: HarperSanFrancisco, 1995). Many of Gorbachev's themes here—from an "integral" global civilization, to the language of actualizing potentials that can be found in the world religions and in modern humanism—are classical Esalen tropes.

18. EC, Summer 1974, 3.

19. See especially Jeremy Carrette and Richard King, *Selling Spirituality: The Silent Takeover of Religion* (London: Routledge, 2005); Kimberly J. Lau, *New Age Capitalism: Making Money East of Eden* (Philadelphia: University of Pennsylvania Press, 2000); and Wade Clark Roof, *Spiritual Marketplace: Baby Boomers and the Remaking of American Religion* (Princeton: Princeton University Press, 1999). I find the whole language of the spiritual marketplace and the cultural essentialism it implies to be unreflective, if not distorting, of the human beings I know, read, and talk to. Much more helpful are Christopher Partridge's notions of a reenchanting *bricolage* and "occulture," that is, a popular cultural practice whereby individuals artistically recreate their worlds through "those often *hidden, rejected* and *oppositional* beliefs and practices associated with esotericism, theosophy, mysticism, New Age, Paganism, and a range of other subcultural beliefs and practices" (Partridge, *The Re-Enchantment of the West: Volume 1, Alternative Spiritualities, Sacralization, Popular Culture, and Occulture* [London: T and T Clark, 2004], 68). In this model, alternative spiritualities are not shady business deals or examples of cultural theft; they are forms of occult art become popular (counter)culture. Similarly, Catherine Albanese has recently traced the elaborate threads of "metaphysical religion" through American history, demonstrating in the process how "combinative practices" are "what everybody [has] been doing all along" (Albanese, *A Republic of Mind and Spirit: A Cultural History of American Metaphysical Religion* [New Haven: Yale University Press, 2006], 515). I could not agree more.

20. Grace Jantzen, *Power, Gender and Christian Mysticism* (Cambridge: Cambridge University Press, 1995).

21. Alex Owen, *The Darkened Room: Women, Power, and Spiritualism in Late Victorian England* (Chicago: University of Chicago Press, 1989); Ann Braude, *Spiritualism and Women's Rights in Nineteenth-Century America* (Bloomington: Indiana University Press, 1989).

22. David J. Hess, *Science in the New Age: The Paranormal, Its Defenders and Debunkers, and American Culture* (Madison: University of Wisconsin Press, 1993). Hess is actually writing about polemics directed against nineteenth-century Spritualists here, but he then goes on to apply the same insight to the modern case of professional skeptics and practicing psychics.

Chapter 18

1. JA, 69.

2. Russell Targ, *Limitless Mind: A Guide to Remote Viewing and Transformation of Consciousness* (Novato, CA: New World Library, 2004), 5.

3. The erotic and the psychical are often correlates of one another. Given what we know about sublimation, the apparent fact that he and Annie never seem to have consummated their love renders the mystico-erotic connection more, not less, probable.

4. See Alan Gauld, *Founders of Psychical Research* (London: Routledge and Kegan Paul, 1968), 153. My thanks to Emily Williams Kelly for this reference, and so much else.

5. HP, 1:6.

6. HP, 1:24.

7. Hodgson likened these telepathic communications to long-distance telephone calls, just as Upton Sinclair would later use the metaphor of the radio and Russell Targ would even later speak of a kind of psychic Internet to which we are all already connected nonlocally. Contemporary technology, it seems, largely determines the use of psychical metaphor.

8. Gerald Heard had also written of evolutionary "buds" (see his *Pain, Sex and Time*, 63), although in a slightly different sense. Myers's notion of "preversion," defined as "a tendency to characteristics assumed to lie at a further point of the evolutionary progress of a species" is also relevant here (HP, 1:xx).

9. HP, 1:5. See also HP, 1:xxii.

10. HP, 2:277.

11. HP, 1:72.

12. Hence "there are coincidences of dream with truth which neither pure chance nor any subconscious mentation of any ordinary kind will adequately explain" (HP, 1:135). The first occurrence of "supernormal" in HP is linked to "coincidental" apparitions occurring at the time of a real death (HP, 1:xvi).

13. HP, 48.

14. Taves, "The Natural History of Supernormal Human Attributes," OTE, 228.

15. Ann Taves, "Religious Experience and the Divisible Self: William James (and Frederic Myers) as Theorist(s) of Religion," *Journal of the American Academy of Religion* 71, no. 2 (2003). The phrase "psychology of mystical trauma" is my own gloss on Myers's system.

16. HP, 2:260.

17. HP, 2:87.

18. HP, 2:254.

19. HP, 1:19.

20. HP, 1:23, 1:219. It is also worth mentioning in this context that Myers operated with a very clear notion of the religion of no religion, in which all religions are both literally false and metaphysically true to the extent that they all operate through the same psychological mechanisms, that is, the symbolic "artifice" of culture and creed as truly effective "schemes of self-suggestion" (HP, 1: 198–219). He also insisted that the "primary passion" of *eros* is no "planetary impulse" but "the inward aspect of the telepathic law," and that the controversy regarding the strictly biological or cosmic nature of sexual love is "central to our whole subject" (HP 1:112; 1:176–77). Finally, Myers set out a double model of subliminal intelligence and subliminal power that echoes my own consciousness-energy paradigm (HP 1:216–19). The correspondences with the Esalen gnosis are truly remarkable.

21. Herbert Thurston, S.J. *The Physical Phenomena of Mysticism,* ed. by J. H. Crehan, S.J. (London: Burns Oates, 1952).

22. I find at least one other important move in Thurston, namely: his keen insight (based again on the Church's canonization process) that there is no necessary relationship between the mystical and the ethical, that is, that rogues as well as saints can manifest powerful psychical phenomena.

23. Ibid., preface. See also Joseph Crehan, S.J., *Father Thurston: A Memoir with a Bibliography of His Writings* (London: Sheed and Ward, 1952).

24. The word "hysteria" is derived from *hysteros*, Greek for "womb." We are back to the *yoni* as source of altered state.

25. For the story, philosophy, and practice of ITP, see George Leonard and Michael Murphy, *The Life We Are Given: A Long-Term Program for Realizing the Potential of Body, Mind, Heart, and Soul* (New York: Jeremy P. Tarcher/Putnam, 1995).

26. James Hickman and Michael Murphy, "Human Potential Interests in the Soviet Union and the Esalen Institute Soviet-American Exchange Program,"

November 1, 1980 (Mill Valley, CA: Esalen Institute Center for Theoretical Studies), 3.

27. Personal letter: Michael Murphy and Steven Donovan to Mr. Michael Witunski, January 7, 1985.

28. EC, April–June 1977, 4.

29. Unpublished document, "The Transformation Project Book Series," n.d.

30. Spiegelberg's stunning view of the Bay, Alcatraz, Angel Island, much of Sausalito and Tiburon, and the Golden Gate Bridge can be seen in the film *Frederic Spiegelberg and the Religion of No Religion.*

31. An early version of this title appears as a subsection title, "The Body of the Future," in Murphy's 1980 essay, "The Body," in A. Villoldo and D. Dychtwald, eds., *Millennium: Glimpses into the 21st Century* (Los Angeles: J. P. Tarcher, 1980).

32. JA, 125.

33. FB, 38.

34. FB, 26.

35. FB, 27.

36. FB, 171–73.

37. FB, 37.

38. For a particular philosopher of science with whom Murphy finds much to agree, see Philip Clayton, *Mind and Emergence: From the Quantum to Consciousness* (New York: Oxford University Press, 2004). Clayton was a regular at the evolutionary theory symposia held at Esalen.

39. FB, 188; LD, 8.

40. FB, 173.

41. Fred M. Frohock, *Lives of the Psychics: The Shared Worlds of Science and Mysticism* (Chicago: University of Chicago Press, 2000), 70–71.

42. FB, 444–47.

43. FB, 478–82.

44. FB, 234, 493–99.

45. FB, 149.

46. FB, 150–51. See also FB, 212.

47. See especially "The Philosophy of Rebirth" in LD, 773–96.

48. Michael Murphy, "The Evolution of Embodied Consciousness," in James Ogilvy, ed., *Revisioning Philosophy* (Albany: SUNY, 1992), 85. This notion of "quicker" is a classical feature of Tantric systems in Asia, most of which promise much faster results than the traditional methods, which, unlike the Tantric techniques, might take many lives to take full effect. The correspondences here with Murphy's model of slow biological evolution "over many lives" and transformative practice "in a single life" is striking and, again, suggest a Tantric transmission.

49. The latter language is from Dean Radin, who makes a very similar case for the reality of psi and supernormal capacities in *Entangled Minds: Extrasensory Experiences in a Quantum Reality* (New York: Paraview, 2006).

50. FB, 551.

51. Pascal Boyer, *Religion Explained: The Evolutionary Origins of Religious Thought* (New York: Basic Books, 2001); Steven Pinker, *How the Mind Works* (New York: W. W. Norton and Company, 1997); and Robert Wright, *The Moral Animal: Why We Are the Way We Are: The New Science of Evolutionary Psychology* (New York: Vintage Books, 1994).

52. Kelly Bulkeley, *The Wondering Brain: Thinking about Religion with and beyond Cognitive Neuroscience* (New York: Routledge, 2004).

53. Frohock, *Lives of the Psychics*, 110.

54. FB, 217–18.

Chapter 19

1. This essay appears as chapter 9 of John Heider, *The Human Potential Papers: 1968–1997*, unpublished manuscript.

2. This experiment, by the way, was a disaster. Heider writes, "Steve [Stroud] asked how many of the women would like to see the inside of their vaginas. Nearly all raised their hands. Then I said, 'Well, we just happen to have with us . . . ' I brought out a speculum. The group froze, the energy went into stasis. At this point, too late, I re-centered and saw that I'd made a mistake, a bad mistake" (HJ, 24).

3. Ironically and tragically, John Heider pointed out to me that Leo Litwak's famous Esalen essay in the *New York Times Magazine*, "Joy Is the Prize" (December 31, 1967), carries a photo of Art [Rogers] with the caption, "Death Trip."

4. There were others as well, including Lois Delattre, who first introduced George Leonard to Michael Murphy and worked in the San Francisco office (she died in January of 1968 during a psychedelic session with MDA); Judith Gold, who drowned herself in the baths early in 1969; and Jeannie Butler, whose clothes were found above the cliff behind the Big House. Anderson's discussion of the suicide issue is balanced and insightful (US, 174, 180–81, 199–202, 236–37).

5. Abraham H. Maslow, *Toward a Psychology of Being* (New York: D. Van Nostrand Company, 1968), iv.

6. Personal communication to Dirk Dunbar, quoted in Dunbar, "Eranos, Esalen, and the Ecocentric Psyche: From Archetype to Zeitgeist," *The Trumpeteer* 20, no. 1 (2004): 21–43. I am entirely indebted to Dunbar for my discussion of Roszak and the 1994 Esalen symposium on ecopsychology.

7. Theodore Roszak, *The Voice of the Earth: An Exploration of Ecopsychology,* 2nd ed. (Grand Rapids, Thanes, 2001), 289.

8. Ibid., 305.

9. For more on Olatunji's life and music, see his official Web site, www.babaolatunji.com.

10. *Esalen Planning Manual,* final draft, January 31, 2000.

11. See especially, Gordon Wheeler, *Gestalt Reconsidered: A New Approach to Contact and Resistance* (Cleveland: Gestalt Institute of Cleveland Press, 1991); and *Beyond Individualism: Toward a New Understanding of Self, Relationship, and Experience* (Hillsdale, NJ: Analytic Press, 2000).

12. "Contributing to Esalen: A Conversation with Ann Knoll Downing, Director of Development," *Friends of Esalen Newsletter,* fall/winter 2004, 5.

13. For two interviews with me and the Muslim journalist Anisa Mehdi on these two events, see *Friends of Esalen Newsletter,* "Beyond Fundamentalism: Threat and Opportunity," parts 1 and 2, vols. 17–18, issue 1, spring 2005 and winter 2006.

14. Quoted with permission from his unpublished paper, "A Polytheistic Conception of the Sciences and the Virtues of Deep Variety," prepared for New York Academy of Sciences Conference on "Unity of Knowledge: The Convergence of Natural and Human Science," June 23–25, 2000. Shweder's paper is a robust critique of E. O. Wilson's sociobiology and its notion of "consilience."

15. I am creatively (mis)reading Shweder here. As applied to Esalen's history, the key word in Shweder's Confusionism is certainly *empty*—whereas Shweder appears to understand the term negatively, Spiegelberg would have almost certainly understood it as a kind of fertile artistic void, that is, as something positive. In any case, Shweder's existential point stands: even with the religion of no religion, one must take a particular perspective, a position, a path, and have one's world "appear" accordingly. Thus Price turned to Buddhist meditation, Murphy to Aurobindo, Spiegelberg to art, Rolf to Rolfing, Leonard to aikido, Donovan to native indigenous practices, and so on.

16. Stevenson's corpus is immense. For an accessible introduction to his lifework, see Jim B. Tucker, *Life Before Life: A Scientific Investigation of Children's Memories of Previous Lives* (New York: St. Martin's Press, 2005). Serious readers of this research, however, should consult Stevenson's *Cases of the Reincarnation Type, Four Volumes* (Charlottesville: University Press of Virginia, 1983).

17. Ian Stevenson, *Reincarnation and Biology: A Contribution to the Etiology of Birthmarks and Birth Defects,* 2 vols. (Westport, CT: Praeger Publishers, 1997). An abridged version of this work has also been published: *Where Reincarnation and Biology Intersect* (Westport, CT: Praeger, 1997).

18. Emily Frazer Williams Cook, "Frederic W. H. Myers: Parapsychology and Its Potential Contribution to Psychology," PhD dissertation, University of Edinburgh, 1992.

19. Edward F. Kelly, Emily Williams Kelly, Adam Crabtree, Alan Gauld, Michael Grosso, and C. Bruce Greyson, *Irreducible Mind: Toward a Psychology for the 21st Century* (Lanham, MD: Rowman and Littlefield, 2006).

20. My thanks to Robert C. Gordon for sharing this unpublished typescript with me.

21. There is some evidence that this may be happening. I am told, for example, that a good chunk of the income Esalen generates today comes from individuals not participating in any workshop.

(In)Conclusion

1. JA, 56.

2. Henry Corbin, prologue to *Spiritual Body and Celestial Earth: From Mazdean Iran to Shi'te Iran* (Princeton: Princeton University Press, 1977), xxix..

3. Frederic Spiegelberg, *The Religion of No-Religion* (Stanford: James Ladd Delkin, 1953), 55.

4. EC, September 26, 1967.

5. Russell Targ, *Limitless Mind: A Guide to Remote Viewing and Transformation of Consciousness* (Navato, CA: New World Library, 2004), xii; italics in original.

6. Although Ian Stevenson's reincarnation memory research has some fascinating things to suggest about transgenderism, that is, gender phenomena like the classic case of "being a man in a woman's body."

7. See EC, June 6, 1972; April 28–June 7, 1972; October 14, 1973; and Fall 1973, 12.

8. Don Hanlon Johnson, *Body, Spirit and Democracy* (Berkeley: North Atlantic Books, 1994), 133.

9. Thomas Jefferson did this. For a lovely essay on the teachings of Jefferson's rational Jesus wedded to Emerson's Transcendentalism as an American gnostic gospel reminiscent of the ancient Gospel of Thomas, see Erik Reece, "Jesus without the Miracles: Thomas Jefferson's Bible and the Gospel of Thomas," *Harper's* (December 2005): 33–39. Significantly, Reece also observes that legend has Thomas traveling to India and notes that Thomas's Jesus "seems so Taoist or Buddhist" (38). We are back to the Esalen gnosis: "Emerson," Reece writes, "did not, like Jefferson, deny Jesus' divinity; he simply said the same potential resides in every human heart" (40).

10. For the founders' understanding of faith as a personal choice beyond all government interference or public orthodoxy, see Jon Meacham, *American Gospel: God, the Founding Fathers, and the Making of a Nation* (New York: Random House, 2006). For Thomas Jefferson's fierce fight against tyranny of organized piety and his reading of traditional Christian doctrines as "so much ignorance, so much absurdity, so much untruth, charlatanism, and imposture," see Andrew Burstein, *Jefferson's Secrets: Death and Desire at Monticello* (New York: Basic Books, 2005), especially ch. 9, "Disavowing Dogma."

11. Quoted by George Moreby Acklom, "The Man and the Book," in Richard Maurice Bucke, *Cosmic Consciousness: A Study in the Evolution of the Human Mind* (1901; New York: Penguin, 1991). Bucke's thought, it must be said, was as undisciplined as it was visionary and intuitive.

12. Harold Bloom, introduction to Walt Whitman, *Leaves of Grass: 150th Anniversary Edition* (New York: Penguin, 2005), viii.

13. "Song of Myself," lines 1261–62.

14. Ibid., line 661.

15. Ibid., lines 1329–30.

16. Ibid., lines 503–8.

17. Ibid., lines 518–20.

18. This is a line from the early notebook portfolios, quoted in Bloom, introduction, xx.

19. Ibid., xxi.

20. Ibid., x.

On Rare Things

THE ORAL, VISUAL, AND WRITTEN SOURCES

The present bibliography is selective instead of exhaustive. Full references to all of the secondary sources employed in the chapters can be found in the chapter endnotes. I have thus focused here instead on recording primary and archival material, some of it relatively accessible, some of it extremely rare and existing only in private collections.

Private, Unpublished, or Privately Published Archival Material

"Association of Space Explorers—USA, Annual Report." Fifth Planetary Congress, November 1989, Riyadh, Saudi Arabia.

"A Benefit for the Claire Nelson Scholarship Fund and the Elaine Farber Research and Development Fund of Esalen Institute." April 17–19, 1970, Hotel Diplomat, 108 West 43rd Street, New York, New York. Esalen benefit brochure.

Brown, George I. "A Research Proposal to the United States Office of Education from the Esalen Institute, Big Sur, California." February 28, 1966 (typescript).

Carter, Seymour. "Presence and Absence: Seymour Carter Shares His Experiences Exploring the Elusive 'I' through Sensory Awareness and Psychotherapy." Unpublished essay by self-described "Artifact of the '60s."

Chaudhuri, Haridas. "Yogic Potentials and Capacities, or siddhis, in Hindu-Buddhist Psychology." Private typed letter-list of Sanskrit terms and definitions written for Michael Murphy.

Donovan, Steven. "Transformation Project Notebook." Private three-ring binder.

Esalen Planning Manual: Final Draft. January 31, 2000.

Gunther, Bernard. "Procedure for Massage." Mimeographed typescript, c. 1967.

Heider, John. "The Enhancement of Perceptual Acuity as a Result of Meditation."
Major paper, Department of Psychology, Duke University, 1965.

———. "Esalen Journals: 1968–1971."

———. *Human Potential Papers: 1968–1997.*

———. *Life on the Group Room Floor: An Introduction to Human Potential Theory and Practice* (Mendecino, CA, 1976).

———. *Living in Paradox: A Utopian Soap Opera.* Unpublished novel.

———. *Mari: The Woman Who Smelled Like the Sea.* Unpublished novel.

Hickman, James and Michael Murphy. "Human Potential Interests in the Soviet Union and the Esalen Institute Soviet-American Exchange Program." November 1, 1980. Mill Valley, CA: Esalen Institute Center for Theoretical Studies.

Hofmann, Albert. "The Transmitter-Receiver Concept of Reality." Lecture delivered at the University of California, Santa Barbara, May 14, 1983.

Maupin, Edward. *The Gods and Other Men: The Myths of Male Attraction.* Unpublished monograph in galleys.

Murphy, Michael. "The Future Evolution of the Body: Possibilities for Human Transformation Revealed by Sport and Other Disciplines." Mill Valley, CA: Esalen Institute Center for Theoretical Studies, September 1980.

"Session with Jenny O'Connor Channeling the Nine, with Maurica Anderson and Dick Price, Wednesday, April 28, 1982, At South Coast, Esalen." Typescript, no author, Esalen archives.

Sivananda in Stanford University, A Review of Sri Swami Sivananda's Works by the Students of the Stanford University, America. Rishikesh, India: Yoga-Vedanta Forest University, 1958.

Esalen Catalog Pieces

The early Esalen pamphlets and later catalogs constitute a rich and reliable source for tracing the outlines of Esalen's institutional history both in Big Sur and in San Francisco. Beginning in the winter issue of 1970, the Esalen catalogs began to feature news items and short essays on important Esalen figures and events. Taken together, these catalogs are an invaluable source of the community's own developing understanding of its mission and history. The following feature stories were used in the present study and deserve mention here.

Grof, Christina and Stanislav Grof. "Spiritual Emergency: Understanding and Treatment of Transpersonal Crises." EC September 1984–February 1985, 4–5.

Murphy, Michael. "Sport as Yoga: Altered States of Consciousness and Extraordinary Powers." EC Fall 1974, 4–5.

Murphy, Michael, and Jack Sarfatti. "Physics and Consciousness: Consciousness Shift toward a 'State-Specific' Physics." EC January– March 1976, 3.

Thompson, Keith. "The Astonishment of Being." EC September 1993–February 1994, 6.

———. "Diplomacy as Psychology." EC September 1984–February 1985, 9.

———. "Games Soviets and Americans Play." EC January–May 1985, 5–8.

———. "The Hot Springs." EC January–June 1991, 4–9.

Audio and Video Tapes

Paul Herbert recorded many of the early Esalen seminars. Many of these are now available under the rubric of Dolphin Tapes. As the technology developed, this early oral history later blended into a videotape collection, much of it recorded by Daniel Bianchetta and all of it presently archived at Esalen. Most of the following audiocassettes and videotapes are housed in the Esalen archives.

Bateson, Gregory. "Cultural Relativity and Belief Systems." A lecture at Grof Workshop at Esalen in November 1976. Dolphin Tapes.

Esalen Massage. Looking Glass Home Video, 1997.

Fadiman, James and Arthur Hastings. "Psychedelics and Paranormal Psychology." A lecture at Esalen in 1971. Dolphin Tapes.

Hofmann, Albert. "LSD and the Nature of Reality." A lecture on Hallucinogens in San Francisco in 1978. Dolphin Tapes.

Huxley, Aldous. "Human Potentialities." A lecture at MIT in 1961. Dolphin Tapes.

Leary, Timothy. "American Culture: 1945–1985." A lecture at College Marin in March 1977. Dolphin Tapes.

Leonard, George. "Ecstasy and Education." A lecture at San Francisco/Esalen in March 1970. Dolphin Tapes.

Lilly, John C. "Dolphin Behavior with Humans." Berkeley: Nyingma, 1976. Audiocassette.

Maslow, Abraham H. "Self-Actualization." A lecture at Esalen in September 1966. Dolphin Tapes.

———. "Psychology of Religious Awareness." A lecture at San Francisco/Esalen in 1967. Dolphin Tapes.

McKenna, Terence. "Always Coming Home." October 20, 1999. Dolphin Tapes.

———. "Hot Concepts and Melting Edges." June 1994. Dolphin Tapes.

———. "Laws and Freedom, Habits and Novelty." June 1994. Dolphin Tapes.

———. "Personal Update, Complexity and Meaning." March 10, 1996. Dolphin Tapes.

Miller, Sukie. "Death and the Afterlife." A lecture in Exploring the Frontiers of Consciousness Lecture Series on November 18, 1998. Institute of Noetic Sciences. Audiocassette.

Munthe, Katriona, and Ted Helminski, *Frederic Spiegelberg and the Religion of No Religion*. Videotape, 1995.

Murphy, Michael. *Tour of the Big and Little House*. Videotape.

Osmond, Humphrey. "Early Psychedelic History." A lecture during the Grof Workshop at San Francisco/Esalen in May 1976. Dolphin Tapes.

Perls, Fritz. "Gestalt Therapy and How It Works." A lecture at Esalen in 1966. Dolphin Tapes.

Rogers, Carl. "My Philosophy and How It Grew." A lecture at AHP Annual Meeting in Honolulu, HI in 1972. Dolphin Tapes.

Schutz, Will. "Principles and Philosophy of Encounter." A lecture at Esalen in 1970. Dolphin Tapes.

———. "Rules of Thumb for Open Encounter." A lecture at Esalen in 1970. Dolphin Tapes.

Schwartz, Gary. "The Afterlife Experiments—Breakthrough Scientific Evidence." A lecture at Exploring the Frontiers of Consciousness Lecture Series on November 13, 2002. Institute of Noetic Sciences. 2 Audiocassettes.

Smith, Huston. "The Nature of Reality." A lecture at ITA Conference in Boston in 1979. Dolphin Tapes.

Spiegelberg, Frederic, "Donovan Apartment Lectures, 1979–1983." 39 audiocassettes in the private collection of Steven Donovan.

Targ, Russell. "The Spiritual Implications of Psychic Ability." A lecture at Exploring the Frontiers of Consciousness Lecture Series on November 17, 1999. Institute of Noetic Sciences. Audiocassette.

Tart, Charles. "On the Paranormal." A lecture at San Francisco/Esalen in February 1971. Dolphin Tapes.

———. "Our Fear of Psychic Abilities." An invitational lecture at Esalen in June 1984. Dolphin Tapes.

Weil, Andrew. "Psychoactive Drugs through Human History." A lecture at UCSB Conference in May 1983. Dolphin Tapes.

Newspaper and Periodical Pieces

In many ways, it was the media of the late 1960s and early '70s that made Esalen famous (with a second "spike" in September of 1989 with Yeltsin's tour).

This media attention was both a blessing and a curse for the young institute, as journalists, with few exceptions, tended to focus on the sensationalistic and the sensuous at the expense of the intellectual and the philosophical. Here is a select list of some of the most relevant pieces.

Associated Press (Miami). "Yeltsin ends his U.S. tour at supermarket." *Anchorage Times*, Monday, 18 September 1989.

Barringer, Felicity. "Soviet Lawmaker Meets with Bush: Yeltsin Offers Suggestions on U.S. Support for Changes in Kremlin Economy." *New York Times*, Wednesday, September 13, 1989.

Brady, Mildred E. "The New Cult of Sex and Anarchy," *Harper's Magazine* (April 1947).

Bohlen, Celestine. "Soviet Populist Takes Manhattan (in Stride)," *New York Times*, September 11, 1989.

Clines, Francis X. "Now Pravda Eats Those Unkind Words About Yeltsin: Times Change. Readers Protest and the Party Paper 'Grovels.'" *New York Times*, September 22, 1989.

———. "Yeltsin in U.S.: Pravda's Ugly Profile." *New York Times*, Tuesday, September 19, 1989.

Firmite, Ron. "The Day We Blasted Moscow." *Sports Illustrated*, June 19, 1989: 46–54.

Friedman, Thomas L. "Baker to See Visiting Soviet Politician." *New York Times*, September 12, 1989.

Gagarin, Nicholas. "Big Sur, California: Tripping Out at Esalen," "In the New Pastures of Heaven," "Into the Center of the Circle," and "Esalen and Harvard: Looking at Life from Both Sides Now." Four-part series. *Harvard Crimson*, February 10, 12, 13, 14, 1969.

"German Savant in India: An Interview with Dr. Frederic Spiegelberg." *Mother India*, April 30, 1949.

Goldman, John J. "Yeltsin Sees Discontent but No Soviet Coup." *Los Angeles Times*, September 11, 1989.

Hamilton, Masha. "Yeltsin: Pravda Apologizes for Story." *Los Angeles Times*, September 22, 1989.

Hendrickson, Paul. "Boris's Borscht Belting: Yeltsin's Boozy Bearhug for the Capitalists." *Washington Post*, September 13, 1989.

Hickman, Jim. "Negotiating with the Russians: A Matter of Trust." *Root Beer Rag*, Spring/Summer 1988.

Howard, Jane. "Inhibitions Thrown to the Gentle Winds: A New Movement to Unlock the Potential of What People Could Be—But Aren't." *Life* 65, no. 2 (July 12, 1968): 48–65.

Klien, J. "Esalen Slides off the Cliff." *Mother Jones IV*, December 1979: 26–33.

Leonard, George. "Encounters at the Mind's Edge." *Esquire,* June 1985.

———. "Where the California Game is Taking Us." *Look,* June 28, 1966.

Litwak, Leo E. "A Trip to Esalen Institute—Joy Is the Prize." *New York Times Magazine,* December 31, 1967.

McAuliffe, Bill. "Yeltsin Pays Call on Reagan in Rochester." *Star Tribune,* September 15, 1989.

Murphy, Michael, "Esalen Has Been Changing." *Association for Humanistic Psychology Newsletter* 7, no. 4 (January 1971): 1–2.

———. "Esalen: Where It's At." *Psychology Today* (December 1967): 34–39.

Music: Together for Our Children. A Worldwide Television Special to Celebrate the End of the Cold War and to Raise Funds to Immunize Children in the United States, Former Soviet Union, and the Rest of the World. Concert brochure cosponsored by Gorbachev Foundation/USA, the Children's Health Fund, and Children Now. Royce Hall, UCLA, June 23, 1993.

Oberdorfer, Don. "Soviet Populist Enthusiastic After First View of U.S." *Washington Post,* September 11, 1989.

———. "Yeltsin: Gorbachev Has Year to Prove Self: Soviet Maverick Cites Possible Revolution From Below," *Washington Post,* September 12, 1989.

Rosenzweig, Rosie, "Rebirth at Esalen." *Boston Herald Magazine,* March 15, 1970, 20–22, 45–48.

Saldich, Virginia Vaughan. "Starbucks Early Contributor: Steve Donovan." *Overseas Brats,* May 2004 14.

Sieff, Martin. "Boris Yeltsin Is Soviet Paradox: A Democratic Communist." *Washington Post,* September 12, 1989.

Thompson, Keith. "Soviet Adventures in Consciousness: A *New Age* Interview with Michael Murphy." *New Age,* March 1982.

Tomkins, Calvin. "Profiles: New Paradigms." *New Yorker.* January 5, 1976, 30–50.

Toth, Robert C. "Apparently Reluctant Bush Has Meeting with Yeltsin." *Los Angeles Times,* September 13, 1989.

Trejo, Frank. "Yeltsin Calls for Outsers: Politburo Should Drop 5, Reformer Says in Dallas." *Dallas Morning News,* September 16, 1989.

Valenta, Jiri. "Yeltsin's Soviet Vision." *Miami Herald,* September 17, 1989.

Waite, Juan J. "Boris Yeltsin: A Star is Born." *USA Today,* September 15, 1989.

Wasson, R Gordon. "Seeking the Magic Mushroom." *Life,* May 27, 1957.

Wernick, Robert. "Big Sur: Life on the Edge." *Smithsonian* (November 1999): 98–111.

Whitaker, Mark, with Gerald C. Lubenow and Joyce Barnathan. "Esalen's Hot-Tub Diplomacy." *Newsweek,* January 10, 1983, 32.

Wright, Lawrence. "Believing is Seeing." *Rolling Stone*, November 16, 1989, 155–99.

———. "Peace." *Rolling Stone*, November 16, 1989.

Young, John V., "'The Road between the Devil and the Deep,'" *New York Times*, Travel Section, November 22, 1970, 7.

Esalen-Viking Book Series

In the late 1960s, Esalen contracted with Viking Press (New York) to publish its own book series under the editorial guidance of Stuart Miller. Beginning with Lederman's 1969 *Anger and the Rocking Chair* (published through McGraw-Hill, before the series was taken over by Viking), seventeen books in all were finally published under Esalen's logo, including the first edition of Murphy's *Golf in the Kingdom*.

Adams, Joe K. *Secrets of the Trade: Madness, Creativity, and Ideology*, 1971.

Assagioli, Roberto. *The Act of Will*, 1974.

———. *Psychosynthesis*, 1971.

Brooks, Charles V. W. *Sensory Awareness: The Rediscovery of Experiencing*, 1974.

Brown, George I. *Human Teaching for Human Learning: An Introduction to Confluent Education*, 1971.

———. *The Live Classroom: Innovation through Confluent Education and Gestalt*, 1975.

Grof, Stanislav. *Realms of the Human Unconscious: Observations from LSD Research*, 1975.

Lederman, Janet. *Anger and the Rocking Chair*(New York: McGraw-Hill, 1969).

LeShan, Lawrence. *The Medium, the Mystic, and the Physicist: Toward a General Theory of the Paranormal*, 1974.

Maslow, Abraham H. *The Farther Reaches of Human Nature*, 1971.

Miller, Stuart. *Hot Springs: The True Adventures of the First New York Jewish Literary Intellectual in the Human Potential Movement*, 1971.

Murphy, Michael. *Golf in the Kingdom*, 1972.

Naranjo, Claudio. *The One Quest*, 1972.

Naranjo, Claudio and Robert E. Ornstein, *On the Psychology of Meditation*, 1971.

Needleman, Jacob, and Dennis Lewis. *Sacred Tradition and Present Need*, 1975.

Ornstein, Robert. *The Psychology of Consciousness*, 1973.

Payne, Buryl. *Getting There Without Drugs: Techniques and Theories for the Expansion of Consciousness*, 1973.

Esalen Institute/Lindisfarne Press Library of Russian Philosophy

In the mid-1980s, Esalen contracted with Lindisfarne Press (Hudson, NY) to publish a second book series, this one on major Russian philosophers and theologians considered to be Russian analogues to the later human potential authors.

Andreev, Daniel. *The Rose of the World*, 1996.

Berdyaev, Nikolai. *The Russian Idea*, 1992.

Bulgakov, Sergei. *The Holy Grail and the Eucharist.* Translated and edited by Boris Jakim, 1997.

———. *Sophia: The Wisdom of God, An Outline of Sophiology*, 1993.

Khomiakov, Aleksei and Ivan Kireevsky. *On Spiritual Unity: A Slavophile Reader.* Translated and edited by Boris Jakim and Robert Bird, 1998.

Solovyov, Vladimir. *The Crisis of Western Philosophy (Against the Positivists)*, 1996.

———. *Lectures on Divine Humanity.* 1995.

———. *The Meaning of Love.* Introduction by Owen Barfield. 1985.

———. *War, Progress, and the End of History: Three Conversations Including a Short Story of the Anti-Christ.* Introduction by Czeslaw Milosz. Afterword by Stephan Hoeller. 1990.

Select Books and Essays

The following books and essays should be considered primary for any full study of Esalen and its history. This again, however, is a highly selective list designed for the reader who is looking to pursue particular themes or figures.

Anderson, Walter T. *The Upstart Spring: Esalen and the American Awakening.* Reading: Addison-Wesley, 1983.

———. *The Upstart Spring: Esalen and the Human Potential Movement: The First Twenty Years.* Lincoln, NE: iUniverse, 2004.

Badiner, Allan H. and Alex Grey, eds. *Zig Zag Zen: Buddhism and Psychedelics.* San Francisco: Chronicle Books, 2002.

Bateson, Gregory. *Mind and Nature.* New York: Bantam, 1979.

Capra, Fritjof. "Bootstrap and Buddhism." *American Journal of Physics* 42, no. 1 (Jan. 1974).

———. "The Dances of Siva." *Main Currents in Modern Thought*, Sep.–Oct. 1972.

———. *The Tao of Physics: An Exploration of the Parallels between Modern Physics and Eastern Mysticism.* Boston: Shambala, 2000 [1975].

————. *Uncommon Wisdom: Conversations with Remarkable People.* New York: Bantam Books, 1988.

Castaneda, Carlos. *The Teachings of Don Juan: A Yaqui Way of Knowledge.* Berkeley: University of California Press, 1998 [1969].

Chaudhuri, Haridas. "The Integral Philosophy of Sri Aurobindo." In Chaudhuri, Haridas and Frederic Spiegelberg, eds. *The Integral Philosophy of Sri Aurobindo: A Comparative Symposium.* London: George Allen and Unwin, Ltd., 1960.

————. *Integral Yoga: The Concept of Harmonious and Creative Living.* London: Unwin Hyman, Ltd., 1990 [1965].

Chaudhuri, Haridas and Frederic Spiegelberg, eds. *The Integral Philosophy of Sri Aurobindo: A Comparative Symposium.* London: George Allen and Unwin, Ltd., 1960.

Davidson, William D., and Joseph V. Montville. "Foreign Policy According to Freud." *Foreign Policy* 45 (Winter 1981–82): 145–57.

Erikson, Barclay J. "A Psychobiography of Richard Price: Co-founder of Esalen Institute." PhD dissertation. Fielding Graduate Institute, 2003.

Feitis, Rosemary. "Ida Rolf Talks about Rolfing and Physical Reality." Introduction to Don Hanlon Johnson, ed., *Bone, Breath, and Gesture: Practices of Embodiment.* Berkeley: North Atlantic Books, 1995.

Ferrer, Jorge N. "Integral Transformative Practice: A Participatory Perspective." *Journal of Transpersonal Psychology* 35, no. 1 (2003): 21–42.

Forte, Robert., ed. *Entheogens and the Future of Religion.* San Francisco: Council on Spiritual Practices, 1997.

————. ed. *Timothy Leary: Outside Looking In.* Rochester: Park Street Press, 1999.

Gindler, Elsa. "Gymnastik for People Whose Lives Are Full of Activity." In Don Hanlon Johnson, ed,. *Bone, Breath, and Gesture: Practices of Embodiment.* Berkeley: North Atlantic Books, 1995.

Gorbachev, Mikhail. *The Search for a New Beginning: Developing a New Civilization.* New York: HarperSanFrancisco, 1995.

Grof, Christina. *The Thirst for Wholeness: Attachment, Addiction, and the Spiritual Path.* New York: Harper Collins, 1993.

Grof, Stanislav. *The Cosmic Game: Explorations of the Frontiers of Human Consciousness.* New York: SUNY Press, 1998.

————. *LSD Psychotherapy.* Auburn Hills: Multidisciplinary Association for Psychedelic Studies, 2001.

————. *Psychology of the Future: Lessons from Modern Consciousness Research.* Albany: SUNY Press, 2000.

———. ed. *Ancient Wisdom and Modern Science*. Albany: SUNY Press, 1984.

Grof, Stanislav, and H. Zina Bennett. *The Holotropic Mind: The Three Levels of Human Consciousness and How They Shape Our Lives*. New York: Harper Collins, 1993.

Grof, Stanislav, and Christina Grof, eds. *Spiritual Emergency: When Personal Transformation Becomes a Crisis*. New York: Penguin Putnam Inc., 1989.

Gustaitis, Rasa. *Turning On*. New York: Macmillan, 1969.

Hanna, Thomas. "Interview with Carola Speads." In Don Hanlon Johnson, ed., *Bone, Breath, and Gesture: Practices of Embodiment*. Berkeley: North Atlantic Books, 1995.

———. "Interview with Mia Segal." *Somatics* (Autumn/Winter 1985–86).

Heard, Gerald. *The Five Ages of Man: The Psychology of Human History*. New York: Julian Press, 1963.

———. *The Human Venture*. New York: Harper and Brothers, 1955.

———. *Pain, Sex and Time: A New Outlook on Evolution and the Future of Man*. New York: Harper and Brothers, 1939.

Heider, John. "The Flexibility and Rigidity of Perceptual/Cognitive Constructs: A Study of Creative Awareness." PhD dissertation, Duke University, 1968.

Hickman, James. "How to Elicit Supernormal Capabilities in Athletes." In P. Klavora and J. Daniel, eds., *Coach, Athlete, and the Sport Psychologist*. University of Toronto School of Physical and Health Education, n.d.

Hickman, James, Michael Murphy and Michael Spino. "Psychophysical Transformation through Meditation and Sport." *Simulation and Games* 8, no. 1 (March 1977).

Huxley, Aldous. *The Doors of Perception and Heaven and Hell*. New York: Harper and Row, 1963.

———. *The Perennial Philosophy*. Cleveland: World Publishing Company, 1962.

Keen, Sam. *Face of the Enemy: Reflections of the Hostile Imagination*. New York: Harper and Row, 1986.

———. *Voices and Visions*. New York: Harper and Row, 1970.

Kelly, Edward F., Emily Williams Kelly, Adam Crabtree, Alan Gauld, Michael Grosso, and C. Bruce Greyson. *Irreducible Mind: Toward a Psychology of the 21st Century*. Lanham: Rowman and Littlefield, 2006.

Kripal, Jeffrey J. and Glenn W. Shuck, eds. *On the Edge of the Future: Esalen and the Evolution of American Culture*. Bloomington: Indiana University Press, 2005.

Leary, Timothy. *Flashbacks: A Personal and Cultural History of an Era*. New York: Tarcher/Putnam Book, 1990.

———. *High Priest*. New York: College Notes and Texts, Inc., 1968.

———. *The Politics of Ecstasy*. Berkeley: Ronin Publishing, 1990 [1965].

————. *Psychedelic Prayers and Other Meditations*. Berkeley: Ronin Publishing, 1997.

Leary, Timothy, Ralph Metzner, and Richard Alpert. *The Psychedelic Experience: A Manual Based on the Tibetan Book of the Dead*. New York: Citadel Press, 1995.

Leary, Timothy, Ralph Metzner, and Gunter M. Weil, eds. *The Psychedelic Reader*. Secaucus: A Citadel Press Book, 1997.

Leonard, George. *Education and Ecstasy*. New York: Delta, 1968.

————. *The End of Sex: Erotic Love After the Sexual Revolution*. Los Angeles: J. P. Tarcher, 1983.

————. *The Silent Pulse: A Search for the Perfect Rhythm That Exists in Each of Us*. New York: Penguin, 1986.

————. *The Transformation: A Guide to the Inevitable Changes in Humankind*. Los Angeles: J. P. Tarcher, 1978.

————. *Walking on the Edge of the World: A Memoir of the Sixties and Beyond*. Boston: Houghton Mifflin Company, 1988.

Lowen, Alexander. *Bioenergetics*. New York: Penguin Compass, 1994.

Marks, John. *The Search for the "Manchurian Candidate": The CIA and Mind Control*. New York: Times Books, 1979.

Maslow, Abraham H. *Religions, Values, and Peak-Experiences*. New York: Viking Press, 1973.

————. *Toward a Psychology of Being*. New York: D. Van Nostrand Company, 1968.

Masters, R. E. L and Jean Houston, *The Varieties of Psychedelic Experience*. New York: Holt, Rinehart and Winston, 1966.

Maupin, Edward W. "Somatic Education: Its Origins, Ancestors, and Prospects." http://www.edmaupin.com/somatic/somatic_origins.htm.

Miller, Henry. *Big Sur and the Oranges of Hieronymus Bosch*. New York: New Directions Publishing Co., 1957.

Montville, Joseph, "The Arrow and the Olive Branch: A Case for Track Two Diplomacy." In John W. McDonald, Jr., and Diane B. Bendahmane, eds., *Conflict Resolution: Track Two Diplomacy*. Center for the Study of Foreign Affairs, Foreign Service Institute, GPO, 1987.

————. with William D. Davidson. "Foreign Policy According to Freud." *Foreign Policy* 45 (Winter 1981–82): 145–57.

————. Foreword to Abdulaziz Sachedina, *The Islamic Roots of Democratic Pluralism*. New York: Oxford University Press, 2000.

————. ed. "A Notebook on the Psychology of the U.S.-Soviet Relationship." A special issue of *Political Psychology* 6, no. 2 (1985).

Murphy, Dennis. *The Sergeant*. New York: Macfadden-Bartell Book, 1968.

Murphy, Gardner and Robert O. Ballou, eds., *William James on Psychical Research*. New York: Viking Press, 1960.

Murphy, Michael. "The Body." In A. Villoldo and D. Dychtwald, eds. *Millenium: Glimpses into the 21st Century*. Los Angeles: J. P. Tarcher, 1980.

———. *An End to Ordinary History*. Los Angeles: J. P. Tarcher, 1982.

———. "The Esalen Institute Transformation Project: A Preliminary Report." *Journal of Transpersonal Psychology* 12, no. 2 (1980): 3–6.

———. *The Future of the Body: Explorations into the Further Evolutions of Human Nature*. New York: Tarcher/Putnam Book, 1992.

———. *Jacob Atabet: A Speculative Fiction*. Los Angeles: J. P. Tarcher, Inc., 1977.

———. *The Kingdom of Shivas Irons*. New York: Broadway Books, 1995.

———. "Sport as Yoga." *Journal of Humanistic Psychology* 17, no. 4 (Fall 1977).

Murphy, Michael, and Steven Donovan. *The Physical and Psychological Effects of Meditation*. Sausalito, CA: Institute of Noetic Sciences, 1999.

Myers, F. W. H. *Human Personality and Its Survival of Bodily Death*. 2 vols. London: Longmans, Green, and Co., 1903.

Ogilvy, James, ed. *Revisioning Philosophy*. Albany: SUNY, 1992.

Ostrander, Sheila and Lynn Schroeder. *Psychic Discoveries Behind the Iron Curtain*. EngleWood Cliffs, NJ: Prentice Hall, 1970.

Perls, Frederick. *Ego, Hunger and Aggression: A Revision of Freud's Theory and Method*. Highland, NY: Gestalt Journal Press, 1992 [1947].

———. *The Gestalt Approach and Eye Witness to Therapy*. Science and Behavior Books, 1973.

———. *In and Out the Garbage Pail*. Lafayette, California: Real People Press, 1969.

Perls, Frederick, Ralph Hefferline, and Paul Goodman. *Gestalt Therapy: Excitement and Growth in the Human Personality*. New York: Dell Publishing Co., 1951.

Peterson, Severin. *A Catalog of the Ways People Grow*. New York: Ballantine, 1971.

Pike, James A. *If This Be Heresy*. New York: Harper and Row, 1967.

———. *What Is This Treasure*. New York: Harper and Row, 1966.

Pike, James A., and Diane Kennedy. *The Other Side: An Account of My Experiences with Psychic Phenomena*. Garden City: Doubleday and Company, 1968.

Puthoff, Harold and Russell Targ. "A Perceptual Channel for Information Transfer over Kilometer Distances: Historical Perspective and Recent Research." *Proceedings of IEEE* 64, no. 3 (March 1976).

Reich, Wilhelm. *Character Analysis*. New York: Farrar, Straus and Giroux, 1990 [1945].

————. *The Function of the Orgasm.* New York: Farrar, Straus and Giroux, 1973 [1942].

————. *The Mass Psychology of Fascism.* New York: Farrar, Straus and Giroux, 1970 [1946].

————. *The Murder of Christ.* New York: Farrar, Straus and Giroux, 1970.

————. *The Sexual Revolution: Toward a Self-Regulating Character Structure.* New York: Farrar, Straus and Giroux, 1974 [1945].

Rolf, Ida. P. *Rolfing: Reestablishing the Natural Alignment and Structural Integration of the Human Body for Vitality and Well-Being.* Rochester, VT: Healing Arts Press, 1989.

Romero, Marina T. and Ramon V. Albareda, "Born on Earth: Sexuality, Spirituality, and Human Evolution." *Revision* 24, no. 2 (Fall 2001): 5–14.

Roszak, Theodore, Mary E. Gomes, and Allen D. Kanner. *Ecopsychology: Restoring the Earth, Healing the Mind.* San Francisco: Sierra Club Books, 1995.

Smith, Huston. *Cleansing the Doors of Perception: The Religious Significance of Entheogenic Plants and Chemicals.* New York: J. P. Tarcher/Putnam, 2000.

Spiegelberg, Frederic. *The Religion of No-Religion.* Stanford: James Ladd Delkin, 1953.

————. *Spiritual Practices of India.* Introduction by Alan W. Watts. San Francisco: Greenwood Press, 1952.

Spino, Mike. *Poems of a Long Distance Runner.* San Francisco: Community Press, 1973.

Stevenson, Ian. *Cases of the Reincarnation Type.* 4 vols. Charlottesville: University Press of Virginia, 1975.

Sutherland, William. *The Cranial Bowl.* Mankato: Free Press, 1939.

"Tantrik Worship: The Basis of Religion." *International Journal [of the] Tantric Order* 5, no. 1 (1906).

Targ, Russell. *Limitless Mind: A Guide to Remote Viewing and Transformation of Consciousness.* Novato: New World Library, 2004.

Targ, Russell, Phyllis Cole, and Harold Puthoff. "Development of Techniques to Enhance Man/Machine Interactions." *SRI Final Report for NASA*, 1976.

Targ, Russell and Keith Harary. *The Mind Race.* New York: Villard, 1994.

Targ, Russell and David Hurt. "Learning Clairvoyance and Precognition with an ESP Teaching Machine." *Parapsychology Review*, July–August 1972.

Targ, Russell and Jane Katra. *Miracles of Mind: Exploring Nonlocal Consciousness and Spiritual Healing.* Novato: New World Library, 1999.

Targ, Russell, E. C. May, and Harold E. Puthoff. "Direct Perception of Remote Geographic Locations." *Mind At Large: Proceedings of IEEE Symposia on Extrasensory Perception.* New York: Praeger, 1979.

Targ, Russell and Harold E. Puthoff. "Information Transmission under Conditions of Sensory Shielding." *Nature* 252 (Oct. 1974): 602–7.

———. "Information Transfer under Conditions of Sensory Shielding." *Nature* 251 (1974).

———. *Mind-Reach: Scientists Look at Psychic Abilities.* New York: Delacorte, 1977.

Targ, Russell, Elisabeth Targ, and Keith Harary. "Moscow – San Francisco Remote Viewing Experiment." *Psi Research* 3, nos. 3–4 (September/December 1984).

Thompson, Keith. *Angels and Aliens: UFOs and the Mythic Imagination.* Reading: Addison-Wesley Publishing Company, Inc., 1991.

Thompson, William Irwin. "Going Beyond It at Big Sur." Chapter 2 of *At the Edge of History.* New York: Harper and Row, 1970.

Thurston, Herbert. *The Physical Phenomena of Mysticism.* London: Burns Oates, 1952.

Uplegedger, John. *Craniosacral Therapy.* Chicago: Easland Press, 1983.

Vest, D. B. (Gerald Heard). *Homophile Studies: One Institute Quarterly* 1, no. 2 (summer 1958).

———. *The Homosexual Magazine* 1, no. 11 (November 1953) and 3, no. 3 (March 1955).

Watts, Alan W. *The Culture of Counter-Culture.* Boston: Charles E. Tuttle Co., Inc, 1998.

———. *In My Own Way: An Autobiography 1915–1965.* New York: Vintage Books, 1973.

———. *The Joyous Cosmology: Adventures in the Chemistry of Consciousness.* New York: Pantheon Books, 1962.

———. *Psychotherapy East and West.* New York: Ballantine Books, 1974 [1961].

———. *This Is It: And Other Essays on Zen and Spiritual Experience.* Toronto: Collier Books, 1969.

———. *Zen and the Beat Way.* Boston: Charles E. Tuttle Co, 1997.

Wheeler, Gordon. *Beyond Individualism: Toward a New Understanding of Self, Relationship, and Experience.* Hillsdale, NJ: Analytic Press, 2000.

———. *Gestalt Reconsidered: A New Approach to Contact and Resistance.* Cleveland: The Gestalt Institute of Cleveland Press, 1998.

White, Rhea A. "Gerald Heard's Legacy to Psychical Research." Academy of Religion and Psychical Research, *Annual Conference Proceedings* 7 (1982): 56–69,

Zukav, Gary. *The Dancing Wu Li Masters: An Overview of the New Physics.* New York: Bantam, 1979.

Index